P9-DNQ-727

TUDORS

Also by Peter Ackroyd

Fiction

The Canterbury Tales: A Retelling
The Trial of Elizabeth Cree
The Last Testament of Oscar Wilde
Chatterton
First Light
English Music
Dan Leno and the Limehouse Golem
Milton in America
The Plato Papers
The Clerkenwell Tales
The Lambs of London
The Fall of Troy
The Casebook of Victor Frankenstein
The Death of King Arthur

Nonfiction

The Collection: Journalism, Reviews, Essays, Short Stories, Lectures
(edited by Thomas Wright)
London Under: The Secret History Beneath the Streets
Dressing Up: Transvestism and Drag: The History of an Obsession
London: The Biography
Albion: The Origins of the English Imagination
Thames: Sacred River
Venice: Pure City
T. S. Eliot
Dickens
Blake
The Life of Thomas More
Shakespeare
Chaucer
J. M. W. Turner
Newton
Poe: A Life Cut Short
Foundation

Peter Ackroyd

THE HISTORY OF ENGLAND
FROM HENRY VIII TO ELIZABETH I

TUDORS

Thomas Dunne Books
St. Martin's Press
New York

THOMAS DUNNE BOOKS.
An imprint of St. Martin's Press.

TUDORS. Copyright © 2012 by Peter Ackroyd. All rights reserved.
Printed in the United States of America. For information, address
St. Martin's Press, 175 Fifth Avenue, New York, N.Y. 10010.

www.thomasdunnebooks.com
www.stmartins.com

ISBN 978-1-250-00362-1 (hardcover)
ISBN 978-1-250-03759-6 (e-book)

St. Martin's Press books may be purchased for educational,
business, or promotional use. For information on bulk purchases, please contact
Macmillan Corporate and Premium Sales Department at 1-800-221-7945,
extension 5442, or write specialmarkets@macmillan.com.

First published in Great Britain by Macmillan,
an imprint of Pan Macmillan, a division of Macmillan Publishers Limited

First U.S. Edition: October 2013

10 9 8 7 6 5 4 3 2 1

Contents

List of illustrations vii

1. Hallelujah 1

2. All in scarlet 14

3. Heretic! 25

4. The woes of marriage 34

5. Into court 46

6. Old authentic histories 62

7. The king's pleasure 78

8. A little neck 91

9. The great revolt 105

10. The confiscation 118

11. The old fashion 129

12. The body of Christ 139

13. The fall 145

14. War games 157

15. A family portrait 168

16. The last days 176

17. The breaking of the altars 184

18. Have at all papists! 193

19. The barns of Crediton 206

20. The lord of misrule 222

21. The nine-day queen 235

22. In the ascendant 245

23. Faith of our fathers 262

24. An age of anxiety 272

25. Nunc Dimittis 281

26. A virgin queen 287

27. Two queens 297

28. The thirty-nine steps 311

29. The rivals 325

30. The rites of spring 337

31. Plots and factions 354

32. The revels now are ended 371

33. The frog 384

34. The great plot 400

35. The dead cannot bite 418

36. Armada 428

37. Repent! Repent! 436

38. The setting sun 444

39. A disobedient servant 454

40. The end of days 463

41. Reformation 467

Further reading 473

Index 483

List of illustrations

1   Portrait of Henry VIII, *c.*1509 (© The Berger Collection at the Denver Art Museum, USA / The Bridgeman Art Library)

2   Portrait of Katherine of Aragon, sixteenth century (© Philip Mould Ltd, London / The Bridgeman Art Library)

3   A woodcut showing King Henry's knights after the English victory over the Scots at Flodden Field, 1513 (© Private Collection / The Bridgeman Art Library)

4   Detail from a depiction of the Field of the Cloth of Gold, *c.*1545 (The Royal Collection © 2011 Her Majesty Queen Elizabeth II / The Bridgeman Art Library)

5   Letter from King Henry VIII to Cardinal Wolsey ('Mine own good cardinal'), thanking him for his hard work and urging him to take some 'pastime and comfort', *c.*1518 (© Private Collection / The Bridgeman Art Library)

6   Cardinal Thomas Wolsey, *c.*1520 (© Hulton Archive / Getty Images)

7   Chalk drawing of Thomas More by Hans Holbein the Younger, *c.*1527 (The Royal Collection © 2011 Her Majesty Queen Elizabeth II / The Bridgeman Art Library)

8   Engraving of the pope being suppressed by King Henry VIII, 1534 (© Private Collection / The Bridgeman Art Library)

9   Portrait of Anne Boleyn, 1534 (© Hever Castle, Kent / The Bridgeman Art Library)

10 Sixteenth-century portrait of Thomas Howard, third Duke of Norfolk, by Hans Holbein the Younger (© Arundel Castle / The Bridgeman Art Library)

11 Detail from a contemporary engraving depicting the martyrdom of the Carthusians (© Private Collection / The Bridgeman Art Library)

12　Engraving showing the Pilgrimage of Grace, nineteenth century (© The Stapleton Collection / The Bridgeman Art Library)

13　Portrait of Jane Seymour by Hans Holbein the Younger, 1536 (© Kunsthistorisches Museum, Vienna / The Bridgeman Art Library)

14　Bishop Latimer's arguments against the Catholic doctrine of Purgatory, with marginal notes by Henry, c.1538 (© Private Collection / The Bridgeman Art Library)

15　Sixteenth-century portrait of Lord Cromwell by Hans Holbein the Younger (© The Trustees of the Weston Park Foundation / The Bridgeman Art Library)

16　Portrait of Anne of Cleves by Hans Holbein the Younger (© Hever Castle, Kent / The Bridgeman Art Library)

17　The title page of the Great Bible, 1539 (© Universal History Archive / Getty Images)

18　Engraving after Holbein portrait of Katherine Howard, 1796 (© The Stapleton Collection / The Bridgeman Art Library)

19　Contemporary portrait of Katherine Parr (© National Portrait Gallery, London / Roger-Viollet, Paris / The Bridgeman Art Library)

20　Allegory of the Tudor succession by Lucas de Heere, c.1570–75 (© Sudeley Castle, Gloucestershire / The Bridgeman Art Library)

21　Portrait of Edward VI at the time of his accession (© Boltin Picture Library / The Bridgeman Art Library)

22　Portrait of Lady Jane Grey, c.1547 (© Yale Center for British Art, Paul Mellon Collection, USA / The Bridgeman Art Library)

23　Queen Mary I, 1554 (© Society of Antiquaries of London / The Bridgeman Art Library)

24　Sixteenth-century portrait of Philip II of Spain (© Philip Mould Ltd, London / The Bridgeman Art Library)

25　Anti-Catholic allegory depicting Stephen Gardiner, Bishop of Winchester, 1556 (© Christie's Images / The Bridgeman Art Library)

26　Woodcut illustration of the burning of Thomas Cranmer, Archbishop of Canterbury, taken from *Foxe's Book of Martyrs*, pub. 1563 (© Lambeth Palace Library, London / The Bridgeman Art Library)

27 Elizabeth I as a young princess, *c.*1546 (The Royal Collection © 2011 Her Majesty Queen Elizabeth II / The Bridgeman Art Library)

28 Page of a manuscript showing the signature of Queen Elizabeth I (© Private Collection / The Bridgeman Art Library)

29 Portrait of Queen Elizabeth I in coronation robes (© National Portrait Gallery, London / The Bridgeman Art Library)

30 Robert Dudley, first earl of Leicester, *c.*1560s (© Yale Center for British Art, Paul Mellon Collection, USA / The Bridgeman Art Library)

31 Thomas Howard, fourth duke of Norfolk, 1562 (© His Grace The Duke of Norfolk, Arundel Castle / The Bridgeman Art Library)

32 Contemporary engraving of Queen Elizabeth I and Parliament (© Private Collection / The Bridgeman Art Library)

33 Mary Queen of Scots in white mourning (© Scottish National Portrait Gallery, Edinburgh / The Bridgeman Art Library)

34 The Execution of Mary Queen of Scots, painted after her death *c.*1613 (© Scottish National Portrait Gallery, Edinburgh / The Bridgeman Art Library)

35 Engraving depicting the pope's bull against the Queen in 1570 (© Private Collection / The Bridgeman Art Library)

36 Hand-coloured copper engraving of the arrival of Queen Elizabeth I at Nonesuch Palace, 1582 (© Private Collection / The Bridgeman Art Library)

37 Map showing the route of the Armada fleet, 1588 (© Private Collection / The Bridgeman Art Library)

38 Portrait of Sir Francis Drake by Nicholas Hilliard, 1581 (© Kunsthistorisches Museum, Vienna / The Bridgeman Art Library)

39 Illustration of the *Ark Royal*, the English fleet's flagship against the Spanish Armada (© Mansell / Time & Life Pictures / Getty Images)

40 Sixteenth-century portrait of William Cecil, first baron Burghley (© Burghley House Collection, Lincolnshire / The Bridgeman Art Library)

41 Engraving of Sir Francis Walsingham (© Private Collection / The Bridgeman Art Library)

42   Contemporary portrait of Sir Robert Cecil (© Bonhams, London /
     The Bridgeman Art Library)
43   Portrait of James VI of Scotland, later James I of England, 1586
     (© Falkland Palace, Fife / Mark Fiennes / The Bridgeman Art
     Library)

TUDORS

1

Hallelujah

The land was flowing with milk and honey. On 21 April 1509 the old king, having grown ever more harsh and rapacious, died in his palace at Richmond on the south bank of the Thames. The fact was kept secret for two days, so that the realm would not tremble. Yet the new Henry had already been proclaimed king.

On 9 May the body of Henry VII was taken in a black chariot from Richmond Palace to St Paul's Cathedral; the funeral car was attended by 1,400 formal mourners and 700 torch-bearers. But few, if any, grieved; the courtiers and household servants were already awaiting the son and heir. When the body, having been taken to the abbey of Westminster, after the funeral service was over, was lowered into its vault the heralds announced 'le noble roy, Henri le Septième, est mort'. Then at once they cried out with one voice, '*Vive le noble roy, Henri le Huitième*'. His title was undisputed, the first such easy succession in a century. The new king was in his seventeenth year.

Midsummer Day, 24 June, was chosen as the day of coronation. The sun in its splendour would herald the rising of another sun. It was just four days before his eighteenth birthday. The ceremony of the coronation was considered to be the eighth sacrament of the Church, in which Henry was anointed with chrism or holy oil as a token of sacred kingship. His robes were stiff with jewels, diamonds and rubies and emeralds and pearls, so that a glow or light hovered about him. He now radiated the power and the glory. He may have acted and dressed under advice, but he soon came to understand the theatre of magnificence.

Henry had taken the precaution, thirteen days before the coronation, of marrying his intended bride so that a king would be accompanied by a queen; it was thereby to be understood that he was an adult rather than a minor. Katherine of Aragon was the child of Isabella of Castile and Ferdinand of Aragon, in whose reign Spain was united. She had come from that country in order to marry Prince Arthur, Henry's older brother, but events conspired against her. Arthur died less than six months after their wedding, of consumption or the sweating sickness, and Katherine was left at the English court in the unenviable position of a widow whose usefulness had gone. It was said that the king himself, Henry VII, might wish to marry her. But this was unthinkable. Instead she was betrothed to Prince Henry, and was consigned to some years of relative penury and privation at the hands of a difficult father-in-law who was in any case pursuing a better match for his son and heir. Yet, after seven years of waiting, her moment of apotheosis had come. On the day before the coronation she was taken in a litter from the Tower of London to Westminster, passing through streets draped in rich tapestry and cloth of gold. A contemporary woodcut depicts Henry and Katherine being crowned at the same time, surrounded by rank upon rank of bishops and senior clergy.

Henry's early years had been spent in the shadow of an anxious and over-protective father, intent before anything else on securing the dynasty. The young prince never spoke in public, except in reply to questions from the king. He could leave the palace at Greenwich or at Eltham only under careful supervision, and then venture into the palace's park through a private door. Much care was bestowed on his early education, so that he acquired the reputation of being the most learned of princes. Throughout his life he considered himself to be a great debater in matters of theology, fully steeped in the scholarship of Thomas Aquinas. He took an early delight in music, and composed Masses as well as songs and motets; he sang, and played both lute and keyboard. He had his own company of musicians who followed him wherever he walked, and by the time of his death he owned seventy-two flutes. He was the harmonious prince. Thomas More, in a poem celebrating the coronation, described him as the glory of the era. Surely he would inaugurate a new golden age in which all men of goodwill would flourish?

Henry was himself a golden youth, robust and good-looking. He was a little over 6 feet in height and, literally, towered over most of his subjects. It was written that 'when he moves the ground shakes under him'. He excelled in wrestling and archery, hawking and jousting. Nine months after the coronation, he organized a tournament in which the feats of chivalry could be celebrated. He rode out in disguise, but his identity was soon discovered. He had read Malory as well as Aquinas, and knew well enough that a good king was a brave and aggressive king. You had to strike down your opponent with a lance or sword. You must not hesitate or draw back. It was a question of honour. The joust offered a taste of warfare, also, and the new king surrounded himself with young lords who enjoyed a good fight. The noblemen of England were eager to stiffen the sinews and summon up the blood.

When he was not master of the joust, he was leader of the hunt. He spoke of his hunting expeditions for days afterwards, and he would eventually own a stable of 200 horses. Hunting was, and still is, the sport of kings. It was a form of war against an enemy, a battleground upon which speed and accuracy were essential. Henry would call out 'Holla! Holla! So boy! There boy!' When the stag was down, he would slit its throat and cut open its belly before thrusting his hands into its entrails; he would then daub his companions with its blood.

Older and more sedate men were also by his side. These were the royal councillors, the majority of whom had served under the previous king. The archbishop of Canterbury, William Warham, remained as chancellor. The bishop of Winchester, Richard Foxe, continued to serve as lord privy seal. The other senior bishops – of Durham, of Rochester and of Norwich – were also in place. The young king had to be advised and guided if the kingdom were to continue on its settled course. Whether he would accept that advice, and follow that guidance, was another matter.

The surviving members of the House of York were restored to favour, after they had endured the indifference and even hostility of the previous king. Henry VII had identified himself as the Lancastrian claimant to the throne. Even though he had married Elizabeth of York after his coronation, he was suspicious and resentful of the rival royal family. The essential unity of the realm was now being proclaimed after the dynastic struggles of the previous century.

The older councillors now took the opportunity of destroying some of the 'new men' whom Henry VII had promoted. His two most trusted advisers, or confidential clerks, were arrested and imprisoned. Sir Richard Empson and Sir Edmund Dudley had been associated with the previous king's financial exactions, but they were in general resented and distrusted by the bishops and older nobility. They were charged with the unlikely crime of 'constructive treason' against the young king, and were duly executed. It is not at all clear that Henry played any part in what was essentially judicial murder, but his formal approval was still necessary. He would employ the same methods, for removing his enemies, in another period of his reign.

Henry was in any case of uncertain temper. He had the disposition of a king. He could be generous and magnanimous, but he was also self-willed and capricious. The Spanish ambassador had intimated to his master that 'speaking frankly, the prince is not considered to be a genial person'. The French ambassador, at a later date, revealed that he could not enter the king's presence without fear of personal violence.

An early outbreak of royal temper is suggestive. In the summer of 1509 a letter arrived from the French king, Louis XII, in reply to one purportedly sent by Henry in which the new king had requested peace and friendship. But Henry had not written it. It had been sent by the king's council in his name. The youthful monarch then grew furious. 'Who wrote this letter?' he demanded. 'I ask peace of the king of France, who dare not look me in the face, still less make war on me!' His pride had been touched. He looked upon France as an ancient enemy. Only Calais remained of the dominion that the English kings had once enjoyed across the Channel. Henry was eager to claim back his ancient rights and, from the time of his coronation, he looked upon France as a prize to be taken. War was not only a pleasure; it was a dynastic duty.

Yet the pleasures of peace were still to be tasted. He had inherited a tranquil kingdom, as well as the store of treasure that his father had amassed. Henry VII bequeathed to him something in excess of £1,250,000, which may plausibly be translated to a contemporary fortune of approximately £380,000,000. It would soon all be dissipated, if not exactly squandered. It was rumoured that the young king was spending too much time on sports and entertainments, and was as a result neglecting the business of the realm. This need not be taken at face value. As the letter to the French king demonstrated, the learned bishops preferred their master to stay away from their serious deliberations.

There were in any case more immediate concerns. Katherine of Aragon had at the end of January 1510 gone into painful labour. The result was a girl, stillborn. Yet Katherine remained evidently pregnant with another child, and the preparations for a royal birth were continued. They were unnecessary. The swelling of her belly subsided, caused by infection rather than fruitfulness. It was announced that the queen had suffered a miscarriage, but it was rumoured that she was perhaps infertile. No greater doom could be delivered upon an English queen. She disproved the rumours when she gave birth to a son on the first day of 1511, but the infant died two months later. Katherine may have been deemed to be unlucky, but the king would eventually suspect something much worse than misfortune.

Henry had already strayed from the marriage bed. While Katherine was enduring the strains of her phantom pregnancy in the early months of 1510, he took comfort from the attentions of Anne Stafford. She was one of the queen's ladies-in-waiting, and was already married. She was also a sister of the duke of Buckingham, and this great lord was sensitive of his family's honour. Anne Stafford was sent to a nunnery, and Buckingham removed himself from court after an angry confrontation with the king. Katherine of Aragon was apprised of the affair and, naturally enough, took Buckingham's part. She had been shamed by her husband's infidelity with one of her own servants. The household was already full of deception and division. Other royal liaisons may have gone unrecorded. Mistress Amadas, the wife of the court goldsmith, later announced the fact that the king had come secretly to her in a Thames Street house owned by one of his principal courtiers.

Yet all sins of lust could be absolved. In the early days of 1511 Henry went on pilgrimage to the shrine of Our Lady of Walsingham in Norfolk. It was reported that he trod, barefoot and in secret, along the pilgrims' road in order to pray for the life of his struggling infant boy. In the summer of the same year he made a pilgrimage to the shrine of Master John Schorne at North Marston in Buckinghamshire. Master Schorne was the rector of that village who had acquired a reputation for saintliness and whose shrine became a centre of miraculous healing. He was said to have conjured the devil into a boot.

In all matters of faith, therefore, Henry was a loyal son of the Church. In that respect, at least, he resembled the overwhelming majority of his subjects. The Venetian ambassador reported that 'they all attend Mass every day and say many paternosters in public – the women carrying long rosaries in their hands'. At the beginning of Henry's reign the Catholic Church in England was flourishing. It had recovered its vigour and purpose. In the south-west, for example, there was a rapid increase in church building and reconstruction. More attention was paid to the standards of preaching. Where before the congregation knelt on rush-covered floors, benches were now being set up in front of the pulpits.

It was the Church of ancient custom and of traditional ceremony. On Good Friday, for example, the 'creeping to the cross' took place. The crucifix was veiled and held up behind the high altar by two priests while the responses to the versicles were chanted; it was then uncovered and placed on the third step in front of the altar, to which the clergy now would crawl on their hands and knees before kissing it. Hymns were sung as the crucifix was then carried down to the congregation, who would genuflect before it and kiss it. The crucifix was then wreathed in linen and placed in a 'sepulchre' until it re-emerged in triumph on the morning of Easter Sunday. This was an age of carols and of holy days, of relics and pilgrimages and miracles.

The old faith was established upon communal ritual as much as theology. The defining moment of devotion was the miracle of transubstantiation at the Mass, when the bread and wine were transformed into the body and blood of Christ. The religious life was nourished by the sacraments, which were in turn administered by a duly ordained body of priests who owed their primary allegiance to the pope. The faithful were obliged to attend Mass on Sundays and holy days, to fast on appointed days, to make confession and receive communion at least once a year. The most powerful of all beliefs was that in purgatory, whereby the living made intercession for the souls of the dead to bring a quicker end to their suffering; the old Church itself represented the communion of the living and the dead.

The saints were powerful intercessors, too, and were venerated as guardians and benefactors. St Barbara protected her votaries against thunder and lightning, and St Gertrude kept away the mice and the rats; St Dorothy protected herbs, while St Apolline healed the toothache; St Nicholas saved the faithful from drowning, while St Anthony guarded the swine. The supreme intercessor was the Virgin Mary, Mother of God, whose image was to be found everywhere surrounded by candles and incense.

The churches were therefore filled with images and lights. Those of London, for example, were treasure-chests of silver candlesticks and censers, silver crucifixes and chalices and patens. The high altar and the rood screen, separating the priest from the congregation, were miracles of art and workmanship. Images of Jesus and of the Holy Virgin, of patron saints and local saints, adorned every available space. They wore coronets and necklaces of precious stones; rings were set upon their fingers and they were clothed in garments of gold. Some churches even exhibited the horns of unicorns or the eggs of ostriches in order to elicit admiration.

The human representatives of the Church were perhaps more frail. Yet the condition of the clergy was sound, as far as the laws of human nature allowed. Incompetent and foolish priests could be found, of course, but there was no general debasement or corruption of the clerical office. More men and women were now in religious orders than at any time in the previous century, and after the invention of printing came a great flood of devotional literature. In the years between 1490 and 1530, some twenty-eight editions of the *Hours of the Blessed Virgin* were issued. The religious guilds, set up to collect money for charity and to pray for the souls of the dead, had never been so popular; they were the institutional aspect of the religious community.

There were eager reformers, of course, who wished for a revival of the Christian spirit buried beneath the golden carapace of ritual and traditional devotion. It is in fact a measure of the health of the Church at the beginning of the sixteenth century that such fervent voices were heard everywhere. In the winter of 1511 John Colet stepped into the pulpit, at his own cathedral church of St Paul's in London, and preached of religious reform to the senior clergy of the realm. He repeated his theme to a convocation of clergy in the chapter-house of Canterbury. 'Never', he said, 'did the state of the Church more need your endeavours.' It was time for 'the reformation of ecclesiastical affairs'. The word had been spoken, but the deed was unthinkable. What Colet meant by 'reformation' was a rise in the quality and therefore the renown of the priesthood.

He despised some of the more primitive superstitions of the Catholic people, such as the veneration of relics and the use of prayer as a magical charm, but he had no doubt on the principles of faith and the tenets of theology. On these matters the Church was resolute. In May 1511 six men and four women, from Tenterden in Kent, were denounced as heretics for claiming among other things that the sacrament of the altar was not the body of Christ but merely material bread. They were forced to abjure their doctrines, and were condemned to wear the badge of a faggot in flames for the rest of their lives. Two men were burned, however, for the crime of being 'relapsed' heretics; they had repented, but then had taken up their old opinions once more. The Latin secretary to Henry, an Italian cleric known as Ammonius, wrote with some exaggeration that 'I do not wonder that the price of faggots has gone up, for many heretics furnish a daily holocaust, and yet more spring up to take their place'.

The career of Ammonius himself is testimony to the fact that the Church was still the avenue for royal preferment. This was a truth of which Thomas Wolsey was the supreme embodiment. Wolsey arrived at court through the agency of Bishop Foxe, the lord privy seal, and seems almost at once to have impressed the

young king with his stamina and mastery of detail. By the spring
of 1511 he was issuing letters and bills directly under the king's
command, thus effectively circumventing the usual elaborate procedures. He was still only dean of Lincoln, but he was already
advising Henry in affairs international and ecclesiastical.

He had the gift of affability as well as of industry, and was
infinitely resourceful; he did what the king wanted, and did it
quickly. The king's opinions were his own. Wolsey was, according to his gentleman usher, George Cavendish, 'most earnest
and readiest in all the council to advance the king's only will and
pleasure, having no respect to the case'. He was thirty-eight years
old, and a generation younger than the old bishops of the council.
Here was a man whom the young king could take into his
confidence, and upon whom he could rely. Wolsey rose at four in
the morning, and could work for twelve hours at a stretch without
intermission. Cavendish relates that 'my lord never rose once to
piss, nor yet to eat any meat'. When he had finished his labours he
heard Mass and then ate a light supper before retiring.

Wolsey therefore became the instrument of the king's will, and
no more forcefully than in the prosecution of Henry's ambitions
against France. In November 1511 Henry joined a Holy League
with the pope and with his father-in-law, Ferdinand of Spain, so
that they might with papal approval attack France. Henry longed
for war, and of course an excuse for combat could always be found.
In this instance the incursion of French troops into Italian territories was cited as the reason for hostilities. In the following month
a Christmas pageant was devised for the king at the house of the
black friars in Ludgate, in which were displayed an artificial lion
and an antelope. Four knight challengers rode out against men in
the apparel of 'woodwoos', or wild men of the forest. It was a
spectacle in praise of battle. A few months later it was decreed by
parliament that all male children were obliged to practise the skills
of archery.

Contrary advice was being given to the king at this juncture.
The bishops and statesmen of the royal council advised peace
against the hazard and cost of war with the French. Many of the
reformist clergy were temperamentally opposed to warfare, and
regretted that a golden prince of peace should so soon become a

ravening lion of war. Colet declared from the pulpit of St Paul's that 'an unjust peace is better than the justest war'. Erasmus, the Dutch humanist then resident at Cambridge, wrote that 'it is the people who build cities, while the madness of princes destroys them'.

Yet the old nobility, and the young lords about the king, pressed for combat and glory in an alliance with Spain against the old enemy. Katherine of Aragon, who had assumed the role of Spanish ambassador to the English court of her husband, was also in favour of war against France. In this she was fulfilling the desire of her father. It was an unequal balance of forces, especially when it was tilted by Henry's desire for martial honour. He desired above all else to be a 'valiant knight' in the Arthurian tradition. That was the destiny of a true king. What did it matter if this were, in England, the beginning of a run of bad harvests when bread was dear and life more precarious? The will of the king was absolute. Had he not been proclaimed king of France at the time of his coronation? He wished to recover his birthright.

In April 1512 war was declared against France; a fleet of eighteen warships was prepared to take 15,000 men to Spain, from where they were to invade the enemy. In the early summer the English forces landed in Spain. No tents, or provisions, had been prepared for them. They lay in fields and under hedges, without protection from the torrential rain. The season was oppressive and pestilential, a menace augmented by the hot wine of Spain. The men wanted beer, but there was none to be found.

It also soon became apparent that they had been duped by Ferdinand, who had no intention of invading France, but merely wanted his border to be guarded by the English troops while he waged an independent war against the kingdom of Navarre. His words were fair, one English commander wrote back to the king, but his deeds were slack. Dysentery caused many casualties and, as a result of disease and poor rations, rumours and threats of mutiny began to multiply. In October 1512 the English sailed back home. 'Englishmen have so long abstained from war,' the daughter of the emperor Maximilian said, 'they lack experience from disuse.' The young king had been dishonoured as well as betrayed. Henry was furious at the hypocrisy and duplicity of his father-in-law, and seems in part to have blamed Katherine for the fiasco. A report soon emerged in Rome that he wished to 'repudiate' his wife, largely because she had proved incapable of bearing him a living heir, and to marry elsewhere.

Yet he refused to accept the humiliation in Spain, and at once began planning for a military expedition under his own leadership. He would lead a giant campaign, and emulate Henry V in the scale of his victories. Henry summoned his nobles, and their armed retainers, as their feudal master. The days of Agincourt were revived. He soon restored Thomas Howard to his father's title of duke of Norfolk and created Charles Brandon, his partner in the jousts, duke of Suffolk; the two warlords were thereby afforded sufficient dignity. If he were to imitate the exploits of the medieval king, however, he would need men and materials. Wolsey in effect became the minister of war. It was he who organized the fleet, and made provisions for 25,000 men to sail to France under the banner of the king. Henry now found him indispensable. He was made dean of York, another stage in his irrepressible rise.

The main body of the army set sail in the spring of 1513, followed a few weeks later by the king. He landed in Calais with a bodyguard of 300 men and a retinue of 115 priests and singers of the chapel. His great and ornate bed was transported along the route eastward, and was set up each night within a pavilion made from cloth of gold. The king had eleven tents, connected one with another; one was for his cook, and one for his kitchen. He was escorted, wherever he walked or rode, by fourteen young boys in coats of gold. The bells on his horse were made of gold. The most elaborate of the royal tents was decorated with golden ducats and golden florins. He was intent on displaying his magnificence as well as his valour. Henry had allied himself with the Holy Roman Emperor Maximilian I, whose nominal empire comprised most of central Europe, but he also wished to claim imperial sovereignty for himself. He had already caused to be fashioned a 'rich crown of gold set with full many rich precious stones' that became known as the Imperial Crown; it would in time signify his dominion over the whole of Britain, but also over the Church within his domain.

The fighting in France itself was to a large extent inconsequential. In the summer of 1513 the English forces laid siege to the small town of Thérouanne in the county of Flanders; a body of French cavalry came upon them, exchanged fire, and then retreated. They rode away so hard that the encounter became known as the battle of the Spurs. Henry himself had remained in the rear, and had taken no part in the action. It was not a very glorious victory, but it was still a victory. When Thérouanne itself eventually submitted, the king's choristers sang the Te Deum.

The English infantry and cavalry moved on to besiege Tournai, a much bigger prize that Edward III had failed to capture in the summer of 1340. It fell within a week of the English arrival. Henry established a garrison in Tournai and strengthened its citadel; he also demanded that Thomas Wolsey be appointed as bishop of the city. Three weeks of tournaments, dances and revels marked the victory in which the courts of Maximilian and Henry freely mingled. The king then sailed back to England in triumph.

Yet the cost of the brief wars was enormous, comprising most of the treasure that Henry VII had bequeathed to his son. Wolsey persuaded parliament to grant a subsidy, in effect a tax upon every adult male, but this proved of course unpopular and difficult to collect. It became clear enough that England could not afford to wage war on equal terms with the larger powers of Europe. The French king had three times as many subjects, and also triple the resources; the Spanish king possessed six times as many subjects, and five times the revenue. Henry's ambition and appetite for glory outstripped his strength.

The true palm of victory, in 1513, was in any case to be found elsewhere. The Scots were restive, and ready once more to confirm their old alliance with the French. It was feared that James IV was prepared to invade England while its king was absent on other duties. And so it proved. Katherine herself played a role in the preparations for battle. She wrote to her husband that she was 'horribly busy with making standards, banners and badges', and she herself led an army north. Yet the victory came before she arrived. James IV led his soldiers over the border but, under the command of the elderly earl of Surrey, the English forces withstood and defeated them. James himself was left dead upon the field, and John Skelton wrote that 'at Flodden hills our bows and bills slew all the flower of their honour'; 10,000 Scots were killed.

The torn surcoat of the Scottish king, stained with blood, was sent to Henry at Tournai. Katherine wrote to her husband with news of the victory, and declared that the battle of Flodden Field 'has been to your grace and all your realm the greatest honour that could be, more than if you should win the crown of France'. Henry was truly the master of his kingdom.

2

All in scarlet

Richard Hunne was a wealthy merchant whose infant son Stephen died in the spring of 1511. The rector of his parish church in Whitechapel, Thomas Dryffield, asked for the dead baby's christening robe as a 'mortuary gift'; this was a traditional offering to the priest at the time of burial. Hunne declined to follow the custom. A year later he was summoned to Lambeth Palace, where he was judged to be contumacious; he still refused to pay what he considered to be an iniquitous fee. When he entered his parish church for vespers, at the end of the year, Dryffield formally excommunicated him. 'Hunne,' he shouted, 'you are accursed, and you stand accursed.'

This was a serious matter. No one was permitted to engage in business with Hunne. He would be without company, because no one would wish to be seen with an excommunicate. He would also of course be assigned to the fires of damnation for eternity. Yet Hunne struck back, and accused the rector of slander. He also challenged the legality of the Church court that had previously deemed him guilty. The case then entered the world of law, where it remained suspended for twenty-two months. In the autumn of 1514 the Church authorities raided Hunne's house, and found a number of heretical books written in English. He was taken to the Lollards' Tower in the west churchyard of St Paul's where in the winter of that year he was found hanged. The bishop of London declared that the heretic had, in a mood of contrition and guilt, committed suicide. Hunne's sympathizers accused the Church of murder. In the words of John Foxe, the martyrologist, 'his neck was broken with an iron chain, and he was wounded in other parts of his body, and then knit up in his own girdle'.

Even before Hunne's corpse was being burned at Smithfield, as a convicted and 'abominable' heretic, a coroner's inquest was convened to judge the manner of his death. In February 1515 the jury decided that three clerics − among them the bishop of London's chancellor, William Horsey − were guilty of murder. The bishop wrote immediately to Thomas Wolsey and called for an inquiry by men without bias; he told Wolsey that Londoners were so 'maliciously set in favour' of heresy that his man was bound to be condemned even if he were 'as innocent as Abel'.

The king then ordered an inquiry, to take place at Baynard's Castle on the north bank of the Thames by Blackfriars, where the bishop of London took the opportunity of condemning the members of the jury as 'false perjured caitiffs'. Henry then intervened with a decision to pardon Horsey and the others; he instructed his attorney to declare them to be not guilty of the alleged crime. Horsey then left London, and travelled quickly to Exeter. This might have seemed to be the end of the matter.

Yet there were important consequences. Three years before, in the parliament of 1512, a bill had been passed requiring that 'benefit of clergy' be removed from those in minor orders convicted of murder; the 'benefit' had meant that clerics would be tried in Church courts and spared the penalty of death. Minor orders represented the lower ranks of the clergy, such as lector or acolyte. In the charged circumstances of the Hunne affair, this measure acquired new significance. The abbot of Winchester now declared to the Lords that the Act of 1512 stood against the laws of God and the freedoms of the Church. The text upon which he preached came from the First Book of Chronicles, 'Touch not mine anointed'.

Henry Standish, warden of the mendicant friars of London and one of the king's spiritual advisers, disagreed. He asserted that no act of the king could be prejudicial to the Church, and that the Church effectively came under the king's jurisdiction. A fundamental issue was raised. Could a secular court call the clergy to account? Could a temporal leader restrain a bishop ordained by God? Standish was summoned to appear before a convocation of the senior clergy, to answer for his opinions, and he appealed to the king for protection.

A great conference of learned men, including all the judges of the land, met at Blackfriars in the winter of 1515 and after much deliberation took the part of Henry Standish; they accused the senior clergy of *praemunire*, by which was meant the appeal to a foreign court or authority. The foreign authority, in this case, was the pope and the papal court. Thomas Wolsey – made a cardinal only three months before – offered a formal submission to the king, and asked him to submit the case to Rome. This might seem an oddly inappropriate response, but it is likely that Wolsey and the king were working together. All now waited for the king's verdict. It was time for Henry to give judgment in the affair of Henry Standish.

He addressed an assembly of lawyers and clergy at Baynard's Castle in November and made the following declaration. 'By the ordinance and sufferance of God we are king of England, and the kings of England in time past have never had any superior but God alone. Wherefore know you well that we shall maintain the right of our crown and of our temporal jurisdiction as well in this point as in all others.' The opinions of Standish were upheld.

This could perhaps be seen as the first movement of the great reformation of the sixteenth century, but the king was saying nothing new. The Statute of Provisors, in 1351, spoke of the 'Holy Church of England' in the reign of Edward III as distinct from 'the pope of Rome'. Richard II, at the end of the fourteenth century, was declared to be absolute emperor within his dominion. In 1485 Chief Justice Hussey declared that the king of England was answerable only to God and was superior to the pope within his realm. In fact Henry VII had repeatedly challenged the status of the Church by citing senior clergy for *praemunire*; he made it clear that he did not want another sovereign power within his kingdom, and in the appointment of bishops he preferred lawyers to theologians. The pope did not intervene.

It was perhaps odd that in his letter to Wolsey the bishop of London should accuse his flock of being altogether heretical, but under the circumstances it was a pardonable exaggeration. The bishop was simply adverting to the fact that among Londoners there was a long and persistent tradition of anti-clericalism. There had always been calls for the Church to be reformed or to come under the command of the king, and the clergy had been under attack from at least the fourteenth century. The parliaments of the 1370s and 1380s wished to remove clerics from high office, and in the Peasants' Revolt of 1381 the archbishop of Canterbury was beheaded by the mob. The clergy, high and low, were accused of fornication and adultery; they spent their time hawking and hunting; they wore their hair long, and they lounged in taverns; they carried swords and daggers. It was a familiar litany of complaint, taken up in an earlier century by Chaucer and by Langland. Yet such abuse, such strident denunciations, were natural and inevitable in the case of an ancient institution. The Church of Rome was always in need of renovation and renewal.

The king had spoken, on a winter's day in Baynard's Castle, and Wolsey knelt before him. Yet the prelate had already become mighty. In the autumn of 1515, at the king's urgent request, Pope Leo X had conferred the red hat of a cardinal upon him. From this time forward he dressed in scarlet. He was the king's cardinal rather than the pope's cardinal, however, and thus could only assist the cause of royal supremacy. At the end of this year Wolsey was also appointed by Henry to be his new lord chancellor, the leading minister of the realm and holder of the Great Seal. He dominated the council of the king. All dispatches, to local justices or to ambassadors, now passed through his hands. No act of policy could be formulated without his active engagement. No senior post could be filled without his intervention. 'Were I to offer to resign,' he said, 'I am sure neither the king nor his nobles would permit it.'

In his command of domestic and international affairs, he needed much subtlety and dexterity. The death of Ferdinand of Spain in February 1516, and the succession of his grandson Charles at the age of sixteen, posed delicate problems of balance and influence. Charles's own titles bear evidence of the complexities of continental politics. He had been nominal ruler of Burgundy for ten years, and assumed the crown of Spain as Charles I; three years later, he became ruler of the Holy Roman Empire as Charles V. His lands, in the south and centre of Europe, comprised the Habsburg inheritance that would dominate English foreign policy for the next hundred years. Another young monarch also claimed the ascendancy. Francis I had assumed the crown of France in 1515, at the age of twenty, and within nine months he had taken an army into northern Italy and captured Milan. This was a feat that Henry could only dream of accomplishing.

On May Day 1515, Henry asked for details about Francis from a Venetian envoy. 'Talk with me awhile,' he said. 'The King of France, is he as tall as I?' There was very little difference. 'Is he as stout?' No, he was not. 'What sort of legs has he?' They were thin or 'spare'. At this point the king of England opened his doublet, and placed his hand on his thigh. 'Look here. And I also have a good calf to my leg.' He said later that Francis was a Frenchman, and therefore could not be trusted.

Until the death of Henry these three young monarchs would vie for mastery, or at least temporary supremacy, and the international history of the time consists of their moves and countermoves. There were treaties and secret agreements, skirmishes and wars, invasions and sieges. Europe became their playing field. In their respective courts, hunts and jousts and tournaments became the theatrical expression of power. But when three young men fight, the results are always likely to be bloody.

The emergence of these three powerful sovereigns also altered the whole balance of European power and, in particular, led inevitably to the relative decline in the authority of the pope. The power of kings was considered to be supreme, dominating Church and nobility. Charles and Francis were always to be engaged in contention, since their territories were adjacent one to another, and it was Henry's part to derive maximum benefit from their rivalry. They were not always engaged in open hostility, however, but tried to benefit from convenient betrothals and dynastic marriages. The birth of a daughter to Henry, on 18 February 1516, at last gave him a pawn in the great game. Nevertheless, Princess Mary was a severe disappointment to her father; he had hoped and prayed for a son and heir, but he disguised his dismay. 'We are both young,' he said, 'if it be a girl this time, by the grace of God, boys will follow.' In this he was mistaken.

In the spring of 1517 a bill was posted upon one of the doors of St Paul's, complaining that 'the foreigners' were given too much favour by the king and council and they 'bought wools to the undoing of Englishmen'. This helped to inspire the riots of 'Evil May Day' in which the radicalism or insubordination of the London crowd became manifest. At the end of April a preacher had called upon Englishmen to defend their livings against 'aliens', by whom he meant the merchants from Florence and Venice, from Genoa and Paris. Wolsey had sent for the mayor on hearing news that, as he put it, 'your young and riotous people will rise and distress the strangers'. A disturbance of this kind was deeply troubling for an administration that had no police force or standing army to enforce its will.

The mayor denied any rumours of sedition but on the evening of 30 April 2,000 Londoners – with apprentices, watermen and serving men at their head – sacked the houses of the French and Flemish merchants. They also stormed the house of the king's secretary and threatened the residents of the Italian quarter. Wolsey, wary of trouble despite the assurances of the mayor, called in the armed retainers of the nobility as well as the ordnance of the Tower. More than 400 prisoners were taken, tried and found guilty of treason. Thirteen of them suffered the penalty of being hanged, drawn and quartered; their butchered remains were suspended upon eleven gallows set up within the city.

In a suitably elaborate ceremony the other rioters, with halters around their necks, were brought to Westminster Hall in the presence of the king. He was sitting on a lofty dais, from which eminence he condemned them all to death. Then Wolsey fell on his knees and begged the king to show compassion while the prisoners themselves called out 'Mercy, Mercy!' Eventually the king relented and granted them pardon. At which point they cast off their halters and, as a London chronicler put it, 'jumped for joy'.

It had been a close-run thing, but there is no disguising the real scorn and even hatred between the court and the citizens. The nobility distrusted and despised the commonalty, a feeling returned in equal measure. It was believed, with some reason, that the bishops and the clergy took the nobles' part; the city's animus against them would play some role in the religious changes of later years. London itself had the capacity to stir riot and breed dissension, and was a constant source of disquiet to the king and his council.

Two or three weeks after the riots, a distemper fell upon the city and the country. In the early summer of 1517 a fever, accompanied by a profuse and foul-smelling sweat, began its progress. It was accompanied by sharp pains in the back and shoulders before moving to the liver; lethargy and drowsiness ensued, with a sleep that often led to death. Swift and merciless, it became known as the sweat or the sweating sickness; because it seems only to have attacked the English, in cities such as Calais and Antwerp, it was called 'sudor Anglicus' or 'the English sweat'. It was also called 'Know Thy Master' or 'The Lord's Visitation'. Tens of thousands died. A physician of the time, Dr Caius, described how it 'immediately killed some in opening their windows, some in playing with children in their street doors; some in one hour, many in two, it destroyed; and at the longest to them that merrily dined, it gave a sorrowful supper'. A chance encounter in the street, a beggar knocking at the door, a kiss upon the cheek, could spell death.

The houses themselves might harbour the pestilence. Erasmus complained that the floors of English dwellings were covered with rushes that harboured 'expectorations, vomitings, the leakage of dogs and men, ale-droppings, scraps of fish and other abominations not to be mentioned'. Whenever there was a change in the weather, vapours of foul air were exhaled. In the streets the open sewers rolled their stagnant and turbid discharge down to the Thames.

In the summer of that year Thomas Wolsey himself fell sick of the sweat, with many of his household dying. Yet he was robust and determined. He could shake off any sickness without permanent injury to his strong constitution. On his recovery he made a pilgrimage to Walsingham; when he had faced death, he had made a vow to pray at the shrine of Our Lady there, a replica of the house in Nazareth where Gabriel had appeared to Mary. After he had meditated and fasted, he continued with the business of the realm.

In the spring of the previous year he had spoken at length, to Henry and to the council, of the inefficiencies and enormities in the administration of justice. He was not a lawyer and had no training in the law, but his intelligence and self-reliance easily surmounted any doubts about his ability. He had decided, with the king, to reinforce the procedures of the law by means of a body known as the Star Chamber; in its judicial capacity, the king's council met in a chamber the roof of which was studded with stars.

Under the stars the lord chancellor could question and punish, in particular, the great ones of the realm. 'I trust,' he wrote, 'to learn them next term the law of the Star Chamber.' He punished lords for maintaining too many retainers, and knights for 'bearing' (bearing down on) their poorer tenants; he investigated cases of perjury and forgery; he regulated prices and food supplies, on the understandable assumption that scarcity might provoke riot. One of the principal functions of the chamber was to suppress or punish public disorder. He investigated the behaviour of the sheriffs. In the previous reign the Star Chamber had heard approximately twelve cases a year; under the direction of Wolsey it heard 120 in the same period.

Wolsey had his own court, too, known as the court of Chancery. This was a civil rather than a criminal court, where disputes over such matters as inheritance and contract were resolved. The plaintiffs could state their case in the vernacular, and defendants were obliged to appear by means of a 'subpoena writ'. It was an efficient way of hearing appeals against judgments in common law. It also provided a method by which the cardinal could keep a tight grip upon the business of the land. Wolsey went in procession to Westminster Hall each day, with two great crosses of silver carried before him together with his Great Seal and cardinal's hat; he dressed in crimson silk with a tippet or shoulder cape of sable. In his hand he carried an orange, hollowed out and filled with vinegar, pressed to his nose when he walked through the crowd of suitors awaiting him. 'On [*sic*] my lords and masters,' his attendants called out, 'make way for my Lord's Grace!' John Skelton described his behaviour in the court of Chancery itself:

> And openly in that place
> He rages and he raves
> And calls them cankered knaves . . .
> In the Star Chamber he nods and becks . . .
> Duke, earl, baron or lord
> To his sentence must accord.

He was resented by those whom he punished, but his ministrations seem to have been effective. In the late summer of 1517 he wrote to Henry with a certain amount of self-congratulation on the blessed state of the realm. 'Our Lord be thanked,' he said, 'it was never in such peace nor tranquillity.'

In this year, too, Wolsey established an inquiry into the causes of depopulation in the counties of England. The countryside had been changing for many generations, so slowly that the alteration had not been discernible until it was too late to do anything about it. By the time that the enclosure of land by the richer or more efficient farmers was recognized as a manifest injustice, it had become a simple fact that could not be reversed. A society of smallholders gave way to one of large tenant farmers with a class of landless labourers. So it is with all historical change. It proceeds over many decades, and many centuries, before becoming irrevocable.

Many tracts and pamphlets were written in the sixteenth century concerning the evils of enclosure. Thomas More's *Utopia* is in part directed against it. The enclosed land was used for the rearing of sheep rather than for the production of crops. More wrote that the sheep were now eating the people rather than the reverse. One shepherd took the place of a score of agricultural workers in the process, thus leading to the depopulation of large parts of the countryside. A bishop wrote to Wolsey that 'your heart would mourn to see the towns, villages, hamlets, manor places in ruin and decay, the people gone, the ploughs laid down'. When labourers were not needed, they moved on. The simple houses of the rural tenantry, once abandoned, were dissolved by

wind and rain; the walls crumbled, and the roofs fell, leaving only
hillocks of earth to show where they had once stood. The village
church might become a shelter for cattle. Yet it was hard, then
and now, to identify the causes of this decay. The distress of the
early sixteenth century may have been caused by a series of bad
harvests and a steadily growing population, for example, rather
than a suddenly accelerated rate of enclosure. A population of
approximately three million was below the peak of the early
fourteenth century, but it was increasing all the time.

Enclosure itself had been a fact of farming ever since the
fourteenth century, when the 'pestilence' or 'black death' took a
large toll upon the population. With the lowered demand for corn,
the land had to be put to different uses. Fields lying idle were
cheap, also, and a steady process of purchase began that continued
well into the eighteenth century. There were barters and exchanges
between farmers, with the wealthiest or the most resourceful
getting the best of the bargain. Many of the once open fields
were enclosed with hedges of hawthorn. It was estimated that the
value of enclosed land was one and a half times that of the rest.
The process could not be prevented or halted. It came to a crisis,
as we shall see, a generation later.

The state of the realm was still very largely the state of an
agricultural society. It was comprised of freeholders and leasehold-
ers, customary tenants and labourers, all owing allegiance to their
lord. Their houses were grouped closely together, with the fields
stretching around them. It was a society immensely susceptible to
the vagaries of the weather, where one bad harvest could spell
disaster.

In what had always been a world of tradition and of custom,
the previous ties of the manor system were now giving way to the
new laws of the market. Custom was being replaced by law and
contract. Communal effort was slowly supplanted by competition.
'Now the world is so altered for the poor tenant,' one contemporary
wrote, 'that he stands in bodily fear of his greedy neighbour – so
that, two or three years before his lease ends, he must bow to his
lord for a new lease.' The larger farmers wished to sell their
produce to the rising populations of the towns and the cities; the
smaller farmers were reduced to subsistence agriculture, by which

they ate what they grew. Land was no longer the common ground of society, the management of which entailed social responsibilities. It had become a simple investment. So the customary rent for a tenant was replaced by what was known as the 'rack rent' or market rent. The process was very slow and very long, not really coming to an end until the eighteenth century. Yet the communal farming of the past, with its own co-operative rituals and customs, was not destined to endure. In this respect the movement of agriculture may be compared with the movement of religion.

There is indeed an affinity. The common fields along the coastal plains of Westmorland and Northumberland, for example, harboured an attachment to the old religion. The corn-growing villages of East Anglia and eastern Kent, engaged in the commercial production of food, were committed to the reform of faith. It seems clear enough that religious radicalism prospered in the eastern counties, and was held back in the north and in the west. Yet there are so many exceptions and special cases that even these generalizations are susceptible to doubt. The eastern part of Sussex espoused the new faith, for example, while the western part supported the old. It can only be said with some degree of certainty that the time of the 'new men' was approaching.

3

Heretic!

In 1517 or 1518 some Cambridge scholars began to meet at the White Horse tavern in that city where, like undergraduates before and since, they debated the intellectual issues of the time. The pressing matters of this time, however, were all concerned with religion; it was at the heart of sixteenth-century debate. Some of these scholars, with all the ardour of youth, were attracted to new and potentially subversive doctrines. Reform was in the air. Some of them wished to return to the simple piety of the movements known as the Poor Catholics or the Humiliati; they wished to eschew the pomp and ceremony of the medieval Church, and to cultivate what was called *devotio moderna*, 'modern devotion'. Others wished to return to the word of the Scriptures, and in particular of the New Testament.

The published work of Desiderius Erasmus had already brought a purer spirit into theological enquiry. While Lady Margaret Professor of Divinity at Queens' College, Cambridge, he completed a Greek and Latin translation of the New Testament which seemed destined to supersede the old 'Vulgate' that had been in use for a thousand years. Erasmus, by an act of historical scholarship, brought back something of the air of early Christian revelation.

He believed that the rituals and the formal theology of the Church were less important than the spiritual reception of the message of the Scriptures; an inward faith, both in God's grace and in the redemptive power of His Son, was of more efficacy than conformity to external worship. 'If you approach the Scriptures in all humility,' he wrote, 'you will perceive that you have been breathed upon by the Holy Will.' By means of satire he also attacked the excessive devotion to relics, the too frequent resort to pilgrimages, and the degeneration of the monastic orders. He rarely mentions the sacraments that were part of the divine machinery of the orthodox faith.

He never advanced into heretical doctrine, but he was as much a dissolvent of conventional piety as Luther or Wycliffe. Without Erasmus, neither Luther nor Tyndale could have translated the Greek testament. He also entertained the hope that the Scriptures would be freely available to everyone, an aspiration that, at a later date, would be deemed almost heretical. One of the scholars who attended the meetings in the White Horse tavern, Thomas Bilney, declared that on reading Erasmus 'at last I heard of Jesus'. Bilney was later to be burned at the stake.

Erasmus has conventionally been described as a 'humanist', although the word itself did not appear in this sense until the beginning of the nineteenth century. In general terms humanism, or the 'new learning' at the beginning of the sixteenth century, concerned itself with a renovation of education and scholarship by the pursuit of newly found or newly translated classical models. It brought with it a profound scepticism of medieval authority, and of the scholastic theology that supported it. The new learning opened the windows of the Church in search of light and fresh air. The somewhat commonplace anti-clericalism of the Lollards had become outmoded in an age of constructive criticism and renovation, and it seemed likely that the universal Church would be able to renew itself.

In the autumn of 1517 Martin Luther spoke out, lending a more fiery and dogmatic charge to the general calls for reform. He was close to Erasmus in many respects, but he quickly moved beyond him in his assertion of justification by faith alone. Faith comes as a gift from God to the individual without the interference of rituals and priests. The Church cannot, and should not, come between Christ and the aspiring soul. A person saved by the sacrifice of Christ will be granted eternal life. Grace will lift the soul to heaven. For those not saved by faith, the only destination is the everlasting fire.

In a series of pamphlets Luther attacked the beliefs and hierarchies of the orthodox faith. The pope in Rome was the Antichrist. There were only two sacraments, those of baptism and holy communion, rather than the seven adumbrated by the Church. Every good Christian man was already a priest. Grace and faith were enough for salvation. The words of Scripture should stand alone. 'I will talk no more with this animal,' Cardinal Cajetan wrote after conferring with him in 1518, 'for he has deep eyes, and wonderful speculations in his head.'

Luther had been read and discussed in Cambridge ever since the monk had nailed his ninety-five theses to the door of the castle church in Wittenberg. The White Horse tavern was nicknamed 'Germany' as the Lutheran creed was discussed within its walls, and the participants were known as 'Germans'. They were, however, an eclectic group; among them were Thomas Cranmer and William Tyndale, Nicholas Ridley and Matthew Parker. Two of them became archbishops, seven became bishops, and eight became martyrs burned at the stake. This was an exhilarating, and also a dangerous, time.

The reading of Luther deepened the instinctive beliefs of some who debated in the White Horse. The doctrine of justification by faith alone has no parallel in Wycliffe, but many of the other anti-clerical doctrines had been expressed for the previous two centuries. Never before, however, had they been shaped with such cogency and coherence. The pulpit of the little Cambridge church of St Edward, King and Martyr, became the platform from which preachers such as Thomas Bilney, Robert Barnes and Hugh Latimer proclaimed the new truths. Faith only did justify, and works did not profit. If you can only once believe that Jesus Christ shed His precious blood, and died on the cross for your sins, the same belief will be sufficient for your salvation. There was no need for priests, or bishops, or even cardinals.

In the spring of 1518, at the urgent instigation of the king, Wolsey was appointed as papal legate; he became the representative of Rome at the court of which he was already chief minister. He embodied everything that the reformers abhorred; he was the whore in scarlet. Whenever he made a submission as the pope's envoy he left the court and then ceremonially reappeared in his fresh role. Yet there was no disguising the fact that the Church and the royal council were now being guided by the same hand. The truth of the matter was not lost upon the king, who would at a later date assert his royal sovereignty over both. Wolsey taught Henry that it was possible to administer and effectively run the Church without the interference of any external power. The king would at a later date, therefore, take over the cardinal's role and in the process greatly enlarge it.

Wolsey's status as papal legate gave him additional power to reform the English Church. He began in the spring of 1519 by sending 'visitors' to various monasteries in order to record the conditions and habits of the monks, where of course they found various levels of disorder and abuse. The abbot brought his hounds into the church; the monks found solace in the tavern; the prior had been seen with the miller's wife. This had always been the small change of monastic life, and had largely become accepted as the way of the world. But Wolsey punished the principal offenders and sent out strict regulations or statutes to guide future conduct.

His severity did not of course prevent him from growing rich in his own manner with a collection of ecclesiastical posts. He was in succession bishop of Bath and Wells, bishop of Durham and bishop of Winchester; these were held in tandem with the arch-bishopric of York, and in 1521 he obtained the richest abbey of the land in St Albans. His tables groaned with gold and silver plate and the walls of his palaces were hung with the richest tapestries. Wolsey was without doubt the richest man in England – richer even than the king, whose income was curtailed by large responsi-bilities – but he always argued that his own magnificence helped to sustain the power of the Church.

At a slightly later date he suppressed some twenty-nine monas-tic houses and used their revenues to finance a school in Ipswich and a college, Cardinal's College, which he intended to build at Oxford. The obscure devotions of a few monks and nuns should not stand in the way of a great educational enterprise. He was interested in good learning as well as good governance; indeed they could not properly be distinguished. So the work of the Church continued even as it was being denounced and threatened by the 'new men', otherwise called 'gospellers' and 'known men'.

At the end of 1520 the doctrines of Luther were deemed to be heretical and his books were banned. They 'smelled of the frying pan', resting on the fires of Smithfield and of hell itself. In the spring of the following year, Wolsey in a great ceremony burned Luther's texts on a pyre set up in St Paul's Churchyard. Yet it was already too late to staunch the flow of the new doctrines. The known men were, according to Thomas More, 'busily walking' in every alehouse and tavern, where they expounded their doctrines. More was already a privy councillor and servant of the court. The supposed heretics were present at the Inns of Court where fraternal bonds could be converted to spiritual bonds. They were 'wont to resort to their readings in a chamber at midnight'. They began to congregate in the Thames Valley and in parts of Essex as well as London. In the parish church of Rickmansworth, in Hertfordshire, certain people flung the statues and the rood screen upon a fire. It was a portent of later iconoclasm in England.

Luther's books came into the country, from the ports of the Low Countries and from the cities of the Rhineland, as contraband smuggled in sacks of cloth. Yet the tracts did not only reach the disaffected. They also reached the king. On 21 April 1521 Henry was seen to be reading Luther's *De Captivitate Babylonica Ecclesiae* ('On the Babylonian Captivity of the Church') and in the following month he wrote to Pope Leo X of his determination to suppress the heresies contained in that tract. Wolsey suggested to the king that he might care to be distinguished from other European princes by showing himself to be erudite as well as orthodox. So with the help of royal servants such as More the king composed a reply to Luther entitled *Assertio Septem Sacramentorum*, 'In Defence of the Seven Sacraments'.

It was not a brilliant or enthralling work, but it served its purpose. The pope professed to be delighted by it, and conferred on Henry the title of *Fidei Defensor*, 'Defender of the Faith'. It was not supposed to be inherited, but the royal family have used it ever since. Luther composed a reply to the reply, in the course of which he denounced Henry as 'the king of lies' and a 'damnable and rotten worm'. As a result Henry was never warmly disposed towards Lutheranism and, in most respects, remained an orthodox Catholic.

The pope died two months after conferring the title upon the king, and there were some who believed that Wolsey himself might ascend to the pontificate. Yet the conclave of cardinals was never likely to elect an Englishman, and in any case Wolsey had pressing business with the Church in England alone. His visitations of the monasteries were only one aspect of his programme for clerical reform. He devised new constitutions for the secular or non-monastic clergy and imposed new statutes on the Benedictine and Augustinian monks. He guided twenty monastic elections to gain favourable results for his candidates, and dismissed four monastic heads.

In the spring of 1523 he dissolved a convocation of senior clergy at Canterbury and summoned them to Westminster, where he imposed a new system of taxation on their wealth. Bishops and archbishops would in the future be obliged to pay him a 'tribute' before they could exercise their jurisdictions. He proposed reforms in the ecclesiastical courts, too, and asserted that all matters involving wills and inheritances should be handled by him. The Church had never been so strictly administered since the days of Henry II. The fact that, in pursuit of his aims, Wolsey issued papal bulls, letters or charters sanctioned by the Vatican, served further to inflame the English bishops against him.

Yet he was protected by the shadow of the king. Wolsey was doing Henry's bidding, so that his ascendancy virtually guaranteed royal supremacy. There was no longer any antagonism between what later became known as 'Church' and 'State'; they were united in the same person. At this stage, however, the question of doctrinal reform did not arise, and Wolsey paid only nominal attention to the spread of heresy in the kingdom. He was concerned with the discipline and efficiency of the Church, and in particular with the exploitation of its wealth.

Wolsey's role as papal legate involved other duties. It was his responsibility as the pope's representative to bring peace to the Christian princes of Europe, as a preliminary to a united crusade against the Turks. In matters of diplomacy the cardinal was a master and through 1518 he continued negotiations with Maximilian of the Holy Roman Empire, Francis of France and Charles of Spain. Their representatives came to London in the autumn of that year and swore a treaty of universal peace that became known as the Treaty of London. The cardinal had engineered it, and the cardinal took the credit. There was a passing allusion to the possibility of a crusade and the pope was named only as *comes* or 'associate' in the negotiations. 'We can see,' one cardinal wrote, 'what the Holy See and the pope have to expect from the English chancellor.'

The English chancellor was in the ascendant. In the fourteen years of his authority as lord chancellor he called only one parliament. When the Venetian ambassador first arrived in the kingdom, Wolsey used to declare to him that 'His Majesty will do so and so'. The phrase then changed to 'We shall do so and so' until it finally became 'I will do so and so'. Yet he was always aware of where the real power and authority lay; he remained in charge of affairs as long as he obeyed the king's will. The achievement of the cardinal, with the Treaty of London, was also the triumph of his sovereign. The king's honour was always the most important element in foreign calculations. Henry himself seemed pleased with the accomplishment. 'We want all potentates to content themselves with their own territories,' he told the Venetian ambassador, 'and we are satisfied with this island of ours.' He wrote some verses in this period that testify to his contentment.

> The best ensue; the worst eschew;
> My mind shall be
> Virtue to use, vice refuse,
> Thus shall I use me.

Yet he was considerably less contented when, in February 1519, the Holy Roman Emperor died and was succeeded in that title by his grandson Charles of Spain. At the age of nineteen Charles was now the nominal master of Austria, Poland, Switzerland, Germany and the Low Countries as well as Spain itself; he thus decided the fate of half of Europe.

The three young kings now engaged in elaborate ceremonies

of peace that could also be construed as games of war. In the summer of 1520 Henry set sail for France in the *Great Harry*, with a retinue of 4,000, on his way to meet the king of France. He sailed in splendour, and the place of their encounter became known as the Field of Cloth of Gold. The Vale of Ardres, close to the English enclave of Calais, had been decorated with pavilions and palaces, towers and gateways, artificial lakes and bridges, statues and fountains that gushed forth beer and wine. Henry was arrayed in what was called 'fine gold in bullion', while Francis in turn was too dazzling to be looked upon. Masses were combined with jousts and feats and wrestling matches, with the celebrations lasting for seventeen days. The event was described as the eighth wonder of the world. A rich tapestry had come to life. The importance of treaties lay not in their content but in the manner of their making. They were expressions of power rather than of amity.

Yet there were secret dealings behind the arras. Even before Henry sailed to France, Charles of Spain had arrived at Dover, to be greeted by Henry himself. Charles was escorted with great ceremony to Canterbury, where he met his aunt Katherine of Aragon for the first time. Three days of dancing and feasting also included hours of negotiation. After meeting the French king at the Field of Cloth of Gold, Henry moved on to Calais, where he colluded once more with Charles. All their plans were against France. Henry himself wished once more to claim the French crown as part of his inalienable birthright.

On these same summer nights, when sovereigns slept in their pavilions of gold, the London watch was searching for 'suspected persons'. They reported that a tailor and two servants played cards and dice until four in the morning, when the game was forcibly suspended and the players mentioned to the constable. In South-wark and Stepney, in pursuit of 'vagabond and misdemeanoured persons', the watch found many 'masterless men' living in ragged tenements. Ten Germans were taken up in Southwark. An 'old drab and a young wench' were found lying upon a dirty sheet in a cellar; on the upstairs floor Hugh Lewis and Alice Ball were 'taken in bed together, not being man and wife'. Anne Southwick was questioned in the Rose tavern at Westminster on suspicion of being a whore. Carters were found sleeping against the walls of a tavern. Mowers and haymakers, makers of tile and brick, were duly noted as dwelling peaceably in the inns of the suburbs. Men and women went about their business, legal or otherwise. And so the summer passed.

4

The woes of marriage

Rumours of the king's infidelities were always in the air. His liaison with Anne Stafford was followed by others, and in the autumn of 1514 he had begun an affair of five years with Elizabeth or Bessie Blount; their trysting place was a house called Jericho in Essex. His entourage was commanded to maintain a strict silence concerning his visits, and the grooms of the privy chamber were obliged 'not to hearken or enquire where the king is or goeth'; they were forbidden to discuss 'the king's pastime' or 'his late or early going to bed'. The fruit of the union was born in 1519, and was named Henry FitzRoy or 'Henry son of the king'; he would eventually become the duke of Richmond. Elizabeth Blount was then duly rewarded with a prestigious marriage, and retained a secure place in Henry's affections.

Other young women were no doubt installed in Jericho for the king's delectation, but the next one to be named by history is Mary Boleyn. She had been conveniently married to a gentleman of the king's household, and under the cover of the court she became the king's mistress in 1520. Now she is best known as the sister of the other Boleyn girl, but her relationship with Henry lasted for approximately five years. In 1523 he named one of the new royal ships the *Mary Boleyn*, and two years later he promoted her father to the peerage as Viscount Rochford.

By this time, however, the king had become enamoured of the younger daughter. The date of his first encounter with Anne Boleyn is not known precisely, but by 1523 she had already come to the attention of Thomas Wolsey. Her attachment to Henry Percy, heir to the earldom of Northumberland, was considered to be a step too far; Percy went back to the north, and Anne was expelled from court. Wolsey's usher, George Cavendish, reports that she was so angry that 'she smoked' red-hot with rage. Only after this date, therefore, is it likely that she caught the eye of the king.

Yet he was soon enthralled by her. Her complexion was considered to be 'rather dark' but she had fine eyes and lustrous hair; her narrow oval face, high cheek-bones and small breasts would be inherited by her eminent daughter. In the early portraits she appears to be pert and vivacious, but at a slightly later date there is evidence of wariness or watchfulness. So many disparate reports exist of her character that it is impossible to form a true judgement. There can be no doubt, however, that she was resourceful and quick-witted; she could not otherwise have survived the life of the court. She loved music and danced very well. It has often been suggested that by charm and persuasion she managed to avoid intercourse with the king until she was certain of becoming his wife, but it is equally likely that Henry himself wished to make sure of a formal union that would render any children legitimate.

All this was known or suspected by Katherine of Aragon, who asked Erasmus to write a treatise entitled *De Servando Conjugio* – 'On Preserving Marriage'. She was aware of Henry FitzRoy, and was deeply offended when he was brought to court at precisely the time when it was clear that she could no longer bear children. Henry had in any case turned away from her. She was approaching the age of forty; all her early grace had faded, and the young king of France described her as 'ugly and deformed'. As a consequence, perhaps, Henry no longer frequented her bed. Most importantly she had failed in her primary duty to bear a son and heir.

Certain doubts had already entered Henry's mind. He had read the text in Leviticus that prohibited any man from marrying the widow of a dead brother. It declares that 'thou shalt not uncover the nakedness of your brother's wife; it is thy brother's nakedness', for which the penalty will be that of bearing no children. He had quoted Leviticus in his treatise against Luther, in which text he had also adverted to 'the severe and inflexible justice of God'. What if his marriage flouted divine decree? In Leviticus itself God speaks: 'I will even appoint over you terror, consumption, and the burning ague . . . and ye shall sow your seed in vain.' God had perhaps denied him a royal heir as a punishment for his sin.

In matters of succession Henry could be savage. He had already demonstrated that the wrath of the king meant death. In the event of the king's own demise Edward Stafford, third duke of Buckingham, was considered the favourite to succeed him; he was after all descended from Thomas Woodstock, one of the sons of Edward III. He was, therefore, an object of suspicion. In the spring of 1521 the king himself had interrogated the duke's servants in order to find evidence of treason. It was alleged as the principal charge that the duke had consulted with a monkish necromancer who had told him that Henry would have no male issue and that 'he should have all'. Buckingham had bought inordinate amounts of cloth of gold and cloth of silver. It was even stated by one of his servants that he had planned to come into the royal presence 'having upon him secretly a knife'. He was of course found guilty by seventeen of his peers and beheaded on Tower Green. It was widely believed at the time that Wolsey – who was known to Londoners as 'the butcher' – had engineered Buckingham's fall but Henry's overwhelming need to preserve his dynasty was the root cause of all.

He may have now rested all his hopes on his bastard son, Henry, but there was no precedent for an illegitimate heir to the throne except for the improbably distant Harold Harefoot in 1037. There was always Princess Mary, already given her own court, but there had been only one queen regnant in English history; and Matilda had in fact been known as 'lady of England'. So a proper male heir would have to be found. Already, then, Henry was contemplating the possibility of a new bride.

Mary could, in the interim, be put to other uses. At the age of two she had been promised to the son of Francis I but then, only four years later, she was formally betrothed to Charles V. What could be more fitting than to be the wife of the Holy Roman Emperor and sovereign of Spain? These were games of war, however, rather than of betrothal.

In the summer of 1521 Henry entered into a treaty with Charles against Francis I, and promised to send a great army of 30,000 foot and 10,000 horse into the French dominion. Yet the stomach for war breeds an appetite for money. That is why Wolsey was soon demanding, and obtaining, new revenues from the Church. In March 1522 he set in motion a great national inquiry to assess the wealth of each individual and the military capacity of every male; it was characteristic of his direct and inclusive style of government. The taxes raised were nominated as 'loans', but in fact they were never repaid. Two months later the earl of Surrey, with a large force of men, invaded northern France to no obvious effect. Charles sailed to England and was formally affianced to Princess Mary. On the journey upriver from Gravesend to Greenwich, the emperor's barges were perfumed with 'sweet herbs' to conceal the offensive odours of the Thames.

In the spring of the following year parliament was convened to treat of what Wolsey called 'the grand invasion of France' or, rather, to provide the funds for it. 'There has been,' a contemporary reported, 'the greatest and sorest hold in the Lower House for payment of two shillings of the pound that ever was seen, I think, in any parliament. This matter has been debated and beaten fifteen or sixteen days together . . .' The tax on the value of land was a precedent never 'seen before this time'. The Speaker of the House, Thomas More, was able by his powers of calm persuasion to pass the measure.

This was the meeting of parliament in which Thomas Cromwell first came to notice. He was already a merchant and a scrivener, a dyer of cloth and a moneylender, his various employments testifying to his skill and facility in the affairs of the world. He would soon also enter Gray's Inn as a lawyer. In his speech to his colleagues he volunteered 'to utter my poor mind'. He urged the king to stay in England and not to risk himself by campaigning in France; he also argued for caution and vigilance in maintaining the supply lines or 'victualling'. In conclusion he recommended that Scotland should be the principal target of the king's army. He used an old maxim, 'who that intendeth France to win, with Scotland let him begin'.

Cromwell was not enthusiastic about the parliamentary debates.

He wrote to a friend that 'for sixteen whole weeks wherein we communed of war, peace, strife, contention, debate, murmur, grudge, riches, poverty, penury, truth, falsehood, justice, equity, deceit, oppression, magnanimity, activity, force ... as well as we might, and left where we began'. He did admit, however, that the Commons had granted the king 'a right large subsidy, the like whereof was never granted in this realm'.

So, in the summer of 1523, the great enterprise was undertaken. Under the command of Suffolk, Henry's jousting partner, 10,000 men sailed to Calais. In girth as well as in splendour, he was a good substitute for the king. He had intended to lay siege to Boulogne and thus gain another port for England. But the king and the cardinal urged him to march upon Paris and, with the help of Charles V and other allies, destroy the heart of France. Yet war is fickle. The allies were captured, or surrounded, or fled from battle. Rain, mud and disease reduced the English forces outside Paris, and eventually they were forced to retreat.

In the vortex of this war strange mischances and collisions were destined to occur. The city states of Renaissance Italy, the true cause of the confrontation between Francis and Charles, were put at great peril; Scotland, as part of its old alliance with France, was threatening invasion with the assistance of French troops; and, with the princes of Europe fighting one another, the Turks came much closer to their goal of conquering the eastern parts of that continent. No one could see a path through the wood because, in truth, there was no path. It was a wearisome story of battles and sieges, of invasions and retreats, which left all the participants in approximately the same position as before.

Yet there was to be one more tremor of martial fervour. At the beginning of 1525 the Spanish imperial army won an overwhelming victory at the battle of Pavia, taking the French king prisoner and destroying much of his nobility. In his excitement Henry projected another grand coalition with Spain for the purpose, as he put it, 'of getting full satisfaction from France'. Charles V was disinclined to share the proceeds of victory; he was now the master of Europe, and felt less need for the support of Henry. Yet the English king continued to dream and to conspire.

He and Wolsey intended to raise money for the further cam-

paign by a forced loan that he called an 'amicable grant'. There was
nothing amicable about it. By virtue of the royal prerogative a tax
of a sixth on wealth was demanded from the laity, and a fourth
from the clergy. The people of England, however, were tired of a
war that was driven only by the desire of the king for honour and
glory. War put at risk commerce between the nations of Europe
and, by artificially raising prices on basic commodities such as meat
and drink, it disturbed the patterns of national trade and industry.
Since the soldiers of England were largely taken from the land,
their deployment severely affected agricultural prosperity. War may
have been in the interest of the king, but it was not waged to the
benefit of the country. What was the point, in any case, of invading
and conquering France? A ballad-writer wrote against Wolsey:

> By thee out of service many are constrained
> And course of merchandise thou hast restrained
> Wherefor men sigh and sob.

War was bad for business. Much foreign trade was directed
through Antwerp, where the major English export was that of
manufactured woollen cloth. The Flemish used to say that 'if Englishmen's fathers were hanged at the gates of Antwerp, their
children would creep between their legs to come into the town'.
The trade in manufactured cloth doubled in the course of Henry's
reign, thus lending power and authority to the guild of the cloth
exporters known as the Merchant Adventurers. From this period,
therefore, we can date the rise of the English merchant. Anything
that endangered or disrupted trade was deplored.

So the resistance to the tax was open and sometimes violent:
4,000 men took up arms in Suffolk, and the tax commissioners
were beaten off in Kent. The citizens of London refused to pay on
the ground that the exactions were unlawful. In Cambridge and in
Lincolnshire the people were 'looking out for a stir'. When the
duke of Norfolk asked to consult with the 'captain' of the rebels in
his own shire, he was told that 'his name is Poverty; for he and his
cousin Necessity have brought us to this doing'.

The risk of another general revolt, like that of 1381, was too
great to be contemplated. Such an uprising was about to break out
in Germany, where a hell of violence and anarchy descended upon

the land; 300,000 rebels took up arms, and 100,000 peasants died. So the king retreated. He issued a proclamation in which he denied knowing anything at all about the tax demands; he then graciously remitted them and issued pardons to the rebels. He had learned a lesson in the limitations of regal power. Yet the cardinal was considered to be more greatly at fault. There was no end, one chronicler wrote, to the 'inward grudge and hatred that the commons bore to the cardinal'. Henry knew that Wolsey had failed. This was no longer the quiet and joyful country at the time of his accession. And the cardinal, well, he was only one man.

The false stridency of the war policy was further exposed when in 1525 the cardinal began to explore the possibilities of an accord with France against the erstwhile ally of Spain. Charles was now so powerful as to become a menace. A treaty 'of perpetual peace' with France was signed in the summer, just six months after the cardinal had proposed a great war against her. Charles V demanded that he be released from his betrothal to the young Princess Mary. All was undone. All must be done again.

Henry was engaged in affairs of the heart as well as those of the battlefield. He had, in his own phrase, been 'struck with the dart of love'. A new ship was commissioned in 1526, to be named the *Anne Boleyn*. In the spring of that year the royal goldsmiths fashioned four brooches for him to bestow upon a certain lady. One was formed in the image of Venus, while another was of a lady and a heart; the third was of a man lying in a woman's lap, while the fourth showed the same woman with a crown. It was noted that in this period he was more than usually boisterous and energetic. The new-found friendship with France was the excuse for any number of revels and banquets and jousts and pageants. In the summer of 1526 Henry hunted with ferocity and passion. He wanted to win the prize.

He had begun to write letters to Anne Boleyn in French, the language of courtly romance. One eighteenth-century historian has described them as 'very ill writ, the hand is scarce legible and the French seems faulty'. Nevertheless they served their purpose. The first of them was presented with the gift of a buck that the king had killed the evening before, and soon enough another followed in which he thanked her 'right heartily, for that it pleaseth you to

still hold me in some remembrance'. This was not the conventional
letter of a king to a royal mistress.

In a subsequent letter he professes himself confused about her
feelings, 'praying you with all my heart that you will expressly tell
me your whole mind concerning the love between us'. He then
proposes that he will take her 'as his only mistress, rejecting from
thought and affection all others save yourself, to serve you only'.
Yet Anne Boleyn had already retreated to her parents' house, at
Hever in Kent, and refused to come to court. 'I could do none
other than lament me of my ill fortune,' he wrote to her, 'abating
by little and little my so great folly.' There is no doubt that he had
conceived an overpowering passion for her, and she in her turn
was doing her best to retain his affection without alienating him.
It was a difficult task, and must have brought her close to nervous
prostration.

In another letter Henry longed for their meeting which 'is on
my part the more desired than any earthly thing; for what joy
in this world can be greater than to have the company of her who
is the most dearly loved'. How do you gently refuse a great and
powerful king? She sent him a diamond, which was decorated with
an image of a lady in her ship. The lady was tossed about on the
waves, but the diamond is a symbol of an imperishable and steadfast heart.

Katherine herself was being cast aside. After the treaty with
France it was no longer necessary to appease her nephew, Charles
V. When three of her Spanish ladies complained of the dukedom
given to Henry's illegitimate son, Henry FitzRoy, they were
dismissed from court. Katherine's letters were being opened and
read by Wolsey. The cardinal, or the king, placed spies among
her entourage. Wolsey insisted that he should be present at any
interview between her and Charles's representatives. Yet the king's
displeasure was not visited upon the child, who might still become
queen of England. Mary now had her own household of more
than 300 servants; at dinner she could choose between thirty-five
courses. She hawked and hunted; she played cards and gambled
with dice.

There was, of course, always the possibility of a son. It seems
fair to assume that Henry had at first wanted Anne as a mistress

but, after the first infatuation, decided that she should be his wife. With Anne Boleyn as the prospective bride, the future of the dynasty might soon be secured. Without a son, as Henry claimed soon after, the kingdom would be overwhelmed by 'mischief and trouble'. His doubts about the union with Katherine of Aragon were undoubtedly genuine. He was not acting out of lust for Anne Boleyn alone. If he had married Katherine despite the injunction of Leviticus, to refrain from the widow of a dead brother, he might truly have been cursed. Twenty-four years before, a papal dispensation had been obtained for the union. It was his duty now to have that original dispensation declared null and void so that he could be properly married for the first time. The pope could not, and should not, waive divine law as expressed in the Bible itself. The conscience of the king was the important matter; the word appears in many of his letters as a way of justifying himself to heaven. He once declared that conscience 'is the highest and supreme court for judgement or justice'. He knew that he was right.

So, in the spring of 1527, Henry began his first attempt to have his marriage to Katherine annulled by Pope Clement VII. He told his wife that he was only exploring the questions raised by certain lawyers and theologians, at which point she wept and swore that her union with Prince Arthur had never been consummated. She knew which way the wind was blowing. In May 1527, Wolsey called the king to appear before him and the archbishop of Canterbury in order to discuss the status of the marriage. It was a piece of stage management, the king himself having already determined that the cardinal would declare the marriage null and void. Yet as papal legate Wolsey could not decide the matter without putting the case to the pope. He adjourned the proceedings and declared that he would consult more widely. This was the beginning of all the troubles that led eventually to the break with Rome.

Wolsey was not sure of the identity of the king's intended bride. He assumed that it would be a diplomatic marriage, perhaps to a female of the French royal house. Anne Boleyn seemed to him to be another court mistress. Yet now Henry went behind his back; taking advantage of Wolsey's absence on a diplomatic mission in France, he sent one of his secretaries to Rome with the draft of a papal bull allowing the king to marry another and unnamed woman with the blessing and authority of the Church. The king told his secretary that the matter would remain secret 'for any craft the cardinal or any other can find'. This is a significant reference to his chief minister, suggesting that their early intimate relations had come to an end. Henry now also began to employ scholars and divines to research all precedents, and to press his case in print. At some point in 1527 work began on collecting and collating a set of arguments for the king's divorce; Henry called it '*liber noster*' or 'our book'.

There now ensued a process of endless false starts, vain hopes, obfuscations and delays that left the king confused and demoralized. Katherine of Aragon managed to alert her nephew, Charles V, to the dangers of her situation. Charles's troops had sacked Rome in May with every form of barbarity, and the pope had become a virtual prisoner in the Castel Sant'Angelo. If the pontiff was at the mercy of Charles, what hope was there of successfully dealing with the marriage of the emperor's aunt? The matter of the divorce was now becoming part of a much larger action.

In May 1527 the young Princess Mary danced before her father at a banquet. The movement of the formal dance was always construed as an allegory, with the final curtsy seen as a gesture of 'fear, love and reverence'. In the following month, the king formally separated himself from Katherine's bed; the Spanish ambassador, no doubt informed by Katherine herself, revealed that the king 'had told her they had been living in mortal sin all the years they had been together'. She burst into tears, and Henry tried to comfort her by remarking that all would turn out for the best. He also begged her to keep the matter secret, but it was already too late. The reports of the separation soon reached the people. It was, the ambassador said, 'as notorious as if it had been proclaimed by the town crier'. The people took the side of the wronged wife, of course, and refused to believe that the king would persist in such a 'wicked' project. The queen, meanwhile, kept her place at court and sat by her husband's side on public occasions, when she smiled and seemed cheerful. 'It is wonderful to see her courage,' the duke of Norfolk said, 'nothing seems to frighten her.'

The matter of the king's marriage was being endlessly debated at Rome. Pope Clement had pleaded ignorance of the canon law to one of Wolsey's ambassadors, only to be told that the whole of canon law was locked in the bosom of his Holiness. 'It may be so,' the pope replied, 'but, alas, God has forgotten to give me the key to open it.' By the end of 1527, however, after much prevarication, he agreed that cardinals Wolsey and Campeggio would examine the facts and pass a verdict without possibility of appeal; Campeggio had been chosen because he was the second and inferior papal legate for English affairs. Wolsey at once wrote to him and asked him to hasten from Rome. 'I hope,' he told him, 'all things shall be done according to the will of God, the desire of the king, the quiet of the kingdom, and to our honour, with a good conscience.' He then crossed out the last four words. The cardinals of the Church always had a good conscience. The pope, still in thrall to Charles, had already commanded Campeggio to weave infinite delays so that no verdict on the king's marriage would ever be given. The cardinal assented, and began to make plans for a very slow progress towards England.

At the beginning of 1528 Anne Boleyn wrote to Wolsey to thank him for 'the great pains and troubles that you have taken for me both day and night'. In a second letter she stated that 'I am most bound of all creatures, next the king's grace, to love and serve your grace'. It is clear that she and Henry now intended her to be queen. Yet not all was what it seemed. Three months after his arrival in England Campeggio wrote to Rome that the cardinal 'is actually not in favour of the affair'; he 'dare not admit this openly, nor can he help to prevent it; on the contrary he has to hide his feelings and pretend to be eagerly pursuing what the king desires'.

In private conversations with Campeggio, Wolsey simply shrugged his shoulders. 'I have to satisfy the king,' he told him, 'whatever the consequences. In time a remedy will be found.' It may be that Henry was beginning to suspect Wolsey. In this period he began to show his chief minister's letters to other members of his council, among them the father of Anne Boleyn. Wolsey was falling into a trap from which he would never be able to extricate himself. There was one occasion, in 1528, when it was recorded that the king 'used terrible language' to the cardinal, leaving Wolsey unhappy and uncertain. When the cardinal named a new abbess for a certain convent, despite the protests of the king at the choice of candidate, Henry wrote him a bitter letter in reply to his excuses. 'Ah, my lord, it is a double offence both to do ill and colour it too . . . wherefore, good my lord, use no more that way with me, for there is no man living who more hates it.' The words might also be construed as a more general warning.

In the spring of 1528 the royal family spent some time together at Wolsey's house, Tyttenhanger, near St Albans. Princess Mary described it as a happy occasion. Yet in this year it was reported that the marriage between Henry and Anne Boleyn was 'certain' and that the preparations for the wedding were already being made. Wolsey wrote at this time that, if the pope did not comply with the wishes and desires of the king, 'I see ruin, infamy, and subversion of the whole dignity and estimation of the see apostolic'. In this, at least, he was proved to be right.

5

Into court

The threat to the papacy also came from other quarters. Luther's tracts, smuggled into England after he was denounced as a heretic, were followed by William Tyndale's translation of the New Testament. Tyndale was a young cleric who had become disillusioned with the pomp and power of the Church; he was ascetic and scholarly by nature, and was instinctively attracted to the purer faith associated with the Lollards and the 'new men' who were even then in small conventicles proclaiming Lutheran doctrine.

He had found no employment in London, after he migrated there from Cambridge, and had travelled to Germany in quest of a more tolerant atmosphere. It was here that he translated the Scriptures from the Greek and Hebrew originals. It was said that his passage was assisted by German merchants who were already imbued with Lutheran learning.

Once he had arrived in Wittenberg, he began his task of translating the Greek into plain and dignified English, in a language that the ploughman as well as the scholar could understand. The more orthodox clerics, however, believed that the Scriptures were too sacred to be left in the hands of the laity and that any interpretation of them should only be under clerical supervision. They also believed that the key words of the Greek were in themselves holy, and would be profaned by translation.

It was here that Tyndale most transgressed, by altering the meaning of certain important concepts. 'Congregation' was employed instead of 'church', and 'senior' instead of 'priest'; 'penance', 'charity', 'grace' and 'confession' were also silently removed. Tyndale later remarked that 'I never altered one syllable of God's word against my conscience', but it was clear enough to the authorities that his conscience was heavily influenced by the writings of Martin Luther. In effect Tyndale was exorcizing the role of the Church in spiritual matters and placing his faith in an invisible body of the faithful known only to God. He also included a translation of Luther's 'Preface to the Epistle to the Romans', and one young man, Robert Plumpton, wrote to his mother that 'if it will please you to read the introducement, you shall see marvellous things hid in it'. The English Bible came as a sensation and a revelation; its translation was an achievement beyond all the works of 'new' theology and pamphlets of anti-clerical disquisition. It hit home, as if God's truth had finally been revealed. The Bible was no longer a secret and mysterious text, from which short phrases would be muttered by priests; it was now literally an open book.

The book had been published in the free city of Worms, on the Rhine, and soon after found its way to England where it was secretly distributed. Copies were being sold for 3s 2d. This was the book that the bishop of London described as 'pestiferous and pernicious poison' and, in the winter of 1526, it was solemnly burnt in St Paul's Churchyard. For the first time in London the Scriptures were consigned to the fire. The prelates would have burnt Tyndale, too, if they could have caught him. The bishop of London bought and burned the entire edition on sale in Antwerp, the principal source of supply, only to discover that he had merely put money in the pockets of the printers and stimulated them to publish another edition.

There were little groups in Coleman Street, Hosier Lane and Honey Lane of London who eagerly took up the new translation, some among them bold enough to proclaim their beliefs. The reformers, known sometimes as 'gospellers', took advantage of the printing press to issue texts, pamphlets and treatises on religious reform. In his role as a royal councillor Thomas More led a raid against the Hanseatic merchants who were lodged in a building known as the Steelyard. 'There is no need to be alarmed at our coming here,' he told the merchants as they were just sitting down for dinner. 'We have been sent by the council and by his grace the lord cardinal.' He went on to say that 'we have received reliable news that many of your number possess books by Martin Luther'. He even accused some of importing those books. Three merchants were immediately arrested, and eight others brought before Wolsey.

In the early weeks of 1526 Robert Barnes had been accused of preaching heresy after he had openly denounced the pomp and wealth of the Church from the pulpit of St Edward's Church in Cambridge. He was brought before the cardinal.

> *Wolsey:* Were it better for me, being in the honour and dignity that I am, to coin my pillars and pole axes and to give the money to five or six beggars, than for to maintain the commonwealth for them as I do? Do you not reckon the commonwealth better than five or six beggars?
>
> *Barnes:* The coining might be for the salvation of your grace's soul and as for the commonwealth, as your grace knew, the commonwealth was before your grace and must be when your grace is gone. I only damned in my sermon the gorgeous pomp and pride of all exterior ornaments.
>
> *Wolsey:* Well, you say very well.

When he was told that the man was 'reformable', the cardinal promised 'to be good unto him'. In a subsequent letter to the king, Barnes characterized himself as a 'poor simple worm and not able to kill a cat'. Yet he also declared that 'there are certain men like conditioned to dogs; if there be any man that is not their countryman, or that they love not, or know not, say anything against them, then cry they: an heretic, an heretic, to the fire, to the fire. These be the dogs that fear true preachers.' Barnes did not go to the fire. He was brought to St Paul's on 11 February, and forced to kneel in the aisle. On a platform in front of him sat the cardinal, on a throne of gold, flanked by eighteen bishops and eighteen abbots and priors. Faggots had been tied to his back, the wood as a symbol of the flames around the stake. In the autumn of that year, provoked by the wide circulation of Tyndale's New

Testament, the bishop of London issued another formal warning against the reading of heretical books.

There is an interesting sequel to the interrogation of Barnes. He was placed under a form of 'house arrest' in a monastery in Northampton, where a friend devised a plan for his escape. Barnes wrote a letter to the cardinal in which he declared that he was so desperate that he was going to drown himself; he named the place, and then deposited a pile of clothes by the river bank. He also left another letter to the mayor of Northampton, asking him to search the river; he said that he had written a private letter to the cardinal that was tied with wax around his neck. The search was duly undertaken and, despite the absence of a body, the welcome news that a heretic had killed himself out of despair was published abroad. Yet Barnes had disguised himself as a 'poor man', travelled secretly to London, and then taken ship to the Low Countries where he composed two tracts under the name of Antonius Anglus.

The 'known men' were becoming of serious concern to those, like Thomas More, who were certain of the perils of their teaching. In the autumn of 1527 a Cambridge scholar, Thomas Bilney, preached against the cults surrounding certain images of the Virgin and of the saints; they were nothing but stocks and stones. Twice he was pulled from his pulpit by an irate congregation. Yet he persisted in his attacks upon what he called idolatry and 'vain worship'. 'Saints in heaven need no light,' he said, 'and the images have no eyes to see.' He was brought before the bishop of London, and made a formal recantation. Yet that was not the end of the matter. He reverted to his earlier unorthodox beliefs, and was eventually burned in the Lollards' Pit outside Norwich. 'Little Bilney', as he was called, became an early Protestant martyr.

Another presumed heretic from Cambridge, George Joye, was called before Wolsey. He was asked to attend 'the chamber of presence' for questioning, but he had never before heard the phrase. 'I was half ashamed to ask after it, and went into a long entry on the left hand, and at last happened upon a door, and knocked, and opened it; and when I looked in, it was the kitchen. Then I went back into the hall and asked for the chamber of presence: and one pointed me up a pair of stairs.' It is trifling, perhaps, but it suggests the fear and trembling that would descend upon one not used to court or to interrogation.

Within three months of Bilney's trial the Church began a concerted effort to discover and apprehend the heretics. The houses of suspected merchants were searched. Close inquiries were made among leather-sellers and tailors, shoemakers and printers. An Oxford scholar, Thomas Garrett, was taken for questioning by the university authorities. He told a friend that he was now 'undone'. His principal interrogator, Dr London, was described as 'puffing, blustering and blowing, like an hungry and greedy lion seeking his prey'. Garrett managed to escape, no one knew whither. So Dr London consulted an astrologer who told him that he had 'fled in a tawny coat south-eastward'. In fact, when he was finally captured at Bedminster on the south bank of the Avon, he was dressed 'in a courtier's coat and buttoned cap'.

As a result of Garrett's evidence the rooms of other scholars were searched and over 100 banned books discovered. Six Oxford men were imprisoned for some months in the fish cellar of Cardinal College, Wolsey's own creation, where it is reported that three of them died. It is significant that all of these 'new named brethren', as More called them, came from the universities; they were a small elite fraternity, but the authorities were afraid that their questions and their opinions might filter through the general population. They were nevertheless a minority, and their beliefs might not have strayed very far beyond the walls of their colleges. It would take the catalyst of the king's divorce, the 'great matter', to quicken the process of religious reform.

Cardinal Campeggio, appointed by the pope to consider the case, made his weary and painful journey to England in the summer of 1528; he suffered from gout, and needed many halts along the way. He was awaited with impatience and, as soon as he was lodged at Bath House in London, Wolsey came to importune him. 'They will endure no procrastination,' Campeggio told Rome, 'alleging that the affairs of the kingdom are at a standstill, and that if the cause remains undetermined it will give rise to infinite and imminent perils.' Unfortunately he was under instruction to delay at all costs.

Soon enough he was granted an audience with the king at the palace of Blackfriars, where the cardinal advised him 'against attempting this matter'; if necessary the pope would grant Henry a fresh dispensation to unite himself with Katherine. The king listened patiently and then gave what Campeggio described as a 'premeditated' answer on the total invalidity of the marriage. It was clear that he was not about to be moved. Then Campeggio offered the suggestion that Katherine should enter a religious house; if she were wedded to God, then Henry would be free to remarry.

So Campeggio and Wolsey visited the queen who, after much reflection, rejected the idea. 'I intend,' she told them, 'to live and die in the state of matrimony, to which God has called me. I will always remain of this opinion, and will never change it.' Her dignity and self-possession, in the face of intolerable pressure, were remarkable. In this impasse Rome repeated its instructions that nothing should be said or done 'without a new and express commission from this place'.

The threat to Katherine took a more definite form. It was alleged in the king's council that a plot, to poison the king and the cardinal, had been discovered; a letter was sent to her on the subject 'in which if she had any hand, she must not expect to be spared'. It was a crude attempt to subdue her, but it did not succeed. The council also complained that 'she showed herself much abroad, and by civilities, and by gracious bowing her head, which had not been her custom formerly, did study to work upon the people'. But the crowds of London were already supporting her. Wolsey ordered a search to be made for hackbuts and cross-bows, the material of insurrection. The situation had reached a point of crisis, not at all helped by the sudden discovery of what became known as 'the Spanish brief'; this was another papal dispensation, permitting the marriage of Katherine and Henry.

As the weeks of autumn and winter passed without any progress, Anne Boleyn and Henry became increasingly angry and impatient. The king was besotted by her; he lodged her in the palace at Greenwich and lavished jewels and other presents on her. 'He sees nothing,' Campeggio told Rome, 'he thinks of nothing but Anne.' In their irritation and anxiety they turned their fire upon the cardinal. In turn Wolsey berated Campeggio with the threat that, if nothing were done, such a storm would burst that 'it were better to die than to live'. One of the king's envoys, Stephen Gardiner, knelt before the pope. 'You who should be as simple as doves,' he said in a remarkable act of impropriety, 'are full of all deceits, and craft, and dissembling.' The pope had informed Henry that he could not act without hearing the arguments of both sides, and in the spring of 1529 Sir Francis Bryan, a cousin of Anne Boleyn, wrote from Rome that 'who so ever hath made your grace believe that he would do for you in this cause hath not, I think, done your grace the best service'. He was clearly alluding to the cardinal. Wolsey himself was saying to his confidential servants that he would pursue the matter as far as he could, and then retire voluntarily in order to devote himself to spiritual affairs. He knew well enough, in any case, that his end might be approaching.

On the last day of May 1529, the legatine court under the direction of Wolsey and Campeggio was convened in the parliament chamber at Blackfriars; the king and queen were staying at the palace of Bridewell, close by, and crossed a wooden bridge over the Fleet river to attend the court. They were both summoned to appear on Friday 18 June, but two days before that date Katherine asked to meet the archbishop of Canterbury and eight bishops; she protested against the whole notion of a trial and told them that she wished to refer the matter to Rome. This would ensure an endless process of debate and questioning. She also delivered a formal protest to the two cardinals at Blackfriars, declaring that they were incompetent judges.

On the day appointed the king and queen came to the legatine court, where Henry took his seat under a cloth of state. Campeggio then delivered an oration on the 'intolerable' matter of 'adultery, or rather incest' that they must now adjudicate.

'King Harry of England, come into the court!'

'Here,' he replied.

'Katherine queen of England, come into the court!'

She rose without replying and, leaving her small circle of advisers and lawyers, she went over to the king; she knelt at his feet and spoke to him so that all could hear her. 'I am a poor woman, and a stranger in your dominions, where I cannot expect good counsel or indifferent judges. I have been long your wife, and I desire to know wherein I have offended you.' She then pleaded her virginity when she met him, and the fact that she had borne him several children (only one of which, of course, had lived). 'If I have done anything amiss, I am willing to be put away in shame.' She spoke a little more, saying that no lawyer in England would, or could, speak freely for her. 'I desire to be excused until I hear from Spain.' With that she rose, and made a low curtsy to the king before leaving the court. The cardinals called after her but she made no answer.

The king then spoke to those assembled, stating that she had always been a true and obedient wife. Wolsey rose and denied the reports that he had been the first mover in the matter of the divorce. The king vindicated him and declared that his own scruples of conscience had prompted him. If his marriage were found to be lawful, he would be happy to continue living with the queen. Few in the court believed him.

In succeeding days a number of witnesses were called, the principal among them testifying that Katherine and Prince Arthur had consummated the marriage after their wedding. On leaving the bedroom on the following morning, Arthur had been heard to say that 'I have been in Spain all night'. One of Katherine's supporters, John Fisher, the bishop of Rochester, protested against 'things detestable to be heard'; Wolsey rebuked him and sharp words were exchanged between them.

Charles V sent an envoy to Rome, saying that a verdict against his aunt would be a great dishonour to his family. He insisted that the matter be 'avocated' or recalled to Rome, where a more fair investigation would be held; he had also given an undertaking that the pope's immediate family would be established as the rulers of Florence. An agent for Wolsey, Dr Bennet, threw himself at the feet of the pope and declared, in tears, that then 'the king and kingdom of England will be certainly lost'. It was unthinkable that his master would appear at a Roman court as a suppliant. Pope Clement wept, and begged for death. On 9 July he called the English ambassadors and told them that the hearing had been recalled to Rome. 'I am between the hammer and forge,' he said. 'It is impossible to refuse what the emperor now demands, whose forces so surround me.'

Meanwhile Campeggio had been drawing out the process of judgment with a series of delays and procedural questions. By Friday 23 July, it seemed that the end was in sight. But on that day Campeggio adjourned the proceedings until October, on the pretence that he must follow the Roman system of justice. He hoped that a favourable verdict might then be announced. The duke of Suffolk was among those who loudly announced their discontent. 'By the Mass,' he said, 'I see now the truth of what is commonly said, that never cardinal yet did good in England!' A few days later the letter from the pope, declaring that the court had been recalled to Rome, arrived for the king. The failure of the legatine court to deliver a favourable verdict to Henry was the decisive moment in Wolsey's career. It is clear enough that he was no longer conducting the affairs of the realm; his last warrant for a royal payment was signed on 18 July, and his last letter to any English envoys was sent on 27 July. He had not yet been dismissed, but the shadow had fallen upon him. Anne Boleyn wrote to him an angry letter, in which she accused him of secretly supporting Katherine's cause; she now relied only on heaven and the king 'to set right again those plans which you have broken and spoiled'. One of the attendants at a royal banquet heard a conversation between Anne and the king which he later reported to the cardinal's usher. 'There is never a nobleman within this realm,' she said, 'that if he had done but half so much as he has done, but he were well worthy to lose his head.'

A book was prepared in which the failures of the cardinal's administration were outlined; this account of pride and waste and folly was signed by thirty-four of the royal council. The French ambassador was sure of their real intentions. 'These lords', he wrote, 'intend after Wolsey is dead or ruined, to impeach the state of the Church, and take all their goods.'

Henry was not sure how to proceed after the failure of his attempt to procure a favourable court verdict, and so he gathered together a team of scholars and clerics in pursuit of his 'great matter'. Among these was Thomas Cranmer. The young reader of divinity at Cambridge suggested that the king could avoid long and fruitless negotiations at Rome by appealing directly to the scholars and universities of Europe; if they declared in his favour, the pope would be obliged to act. As soon as he was informed of Cranmer's plan the king declared that the cleric 'had the sow by the right ear'. In time Cranmer became the man to guide the English Reformation.

The king's envoys visited the universities of Europe in order to gain the opinions of eminent canonists on the prohibitions of Leviticus against marrying a brother's widow. Some of them could be persuaded by the liberal use of bribes to declare in his favour, but others proved recalcitrant. It was not a wholly successful enterprise. Paris and Bologna, together with six other universities, supported his position. But the divines of Padua, Ferrara and Venice were against him. Poitiers and Salamanca also favoured Katherine. When it was rumoured that even the doctors and proctors of Oxford were opposed, the king wrote a harsh letter to them from Windsor that ended with the words *'non est bonum irritare crabrones'*, 'It is not good to stir a hornets' nest'. The king also arranged for a sympathetic letter, signed by all the peers and prelates of England, to be dispatched to the pontiff. He had not yet decided to defy the pope and was still willing to persuade him.

By the early autumn of 1529 it was clear to all observers that the time of Wolsey had come to an end. He was no longer one of the king's confidential councillors, and Henry had been alerted to secret correspondence between Wolsey and the pope. Wolsey's usher reported that, on one of the last occasions the cardinal was at court, the king took out a letter and was overheard asking him 'how can that be: is not this in your own hand?' The nature of the letter is not known, yet it must have contained something to the cardinal's disadvantage.

On 9 October the first formal charges were laid against Wolsey. He was accused of *praemunire*, or of placing the interests of the pope before those of the king. Since he had become papal legate at Henry's urgent instigation, this was not the principal issue. The king was attacking the pretensions of the pope as well as the supposed malfeasance of the cardinal. When the writ was issued against Wolsey, it was decreed that all of his lands and goods were also forfeited to the Crown. His days of glory had come to an end. The cardinal then wrote to Henry pleading for 'grace, mercy, remission and pardon'. The French ambassador visited him and found him scarcely able to speak. His countenance 'has lost half of its life'.

Two weeks after Wolsey's dismissal the king was pleased to invite Thomas More to become the new chancellor. Since More was known to be an avid hunter of heretics, it was evident proof that Henry did not wish to disavow the orthodox Church. In fact More started his pursuit within a month of taking his position; he arrested a citizen of London, Thomas Phillips, on suspicion of heresy. Phillips was interrogated many times and yet refused to admit any guilt; More consigned him to prison, where he remained for three years. It was the beginning of the new chancellor's campaign of terror against the 'known men'.

Yet ambiguous words were still coming from the king himself. Even as he was working to obtain papal consent for his separation from Katherine, he was reflecting upon the alternatives. In a heated argument with the queen he had declared that if the pope did not judge the marriage to be null and void, he 'would denounce the pope as a heretic and marry whom he pleased'. He told the imperial ambassador that Luther had been right to attack the pomp and circumstance of the Church. Yet he saw no certain way forward, and had no grand strategy for religious reformation. He was in any case perplexed and anxious after the uncertain ending of the legatine court. It was reported that he was suffering from insomnia, and was ill in bed 'in consequence of the grief and anger he had lately gone through'. He spent four hours closeted with the French ambassador, talking over the options and perils that faced him.

Nevertheless Henry now took over the direction and administration of the country. He would never again allow any one minister to determine policy in the manner of Wolsey. Eleven days after the cardinal's dismissal the king applied the Great Seal, the sign and symbol of royal power, to certain documents in an inner chamber at Windsor; it was a ceremonial occasion, and was duly recorded as such. He gathered a new inner group around him, among them the dukes of Norfolk and of Suffolk. Even the lord chancellor was a layman, thus breaking an ancient precedent.

One other member of the administration was recruited. Thomas Cromwell had been previously in the service of Wolsey, particularly in the work of dissolving smaller monasteries and nunneries. On his master's fall he was seen weeping, with a book of prayers to the Virgin in his hand; yet he inveigled himself into the king's good grace and was nominated for a place in parliament. Soon enough his talent and self-assurance helped him to rise, in a career that has been compared to that of a grand vizier in an eastern despotism, and he became successively royal councillor, master of the king's jewels, chancellor of the exchequer for life, master of the rolls and secretary of state. Yet he never repudiated his old patron and when granted his own coat-of-arms he adopted Wolsey's device of the Cornish chough.

It had been intimated to the cardinal that he should retire to a small episcopal palace in Esher and, as he rode there on his mule, a messenger came from the king bearing with him a ring and a letter. Henry had written to tell him that he need not despair and that he could at any time be raised higher than before. The cardinal alighted from his mule and knelt down on the earth in prayer. The motives of the king are not immediately apparent. It was said at the time that there was a mystery or secrecy about royalty that no observer should attempt to penetrate. Yet it may be that Henry wished to test the success of his new council before irrevocably destroying the cardinal.

A parliament was summoned at the beginning of November as a way of informing the nation of the king's will. The members of the Commons, in large part lawyers and country gentlemen, were quite at ease with the royal prerogative; their role was to register the king's decrees and to shield him from blame for unpopular measures. When Thomas Cromwell was first nominated as a member of parliament he was told to consult with the duke of Norfolk 'to know the king's pleasure how you shall order yourself in the parliament house'. The Speaker was a royal official whose salary was paid by the king and, as Edward Hall states in his *Chronicle*, 'the most part of the Commons were the king's servants'.

The parliament of 1529 was no different from its predecessors. The king sat upon his throne while the lord chancellor, Thomas More, standing at his right hand, delivered an oration on the causes for its summons. He adverted to Wolsey as 'the great wether [a castrated ram] which is of late fallen'. The members of the Commons soon showed their loyalty with an Act 'to release the king from repayment of the loans he borrowed'. When one member opposed the measure the king wondered aloud whether he was 'on my side'. The parliament passed bills on the rearing of calves and the price of woollen hats beyond the sea, but its attention was largely trained on the economic exactions of the Church. It was riding in the wake of the anti-clerical anger released at the fall of Wolsey. A general petition was drawn up in which the vices and corruptions of the clergy were denounced in strident terms as the fruit of the seven deadly sins; the 'ordinaries' or secular clergy were vicious and ravenous and insatiable and idle and cruel.

The clamour was then given the shape of formal bills against the payments demanded by clerics for proving wills and for funerals; the clergy were also to be prohibited from holding any land on lease and from engaging in trade. It is quite clear that the royal council had inspired, if not exactly orchestrated, these complaints. It was another way of striking at the pope by reminding him that parliament would always uphold the wishes of the king. He had his people behind him. It is characteristic of the early reform of religion in England, however, that it should begin with pragmatic and financial concerns. The English instinct has always been towards practice rather than theory.

When their bills were sent to the upper house John Fisher, the bishop of Rochester, complained that the Commons were trying to destroy the Church and that they acted 'for lack of faith'; when the Commons complained to the king, Fisher was obliged to withdraw his remarks. It was generally believed, however, that the bishops of England were too eager to defend the financial abuses that had been condemned. When they claimed that their practices were based on prescription and custom, a lawyer from Gray's Inn remarked: 'The usage hath ever been of thieves to rob on Shooter's Hill, *ergo*, is it lawful?' The hunt had begun.

In the autumn of this year Anne Boleyn gave to her royal

master a copy of a pamphlet that had recently been issued. It has been argued that Anne was a Lutheran in all but name, but it may be that she simply wished to advise Henry on a possible extension of his powers and of his income. Simon Fish's *A Supplication for the Beggars* was an anti-clerical manifesto in which the author directly addresses the king on the scandalous practices of the 'ravenous wolves' of the clergy who are devouring his kingdom. From the bishop to the summoner, this 'idle ravenous sort . . . have gotten into their hands more than the third part of all your realm'. They had also debauched 100,000 women. What was the remedy? Make laws against them. Fish added that 'this is the great scab, why they will not let the New Testament go abroad in your mother tongue'. It is reported that Henry 'kept the book in his bosom three or four days', and he is likely to have agreed with much of its contents. The bishop of Norwich wrote in alarm to the archbishop of Canterbury that 'wheresoever they go, they hear say that the king's pleasure is, the New Testament in English should go forth, and men should have it and read it'. Did not Anne Boleyn have a French translation of the New Testament?

Throughout the autumn and winter of 1529 the king's team of scholars were busily investigating volumes of forgotten lore in order to find precedents for Henry's separation from Katherine. But in the course of their work Cranmer and others came upon, or were invited to consider, material that might entirely change the relations between king and pope. In an ancient book entitled *Leges Anglorum* they discovered that in AD 187 a certain Lucius I became the first Christian king of England; Lucius had asked the pope to entrust him with Roman law, whereupon the pope had replied that the king did not need any Roman intervention because 'you are vicar of God in your realm'. This of course was highly significant in the charged atmosphere of the time. By invoking ancient precedent Henry might be able to claim spiritual suprem- acy as well as secular power. The canons of various Church councils were scrutinized to elicit the opinions that no bishop could assume the title of 'universal bishop' and that no see need defer to the authority of Rome. The papers were eventually given the title of *Collectanea satis copiosa*, or a 'large enough collection'.

The document was given to Henry in the summer of 1530 and

he examined it very carefully; he made notes on forty-six separate points. In a conversation with an envoy from the king of France he declared that the pope was an ignorant man and not fit to be any kind of universal pastor. Henry was also well informed about the anti-clerical works coming out of Antwerp and Hamburg. After he had read William Tyndale's *The Obedience of a Christian Man*, in which it is argued that the king's authority should be extended over ecclesiastic affairs, he is reported to have said that 'this is the book for me and all kings to read'.

In that summer the king's ambassadors in Rome declared to the pope that no Englishman could be cited in a foreign court. When Anne Boleyn's father, the earl of Wiltshire, came as an envoy before the pontiff he refused to kiss the pope's foot even though it was graciously stretched out to him. In this year Henry himself wrote to the pope expostulating with him for using ignorant counsellors. 'This truly is a default, and verily a great fault, worthy to be alienate and abhorred of Christ's vicar, in that you have dealt so variably, yes rather so inconstantly and deceivably.' He went on to declare that 'never was there any prince so handled by a pope as your holiness has treated us'. The question at the English court now concerned the best path by which to advance.

The last days of Wolsey were at hand. He was harried north, to his archbishopric of York. The duke of Norfolk advised Thomas Cromwell to 'tell him if he go not away shortly, but shall tarry, I shall tear him with my teeth'. When he was informed that his proposed school at Ipswich was being deferred, and that the construction of Cardinal College in Oxford had been diverted for the king's purposes, the cardinal told Cromwell that 'I cannot write more for weeping and for sorrow'. Yet he still asserted his own power. He set the date for his enthronement as archbishop of York and wrote to the king asking for his mitre and pall. Henry then spoke aloud of his 'brazen insolence'. 'Is there still arrogance in this fellow,' he asked, 'who is so obviously ruined?' On 4 November, three days before the planned enthronement, Wolsey was arrested. It was alleged that he had engaged in secret correspondence with the pope and with the French and Spanish sovereigns. There may have been some truth in this, since in his extremity he had sought assistance wherever he could find it, but it is most unlikely that he had committed treason. It is also possible that he was trying to promote the cause of Katherine and to hinder that of the woman whom he called 'the night crow'.

After his arrest he was taken south at a slow pace, stopping at the abbeys and monastic houses along his route. His once sturdy constitution was by now fatally undermined, and on his journey he was attacked by a violent case of dysentery. It was said to have been brought on by a surfeit of Warden pears, but there were other reasons for his dissolution. The keeper of the Tower, Sir William Kingston, was ordered to meet Wolsey at Sheffield; his destination was now in sight. When Wolsey heard of Kingston's arrival, he clapped his hand on his thigh and gave a great sigh. His gentleman usher tried to put the best interpretation on the events, saying that Kingston had come to conduct the cardinal into the presence of the king. The cardinal was not convinced. 'I perceive,' he said, 'more than you can imagine or can know. Experience of old has taught me.'

Kingston was then introduced to the prelate and knelt before him. 'I pray you, stand up,' Wolsey said, 'kneel not unto a very wretch, replete with misery, not worthy to be esteemed, as a vile object, utterly cast away.' Kingston also tried to reassure him, but the cardinal was not to be comforted. 'I know', he said, 'what is provided for me.' He knew that it would be a traitor's death, with beheading as the best fate he could expect. His dysentery became more violent still, and by the time he reached Leicester Abbey most of his strength had gone. 'Father Abbot,' he said on his arrival, 'I am come hither to leave my bones among you.' He was laid in a bed, where he waited for his end. He spoke of the king. 'He is a prince of royal courage, and has a princely heart; and rather than he will miss or want part of his appetite he will hazard the loss of one half of his kingdom.' At the stroke of eight in the evening, Wolsey lost consciousness and died. He still lies buried somewhere within the ruins of Leicester Abbey, and a monument stands on the supposed site of his grave. Yet this was more than the passing of an individual life. The fall of Wolsey was intimately associated with the demise of the Church.

6

Old authentic histories

Henry had determined to act on behalf of what he called 'entire Englishmen' against 'Englishmen papisticate'. In the early autumn of 1530 he claimed that fourteen senior clerics, among them eight bishops and three abbots, were guilty of *praemunire*; they were accused of colluding with Wolsey in his role as papal legate. Only days after the death of the cardinal, the same 'information' was filed against all of the clergy of England; they were charged with the offence because they had administered canon law or Roman law in the ecclesiastical courts, a crime which of course they had been committing for many centuries. The Spanish ambassador reported that the bishops and abbots were 'terrified'. No one understood the workings of this new-found principle, and its interpretation was widely believed to reside only in the king's head. Parliament was recalled at the beginning of 1531, and at the same time the convocation of the clergy was transferred from St Paul's to Westminster. Both bodies would be under the king's thumb.

In this atmosphere of fear and threat it was learned that the king would graciously accept a large sum of money to allay the offences of the clergy. In effect they were being forced to pay a subsidy. The province of Canterbury duly obliged by offering £100,000 but the offer was accompanied by a series of conditions. The bishops and abbots asked for a clear definition of *praemunire*, in case of future difficulties, and demanded that the Church itself be confirmed in all its ancient privileges as stated in Magna Carta. These proposals seem to have infuriated the king, who did not wish to bargain with his subjects. The invocation of Magna Carta also posed a threat to any unilateral action he might wish to take on religious matters.

So he attacked. In February 1531 he sent five articles to be added to the proposal on the clerical subsidy. In the first of them he called upon convocation to recognize him as 'sole protector and supreme head of the English church and clergy'. This was the fruit of his reading the ancient sources, suggested to him by Cranmer and others, where the supreme leadership of the Church in England was first bestowed upon King Lucius. In the second article the king proposed the theory that it was he who truly had the 'cura animarum' or 'cure of the souls' of his subjects. No king had ever proposed such sweeping powers; no king had ever presumed so much.

Consternation ensued among the leaders of the clergy. They may not have had the opportunity of reading *Leges Anglorum*, as well as the other sources made available to the king, and so Henry's assumption of sovereignty over the Church was an extraordinary and almost unthinkable innovation. He wished to replace the papacy that had governed the Church for more than a thousand years. And what did he mean by the 'cure' or 'care' of souls? That was the office of a priest duly ordained.

They were also aware that there would be some intimate connection with the king's wish to separate himself from Katherine. Of this, too, they could know nothing certain. They could only look on with trepidation. The country, and the capital, were deeply divided on the 'great matter'. When a minister of the church of Austin Friars in London asked for prayers to be said on behalf of Anne Boleyn, 'queen', most of the congregation rose from their seats and walked out. It was said that the women of the country took the queen's part – all of them, that is, except for Anne Boleyn. The Spanish ambassador wrote that 'the Lady Anne is braver than a lion ... She said to one of the queen's ladies that she wished all Spaniards were in the sea. The lady told her such language was disrespectful to her mistress. She said she cared nothing for the queen, and would rather see her hang than acknowledge her as her mistress.'

Agonized debate now took place among the members of the convocation, torn between their duties to the pope and their loyalty to the king. They also knew that it would be dangerous, and even fatal, to incur the wrath of the sovereign. Yet under the nominal leadership of John Fisher, the bishop of Rochester, who had already spoken out on behalf of the queen, they tried to withstand the pressure of the king. In this period Fisher was under severe threat from person or persons unknown. A gun was fired at his episcopal palace beside the Thames, and the shot seemed to have come from the house of the earl of Wiltshire on the other side of the water; the earl of Wiltshire was of course the father of Anne Boleyn. One of Fisher's early biographers says that the bishop decided to return to Rochester at the earliest opportunity.

Another odd event increased his alarm. A porridge had been prepared for the bishop's household, of which several of his servants had partaken. Fisher himself had not been hungry and had not tasted it. In the event one servant, and a poor woman fed out of charity, died; many others became ill. The porridge had been poisoned by the cook, who confessed that he had added laxatives to the food; but he insisted that it was simply a joke, or prank, that had misfired. The king's reaction was ferocious. He determined that an Act should be passed through parliament rendering murder by poisoning an act of treason, for which the penalty was to be boiled alive. The cook was duly placed in a boiling cauldron at Smithfield. Some at court whispered that Anne Boleyn, or one of her supporters, had persuaded him to commit the crime. Henry may have acted with sudden ferocity in order to remove any such suspicions.

The king's own advisers were uncertain about the full consequences of his demands upon the convocation, and they were divided into what might be called radical and conservative factions. The Boleyns wished to press forward very quickly. If the king were head of the Church, the pope's opinion on the matter of the separation would be of no consequence; the marriage with Anne could be duly solemnized. Others feared that a papal interdict, or excommunication of the nation, might bring war with Spain and a general disruption of trade with the Catholic powers of Europe. The king himself was not clear about his future strategy; he was proceeding by degrees, testing his ground with every step.

That is why he came to an agreement with the convocation that seemed to take away the spirit of their submission. After much debate, and much consultation between the archbishop of Canterbury and the king, it was agreed that Henry would be the supreme head of the Church in England *'quantum per Christi legem licet'* – 'so far as the law of Christ allows'. Some sources render it as *'Dei legem'*, 'the law of God', but the purport is the same. When this proposal was put to the convocation, a general silence followed. 'Whoever is silent,' the archbishop told them, 'seems to consent.' A voice called out that 'then we are all silent'. So the proposal was agreed. It was one of the defining moments in the reformation of the Church and opened a schism that has lasted ever since. It also threw into doubt the concept of a united Christendom. The Turks, then pressing down upon the eastern borders of Europe, might have taken comfort from that fact.

Yet the phrase invoking Christ's law was open to manifold interpretations, and in extreme form might be thought to cancel any spiritual sovereignty that the king claimed. It was not at all clear whether Henry had decided finally to supplant the papacy; he had, as it were, issued a warning to Rome. In any future confrontation, the clergy of England would be bound to him. As everyone knew, no one would in practice be able to defy his authority. Now that he had been granted the money from the clergy, however, he seemed disinclined to pursue the matter – for the time being, at least.

Henry had withdrawn further into a private set of rooms that were known as the 'privy chamber', the 'privy lodgings' and the 'secret lodgings' at his palace in Whitehall, and in Hampton Court. He had now also withdrawn himself from Katherine. She wrote to her nephew that her life was 'now so shattered by misfortune that no human creature among Christians ever suffered so intense an agony'. Her agony materially affected her daughter, Princess Mary, who in the spring of 1531 fell ill for three weeks with some kind of stomach disorder; her physicians diagnosed it as 'hysteria', by which they meant a fault within the womb. When Katherine asked permission to visit her, the king suggested that she should stay with her permanently. At the end of May a delegation from the privy council was dispatched to her, imploring her to be 'sensible' in the matter of the separation. She turned upon them with all the fervour of an unjustly maligned woman. 'I am his true wife,' she told them. 'Go to Rome and argue with others than a lone woman!'

Two months later he formally renounced her. In midsummer she accompanied Henry to Windsor, but then without warning he rode to Woodstock after ordering her to stay where she was. Having received an indignant letter from her, he replied in some-what abusive terms. She had subjected him to the indignity of a citation to Rome. She had turned down the advice of his counsel-lors. He wanted no more letters. She was removed to the More, a large house in Hertfordshire that had previously belonged to the cardinal; then she was dispatched to Ampthill Castle in Bedford-shire. Her large court remained with her, and she was inevitably seen as the central figure for those opposed to the Boleyns and to the radical religious strategy they pursued. The queen herself became more strict in her observances. She rose at midnight to attend Mass; she confessed and fasted twice a week; she read only works of devotion and beneath her court dress she wore the habit of the third order of St Francis.

A marked signal of the popular mood emerged in the winter of this year. On 24 November Anne had gone with a few others to dine at a friend's house beside the Thames. The word of her arrival soon spread through the city, and a mob of 7,000 or 8,000 women (or, perhaps, men dressed as women) descended upon the location with the intention of frightening her or seizing her. Fortunately she heard the rumour of their approach and left quickly by means of the river. The king ordered that the whole incident should remain unreported, but the Venetian ambassador had already recorded the event.

The animus against Anne grew. She was commonly known as the 'goggle-eyed whore', and the abbot of Whitby was arrested and prosecuted for calling her 'a common stewed whore'. General excitement and contention arose in the parishes of the kingdom, as the people debated every aspect of the king's 'great matter' in respect of the separation from Katherine and the supremacy of the pope. It is reported that the air was filled with wild rumour and speculation, with talk of witches and devils and stories of saints and apparitions. Thomas Cranmer himself saw a portent in the sky. He observed a blue cross above the moon, together with a horse's head and a flaming sword. 'What strange things do signify to come hereafter,' he wrote, 'God alone knows.'

In the winter of 1531 a young woman appeared in the role of an inspired prophet forecasting doom. Elizabeth Barton was a young serving girl from Kent who worked in the household of a steward for the archbishop of Canterbury. She had previously been invaded by an unknown ailment and, after some months of suffering, began to fall into clairvoyant trances in which 'she spoke words of marvellous holiness'. Her reputation began to spread until it was magnified beyond measure; she announced that she had been visited by the Virgin, who had promised her release from suffering on a certain day. On that day she was conducted in a procession of 2,000 people to a chapel of the Virgin, where she fell into a trance; a voice issued from her belly speaking 'so sweetly and so heavenly' of religious joy but 'horribly and terribly' of sin.

A book of her oracles was sent to the king, who did not take it seriously. An angel commanded her to seek an audience with him, and it seems that she was granted an interview on three separate occasions. In 1528 she had also held a private interview with Thomas Wolsey. For the time being, at least, the king left her alone. But she proved to be more dangerous than he thought. By 1531 her prophecies touched Henry himself. If he divorced his wife he should not 'reign a month, but die a villain's death'. He must address himself to three matters, the first 'that he take none of the pope's right, nor patrimony from him, the second that he destroy all those new folks of opinion and the works of their new learning [religious reform], the third that if he married and took Anne to wife the vengeance of God should plague him'.

She made other declarations of a similar nature, all of which served only to inflame the people who believed implicitly in divine revelation. A network of priests and friars was now gathered around her, carrying her message in the pulpit and beside the market cross. She began to converse with the courtiers around Katherine; John

Fisher wept as he listened to her, believing that he heard the words of God. The young woman was becoming dangerous. As Thomas Cranmer confessed at a later date, 'Truly, I think, she did marvellously stop the going forward of the king's marriage by the reasons of her visions.'

More unwelcome words came from the pulpit. On Easter Sunday 1532 a Franciscan friar preached before Henry and Anne Boleyn at Greenwich; Father Peto bravely denounced the king for his behaviour and prophesied that if he should marry Anne he would be punished as God had punished Ahab: 'The dogs would lick up your blood – yes yours!' It was fortunate that the friar did not lose his life for imagining the king's death; instead he was eventually banished from the realm.

Against this background of unrest parliament was once more convened, in which the king determined to continue his campaign against Pope Clement VII. An Act was introduced effectively to cancel what were known as 'annates', the payments made to Rome by newly elected bishops and archbishops. The measure was delayed for a year, to be introduced at the king's discretion; it was in other words a bribe for the pope's good behaviour. The Act met very strong resistance in the Lords, particularly among the spiritual peers who were deeply concerned about Henry's ultimate intentions. Yet they were in the minority.

Then the Commons, more compliant to the court's wishes, presented to the king a long petition containing its grievances against the Church; in particular it questioned the right of the clergy to pass legislation in convocation. The Commons also complained about such matters as the ecclesiastical courts, the trial of heretics and the size of ecclesiastical fees. These were familiar complaints, but they were given added force in the light of the king's new role as supreme head of the Church.

In the early days of April the king dispatched the petition to the archbishop of Canterbury, already sitting in convocation, and demanded a swift reply. He received it a week later. The clergy denied all the charges raised against them and asserted that their power of legislation was based upon the Scriptures; their activities were in no way detrimental to the royal prerogative. The king then summoned the representatives of the Commons into his presence, and gave them the clerical response. 'We think this answer will smally please you,' he told them, 'for it seemeth to us very slender. You be a great sort of wise men; I doubt not but you will look circumspectly in the matter, and we will be indifferent between you.' The king had therefore implicitly pitted the Commons against the Church.

The bishops knew that their answer had failed to satisfy the king or the parliament, and so they immediately offered one concession. They pledged that in the king's lifetime they would never introduce legislation in matters unconnected with faith; the qualification was a very slender one, and did not resolve anything. On 11 May the king once more invited a delegation for a formal interview. 'I have discovered,' he said, 'that the clergy owe me only one half of an allegiance. All the prelates at their consecration make an oath to the pope clean contrary to the oath they make to us so that they seem his subjects and not ours.' This was disingenuous, but the king's intention was becoming clear. He was intent upon fundamentally destroying the power and the authority of the pope.

He sent another memorial to the convocation or, rather, he issued a series of demands. No new canons, or legislative orders, were to be proposed or enacted without royal licence. All existing ecclesiastical laws were to be reviewed by a panel of ecclesiastics and parliamentarians, sixteen on either side, and a majority verdict would suffice for abolition. Any such majority verdict would then be upheld by the king, whose authority was supreme.

The convocation debated the matter for five days, but by that time the king had grown impatient. He demanded an answer. With one exception, the bishop of Bath, all the clergy then replied that they accepted the proposals in full knowledge of the king's 'excellent wisdom, princely goodness and fervent zeal to the promotion of God's honour'. Their answer, or surrender, became known as the 'Submission of the Clergy'. The Spanish ambassador wrote that 'churchmen will now be of less account than shoemakers, who at least have the power of assembling and making their own statutes'. At a later date the great historian Lord Acton would describe the 'Submission' as representing 'the advent of a new polity'. The independent nation state of England could not truly have emerged without this radical separation from the authority of

Rome. Yet the change can be put in more immediate terms. An absolute monarch needed absolute rule over all his subjects, lay and clerical.

On the day after the 'Submission' Thomas More resigned, or was forced to resign, as chancellor. He had become too prominent a supporter of the pope, and of the old rights of the Church. 'If a lion knew his own strength,' he had once said of the king, 'hard were it for any man to rule him.' There was one other who still resisted the wishes of the king. John Fisher, bishop of Rochester, was in secret communication with the Spanish ambassador; they agreed that, if they accidentally met in public, they would ignore one another. Yet within months Fisher was suggesting that a Spanish invasion force should sail to England and overthrow the king. The archbishop of Canterbury, William Warham, dictated to his scribes a testament in which he denounced the legislation against the Church. 'By these writings,' he said, 'we do dissent from, refuse, and contradict them.' Then he lay down and died, beyond the reach of the king at last. Out of the habit of obedience, and of loyalty to the throne, all the other bishops acquiesced. It is probable, also, that they feared the wrath of the king.

Henry sought the support of parliament at every stage in these proceedings largely for the sake of safety. The king himself went to parliament on three separate occasions in order to sway the vote. He could not be sure how the country would receive the great changes he was preparing. So he tried to make it seem that the Commons, in particular, were instigating or seeking the measures against the Church. Although he was in effect the sole mover of the anti-clerical legislation, he deemed it best to appear above the fray.

In the process the Commons itself acquired additional authority and came to be regarded as a partner to the king. In a later address the king told parliament that 'we be informed by our judges that we at no time stand so highly in our estate royal as in the time of parliament, wherein we as head and you as members are conjoined and knit together in one body politic'. This was effectively a new doctrine of state whereby 'the king in parliament' wielded supreme authority in a newly united nation.

*

In the early autumn of 1532 the king placed a mantle of crimson velvet, and a golden coronet, upon Anne Boleyn. She had been given a hereditary peerage, as marquess of Pembroke, the first woman to be so honoured in England. It was clear that she was soon to be further exalted. A number of the queen's jewels were now transferred to her, despite Katherine's vehement protests. Yet all was not well. When the king took her on progress through the southern counties the response of the people was at best sullen when not overtly hostile. Henry scrutinized the faces of all the members of the court, when they were in her presence, to ensure that they paid her the right measure of respect. It was reported that the king 'begged the lords to go and visit and make their court to the new queen'.

A number of tracts were published around this time by the king's printer, Thomas Berthelet, supporting the king's 'great matter'. One of them, *A Glass of the Truth*, may have in part been written by the king himself. It defended Henry's decision to separate from Katherine by reason of biblical injunction, but also included some private details about her supposed wedding night with Prince Arthur.

He took Anne with him on a journey to France; now that he had come close to an open breach with Charles V, the nephew of the queen, he was obliged to maintain his alliance with Francis I. But the sister of the French king, and other ladies of the court at Paris, declined to meet her; Henry's own sister, Mary, had also refused to accompany them across the Channel. Anne was obliged to remain in Calais, while Henry proceeded to Boulogne for his interview with the French sovereign. Their visit lasted far longer than they intended, when severe gales and storms prevented them from embarking in the *Swallow* for a fortnight. When they did eventually return to England they were confronted at Canterbury by Elizabeth Barton, 'the mad nun of Kent', who once more lectured them on their transgressions and prophesied calamity.

Yet the mind and intention of the king could not now be changed. It seems that, a few days later, he slept with Anne Boleyn. Certainly, by the beginning of December, she was pregnant. The birth of Elizabeth occurred nine months later. The only possible reason for the decision to begin sexual relations was the certainty that the two had now agreed upon an immediate marriage. There are reports that a secret ceremony took place two days after their return from France, with only Anne's close family as witnesses, but they cannot be proven. It is likely, however, that the king would have taken the precaution of some official ritual before inseminating his lover. The risk of an illegitimate child was too great.

A formal marriage did take place in the following month when, just before dawn on 25 January 1533, they were united by the king's chaplain in the 'high chamber' above the newly built Holbein Gate at Whitehall Palace. The other circumstances of the marriage are not known, but it is believed that two or three of the king's privy chamber were present. Soon afterwards the preachers of the court began to pray for 'Anne, the queen', and Katherine was ordered to omit the title. By the following month the condition of Anne Boleyn was widely known, and the lady herself began to joke about her new-found craving for apples; her laughter rang around the hallways. She told the Venetian ambassador that 'God had inspired his Majesty to marry her'.

Their union took place in the full anticipation of a final break with Rome. A parliament had been called at the beginning of February. Its first measures were concerned with the quality of shoe leather and the fair price of goods; crows and ravens were to be destroyed, and the road from the Strand to Charing Cross should be paved. Only then did the members direct their attention to more spiritual matters. The Act in Restraint of Appeals declared that all ecclesiastical cases should be determined within England itself with no reference to any supposed higher authority; this meant that the matter of the king's separation would be adjudicated in London and Canterbury rather than in Rome. It has been described as the most important statute of the sixteenth century, for it was the one that effectively destroyed the polity of the Middle Ages.

The prologue to the Act itself sufficiently emphasized the king's imperial longings. It declared that 'whereas, by divers sundry old authentic histories and chronicles, it is manifestly declared and expressed that this realm of England is an empire, and so hath been accepted in the world, governed by one Supreme Head and

King ... unto whom a body politic, compact of all sorts and degrees of people, divided in terms and by names of spirituality and temporality, be bounden and owe to bear, next to god, a natural and humble obedience'. So the reformation of religion was to be conceived as a welcome return to the past. All the changes and novelties claimed the authority of ancient law and practice. There is no mention of 'the pope's holiness', as there had been in previous statutes, only of 'the see of Rome'. Henry had recovered his imperial dignity as absolute ruler, with the expectation that he would acquire control over the entire British Isles. Twenty years earlier he had named two new ships the *Henry Imperial* and the *Mary Imperial*. Seals and medals were issued showing him sitting in state.

It is often suggested that Thomas Cromwell was the minister who oversaw or even devised these constitutional changes, but many hands were behind the proposals. Cranmer was naturally among them, but lawyers in parliament were also willing to help with drafts of the legislation. Many of them had been opposed to the powers of the ecclesiastical courts and had consistently favoured common law over canon law. It was, after all, their profession. A further consequence ensued. If canon law was subordinate to common law, it was also subordinate to the king. So by degrees the concept of *imperium* was formed. That concept is more properly known as 'caesaro-papism'; the king was now both Caesar and pope. Henry was described as a king with a pope in his belly. Material consequences also arose from this dual authority. The imperial ambassador reported in the spring of this year that the king 'was determined to reunite to the Crown the goods which the churchmen held of it'.

Thomas Cranmer had been chosen by Henry for the archbishopric of Canterbury, on the death of William Warham, but it was still deemed necessary that he receive his authority from the pope. The old dispensation had to be observed for a little longer, if only to guarantee Cranmer's legitimacy. So Henry withheld royal consent to the Act in Restraint of Appeals, just as he had resisted seizing the annates destined for Rome. To Pope Clement VII he still posed as the defender of the faith against a disobedient and anti-ecclesiastical Commons. He even asked the papal nuncio to accompany him on a visit to parliament.

The pope obliged with a bull confirming Cranmer but, before the new archbishop swore his formal oath to Rome as legate of the Holy See, Cranmer declared that he was determined to fulfil only his obligations to God and to the king. At the end of March he was duly consecrated. It was time now for the next steps. The clergy, assembled at their convocation, declared the marriage between Henry and Katherine of Aragon to have been invalid. Only 19, out of 216, dissented. The rout of the Church was complete. John Fisher was placed under house arrest and was not released until the status of Anne Boleyn was finally confirmed.

At an ecclesiastical court meeting in Dunstable, on 23 May, Cranmer issued a decree stating that the marriage with Anne Boleyn was fully lawful. The archbishop had previously written to Thomas Cromwell, pleading that the meeting of the court be kept a close secret; he did not want to run the risk of Katherine's attendance. When Pope Clement VII heard of the verdict delivered by 'my lord of Canterbury' he declared that 'such doings are too sore for me to stand still and do nothing. It is against my duty to God and the world to tolerate them.' The bishop of London, present for the occasion, remonstrated with the pontiff. Whereupon Clement threatened to burn him alive or boil him in a cauldron of lead. The bishop told the king that the pope was 'continually folding up and unwinding of his handkerchief, which he never does except when he is tickled to the very heart with great anger'.

On the morning of 31 May Anne Boleyn was carried from the Tower to Westminster in a white chariot drawn by two palfreys in trappings of white damask; above her head was a golden canopy stringed with silver bells. The citizens and their wives had dressed the fronts of their houses with scarlet arras and crimson tapestries, so that the streets seemed to have become clouds of colour. The mystery plays were performed on special stages, and the fountains of London poured forth wine. On the following day she was taken from Westminster Hall to the abbey, where she was crowned as queen of England. 'I did set the Crown on her head,' Cranmer wrote, 'and then was sung Te Deum.'

Despite the grandeur of the ceremony, the feelings of the population might not be so adulatory. During her procession into the city the constables of each parish had stood on guard with their staves at the ready 'for to cause the people to keep good room and order'. The monogram of the king and his new queen, 'HA', was interpreted by some as a ribald 'Ha! Ha!' Yet the Venetian envoy witnessed 'the utmost order and tranquillity' of the large crowds, even if part of that tranquillity might be better interpreted as silent hostility. The people had come out of curiosity, perhaps, rather than respect. It is reported that Anne herself counted only ten people who shouted out the customary greeting of 'God save your Grace'. A contemporary writer, commenting on the intricate patterns of her coronation garments, suggested that 'her dress was covered with tongues pierced with nails, to show the treatment which those who spoke against her might expect'. Power may be glorious but it can quickly become fierce; three years later the radiant new queen would experience this herself.

A deputation of councillors came to Katherine, now officially titled as princess dowager rather than queen. They informed her of the decision of the court at Dunstable and of the king's marriage. 'Oh yes,' she replied, 'we know the authority by which it has been done, by power rather than justice.' She asked to see a copy of the proposals they had brought to her and, when she saw the phrase 'princess dowager', she took a pen and struck it out. In retaliation Henry reduced the size of her household. In the summer of that year two women were stripped and beaten with rods, their ears nailed to a wooden post, for having said that 'queen Katherine is the true queen of England'.

The king and his councillors now moved against Elizabeth Barton. In the summer of 1533 Henry asked Cranmer and Cromwell to investigate the claims and the behaviour of the nun, who is then said to have confessed 'many mad follies' to the archbishop. She was accused of high treason, by reason of her prophecies of the doom of the Tudors, and was taken to the Tower of London for questioning. It may be that she was put on the rack. In any case it was declared that she had confessed that all her visions and revelations had been impostures, and in a subsequent meeting of the Star Chamber 'some of them began to murmur, and cry that she merited the fire'. It was then determined that the nun should be taken throughout the kingdom, and that she should in various places confess her fraudulence. At the beginning of 1534 she was 'attainted' in parliament of treason, and was later dragged through the streets from the Tower to Tyburn where she was beheaded. It was sufficiently clear that anyone who opposed the king was in mortal danger. The traditional pieties of the faithful, which had once blessed and sustained the nun, were not enough to save her.

At the time of Elizabeth Barton's arrest and confession the king was reported to be 'very merry'. He had come through. He was pope and Caesar. He was compared to Solomon and to Samson. 'I dare not cast my eyes but sidewise,' a contemporary wrote, 'upon the flaming beams of the king's bright sun.' He was building a new cock-pit for his palace at Whitehall, and his new queen was pregnant with what was hoped to be a male heir. The dynasty was at last secure.

During the queen's pregnancy, however, he was unfaithful. The identity of the woman is not known, but she was described by the imperial ambassador as 'very beautiful'; he also said that 'many nobles are assisting him in this affair', perhaps as a way of humiliating Anne Boleyn. On discovering the relationship Anne confronted Henry and used 'certain words which the king very much disliked'. His royal temper flared up and he is reported to have told her to 'shut her eyes and endure as her betters have done'; he also declared that he could lower her as well as raise her.

The storm passed, and Anne Boleyn still held the future within her. The astrologers and physicians of the court prognosticated the birth of a son, and Henry was hesitating between the names of Henry and Edward for his heir. Yet on 7 September, in a room known as the Chamber of the Virgins, Anne was delivered of a girl. 'God has forgotten him entirely,' the imperial ambassador wrote to his master. The infant was named Elizabeth after the king's mother, Elizabeth of York. Henry was disappointed, but he professed to be hopeful that a son would soon follow. A week after the birth, Princess Mary, now seventeen, was stripped of her title; she was to be known now as 'the Lady Mary, the king's daughter'. She wrote a letter of gentle complaint, declaring that she was 'his lawful daughter, born in true matrimony'. In his reply the king accused her of 'forgetting her filial duty and allegiance' and forbade her 'arrogantly to usurp' the title of princess. Three months later Elizabeth was taken in state to Hatfield House, in Hertfordshire, where her court was established. On the following day Mary was ordered to Hatfield, also, but only to enter 'the service of the princess'. It was said that the king wished her to die of grief.

Yet all was not well within the royal palace. The unanticipated birth of a daughter, and the emergence of a royal mistress, made it plain to Anne Boleyn that her position was not as secure as it once had been. At a banquet she told a French envoy that she dared not speak as freely as she wished 'for fear of where she was, and of eyes that were watching her countenance'. The royal court was a fearful and suspicious place, full of whispers and devices. She knew also that she was far from popular with the people. Her time of lamentation would soon come.

7

The king's pleasure

The pace of religious change was quickened by the king's statutes against the pope. Henry wanted no innovations in belief or in worship, but his first measures would surely lead to others. The papacy was the keystone of the arch of the old faith; once it was removed, the entire structure was likely to weaken and to fall. The emergence of a national Church would in the end result in a national religion. A radical preacher, Hugh Latimer, had been intoning in Bristol against 'pilgrimages, the worshipping of saints, the worshipping of images, of purgatory'; but he had also been a prominent supporter of the separation from Katherine, and in 1533 Cromwell enlisted him in the court's service. Latimer was soon dispatching preachers of his persuasion to several parts of the country. It was enough for Henry's purposes that they were opposed to the pope, but they advocated more radical measures in other aspects of devotion. So the causes of religious reform and of the royal supremacy were associated.

Some occasions of iconoclasm were also reported. John Foxe, the author of *Actes and Monuments of these Latter and Perillous Dayes, Touching Matters of the Church*, more commonly known as *Foxe's Book of Martyrs*, records that in 1531 and 1532 religious images were 'cast down and destroyed in many places'. The rood – the image of Christ on the cross that hung between the nave and the chancel – was seized from the little church of Dovercourt, a village in Essex. It was then carried for a quarter of a mile before being burned 'without any resistance of said idol'. Since the rood was reported to have the miraculous power of keeping the door of the church open, this was a signal defeat for those who venerated it. Three of the perpetrators were apprehended and hanged.

In the autumn of 1533 it was reported that statues were being thrown out of churches as mere 'stocks and stones'; the citizens and their wives pierced them with their bodkins 'to see whether they will bleed or no'. These were not simply incidents of random destruction. It was said that if you take off the paint of Rome, you will undo her. There must have been some who saw religious imagery as one of the instruments of their slavery, but many people also regarded the gilded statues and paintings as an affront to the poor. 'This year,' an Augustinian canon wrote in 1534, 'many dreadful gales, much rain, lightning, especially in summertime, and at odd times throughout the year; also divers sudden mortal fevers and the charity of many people grows cold; no love, not the least devotion remains in the people, but rather many false opinions and schisms.' The times were out of joint. Henry was denounced by some as the Mouldwarp of English legend who would be 'cursed with God's own mouth'.

Parliamentary work had still to be done in matters of religion. At the end of 1533 the royal council was meeting daily in order to prepare policy, and summoned several learned canonists for their advice. Parliament was called and assembled at the beginning of the new year. It sat for the first three months of 1534, during the course of which it confirmed and ratified all of the measures proposed by the king and his council. The Submission of Clergy Act recognized the previous submission of the clergy; the Absolute Restraint of Annates Act prohibited the sending of moneys to the pope and concurred with the election of bishops; the Dispensation and Peter's Pence Act confirmed that the archbishop of Canterbury was now in charge of dispensations from canon law.

In March 1534 Pope Clement VII decreed that the king's first marriage to Katherine was still valid, thus consigning Anne Boleyn and Elizabeth to oblivion. It is reported that Henry took no account of it. Yet in retaliation the pope's name was removed from all prayer books and litanies; it was further ordered that it should be 'never more (except in contumely and reproach) remembered, but perpetually suppressed and obscured'. If the pope was ever mentioned at all, it was only as the bishop of Rome. This is the period when the word 'papist' became a term of contempt. In the winter of that year a priest, supporting the royal supremacy, fashioned an image of the pope out of snow; 4,000 people came to watch as it slowly melted away.

Just days after the papal decision an Act of Succession was passed by parliament, by which the royal inheritance was settled on the children of Anne Boleyn. Yet the Act was also enforced by an oath, whereby every person of full age was sworn to defend its provisions. It was in effect an oath of loyalty, so that any refusal to swear was deemed to be an act of treason. It passed through parliament after some debate, and the removal of certain ambiguous words, but there is no doubt that it was generally supported. Such was the measure of co-operation with the king, in fact, that a new subsidy Act guaranteed him revenue from taxation in times of peace as well as war. So the Commons supported him; the nobility supported him, or at least did not speak out publicly against him; the bishops supported him, albeit with secret doubts and reservations. A popular phrase of the time was that 'these be no causes to die for'. Two men, in particular, refused to follow this advice.

Yet there was genuine fear, with some people denounced for speaking ill of the king and his new marriage. They could now be condemned as traitors. One villager complained that if three or four people were seen walking together 'the constable come to them and will know what communication they have, or else they shall be stocked'. A fragment of a conversation is recorded in a court document: 'Be content, for if you report me I will say that I never said it.' Erasmus wrote that 'friends who used to write and send me presents now send neither letters nor gifts, nor receive any from any one, and this through fear'. He went on to say that the people of England now acted and reacted 'as if a scorpion lay sleeping under every stone'. Between 1534 and 1540 over 300 executions were ordered on the charge of treason. A large number of people fled the realm.

Thomas Cromwell himself took up the investigation of those who were accused. A letter from him to a priest in Leicestershire stated: 'The king's pleasure and commandment is that, all excuses and delays set apart, you shall incontinently upon the sight hereof repair unto me . . .' It was one of many unwelcome invitations. To speak of a surveillance state would be anachronistic and wrong, but it is apparent that Cromwell and his agents had created an effective, if informal, system of control. 'I hear it is your pleasure,' one lord wrote, 'that I should go into the country to hearken if there be any ill-disposed people in those parts that would talk or be busy any way.' There was in any case no sense of privacy in the sixteenth-century world; men commonly shared beds, and princes dined in public. The individuals of every community were under endless scrutiny from their neighbours, and were subject to ridicule or even punishment if they breached generally accepted standards. There was no notion of liberty. If it was asked, 'May I not do as I wish with what belongs to me?', the answer came that no man may do what is wrong. In every schoolroom, and from every pulpit, the virtue of obedience was emphasized. It was God's law, against which there could be no appeal.

The clergy were asked to supervise their parishioners, and the local justices were supposed to watch the bishops to see if they 'do truly, sincerely, and without all manner of cloak, colour or dissim-ulation execute and accomplish our will and commandment'. 'Tale-tellers' and 'counterfeiters of news' were to be apprehended. The Act of Succession was nailed to the door of every parish church in the country, and the clergy were ordered to preach against the pretensions of the pope; they were forbidden to speak of disputed matters such as purgatory and the veneration of the saints. The royal supremacy was to be proclaimed from every pulpit in the land. Henry demanded no more and no less than total obedience by methods which no king before him had presumed to use. He made it clear that, in obeying their sovereign, the people were in effect obeying God. In the same period the king and Cromwell were reforming local government by placing their trusted men in the provincial councils. In Ireland and Wales and northern Eng-land, the old guard was replaced by new and supposedly more loyal men. The country was given order by a strong central authority supervised by Thomas Cromwell, who sent out a series of circular letters to sheriffs and bishops and judges.

The oath attendant upon the Act of Succession was rapidly imposed. The whole of London swore. In Yorkshire the people were 'most willing to take the oath'. The sheriff of Norwich reported that 'never were people more willing or diligent'. In the small village of Little Waldingfield in Suffolk, ninety-eight signed with their name, and thirty-five with a mark.

A few refused to sign, however, believing that it was contrary to the will of the pope and of the whole Church. Among these brave, or stubborn, spirits were the Carthusian friars of Charterhouse. It is reported on good authority that the king himself went in disguise to the monastery, in order to debate with them on the matter. Those who stood firm were soon imprisoned. On 15 June 1534 one of the king's men reported to Thomas Cromwell that the Observant Friars of Richmond were also refusing to conform; 'their conclusion was,' he wrote, 'they had professed St Francis's religion, and in the observance thereof they would live and die'. And, yes, they would die. Two days later, two carts full of friars were driven through the city on their way to the Tower.

The recalcitrant bishop of Rochester, John Fisher, refused to take the oath and was also consigned to the Tower; from his prison he wrote to Cromwell beseeching him to take pity and 'let me have such things as are necessary for me in mine age'. A visitor reported that he looked like a skeleton, scarcely able to bear the clothes on his back.

Thomas More was also summoned before Cranmer and Cromwell at Lambeth Palace, where the oath was given to him for his perusal; but he also refused to subscribe. He was happy to swear that the children of Anne Boleyn could succeed to the throne, but he could not declare on oath that all the previous Acts of Parliament had been valid. He could not deny the authority of the pope 'without the jeoparding of my soul to perpetual damnation'. He too was consigned to the Tower, where he would remain until his execution. Another notable refusal came from the king's first daughter, Mary, who could not be persuaded to renounce her mother. She was not yet put to the test of formal signature, but her position was clear enough. When Anne Boleyn heard the news she declared that the 'cursed bastard' should be given 'a good banging'. Mary was in fact confined to her room, and one of her servants was dispatched to prison. She soon became ill once more and the king's physician, after visiting her, declared that the sickness came in part from 'sorrow and trouble'.

Some last steps had to be taken in the long separation from the pope. The final Act of the parliament, assembled at a second session in November, was to bring to a conclusion and a culmination all of its previous work. The oath of succession was refined, in the light of experience with More and others, and a new Treasons Act was passed that prohibited on pain of death malicious speech against the king and the royal family. It would be treason, for example, to call the king a heretic or a schismatic or a tyrant. Now it was a question of loyalty rather than theology.

A Supremacy Act was also passed that gave legal and coherent form to all of the powers that the king had assumed, with the statement that 'the king our sovereign lord, and his heirs and successors, shall be taken, accepted and reputed as the only supreme head on earth of the Church of England, called *Anglicana Ecclesia*'. He could reform all errors and correct all heresies; his spiritual authority could not be challenged. He lacked only *potestas ordinis*; because he was not a priest, he had no right to administer the sacraments or to preach. He was the Catholic head of a Catholic Church. Thus, in the words of John Foxe, the pope was 'abolished, eradicated and exploded out of this land'. The king was effectively acting upon a principle of English thought and practice that had first manifested itself in the twelfth century. The opposition between William Rufus and Anselm of Canterbury was similar to that between Henry and Archbishop Warham. One of the servants of the king's father, Edmund Dudley, had stated twenty years before that 'the root of the love of God, which is to know Him with good works, within this realm must chiefly grow by our sovereign lord the king'. This veneration of the Crown was one of the abiding aspects of English history.

The frontispiece to Miles Coverdale's translation of the Bible, published in 1535, displayed an image of the king sitting on his throne beneath the Almighty. Henry holds in each hand a book on which is written 'The Word of God'; he is giving copies to Cranmer and to another bishop, saying 'Take this and preach'. In the lower part of the frontispiece the people are shouting *'Vivat Rex! Vivat Rex!'* while children who know no Latin are saying 'God save the King!'

In retaliation for the Act of Supremacy the pope issued a bull of interdict and deposition against the king. Henry was now a thing accursed; on his death his body should be denied burial, while his soul could be cast into hell for ever. The people of England would be declared contumacious unless they rose in instant rebellion; their marriages would be deemed illegal and their wills invalid. No true son of the Church should now trade, or communicate, with the island. On the urgent wish of the French king, however, the pope did not publish this general excommunication for three years. At this juncture, foreign politics came to the assistance of Henry.

The more conservative of the bishops believed that Henry would now be the bulwark against German heresy, while Cranmer hoped that the king would be the instrument of reform. In this expectation he was joined by Thomas Cromwell, who knew that his master could now grow rich as well as powerful. A document had been prepared entitled 'Things to be moved for the king's highness for an increase and augmentation to be had for the maintenance of his most royal estate'. It was proposed that the lands and incomes of the Church should in large part be diverted to the king's treasury.

At the beginning of 1535, therefore, a survey of the Church's worth was undertaken. It was the largest such report since the Domesday Book of the eleventh century. The officials from every cathedral and every parish church, every monastery and every hospital, every convent and every collegiate church, were obliged to open their estate books and their accounts; they were questioned on oath about their income from tithes and from lands. They were asked to give an account of their gold chalices and their silver candlesticks. Within a short time the king knew exactly how much he could expect from church revenue, having already laid down that a tenth of its income should be his. In the process he took much more than the pope ever did.

In the same period Thomas Cromwell had been appointed

'vicegerent', or administrative deputy in spiritual matters, precisely in order to supervise the collection of revenue. He was accustomed to questions of church money; it had been he who, under Wolsey, had appropriated the incomes of certain monasteries for the sake of the cardinal's new college at Oxford. In the summer of the year the 'visitations' of the smaller monasteries began in the west of England, seeking out instances of venality and immorality among the monks and abbots; the visitors were given power to discipline or remove recalcitrant clergy, and encouraged the brothers to denounce one another for various sins. It was said of one prior that he 'hath but six children and but one daughter . . . he thanks God he never meddled with married women, but all with maidens the fairest that could be got . . . the pope, considering his fragility, gave him licence to keep an whore'. It was decreed that no abbot or monk should be permitted to walk outside the walls of the monastery. It was also determined that all religious under the age of twenty-four were to be dismissed. Some novices had appeared at service in top-boots and hats with satin rosettes.

The visitors then turned their attention to the universities, where it was decided that the learning of the scholastics and the medieval doctors should be abandoned in favour of the humanist learning approved by Erasmus and other reformers. Daily lectures in Latin and in Greek, central to the principles of Renaissance learning, were instituted. The study of canon law was discontinued. If the visitations were primarily concerned with the raising of revenue, they also engaged themselves with matters of religious and educational renovation.

This was also the dying time. The monks of the Charterhouse were the first to be executed, having been arraigned under the Treasons Act just passed by parliament. The jury were not eager to sentence to death such holy men, but Cromwell told them that they would themselves suffer death if they refused. When their prior, John Haughton, heard the verdict he simply said, 'This is the judgment of the world.' On 4 May 1535, they were brought in their habits to the scaffold, the first time in English history that clergy have suffered in their ecclesiastical dress. Haughton was the first to die. He was partially hanged before his heart was ripped out and rubbed in his face; his bowels were then pulled from his stomach, while he still lived, and burned before him. He was beheaded and his body cut into quarters. Two more followed, and then three in the next month. Many lords and courtiers were part of the crowd, including two dukes and an earl, and it was reported that 'the king himself would have liked to see the butchery'. It was an image of his power over the Church and the people.

The citizens of London were less sanguine about the punishment and many were horrified that monks should suffer in their habits. It was observed that, since the day of their death, it had never ceased to rain. The corn harvest was a failure, yielding only a third of the usual crop. All this was conceived to be a sign of divine displeasure. Yet who now would dare to speak out against the king? Certain noblemen, however, sent secret messages to Spain in an effort to spur an invasion; it was said that the king had lost the hearts of all his subjects.

In a memorandum book belonging to Thomas Cromwell are the following notes:

Item – to advertise with the king of the ordering of Master Fisher.

Item – to know his pleasure touching Master More.

Master Fisher was indeed put on trial in the middle of June, accused of high treason for having said that 'the king our sovereign lord is not supreme head in earth of the Church of England'. His fate was not averted by the decision of the pope to grant him the red hat of a cardinal. To Henry this seemed to be mere meddling in the affairs of England, and he promised that his head would be off before the hat was on. The hat got as far as Calais.

A jury of twelve freeholders condemned the aged cleric to a traitor's death, in the manner of the Carthusians, but true to his word Henry commuted the punishment to a simple beheading. Five days later, on 22 June 1535, Fisher was taken to the scaffold; emaciated and ill, he was too weak to walk to the site of execution on Tower Hill, and so he was carried in a chair where before his execution he besought those present to pray for him. 'I beseech Almighty God,' he said, 'of His infinite goodness to save the king and this realm . . .' His head was taken off at the first stroke, and the observers were astonished that so much blood should gush from so skeletal a body.

The day after the execution the king attended an anti-papal pageant, based upon the Book of Revelation. Such spectacles and dramas were becoming more frequent. The imperial ambassador observed that the king sat retired 'but was so pleased to see himself represented as cutting off the heads of the clergy that, in order to laugh at his ease and encourage the people, he discovered himself'.

Thomas More followed John Fisher to the scaffold. Four days after Fisher's death a special commission was established to consider his case. Ever since his imprisonment in the Tower he had been cajoled and bullied by Cromwell, in the hope that he might relent. Cromwell even insinuated that More's obstinacy, by providing a bad example, had helped to bring the Carthusians to destruction. This proved too much for even his patience to bear. 'I do nobody harm,' he replied, 'I say none harm, I think none harm, but wish everybody good. And if this be not enough to keep a man alive, in good faith I long not to live.'

The trial was held in Westminster Hall, where he conducted himself with acuity and dignity. But the verdict was never for a moment in doubt. He was convicted of treason and five days later was led to Tower Hill where the axe awaited him. His last words were a jest to the executioner. 'You will give me this day,' he told him, 'a greater benefit than ever any mortal man can be able to give me. Pluck up thy spirits, man, and be not afraid to do thine office. My neck is very short; take heed, therefore, thou strike not awry for saving of thine honesty.'

Katherine of Aragon, witnessing the destruction of those whom she considered saints, sent an urgent letter to the pope with the message that 'if a remedy be not applied shortly, there will be no end to ruined souls and martyred saints. The good will be firm and suffer. The lukewarm will fail if they find none to help them.' But no help was at hand. The execution of More and Fisher, together with that of the Carthusian monks, was considered by the Catholic countries of Europe to be an act of barbarism, the Christian princes conveniently forgetting their own savage measures against supposed heretics. There was no Inquisition in England.

In the search for allies, therefore, it became advisable to reach some accord with the Protestant leaders of Germany. In a message to the elector of Saxony, for example, Henry congratulated him for his 'most virtuous mind' and declared that the two countries 'standing together would be so much stronger to withstand their adversaries'. It was hoped that a league of the reforming nations of Europe might then be formed. It was also hoped that the king might be persuaded to sign the Lutheran confession of faith, known as the Confession of Augsburg, that had been drawn up five years before by the German princes. The proposals came to nothing.

The scope of the 'visitations' of the smaller monasteries was extended in the autumn of 1535. The visitors had previously confined their attentions to the west of England; when their work was completed there, they moved on to the east and to the south-east before travelling to the north at the beginning of 1536. The speed of their researches did not augur well for their reliability. Yet the visitors continually questioned and investigated the priors, the abbots, the monks and their servants: 'Whether the divine service was kept up, day and night, in the right hours? And how many were commonly present, and who were frequently absent?' 'Whether they kept company with women, within or without the monastery? Or if there were any back-doors, by which women came within the precinct?' 'Whether they had any boys lying by them?' 'Whether any of the brethren were incorrigible?' 'Whether you do wear your religious habit continually, and never leave it off but when you go to bed?'

There were in all eighty-six questions. One prior was accused of preaching treason and was forced to his knees before he confessed. The abbot of Fountains kept six whores. The abbot of Battle was described to Cromwell as 'the veriest hayne, beetle and buserde, and the arrentest chorle that ever I see'. A hayne was a wretch; a beetle was a blockhead; and a buserde was a stupid person. An arrentest chorle may be described as a thoroughly boorish wretch. The canons of Leicester Abbey were accused of buggery. The prior of Crutched Friars was found in bed with a woman at eleven o'clock on a Friday morning. The abbot of West Langdon was described as the 'drunkenest knave living'. The visitor, Richard Leyton, described to Cromwell how he had entered the abbot's lodging. 'I was a good space knocking at the abbot's door; no voice answered, saving the abbot's little dog that within his door fast locked bayed and barked. I found a short poleaxe standing behind the door, and with it I dashed the abbot's door in pieces . . . and about the house I go, with that poleaxe in my hand, for this abbot is a dangerous desperate knave, and a hardy.'

The visitors also noted the number of shrines and relics that they observed in the course of their labours; they marked them under the heading of '*superstitio*', a sign of the direction in which Cromwell and his servants were moving. At the abbey of Bury St Edmunds, for example, they found one of the stones with which St Stephen was killed and one of the coals with which St Lawrence was roasted. In the same establishment they came across the skull of St Petronilla that people sick of the fever placed on their heads. The monasteries were therefore considered to be beds of papistry, and it was said that the monks were in a sense the reserve army of Rome. Thomas Cromwell described them as 'the pope's spies'. If there was no evidence of wrongdoing, the visitors merely concluded that the monks were engaged in a conspiracy of silence. When sins are being actively looked for, they can always be found.

A parliament was called in February 1536, the last session of a body that had been assembled seven years before. It has since become known as the Reformation Parliament, and can perhaps be called the most important in all of English history. The king came into the House of Lords with a 'declaration' about the state of the monasteries, no doubt based upon the various reports of the visitors. Hugh Latimer, appointed bishop of Worcester in the previous year, was present on the occasion and records that 'when their enormities were first read in the parliament house, they were so great and abominable that there was nothing but down with them'. Some dissent may have been expressed. According to one report the king summoned members of the Commons to the royal gallery. 'I hear,' he said, 'that my bill will not pass, but I will have it pass, or I will have some of your heads.'

An Act for the Dissolution of Monasteries was indeed passed, by which all religious houses with an annual income of less than £200 were to be 'suppressed'. This was a large sum of money, and in theory 419 monastic houses were obliged to close; yet the abbots made petitions for exemptions, and 176 of the monasteries were granted a stay of execution. It is also clear Cromwell and his servants were bribed in money or in goods. Yet this was not a general dissolution. The larger monasteries had not been touched, and the monks of the smaller establishments were given leave to transfer to them. All was still well in the 'great and solemn monasteries wherein (thanks be to God) religion is right well kept and observed'. It is hard to believe, however, that piety only began at £200 per year.

As a consequence the protests were few and uncoordinated. It might be thought that Cromwell's strategy was to proceed slowly and cautiously, removing one obstacle at a time. It is more likely, however, that the king and his chief minister were trying to find their way in unfamiliar territory; they were not yet clear about their final objective and fashioned their policy as they went along. The senior clergy in convocation were in the meantime formulating the principles of the new faith under the royal supremacy. The imperial ambassador noted that 'they do not admit of purgatory nor of the observance of Lent and other fasts, nor of the festivals of saints, and worship of images which is the shortest way to arrive at the plundering of the church of St Thomas of Canterbury and other places of resort for pilgrims in this country'. In this conclusion, the ambassador was correct. It was a practical and financial, rather than a dogmatic and doctrinal, decision.

Parliament, in its last session, also established a Court of Augmentations through which all the revenues from the dissolution of the monasteries – all the rents and tithes – were to be adjudicated and passed to the Crown. Other parties were also interested in the spoils. One lord wrote to Cromwell 'beseeching you to help me to some old abbey in mine old days'. The court was duly set up in the spring of 1536. This was, in a word Thomas Cranmer now used for the first time, the 'world of reformation'.

8

A little neck

On 7 January 1536 Katherine of Aragon died. Rejected and humiliated by her husband, deprived of the company of her daughter, her last years had not been happy ones. She had been alternately abused and threatened, but she could not be moved from the fact that Henry was her lawful husband. She clung to this certainty as the world around her shifted. It was even rumoured that the king was ready to behead her, but it is unlikely that he would have made so egregious a mistake. She had written to her daughter, Mary, that 'he will not suffer you to perish, if you beware to offend him'; it is not exactly a ringing endorsement of his clemency. She also advised her daughter that 'in whatsoever company you shall come, obey the king's commandments, speak few words and meddle nothing'. She had not meddled; she had simply endured. The Spanish were always associated, in this period, with formality and self-control; she had those qualities to the highest degree. In a letter written to her husband, hours before her death, she implored him to preserve his soul from the peril of sins 'for which you have cast me into many miseries and yourself into many cares'. She signed it as 'Katherine the Queen'. It was suspected by some that she had been poisoned, but in fact a cancerous tumour was found around her heart.

On hearing the news of her death the king rejoiced. 'God be

praised,' he said, 'we are free from all suspicion of war!' He had been concerned that her nephew, Charles V, might form a Catholic league with France and the pope against the infidel of England. On the following day he and Anne Boleyn appeared at a ball, both of them dressed in brilliant yellow.

It is not known how Mary learned of the death of her mother, but the news provoked another bout of illness. She was once more threatened by Anne Boleyn. 'If I have a son, as I hope shortly,' Anne wrote, 'I know what will happen to her.' 'She is my death,' Anne had once said, 'and I am hers.' Mary was now alone in the world, and her thoughts turned to the prospect of escape to her mother's imperial family in Brussels. She spoke to the imperial ambassador about the possibility of fleeing across the Channel, but he advised caution and circumspection. In the meantime, he said, 'she is daily preparing herself for death'. She was in a most invidious position. In certain circumstances she might be considered a pretender to the throne. Those who wished to rebel against the new order of religion, for example, would welcome her at their head. She was surrounded by perils.

On the day of Katherine's burial in the abbey church of Peterborough, 29 January, Anne Boleyn miscarried a male child; it was one more link in the chain of fate that bound together the two women. Anne blamed the accident on the shock she had received, five days before, on hearing the news that the king had fallen from his horse during a jousting match at the tiltyard in Greenwich; he had lain unconscious on the ground for two hours. Yet the king believed, or chose to believe, that the hand of divine providence lay behind the event. 'I see,' he is reported to have said, 'that God will not give me male children.'

The king's attentions were already wandering once more. Thomas Cromwell had told the imperial ambassador that 'in future he was to lead a more moral life than hitherto – a chaste and marital one with his present queen'. Yet the minister had put a hand to his mouth in order to hide his smile, so the ambassador concluded that he was not necessarily telling the truth. Henry was in fact pursuing Jane Seymour, a young lady in the household of Anne Boleyn herself, whose rather sharp features were later bequeathed to her son. It was reported that Anne Boleyn found the girl on her husband's knee and flew into a rage, but this may just be later gossip.

The ambassador also tells another story that hints at the complications of the court. While speaking to 'the brother of the damsel the king is now courting', he witnessed an argument when 'angry words seemed to be passing between the king and Cromwell for, after a considerable interval of time, the latter came out of the embrasure of the window where the king was standing, on the excuse that he was so thirsty he could go on no longer, and this he really was, from sheer annoyance, for he went to sit on a chest, out of the king's sight, and asked for something to drink'. Eventually Henry came looking for him.

A courtier once described how 'the king beknaveth him [Cromwell] twice a week, and sometimes knocks him well about the pate; and yet when he hath been well pummelled about the head and shaken up as it were a dog, he will come out of the Great Chamber . . . with as merry a countenance as though he might rule all the roost'. This is the human aspect of court life, rarely observed, where we are able to glimpse the constant personal tensions that fashioned the decisions we now call history.

Great and malign changes, indeed, were soon to occur at the court. It was reported that the king had expressed his horror of Anne Boleyn to an intimate in the privy chamber, and accused her of luring him into marriage through the use of witchcraft. That is why he had been abandoned by God. So the story goes. Yet in practice he still behaved to her with every courtesy and attention, and the records show that she was spending a great deal of money on fine garments for herself and her daughter. There was every reason to suppose, despite the fears of the king, that she might bear another child. Anne Boleyn herself professed to believe so.

But then the calamity struck. On 24 April two separate commissions, under the conditions of utmost secrecy, were established to search into occasions and suspicions of treason. On one of them sat Thomas Cromwell and the duke of Norfolk, Anne Boleyn's uncle but no longer her friend. Three days later it was suggested that the king might wish for a divorce. What had happened? One of the ladies at the court had spoken unwisely about the queen's affairs and had mentioned a certain 'Mark'. Once it had been spoken, it could not be unsaid. To conceal or to attempt to suppress information about the queen's alleged infidelity would be equivalent to treason – or, in the phrase of the time, misprision or conceal-ment of treason. The rumour or report had immediately taken on a life of its own.

On 30 April Mark Smeaton, a court musician and a groom of the privy chamber, was taken from Greenwich to the Tower where he confessed to having been Anne's lover; that confession may have smelled of the rack, but it might have been a true account prompted by terror. He never retracted it and repeated it at the foot of the gallows. On the following day at the May Day jousts Anne's brother, George Boleyn, Viscount Rochford, rode against Sir Henry Norris; Norris was the intimate friend of the sovereign and the chief gentleman of the privy chamber. They were both soon to die for the suspicion of having lain with Anne Boleyn.

After the joust was over the king rode from Greenwich to Whitehall, taking Norris with him as one of a small company. During the journey he turned on Norris and accused him of pursuing an affair with his wife. To meddle with the queen of England was treason. The king promised him a pardon if he confessed the truth, but Norris vehemently denied the charge. He was taken to the Tower at dawn on the following day. George Boleyn had already been arrested, and charged with having sexual relations with his own sister. The evidence for the incest came from his wife, Lady Rochford, who may have spoken out of malice towards her promiscuous husband. The ladies of the queen's house-hold had also been interrogated and may have revealed interesting information. Some five men were accused of having slept with her – Mark Smeaton, George Boleyn, Henry Norris, William Brereton, Francis Weston – and were executed. Three others, including Thomas Wyatt the poet, were acquitted. These commissions of inquiry were not necessarily show trials.

The queen herself was interrogated by the king's council. At one point Anne Boleyn was seen entreating the king in Greenwich Palace, with her baby daughter in her arms; but this was not enough. The cannon was soon fired, as a token that a noble or a royal had been taken to the Tower. When she arrived at that place she fell on her knees and prayed 'God to help her, as she was not guilty of the thing for which she was accused'. When she was told that Smeaton and Norris were among those incarcerated she cried out: 'Oh Norris have you accused me? You are in the Tower with me, and you and I will die together; and Mark, so will you.'

She had spoken with her gaoler in the Tower, Sir William Kingston, about certain earlier conversations:

Anne Boleyn: Why don't you get on with your marriage?
Henry Norris: I will wait a while.
Anne Boleyn: You look for dead man's shoes; for if anything happens to the king, you would look to have me.
Henry Norris: If I had any such thought, let my head be cut off.

A dialogue with Mark Smeaton was also remembered:

Anne Boleyn: Why are you so sad?
Mark Smeaton: It does not matter.
Anne Boleyn: You must not expect me to speak to you as if you were a nobleman, since you are an inferior person.
Mark Smeaton: No, no, madam. A look suffices me.

The remarks were not proof of guilt, by any means, but they do not appear to be entirely innocent. 'Imagining the king's death', as Anne had done, was in itself an act of treason. It would not be difficult for a jury to convict her. The royal court had now turned against her, sensing in which direction the wind was blowing. Only Cranmer had doubts. 'I am in such perplexity,' he told the king, that 'my mind is clean amazed; for I never had better opinion in woman than I had in her.'

Four of the accused were brought to trial in the middle of May, in Westminster Hall, while George Boleyn was to be arraigned before his peers in the Tower. Only Smeaton acknowledged his crime by repeating his confession that he had known the queen carnally on three occasions. The others pleaded not guilty. It is reported that Norris had also confessed, on first being questioned, but then withdrew the confession. They were all sentenced to death.

On her first arrival the queen had asked the lieutenant of the Tower, Sir William Kingston, if she would die without being shown justice. 'The poorest subject the king has,' he replied, 'has justice.' And, at that, she laughed. She knew well enough that she would not survive the anger and suspicion of the king. She and her brother were taken to the Great Hall of the Tower before twenty-seven peers of the realm, as a mark of respect to their rank, and were questioned. 'I can say no more but "nay",' the queen said, 'without I should open my body. If any man accuse me, I can say but "nay", and they can bring no witnesses.' The pair were duly convicted of high treason, for which the penalty in the queen's case was death by burning. Yet a beheading was penalty enough. The lieutenant of the Tower told her that 'it will be no pain, it was so subtle'.

'I have heard say,' she replied, 'that the executioner is very good, and I have a little neck.' Then she put her hands about her neck, and laughed. On 19 May, just before noon, she was brought to the scaffold within the walls of the Tower. In her nervousness she continually glanced behind her, as if she might be taken unawares. She was the first queen of England ever to be beheaded. Her exact age at the time is unknown, but it is estimated that she was in her early thirties. When the executioner held up the head, its eyes and lips moved. Her body was then thrown into a common chest of elm-tree, made to hold arrows.

Henry had also taken the precaution of having his marriage to Anne annulled, on the grounds that she had been involved in a liaison nine years before, without seeming to realize that if she had not been his wife she could not have committed adultery. But he wished to expunge her, to blot her out. Whether he was right to do so has been a matter of controversy ever since the events themselves. It has been supposed, for example, that Anne Boleyn was the victim of a conspiracy managed by Cromwell or by the 'conservative' faction at the court.

Yet common sense would suggest that this would be a perilous undertaking indeed. All of the men accused were well known at court; George Boleyn was her brother, in high estate, and Henry Norris was the intimate of the king. It would have been madness to implicate such men in a scheme that had no foundation. At the trial all the details of the times and places were read out, as, for example, in the first indictment that 'the queen [on the] 6th October 25 Hen. VIII [1533] at Westminster, by words etc.,

procured and incited one Henry Norris, Esq., one of the gentlemen
of the king's privy chamber, to have illicit intercourse with her;
and that the act was committed at Westminster, 12th October,
25 Hen. VIII'. The details may not have been entirely accurate,
but the fact that they were given suggests a strong and definitive
case was being made. This was not some nebulous charge built
upon rumour and false report. Why accuse five men, four of them
known and respected, when one would have been sufficient?

And the charges were believed. It is true enough that no one
would willingly defy the wishes of the king, but it is still the case
that twenty-seven peers unanimously decided that the queen had
indeed committed incest with her brother. Two grand juries and a
petty jury had concluded the cases of the other men.

It is at least possible that Anne Boleyn was not as innocent as
she claimed. It may be that she pursued other men in desperate
search for a male child who could be hailed as the heir to the
throne, thereby saving herself and her family for the foreseeable
future. Another aspect of the trial was suppressed. It was alleged
against her that she had spoken to George Boleyn's wife about the
king's impotence. A piece of paper detailing the matter was handed
to George Boleyn, during the course of the trial, that he was
supposed to read in silence. 'The king was not skilful in copulating
with a woman and he had not virtue or power.' In scorn, and
bravado, he read it out aloud. That is not necessarily the action of
an honest man. It is the action of a defendant daring the court to
do its worst. Boleyn also did not deny that he had spread rumours
about the princess Elizabeth's true paternity. It was in fact rumoured that the real father was Sir Henry Norris. No one can at
this late date be certain of anything. The truth, as always, lies at the
bottom of the well. The best epigraph of the events in the spring
of 1536 comes from one of those briefly accused, Thomas Wyatt:

> These bloody days have broke my heart,
> My lust, my youth, did then depart . . .

The king dressed in white on the day of Anne Boleyn's
execution, and on the following morning he married again. He
must have been thoroughly convinced of her guilt, or had come
upon another offence that he never disclosed, or both. When his

illegitimate son, Henry of Richmond, visited him the king greeted him with tears saying that he and Mary 'ought to thank God for having escaped from the hands of that woman, who had planned their deaths by poison'. He was said to have behaved with an almost defiant gaiety, and to have composed a verse tragedy in which Anne Boleyn had 100 different amours.

The king had a further reason to remarry. He was now forty years old and he was desperate for a male heir. He had in effect already bastardized Mary and Elizabeth. The duke of Richmond was illegitimate and therefore ineligible.

The death of Anne Boleyn was not greeted with any great dismay by the people of England. Anne had been in large part disparaged by the populace, at least in private, and a contemporary described the joy evinced 'at the ruin of the concubine'. Henry's new wife, Jane Seymour, was not herself universally popular. 'There is a ballad made lately of great derision against us,' Henry told her, 'which if it go abroad and is seen by you, I pray you to pay no manner of regard to it. I am not at present informed who is the setter forth of this malignant writing; but if he is found, he shall be straitly punished for it.' The man was in fact never found.

The joy of the people was also part of a general belief that Lady Mary would now be restored to royal favour. Yet this was too optimistic an interpretation of events at court. Thomas Cromwell now moved against Mary's supporters on the grounds that they had been trying to engineer the succession on her behalf. It seems that Jane Seymour herself urged her new husband to reconcile himself with his oldest daughter, but instead Henry subjected Mary to even more pressure.

He sent a delegation to her, under the leadership of the duke of Norfolk, urging her to take the oath of allegiance; this would entail repudiating the marriage of her mother and her own legitimacy. It would also require her to accept the king as supreme head of the Church. On all these matters, she declined to swear. The duke of Norfolk then declared that she was guilty of treason. It was clear enough that Henry was willing to prosecute her, with all the unhappy and perhaps even unbearable consequences. Thomas Cromwell wrote to her that 'I think you the most obstinate and obdurate woman . . . that ever was'; he urged her to repent 'your ingratitude and miserable unkindness'. He warned that otherwise she would reach 'the point of utter undoing' which might include a traitor's death. She was now twenty-one years of age.

A short while after, she surrendered. The imperial ambassador had remonstrated with her, telling her that it was her duty to survive the chaos and the terror. He persuaded her that her destiny might lie in rescuing the nation for the true faith, and that nothing in the world should prevent this. Martyrdom would be a failure of responsibility. She did not read the declaration of submission, but simply signed it. She had declared 'the King's Highness to be the supreme head in earth under Christ of the Church of England' and that the marriage between her mother and the king 'was by God's law and man's law incestuous and unlawful'.

She could go no further. In her abject state she wrote to her father declaring that 'my body I do wholly commit to your mercy and fatherly pity, desiring no state, no condition nor no manner or degree of living but such as your grace shall appoint unto me'. She was at once welcomed back into royal favour, but the damage to her conscience and sense of self had been done. She would never bend, or weaken her will, again. The guilt of repudiating her mother would remain with her, perhaps to be in part allayed by the fires of Smithfield. It is reported that she was overcome with sorrow and remorse, immediately after signing the document, and asked the imperial ambassador to obtain for her a special dispensation from Rome. Yet she seems to have adjusted to her return to court very well, purchasing jewellery and fine clothes; she gambled, modestly but continuously, and had her own group of minstrels. She also had her own 'fool', a lady called Jane, with a shaven head.

After the beheading of Anne Boleyn it was clear that the party of religious change, which had profited by her intervention in the affairs of the realm, might be destined for an eclipse. In Rome dislike of the king was replaced by something like sympathetic pity, in the pious hope that Henry might now return to the embrace of the Church after his experiences with the 'witch'. That was of course entirely to misunderstand the nature of Henry's reform. He had never been opposed to the doctrines of the Church, only to its leadership. His understanding of the power, and profits, he had thereby gained was enough to prohibit any return to Rome. He believed also that religious unity was the prerequisite of political unity.

He saw himself in the role of the Old Testament kings who were determined to enforce the law of God upon their kingdoms in the fear that they might be consumed by divine wrath. Had not Jehoash, king of Israel, stripped the priests of their gold? Had not Josiah renovated the Temple of the Lord? Had not Solomon sat in judgment? The bishop of Durham, Cuthbert Tunstall, declared that Henry acted 'as the chief and best of the kings of Israel did, and as all good Christian kings ought to do'.

His assertion of royal supremacy, however, was aligned with a desire for reform of the monasteries and the colleges. The king attended several Masses each day and never proclaimed or believed himself to be a Lutheran. He was also attached to various forms of popular piety, including the ritual of 'creeping to the cross'. All his life he fingered a personal rosary, now in the possession of the duke of Devonshire, and ordained many requiem Masses at the time of his death. He was in most respects an orthodox Catholic.

A meeting of parliament was called at the beginning of June in order to discuss the circumstances of the realm after the recent execution of Anne Boleyn. It cancelled the two Acts favourable to Anne Boleyn and her offspring, thus reducing Elizabeth to the same status as Mary. The lord chancellor extolled the third marriage of the king, who, 'at the humble entreaty of his nobility, has consented once more to accept that condition and has taken to himself a wife who in age and form is deemed to be meet and apt for the procreation of children'.

The key was the begetting of a male heir and, if the king should die (which God forbid!) or the new queen prove infertile, 'he desires you therefore to nominate some person as his heir apparent'. Their answer may already have been agreed and rehearsed. In the absence of a legitimate male heir, parliament granted the king the power to bequeath his crown at his will. The way, therefore, was open to the illegitimate duke of Richmond. He was the least bad alternative. Yet the frailty of the dynasty was confirmed when, in the summer of 1536, Richmond died of tuberculosis or some other undiagnosed lung complaint; Henry ordered that the body should be buried secretly, to prevent public disquiet, but nothing could conceal the fact that the succession now rested on two daughters who had been declared illegitimate. The young man's ornate tomb is still to be seen at the church of St Michael the Archangel in Framlingham, Suffolk.

The evidence of the king's anxiety at this time emerged when in the summer Lord Thomas Howard, the younger brother of the duke of Norfolk, was accused of treason; his crime was to contract himself to Lady Margaret Douglas, the daughter of the queen of Scots. Since the queen was Henry's sister, Henry suspected that Howard was aiming at the succession. Howard was confined to the Tower where he died in the following year.

In June 1536 the convocation of the senior clergy had been assembled at St Paul's. Hugh Latimer, the recently consecrated bishop of Worcester and principal reformer, had been chosen to preach to them. His text came from the sixteenth chapter of St Luke's Gospel, namely 'the children of this world are in their generation wiser than the children of light'. He asked them to examine their hearts and enquire what they had achieved in convocation after convocation. The odious fictions of Rome survived even still, including 'the canonizations and beatifications, the totquots and dispensations, the pardons of marvellous variety' as well as 'the ancient purgatory pickpurse'. You know the proverb, he told them. An evil crow, an evil egg. At the end of his sermon he warned them that 'God will visit you. He will come. He will not tarry long.'

The reaction of the 500 clerical delegates is not known, but two weeks later they presented the king with a petition of complaint against the numerous blasphemies and heresies that were now circulating through the kingdom. It was a barely disguised attack on Latimer and other radicals. They were aggrieved that the sacrament of the altar was being described as a 'little pretty piece Round Robin'. The hallowed oil of extreme unction was 'the bishop of Rome's grease and butter'. Our Lady was only a woman 'like a bag of saffron or pepper when the spice was out'. Mass and matins were 'but roaring, howling, whistling, mumming, conjuring and juggling'. It was an implicit invitation to the king to bring to a halt the process of reform. There was no question of 'toleration'. The concept was only rarely mentioned. Matters of religion were too powerful and too important to be treated with circumspection. Falsehood was to be prosecuted by every means available.

In response Henry, with the help of Cranmer and others, drew up a summary of the articles of faith that the people of England were required to believe. The preface to the Ten Articles declared that their purpose was to bring 'unity and concord in opinion'. In truth the king wished to assert the royal supremacy, and the general renovation of the Church, without embracing Lutheran doctrine. He seems to have concurred with the reformers' emphasis upon only three of the sacraments – those of baptism, penance and the Eucharist – without denying the efficacy of the other four. Purgatory was denounced as a pernicious invention of the bishop of Rome, but it was also declared that 'custom of long continuance approving the same, we agree that it is meet and expedient to pray for the souls departed'. It was a question of balance. A manuscript draft of one page survives; it shows the rival scribblings of the reformer Cranmer and the conservative Tunstall vying for authority.

There are other examples of compromise or mediation. The habit of kneeling and worshipping images of the saints was considered to be unnecessarily superstitious. But other customs and ceremonies of the Church, such as the giving of ashes on Ash Wednesday and the carrying of palms on Palm Sunday, were deemed to be 'good and laudable'. Even as the Articles were being drawn up the king and his new queen, Jane Seymour, took part in a Corpus Christi procession celebrating the Eucharist consecrated in the Mass. The question of reform was raised but by no means answered, and the English Church was still in almost all respects a Catholic Church. You may go so far, but you can go no further. The process of religious change was fitful, improvised and still uncertain. The Ten Articles were therefore described by the German reformer Melanchthon as '*confusissime compositi*'.

There was no confusion, however, in the prosecution of Henry's immediate purpose. In the late spring and early summer of 1536, the smaller monasteries came under the hand of Thomas

Cromwell. Parliament had already passed the Act for the Dissolution of the Monasteries in the early months of the year, and now the royal commissioners began their work of suppression. It took a period of six or more weeks to dissolve a small monastery. The bells were taken from the towers and the lead was stripped from the roofs; all the plate and jewellery were carried off, and the disposable corn sold. In the work of despoliation, 2,000 monks and nuns were dispossessed and sent back into the world. How they lived, on their return, is unknown.

The process, however, was not always a swift or quiet one. When the visitors determined that the rood loft in the priory of St Nicholas in Exeter should be pulled down, a crowd of angry women entered the church to seize the workman 'and hurled stones at him, insomuch that for his safety he was driven to take to the tower for refuge'. Yet they pursued him so eagerly that he was forced to leap out of a window and 'very hardly he escaped the breaking of his neck, but yet he brake one of his ribs'.

At the end of September the monks of Hexham in Northumberland also resisted the encroachments. When the commissioners came into the town they saw 'many people assembled with bills, halberds and other defenceable weapons, ready standing in the street, like men ready to defend a town of war'. As the commissioners rode towards the monastery the common bell of the town and the great bell of the monastery were rung; the doors were shut against them and several monks were gathered on the roof and steeple with swords, bows and arrows. 'We be twenty brethren in this house,' one canon shouted, 'and we shall die all before you shall have the house!'

They also had another weapon besides swords and bows. The archbishop of York had begged the king to spare the monks of Hexham and had indeed received a grant to that effect under the Great Seal. When the commissioners saw this grant, they withdrew. On the following day the monks came out of their house, two by two, and with their weapons joined the people of Hexham in 'a place called the green'. From there they watched until the commissioners 'were past out of sight of the monastery'. Yet they were punished at a later date. The king mentioned Hexham by name in a letter to the duke of Norfolk in which he states that the monks 'are to be tied up [executed] without further delay or ceremony'.

Popular anger or frustration was further created by the publication of certain 'injunctions'. These were issued as a result of the rulings of the Ten Articles and, among other matters, forbade the mention of purgatory and abolished many saints' days that had hitherto been celebrated as holidays. In this year Thomas Cromwell also ordered the destruction of the shrine of Edward the Confessor in Westminster Abbey. It was another attack upon the 'superstitions' maintained and exploited by the monks. To many people, and perhaps especially to the citizens of London, these were matters of indifference. But the more orthodox, and the more devout, were angry. Their resentment soon turned to open rebellion.

9

The great revolt

By the spring and summer of 1536 rumours and whispers were circulating through the kingdom. A priest from Penrith in Cumberland had travelled as far south as Tewkesbury, where he said in an alehouse that 'we be kept bare and smit under, yet we shall rise once again, and 40,000 will rise upon a day'. He may have been in his cups but the people of the north, in particular, were aggrieved at the dissolution of the smaller monasteries. They had been providing food and comfort, in somewhat bleak circumstances, for many generations.

An Essex priest went with a labourer, by the name of Lambeles Redoon, to gather the sheaves of corn. 'There shall be business in the north,' the priest said before adding that he, and 10,000 others, would flock there.

'Little said,' the labourer wisely replied, 'is soon amended.'

'Remember you not what I said unto you right now, care you not for that, for before Easter comes, the king shall not reign long.'

Rumours abounded that all the jewels and vessels of the parish churches were to be removed and replaced by tin or brass. The sack of the shrines lent a certain credit to the reports. It was whispered that parish churches were to be situated at least five miles apart, and that any in closer proximity were to be pulled down. It was said that all christenings, burials and marriages were to be taxed, and that no poor man was to be allowed to eat white bread or goose without paying tribute to the king. Edward Brocke, 'an aged wretched person', had said that there would be no end to bad weather while the king still reigned.

The fall of Anne Boleyn was believed to have been prophesied by Merlin. Other signs and portents were scrutinized. The word passed among the monasteries that 'the decorate rose shall be slain in his mother's belly', which was said to mean that Henry would be killed by the priests since the Church he oppressed was his mother. The language of prophecy was the language of the people pitched against the language of royal proclamations.

Intimations of revolt emerged in the summer. When a priest in Windsor had preached rebellion, he was hanged on the spot. When fifty or sixty men and women in Taunton rose up in riot, twelve were sentenced to death and dispatched in different places for their executions to act as a warning. No priest or friar, between the age of sixteen and sixty, was permitted to carry any weapon save for his meat knife.

The first large revolt erupted at the beginning of October 1536, after three groups of royal councillors had descended upon Lincolnshire with a variety of purposes; one was set upon the suppression of the smaller monasteries, while the two others were concerned with gathering taxes and interrogating the clergy. This interference from London was considered to be too grievous to bear. In the market town of Louth a procession had gathered behind three silver crosses when a singing-man, Thomas Foster, cried out, 'Masters, step forth and let us follow the crosses this day: God knows whether ever we shall follow them again.' The fear was of confiscation, and that evening a group of armed villagers arrived at the parish church in order to guard its treasures.

The news of these 'rufflings' in Louth soon spread, and bands of armed men under the leadership of one who called himself Captain Cobbler began to ride through the county to impede or stop the work of the royal commissioners; the common bells of the various parishes were rung in order to raise the people. The rebels were demanding that the king 'must take no more money of the commons during his life and suppress no more abbeys'; they also wanted Thomas Cromwell and various 'heretic' bishops to be surrendered to them for condign punishment. The vicar of Louth added that the people were dismayed at 'the putting down of holy days . . . and putting down of monasteries' as well as 'the new erroneous opinions touching Our Lady and purgatory'. Religion was at the heart of their protest.

They co-opted the support and leadership of the 'gentlemen', willing or unwilling, so that their revolt could have a more legitimate air. Yet when the chancellor of Lincoln was pulled from his horse and murdered by a mob, with the priests calling out 'Kill him! Kill him!', the affair became much more serious. The signal came for a general arming of the people, and beacons were lit along the south shore of the Humber. The people of Yorkshire saw the fires and understood the message. A large army of 10,000 men, made up of bands from different parts of Lincolnshire, met at Hambleton Hill. They gathered strength, and it was reported that 20,000 of them were advancing upon Lincoln itself.

The court had of course been informed of these events, and Henry called upon the duke of Norfolk to lead a force against the rebels. Such was his uncertainty that he brought his two daughters, Mary and Elizabeth, to Whitehall, and ordered the Tower of London to be reinforced. It was possible that the whole country might rise against him. Had he miscalculated the effects of his religious policy? Stephen Gardiner, then bishop of Winchester, recalled at a later date that 'when the tumult was in the north, in the time of King Henry VIII, I am sure the king was determined to have given over the supremacy again to the pope, but the hour was not then come'. Various reports now reached Cromwell and the king. The apprentices were leaving their masters. The towns were defenceless. The tenants were rising against their lords. There were 40,000 men on the march. The king gathered a group of fifteen councillors around him.

When the rebels arrived in Lincoln, the gentlemen were lodged in the cathedral close; the chapter-house became their meeting place. By now the king's men had mustered many horsemen, and royal forces had gathered at Nottingham, Huntingdon and Stamford. The rebels were also intent upon battle and demanded that the gentlemen should lead them forward. It would mark the beginning of a civil war, a religious war that might destroy the country. It was reported that 'all the gentlemen and honest yeomen of the county were weary of this matter, and sorry for it, but durst not disclose their opinion to the commons for fear of their lives'. They were in a sense now being held hostage by the 'churls'.

They sent a message to the king seeking pardon, and then walked from the cathedral to the fields beyond the town where the commons were gathered; they told them that they would not go forward with them but would wait for the king's reply. The news bewildered the rebels, who now began to fear that all was in crisis. A large party of them slipped back to their villages, and it was reported that half of their number left Lincoln. A royal herald now arrived at the town, demanding surrender, and in the face of the king's power the insurgents dispersed. In answer to a petition from the commons Henry had sent a defiant message. 'How presumptuous then are you, the rude commons of one shire,' he wrote with more vehemence than tact, 'and that one of the most brute and beastly of the whole realm ... to find fault with your Prince?' Clemency was offered to the largest number of them, and only a few local leaders were hanged. The abbots of Kirkstead and of Barlings were also executed for their part in fomenting the troubles. The rebellion had lasted a fortnight.

But if the rebellion in Lincolnshire was over, it was merely a prelude to a much larger and more dangerous movement elsewhere. 'This matter hangeth yet like a fever,' an official wrote to Cromwell, 'one day good, one day bad.' The men of Yorkshire had seen the beacons beside the Humber and eagerly took up the standard of revolt. If they had not risen in Lincolnshire, a royal commissioner told Cromwell later, they would not have risen in the north. The revolt in the East Riding was essentially a northern drift of the original rebellion, but it took a more organized form. The monasteries had played an important part in the life of Yorkshire, and the suppression of the smaller of them had been widely denounced.

The rebellion under the nominal leadership of Robert Aske, a gentleman, was begun by the bells of Beverley; a proclamation was made to the effect that all should swear an oath to maintain God, the king, the commons and the holy Church. The bishops and the nobles were of course omitted, because it was widely believed that their 'wicked counsels' had misled the sovereign. The king, and the common people, and the Church, were deemed to be the bedrock of England. In any case nothing could touch Henry adversely; that would be treason.

It was known as 'the Pilgrimage of Grace'. Its token was a badge or banner depicting the five wounds of Christ, the holy wounds inflicted at the time of the crucifixion. It is perhaps sufficient indication that the rebels were in large part engaged in a religious protest. Their demands included the return of the 'old faith' and the restoration of the monasteries; another condition, interestingly enough, was that 'the Lady Mary may be made legitimate and the former statute [of her illegitimacy] therein annulled'. So Mary was seen as the unofficial representative of the orthodox Catholic cause.

When the bells rang backwards at Beverley the people flocked into the fields and under Aske's direction they agreed to meet fully armed at West Wood Green; the whole county was stirred and Aske published a declaration obliging 'every man to be true to the king's issue, and the noble blood, and preserve the Church of God from spoiling'. Lord Darcy, the king's steward in Yorkshire, was informed of certain 'light heads' stirring up rebellion in Northumberland, Dent, Sedbergh and Wensleydale; he rode at once to Pontefract Castle and dispatched his son to the court at Whitehall. The rebellions in the North Riding and County Durham were guided by Captain Poverty, a principle rather than a person; it seems likely that the men of these areas, as well as Cumberland and Westmorland, were animated by agrarian and economic concerns as much as matters of religion. In Cumberland the four 'captains' – Faith, Poverty, Pity and Charity – marched in solemn procession around the church at Burgh before hearing Mass there.

Robert Aske's pilgrims were by the middle of October intent upon marching to York. Others had been drawn off to besiege Hull, a trade rival to Beverley, which quickly fell without a fight. Darcy wrote to the king asking for money and weapons to save the king's treasure in York, where the citizens were 'lightly disposed'. On 15 October Aske led 20,000 men to the gates of the city and issued a proclamation in which he stated that 'evil disposed persons' about the king had been responsible for innovations 'contrary to the faith of God'; they also intended to 'spoil and rob the whole body of this realm'. This was a reference to the suppression of the smaller monasteries and to fears about the parish churches; but it also bears some relation to the burden of taxation levied on the people.

The lord mayor of York opened the gates, and Aske entered with his men; the great requirement was order, and it was decreed that the rebels or 'pilgrims' should pay twopence for any meal they consumed. Aske brought with him a petition to be sent to the king. This repeated all the earlier complaints and discontents, of which 'the suppression of so many religious houses' came first. It also denounced Thomas Cromwell and many bishops 'who have subverted the faith of Christ'. On the door of York Minster Aske set up an order for 'the religious persons to enter into their houses again'. Many small monasteries had been established in and around the city. The people escorted the monks by torchlight back to their old homes with much cheering and rejoicing. Wherever they were restored 'though it were never so late they sang matins the same night'.

The Yorkshire rebels had been sadly disappointed by the failure of the Lincolnshire men, but they were now acting in a far more disciplined and determined manner. They had also gathered the willing or unwilling support of the gentry of the county, to whom they administered an oath stating that 'you shall not enter into this our pilgrimage of grace for the commonwealth but only for the love you bear unto Almighty God his faith and to the Holy Church militant and the maintenance thereof, to the preservation of the king's person and his issue, to the purifying of the nobility, and to expel all villein blood and evil counsellors'. The dispersal of all those of 'villein blood' was another sign of anxiety; it was believed that the traditional social order, and the respect for social degree, were being fatally undermined. The gentry and commons alike were deeply conservative. Aske and his followers seem to have genuinely believed that they were acting on behalf of the king, and that he would in the end thank them for their endeavours.

Aske now marched to Pontefract Castle with only 300 men. He sent in a letter to the lords gathered there that they must surrender or be threatened with an assault; he knew well enough that thousands of his men were not far behind. Darcy decided to treat with him and invited Aske to enter the state chamber where he might debate the grievances of the pilgrims with the archbishop of York and others. Aske stood in front of these great lords and explained to them that 'first, the lords spiritual had not done their duty'. Two days later Darcy surrendered the castle. It was believed by Henry, and by others, that he had failed in his responsibilities.

The revolt had already spread beyond the bounds of Yorkshire into Cumberland and Westmorland, Durham and Northumberland; or rather it would be more exact to say that existing turmoil and suspicion were exacerbated by the events in the East Riding. Berwick and Newcastle held out for the king, as did the royal castles at Skipton and Scarborough. There was no general campaign, and only a few skirmishes; a large number of people had been mobilized with uncertain consequences.

A royal herald had arrived at Pontefract Castle and was taken to Robert Aske; the herald described him as 'keeping his port and countenance as though he had been a great prince'. The king's proclamation was given to him, but it seems to have contained nothing but high words. Then the report came that a royal army, under the earl of Shrewsbury, had gathered just 12 miles south of Doncaster; the soldiers were 25 miles from Pontefract Castle. It was agreed that Aske and his men should move down to the Don and oppose their crossing. It was also proposed that the commons should bear with them into any battle the sacred banner of St Cuthbert, the patron saint of the north. Other bands of armed men now joined Aske in Pontefract and the whole area was in arms.

As the rebels approached Doncaster, the royal herald arrived with a message from the earl of Shrewsbury. He said that the blood of a civil war must be averted, and suggested that 'four of the discreetest men of the north parts' should come to Doncaster and explain to the lords assembled there the reasons for their rising. There ensued much debate between Aske and his colleagues. If they failed in battle with the king's men, their cause would be lost irrevocably. If they won the fight a religious war would ensue, fought largely in the south. Yet this was their best opportunity. The royal army was small and might easily be defeated, leaving the road open to London. The rebels did not know that the king's men were in disarray and were not sure of the strength or the position of their enemy. But Aske was no Napoleon or Cromwell; he hesitated, and chose the safer option. The lords and the rebels would meet in a chosen place.

The men of Yorkshire and Durham marched towards Doncaster, the priests and monks moving along the lines with words and prayers of encouragement; they proceeded behind the banner of Cuthbert and sang a marching song:

> God that rights all
> Redress now shall
> And what is thrall
> Again make free . . .

They chose four delegates, who proceeded to the royal camp, where Shrewsbury had been joined by the duke of Norfolk and other grandees. The delegates had memorized their articles of complaint, about maintaining the old faith and preserving the ancient liberties of the Church, which Norfolk wrote down. It was then agreed that a conference of approximately thirty on each side would meet on Doncaster bridge, where they would discuss all of these matters. The details of their debate are not known, but it is possible that Norfolk intimated that he took their part in religious matters; he was known to be orthodox in his attachment to the old faith.

A truce was then agreed, whereby the pilgrims agreed to disperse on condition that all their complaints were put before the king. Henry himself was furious that Norfolk had come to terms with what he considered to be pernicious rebels; he had wanted them to be destroyed by the royal army. Yet the advantage now lay on his side. The pilgrims were hardly likely to rise again. He now had the indisputable benefit of time to wear down any opposition. Aske and his men continued to believe that the king would gratefully accept their proposals; once the evil counsels of Thomas Cromwell and Archbishop Cranmer were removed he would see the light once more.

On 2 November general pardons were issued for all rebels dwelling north of Doncaster, with the exception of Robert Aske and nine other instigators of the revolt. In a sermon at St Paul's

Cross, on the previous Sunday, Hugh Latimer had preached about those who wore 'the Cross and the Wounds before and behind' in order to 'deceive the poor ignorant people and bring them to fight against both the King, the Church and the Commonwealth'.

When Norfolk and the other negotiators came into the king's presence at Windsor he was at first in a furious rage against them for sparing the blood of traitors; eventually he had calmed himself enough to write down his responses to the complaints of the pilgrims. 'First,' he wrote, 'as touching the maintenance of the Faith, the terms be so general, that hard they be to be answered.' Yet he took advantage of their generality to protest that he, more than any other king, had preserved the purity of the true faith. He defied them and offered no hint of retreat. 'Wherefore,' he warned them, 'henceforth remember better the duties of subjects to your king and sovereign lord, and meddle no more of those nor such like things as you have nothing to do in.' Yet a day's reflection convinced him that it was better to temporize with, rather than to confront, the men of Yorkshire. They were still in arms, and the 'wild men' of the far north were ready to join them.

The king sent a message to Lord Darcy, suggesting that by some stratagem he should kidnap or kill Aske; Darcy refused on the grounds that it was against his honour to 'betray or disserve any living man'. It was a bold reply, but a foolish one. His loyalties were already highly suspect and he was believed to side with those of the old faith. It was alleged that he had surrendered Pontefract Castle too easily. The king suspected that many of the northern gentry were covertly engaged in rebellion, and he reacted accordingly. It was reported by two witnesses that Darcy, on hearing the news of the Lincolnshire rebellion, had said: 'Ah, they are up in Lincolnshire. God speed them well. I would they had done this three years past, for the world should have been better than it is.' His reckoning would soon come.

Rumours of disturbances and meetings were still coming from the northern counties; more alarming, from the court's perspective, was the news that copies of the pilgrims' petition were circulating in London. Aske and his men met at York and at Pontefract. Henry ordered Norfolk to return to the north where he was to demand the outright submission of the rebels; when the duke informed him that such a favourable resolution was impossible, the king grew very angry. His wrath was directed at Norfolk as much as the rebels themselves; he believed the duke to be weak and vacillating, and even half suspected him of siding with the men of the north. Yet he knew that their threat remained. He promised a free pardon, and even a meeting of parliament at York to consider their demands; he was playing for time, secretly preparing an army to defeat them in the field.

Norfolk met Aske and his colleagues once more. He agreed that the king had been misled by Cromwell and the witch, Boleyn; the 'pilgrimage' had shown him the right path after their crooked dealings; but the monarch could not be seen to grant petitions that were exerted by force. If the pilgrims dispersed peacefully, he would consider all their requests sympathetically. On the question of the suppressed monasteries, Norfolk stated that they would be restored until the meeting of the next parliament, where their fate would be decided. This was in fact a lie, but Henry had already made it clear that he could promise anything. The rebels were also offered a free pardon. This was enough. Aske rode to Pontefract and convinced the assembled commons that they had achieved their aims. He tore off the badge of the Five Wounds he was wearing and declared that he was no longer a captain of rebels. The revolt was at an end.

Yet deceit and dissembling were still the customs of the day. On Friday 15 December the king sent a message to Robert Aske by means of one of the gentlemen of the privy chamber. He wrote that he had a great desire to meet Aske, to whom he had just offered a free pardon, and to speak frankly about the cause and course of the rebellion. Aske welcomed the opportunity of exonerating himself. As soon as Aske entered the royal presence the king rose up and threw his arms around him. 'Be you welcome, my good Aske; it is my wish that here, before my council, you ask what you desire and I will grant it.'

'Sir, your majesty allows yourself to be governed by a tyrant named Cromwell. Everyone knows that if it had not been for him the 7,000 poor priests I have in my company would not be ruined wanderers as they are now.'

The king then gave the rebel a jacket of crimson satin and

asked him to prepare a history of the previous few months. It must have seemed to Aske that the king was in implicit agreement with him on the important matters of religion. But Henry was deceiving him. He had no intention of halting or reversing the suppression of the monasteries; he had no intention of repealing any of the religious statutes in force; and he would never hold a parliament in York. Yet Aske could still prove useful. Rumours of more disturbances in the north had reached the council; the king asked Aske to confirm his new-found loyalty by helping to suppress them. Henry had indeed cause for alarm. Reports of new risings in Northumberland had been received. Bills had been set up on the doors of churches. 'Commons, keep well your harness. Trust you no gentleman. Rise all at once. God shall be your governor and I shall be your captain.'

One of these captains now rode out. Sir Francis Bigod came from a great northern family, whose castle was 3 miles north of Whitby. But he was also a debt-ridden scholar who protested that he was 'held in great suspect and jealousy because of his learning'. He had witnessed the events of the 'pilgrimage' and did not trust the promises of the king. He is perhaps best considered as an old-fashioned Lollard, and in particular he detested the monastic system; yet he feared for the northern lands and wished to protect them. He may also have had rebellion in his blood; his ancestors had formerly fought Henry I and Edward III.

Bigod addressed a crowd on the grievances of the north, and many of them called back to him: 'Forward now or else never!' It was determined that Hull and Scarborough should he held by the rebels until a parliament was assembled at York, but Bigod's followers were repulsed in both places. Thomas Cromwell sent an observer to the north who wrote back to him: 'I assure your lordship the people be very fickle, and methinks in a marvellous strange case and perplexity; for they stare and look for things, and fain would have what they cannot tell what.'

So this belated wave of rebellions failed in its purpose. The local gentry, keen to display their loyalty to the king, mustered their troops of followers. The duke of Norfolk raised an army of 4,000 men, most of whom had previously ridden with Robert

Aske; they were eager now to atone for their previous faults. The rebels were hunted down, ambushed and slain. A group of them attempted an assault on Carlisle, but they were beaten back and captured. Norfolk also issued a proclamation that commanded all rebels to come to Carlisle where they must submit to the royal mercy. So the 'poor caitiffs', as they were called, duly made their pleas. 'I came out for fear of my life.' 'I came forth for fear of loss of all my goods.' 'I came forth for fear of burning of my house and destroying of my wife and children.'

Yet there was no way of mitigating the wrath of the king. He ordered the duke of Norfolk to 'cause such dreadful execution to be done upon a good number of the inhabitants of every town, village and hamlet ... as they may be a fearful spectacle to all others hereafter that would practise any like matter; which we require you to do, without any pity or respect'. In a further twist of malign fate it was decreed that certain prisoners should be tried by juries made up of their own relations; the uncle might agree to a sentence of death upon a nephew and then see his head impaled upon a stake. Many of the rebels were hanged in their home villages, from the trees in their own gardens, as a memorial of their treason. Others were hanged in chains. The king had demanded the most severe retribution as a warning to future generations.

The brutality, and the subsequent terror, worked. There were no more rumours and whispers of revolt. There were no more complaints about the suppression of the monasteries. The people had fallen silent. The leaders of the revolt had already been dispatched to London and were lodged in the Tower. Lord Darcy was brought to trial in Westminster Hall for treason, and was beheaded on Tower Hill. Robert Aske, despite the king's previous hospitality, was tried and found guilty. He was hanged at York.

If the rebels had held together more tightly, and seized the initiative, they might have reached London and the court. They had failed to do so but, in the process, they had revealed a strong current of popular protest against the religious policies of the king and Cromwell. The majority of the people wished to maintain their parish churches in good order and were opposed to any innovation. They argued, for example, that the *cura animarum* or 'care of souls' should be returned to the pope. They denounced Luther and others whom they called heretics. Yet Henry had faced them down; by duplicity and cunning he had defeated their leaders. He had broken the promises made on his behalf by the duke of Norfolk. But he might have said with some justification – what other way to deal with traitors? And he had won. Cranmer wrote that the enemies of reform 'now look humbled to the ground and oppose us less'. Henry could move forward with impunity.

10

The confiscation

Any monks or abbots complicit in the late rebellion were seized and executed, their houses surrendered to the king. The abbots of Kirkstead and Barlings, of Fountains and Jervaulx and Whalley, were all hanged; they were followed a year later by the abbots of Glastonbury, Colchester and Reading. This was merely the prelude to a more general confiscation. The fact that the king had prevailed over the Pilgrimage of Grace meant that he and Cromwell felt emboldened to continue, and to widen, their policy of suppression. Within three years the monasteries, the friaries, the priories and the nunneries would be gone.

Yet Henry still feared popular discontent. He described his method to the rulers of Scotland as they began their own policy of dissolution. He advised them to keep their intentions 'very close and secret' in order to thwart any delays from the clergy. He then suggested that commissioners be dispatched 'as it were to put good order in the same' but really 'to get knowledge of all their abominations'. The Scottish leaders should consult among themselves on the distribution of the monastic lands 'to their great profit and honour'. The monks and abbots should then be offered some financial settlement. This was indeed the policy he followed.

Some of the great abbots were first obliged to surrender their houses, signing a declaration that 'they did profoundly consider that the manner and trade of living, which they and others of their pretended religion, had for a long time followed, consisted in some dumb ceremonies . . . by which they were blindly led, having no true knowledge of God's laws'. This might charitably be called a voluntary surrender, although the threat of death or imprisonment lay behind it. These submissions were then followed by induced surrenders as one by one the greater monasteries fell. In the first eight months of 1538, for example, thirty-eight of them were appropriated by the Crown.

Cromwell's agent at the priory of Lewes described 'how we had to pull the whole down to the ground'. The vault on the right side of the high altar was the first to be destroyed, followed by the groined roof, walls and pillars of the church. 'We brought from London,' he wrote, 'seventeen persons, three carpenters, two smiths, two plumbers, and one that keepeth the furnace.' The furnace was used to melt down the lead stripped from the roof. Nothing went to waste. The pages of the books from the monastic libraries, once one of the glories of England, were employed to scour candlesticks or clean shoes; they also had another use since the pages could become 'a common servant to every man, fast nailed up upon posts in all common houses of easement'. A house of easement was a latrine.

A young man who lived in the neighbourhood of Roche Abbey, in south Yorkshire, spoke to one of the workmen who were destroying the abbey church.

'Did you,' he asked, 'think well of the religious persons and of the religion then used?'

'Yes,' the man replied, 'for I saw no cause to the contrary.'

'Well, then how comes it to pass that you are so ready to destroy and spoil what you thought so well of?'

'Might I not as well as others have some profit from the spoil of the abbey? For I saw all would away, and therefore I did as others did.'

There speaks the representative voice of the Englishman at a time of reformation.

The Carthusians were the most roughly handled, and in the summer of 1537 a list was drawn up detailing their fates under the headings of 'there are departed', 'there are even at the point of death' and 'there are sick'. The Charterhouse at Smithfield was turned into a venue for wrestling matches, and the church became a warehouse for the king's tents; the altars were turned into gaming tables.

As the certainty of suppression became more evident, the monasteries were eager to sell or to lease whatever property they possessed. At Bisham the monks sold their vestments in the chapter house while at a market set up in the cloister they brought their own cowls to sell.

Yet some provision was made for the lives of the monks themselves. At the priory of Castle Acre, for example, the religious were given a payment of £2 together with a small quarterly pension; this became general practice. As a result some monks were willing and even eager to go. 'Thank God,' said the former abbot of Beaulieu, 'I am rid of my lewd monks.' The former abbot of Sawtry revealed that 'I was never out of debt when I was abbot'. Certain abbots became diocesan bishops and were more prosperous than ever; the prior of Sempringham became bishop of Lincoln, for example, and the abbot of Peterborough became the see's bishop. The monks themselves often became the canons or prebendaries of the cathedrals.

Resistance was maintained by the brave or the foolish. When one monk at the Carthusian house of Hinton denied the royal supremacy, the others explained that he was a lunatic. The royal commissioners sometimes moved on from recalcitrant houses, leaving them isolated and unprotected until the commissioners returned on a future occasion. Yet sometimes the seizures were sudden and immediate. The monks at Evesham were at evensong in the choir when they were told to 'make an end'.

Where did the spoils go? It had previously been proposed that the dissolution of the monasteries was for the higher good of the nation. The incomes of the various priories would be spent on colleges and hospitals and schools 'whereby God's work might the better be set forth, children brought up in learning, clerks nourished in the universities, old servants decayed to have livings, almshouses for poor folk to be sustained in, readers of Greek, Hebrew and Latin to have good stipends, daily alms to be ministered, mending of highways . . .' It never happened. The only deity worshipped was that of Mammon.

It is difficult to estimate the size of monastic occupation. At the time it was believed that the clergy owned one third of the land, but it may be safe to presume that the monks controlled one sixth of English territory. This was of immense benefit to the Crown, and represents the largest transfer of land ownership since the time of the Norman conquest.

The greater parts of the monastic lands were sold to the highest bidder or the highest briber; many went to the local gentry or to newly rich merchants who were eager to secure their status in a society based solidly on land ownership. It was a way of binding the rising families both to the cause of the reformation and to the Tudor dynasty. City corporations sometimes made purchases, as did syndicates of investors that included doctors and lawyers. The parlours of successful men were hung with altar-cloths, their tables and beds covered with copes instead of carpets. The once sacred chalices and patens were now in secular use. It is reported that, in Berwick, a baptismal font was used as a basin 'in which they did steep their beef and salt fish'.

Many of the monasteries and priories fell into the pockets of the courtiers. Cromwell and the duke of Norfolk, for example, shared between them the lands and revenues of the wealthy Cluniac priories at Lewes in Sussex and at Castle Acre in Norfolk. Cromwell eventually appropriated the land and revenue of six religious houses, and was widely reputed to be (after the king) the richest man in England. The duke of Northumberland secured eighteen monastic properties, while the duke of Suffolk became master of thirty foundations. Cartloads of plate and jewels were taken to the royal treasury.

From the ruins of the plundered monasteries and abbeys arose new buildings. Sir William Paulet purchased Netley Abbey and built a fine residence from the remains of the church and cloisters; Sir Thomas Wriothesley fashioned a gatehouse in the nave of Titchfield Abbey, and Sir Edward Sharington turned a nunnery into a family house. It was reported at the time that a Lancashire gentleman, having purchased an abbey, 'made a parlour of the chancel, a hall of the church and a kitchen of the steeple'. The steeple of Austin Friars, in London, was used to store coal. The Minories, an abbey of nuns of the order of St Clare, was turned into an armoury and St Mary Graces became a naval depot where great ovens were introduced for baking bread. The house of the Crutched Friars, in the street near Tower Hill which still bears the name, was changed into a glass manufactory. Other churches were converted into stables, cook-houses and taverns. The abbeys of Malmesbury and Osney became clothing factories.

Some of the great men of the realm openly asked for the spoils. Sir Richard Grenville, the marshal of Calais, wrote to Cromwell that 'if I have not some piece of this suppressed land by purchase or gift of the king's majesty I should stand out of the case of few men of worship of this realm'. He was, in other words, following the example of everyone else.

Much haggling and bargaining took place with the monks themselves. The abbot of Athelney was offered 100 marks, and another ecclesiastical post. He threw up his hands and declared that 'I will fast three days on bread and water than take so little'. One monk tried to sell his cell door for two shillings, and said that it had cost more than five shillings. So within three years the life of ten centuries was utterly destroyed.

It was perhaps a saving grace that eight cathedral churches, once staffed by monks and nuns, were now turned into secular cathedrals; the most important cathedrals in England became Canterbury, Rochester, Winchester, Ely, Norwich, Worcester, Durham and Carlisle. Only the monastic cathedral of Coventry was torn down. The others remained as centres of music and sung liturgy in a reformed world that became increasingly wary of their power.

It is difficult to calculate the effect of the dissolution on the educational life of the country. Some effort was made to replace religious with secular training. There had been a rise in the number of educational foundations in the decades around 1500, but the appetite for formal education was by no means diverted or diminished. Henry and his ministers, for example, endowed twelve permanent grammar schools in the cathedral cities, and it can be said with some certainty that the sixteenth century remained the age of the grammar school. The richer tradesmen endowed schools in their own towns, and borough institutions took the place of monastic institutions. Christ's Hospital was established, for example, within the former Greyfriars Convent in London.

The leading reformer, Hugh Latimer, urged upon the clergy of Winchester their duty to educate children in the learning of English, while Cranmer proposed a collegiate foundation at Canterbury to take the place of the monastic cathedral school. At a later date, the archbishop of York declared the foundation of schools to be 'so good and godly a purpose'. Yet the old faith could still prove useful: some monks began life again as schoolmasters in village or town; chapels became schoolrooms.

Some of the last monasteries to be dissolved were those of Colchester, Glastonbury and Reading, where the abbots were denounced as seditious. The abbot of Glastonbury was accused of concealing or taking away the treasures of his house and is reported to have said that 'the king shall never have my house but against my will and against my heart'. More seriously, perhaps, he is reported to have previously expressed support for the northern rebels of the Pilgrimage of Grace. He declared them to be 'good men' and 'great crackers'. It was also discovered that he, together with the abbot of Reading, had supplied the pilgrims with money. When the abbey itself was searched, gold and silver, vessels and ornaments, were found in walls, vaults and other 'secret places'. The commissioners searched the abbot's rooms and found there such suspicious items as papal bulls and arguments against the king's divorce. He was questioned and his answers were deemed to be 'cankered and traitorous'.

The abbot was charged and sentenced; he was dragged through the streets of Glastonbury before being taken to the conical hill known as Glastonbury Tor where he was hanged. His head was then placed on the abbey gate, and his quarters distributed through Somerset. So was dissolved one of the greatest of English shrines, supposedly the home of the Holy Grail and the last resting place of King Arthur. The abbots of Reading and Colchester suffered the same fate in their own towns.

The convents and friaries were the next to fall. Some 140 nunneries had been established in England, with perhaps 1,600 women, the majority of them belonging to the Benedictine order. It was much harder for a nun than a monk to make her way in the secular world; she could earn no obvious living, and as an unmarried woman would endure many more hardships in a society that considered marriage to be the only proper fate of the female. Nuns and monks were in any case still bound to their vows of chastity.

The nuns of Langley were according to the commissioners 'all desirous to continue in religion'. The prioress 'is of great age and impotent' while 'one other is in regard a fool'. Yet they were not spared. The nunneries were genuinely missed in their immediate neighbourhoods. They had become guest houses for the more important gentry. At the nunnery in Langley, for example, Lady Audeley used to attend church accompanied by twelve dogs. The convents had also offered a simple education for the daughters of the gentry, where they learned surgery, needlework, confectionery, writing and drawing. The great ages of female spirituality, evinced by such women as Dame Julian of Norwich, now also came to an end.

In the autumn of 1538 the friaries were destroyed. They were all situated within or close to towns, the friars themselves devoted to an active ministry of preaching in the world; 200 of them were in existence, and the number of friars can be estimated at 1,800. They had very little wealth or treasure, but it was considered fitting that they should also submit to the king's authority. In many cases their surrender took the form of a confession to unnamed 'crimes and vices'. Particular charges were sometimes raised against them. They were accused of dabbling in necromancy. The community of Austin Friars in London was compared to a herd of wild beasts in Sherwood Forest, and it was reported that they sat in the beerhouse from six in the morning until ten at night 'like drunken Flemings'. But in truth the principal offence of the friars was their resistance to reform. The Observant friars, in particular, had been vociferous in the cause of Katherine of Aragon. Some of the friars changed their clothes and became secular priests, while others went back into the world. Thomas Cromwell came across one friar, however, who was still wearing his old habit. 'If I hear by one o'clock that this apparel be not changed,' he warned him, 'you will be hanged immediately for example to all others.'

While the monasteries were suppressed, their shrines and relics were destroyed. The 'rood of grace' at Boxley Abbey, in Kent, was one such holy image, which was also known, to the men of the new faith, as the Dagon of Ashdod or the Babylonish Bel. It was a wooden crucifix upon which the eyes and the head of Jesus sometimes moved; on some occasions the whole body on the cross trembled to express the reception of prayers. Many offerings were of course made to such a miraculous figure. A man named Partridge suspected a fraud and, laying hands on the rood, exposed a number of springs that had made the motions. It was brought to London, and pieces of it were tossed to the crowd outside St Paul's Cathedral.

In the summer of 1537 the cult statue of Our Lady of Worcester was stripped of its clothes and jewels, to reveal that it was a doll-like effigy of an early medieval bishop. The images of the Virgin were taken down from shrines in Ipswich, Walsingham and Caversham; they were carried in carts to Smithfield and burned. The blood of Hailes, popularly believed to be the blood of Christ, was revealed to be a mixture of honey and saffron. The bishop of Salisbury, Nicholas Shaxton, urged the destruction of all 'stinking boots, mucky combs, ragged rochets [vestments], rotten girdles, pyld [threadbare] purses, great bullocks' horns, locks of hair, and filthy rags, gobbets of wood under the name of parcels of the holy cross . . .' It was soon decreed that there must be no more 'kissing or licking' of supposed holy images.

These were only preliminaries to the greatest act of destruction, or desecration, in English history. The shrine of St Thomas Becket at Canterbury was probably the richest in the world. The least costly of its materials was pure gold, and Erasmus once described how 'every part glistened, shone and sparkled with rare and very large jewels, some of them exceeding the size of a goose's egg'. It was a treasure house of devotion, a bright worker of wonders and miracles. This was now dismantled, with the jewels and gold packed into wooden chests before being transported to London in twenty-six ox-wagons. One great ruby donated to the saint by a king of France, Louis VII, was fashioned into a ring that Henry wore on his thumb.

The saint himself was demoted and was only to be known as Bishop Becket; all of his images were removed from the churches and his festival day was no longer observed. He was tried in his absence, as it were, and was attainted of treason. He had not been a martyr but a traitor to his prince. It was in the king's gift, therefore, to make and unmake saints. The bones of Becket were disinterred and burned on a fire lit in the middle of the city; the ashes were then discharged into the air from a cannon. It was at this moment that the pope decided to publish his Bill of Deposition against the English king, deeming him to be excommunicate and releasing his people from the duty of obeying him. It was of no practical consequence.

This demolition of holy sites did encourage, in the more profane sort, a tendency to ridicule and scoff at all the old certainties. It was said that 'if our lady were here on earth, I would no more fear to meddle with her than with a common whore'. When a priest raised the sacred host, during the Mass, one of the parishioners held up a small dog. Some townspeople of Rye were reported as saying that 'the mass was of a juggler's making and a juggling cast it was' and that 'they would rather have a dog to sing to them than a priest'.

The dissolution of the friaries was followed by the burning of a friar. John Forrest, an Observant friar, had been imprisoned four years before on the charge of denying royal supremacy. On 22 May 1538, a cradle of chains was placed above a pile of wood in Smithfield. Upon the pyre would soon be placed the desecrated image of a saint, known as Darvel Gadarn, that had been esteemed by the people of North Wales. The image was that of a military saint, with a sword and spear. It was said that those who made offerings of money or animals to the wooden statue would be snatched from hell itself by the saint. It was also said that the image could set alight a forest. Now Darvel himself would erupt in flames.

The ceremony of execution itself was typical. Forrest was dragged on a hurdle from Newgate to Smithfield, where a crowd of 10,000 were in attendance. The bishop chosen to read the sermon was Hugh Latimer, who had written to Thomas Cromwell in high spirits that 'if it be your pleasure that I shall play the fool after my customary manner when Forrest shall suffer, I would wish that my stage stood near to Forrest'. So his pulpit was placed next to the scaffold, from which height he preached for three hours. When he exhorted the friar to repent Forrest replied in a loud voice that 'if an angel should come down from heaven and show me any other thing than that I had believed all my lifetime, I would not believe him'.

'Oh,' Latimer replied, 'what errors has the pope introduced into the Church! And in order that you may the better understand this, you shall presently see one of his idolatrous images, by which the people of Wales have long since been deceived.' On a signal from Cromwell eight men carried the image of Darvel Gadarn into the open space, eliciting a great yell from the citizens, and then the three executioners continued the comedy by tying it with ropes and chains to prevent its escape.

'My lord bishop,' Cromwell called out, pointing to Forrest, 'I think you strive in vain with this stubborn one. It would be better to burn him.' He turned to the soldiers. 'Take him off at once.'

He was led to the cradle of chains and hoisted into the air. The wooden image, and other piles of wood, were placed beneath him and lit with torches.

The friar was suspended above the fire, and when he began to feel the flames he beat his breast and called out *Domine miserere me* – 'Lord have mercy on me'. He took two hours to die. In his mortal agony he clutched at a ladder to swing himself out of the blaze, but he did not succeed. The chronicler Edward Hall, remarked without pity that 'so impatiently he took his death as never any man that puts his trust in God'. A ballad was soon circulating through the streets of London:

> But now may we see,
> What gods they be,
> Even puppets, maumets and elves;
> Throw them down thrice
> They cannot rise,
> Not once, to help themselves.

A few hours later the holy rood or crucifix close to the church of St Margaret Pattens, in Rood Lane, was attacked and demolished. It would not be so easy to remove or destroy the tenets of the old faith.

11

The old fashion

At the beginning of 1537 the bishops were ordered to draw up a statement of belief that would broadly fit Henry's scheme for a middle way between orthodoxy and reform; the bishops themselves were divided on almost every matter under discussion, with the result that they produced what the bishop of Winchester called 'a common storehouse, where every man laid up in store such ware as he liked'. Some said that there were three sacraments, others insisted that there were seven, and yet others believed that there were one hundred. They sat at a table covered with a carpet, while their priestly advisers stood behind them. Once they had agreed tentatively on a closing statement, they dispersed with alacrity; the plague had struck London, and the dead were lying close to the doors of Lambeth Palace.

The king went through the document and made copious emendations to the text. Thomas Cranmer then supervised the king's work and was bold enough to correct his sense and his grammar. He told his sovereign that one word 'obscureth the sentence and is superfluous' and reminded him that 'the preter tense may not conveniently be joined with the present tense'. It seems that Henry did not take offence at the archbishop's presumption.

It was entitled *The Institution of a Christian Man* but it became better known as *The Bishops' Book*. It was essentially a series of popular homilies to be preached from the pulpit, and was close enough to the injunctions of the old faith to be accepted and acceptable. The major difference of belief lay in the controversy between faith and works; those of a Lutheran persuasion believed that the only hope of human redemption reposed in the faith of Christ; all mankind was utterly corrupt, but Christ's sacrifice upon the cross was sufficient to save the erring soul. If the individual placed all his or her faith and hope in Christ he or she would be saved. No work or act made any difference. It was a question of being reborn by God's act of grace as if by a lightning flash, with the sinner then becoming utterly reliant upon divine mercy. Those who followed the tenets of the old Church profoundly disagreed with this doctrine, believing that acts of charity and good works were essential for salvation; they also reinforced the fervent belief that the administration of the seven sacraments by the Church was part of the process of redemption.

In *The Bishops' Book* the issue was avoided in what may be called an act of creative ambiguity. In particular the king's revision deleted and amended passages that Cranmer had written on justification by faith alone. Where Cranmer had stated that the believer became God's 'own son through adoption and faith' Henry added the words 'as long as I persevere in His precepts and laws'. The final text emphasized faith without endorsing Lutheran doctrine while at the same time reducing the role of good works without repudiating Catholic beliefs. But the book also supported such ancient practices as the bearing of candles at Candlemas and the hallowing of the font. Henry also demanded that the section on the three sacraments should be altered to include the missing four. It seems likely that, for most people, there was no reason to doubt that the 'old ways' would continue indefinitely.

It was said by a magistrate from Rainham in Kent that the new book 'alloweth all the old fashion and putteth all the knaves of the New Learning to silence so that they dare not say a word'. Cranmer rebuked the magistrate by saying that 'if men will indifferently read those late declarations, they shall well perceive that purgatory, pilgrimages, praying to saints, images, holy bread, holy water, holy days, merits, works, ceremony, and such other be not restored to their late accustomed abuses'. *The Bishops' Book*, therefore, was open to interpretation.

In a set of injunctions, published in the following year, an English Bible was introduced to the people. Thomas Cromwell decreed that within a period of two years every church must possess and display a copy of the Bible in the native tongue; it was to be chained in an open place, where anyone could consult it. The edition used was that of Miles Coverdale, published in 1535 and essentially a reworking of Tyndale's original. Thus the man who had been denounced as a heretic, and whose translation had been burned by royal decree eleven years before, was now the unheralded and unsung scribe of the new English faith. It was also ordered that one book comprising the Pater Noster, the Ave Maria, the Creed and the Ten Commandments was to be set upon a table in the church where all might read it; this also was to be in the English tongue.

The translation has been described as one of the most significant moments in the history of reformation. It immediately identified the English Bible with the movement of religious change, and thus helped to associate what would become the Protestant faith with the English identity. In the seventeenth century, in particular, cultural history also became religious history. The career of Oliver Cromwell, for example, cannot be understood without a proper apprehension of the English translation of the Scriptures; it is perhaps worth remarking that Oliver Cromwell was a distant relation, through the marriage of his great-grandfather, to Thomas Cromwell. The translated Bible also introduced into England a biblical culture of the word, as opposed to the predominantly visual culture of the later medieval world; this refashioned culture was then to find its fruits in Milton and in Bunyan, in Blake and in Tennyson.

The English Bible also helped to fashion a language of devotion. Coverdale was the first to introduce such phrases as 'loving kindness' and 'tender mercy'. A tract of the time declared that 'Englishmen have now in hand, in every church and place, the Holy Bible in their mother tongue'. It was said that the voice of God was English. A seventeenth-century historian, William Strype, wrote that 'everybody that could bought the book, or busily read it, or got others to read it to them'. It was read aloud, in St Paul's Cathedral, to crowds who had gathered to listen. The king's men also hoped that the reading of the Bible would inculcate obedience to the lawful authorities, except that obedience was now to the king rather than to the pope.

In the same set of injunctions Thomas Cromwell decreed that every parson or vicar 'should keep one book or register, wherein he shall write the day and year of every wedding, christening and burying'. The parish register has been kept ever since, and must mark one of the most notable innovations of the reformed faith. It was also decreed that the images of the saints were no longer to be regarded as holy, and that the lights and candles placed before them should be removed. The Catholic Church of England was to be cleansed and renovated, but not overturned.

Cromwell also ordered the clergy to keep silent on matters of biblical interpretation, not to be 'babblers nor praters, arguers nor disputers thereof; nor to presume that they know therein that they know not'. It was of the utmost importance to be quiet on matters of doctrine for fear of provoking more discord and discontent in a country that had narrowly avoided a damaging religious war.

The deliberate ambiguity of the religious reforms was itself enough to reduce the possibility of any endorsement of Lutheranism. In the summer of 1538 some Lutherans arrived from Germany to explore the possibility of a union on matters of faith; they had been lured to London by the king in the belief that it might be possible to reach an agreement with German leaders, such as the elector of Saxony and the landgrave of Hesse, in opposition to the pope and the emperor. One problem, however, could not be removed. One of Henry's own negotiators, Robert Barnes, had once told Luther himself that 'my king does not care about religion'. And so it seemed.

The German embassy of three got precisely nowhere. They were lodged in poor accommodation and complained that 'multitudes of rats were running in their chambers day and night, which is no small disquietness, and their kitchen was so near the parlour that the smell was offensive to all that came to them'; one of them fell seriously ill. On matters of faith the king was polite but unmoving; they wished to extirpate such abuses as private Masses and the enforced celibacy of the clergy, but Henry could not be persuaded. They stayed for almost five months before returning with relief to Germany. The Lutheran reformer Melanchthon sent a private letter to Cranmer deploring the maintenance of popish superstition.

From Germany, too, arrived the first Anabaptists; they believed that infant baptism is not New Testament baptism, and that they were the true elect of God who did not require any external authority. All goods (including wives) should be held in common, in preparation for an imminent Second Coming. In a proclamation of November 1538, they were ordered by the king to leave the realm; those who remained were persecuted and burned.

The king's distaste for anyone tainted with unorthodox doctrine became amply evident during proceedings in the same month against a schoolmaster, John Lambert, who was prosecuted for denying Christ's presence in the consecrated bread and wine of the Mass. Henry himself presided at the heresy trial, dressed entirely in white silk as a token of purity; his guards also wore white. Cromwell wrote that 'it was a wonder to see how princely . . . and how benignly his grace assayed to convert the miserable man, how strong and manifest reasons his highness alleged against him'.

The trial took place in the banqueting house of the palace at Westminster. 'Ho, good fellow,' the king began, 'what is your name?' He sat beneath a canopy with his lords on the left side and with his bishops on the right. Lambert had in fact used an alias to avoid official detection, and tried to explain this to the king. Henry stopped him with a voice of thunder. 'I would not trust you, having two names, although you were my brother.' The trial, from Lambert's point of view, was of course already lost:

'Tell me plainly whether *you* say it is the body of Christ.'

'It is not his body. I deny it.'

'Mark well – for now you shall be condemned even by Christ's own words. "*Hoc est enim corpus meum.*" This is my body.'

The interrogation lasted for five hours. 'Will you live or die?' the king asked the prisoner at the conclusion. 'You have yet a free choice.'

'I commit my soul to God and my body to the king's mercy.'

'That being the case, you must die. I will not be a patron to heretics.'

Six days later Lambert was executed at Smithfield. The flames took off his thighs and legs, but the guards lifted up his still living body with their halberds and thrust it into the fire. 'None but Christ!' he called out. 'None but Christ!' Then he expired.

A religious envoy also came from another quarter. An English cardinal, Reginald Pole, had been sent from Rome as a papal legate but, hearing of his mission, the king naturally refused him entry to the country; he also surrounded him with spies and assassins. Henry himself sent a letter to Charles V, in which he warned that the cardinal was eager to promote discord among nations; his disposition is 'so cankered that from it can no good thing proceed, but weeping crocodile tears he will, if it be possible, pour forth the venom of his serpent nature'.

When the cardinal arrived in France Henry wrote to his ambassador there that 'we would be very glad to have the said Pole trussed up and conveyed to Calais'; Pole himself was informed that 100,000 pieces of English gold would be given to the man who brought him to England dead or alive. He was not killed, but he returned to Rome with his mission thwarted.

The king also proceeded against the members of Pole's family. 'Pity it is,' Cromwell wrote, 'that the folly of one brainsick Pole, or to say better of one witless fool, should be the ruin of so great a family.' Pole was one of a distinguished line that issued directly from the Plantagenet dynasty; his mother, Margaret Pole, the countess of Salisbury, was the daughter of the duke of Clarence who was popularly supposed to have been drowned in a butt of malmsey in the Tower on the orders of Edward IV. Their lineage alone would have been enough to place the cardinal and his relatives under grave suspicion. The fact that they were of the old faith only increased the risks against them. They themselves were aware of their peril and made some effort to avoid one another in public for fear of supposed conspiracy. But they were undone by the open sedition of Reginald Pole.

The cardinal's younger brother, Sir Geoffrey Pole, was arrested and interrogated; he was of unstable temper and at the first sign of pressure he conceded. He revealed all that he knew of his family's activities and perhaps embellished certain details. As a result another of his brothers, Henry, Lord Montague, was arrested together with his cousin, the marquis of Exeter. Geoffrey Pole then tried to suffocate himself with a cushion while incarcerated in the Tower. Margaret Pole herself was questioned and fiercely denied any imputations against her. 'We have dealt with such an one,' her interrogator said, 'as men have not dealt with tofore; we may rather call her a strong and constant man than a woman.' She was eventually imprisoned and taken to her death.

On coming to the scaffold she told the executioner that she would not lay her head upon the block, saying that she had received no trial. When she was forcibly held down the man, apparently not very experienced in his task, hacked away at her head and neck for several minutes. It was weary work but ultimately the head was off. On hearing the news of his mother's death, Cardinal Pole declared that 'I am now the son of a martyr'. He continued in a similar vein. 'Let us be of good cheer,' he said. 'We have now one more patron in heaven.'

Geoffrey Pole testified that Lord Montague had said that the king 'will one day die suddenly – his leg will kill him – and then we shall have jolly stirring'. Montague had also feared that, when the world 'came to stripes', there would be 'a lack of honest men'. He said that 'I trust to have a fair day upon those knaves that rule about the king; and I trust to see a merry world one day'. A 'merry world' was a truism of the period, meaning whatever the speaker wished it to mean. There was much more to the same effect. It was also revealed that the Poles had stayed in contact with their brother overseas, and had even warned him that his life was in danger. It was professed at the time that this was a serious Catholic conspiracy to depose the king, but it looks like the isolated murmurings of a disaffected, if distinguished, family. Yet the king was not likely to overlook any sign of dissent to his religious policy. If the sovereign does not feel secure, then no one is secure. Montague and Exeter were duly condemned to death and hanged as traitors. Against their names in the register of the Order of the Garter was written '*Vah, proditor!*' – 'Oh, traitor!' Exeter's son, Edward Courtenay, was consigned to the Tower, where he remained for the next fifteen years. He was freed only when Mary became sovereign. This was the way to deal with potential claimants to the throne.

Yet Henry's dynastic ambitions were already secure. By the spring of 1537 Henry's new wife was pregnant, and on 12 October gave birth to a healthy boy. The child was named Edward, since he had been born on the day dedicated to St Edward the Confessor. The line of kings would continue. Jane Seymour herself, however, became sick with puerperal fever, perhaps from an injury at the time of delivery, and died twelve days after giving birth. She was twenty-nine years old.

The period of court mourning lasted for almost three weeks, and on 12 November her body was laid in St George's Chapel at Windsor. The king ordered that 12,000 Masses should be said in the churches of London in order to intercede for her soul, a striking instance of Henry's attachment to the beliefs and rituals of the old faith. The king wore purple, the colour of royal mourning; Lady Mary wore black with a white headdress, as a token of the fact that the queen had died in childbed. A man was arrested for repeating a prophecy, in the Bell Inn on Tower Hill, that the prince 'should be as great a murderer as his father' since he had already murdered his mother at his birth.

A macabre scene was enacted a few months later when some idlers were watching the funeral of a child in a London churchyard. A priest in their company found the demeanour of the mourners to be peculiar and, hastening over to them, he opened the shroud; there was no baby in the folds, but the image of a child made out of wax with two pins stuck through it. The death anticipated was said to be that of the infant prince, and the news of the magical funeral spread through the kingdom.

Elaborate precautions and regulations were in any case established within the royal nursery. No one could approach the cradle of the infant prince without a royal warrant in the king's own hand. The baby's food was to be tested in case of poison. His clothes were to be washed by his own servants, and no one else was allowed to touch them. All the rooms of the prince's quarters had to be swept and scrubbed with soap three times a day. The fear of disease was always present for infants and small children. A charming cameo can be found, in the Royal Collection, of Henry with his arm around the infant boy; it is one of the few images that show the king as a natural human being. In the spring of the following year the king spent much time with his son 'dallying with him in his arms . . . and so holding him in a window to the sight and great comfort of all the people'. For the next six years Lord Edward would be brought up, as he himself put it in his diary, 'among the women'. This had also been the fate of his father.

Henry was soon in active pursuit of another wife. He told his ambassadors at the imperial court in Brussels that 'we be daily instanted by our nobles and Council to use short expedition in the determination of our wife, for to get more increase of issue to the assurance of succession, and upon their admonitions of age coming fast on, and that the time slippeth and flyeth marvellously away, we be minded utterly to be within short space at a full resolution, one way or other, and no longer to lose time'. 'Marvellously' is an appropriately sixteenth-century word. 'I marvel' may mean 'I wonder' or 'I am amazed'. So a short dialogue might be: 'I marvel that . . .'; 'I marvel that you marvel . . . '

Although he was preparing himself for a fourth marriage, Henry never wholly forgot Jane Seymour. He made two subsequent journeys to her familial home, Wolf Hall, and in his will he ordained that 'the bones and body of our true and loving wife Queen Jane' be placed with his in the tomb. He himself might have been placed in it sooner than he intended. In the spring of 1538 the ulcers on his swollen legs became blocked, and it was said that 'the humours which had no outlet were like to have stifled him'. It seems possible that a blood clot entered his lungs; for twelve days he lay immobile and scarcely able to breathe, his eyes and veins standing out with the protracted effort. Rumours spread that the king of England was dead, and arguments arose over the relative claims of Edward and Mary to the throne. Yet the fury of the fit eventually passed. Soon enough, he was recovered.

He began another phase of his royal building. He enlarged the palace at Hampton Court so that it eventually encompassed more than a thousand rooms and was the largest structure in England since the time of the Romans. In the autumn of 1538, too, he began work in Surrey on an architectural conceit or fantasy known as Nonsuch Palace, so named because there was none such like it in the entire kingdom. It was made up of turrets and towers, cupolas and battlements; the upper part was framed in timber and decorated with stucco panels and carved slates. The gardens were filled with statues and waterfalls, with images of birds and pyramids and cupids from which gushed water. It was fit for an extravagant and conceited king, but it was not completed in his lifetime. Henry would reign for only nine more years.

12

The body of Christ

At the beginning of 1539 fears emerged over the threat of invasion, encouraged by the papal edict against the king; the French king and the Spanish emperor were rumoured to be in alliance with the pope, while the king of Scotland, James V, promised to support them. 'We will be', one courtier wrote, 'a morsel among choppers.' It was said that 8,000 mercenaries were gathering in the Low Countries. A fleet of sixty-eight ships was sighted off Margate. This would be the first concerted attack since the time of the Norman invasion. Henry had been excommunicated but his enemies declared that the people were still in slavish obedience to a heretic king; one merchant wrote from London that they would all be taken 'for Jews or infidels' and could lawfully be enslaved by the enemy.

Henry reviewed his fleet, consisting of 150 ships, and ordered military musters to be summoned throughout the country; he then toured the more vulnerable areas along the south coast and ordered new fortifications. The fortresses along the border with Scotland were strengthened. The king's ships left the Thames for Portsmouth. The building stone from the abandoned monasteries was employed to build defences. The privy council met daily in preparation for war. The bodyguard of the king were known as 'gentlemen pensioners'; they wore velvet doublets and coats, complete with gold chains, and each gripped a large pole-axe in his right hand.

At the beginning of May thousands of men, from the age of sixteen to sixty, mustered whatever armour and weapons they possessed before marching from Mile End, the traditional meeting point of armed bands, into the city; the fields of Stepney and Bethnal Green 'were covered with men and weapons', with the battalions of pikes 'like a great forest'. In the following month Thomas Cromwell staged a battle between two barges on the Thames; one was commanded by men dressed as the pope and his cardinals, while in the other stood figures representing the king and the court. The Vatican was of course overpowered and ditched into the river.

Henry himself was in a state of high anxiety. It was the one eventuality he had most feared. The French ambassador in London wrote in alarm to his court, begging to be relieved of his duties on the grounds that he feared the wrath of the king; he was 'the most dangerous and cruel man in the world', and seemed to be in such a state of fury that he had 'neither reason nor understanding'. The ambassador professed to believe that the king might attack or even kill him in the course of an audience.

Yet the enterprise against England was prevented by quarrels between France and Spain. It is also likely that the spies of those nations had reported to their masters that there was little evidence of internal disaffection; the people would not rise up in arms against their king. No invading navy arrived, and the general alarm soon subsided. But the king knew very well that it would be unwise to stir up domestic discontent any further; he had pushed the people to the edge of their religious tolerance. He deemed it wise, therefore, to placate the conservative or orthodox faithful who comprised the majority of the population. In that spirit, too, he was following his own instincts.

Henry was clearly moving away from the path of religious reform. In a declaration for 'unity of religion', devised in the spring of 1539, the king blamed the indiscriminate reading of the English Bible for the incidence of 'murmur, malice and malignity' within the realm. He had hoped that the Scriptures would be read 'with meekness' but instead they had provoked rivalry and dissension.

The people disputed 'arrogantly' in taverns and even in churches, angrily denouncing rival interpretations as heretical or papistical. The Bible should, in future, only be read in silence. The declaration was in fact never issued, and was replaced by a more formal proclamation.

Evidence of religious disputes can be found in the records of the church courts. Mrs Cicely Marshall of St Albans parish was accused of 'despising holy bread and holy water', while a fellow parishioner was blamed for 'despising our Lady'. John Humfrey of St Giles, Cripplegate, was summoned for 'speaking against the sacraments and ceremonies of the church'. A woman from the parish of St Nicholas in the Flesh Shambles was presented 'for busy reasoning on the new learning, and not keeping the church'. Margaret Ambsworth of St Botolph without Aldgate was summoned 'for instructing of maids, and being a great doctress'. Robert Plat and his wife 'were great reasoners in scripture, saying they had it of the Spirit'. All of these people, and many more, were given the common name of 'meddlers'.

A parliament was also summoned in the spring of 1539 to consider matters of religion. A contemporary reported that it was assembled to negotiate 'a thorough unity and uniformity established for the reformation of the church of this realm'. Unity was not easily to be won.

Various opinions, for example, were maintained over the bread and the wine offered in the Mass. The orthodox Catholic faithful upheld the doctrine of transubstantiation, whereby the bread and wine became in actual fact the body and blood of Christ. This is a mystery of the faith. It is believed because it is impossible, and proof of the overwhelming power of God. Luther also believed in the real presence of Christ in the sacrament, but denied that He was there 'in substance'; his belief was in something that became known as consubstantiation or sacramental union, whereby the integrity of the bread and wine remain even while being transformed by the body and blood of Christ.

The more radical reformers, intent upon destroying priestly power and what were for them superstitious rituals, declared that the Eucharist was only a commemoration or remembrance of Christ's sacrifice that had been performed once and for ever; it could not be endlessly rehearsed at the altar. '*Hoc est corpus meum*' should therefore be translated as 'This signifies my body'. Christ was in heaven; He was not on the earth, even at Mass.

Endless permutations could of course be devised between these three statements of belief. Thus one reformer declined to believe that the bread and wine are miraculously changed, but conceded that 'the Body and Blood of Christ are truly received by faith' when the worshipper partakes of them in perfect piety. This was known as 'virtualism'. In an age when religion was the single most important aspect of social life, these debates were also matters of state. At the beginning of the parliamentary session a small committee was set up to examine all of the issues, the most tendentious being the question of the Blessed Sacrament.

The committee comprised four conservative and four reforming bishops, with Cromwell presiding as vicegerent in religious matters. Of course they could come to no shared conclusions, and Henry stepped forward. He allowed the conservative duke of Norfolk to present six simple questions to the House of Lords that were so framed as to yield only one possible answer. The result of their deliberations emerged in the document known as the Act of the Six Articles that clearly restated the orthodox position on such matters as confession and clerical celibacy. It was essentially a device to quell religious controversy and forge unity in matters of doctrine. It became known to those who detested it as 'the whip with six strings' or 'the bloody act'.

The Six Articles were a strong rebuff to reformers such as Cranmer and Cromwell, and were a clear victory for the conservative faction. Transubstantiation was upheld in all but name, although Cranmer had finally managed to remove the term itself. But Henry had the last word; in his own hand he amended the draft of the Act so that the bread and wine were now ordained to be 'none other substances but the substance of his foresaid natural body'. After Henry's death Cranmer declared that 'Christ is eaten with the heart. Eating with the mouth cannot give life. The righteous alone can eat the Body of Christ.' But for the moment he was forced to remain silent.

At a later date he also recorded his opinion that the Act of the Six Articles 'was so much against the truth, and common judgements both of divines and lawyers, that if the king's majesty himself had not come personally into the parliament house, those laws had never passed'. Yet they seem to have been welcomed by the populace. The French ambassador wrote to his court that 'the people show great joy at the king's declaration touching the sacrament, being much more inclined to the old religion than to the new opinions'. The people were not even prepared to read their prayers in English. 'How loath be our priests to teach the commandments,' one reformer lamented, 'the articles of faith and the pater noster, in English! Again how unwilling be the people to learn it! Yea, they jest at it calling it the new pater noster...'

The denial of transubstantiation was now to be punished by death in the fire, while the refusal to subscribe to the other five articles led to the forfeiture of all goods and imprisonment at the king's pleasure. It was the most severe religious law in English history. The articles were essentially the king's declaration of faith. It was a faith shaped by the will of the ruler and by the power of punishment. It is reported that some 200 were arrested and held in prison; they had, in the phrase of the period, been 'brought into trouble'. Some free spirits were not hindered. John Harridaunce, known as the inspired bricklayer of Whitechapel, was still preaching out of his window between nine and twelve at night, where he referred to the religious reformers as 'setters forth of light'. When a neighbouring baker warned him that he was breaking the tenets of the Six Articles he replied that 'it is fit for me to be burnt as for thee to bake a loaf'.

The duke of Norfolk remarked to his chaplain, 'You see, we have hindered priests from having wives.'

'And can your grace', the chaplain replied, 'prevent also men's wives from having priests?'

Two bishops were forced to resign their sees as a result of the new measures; Hugh Latimer left Worcester and Nicholas Shaxton left Salisbury. Archbishop Cranmer was obliged to send his wife and children into exile. In the early summer the archbishop summoned a Scottish evangelical, Alexander Alesius, to Lambeth palace. 'Happy man that you are,' he said, 'you can escape! Would that I were at liberty to do the same; truly my see would not hold me back.' He then admitted that he had signed the decree when 'compelled by fear'. The Lutherans of Germany were horrified by the Act, which they regarded as the end of religious reform in England. The king had shown his true colours. He was not in the least evangelical. He only wished to augment his revenues, with the treasures of the old Church, and to increase his power.

There was a significant epilogue to the passing of the Act. Thomas Cranmer, wrestling with his highly developed conscience, made a series of scholarly notes on the mistakes and misjudgements contained in the articles. His secretary, Ralph Morice, took a wherry from Lambeth to deliver the notebook to the king himself. On the south side of the river, at this moment, a bear-baiting was being held. The bear broke loose from its tormentors and plunged into the Thames, hotly pursued by the dogs.

All the passengers in the wherry, with the exception of Cranmer's secretary, leaped into the water. The bear then clambered into the boat, at which point Morice lost his nerve and jumped overboard. All thought of the notebook left him in his desire to be rescued. When he finally reached land, however, he saw the book floating on the water. He called out to the bear-ward to retrieve it. But when the man took up the book, he handed it to a priest. The cleric saw immediately that these were notes against the Six Articles and accused Morice of treason. In the ensuing argument Morice foolishly confessed that the notes had been written by the archbishop of Canterbury himself. The priest refused to hand them back.

Morice now fell into a panic and in his distress called upon Thomas Cromwell. On the following morning Cromwell summoned the priest, who was about to hand the book to one of Cranmer's enemies. Cromwell 'took the book out of his hands, and threatened him severely for his presumption in meddling with a privy councillor's book'. The story is an indication, if nothing else, of the fears and tensions within the court itself. Reports circulated at the time that Cranmer had been sent to the Tower and even that he had been executed. In the same period Thomas Cromwell and the duke of Norfolk had a furious quarrel at Cromwell's house; the subject of the dispute is not known. Could it be that Cromwell himself was now no longer safe?

13

The fall

Henry had been seeking another wife ever since the death of Jane Seymour; another son was likely to guarantee the future of his dynasty. The wives of kings were generally considered to be little more than brood mares. Charles V had proposed the duchess of Milan to him, and the French court had suggested various other ladies for the dubious honour of obtaining his hand. He asked the French ambassador to convey eight of them to Calais, where he could inspect them all at once; the invitation was declined.

Yet Cromwell, favouring a union with the Protestant princes of northern Europe, took the part of Anne of Cleves. Her father, only recently dead, had been a reformer if not precisely a Lutheran; Anne's older sister was already married to the elector of Saxony. They would be invaluable allies. Henry also feared the collaboration between the French king and the emperor, together with the pope, in any future enterprise against England. At that very moment Charles V was travelling from Spain into France. Henry needed friends.

It was whispered that Anne of Cleves was as modest as she was beautiful; a portrait of her, executed by Hans Holbein, was brought to England. The king gazed upon it and pronounced her to be eminently worthy of marriage. It was reported at the time that she spoke no language but German and that she had no ear for music.

Yet in matters of state these are trifles. After the conclusion of some months of negotiation, the lady was shipped to England at the end of 1539. Henry was so eager to see her that he rode incognito to Rochester, where he looked upon her secretly. He did not like what he saw, comparing her to a Flanders mare. He berated the earl of Southampton for having written, from Calais, about her beauty. The earl excused himself on the grounds that he believed matters had gone too far to be reversed. The king's anger then fell upon Cromwell. He told him that the proposed bride was 'nothing so well as she was spoken of'. He then asserted that 'if I had known what I know now, she should not have come into this realm'. At a later meeting he asked him, 'Is there none other remedy but that I must needs, against my will, put my neck in the yoke?'

There was no remedy. He did not dare to renounce her at the cost of alienating his new allies in northern Europe and, as he put it, 'for fear of making a ruffle in the world'. 'I am not well handled,' he told Cromwell. Cromwell would pay the price at a later date. The marriage was duly solemnized on 6 January 1540, even as the king was making it clear to his court that he had taken a great dislike to his bride. He was always scrupulously polite to her and, knowing no English, she may have been unaware of his aversion. The morning after the marriage Cromwell asked him if he now liked her more. No. He suspected that she was not a virgin, and she had such 'displeasant smells' about her that he loathed her more than ever. He doubted if the marriage would ever be consummated. In that speculation he proved to be right. The royal couple were married for a little over six months and, although on occasions they lay in the same bed, there was no progeny. Instead the king told one of his doctors that he had '*duas pollutiones nocturnas in somno*' or, in common parlance, two wet dreams.

A courtier had come up to Cromwell as he stood alone in a gallery, leaning against a window. 'For God's sake,' he told Cromwell, 'devise how his grace may be relieved by one way or another.'

'Yes, but what and how?' Cromwell broke away saying, 'Well, well, it is a great matter.'

Eventually it was proposed that there should be an amicable

separation; Anne of Cleves would not follow the same path as Anne Boleyn or even Katherine of Aragon. The convocation of the clergy were persuaded to declare the marriage null and invalid, on the grounds that there had been no issue, and parliament confirmed the verdict. Anne of Cleves herself did not seem particularly discomfited by the dissolution of her marriage, and was in any case given a generous pension. She learned English quickly enough, and settled down in the country for the next seventeen years with very few regrets. One of the many properties she owned is still to be seen in Lewes.

Henry was all the time attending carefully to the security and education of his only son. Edward was the key to the future. His first portrait, by Hans Holbein, was probably executed in 1540. It shows the infant dressed in rich robes, like a miniature version of his father. Like his father, too, he stares directly and calmly out of the canvas; his right hand is raised, as if he were about to make a declaration, and the rattle in his left hand closely resembles a tiny sceptre.

In this year a tutor, Richard Cox, was appointed to guide the three-year-old boy in all the lessons a virtuous prince must learn; another tutor, John Cheke, was appointed four years later. The two men were humanist scholars in the tradition of Erasmus, and seem to have trodden the same middle path in religion as Henry himself. The teachers of the heir to the throne could never have been Lutherans. Yet the truth remains that Edward endorsed a more radical Protestantism almost as soon as he gained the throne. He was to be called 'the godly imp'.

He was instructed also in Greek and in Latin, of which he soon had a fair command. He would be introduced to the arts of horseriding and of archery, both fit for a king. As he acquired more learning the prince was given his own study, with a writing desk covered in black velvet; various mathematical and astronomical instruments were at his disposal, including a compass and a metal rule. A chess set lay on a shelf, while an hourglass hung from the wall. He had slates on which to write, as well as a variety of pens. In another room beside his bedchamber he kept miscellaneous papers concerning his mother, Jane Seymour, as well as his books;

he also owned a puppet, and two pairs of spectacles. Diverse carved and painted objects, such as a spear and a staff 'of unicorns' horns garnished with silver gilt', were also to be found.

In the spring of 1540 Thomas Cromwell was created earl of Essex; his bright particular star was still in the ascendant. He was conducting the primary affairs of the nation; soon after his elevation he committed the bishop of Chichester to the Tower of London on the charge of favouring those who refused the oath of supremacy. He had also threatened the bishops of Durham, Winchester and Bath with the consequences of royal displeasure.

Yet there were always mutterings against him. He treated the nobles with a high hand, so that the duke of Norfolk in particular became his implacable opponent. He was accused of being over-mighty and over-wealthy, and of recklessly squandering the king's treasure.

On the morning of 10 June 1540, he took his place in the Lords, as usual; at three in the afternoon of the same day he proceeded to his chair at the head of the council table. Norfolk shouted out, 'Cromwell! Do not sit there! That is no place for you! Traitors do not sit among gentlemen.' 'I am not a traitor,' Cromwell replied. Whereupon the captain of the guard, and six other officers, came to him.

'I arrest you.'

'What for?'

'That, you will learn elsewhere.'

In his fury Cromwell threw his cap down on the stone floor of the chamber. 'This, then,' he said 'is the reward for all my services.' The members of the council then erupted in a fury of antagonism, screaming abuse and thumping their fists on the table.

It is impossible to unravel all the private suspicions and antagonisms that led to his fall. He was hated by many of the nobility who resented the fact that the son of a blacksmith should have risen above them. Those of the old faith detested him for his destruction of their shrines and monasteries. The public accusations against him were manifold. He was accused of taking bribes and of encroaching on royal authority in matters like pardoning

6.

1. Henry VIII at the time of his accession:
a golden youth in his prime.

2. Katherine of Aragon, daughter of
Ferdinand of Aragon and Isabella of Castile.
She was Henry's first unhappy wife.

3. A woodcut showing the English knights at Flodden Field,
who fought in the absence of their king.

9. Unlucky Anne Boleyn, who incurred the wrath of her husband.

10. Thomas Howard, third Duke of Norfolk, a courtier eventually charged with high treason.

11. The martyrdom of the Carthusian friars of Charterhouse. Their bowels were ripped open before their eyes.

1. Henry VIII at the time of his accession: a golden youth in his prime.

2. Katherine of Aragon, daughter of Ferdinand of Aragon and Isabella of Castile. She was Henry's first unhappy wife.

3. A woodcut showing the English knights at Flodden Field, who fought in the absence of their king.

9. Unlucky Anne Boleyn, who incurred the wrath of her husband.

10. Thomas Howard, third Duke of Norfolk, a courtier eventually charged with high treason.

11. The martyrdom of the Carthusian friars of Charterhouse. Their bowels were ripped open before their eyes.

9. Unlucky Anne Boleyn, who incurred
the wrath of her husband.

10. Thomas Howard, third
Duke of Norfolk, a courtier eventually
charged with high treason.

11. The martyrdom of the Carthusian friars of Charterhouse.
Their bowels were ripped open before their eyes.

6. Wolsey in all his glory before his fall.

7. Thomas More, England's conscience, who incurred the enmity of the king.

8. The king trampling on the pope, an allegorical depiction typical of the times.

4. The Field of the Cloth of Gold – diplomacy at its height.

5. A letter from Henry to his 'good cardinal', Thomas Wolsey, when they were still close collaborators.

1. Henry VIII at the time of his accession: a golden youth in his prime.

2. Katherine of Aragon, daughter of Ferdinand of Aragon and Isabella of Castile. She was Henry's first unhappy wife.

3. A woodcut showing the English knights at Flodden Field, who fought in the absence of their king.

12. The Pilgrimage of Grace, a northern rebellion for the sake of the 'old faith'.

13. Jane Seymour, mother of Edward VI, the only consort of the king who produced a male heir.

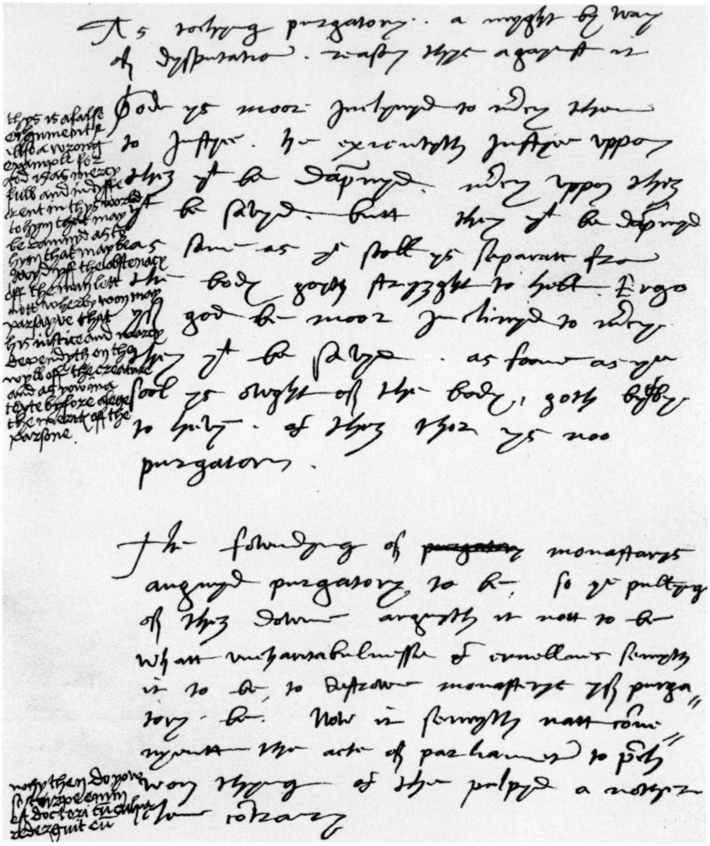

14. Bishop Latimer's arguments against Purgatory, a fiction of the papists. Henry's own thoughts on the matter are annotated in the margin.

15 (*below left*). Thomas Cromwell in his finery before he, too, was disgraced and killed.

16 (*below right*). Anne of Cleves, the king's unsuitable bride who survived her husband.

17. Title page of the Great Bible of 1539, the first authorized edition in the English language.

18 (*below*). Katherine Howard, wedded and beheaded in quick succession.

19 (*below right*). Katherine Parr, the last and most fortunate of Henry's queens.

20. An allegory of the Tudor family, an example of royal propaganda.

21. Edward VI, pale and sickly.

22. Lady Jane Grey, the queen of nine days
before the accession of Mary.

convicted men and issuing commissions. He was indeed guilty of all these, if guilty is the right word. They were really activities that came with the job, and had previously been tolerated by the king. Bribery was the only way, for example, that the system of administration could work.

Another set of charges concerned Cromwell's beliefs; he was accused of holding heretical opinions and of supporting heretics in court and country. It was claimed that he was a Lutheran who had all the while been conspiring to change the religion of the nation; as the king's ambassador to the emperor put it, he had allowed the impression that 'all piety and religion, having no place, was banished out of England'. Letters between him and the Lutheran lords of Germany were discovered, although it is possible that they were forgeries. It was reported to the German princes that he had indirectly threatened to kill the king if Henry should attempt to reverse the process of religious reform; he had said that he would strike a dagger into the heart of the man who should oppose reformation. If such a threat had been made, then Cromwell was guilty of treason. It was of course the principal charge against him.

He was allowed to confront his accusers, but he was not permitted a public trial before his peers. He was instead subject to an Act of attainder for treason, a device that he himself had invented. The bill of attainder passed through both Lords and Commons without a single dissenting vote. Only Cranmer endeavoured to find a good word for him, and wrote to the king remarking on Cromwell's past services. 'I loved him as a friend,' he said, 'for so I took him to be.'

It is sometimes asserted that Cromwell's fate was largely the consequence of the fatal alignment between religion and politics, but the bungled marriage of Henry and Anne of Cleves also played some part in the matter. The French king and the emperor had failed to forge an alliance, so Henry no longer needed the princes of Germany for allies; the marriage had proved to be without purpose. Although Cromwell had expedited the union at Henry's request and with Henry's approval, he could not wholly shield himself from the king's frustration and anger.

Of course the force of the conservative reaction to Cromwell's statutes of religion, for which the Pilgrimage of Grace is evidence, had shaken Henry; the king had colluded with them, but in the popular mind Cromwell was the prime mover of reform. He was the 'evil counsellor' who had given wicked advice to his sovereign. It was politic, therefore, that Cromwell should be given up.

Yet there were darker and deeper reasons for his removal. Cromwell had been arrested and tried as part of a diplomatic dance. The French king, Francis I, had always detested Cromwell as a heretic and as a supporter of the Spanish cause; when the duke of Norfolk came to the French court as a special ambassador, Francis suggested to him that an agreement might be reached if Cromwell were removed from office. Norfolk duly repeated this observation to the king. Henry himself was now happy to be characterized as a religious conservative, to ingratiate himself further with the French, and so it suited him to portray Cromwell as a covert Lutheran heretic who had misled his master. The fact that these charges were largely untrue was not important. In effect Cromwell had served his purpose, having enriched the king with the dissolution of the monasteries, and could now be dispatched from the scene.

Cromwell was removed to the Tower to await his execution by the axe. His house was searched and a hoard of 'crosses, chalices, mitres, vases and other things from the spoils of the Church' were discovered. Henry stripped him of all his titles, and declared that his former servant was to be known only as 'Thomas Cromwell, cloth-carder' in recognition of a former lowly occupation before his royal service. The church bells pealed in rejoicing, and impromptu parties were held in the streets of London.

From his last lodging he wrote a contrite letter to the king in which 'your highness's most heavy and most miserable prisoner, and poor slave' begged for 'mercy, mercy, mercy'. Mercy was not a commodity, however, in which the king traded. On the morning of 28 July Cromwell proclaimed on the scaffold that he was dying in the old faith, and then he bowed his head for the axe. The two executioners were 'ragged and butcherly', and another contemporary account describes how they were 'chopping the Lord Cromwell's neck and head for nearly half-an-hour'.

The fall of Cromwell was the harbinger of a more severe prosecution of those whom Henry and the conservative faction

deemed to be heretics. Robert Barnes, once an Augustinian friar
at Cambridge, was one of the reformers whom Cromwell had
protected; it was he whom Cromwell had used in the past as an
envoy to the German Lutherans. In February 1540, Barnes
preached against the leading conservative Stephen Gardiner,
bishop of Winchester, and accused him of setting 'evil herbs' in
the 'garden of scripture'. At the end of his sermon he had flung
down his glove as a token of defiance against the bishop. Barnes
was taken up, but recanted. Three months later, in the spring of
1540, he once again preached what was considered to be heretical
doctrine at St Mary Spital; on this occasion he was sent to the
Tower. It may be that, at this stage, he was used as part of the
case against Cromwell; one of the viccgerent's closest supporters,
after all, was an arrant heretic. Two days after Cromwell's
execution, Barnes was burned at Smithfield.

He did not die alone. In a triumphant reassertion of his
'middle way' the king burned two other reformers, who were
believed to be part of Cromwell's supposed conspiracy, and hanged
three 'papist' priests who had denied the royal supremacy. Henry
was proclaiming that he was not a sovereign of one faction or
another; he dispensed justice equally to all. There was one difference; it was said that those who supported the papacy were hanged,
while those who opposed it were burned.

From this time forward, in fact, he no longer employed one
pre-eminent minister. The years of Wolsey and of Cromwell were
over. Now the king decided to supervise the affairs of the realm.
He described himself as 'old' but he was not too old to control the
business of the council or to read the dispatches of his ambassadors. The king's council was established upon a more formal basis;
it had a membership of approximately nineteen peers or prelates,
and met each day at court. A minute book was to be kept. The
privy council now fashioned policy in partnership with the king;
it supervised the workings of the law and the operations of the
exchequer. Some counsellors were superior to others, of course,
and the most prominent among them were now Stephen Gardiner,
Thomas Cranmer and the duke of Norfolk.

Norfolk had another advantage. At the end of the previous
year he had brought his pretty niece to court, as one of the

maids-in-waiting to Anne of Cleves. Katherine Howard was perhaps sixteen, perhaps twenty-two – her date of birth is not known
for certain – and not at all demure. It was one of her family's
mottoes that marriage must provide more than 'four bare legs in a
bed'. A marriage, in other words, must bring with it other
advantages. Katherine Howard was schooled in all the arts and
tricks that might appeal to the king, and it seems that she was not
averse to using them. On 28 July, just nineteen days after his union
with Anne of Cleves was formally annulled, Henry married her. It
proved to be her day of doom.

She soon became acquainted with her husband's formidable
temper. The ulcer on his leg once more became infected, and the
pus was drained from it in a sometimes painful operation. He
became morose and depressed. He began to regret the execution
of Cromwell, and complained that he had been deceived about
him by some of his councillors who 'by false accusations had made
him put to death the most faithful servant he ever had'. He often
blamed others for the faults of his own actions. It was reported
that he had 'formed a sinister opinion of some of his chief men',
and dispatched so many people from court that it 'resembled more
a private family than a king's train'. He fell into foul fits of temper,
and refused even to listen to music. He would not allow the new
queen into his presence for ten days.

A respite was at hand. By the spring of 1541 his ulcer had
healed and on 10 April the French ambassador reported that 'the
Queen is thought to be with child'. The rumour proved to be false,
however, and it is possible that Katherine Howard miscarried.
It was the old curse that seemed to hang over the king. It was
reported, by the same ambassador, that Henry was displeased with
his wife and was 'avoiding as much as possible her company'.

On 30 June, however, the king and queen led a great progress
to the north. He had never travelled to those regions before, and
had really known them only in the context of riot and rebellion.
This was his opportunity to impress the northern people with his
might and magnificence. He led 5,000 horse and 1,000 foot-
soldiers so that it seemed an armed camp was on the march from
Grafton to Northampton, Lincoln to Boston, Doncaster and
Pontefract and York. He dressed in cloth of gold, and graciously

accepted the submission of erstwhile rebels. His was the theatre of power.

Yet behind the scenes of this theatre another drama was being performed. Katherine Howard, perhaps vexed and unsatisfied by her ageing lover, was proving to be unfaithful. Even as the progress went further northward she began a liaison with a gentleman, Thomas Culpeper, and with the connivance of her ladies-in-waiting arranged to meet him at secret venues; she sought the back doors and the back stairs to expedite her passion. He became her 'sweet little fool'.

At the same time it was rumoured that, five years before, Katherine had been intimate with her instructor on the virginal. Henry Manox had boasted that she had promised him 'her maidenhead though it be painful to her'. This fault was compounded when another former lover from the same period, Francis Dereham, now came forward. It was believed, at a later date, that he was in fact her common-law husband. It is possible that he threatened her with some disclosure. At all events she appointed him as her private secretary and usher of her chamber. It was a woeful mistake.

Cranmer was approached by an informant who knew all about Katherine Howard's previous indiscretions. The archbishop summoned certain members of her former household, who only confirmed the stories. It was imperative that the king be told, but no one wished to be the messenger of such tidings. If the news proved to be false, the result would be fatal. On 1 November, in the royal chapel, the king gave public thanks to God for having been 'pleased to give me a wife so entirely conformable to my inclinations'. While the service continued the archbishop left a sealed letter for the king with the details of the queen's previous indiscretions.

Henry refused to believe them. He insisted that the reports were the work of a faction determined to bring down the duke of Norfolk as well as the queen. He demanded that Cranmer investigate this plot and 'not to desist until you have got to the bottom of the pot'. Whereupon the king's guards interrupted Katherine and her ladies while they were dancing together, insisting that this was 'no more the time to dance'. The young queen was then confined to her apartments, where she remained in fear and trembling. She must have suspected that certain inconvenient facts were about to emerge.

When Cranmer and the council questioned more deeply into the affair, it was clear that the queen was in fact deeply compromised. Manox and Dereham were interrogated, in the course of which interview Manox confessed how he 'had commonly used to feel the secrets and other parts of the queen's body'. Dereham also confirmed that he 'had known her carnally many times, both in doublet and hose between the sheets and in naked bed'.

Cranmer interviewed Katherine on at least two occasions but found her 'in such lamentation and heaviness as I never saw no creature'. She screamed with panic at her likely fate. There were times when she seemed about to fall 'into some dangerous ecstasy, or else into a very frenzy'. She lied to Cranmer about her previous lovers, alleging that Dereham had raped her 'with importunate force'. She admitted a few days later that he had indeed given her tokens. He knew 'a little woman in London with a crooked back, who was very cunning in making all manner of flowers' out of silk. She also admitted that he called her 'wife'. On their nights of love-making he would bring with him wine, apples and strawberries. But 'as for these words, *I promise you, I do love you with all my heart*, I do not remember that ever I spake them'. She wrote out a full confession to the king, which seems to have cheered him a little. She had, at the very least, never been unfaithful to him in the course of their marriage.

Yet rumour has a thousand tongues, and the royal court is its proper home. Once the queen's former frailties were known, it was hard to conceal more recent examples. The name of Thomas Culpeper was mentioned. The gossip about the young courtier soon reached the ears of the privy council which, in the words of its proceedings, 'weighed the matter and deeply pondered the gravity thereof'. They called some of the queen's ladies and interrogated them about her behaviour. One of them, Margaret Morton, said that there passed a look between the queen and Culpeper 'of such sort that I thought there was love between them'. She also alleged that the two had been alone in the queen's closet for five or six hours, and 'for certain they had passed out' –

the sixteenth-century phrase for orgasm. Another lady-in-waiting confirmed that there was much 'puffing and blowing' between them. The queen's principal lady, Lady Rochford, the perfidious sister-in-law of Anne Boleyn, had already been 'seized with raving madness'; she had eased the passage of Culpeper into her mistress's chamber. She would be brought, insane, to the scaffold.

The privy council next interrogated Culpeper. His was the crucial case, since the queen's adultery would be considered to be high treason. He denied any actual intercourse but agreed that 'he intended and meant to do ill with the queen and that in like wise the queen so minded to do with him'. The privy council did not believe him. He and the queen must have passed out. 'You may see what was done before marriage,' Cranmer told them. 'God knows what has been done since!' It was suggested that Katherine had also been dallying with Dereham on the progress to the north.

Henry attended a secret night session of the council at the London residence of the bishop of Winchester. When the full account was put to him, he raged so violently that it was feared he would go mad. He called for his sword, with the intention of killing his young wife. He swore that she would never 'have such delight in her lechery as she should have pain and torture in her death'. Then he broke down and wept, which was considered 'strange' for one of his 'courage'. The news of the queen's disgrace was soon known everywhere. The duke of Norfolk, her uncle, declared to the French ambassador that she 'had prostituted herself to seven or eight persons' and that she ought to be burned.

On 1 December Culpeper and Dereham were both brought to Westminster Hall on the charge of treason. In the course of the charges Katherine herself was described as a 'common harlot'. The two men were found guilty and sentenced to the traitor's death of hanging and disembowelling. Henry Manox, having offended long before Katherine had become queen, was reprieved. Culpeper, a gentleman, had his punishment commuted to a simple beheading.

On 13 February 1542 Katherine Howard followed him to the scaffold. She had been married to the king for less than two years. She panicked when she embarked on the Thames for her final journey, and had to be manhandled onto the boat. A flotilla of vessels then carried her from Syon to the Tower, where she was received with all the honours due to a queen. She was beheaded three days later, on Tower Green, and was said to have been meek and repentant at the end. She had in fact rehearsed her death and had asked for the block to be brought to her prison chamber so that she could learn how to put her neck upon it gracefully. Her body was buried close to that of Anne Boleyn in the chapel of St Peter ad Vincula. Many of her family were sent to the Tower but were eventually released. The duke of Norfolk stayed on his estates and avoided the court. But from this day forward Henry never really trusted him.

On the day of his wife's execution the king held a great banquet, with twenty-six ladies at his own table, and over the succeeding days gave many such feasts. He was eating so much that his vast bulk grew ever heavier, and his bed was enlarged to a width of 7 feet. Yet in private he was cast down. In the margin of a translation of Proverbs, the king made a double mark beside the following passage: 'For the lips of a harlot are a dropping honeycomb, and her throat is softer than oil. But at the last she is as bitter as wormwood, and as sharp as a two-edged sword.'

14

War games

In the summer of 1542, Pope Paul III established the Holy Office
of the Inquisition, with six cardinals as inquisitors-general. 'Even
if my own father were a heretic,' the pope declared, 'I would
gather the wood to burn him.' The paths of religious faith were
perilous. Henry, now that he had broken with the papacy, was
eager to see Charles V follow his example; it was the English king's
wish to see a great general council held in which the differences of
religion could be debated and perhaps resolved.

The diplomatic situation seemed to be working in his favour.
He was contemplating an alliance with Charles V against France, a
joint invasion that would not in fact take place until the summer of
1544. Yet in the meantime it was important to secure his northern
territories. He had agreed to meet the king of Scotland, James V,
at York towards the end of his northern progress in the summer of
1541; but James, perhaps fearing kidnap or assassination, did not
arrive. The king's father, James IV, had been killed by Henry's
army at Flodden Field less than thirty years before. This rebuff
served only to augment Henry's anger at the increasing number of
border raids by the Scots, who still considered parts of northern
England as their proper home. When a Scottish raiding party
seized one of the king's representatives, in the summer of 1542, the
matter came to open war.

The French king and his court were delighted. Francis I told the English ambassador that 'your majesty [Henry] had begun with the Scots, and the Scots had given you your hands full'. He had nothing to fear from the English while they were distracted by the ancient enemy. The Scots were also now in full cry. 'All is ours,' they said. 'The English are but heretics.' In the autumn of 1542 the duke of Norfolk, partly returned to favour, led 20,000 men into the Lothians where he laid waste to the harvest; he also left towns and villages in ruins. The army then retired to Berwick.

In reprisal, a Scottish army of some 15,000 men advanced into Cumberland in the last week of November. They were not met by English forces, whose commanders were taken wholly by surprise by the Scottish movement, but rather by the farmers and farm labourers of the county who promptly took up their arms and mounted their horses; in this part of England, it was always wise to be prepared for combat. Then they launched a series of attacks upon the Scots, dividing their forces and killing any stragglers. When an unexpected company of horsemen suddenly appeared on the horizon, the cry went up that the duke of Norfolk had come with his men.

Norfolk was not in the vicinity at all; nevertheless the Scots fled towards the border pursued by a few thousand English soldiers hurriedly assembled by a northern magnate, Sir Thomas Wharton. Yet the Scottish forces lost their way and began to flounder in the Solway and its reaches just as the tide began to flow. They drowned, or were killed; most of them met their end in Solway Moss, a quagmire between Gretna and the Esk where they were surrounded and dispatched. Many of the greatest nobles of the land were seized and taken to London. 'Worldly men say that all this came by misorder and fortune,' John Knox said, 'but who has the least spunk of the knowledge of God may as evidently see the work of His hand . . .'

James V, on hearing the news, became disconsolate and pined to death. In a literal sense he suffered from loss of power. On 8 December he heard the news that his wife had given birth to a child, Mary, who became the woeful queen of Scots. 'The devil go with it,' he said. 'It will end as it began. It came from a lass and it will end with a lass.' By this he meant that the Stuart dynasty had been established by the daughter of Robert the Bruce, and would end with his own newborn daughter. But Mary, queen of Scots, was not destined to be the last of the line. It only came to an end with the demise of Queen Anne 172 years later. Ten days after making this semi-accurate prophecy, he was dead. The English king was jubilant. This was what sovereigns were put on earth to achieve. To win glory. To conquer their enemies. All the heaviness that had fallen upon him after the disgrace of Katherine Howard seemed to have left him.

A parliament was called at the beginning of 1543. Its first task was to grant a subsidy to the king to pay for the war in Scotland and 'for his other great and urgent occasions', by which was meant the coming invasion of France. An Act was also passed 'for the advancement of true religion, and abolishment of the contrary'; one more attempt to quell the religious dissension of the country. No plays or interludes could mention the Scriptures; no one could read from the Bible in an open assembly. Merchants and gentle-men might study it in the quietness of their homes 'but no women, nor artificers, apprentices, journey-men, serving-men under the degree of yeomen; nor no husbandmen, or labourers, might read it'.

In the late spring of the year, yet another formulation of the English faith was issued from the press. It was entitled *A Necessary Doctrine and Erudition for any Christian Man; set forth by the King's Majesty of England*. It became known simply as the King's Book. Although it is in essence a conservative document, it promulgated once more the middle way between Catholicism and Lutheranism. The power of the pope was denied, but the sacrifice of the Mass was upheld. Purgatory was not quite abolished, but it was growing ever dimmer. The miracle of transubstantiation was affirmed. Faith and works were equally urgent for salvation; shrines and pilgrim-ages were not.

The king's council was busy with matters of heresy in this period. In a space of some five days, from 15 to 19 March, seven suspects were brought before it or committed to several prisons. On 17 March, for example, one cleric was dispatched to the Fleet for 'evil opinions touching the Sacrament of the Altar'. It was said that the principal member of the conservative faction, Stephen Gardiner, 'had bent his bow to shoot at some of the head deer'. In his Easter Day sermon Gardiner grouped together Anabaptists and those who questioned the cult of Mary, crying out from the pulpit 'Heretics! Faggots! Fire!' When one chaplain of Canterbury was buried in the cathedral, the bell-ringer took the censer from the thurifer and poured its burning coals over the new grave; the dead cleric was suspected of heresy.

Yet one man of Canterbury escaped. Archbishop Cranmer, the chief supporter of the cause of reform, was also suspected. At a sermon in the cathedral he was supposed to have preached that the sacrament of the altar was 'but a similitude'; it was not Christ's body but a token or remembrance. If he had thus spoken, then he was going much further than any other English dignitary dared. Some of the canons at his own cathedral began to whisper against him. The more orthodox members of the king's council were heard to suggest that it was invidious to burn poor men but to allow the principal instigator of heresy to stay in favour. By the spring of 1543 they sent a declaration to the king in which a commission of inquiry into Cranmer's teaching was suggested.

Some evenings later the royal barge was moored at Lambeth, and the king invited the archbishop for a river journey. When they were comfortably seated the king turned to Cranmer. 'Ah, my chaplain, I have news for you. I know now who is the greatest heretic in Kent.' He pulled out the document of accusations, collected from Canterbury by the council. Cranmer read it, and then knelt before the king. He wished the matter to be brought to a trial. He acknowledged that he still opposed the spirit of the Six Articles, but declared that he had done nothing against them. The king had always trusted, and confided in, the archbishop. He also wished to avoid further disunity and controversy in an already troubled Church.

So he asked Cranmer himself to be the judge in the whole matter. The archbishop demurred, but the king insisted. The cleric thereupon appointed his chancellor and his registrar to examine those who had accused him of heresy. The homes of the principals were searched, and papers were found that suggested a conspiracy among them; certain letters from Stephen Gardiner were recovered. Cranmer also learned that some of his apparent allies had been implicated. But he was not a man of vengeance. Quietly he allowed the matter to rest. When the king requested that he call one of his secret enemies a 'knave' to his face, he replied that this was not the language of a bishop.

A further attempt upon Cranmer was made at the end of November. The king now played a game of hazard. He authorized his council to summon the archbishop on the charge of heresy and 'as they saw cause, to commit him to the Tower'. Yet that night he summoned the archbishop into his presence. When Cranmer arrived in haste, Henry told him precisely what the council planned to do.

Cranmer seemed to receive the news meekly enough and said something to the effect that he expected a fair hearing. The king rebuked him. 'Do you not think that if they have you once in prison, three or four false knaves will soon be procured to witness against you and to condemn you, which else now being at your liberty dare not once open their lips or appear before your face?' Henry was acquainted with the nature of trials for heresy.

Henry then gave Cranmer his personal ring, which was a sure token of royal support; it was a sign that he had determined to take the matter into his own hands. With this, Cranmer returned to his palace at Lambeth. On the following morning he was duly summoned to come before the council, but he suffered the indignity of being kept waiting for three-quarters of an hour 'among serving men and lackeys'. The king was informed of this very quickly, and thundered in his rage. 'Have they served me so?' he asked. 'It is well enough. I shall talk with them by and by.' It has all the making of a stage play which, from the pen of Shakespeare, it eventually became.

Cranmer stood before the council, where he was informed by his erstwhile colleagues that he was under arrest on suspicion of heretical teachings. He then showed them the king's ring, at which they were astounded. 'Did I not tell you, my lords?' one of them cried out. The errant councillors were led before the king, who lectured them on the need for amity and unity. 'Ah, my lords,' he told them. 'I had thought that I had had a discreet and wise council, but now I perceive that I am deceived. How have you handled here my lord of Canterbury?'

The duke of Norfolk, one of the leaders of the plot against Cranmer, said that 'we meant no manner of hurt unto my lord of Canterbury in that we requested to have him in durance; that we only did because he might after his trial be set at liberty to his more glory'. It was, at the best, a very weak excuse. 'Well,' the king replied, 'I pray you, use not my friends so. I perceive now well enough how the world goes with you. There remains malice among you one to another. Let it be avoided out of hand, I would advise you.' Cranmer was safe for the rest of the king's reign.

Henry had protected his archbishop out of genuine affection but also out of policy. He did not want his nation, or indeed his religion, to be further divided. It seemed, however, that in essential matters of doctrine the reformers had lost their cause. One of them wrote that a man might journey the length and breadth of the kingdom without finding one preacher who 'out of a pure heart and faith unfeigned is seeking the glory of our God. He [the king] has taken them all away.' The action was of a piece with Henry's new alliance with Charles V, Holy Roman Emperor and the most Catholic king of the Spanish empire.

Yet there was a chance that reform might find a new champion. In the summer of 1543 Henry married his sixth and last wife. In the immediate court environment, to which Katherine Parr belonged, the king had, according to the Spanish ambassador, become 'sad, pensive and sighing'. He pined for female companionship and affection. Katherine Parr – twice widowed and one of Lady Mary's entourage – was in love with one of the king's courtiers, Thomas Seymour. The king, however, dispatched him to Brussels as an ambassador and decided to marry Katherine Parr himself. There was no question of refusal. He may have been fat and infirm but he was the sovereign; it was her duty to accept. 'A fine burden,' Anne of Cleves is reported to have remarked, 'Madam Katharine has taken on herself!'

Katherine Parr was learned, by the standards of the day, and she was also pious; she even wrote two devotional manuals, one of them entitled *The Lamentations of a Sinner*. So she had become interested, to put it no higher, in the case of religious reform.

'Every day in the afternoon for the space of one hour,' it was reported, 'one of her chaplains, in her privy chamber, made some collation to her and to her ladies and gentlewomen . . .' Among these ladies were a number of tacit Lutherans – Lady Elizabeth Hoby, Lady Lisle, Lady Butts and the duchess of Suffolk among them. One of the more interesting features of the late Henrician court lies in this recrudescence of female piety. One contemporary noted that the 'young damsels . . . have continually in their hands either psalms, homilies, or other devout meditations'. Katherine Parr was among them and, according to John Foxe, was 'very zealous towards the Gospel'. In good time this would bring her trouble.

Throughout this year, and the beginning of 1544, preparations were made for the great invasion of France under the combined leadership of Henry of England and Charles of Spain. The cost of the undertaking was so vast, however, that the general coinage of the realm was debased by introducing a larger amount of alloy into its gold and silver coins. By these means the king's mint acquired large sums of money, since the face value of the currency was the same despite the smaller amount of precious metal. Prices naturally rose, at a rate of approximately 10 per cent each year, and the economy took twenty years to recover. These were the results of the king's passion for war.

Other ways of making money were also found. It was decided to exact a 'benevolence' from the nation. Those who owned lands worth more than an annual value of 40 shillings were to be requested to contribute to the king's coffers; it was their duty to the sovereign. Those who refused were punished. One alderman of London was sent as a common soldier to the Scottish border, where his commander was told to subject him to the harshest and most dangerous duties. Another alderman was simply sent to the Tower, where he remained for three months.

The preparation for the invasion had already cost much blood. Scotland had renounced all its promises and agreements with the king, concluded after the disaster at Solway Moss, and once more established the old alliance with France. Henry could not contemplate the prospect of an enemy at his back door, and so he resolved to punish the Scots for what he regarded as their duplicity and faithlessness. At the beginning of May an English fleet sailed up the Firth of Forth and their commander, Edward Seymour, earl of Hertford, was ordered to 'burn Edinburgh town, so razed and defaced when you have sacked and gotten what you can of it, as there may remain forever a perpetual memory of the vengeance of God'. He was commanded to overthrow the castle and beat down Holyrood House, while at the same time putting to the flame all the towns and villages in the immediate vicinity. The campaign of terror was then to continue to Leith and St Andrews, 'putting man, woman and child to fire and sword, without exception, where any resistance shall be made against you'. Once more the wrath of the king meant death.

Hertford duly obeyed the orders of his sovereign and reported on 9 May that he had made 'a jolly fire and smoke upon the town' of Edinburgh. Nine days later he wrote that his mission was accomplished to the effect that 'we trust your Majesty shall hear that the like devastation hath not been made in Scotland these many years'. A French fleet came to the aid of their allies and landed a considerable force which, with the Scottish army, marched to the border country; their campaign of fire and fury was duly challenged by another invasion by the earl of Hertford who in the autumn of the year destroyed 243 villages, five market towns and seven monasteries. This dance of death between the two nations would continue, at intervals, until the time of Oliver Cromwell.

The army of the English set out for France itself in the summer of 1544. The largest invasion force ever was dispatched abroad: 48,000 men took to the Channel. It needed the combined strength of 6,500 horses to drag the guns and carts of ammunition. The bishop of Winchester, Stephen Gardiner, had been appointed somewhat quixotically as Purveyor General; he said that he had been a 'continual purveyor of cheese, butter, herrings and stockfish'. His enemies now referred to him as 'Stephen Stockfish'.

The first scheme of war provided that the armies of the king and the emperor should march upon Paris, but Henry detected flaws in the proposal; it would leave his forces dangerously unprotected in the rear. It was first necessary for him to subdue the towns of Boulogne and Montreuil before passing the Somme on his way to the capital. By the end of June the English army had gathered about Boulogne, and on 14 July Henry crossed the Channel. A few days later he rode out from the gates of Calais, then an English garrison town, and came upon the territories of France; across his saddle he placed a great musket with a long iron barrel. He was travelling 25 miles south to join his army at Boulogne. The siege guns were soon blasting at the castle on the eastern side of the hilltop town.

Diplomatic, as well as military, activities were under way. In the summer of 1544 Francis wrote to the two kings, privately urging each of them to come to terms with him and thus hoping to divide their counsels: Henry sent the letter on to his ally, Charles, and replied to the French king that he was suggesting a policy 'wherein you greatly touch our honour, the which, as you are aware, having always guarded inviolably to this present, I will never consent in my old age that it shall be any way distained'. In the following month he wrote – or rather dictated – a letter to Katherine Parr even as he sustained the siege of Boulogne. He told her that 'we be so occupied, and have so much to do in foreseeing and caring for everything ourself, as we have almost no manner of rest or leisure to do any other thing'. This is the king at war, energetic and ever busy. He was delighted to be once more in arms, and one of his commanders reported that he was 'merry and in as good health as I have seen his grace at any time this seven year'. He was in pursuit of glory, which was really the only reason for warfare.

Charles V was detained at the town of Dizier or St Didier for seven weeks, thus losing half the time that had been calculated for the march upon Paris itself. But the emperor then pressed forward, even though in the process his communications were broken and his supplies cut off. The advance surprised Henry, but the king could not have foreseen the duplicity of his ally. Francis and Charles had settled the terms of a separate peace, leaving out Henry, and needed only an excuse to enact it. With Charles's army in perilous circumstance, the emperor declared himself obliged to make a treaty. The Spaniards and the French once more joined hands in the diplomatic dance.

The siege of Boulogne had been protracted beyond anticipation. The valour of the defenders of the town provoked even the king's admiration. 'They fought hand to hand,' he wrote to the queen, 'much manfuller than either Burgundians or Flemings would have done . . .' Yet finally he prevailed, and the people of the town marched out in surrender. Montreuil still held out, however, and it was clear to all that the English army would never reach the gates of Paris. At this juncture Charles sealed the treaty with Francis, leaving Henry the only belligerent. The king's anger and incredulity at the treachery of his ally are understandable, but the relative failure of the invasion is not in doubt. He had taken Boulogne, but not Paris, at an estimated cost of some £2 million; that was roughly equivalent to ten years of normal spending. The bulk of the crown lands, acquired from the Church, were sold off. This led directly to the frailty of the royal finances in subsequent years, and was one of the contributing factors to the Civil War. Yet this is to move too far forward. In the immediate context of 1544 the treasury was exhausted and Stephen Gardiner was moved to write, in emulation of Colet thirty-three years before, that 'the worst peace is better than the best war'. On the last day of September Henry sailed back to England.

The threat from France remained, more dangerous than ever after the peace with Spain. It became clear by the spring of the following year that Francis was planning an invasion and was gathering a large fleet of ships for the purpose; galleys were even being brought overland from the Mediterranean to join the flotilla. The fortifications along England's shores were strengthened further and the trained bands of local fighters were put on alert. In the event the French force got precisely nowhere; inclement winds propelled the ships back to their own coastline, and the supplies of food began to run low. So the French commanders ordered a retreat. An attempt was made at battle near Portsmouth, when some French galleys fired at the English ships, but once more an unfavourable wind forced them back. A French fleet was sighted off Shoreham, but again it turned around; an outbreak of disease had felled the sailors. In the course of this flurry of maritime activity one ship, the *Mary Rose*, managed to sink itself in Portsmouth harbour. This can be taken as a symbol of the armed struggle between England and France.

15

A family portrait

In 1545 a family portrait had been commissioned by the king from an unknown artist. It displays Henry in full might, sitting on his throne between his heir and the long-dead Jane Seymour; on the right stands Lady Elizabeth, and on the left Lady Mary. Henry's hand rests upon his son's neck. The setting is the king's lodging on the ground floor of the royal palace at Whitehall. Katherine Parr is not a part of this dramatic tableau, but she was now very much part of the family. During the king's absence in France, she had become the regent of England. She stayed generally at Hampton Court, where Mary and then Elizabeth resided with her. They were educated in the broadly based humanism associated with the name of Erasmus that soon became an aspect of early Protestantism.

Katherine also helped to guide the studies of the young Prince Edward. He called her 'his most dear mother', and told her that 'I received so many benefits from you that my mind can hardly grasp them'. She herself was receiving instruction and Edward wrote that 'I hear too that your highness is progressing in the Latin tongue . . . wherefore I feel no little joy, for letters are lasting'. This is a conventional expression, and need not necessarily reflect Edward's real sentiments. Yet he did persevere with his classical studies. He had read and memorized, for example, four books of

Cato. He read Cicero in Latin and Herodotus in Greek. Soon enough he began the study of French; he was, at least in theory, one day to become the king of France. He also became immersed in geography and history as a way of preparing himself for sovereign rule. He informed his tutor, John Cheke, that 'I have only done my duty'. In such a position of eminence, and with such an overweening father, his sense of his role and responsibilities was already immense. It was remarked that, even as a young boy, he had the mannerisms of an adult.

His caps were decorated with diamonds and sapphires, his garments woven from cloth of gold; he possessed a dagger of gold that hung from a rope of pearls, its sheath covered in diamonds, rubies and emeralds. He shone as he walked or rode. A painting of him, from 1546, survives. He stands between a pillar and a window, dressed in all the robes of state. He holds the golden dagger in his right hand while his left hand significantly touches his codpiece as a symbol that the dynasty would continue.

Yet he also had time for the sports of kings. Among his possessions were gloves for hawking, rods for fishing, and swords for fencing. He owned greyhounds and horses. He loved to hunt and draw the longbow; he played rackets and engaged in the noble art of tilting. He also performed upon the lute, like his father.

He had an especial affection for his half-sister Mary, but his love was not unmixed with the same sense of duty. He asked Katherine Parr to ensure that Mary no longer attended 'foreign dances and merriments which do not become a most Christian princess'. He was eight at the time he issued this warning. At a later date the siblings would disagree about the purport of being a 'Christian'. Yet his anxiety suggests a picture of Mary quite different from that of the sour and zealous burner of heretics; she loved dancing; she had a taste for finery and liked to gamble at cards. She had a passion for music, just like her father and her siblings. Music is a key to the Tudor age. An image of Elizabeth survives, dining to the sound of twelve trumpets and two kettledrums together with fifes, cornets and side drums. Everybody sang in the streets or at their work, 'the mason at his wall, the shipboy at his oar, and the tiler on the housetop'. A lute was placed in many barber shops, for customers to while away the time.

But Mary also had a reputation for her studies, and another royal, Mary of Portugal, praised 'the fame of her virtue and learning'. In the last months of 1545, under the supervision of Katherine Parr, she was translating a paraphrase by Erasmus of the Gospel according to St John that was published in the following year.

Edward was matched in his zeal for learning by his other half-sister, who was a precocious student of languages. Elizabeth mastered Greek and Latin with ease, studying Greek in the morning and Latin in the afternoon; late in her realm, when she was by the standards of the time an old woman, she managed an extempore oration in Latin that delighted her court. She also learned Spanish, Italian, Flemish and a little Welsh. At the age of eleven she presented her stepmother with her translation from the French of Margaret of Navarre's long poem, *The Mirror of the Sinful Soul*; her English prose covers twenty-seven pages. Her principal tutor, Roger Ascham, reported that at the age of sixteen 'the constitution of her mind is exempt from female weakness, and she is endowed with a masculine power of application. No apprehension can be quicker than hers, no memory more retentive . . .' A childhood companion of Edward, Jane Dormer, took a less sanguine view of the girl; at the age of twelve or thirteen Elizabeth was 'proud and disdainful'. So we have a fine example of two young women granted a humanist education that rivalled any being offered at the schools or universities. It was not unique – Thomas More had provided the same tuition for his own daughters – but it was unusual.

The happy family, however, was about to be disturbed by tensions concerning religion. Henry himself was still much exercised over matters of faith. When he appeared in parliament, at the end of 1545, he burst into tears when he began to address the divisions in the kingdom. 'I hear', he said, 'that the special foundation of our religion being charity between man and man is so refrigerate as there was never more dissension and lack of love between man and man . . . some are called Papists, some Lutherans, and some Anabaptists; names devised of the devil . . .' He went on to declare that 'I am very sorry to know and hear how unreverendly that precious jewel the Word of God is disputed, rhymed, sung and jangled in every alehouse and tavern'.

Cranmer himself was in the process of modifying his most sacred beliefs. In this transition, by a slow and gradual process of meditation and study, the archbishop repudiated the idea of transubstantiation by which the bread and wine are changed into the body and blood of Christ. Eventually he would come to believe that the miracle took place in the heart of the communicant, whereby he or she is spiritually changed on reception of the host. Everything was in flux.

Argument and debate, therefore, exercised the more acerbic or inquisitive spirits. Henry had wanted a purified Catholic Church, cleansed of its more egregious superstitions; he had also wanted a national Church under his sovereignty. What he had created, however, was a fragile and in some ways inconsistent alternative. The fact that it changed utterly after his death is a measure of its instability. A new English litany was published in the summer of 1545, but the Mass and the other services of the Church were still performed in Latin. In the same year a bill against heretics, more severe than any before, was thrown out by the Commons in parliament; this is another sign of division. The ceremony of 'creeping to the cross' on Good Friday was abolished at the beginning of 1546; when Cranmer sought to remove all ceremonies involving bells and crucifixes the king first agreed, but then changed his mind. He still wanted to preserve the image, to the king of France and to the emperor, of an orthodox sovereign. He was even then in the process of negotiating with them.

After the abortive end of hostilities it became clear that France and England would have to treat with one another before squandering any more resources on useless threats and counter-threats. So there began a process of diplomatic conversations that Henry caustically described as 'interpretations'; he told his envoy that 'you must stick earnestly with them, and in no wise descend to the second degree, but upon a manifest appearance that they would rather break up than assert to the first degree'. It was a matter of subtleties and feints and manoeuvres in a situation of mutual suspicion and distrust. The result was the Treaty of Ardres, signed in the summer of 1546, by which Henry was allowed to occupy Boulogne for eight years before returning it for the sum of 2 million *écus*. It was the last treaty he would ever sign.

That 'charity between man and man', upheld by the king in parliament, was notably lacking among some of Henry's councillors. The more conservative of them held considerable doubts about the nature of Katherine Parr's influence upon the household. The fact that Mary was translating Erasmus is itself significant, and the scholar's paraphrase of the Gospel according to St John played some part in the later reformation under Edward's rule. So Katherine was encouraging the kind of reformed spirituality that humanism inspired.

The king had complained, in the early months of 1546, about the way in which his wife brought up the subject of faith. John Foxe, whose evidence is generally reliable, quotes him as saying sarcastically to Stephen Gardiner that it is 'a thing much to my comfort to come in mine old days to be taught by my wife'. At a later opportunity Gardiner whispered to the king that the queen's opinions were, according to the law, heretical and that 'he would easily perceive how perilous a matter it is to cherish a serpent within his own bosom'. These words also come from Foxe. Henry then allowed Gardiner to interview the ladies closest to the queen.

Such matters emerged at a time when the prosecution of heretics was increased, and in particular the persecution of a woman close to the queen and the queen's ladies. Anne Askew had friends at court, and her brother was gentleman pensioner and cup-bearer; but she was being watched. One spy who had lodgings opposite her own reported that 'at midnight she beginneth to pray, and ceaseth not in many hours after . . .' In March 1546 she was summoned before the commissioners of heresy at Saddlers' Hall in Gutter Lane; here she confessed to having said that 'God was not in temples made with hands'. She was asked whether a mouse, eating a consecrated host, received God. She made no answer, but merely smiled.

She was consigned to a London prison before being brought before the bishop of London, Edmund Bonner, who later earned the nickname of 'Bloody Bonner'. On this occasion he was a mild persecutor and, being approached by her 'good friends', released her on the understanding that she had submitted. Yet then she relapsed into heresy, and in the summer of the year was brought before the council at the palace in Greenwich. She was of 'worshipful stock' but her recalcitrance was therefore all the more notable; it was also hoped by the conservatives on the council that the prospect of torture or of burning might prompt her to implicate some ladies of the court. She was asked to confirm that the Holy Sacrament was 'flesh, blood and bone' to which she replied that 'it was a great shame for them to counsel contrary to their knowledge'. When pressed for her views on the Eucharist she responded that 'she would not sing the lord's song in a strange land'. When Stephen Gardiner charged her with speaking in parables she borrowed some words from Christ and replied, 'if I tell you the truth, you will not believe me.' Gardiner declared that she was a parrot. By now, weary of imprisonment, she was 'sore sick, thinking no less than to die'. When in prison she composed a ballad, of which one verse runs:

> I saw a ryall trone
> Where Justyce shuld have sitt
> But in her stede was one
> Of modye [angry] cruell wytt.

In the Tower she was charged to reveal the others of her sect; when she maintained her silence, she was put on the rack and tortured. Still she did not name her secret allies. She wrote her own account, published in the following year in Germany. 'Then they did put me on the rack because I confessed no ladies or gentlewomen to be of my opinion, and thereon they kept me a long time; and because I lay still and did not cry my Lord Chancellor and Master Rich took pains to rack me with their own hands, till I was nigh dead.' On 15 July she was brought to Smithfield for burning, but she had been so broken by the rack that she could not stand. She was tied to the stake, and the faggots were lit. Rain and thunder marked these proceedings, whereupon one spectator called out 'A vengeance on you all that thus doth burn Christ's member.' At which remark a Catholic carter struck him down. The differences of faith among the people were clear enough.

A month later, Katherine Parr was marked out for investigation. This is the story John Foxe tells, twenty years later, in *Foxe's Book of Martyrs*. It is likely that he heard of it from those who were part of the court at the time; he is hardly likely to have invented it, since it does not serve any essential purpose in his Protestant 'book of martyrs' except to blacken the reputation of Stephen Gardiner. For that purpose, however, he may have embellished the facts of the matter. He reports correctly that, in this period, Henry kept largely to his privy quarters where he saw only his closest advisers. This was the atmosphere in which the king allowed Gardiner secretly to investigate his wife's religious opinions for any taint of heresy. He even permitted certain articles of accusation to be drawn up against her. This is inherently plausible; given the facts of his own mortality, so obvious to him now, he may have been concerned about those in the immediate vicinity of his son after his death.

The articles of accusation were fortunately dropped on the floor of the court, where they were recovered by some 'godly person' who took them at once to Katherine Parr. It is more likely that a 'godly' friend, knowing of the machinations against the queen, privately warned her. Whereupon she fell 'into a great melancholy and agony'; given her husband's treatment of some of his earlier consorts, this is hardly surprising. Her terror was such, however, that one of the king's own doctors was sent to minister to her; this man was also privy to Henry's designs, and gave her further information about the enemies set to destroy her.

Yet the king called her to him one evening, and began to discourse on matters of religion. She took the opportunity of apologizing for her previous 'boldness' which was not done to 'maintain opinion' but to afford him diversion 'over this painful time of your infirmity'. She is reported to have said, in order to assuage him still further, that she had also hoped that 'I, hearing your majesty's learned discourse, might receive to myself some profit thereby'. His vanity appeased, the king graciously condescended to pardon her. 'And is it even so, sweetheart!'

The king and queen, together with some of their retinue, were in the privy garden a day or two later. The lord chancellor, Thomas Wriothesley, then came forward with a guard of forty soldiers to arrest Katherine Parr and some of her ladies on the charge of heresy. But the king interposed. He took the chancellor aside and asked him for an explanation. He was then heard to shout, 'Knave! Arrant knave! Beast! And fool!' before dismissing him and the soldiers.

It is a story from one source, and no other, but authentic touches can be found in it. The life of the court was indeed full of enmity and suspicion concerning the highest in the land, and there can be no doubt that differences over the pace and nature of religious reform were at the centre of the controversies. The rather serpentine conduct of the king, setting one group of courtiers against another, is also in character. It was a means of keeping control and of asserting mastery, even over his wife. It was further reported by Foxe that Henry never afterwards trusted the conservative bishop of Winchester, Stephen Gardiner, who had first started the investigation of Katherine. This mistrust is confirmed by the king's subsequent treatment of the bishop. The queen was back in favour, and dabbled no more in pious discussions. She would very soon be devoted to nursing her husband in his last illness.

16

The last days

The king, in his mid-fifties, wanted no mention of death. He spent most of his time in his privy chamber at Whitehall or at Greenwich; the walls were covered with tapestries, and the furnishings included two or three tables, a cupboard for plate and goblets, and some chairs. Musical instruments were also to be found there for solace and recreation. Outside, in the presence chamber, the courtiers paid their reverences to an empty throne. This was still the site of the king's majesty and must be so honoured.

He was by now ill and ailing. The royal accounts show that large sums were being spent for the purchase of rhubarb, a sovereign specific against the infirmities of a choleric disposition; he had always harboured powerful forces of anger but his fury was compounded by the fact that he was now in almost constant pain. He was obese and had to be transported in chairs called 'trams' through his galleries and chambers. A tram was an early form of wheelchair to ease the burden of his ulcerated legs. The chronicler Edward Hall reports that he 'could not go up or down stairs unless he was raised up or let down by an engine', no doubt some form of pulley or hoist. He was also obliged to wear spectacles, which were then known as 'gazings'; they were clipped to the nose.

Yet he was able to strike out again. He excluded Stephen Gardiner from court for failing to exchange some diocesan lands with the king; that was the explanation proffered at the time, but it may also be that the bishop's disgrace was the result of his intrigue against Katherine Parr. It is reported that although the bishop was banished from the king's presence he would go with the other councillors to the door of the king's bedchamber and wait there until these more honoured councillors returned, only to give the world the impression that he was still in favour. It is in fact easy to conclude that there was a general purge of the 'conservative faction' in this period. The greatest of them, the duke of Norfolk, was soon to be consigned to the Tower.

Norfolk had been a pre-eminent councillor for much of the king's reign but in November 1546 he and his son, the earl of Surrey, fell victim to Henry's fear and suspicion. Surrey had quartered the royal arms with his own, and had advised his sister to become the king's mistress in order to advance the family fortunes; he had been heard to suggest that in the event of the king's death his father should become protector of the realm. They were in double peril because the Howard family, as collateral descendants of the Plantagenets, had some pretension to the throne. In a sheet of charges the king added certain words in his own hand, marked here by capitals. 'HOW THIS MAN'S INTENT IS TO BE JUDGED; AND WHETHER THIS import any danger, peril or slander to the title of the Prince or very Heir Apparent . . .' The succession of Edward had to be protected at all costs.

In the early days of December Norfolk and Surrey were imprisoned. It was now reported that the duke had known about a secret scheme, concocted by Stephen Gardiner, to restore the papacy. It was revealed also that Surrey had said that the 'new men', the religious reformers, would after the king's death 'smart for it'. The earl was brought before a special commission at the Guildhall, on 13 January 1547, and duly sentenced to death. Norfolk escaped a trial, for the time being, but was consigned to the Tower. He was saved from the executioner only because of the king's own demise.

The reports of the various ambassadors tell the same story of decline and decay; the king looks 'greatly fallen away' and is 'so unwell given his age and corpulence that he may not survive'. His physicians were reported to be in despair, and rumours circulated that he was already dead. 'Whatever his health,' one ambassador wrote, 'it can only be bad and will not last long.'

Yet who was to tell the king that he was dying? Even to 'imagine' the death of the sovereign was to incur the charge of treason. It was also unwise to snuff out the last gleam of hope. The doctors gave the charge to Sir Anthony Denny, who had for some time been the principal gentleman of the bedchamber. He approached his master and whispered to him that 'in man's judgement, you are not like to live'. He then encouraged him to prepare for death in a pious Christian manner. The king was advised to call for Thomas Cranmer but replied that he 'would take a little sleep' first. When the archbishop did arrive, he was too late; if Henry was not already dead, he was at least speechless. The king died at two in the morning of 28 January 1547. He had reigned for thirty-seven years and nine months.

It is difficult to assess the king's private religion at the end of his life. He was said to have entertained the idea, according to Foxe, of substituting the Mass with a communion service; but this Lutheran impulse cannot be substantiated. The evidence suggests that he died, as he had lived, a Catholic. His will invoked 'the name of God and of the glorious and blessed virgin our Lady Saint Mary'; he also ordered that daily Masses be said, as long as the world endured, for the salvation of his soul. That is not the language of a Lutheran. It suggests, although it does not prove, that the king still believed in the existence of purgatory despite the denial of it in his own religious articles.

As for the religion of the country, opinions differed at the time and still differ. Was it a predominantly and practically Catholic kingdom, with a king instead of a pope at its head? Or was it in the throes of a singular change to a plainer and simpler worship? It is perhaps best seen as a confused and confusing process of acquiescence in the king's wishes. The habit of obedience was instinctive, especially when it was compounded by fear and threat of force. A French observer said at the time that if Henry were to declare Mahomet God, the English people would accept it. Certain devout people would not be moved from the dictates of their conscience – Thomas More and Anne Askew come to mind – but, for most, the practice of religion was determined by custom and regulated by authority. The rituals of public worship were the same as those practised in the fourteenth and fifteenth centuries; the evidence of wills suggests that the reformed religion had not made great progress with the majority of the people. By establishing the principle of royal supremacy, however, Henry had created an instrument that could be used for the purposes of religious reform.

The chain of stern necessity now bound all the participants in the drama. The death of a king was a momentous event, a rupture in the natural order that had swiftly to be repaired before the forces of chaos spilled out. In the last months of his life access to the king had been granted by Sir Anthony Denny and Sir William Paget, private secretary. Denny and Paget were a powerful influence upon the ailing king, and in this crucial period it is likely that they aligned themselves with the reformers in the king's council.

In the autumn of 1546 the imperial ambassador, in a dispatch to his master, described the unexpected rise in the influence of these reformers. 'The Protestants', he told him, 'have their openly declared champions . . . I had even heard that some of them had gained great favour with the king; and I could only wish that they were as far away from court as they were last year.' He then named the two most prominent among them as 'the earl of Hertford and the lord admiral'. These two men, Edward Seymour and John Dudley, would indeed set the tone of the next reign.

Edward Seymour, earl of Hertford, was Edward's uncle; he was Jane Seymour's elder brother who on his sister's marriage to the king had become a gentleman of the privy chamber. He had been raised to his earldom at the time of the young prince's christening, and steadily climbed in royal favour; he had become warden of the Scottish Marches, or the northern borderlands, where his military skills were evident. He had taken part in the king's campaigns in Scotland and France, and had therefore become part of the king's inner martial band. John Dudley was the son of a royal councillor who had been beheaded at the beginning of Henry's rule; he had quickly proved himself to be a master of the sea, and had progressed from vice-admiral to lord high admiral; he had also participated in the expeditions against Scotland and France, winning Henry's admiration and friendship. Seymour and Dudley were, in effect, warlords.

The pair were deeply concerned, therefore, with the question of the king's last will and testament. It is dated 30 December 1546, a little less than a month before his death. An original had been revised on 26 December by Henry in the presence of some of his councillors. We may see among them Denny and Paget, Seymour and Dudley. Henry bequeathed the crown to his son and to his son's issue; if that failed he named any children born of his own queen, but in that regard he was perhaps over-confident. The throne would then pass to Lady Mary, and then to Lady Elizabeth. All this came to pass. The right to the throne then jumped to the issue of the king's youngest sister, the duchess of Suffolk, thus excluding the claims of the Scottish family of Stuarts into which his older sister had married. This would cause much controversy during the reign of Elizabeth.

Henry then designated sixteen men as members of the regency council that would superintend the early years of the reign of Edward VI. Yet the fact is that he never signed the will. He left it too late, perhaps reserving to himself the possibility of changing its details and thus maintaining discipline in the court. It was subsequently signed with a 'dry stamp' or facsimile on the day before his death, 27 January, a delay that might have allowed for the exercise of creative editing; the signature, which was stamped upon the will and then inked in, was also contrived at a stage when he was no longer capable of reacting to any changes.

All the members of the regency council were 'new men', or what might be called professional men who had gained their ascendancy in the last years of Henry's rule. Those of the nobility had only attained that rank in recent years. Some of them inclined towards the reformed faith, among them Denny and Seymour, but the majority were no doubt happy with the religious settlement that Henry had ordained. The king was actively seeking balance and moderation in the council of the young heir.

That is perhaps why Stephen Gardiner, the leading conservative, was excluded from the council. The king may have suspected Gardiner of papal sympathies, and such a stance would be doubly dangerous during a minority. This was a deliberate decision by the king himself. It is reported that he omitted Gardiner's name with the remark that 'he was a wilful man and not meet to be about his son'. Paget records that he and others tried to persuade the king otherwise but Henry retorted that 'he marvelled what we meant and that we all knew him to be a wilful man'. He is also reported to have said that 'I remembered him well enough, and of good purpose have left him out; for surely if he were in my testament, and one of you [the council], he would cumber you all, and you should never rule him, he is of so troublesome a nature. I myself could use him, and rule him to all manner of purposes, as seemed good unto me; but so shall you never do.' Temperamental, rather than doctrinal, considerations may have ensured his dismissal. It seems likely that the king wished for the continuance of his 'middle' policy of reformed Catholicism. In this, he was to be disappointed.

The heir to the throne, in his own chronicle, reported the events in the immediate aftermath of the king's death. Edward had been staying in Seymour's castle at Hertford, but was then taken to Enfield Palace where he was told of his father's death. 'The next day . . . he [Edward himself] was brought to the Tower of London where he tarried the space of three weeks; and in the mean season the council sat every day for the performance of the will.' He then states that 'they thought best to choose the duke of Somerset to be Protector of the Realm and Governor of the King's Person'. The new duke was none other than Edward Seymour himself, promoted to this title after becoming the protector.

Paget and Seymour had been colluding even as the king approached his death. 'Remember what you promised to me in the gallery at Westminster,' Paget wrote to Seymour later, 'before the breath was out of the body of the king that dead is. Remember what you promised me immediately after, devising with me concerning the place which you now occupy.' Twenty-four hours after Henry's death Seymour wrote to Paget from Hertford. The letter was sent between three and four in the morning, carried by a messenger who was ordered to 'haste, post haste, haste with all diligence for thy life, for thy life'. Among other matters Seymour told Paget that 'for divers respects, I think it not convenient to satisfy the world' about the contents of Henry's will until they had met and so arranged affairs 'as there may be no controversy hereafter'.

So the two men had been scheming about their seizure of power. It is also possible, to put it no higher, that Paget, with the connivance of Denny, had added material to the will itself. There was, for example, a clause known as 'unfulfilled gifts', decreeing that any promise of Henry to reward his courtiers should be implemented after his death; by these means lands and honours were liberally distributed to the 'new men'.

In a contest of high stakes, amid all the fear and ambition released by the king's death, any trick or forgery was acceptable. The members of the court were grasping and unscrupulous, having to act and react in a climate of anxiety and suspicion. It was an atmosphere that Henry had created, perhaps, but in this respect he was not very different from his predecessors and successors.

On 4 February the new council ignored the basic sentiment of the king's will. Henry had ordained a system of majority rule, to preserve the balance of the government, that could only be over-turned if the 'most part' agreed to do so in writing. It was overturned immediately when the council decided that 'some special man' should guide the proceedings of the realm; Seymour, as a man of proven ability and a blood relative of the new king, was chosen as protector of the kingdom and governor of the king's person. The imperial ambassador was not so sanguine; he reported to the emperor's sister that Seymour, or Somerset as we must now call him, was 'a dry, sour, opinionated man'. In the scramble for power, however, he had won.

The body of the dead king was disembowelled and cleansed, but the surgeons discovered that the arteries were so blocked that there was 'hardly half a pint of pure blood in his whole body'. It was then encased in lead, with a coffin that was carried by sixteen men at the time of his burial. An army of 1,000 accompanied the funeral march from Westminster to Windsor, with 250 mourners as well as all the other dignitaries of Church and State; the procession stretched for 4 miles. When the procession stopped for the night at Syon, it is reported that part of the leaden coffin had come apart and that a dog was seen to be licking the spilled blood. It is a striking illustration of a macabre prophecy delivered to

Henry by Father Peto fifteen years before – 'The dogs would lick up your blood – yes yours'. It is perhaps too dramatically appropriate to be true.

The hearse itself was nine storeys high, and the road to Windsor had to be repaved to accommodate it, while on top of the hearse a great wax effigy of the king was displayed to the crowds of spectators. It was dressed in cloth of crimson velvet, and adorned with jewels. The real body, already decomposing, was lowered into the choir vault of St George's Chapel.

17

The breaking of the altars

On 20 February 1547 a solemn little boy proceeded down the aisle of Westminster Abbey; the great lords of the realm held up the crown, the orb and the sceptre. 'Yea, yea, yea,' the congregation called out, 'King Edward! King Edward! King Edward!' On the previous day they boy had been greeted by a London pageant, with images of a phoenix and a lion, of crowns and of flowers. A chant emerged from the crowd, 'Sing up heart, sing up heart, sing no more down, but joy in King Edward that weareth the crown.' He had stopped to watch the acrobatics of a tight-rope dancer.

Edward, coming to the throne of England at the age of nine, was hailed by some as the new Josiah. Josiah, son of Amon, assumed the rule of his country at the age of eight and proceeded to do 'that which was right in the sight of the Lord'. He tore down the graven images of the Assyrian cults and broke the altars into dust. In his reign, the true law of God was providentially found and became the law of Judah. The parallels were clear to those who wished to eradicate the traces of the Romish faith. Edward was seen as a godly king with a fundamental biblical power.

Continuity was assured, also, with the council previously around Henry now preserved around his son. In *Foxe's Book of Martyrs* John Foxe concluded, however, that 'a new face of things began now to appear, as it were in a stage new players coming in, the old being thrust out'. Among the discarded players were the conservatives Stephen Gardiner and the duke of Norfolk, thus tilting the balance in favour of further religious reform. Stephen Gardiner had in fact played a role at the coronation ceremony, but that was his only public duty in the course of the new king's reign. The duke of Somerset, the protector, now dominated the proceedings of the council and had become king in all but name; two gilt maces were always borne in procession before him and he asked Katherine Parr to hand her royal jewels to his wife. He went so far as to call the French king 'brother', in a diplomatic letter; the English ambassador in Paris was advised that this was not good form from one who was not the Lord's anointed.

Somerset's relations with his real brother were tense and difficult. Thomas Seymour had been appointed lord high admiral for life. One early biographer described him as 'fierce in courage, courtly in fashion, in personage stately and in voice magnificent', but had made one other observation; he was, perhaps, 'somewhat empty in matter'. He was one of the hollow men who triumph at court. He now demanded to be made governor to the young king who was, after all, also his nephew. Instead he was given a place on the privy council and promised some of the spoils of office. His ambitions were not so easily satisfied, however, and he began to plot against the rule of his brother Edward.

He also took the precaution of uniting himself with the royal widow. Katherine Parr had wished to marry him in the days when she was being courted by the king and, now that Henry was dead, she and Seymour acted swiftly to secure their alliance. In their quick courtship she wrote to him from her house in Chelsea asking him to come to her early in the morning so that 'you may come without suspect'. The haste was considered by many to be unseemly; if Katherine were soon to prove to be pregnant, it was conceivable that Henry was the father. Any child would be a remarkable dynastic conundrum. The young princesses, Mary and Elizabeth, shared their outrage at 'seeing the ashes, or rather the scarcely cold body of the king our father so shamefully dishonoured by the queen our stepmother'; these were the words of Elizabeth who also urged caution and dissimulation on her older sister. They were dealing with 'too powerful a party, who have got all authority into their own hands'. She herself was obliged to use 'tact' toward Katherine Parr; silence and cunning were always to be her weapons.

Thomas Seymour, snubbed in the matter of the royal governorship, nevertheless connived to win his young nephew's favour. He began to visit him in private, and surreptitiously gave him money while denouncing his brother's meanness. 'You are a beggarly king,' he told the boy. 'You have no money to play or give.' He even elicited from him a letter to Katherine Parr in which it seemed that Edward was asking his stepmother to marry Seymour. 'Wherefore,' he wrote, 'ye shall not need to fear any grief to come, or to suspect lack of aid in need; seeing that he, being mine uncle [the protector], is so good in nature that he will not be troublesome.' He was offering, in other words, to protect Katherine against the obvious wrath of Somerset at any clandestine marriage. The protector was indeed greatly offended.

It seems more than likely that Seymour himself dictated the letter to the young king, which throws into doubt the image of the boy as grave and devout beyond his years. A few weeks after his accession it was noted that Edward began to swear and blaspheme, using such phrases as 'by God's blood'. He told his tutor that one of his classmates, chosen from the sons of the nobility, had advised him that 'kings always swore'. He was made to watch as the schoolfriend was soundly whipped.

The protector was by instinct a religious reformer and his closest associates were also of that persuasion; his personal doctor, William Turner, had published works banned during the previous reign. It was reported that his six daughters had been educated in 'good literature and in the knowledge of God's most holy laws', which was an indirect way of saying that they had been evangelized. In one of his proclamations he warned 'parents to keep their children' from such 'evil and pernicious games' as bowling and tennis, an order which at a slightly later date might have been described as puritanical.

John Bradford, a radical sectary, was questioned by the bishop of Durham at the end of the reign. 'My lord,' he said, 'the doctrine taught in King Edward's days was God's pure religion.' The reply was swift and revealing. 'What religion mean you in King Edward's days? What year of his reign?' The first attempts at change came soon enough. Ten days before the new king's coronation the wardens and curates of St Martin's in London tore down all the images of the saints and whitewashed the paintings on the walls. They were acting too quickly, in fact, and were taken to the Tower for a period.

Yet an alteration in feeling was quickly becoming manifest. In a contemporary diary, for 1547, is the entry that 'this year the archbishop of Canterbury did eat meat openly in Lent, in the hall of Lambeth, the like of which was never seen since England was a Christian country'. Thomas Cranmer had already outlined the nature of the English Church; he said that it was necessary that he and the other bishops should renew their commissions as functionaries of the new king. They were no longer to be seen as the successors of the apostles but as government officials. This was now a state Church in which the pulpits would be used to publish the decrees and desires of the council. It is perhaps well to remember that Edward was the first anointed English king to enjoy the title of supreme head of the English Church.

At the beginning of the new reign Thomas Cranmer grew a beard. This may be seen as a token of mourning for his old master, but in fact the clergy of the reformed Church favoured beards; it may be seen as a decisive rejection of the tonsure and of the clean-shaven popish priests. After long meditation the archbishop, as we have seen, rejected the doctrine of real presence in the Eucharist. He now invited several Protestant reformers to England, where he gave them some of the most important professorial chairs at the two universities.

In the next six years some seventy European divines made their way to England – preachers, scholars, humanists and pastors who maintained a strong and enthusiastic correspondence with their colleagues still overseas. It seemed for a while that the young king Edward might eventually come to be head of a great movement of European Protestantism. Protestant refugees, fleeing from the persecution of Charles V, also came over. A group of Flemish settlers were granted the church of Austin Friars in London for their communion, and a colony of Walloon weavers was established in the ruins of Glastonbury Abbey. The breadth of toleration under Somerset's protectorate was such that not one person was executed, or tortured, for his or her religious opinions; this must be considered a unique period in sixteenth-century English history.

Many of these European refugees and scholars had already come under the influence of Jean Calvin who had now established a reforming movement of great sternness and discipline. He was a French scholar who discovered within himself a gift for systematic thought and a huge capacity for government; in 1536, at the age of twenty-six, he published the *Institutes of the Christian Religion* in which he established the principles of what was essentially a new city of God. Working in relative isolation, and in a short period of time, he created an entire system of theology at once authoritarian and impersonal. There was nothing private about Calvin; he was always a public force. That was the source of his greatness.

He travelled to Basle, and to Strasburg, in order to escape persecution from the French king and church. At Geneva, through the power of an unyielding will yoked with moral fervour, he created a new republic founded upon faith. He regulated worship and created a liturgy; by means of a council he watched over the morals of the city. It can be said that single-handedly he revived the spirit and the progress of the European reformation, at a time when it seemed to be in retreat from the forces of the Catholic powers.

At the heart of Calvinism was the doctrine of predestination, derived ultimately from the texts of Paul and Augustine. Before the foundations of the earth had been created God had decreed that some should be saved for everlasting life and that others should be damned eternally. If God was Almighty, then of course he already knew the identity of the elect and the reprobate. The divine potter had created some vessels of honour and of mercy, and other vessels of wrath and dishonour. Some, on embracing this doctrine, might fear for the fate of their souls and fall into despair. But for most believers the doctrine of foreknowledge and predestination was a sovereign cure for anxiety and apathy; it was an inspiring and animating doctrine that encouraged self-sacrifice and moral courage. What joy was to be found in the knowledge that you are saved? It was the power behind Oliver Cromwell's exultant sense of 'providence'. The true Church consisted of the elect, known only to God; once you had been saved by God's grace you could not relapse into sinfulness. It lent status to those who might have felt themselves to be otherwise deprived.

This was the faith now being promulgated in England, particularly in the churches established by European reformers taking refuge from the depredations of Charles V. It was a doctrine that naturally attracted enthusiasts and idealists; since they are the people who work wonderful changes in the world, Calvinism rapidly spread. It became the dominant theme for the 'hotter' breed of reformers, and soon established itself in Poland and in Bohemia, in the Palatinate and in the Dutch Netherlands.

Now, after the accession of the young king Edward, some of the more ardent radical spirits emerged from the shadow imposed upon them by Henry's religious policy; Thomas Underhill, for example, proclaimed himself to be a 'hoote gospeller' in the parish of Stratford-on-the-Bow. Hugh Latimer, the most influential radical preacher of the age, had been released at the beginning of the reign and had gone to live with Archbishop Cranmer at Lambeth Palace. From the pulpit he denounced those prelates who refused to preach the reformed faith as 'couched in courts, ruffling in their rents, dancing in their dominions, burdened with ambassages, pampering of their paunches, like a monk that maketh his jubilee, munching in their mangers, and moiling in their gay manors and mansions'. He ended his sermon with the two words, 'well, well'.

Dissatisfaction with the old priests sometimes erupted in the streets. The royal council commanded that the serving men and apprentices of London should no longer use 'such insolence and evil demeanour towards priests, as reviling, tossing of them, taking violently their caps and tippets from them'. A vivid picture of these malcontents is given in *The Displaying of the Protestants*, published some years later; of the London apprentices it is said, 'no regard they have at all to repair to the church upon the holy days, but flock in clusters upon stalls, either scorning the passers-by, or with

their testaments utter some wise stuff of their own device'. Such is
the disaffection or moroseness to be found at times of change.

The more committed or devout Catholics now migrated to
France or to Italy, taking with them their threatened relics; among
them were the monks who had been ejected from the Charterhouse of London. One woodcut showed the exodus of the faithful,
with the legend 'Ship over your trinkets and be packing you
Papistes'. One priest threw himself from the steeple of St Magnus
the Martyr, on Lower Thames Street, into the river below.

In the spring of 1547, three months after the coronation, a
set of injunctions was issued for the general purification of the
churches. Every picture was to be removed from the walls, and
every image of saint or apostle was to be put away 'so that there
should remain no memory of the same'. Rosaries were no longer
to be used. The 'lighting of candles, kissing, kneeling, decking of
images' were denounced as superstitious; processions to shrines
were no longer permitted, and in the more radical parishes of
London stained-glass windows were smashed or removed. Other
godly parishes were filled with equal enthusiasm. In Much
Wenlock, Shropshire, the bones of a local saint were thrown onto
a bonfire. In Norwich 'divers curates and other idle persons' visited
the churches in the search for idolatrous images. In Durham the
royal commissioners jumped up and down on the monstrance
paraded at the festival of Corpus Christi. It was decreed that
elaborate polyphonal music was no longer appropriate in a house
of worship. The organs also fell silent. It had been said by
reformers that the music of the old Church was 'but roaring,
howling, whistling, mumming, conjuring and juggling; and the
playing at the organs a foolish vanity'.

The injunctions had also ordered the use of the English litany,
and the reading of the lessons in English. The churchwardens
were required to purchase one copy of the *Paraphrase of the New
Testament* of Erasmus, a key text for the reformers. They were
also obliged to keep within the church an edition of Thomas
Cranmer's *Book of Homilies*, a collection of twelve sermons on the
principal doctrines of the English Church; the sermons were to
be read from the pulpit on successive Sundays, and were largely
Cranmer's own work in which he was able to set out his vision of

the reformed faith. That is why there was no mention of the Mass, and only the most cursory reference to baptism. The sovereign source of strength and power lay in a proper reading of the Bible for 'the Scripture is full, as well of low valleys, plain ways, and easy for every man to walk in, as also of high hills and mountains, which few men can ascend unto'. The graceful cadences and euphonies of Cranmer's style did much to ease the introduction of the new faith.

In May 1547, a general 'visitation' of the churches was announced. The country was divided into six circuits, and the royal commissioners interrogated the parish clergy on their compliance with the injunctions. Was the English litany in proper use? Did any priest still preach the primacy of the pope? Are there still any 'misused images . . . clothes, stones, shoes, offerings, kissings, candlesticks, trindles of wax and such like'? The visitors commanded all parishes to give up their ancient festivals or 'church ales' in which money was raised for the maintenance of the church fabric; festivals in commemoration of the local saint were also forbidden.

One by one the great seasonal festivities of the old Church were silenced. The processions on Corpus Christi in celebration of the holy Eucharist, the May games of Robin Hood, the Hocktide 'bindings' of Easter where the members of one sex tied up the other, only to release them on the promise of a kiss or a small payment – all of these were denounced as relics of popery. There were to be no more rituals involving the 'boy bishops', whereby a young boy was dressed up to parody a divine, and the churches were no longer to be decorated with flowers. The religious guilds were abolished, too, and with them vanished the pageant plays of previous generations. One contemporary wrote that the country, 'once renowned throughout Christendom as merry England, has lost its joy and merriment, and must be called sad and sorrowful England'.

So the interiors of the churches were now whitewashed with lime and chalk; the crucifix was supplanted by the royal arms, and the written commandments took the place of the frescoes. They had been, as one fervent homilist put it, 'scoured of such gay gazing sights'. The conservative faithful compared them to barns rather than to chapels but, for the godly, they were the appropriate setting for psalms, Bible readings and sermons. These more radical and reformed churches were now fundamentally different from any that had come before, and were the harbingers of wholly new forms of worship. In the winter of 1547 the great rood of St Paul's Cathedral, together with all the other images, was taken down in the course of one night. Subsequently the charnel house and chapel were turned into dwelling houses and shops. A decline in lay piety was already sufficiently obvious. When John Leland had toured the south-west of England five years previously, to prepare material for his *Itinerary*, he could find no signs of any church-building; the churches he praised were all the work of earlier generations.

Two bishops spoke out against the changes. Stephen Gardiner, excluded from the councils of the king, denounced the excessive zeal for innovation. 'If you cut the old canal,' he said, 'the water is apt to run further than you have a mind to.' When he was warned that his opposition to the council might put him in danger he replied that 'I am already by nature condemned to death'. Gardiner wrote to the protector asking him not to continue with his work of reform during the minority of the king; he believed that it would endanger public peace. The bishop also wrote to Thomas Cranmer, disputing some of the doctrines upheld in the *Book of Homilies*. Gardiner was summoned to the council and required to obey the new injunctions; when he prevaricated he was sent to the Fleet prison, accompanied by his cook and two servants.

Edmund Bonner, bishop of London, had already preceded him to that place. 'Ah bishop,' the reforming duchess of Suffolk exclaimed as she passed beneath the window of Gardiner's cell, 'it is merry with the lambs when the wolves are shut up!' But the bishops were not the only protesters. The French ambassador reported murmurings of grief and anger 'in the northern parts on account of the novelties which are attempted every day by these new governors against the ancient approved religion'. The murmurings grew louder and louder until eventually a rebellion arose in the land.

18

Have at all papists!

Protector Somerset was, above all else, a soldier; his sphere was war. From the earliest days of the protectorate he was concerned with national defences, along the south coast and in the northern lands where the threat from Scotland was still very strong. He had proved his military capacities in that country, by mounting a successful invasion and an effective border raid in two successive years, and his eyes were turned to Scotland again. In 1543 Prince Edward had been betrothed to Mary, infant queen of Scots, but nothing had transpired. It was most unlikely that anything would. Yet Somerset still publicly expressed hopes of a union between the two countries, a kingdom of 'Great Britain' united in the strength of the reformed religion.

Like many successful military commanders he was rough in speech and inclined to deliver orders rather than to consult; he came to rely upon proclamations, for example, as the method of ordering the nation and issued seventy-seven of them in a little under three years. They varied from decrees against the hoarding of grain to the regulation of the price of meat. These proclamations did not have to be approved by the council, and in almost every case they were accompanied by the threat of severe punishment. It may be that he was uneasy about the source and nature of his power and therefore required the blunt force of the proclamation.

Whatever the reason, he acquired a reputation for arrogance and *froideur*; it was widely reported that he did not truly consult with his colleagues of the council and preferred to rule all from a lonely eminence. 'Of late,' one old courtier wrote to him, 'your Grace is grown into great choleric fashions, whensoever you are contraried in that which you have conceived in your head.' Yet he did possess what might be called a paternalistic concern for the country, as long as its interests coincided with his own.

He was in many respects an avaricious man and acquired an unknown number of church properties and estates. His reformed religion came at a price. Three months after Edward's coronation he began building the palace at the top of the Strand that became known to posterity as Somerset House. Three palaces of bishops, and the parish church of St Mary-le-Strand, were pulled down to make room for it; a chapel, part of the church of St John of Jerusalem in Clerkenwell, was blown up with gunpowder so that it could furnish him with stone and other materials. He also looted St Paul's Cathedral. The French ambassador wrote that 'in a building he is raising in this town they stop work neither Sundays nor feast days; and indeed they worked on it even upon last Ascension Day'. His essential point was not the speed of the erection but the fact that the protector was willing to ignore the ancient holy days. It was said at the time that, on observing this spectacular appropriation of church properties, men's hearts hardened against him. At a later date John Stow, in his *Survey of London*, wrote that 'these actions were in a high degree impious, so did they draw with them both open dislike from men and much secret revenge from God'.

Yet it seemed at the time that the protector was in divine favour. In the late summer of 1547, after much inconclusive negotiation with the Scots, Somerset invaded his northern neighbour. The move had as much to do with France as with Scotland; the new French king, Henry II, was determined to reclaim Boulogne, which had been ceded to Henry VIII the year before at the Treaty of Ardres. The young king of France had come to the throne in the spring, at the age of twenty-eight, and of course aspired to martial glory. Even as he prepared for struggle within the borders of his own kingdom against England he strengthened his ties with the old ally, Scotland; it was reported that the navies of both countries were harassing English vessels. Somerset also wished to punish the Scots for formally repudiating the marriage treaty between the young queen, Mary, and Edward VI. He, too, dreamed of glory.

By the late spring troops and mariners had been assembled on the very slender grounds that the Scots had organized one or two border raids. Cuthbert Tunstall, bishop of Durham, was ordered back to his diocese in order to prepare for war. On 31 August Somerset crossed the border with a proclamation that he had come 'only to defend and maintain the honour of both the princes and realms', and at a place beside Musselburgh known as Pinkie Cleugh he gained a decisive victory over the Scottish forces. The defending army also faced cannon fire from the English ships offshore.

It is estimated that some 10,000 Scots were killed. A contemporary chronicler notes that 'the dead bodies lay as thick as a man may note cattle grazing'. Some of the survivors fled to Edinburgh, flinging away their weapons as they ran; others tried to hide under the willow pollards in the neighbouring bogs, with their mouths above the water like otters. After his victory Somerset promptly returned to England, leaving a force of occupation in what was essentially a defeated nation. It was decided that a number of forts, with appropriate garrisons, should be established to cow and to subdue the people. It was the beginning of a further financial crisis, with the growing realization that the costs of occupation were far greater than any rewards. The Scots were not about to submit.

Somerset had come back in haste because he feared that the French might attempt an invasion on the southern coast; the Scottish nobility had already asked Henry II for assistance against the common enemy. He may also have feared further scheming by his younger brother. The young king later recalled that 'in the month of September 1547 the Lord Admiral told me that mine uncle, being gone into Scotland, should not pass the peace without the loss of a great number of men or of himself, and that he did spend much money in vain'. In that respect, Thomas Seymour was proved to be correct. Edward then went on to write that 'after the return of mine uncle he [Thomas] said that I was too bashful in my matters, and that I would not speak for my right. I said I was well enough.'

But Somerset's return was also the necessary prelude to the first parliament of the new reign. It assembled on 4 November, and was inaugurated with a Mass in which the Gloria, the Creed and the Agnus Dei were sung in English, a sure sign of the way in which matters of faith were to be resolved. One of the first measures was in fact an Act that abolished all chantries, endowments made in wills for the procuring of Masses for the sake of the souls of the dead. They were deemed to be forlorn superstitions connected with the discredited belief in purgatory; they encouraged the people in their ignorance of 'their very true and perfect salvation through the death of Jesus Christ'.

It was piously stated that the funds and lands released from enthralment to vain piety were now to be directed towards schools and other foundations; in fact most of the revenue went straight into the pockets of the treasury for use in the Scottish wars. The number of schools created by Edward VI has been miscalculated. The majority of schools that claim him as their founder did in fact exist long before his reign; he simply continued their foundation by making a fixed payment to the schoolmaster in place of the fees the master had received from the now dissolved chantries. In the course of Edward's rule, however, free schools were established at St Albans, Berkhamsted and Stamford. The same process of secular change affected the universities; the old monastic foundations were dissolved and new colleges took their place. Trinity College in Cambridge, for example, was established in 1546; Emmanuel College, Cambridge, was founded in 1584 on the site of a dissolved Dominican friary that had been purchased for the purpose.

Some of the revenue from the chantries was evidently put to more familiar uses, and the imperial ambassador reported that 'all the gentry, large and small, are . . . on the look out to receive rewards and benefits from the king'. A small group of peers at the centre of power shared the major part of the remaining spoils; the corruption of rulers made up what Thomas More called in his *Utopia* 'a conspiracy of rich men seeking their own commodity under the name of the commonwealth'. It was said that it was better to be in hell than in the court of augmentation, where the monastic revenues were administered. The proverb 'The law is ended as a man is befriended' was on everyone's lips. 'Who passeth on [refrains from] offending and breaking the laws when he hath plenty of money to stop the execution of them?' It is the story of the government of England.

It has been calculated that more than 2,500 chantry foundations were thus removed from the land. The English were no longer permitted to pray for their dead. At the beginning of 1548 it was also proclaimed that no candles should be carried on Candlemas Day, nor ashes be applied on Ash Wednesday, nor palms be borne on Palm Sunday.

In accordance with its reformist inclinations parliament also passed legislation that allowed communion to be taken in both kinds, the bread and the wine; with this change a vernacular Order of Communion was introduced, inserted into the Latin Mass. Muscatel or malmsey wine was given to the 'better sort' while the rest had to make do with claret. It was further resolved that there should be no restrictions on printing, teaching or reading the Scriptures. It was therefore hoped that England would become the land of the Bible. From this time forward bishops were to be made by king's letters patent, making sure that the newly evangelized nation had a staff of permanent officials. Piece by piece, step by step, the religion of the people was changed.

Parliament also issued a new Treason Act that repealed the draconian legislation imposed by the old king on his sometimes fractious realm. It was now no longer considered treason merely to speak against the king; any more heinous acts now needed two witnesses rather than one before matters were taken further. This particular clause on the need for two witnesses has been described by a great administrative historian, Henry Hallam, as 'one of the most important constitutional provisions which the annals of the Tudor family afford'.

In a similar spirit of toleration the Act for the Burning of Heretics, dated 1414, was also removed from the statute book. More importantly, perhaps, the Act of Six Articles was abolished; this had been described, at its inception in 1539, as 'an Act abolishing diversity in Opinions'. It was imposed essentially to uphold orthodox Catholicism and silence active reformers; it was no longer necessary or expedient in the new atmosphere of Edward's reign, and its repeal could of course also be construed as a measure of religious toleration. So parliament had thrown out all the old precautions over treason and heresy, and thus had tacitly dismantled much of the oppressive legislation of the old reign.

One much less liberal measure was introduced. A new Vagrancy Act was passed that ordered into slavery those who were unwilling to work. Two justices of the peace, on hearing about the 'idle living' of any person from two witnesses, could ordain that the guilty party should be branded on the chest with a 'V' and sentenced to two years of slavery; the culprit could be chained or driven with whips. Anyone who tried to flee from this exacted labour would be punished with perpetual slavery for the first offence and with death for the second. The severity of the measure is a token of the anxiety that the vagrants caused in sixteenth-century England. They roved the country in bands, begging or stealing at pleasure; the 'sturdy beggars' were an old order with their own traditions and their own language in 'the canting tongue'. 'The cull has rum rigging, let's ding him, and mill him, and pike' was as much to say that 'the man has very good clothes, let us knock him down, rob him and run'.

The masterless man was also believed to be the sign of a dissolving or deteriorating social order, thus provoking fresh fears of the future. In 1577 William Harrison wrote that 'it is not yet full three score years since this trade began, but how it hath prospered since that time it is easy to judge, for they are now supposed of one sex and another to amount unto about 10,000 persons, as I have heard reported'. Yet the legislation is also evidence of the social discipline that was maintained over the nation by means of church 'visitations' and injunctions and proclamations. Anyone walking free had to be detained or restrained. The fear of disorder was very strong.

A tumult of legislation had indeed been passed in the first months of Somerset's rule. In the spring of 1548 William Paget, once the colluder or conspirator with Somerset, wrote a letter to the protector in which he declared that the country had become restless. 'The use of the old religion is forbidden, the use of the new is not yet printed in the stomachs of eleven of twelve parts of the realm.' He warned the protector to be cautious and to move carefully. 'Commissions out for this matter, new laws for this, proclamations for another, one in another's neck, so thick that they be not set among the people . . . You must take pity upon the poor men's children, and of the conservation and stay of the realm, and put no more so many irons in the fire at once.' But Somerset objected to him as a Cassandra, prophesying woe.

Yet there had never been so much dissension over matters of religion. Some said that Somerset had gone too far, and others complained that he had not gone far enough. An indication of religious controversy can be found among the members of the royal family. Edward professed his 'comfort and quiet of mind' at the changes in religion, and even began writing a treatise in French on the subject of papal supremacy; at the same time his older sister, Mary, was hearing four Masses a week. Fights broke out in churches between the various factions, conservative and reformed. One church favoured the rite of Rome while another practised that of Geneva; neighbouring churches might worship according to the rules of Zurich or Wittenberg. Verse satires, ridiculing conservatives and reformers, were widely circulated; one of them was entitled *Have at all Papists! By me, Hans Hatprick* and another was printed as *A Ballet, declaring the Fall of the Whore of Babylon, intituled 'Tie this Mare, Tom-boy'.*

In the churchwardens' accounts at Stanford in the Vale, then in Berkshire, the date was given as 'the time of Schism, when this realm was divided from the Catholic church' when 'all godly ceremonies & good uses were taken out of the Church'. The parish priest of Adwick le Street, in Doncaster, wrote that at Rogation-tide 'no procession was made about the fields, but cruel tyrants did cast down all crosses standing in open ways despitefully'. At a school in Bodmin the boys set up rival factions of 'the old religion' and 'the new religion' in a series of elaborate battles. When they managed to blow up a calf with gunpowder, the master intervened with a whip. The social and religious order had to be maintained at all costs. A boy of thirteen was whipped naked at the church of St Mary Woolnoth; his offence was to throw his cap at the Blessed Sacrament raised during a Mass.

In the spring of 1548, therefore, all preaching was prohibited except by those especially licensed to do so; this was meant to silence 'rash, contentious, hot and undiscreet' men who were forever stirring the pot of religious dissension. Yet even this was not enough and, later in the year, all preaching came to an end. An exception was made for the conservative bishop of Winchester, Stephen Gardiner. He had been released from the Fleet prison on his promise that he would conform to the new religious polity, and had scarcely returned to his palace in Southwark when he was informed by the council that he was to preach before the king. He was asked to read out, and subscribe to, certain articles concerning the recent changes in religion. He was being ordered, in other words, publicly to assent to such matters as the destruction of images and the administration of communion in both kinds.

He refused, saying that this was 'like a lesson made for a child to learn'. Whereupon he was summoned to court and the protector warned him that he could be deprived of his bishopric for disobedience to the king's highness. Gardiner then relented a little and agreed to compose a sermon touching upon such matters. He consented to preach on St Peter's Day, or 29 June, but the afternoon before he received a message from the protector forbidding him to make any mention of the doctrine of transubstantiation. He was about to send his chaplain with a verbal response, when he broke off. 'You shall not go,' he told him. 'I will do well enough, I warrant.'

On the following afternoon he stepped up to the new 'preaching place', the open pulpit set in the privy garden at Whitehall; the young king sat at a window in the gallery, overlooking the preacher, where assembled in the garden was 'such an audience as the like whereof hath not lightly been seen'. Everyone wished to hear the bishop make his peace with the religious changes. He proceeded to say that 'I will plainly declare what I think of the state of the Church of England at this day, how I like it and what I think of it'. It was in some respects an ambiguous message. He grudgingly agreed to the dissolution of the chantries, but still believed it right to pray for the dead; he accepted that rituals and ceremonies were essentially 'things indifferent' and so did not object to the reforms, but he did believe that priests should retain their vow of chastity; despite the protector's warning to avoid the subject of transubstantiation, the bishop did affirm the power of the sacrament with the phrase 'This is my body'.

After the sermon was over Gardiner was 'merry and quiet' on his way back to Southwark in his barge. When his chaplain heard a rumour that he would be committed to the Tower the bishop replied that 'it was but tales for he thought that he never pleased the Council better in all his life'. On the following day he was arrested and, on the charge of 'wilful disobedience', was sent to the Tower of London where he was kept in close confinement for the next five years.

Somerset, even in the midst of these controversies, was pre-occupied with Scotland. Early in 1548 he issued 'an epistle or exhortation' to the Scottish people in which he pleaded for a bond of common interests 'united together in one language, in one island' which should be given 'the indifferent old name of Britaines again'; the names of England and Scotland would therefore be abolished. Once more he insisted on the marriage of Edward and Mary as the ground for this unity but, once more, the Scots were not listening. It came as a deep shock, therefore, when it was confirmed that Mary, queen of Scots, was in fact to be betrothed to the dauphin, the French king's eldest son. So began the public career of the young princess whose troubled life cast its shadow over English affairs for the next thirty-nine years; even at the age of ten it was said that 'her spirit is already so high and noble that she would make great demonstration of displeasure at seeing herself degradingly treated'. Mary of Guise from Lorraine, the widow of James V, became effectively the dowager queen of Scotland in her daughter's absence in France, where the young girl was to be raised with her future husband. France now brooded on the northern borders of England.

The French king was still eager to regain Boulogne, but the overwhelming victory of the protector's forces at Pinkie Cleugh gave him pause. It was also in the interest of England to avoid war with France; any military campaign would prove ruinously expen-sive. In February 1548 the French ambassador was gracefully received by the young king at Greenwich, where they witnessed a mock siege; they spoke together in Latin, for mutual ease of intercourse. Four months later a French force landed at Leith in order to aid their Scottish allies; sallies and counter-sallies were launched about the town of Haddington in East Lothian, but large-scale fighting was avoided. Nevertheless the presence of French troops on Scottish soil was an irritant, and emphasized the flaws in Somerset's policy of subjugation by means of garrisons.

The younger brother of the protector, Thomas Seymour, had not abandoned his schemes of advancement. Further evidence of his incapacity emerged at the time when the young Lady Elizabeth entered the household of Katherine Parr; she was at the time fourteen but her young age did not deter the man who delighted to be called her 'stepfather'. He would appear in her bedchamber dressed only in his nightgown and slippers; he would engage in playful romps with her, smacking her on the back or buttocks. It was evident, too, that the princess had become infatuated with the handsome lord high admiral. It is said that eventually Katherine Parr found them in each other's arms. Elizabeth left the household. When it was rumoured that the princess was indeed pregnant with Seymour's child, the privy council was obliged to question members of her entourage; there was no truth to the reports, but the foreign ambassadors were happy to pass on any titillating news of Anne Boleyn's daughter. The episode also served to materially increase Elizabeth's natural wariness and secretiveness.

When Katherine Parr died in the early autumn of 1548, six days after giving birth to an infant girl, Seymour found himself with another opportunity of bolstering his state. It soon became clear that he still had designs upon Lady Elizabeth. He asked one of her household servants, Thomas Parry, 'whether her great buttocks were grown any less or no'? More pertinently, perhaps, he began to make enquiries about 'the state of her grace's houses, and how many people she kept'. What houses she had and what lands? Were they good lands or not, and did she hold them for life?

A courtier was out riding with him one day, en route to parliament. 'My lord admiral,' he said, 'there are certain rumours of you that I am very sorry to hear.'

'What are they?'

'I am informed you make means to marry either with my Lady Mary or my Lady Elizabeth. And touching that, my lord, if you go about any such thing, you seek the means to undo yourself, and all those that shall come of you.' When Seymour denied any such intention, the courtier replied that 'I am glad to hear you say so – do not attempt the matter'. He warned Seymour that the two previous kings had been highly suspicious of over-mighty subjects; might not the new king have the same infirmity? Seymour's own brother, Protector Somerset, might also be moved to act against him.

Yet Seymour shook off any such warnings, and decided that it was time to act upon Edward himself. 'Since I saw you last,' he told him, 'you are grown to be a goodly gentleman. I trust that within three or four years, you shall be ruler of your own things.' When the king reached sixteen, he might be able and willing to rule of his own accord and thereby dismiss the protector; Seymour might then rise high in royal favour. Yet at this juncture the king simply said 'no'.

Seymour still plotted. He fortified his dwelling, Holt Castle in Worcestershire, and brought in a great store of beer, beef and wheat; by some means or other he obtained the 'double key' that would grant him access to the privy garden and the king's lodging. He made the journey from Holt Castle to Whitehall many times with a company of his followers. He said that 'a man might steal away the king now for there came more with me than is in all the house besides'. Then, on the night of 16 January 1549, he was surprised by Edward's dog just outside the royal bedchamber; he shot the dog and, as cries of 'Help! Murder!' rang out, he was apprehended by the king's guard. It seems likely that he intended to kidnap the king and raise a civil war in his name. It was alleged later that he had made provision to recruit a private army and that he had planned to take over the royal mint at Bristol; these were also clear tokens of treasonable attempts.

He was arrested on the day after his discovery in the king's quarters and taken to the Tower; soon enough he came to trial for his life on the charge of treason. The protector was now in the unenviable position of prosecuting his younger brother to the death. 'They cannot kill me,' Seymour said, 'except they do me wrong.' But then, a little later, he complained of his 'friends' on the royal council that 'I think they have forgotten me'. The young king himself also turned against him. His recorded words were that 'it were better for him to die before'. It was better for him to be dead.

In the inquiry against him, his designs on Elizabeth were also formally investigated. The young princess herself was questioned together with the more prominent members of her household. 'They all sing one song,' their interrogator wrote to the protector, 'and so I think they would not do, unless they had set the note before.' It seems likely, therefore, that Seymour's advances had gone further than was considered permissible and may have verged on treason. 'There goeth rumours abroad', Elizabeth complained, 'that I am in the Tower, and with child by my lord admiral.' The rumours were false, but three of her entourage were dismissed. There had been smoke, and perhaps there had also been fire.

Even while he remained in the Tower Seymour engaged in more schemes. He made a pen from the point of an aiglet plucked from his hose and, according to Hugh Latimer, fabricated an ink 'with such workmanship as the like has not been seen'; with pen and ink he then wrote two letters, to the princesses Mary and Elizabeth, 'tending to this end, that they should conspire against my lord protector's grace'. He concealed these letters within his shoe but, on his prison lodging being searched, they were discovered.

The king, the fount of justice, was obliged to speak. 'We do perceive', the king said to his council, 'that there is great things objected and laid to my lord admiral mine uncle – and they tend to treason – and we perceive that you require but justice to be done. We think it reasonable, and we will well that you proceed according to your request.' On the following day, 25 February, a bill of attainder for treason was sent to parliament. One of the articles against Seymour charged him to have attempted 'to get into your hands the government of the king's majesty, to the great danger of his highness' person, and the subversion of the state of the realm'.

On 20 March he was taken to Tower Hill, where he was beheaded. The protector had signed the death warrant, with a shaking hand, but had taken no part in the parliamentary proceedings against his younger brother. It has been surmised that some among the council were happy to pit brother against brother, hoping thereby to accomplish the ruin of both of them. Sure enough some denounced Somerset for fratricide. A 'godly and honourable' woman reproached him with the words, 'Where is thy brother? Lo, his blood crieth against thee unto God from the ground.' He was condemned as 'a blood-sucker and a ravenous wolf' and it was predicted that 'the fall of the one brother, would be the overthrow of the other'.

19

The barns of Crediton

In the first years of the young king's reign social, as well as religious, divisions became apparent. 'In times past,' Hugh Latimer, the most popular preacher of the day, said in a sermon, 'men were full of compassion; but now there is no pity; for in London their brother shall die in the streets for cold; he shall lie sick at the door between stock and stock – I cannot tell what to call it – and then perish for hunger.' The coinage had been debased by the authorities, thus unleashing further waves of inflation on a country already impoverished. In the seven years between 1540 and 1547 prices rose by 46 per cent; in 1549 they had risen by another 11 per cent. The trend of an ever-growing population meant that the plight of the poor, and of the agricultural labourer, increased. Food was dear; wages were low. It has become known as the 'price revolution', accompanied by dearth and distress on a national scale. In addition the administration itself could scarcely pay its debts.

Latimer knew where most of the blame might be laid. 'You landlords,' he said, 'you rent-raisers, I may say you step-lords, you have for your possessions too much . . . thus is caused such dearth that poor men which live of their labour cannot with the sweat of their faces have a living.' The principal complaint of the people was raised against the system of enclosure, a term that in fact covered a multitude of practices, which embodied a wholly different concept of land use. One of these movements was 'engrossing' whereby many smallholdings were concentrated in the hands of one person; a second amounted to the enclosure of previous common grounds by a landlord who claimed ownership; a third was the conversion of arable into pasture land. So it was that Latimer intoned against 'these graziers, enclosers, rent-raisers . . . whereas have been a great many house-holders and inhabitants, there is now but a shepherd and his dog'. It has been suggested that the bulk of enclosures actually took place at an earlier date, but the fast rise in prices and the fall in wages created a climate in which all economic woes were magnified.

Hugh Latimer also addressed the problem of debasement. 'We now have a pretty little shilling [12*d*.],' he said, 'the last day, I had put it away almost for a groat [4*d*.].' A shilling was in other words worth only a third of its previous value. John Heywood phrased it differently:

> These testons look red: how like you the same?
> 'Tis a token of grace: they blush for shame.

The copper, in other words, was showing through the thin surface application of silver. When money is not taken seriously, the economy begins to crumble. A reformer, John Hooper, wrote to William Cecil, even then beginning his career at court, that 'the prices of things be here as I tell you, the number of people be great; their little cottages and poor livings decay daily; except God by sickness take them out of the world, they must needs lack. You know what a grievous extreme, yea, in a manner unruly evil hunger is.'

In the summer of 1549 a number of riots were specifically aimed at enclosures, in which the irate crowd pulled down the hedges that had been planted to separate the land. The hedge itself became a symbol of all the ills assailing the people, among them the encroachment upon waste and common land as well as the loss of tenants' rights against landlords who persistently raised their rents. Custom was giving way to contract and competition. In response the government of the protector sent out a number of commissioners to investigate why it was that 'many have been driven to extreme poverty and compelled to leave the places where they were born'; an inquiry would be instituted to ensure that the relevant statutes, from the two previous reigns, were still being obeyed.

It was a measure of the protector's concern that the royal deer park at Hampton Court was 'disparked' or made open and that the common right to land was restored in many parishes. The imperial ambassador observed to his court that 'I have heard in deep secret that the protector declared to the Council, as his opinion, that the peasants' demands were fair and just; for the poor people who had no land to graze their cattle ought to retain the commons and the lands that had always been public property, and the nobles and rich ought not to seize and add them to their parks and possessions'. A further thought may have occurred to him. If the new faith did not help to promote social justice and to uphold the rights of the poor, surely it had failed in some of its first duties?

Yet dissent and discontent continued. In the previous reign 'all things were too strait,' Sir William Paget told Somerset at the end of 1548, but 'now they are too loose'. In the old days 'was it dangerous to do or speak though the meaning were not evil; and now every man hath liberty to do and speak at liberty without danger'. In the reign of a child king, there was disorder.

General discontent was rising. 'All things in manner going backward and unfortunate,' Paget also wrote, 'and every man almost out of heart and courage, and our lacks so well known as our enemies despise us and our friends pity us.' In the spring of 1549 rumours were circulating through the kingdom, and a proclamation was issued against 'lewd, idle, seditious and disordered persons . . . posting from place to place . . . to stir up rumours or raise up tales'.

It was reported that the king was dead. 'In the mean season,' Edward wrote in his journal, 'because there was a rumour that I was dead, I passed through London.' It was said that the war in Scotland was a complete failure. Indeed it had not prospered. It was rumoured that a charge would be levied for weddings, christenings and funerals. It was whispered that the protector and the council were corrupt. The bad harvest of 1549 exacerbated these protests. As a precaution all wrestling matches were forbidden, and all plays or interludes were suspended; it was unwise to allow any large congregation of people. The poor were being accused of sedition, but the reason for discontent might be found elsewhere. Robert Crowley, in a volume entitled *The Way to Wealth*, accused 'the great farmers, the graziers, the rich butchers, the men of law, the merchants, the gentlemen, the knights, the lords, and I cannot tell who' for provoking popular revolt.

In May a rebellion was fostered in Wiltshire, but the forces of a local magnate scattered or slew the protesters. In Oxfordshire the rebels were defeated by an army of 1,500 men led by Lord Gray; some were taken and hanged, befitting a state of war, while others ran back to their homes. Similar abortive risings took place in Sussex and Hampshire, Kent and Gloucestershire, Suffolk and Essex, Hertfordshire and Leicestershire and Worcestershire. Something was gravely amiss in the entire kingdom, even if these pockets of resistance were quickly stifled.

Yet nothing could withstand the force of popular protest that emerged in the early days of June. It has become known as the Western Rising or the Prayer Book Rebellion, attesting to the fact that religious and social ills were not easily to be distinguished. At the beginning of 1549 the second session of Edward's parliament had approved the publication of the Book of Common Prayer. It was authorized as part of the Act of Uniformity 'for the uniformity of service and administration of the sacraments throughout the realm'; it was one of the most important and permanent of parliamentary Acts, effectively prescribing the doctrine and liturgy of the Church of England for future generations.

The Act was largely the work of Thomas Cranmer in consultation with the bishops, and the freedom of debate among the senior clergy in the House of Lords meant that it did not pass without strenuous opposition. One contemporary wrote that there was 'great sticking touching the blessed body and blood of Jesus Christ. I trust they will conclude well in it, by the help of the Holy Ghost.' The Holy Ghost did not intervene and, although the Act was passed, eight out of the eighteen bishops present voted against it.

Cranmer insisted in the course of the great debate that 'our faith is not to believe Him to be in the bread and wine, but that

He is in heaven'. He denied the doctrine of transubstantiation, therefore, and insisted that Christ had only a spiritual presence determined by the faith of the recipient. Neither the Bible nor the holy fathers ever mention the doctrine; Cranmer believed it to be the invention of the Antichrist and his heir, Pope Gregory VII, in whose reign at the end of the eleventh century it had been introduced. Yet the more conservative bishops denounced this in turn as heresy. One reformer, Peter Martyr, wrote at the time that 'there is so much contention about the Eucharist that every corner is full of it; every day the question is discussed among the Lords, with such disputing of bishops as was never heard; the commons thronging the lords' galleries to hear the arguments'. These were days when the principles of religion were debated with the same eagerness as the tenets of politics and economics are now discussed.

The Book of Common Prayer, in revised form, is still in use. It is a breviary, a missal and a ritual liturgy. In time it lent strength and unity to the English Church but, like all great agents of revolution, it was fiercely controversial at the moment of its publication. It was a book of worship, written in solemn and subtle English, of which we may take one example. In the medieval marriage service the wife had pledged to be 'bonner and buxom in bed and in board'. This has the nice alliteration of an older language. Now both partners were asked to 'love and to cherish' 'for better, for worse, for richer for poorer, in sickness and in health'.

Another fundamental alteration became evident in the newly anglicized text. 'Wherefore O Lord and heavenly Father, according to the institution of Thy dearly beloved Son, our Saviour Jesus Christ, we Thy humble servants, do celebrate and make here before Thy divine Majesty with these Thy holy gifts the memorial which Thy Son wished us to make: having in remembrance His blessed passion, mighty resurrection and glorious ascension.' What had previously been deemed a 'holy sacrifice' was now a 'memorial'. The sacrifice of Christ upon the cross was remembered but not repeated or reproduced.

As a result all the more arcane rites of the Mass were removed. There was to be no more 'shifting of the book from one place to another; laying down and licking of the chalice . . . holding up his fingers, hands, or thumbs joined towards his temples; breathing upon the bread or chalice'; no more secret whisperings and sudden turnings of the body. The theatre of piety was being deconstructed. The host and the chalice were not to be elevated at the climax of the drama; the adoration of the sacrament was curtailed as a symptom of idolatry. There were to be no more intimations of sacrifice and the minister, no longer called priest, was ordered simply to place the bread and wine upon the altar. The Mass was therefore stripped of its mystery.

In the old service the priest had at the moment of the elevation of the host turned symbolically to the east as the site of Golgotha, with his back turned towards the congregation as if he were communing with sacred rites; it was from the east that Christ would come on the Day of Judgment. It was now stipulated that the minister should stand at the north side of the communion table and face the people. The rich vestments of the past were forbidden, and he could don only a white surplice. The traditional calendar of the saints' days was also omitted from the Prayer Book as arrant superstition.

Most importantly, however, the sacred service would now be performed in English rather than in Latin. One layman repeated what would become a familiar complaint that the English language could not comprehend the mystery of the Mass; it was better for it to be rendered in a language that the congregation did not understand. It was thereby filled with magic, like the ritual pronunciation of a spell. The old service had been chanted and memorized for ten centuries. The words of the hymns and psalms, the very order of the Mass itself, were part of folk memory. Now, in one parliamentary Act, they were all swept away. All these changes represented the decisive rupture with the world of medieval Catholicism.

Any minister who refused to use the new book would be imprisoned for six months and deprived of his position; on any third offence he would be consigned to life imprisonment. This was indeed an Act for 'uniformity'. Yet if Somerset and Cranmer therefore hoped to stifle dissent, they were soon disabused. A storm of protest arose in the western counties at this break with traditional practice. The new prayer book and service were to be introduced on Whit Sunday 9 June 1549. So they were in the parish of Sampford Courtenay in Devon, where they were greeted with dismay. On the following day the parishioners approached their priest, and asked him what service he intended to use, the new or the old. The new one, he told them. But they informed him that they would have nothing but 'the old and ancient religion'.

The priest himself was not unwilling to accede to their request. He went with them to the church, where he put on his traditional vestments and proceeded to say the Mass, in Latin, with all the now forbidden rites. The news of this development spread from Sampford Courtenay to all parts of Devon and Cornwall. The bells were rung to spread the good news. It was demanded that the old sacrament be 'hung over the altar and worshipped and those who would not consent thereto, to die like heretics'. It was added that 'we will not have the new service, nor the Bible, in English'. This marked the beginning of the Prayer Book Rebellion. The religious discontent turned into social discontent, exacerbated by the general climate of economic hardship. The world was being turned upside down:

> When wrens wear woodknives, cranes for to kill
> And sparrows build churches on a green hill
> And cats unto mice do swear obedience . . .

The rebellion was perhaps only to be expected; one reformer had told a continental colleague that 'a great part of the country is popish'. Another reformer, Martin Bucer, wrote to his home town of Strasburg that 'things are for the most part carried on by means of ordinances, which the majority obey very grudgingly'. This was indeed a major cause of the rebellion; the changes were imposed on the people by parliament in London. At a slightly later date Bucer wrote that 'of those devoted to the service of religion only a small number have as yet addicted themselves entirely to the kingdom of Christ'.

When a local gentleman tried to quell the uprising at Sampford Courtenay and was hacked to death on the steps of the parish church, his body was buried in the alignment of north to south; this testified to the fact that he was considered to be a heretic. The uprising, now touched with blood, soon spread. An historian of Exeter, John Hooker, wrote at the time that the news 'as a cloud carried with a violent wind and as a thunder clap sounding at one instant through the whole country . . . they clapped their hands for joy and agreed in one mind to have the same in every of their several parishes'. The rebels from Devon were joined with those from Cornwall, and the combined force captured Crediton; it was retaken by loyalist troops but only at the expense of burning all the barns in which the rebels had been hiding. 'The barns of Crediton!' became a popular war cry.

A story had just come out of Clyst St Mary, a village 3 miles east of Exeter. Walter Raleigh, the father of the famous mariner, was riding towards the town when he observed an old woman on her way to Mass praying with a set of rosary beads in her hand. He stopped to rebuke her, 'saying further that there was a punishment by the law appointed against her'. The woman hurried on to the church where she denounced the gentleman for his 'very hard and unseemly speeches concerning religion'. She also told her fellow parishioners that he had made the threat that 'except she would leave her beads and give over holy bread and water the gentlemen would burn them out of their houses and spoil therein'. This was a general and impolitic menace to the whole community; Raleigh was found and beaten, while a local mill was burned down. The events became part of the rebellion itself.

At the beginning of July 2,000 rebels marched in procession towards Exeter; they were guided by priests, robed and chanting, and at their head was the sacred pyx, or jewelled container, holding the Blessed Sacrament. They had come to besiege the town as an emblem of detestable heresy. The townsmen of Exeter resisted the siege with valour, despite the restrictions of food and water; one of them said that 'he would eat one arm and fight with the other before he would agree to a surrender'.

The protesters had drawn up a set of articles in which it was stated that 'we will have the holy decrees of our forefathers observed, kept and performed and the sacrament restored to its ancient honour'. They denounced the Book of Common Prayer itself as 'a Christmas play' or 'a Christmas game'; this observation came from the fact that at the time of receiving communion the men and women were supposed to form separate groups. This was uncannily similar to the first movement of a festive dance, and so invited ridicule.

The rebellion could not, or would not, be quelled by the local magnates; as a result, Somerset was obliged to call in his own soldiers, most of whom were mercenaries from Germany and Italy. Never before had an English ruler called in foreign troops against his own people. Six battles were fought against the rebels, the most bloody of which was at the village of Clyst St Mary itself, where on 25 July Lord Russell launched an attack on approximately 2,000 of what must now be termed the enemy; 1,000 rebels died in the action, and 900 were taken only to be massacred on Clyst Heath. It was said that all their throats were slit within ten minutes. The village was put to the torch and many of the villagers were murdered. It may be true that no heretics were burned during the regime of Protector Somerset, but this general carnage must count as one of the horrors of religious warfare. When they heard of the killings another force of rebels marched to Clyst Heath, where 2,000 of them were dispatched.

Russell then moved on to relieve Exeter but, by the time he arrived, the rebels had broken off their siege and departed. Yet retribution could still be exacted. A 'mass priest' was hanged from the steeple of the church of St Thomas, in the south of the city, wearing his vestments and draped with the bell, beads and holy-water-bucket of the old faith. The mayor of Bodmin was summoned to dinner, after which he was invited to inspect the gallows. 'Think you,' he was asked, 'think you it is strong enough?'

'Yes, sir, it is.'

'Well then, get you up, for it is for you.'

The mayor had in fact been forced to participate in the rising by the rebels. But revenge always includes rough justice. A final battle at Sampford Courtenay, where the riots had begun, was enough to dissolve the Prayer Book Rebellion.

Just as one fire was slowly being extinguished another flared up. In the second week of July a group of Norfolk inhabitants threw down the pales and hedges of the enclosed fields and then, under the leadership of Robert Kett, made a camp on Mousehold Heath just outside the walls of Norwich. Other people from the surrounding countryside flocked to them, to protest against what they considered to be the iniquitous oppressive regime of the gentry, and it was estimated that some 16,000 gathered beyond the city walls. One group of villagers from Heydon marched behind their parish banner, thus testifying to their allegiance to the old faith. Somerset and his councillors purported to believe that the revolt was being spread by 'some naughtie papist priests'.

Kett and the other leaders of the revolt sent a series of articles to the protector in which they outlined their complaints; they prayed his grace 'that no lord of no manor shall common upon the commons' and that 'copyhold land that is unreasonably rented may go as it did in the first year of King Henry VII'. No lord of the manor should be able to exploit common land. Private jurisdictions should be abolished. Their demands in general are clear evidence of a belief in the ancient and traditional ways of the countryside; the rebels were not innovators but conservators, protesting against the encroachments of a free market, the rapacity of newly rich landlords, and the steady depreciation in the value of money. They wished to return to what can be called feudalism. That is why they also wished to retain the old faith. It is significant that the rebels in Norfolk had first come together at a play concerning the translation of Thomas Becket to the shrine of Canterbury.

A phrase passed around that they would leave as many gentlemen in Norfolk as there were white bulls – none at all, in other words. 'All power is in the hands of the gentry,' it was reported in the first history of the rising, 'and they so use it as to make it unbearable; while nothing is left for us but the extreme of misery ... What is our food? Herbs and roots. Since we too have souls and bodies, is this all we are to expect from life?' A verse was left on the carcass of a slain sheep:

> Mr Pratt, your sheep are very fat,
> And we thank you for that;
> We have left you the skins to pay for your wife's pins,
> And you must thank us for that.

The protector had told the imperial ambassador that 'all hath conceived a wonderful hate against gentlemen and taketh them all as their enemies ... In Norfolk gentlemen, and all serving men for their sakes, are as evil-handled as may be.' As a precaution a bodyguard of 2,000 horse and 4,000 soldiers was established around the young king. The gates of London were strengthened, and a drawbridge placed upon London Bridge. On 18 July martial law was declared, and even to mention rebellion was to draw down death at the end of the rope. It is a measure of how local revolt could threaten the whole harmony of Tudor administration, based as it was upon an informal pact between the centre and the regions. Untune that string, and hark what discord follows.

The rebels on Mousehold Heath declared themselves to be 'the king's friends and deputies', emphasizing once more their role as traditional loyalists, and brought a semblance of order into their confused ranks. Spokesmen for each hundred were appointed, and Kett ordained that justice would be dispensed beneath a great oak that became known as the Tree of Reformation. Certain gentlemen and landowners were paraded beneath the tree, charged with robbing the poor, and then imprisoned within the camp.

Local camps were set up in other neighbourhoods in Suffolk and elsewhere, creating a network of protest in East Anglia. Some 3,000 Yorkshire men had gathered under the proclamation that 'there should no king reign in England; the noblemen and gentlemen to be destroyed'. This was considerably more radical than any demands made by Kett and his men; but now all were denounced indiscriminately as agents of chaos.

On 31 July the marquis of Northampton brought 1,500 men to the walls of Norwich, where he attempted to break the supply lines between the town and the rebels; his forces made their way through the lanes and alleys of the town, but the decayed and dilapidated walls offered them no protection. The rebels came down from Mousehold Heath, with what one chronicler describes as 'confused cries and beastly howlings', and cut them apart; Northampton fled, leaving Norwich to the mercy of the insurgents. Kett set up an armed camp in the grounds of the cathedral and took command. He and his men were now guilty of treason, having assaulted and slaughtered the king's army.

Somerset and the council met each day for a week, but could come to no decision. The protector first envisaged that he would lead an army against Kett and his men but then, for reasons that are unclear, changed his mind. Instead he sent out John Dudley, earl of Warwick, at the head of a force of 6,000 foot together with 1,500 horse. On 23 August, 3 miles from Norwich, Dudley sent Kett a final summons to surrender or else face certain defeat at the hands of overwhelming strength. When a royal herald approached the rebels with news of the offer a boy pulled down his breeches and did 'a filthy act'; in response Dudley's soldiers shot him.

Uproar now arose in the rebel camp and, when Kett offered to meet Dudley, his followers would not allow him to leave them. Whereupon Dudley now fired Norwich; his forces broke down the portcullis gate and began to roam through the city with their swords in their hands. The knights and gentlemen within the army had drawn their swords and kissed one another's blades, which was according to Holinshed 'an ancient custom used among men of war in times of great danger'. Dudley made for the marketplace, where many of the rebels were encamped, and promptly hanged forty-nine of Kett's men; such was the congestion that the gallows broke apart. The rebels formed themselves into three separate companies and dispersed, launching various sallies and incursions against the army.

With much of the city on fire, and with supplies running low, Kett decided that it was better to evacuate Mousehold Heath and move to the more defensible terrain of Dussindale to the east of Norwich. He took with him the gentlemen, or hostages, who might prove useful in any negotiations. On the following morning Dudley and his army moved onto Dussindale, where a pardon was offered. It was rejected. After a confused preliminary skirmish the guns were trained upon the rebels and, as they wavered, Dudley's horse rode into them; the prominent rebels in the front line, with Kett among them, fled the scene. The remnant of the rebel force formed a barricade out of the carts and carriages closest to hand; they faced almost certain death, on the field of battle or on the gallows at a later date, but Dudley held out to them once more the promise of pardon. It seems that he came in front of them to pledge his word that, if they submitted and surrendered, they would be spared. Most of them took this last opportunity, crying out 'God save King Edward! God save King Edward!' The fighting was over by mid-afternoon, with 2,000 of the rebels lying dead.

Kett had taken refuge in a barn some 8 miles away, but here he was found and taken prisoner. He was returned under armed guard on the following day to Norwich, where 300 of the recalcitrant rebels were hanged. Kett himself, after a trial in London, was eventually hanged in chains from the wall of Norwich Castle. A plaque was set up by that place in 1949 which read: 'in reparation and honour to a notable and courageous leader in the long struggle of the common people of England to escape from a servile life into the freedom of just conditions'.

At the time, however, the verdict upon him was more ambiguous. Kett had been Dudley's tenant, and rumours have survived of an intrigue between the men to bring down the protector. The treasurer of the army, in particular, had been sending money to Kett. It has been rumoured that Lady Mary had also been party to the plot. But the principal participants, if such they were, have successfully covered any tracks they might have made. All is dark and uncertain. We may chronicle the larger movements of the time but the private deeds remain invisible. We may see dark shapes and outlines – the smiler with the knife under the cloak, the intriguer with the open purse – but we can conclude nothing.

The rebellions may have been crushed, but their ubiquity demoralized the government of the protector. He had acted in an inconsistent manner, at one moment trying to ease their discontents while at another relying upon naked force to suppress them; he had attempted both conciliation and violence, so gaining a reputation for both weakness and brutality. But if it was clear that the response of Somerset and his colleagues was confused, it is also evident that the local administrations of both Devon and Norfolk were weak and uncertain. It did not help that the great magnate of East Anglia, the duke of Norfolk, had been confined in the Tower since 1546 on the charge of high treason. It is perhaps significant that Lady Mary, the largest landowner in Norfolk, seems to have done nothing to arrest the disorder.

At this juncture John Dudley, earl of Warwick, stepped forward; he was reputedly a friend and colleague of Somerset but, in matters of politics, the winner takes all. In the reign of Henry he had fought successfully both in Scotland and in France; his reputation as a military commander was now further attested by his victory over the Norfolk rebels where, unlike Somerset, he had taken to the field. He was circumspect and politic; not domineering, he adopted a conciliatory style.

When he returned to London at the head of the conquering army, he was virtually in control of the city. Power was now the spur to action. It was clear enough that the policies of Somerset were failing. It was claimed that he had gone too far in his early appeasement of the rebels; that, in a sequence of letters he had written in the summer, he had come close to a policy of collaboration with them against the 'sheep-owners'. This may have been a negotiating tactic, like that which Henry VIII employed at the time of the Pilgrimage of Grace, but it was cause enough to earn the suspicion and dislike of the landed class. His 'levity' and 'softness' were denounced.

Other evidence of failure could be found. English authority in Scotland, imposed by means of garrisons, was failing. In the summer the resurgent French king, Henry II, declared war against England and began to lay siege to the English colony of Boulogne. He also had in his possession the young queen of Scotland, as his future daughter-in-law, and he seemed likely to claim her country as his own. From rebellion at home to failure abroad, evidence of Somerset's misgovernment was everywhere to be seen.

So, on his arrival in London, Dudley at once began to consult and scheme with the principal councillors of the realm. Lady Mary was soon acquainted with the proposals to depose Somerset, and it seems very likely that she was asked to take part; it was even possible that she might be declared 'regent' in these early years of her brother's rule. While consorting with the conservatives, however, Dudley was also ingratiating himself with the reformers. The council were united against the protector.

The leading members of that council addressed a letter to Charles V in which they stated their reasons for deposing Somerset. He had become 'haught and arrogant'; he had been used 'to taunt such of us as frankly spake their opinions'; he had shown 'wilfulness and insolency'; he had by his proclamations and devices brought the people 'to such a liberty and boldness that they sticked not to rebel and rise in sundry places'; and, in the middle of these disorders, he still built for himself 'in four or five places most sumptuously'.

As soon as he became aware of these stirrings against him, which had first become manifest in late spring or early summer, Somerset tried to mobilize support on his own behalf. He sent out letters and proclamations that were in turn answered by letters and proclamations from the council. On 5 October the young king summoned 'all his loving subjects' to Hampton Court, where he then resided, and to come 'with harness and weapon'; the protector was clearly speaking through him. The young king was even brought before some of Somerset's followers, where he requested that 'I pray you be good to us and to our uncle'. Yet it is unlikely that Edward had any real affection for him, or even resented the turn of events. When he eventually returned to London the imperial ambassador said that the young king 'certainly looked as if he had had a surprise'.

Two days later the protector removed Edward from Hampton Court to the castle at Windsor, where a group of his own men-at-arms were set to guard him. He issued a summons to the lords and to the people asking for their assistance; but no one rose in his defence. Even Cranmer, with whom he had planned the reforms of religion, seems now to have turned against him.

Dudley and the council informed the people by means of proclamation; they wrote to the ambassadors, and to the two princesses. They also took the precaution of sending a letter to the young king himself, professing their loyalty and condemning Somerset for ignoring their advice and exceeding his authority. The protector, seeing the forces now ranged against him, capitulated; any alternative strategy could only lead to civil war. A struggle between the nobles would be an unwelcome reprise of the Wars of the Roses. He surrendered on the understanding that he would be treated leniently. He was, however, together with his partisans, immediately sent to the Tower, where he 'confessed' to twenty-nine articles declared against him.

Although Dudley may have been the guiding hand behind these events, it is not at all clear that he was the immediate beneficiary. It seemed for a time that the conservative faction in the council now held the ascendancy. A proclamation was therefore issued on Christmas Day condemning certain 'evil disposed' persons and denying that 'they should have again their old Latin service, their conjured bread and water, with such like vain and superstitious ceremonies . . .' Somerset had been so closely associated with such innovations as the Book of Common Prayer that his fall was always likely to arouse the hopes of his religious adversaries. Rumours spread that the conservative faction was about to strike at Dudley by accusing him of being complicit in all of Somerset's actions; reports followed that Cranmer had to persuade the king to nominate reformers to the council in order to gain a majority. In the event, through a series of manoeuvres as obscure as they are intricate, Dudley defeated the conservative faction and expelled their principal members from the council. Somerset was released from the Tower in February 1550 and was given a free pardon. Yet the politics of state had changed for ever.

20

The lord of misrule

Dudley did not take the title of protector; he was too cautious to proclaim his primacy in that manner. Instead he determined to act and to govern through his colleagues on the council. The title Dudley assumed was, therefore, that of lord president of the council. The young king was now brought more firmly into the leading role; he attended certain meetings of the council, although it is likely that these were stage-managed for his benefit.

Yet even though Dudley did not take the name of protector he did assume another title. In due course, more confident in his power, he was ennobled as duke of Northumberland. Northumberland's chaplain, John Hooper, hailed him as a 'faithful and intrepid soldier of Christ' and 'a most holy and faithful instrument of the word of God', thus announcing to the world the duke's reformist credentials. It is difficult to search the heart and conscience of any man. At the time of his death Northumberland confessed that he had always in secret believed the old faith of Catholic England, which in turn would suggest that he had used the banner of reform simply to maintain and consolidate his power.

He also favoured the reforms of religion in the hope and expectation that he could profit from the spoils; a new bishop chosen for the see of Winchester was obliged to surrender his lands in exchange for an annual salary and Northumberland then took

these large territories for himself and his followers. The bishopric
of Durham was dissolved and its revenues were directed to sustain
Northumberland's new dukedom. The lands of the bishops were
described as the last course of the feast provided by the Church. A
preacher at St Paul's lamented that 'covetous officers have so used
this matter that even those goods which did serve to the relief of
the poor, the maintenance of learning, and to comfortable necessary
hospitality in the commonwealth be turned to maintain worldly,
wicked, covetous ambition'. Charity had given way to bribery.
In the reign of a boy king the adults in power were free to gorge
themselves upon the kingdom.

Edward remained oddly pliant and passive in his dealings with
the duke. A French observer noted that 'whenever there was
something of importance that he [Northumberland] wanted done
or spoken by the king without anyone knowing that it came from
him, he would come secretly at night into the prince's chamber
after everybody was in bed, unnoticed by anyone. The next morning
the young prince would come to his council and, as if they came
from himself, advocate certain matters – at which everyone marvelled, thinking they were his own ideas.' It was noticed by another
foreign observer that the king always kept his eyes upon the duke,
and would leave a meeting or conversation 'because of signs the
duke of Northumberland had made to him'. Slowly he was being
educated in the ways of the world, and in the ways of government,
but in no sense did he possess independent authority. Northumberland controlled the grant of offices and lands. It was said that he
encouraged the young king in all martial pursuits, including those
of archery and hunting, thus keeping him out of the way.

In the matter of religion, however, Edward may have already
formed his own opinions. At the time of the fall of Somerset he
was twelve years old. That is age enough to be enamoured of faith
and piety, and his condemnation of Mary's religious practices
suggest that he was already something of a martinet in this sphere.
In the previous year he had completed a treatise on papal pretensions, in which he concluded that the pontiff was 'the true son of
the devil, a bad man, an Antichrist and abominable tyrant'. He
may have been instructed by his tutors in this regard, but the tone
is surely his own. When he went through the service of consecration

for a new bishop he came upon an invocation of the saints; with a stroke of his pen he cancelled it as a blasphemous addition. It was he who decided that there should be weekly sermons in his country's churches. 'Believe me,' one reformer wrote, 'you have never seen in the world for these thousand years so much erudition united with piety and sweetness of disposition.'

He was known as the 'godly imp', as we have observed, and there may have been a strong element of youthful idealism in his character. Had he not been hailed as 'the young Josiah'? It was a title that he may have wished to fulfil. Thus he was asked to provide judgement, early in his reign, on the curious case of the bishop's vestments.

John Hooper, Northumberland's chaplain, had been promoted to the see of Gloucester. But the putative bishop saw an obstacle in his path. For the ceremony he would be obliged to wear the ecclesiastical habits, the white rochet and black chimere, that he had in the past denounced as the dress of the harlot of Babylon. He said that he would not become a magpie in white and black. The surplice was the magic robe of the conjuror. He was also supposed to swear obedience to the archbishop of Canterbury, where before he had promised to defer to no authority other than the Scriptures. His opposition threatened to split the new church discipline, and as a result he was confined for a period to the Fleet prison. Cranmer asked for the king's judgement on the matter and, at the behest of Edward, a compromise was agreed. Hooper would don the vestments at the service of consecration, but he would not be obliged to wear them for his diocesan affairs. The bishop has since that time become known as 'the father of nonconformity'. We may say, in the words of St James, 'how great a matter a little fire kindleth'.

A parliament had been summoned towards the end of 1549 that confirmed the movement of religious change. The eight orders of the medieval church were abolished to make way for the less complex order of bishops, priests and deacons. This was now largely to be a simplified preaching ministry. The priest was no longer expected 'to offer sacrifice and celebrate Mass both for the living and the dead', as desired in the past, but to preach the plain gospel and administer the sacraments. Yet many clandestine papists were still to be found among the clergy; they recited the communion office with the same cadences and whisperings as the old Latin Mass; they bent down over the communion table; they genuflected and lifted up their hands; they struck their breasts and made the sign of the cross in the air. These were the vile rags of popery, infinitely comforting to many in the congregation.

An Act was passed prohibiting any statues or figures in the parish church except 'the monumental figures of kings or nobles who had never been taken for saints'; since the Book of Common Prayer provided all necessary instruction, other prayer books, manuals or missals were to be destroyed. If they were not burnt, they could be sold to book-binders as convenient material; they could of course also be used in the jakes. In the spring of the following year it was decreed that stone altars should be removed and replaced by wooden communion tables. 'A goodly receiving, I promise you,' one conservative bishop declared, 'to set an oyster table instead of an altar . . .'

The altar of St Paul's Cathedral was taken down in the dead of night, in case of popular protest, and a table set up at the foot of the steps before a curtain. Yet a chronicle of the time reports that, three days later, 'a man was slain in Paul's church and two frays within the church that same time afterwards'; these 'frays', or disturbances, became so frequent that a royal proclamation was issued against them, lamenting that 'many quarrels, riots, frays and bloodshed have been made in some of the said churches, besides shooting of handguns to doves'. Churches had now become the centre of bitter controversy.

The parish church was now a plain, bare room; no decoration was to be seen except, perhaps, for a memorial text or two and a painted wooden board bearing the royal arms. Where once the altar had stood was now a table and bench for communicants. William Harrison, at a slightly later date, wrote that 'dead cold is our age . . . there is blue ice in our churches'. Yet in these bare churches the laity participated much more openly in the service; Bible reading was given primacy, and the fundamentals of the Christian faith – the creeds, the confession of faith and prayer – were properly and fully emphasized. In the royal court itself biblical and prophetic poetry took the place of sonnets and ballads. Edwardian drama, too, concerned itself with scriptural themes.

It was still possible to go too far. In the spring of 1550 Joan Bocher, known as Joan of Kent, was arrested for preaching the doctrine that Christ was not incarnate of the Virgin Mary; he had passed through her by miracle like a ray of light through a glass. At her interrogation she ably pointed out the changes of doctrine already accommodated by the religious authorities. 'Not long since,' she said, 'you burned Anne Askew for a piece of bread [the denial of transubstantiation] and yet came yourselves to believe and propose the same doctrine for which you burned her . . .' That was true enough. Yet she was sentenced to death by burning and when a preacher intoned against her as she stood at the stake in Smithfield she called out that 'he lied like a knave'. And so she died. She was condemned as an 'Anabaptist', a catch-all title of opprobrium that was attached to anyone with beliefs that might lead to subversion or anarchy within the body politic.

These were nervous times. Fears of another popular rebellion could not be allayed, and the dearth of resources rendered the government weak. Since the treasury was empty, it was necessary to make peace with France; Northumberland promptly managed this by returning Boulogne to the French king, receiving only half of the promised compensation. Henry VIII's one conquest had been a costly mistake. The decision was fiercely criticized at the time, as a sign that England was no longer pre-eminent in the affairs of Europe, but it did bring an end to an expensive policy of aggression. As Paget put it in a letter to Northumberland, 'then was then and now is now'. Calais was the last vestige of what had once been great English possessions in France; that, too, would soon be lost. Northumberland also brought back the English forces from Scotland, thus reversing another of Somerset's favourite policies. The mercenaries who had helped to put down the rebellions, in west and east, were paid off. The period may perhaps be viewed as one in which for the first time English insularity came to the fore.

The impact of the rebellions can also be recognized in a further parliamentary Act 'for the punishment of unlawful assemblies and raising of the king's subjects'. Northumberland also started work on removing other causes of discontent. He began the complex and difficult task of reversing the debasement of the coinage that had occurred in the previous reign and in the protectorate. In this respect he and his fellow councillors achieved only a small measure of success. Under his leadership the privy council was re-established as the governing forum of the realm.

Lady Mary had once described Northumberland as 'the most unstable man in England'. He returned the compliment in his belief that she was a serious threat both to him and to the new religious settlement. She was next in line to the throne and, if Edward were to die, Northumberland would be cast into the wilderness or worse. She was also the single most prominent supporter of the old faith. It would perhaps be convenient to kill her, yet the popular outcry would threaten the unity of the kingdom itself. She was also the cousin of the most powerful monarch in Europe, the emperor Charles V, and Northumberland knew that it would be unwise and dangerous to incur his wrath; the emperor had just subdued the rebellious provinces of Germany, and knew precisely how ill-prepared England was for war. In the spring of 1550, however, her privilege of observing the rites of the old religion was denied to her, and she was asked to submit to the Act of Uniformity. The imperial ambassador at once objected to this privation.

From this time forward Mary felt that she was in danger; she told the ambassador that the councillors were 'wicked and wily in their actions and particularly malevolent towards me'. She believed that they were indeed now planning to murder her. By the summer, therefore, she had drawn up plans to flee by boat to the European mainland, where she might retreat to her cousin's court in Flanders. At the end of June four imperial warships and four smaller ships approached the English coast near Maldon on the coast of Essex but, at this point, it seems that Mary's nerve failed her. She repeated, over and over again, 'What shall I do? What shall become of me?' The ships retreated, and the princess became ever more closely watched by the council. Her chaplains were ordered to refrain from saying Mass, to which she replied that they were covered by her own immunity.

Edward himself then sent her a letter, partly written in his own hand, in which he condemned her misplaced piety and warned her that 'in our state it shall miscontent us to permit you, so great a subject, not to keep our laws. Your nearness to us in blood, your greatness in estate and the condition of this time, maketh your fault the greater.' An implied threat of discipline, or punishment, may be discerned here. In her reply Mary told her brother that his letter had caused her 'more suffering than any illness, even unto death'. The bad blood between them was a source of much grief and suspicion.

When she was summoned to London to account for herself, she was accompanied by fifty knights wearing velvet coats and chains of gold; an entourage of eighty retainers followed her, each of them displaying a set of rosary beads. The message could not be clearer. But apart from proclaiming her attachment to the old faith, the display was also designed to manifest Mary's power. If it should come to a fight, there was every chance that she would be the victor. She had the strength of the old faith with her. Two days later she went in procession to Westminster, where thousands of people came out to greet her. Omens and portents were in the air. It was reported that the earth shook as 'men in harness came down to the ground and faded away'. It was also recorded that 'three suns appeared, so that men could not discern which was the true sun'.

Edward had just begun keeping a journal, and in his entry for March 1551 he notes that 'the lady Mary, my sister, came to me at Westminster'. She was called into a meeting with him and his council where it was made plain that he 'could not bear' her attendance at Mass.

'My soul is God's,' she replied. 'I will not change my faith nor dissemble my opinions with contrary doings.'

'I do not constrain your faith,' the young king replied. 'You cannot rule as a king. You must obey as a subject. Your example may breed too much inconvenience.'

A further exchange is reported:

'Riper age and experience,' she said, 'will teach Your Majesty much more yet.'

'You also may have somewhat to learn. None are too old for that.'

Soon after this a message came from the emperor, Charles V, threatening war if Edward did not allow his sister to hear Mass. He noted that 'to this no answer was given at this time'. Eventually the reply came that Mary was the king's subject and was obliged to obey his laws.

Yet much of Northumberland's time and attention was given to internal dissension and resistance to his own rule. The paramount threat once more was Somerset himself, who, on his return to the council after a brief spell of imprisonment, was devoted to undermining his successor. Somerset had survived the Tower but he had lost most of his authority and significance. For a proud man, this was too much to bear. He began a whispering campaign, or 'popular murmuring', against the lord president's policy.

He established a faction against Northumberland, primarily among his supporters in London, and it is certainly possible that in the last resort he planned some kind of coup against him in parliament; it was said that he had hired an assassin to cut off Northumberland's head, and that he had incited the citizens of London with drums and trumpets and cries of 'Liberty!' The lord president did not wait for him to strike, however, but ordered his arrest in the autumn of 1551. At his subsequent trial he was accused of spreading sedition, by stating, for example, that 'the covetousness of the gentlemen had given the people reason to rise'. The charge of attempted assassination, however, seems to have been fabricated by Northumberland himself. He in fact admitted the manufacture of evidence on the eve of his own execution, and asked pardon from Somerset's son.

Great crowds attended Somerset's execution on Tower Hill. He addressed them from the scaffold, beginning with the words 'Masters and good fellows . . .' As he spoke there was a noise 'as of gunpowder set on fire in a close house bursting out' and at the same time a sound of galloping horses as of 'a great number of great horses running on the people to overrun them'. Panic seized the spectators who fled in bewilderment, crying out 'Jesus save us, Jesus save us' or 'This way they come, that way they come, away, away'. There were no horses, and no gunpowder. One lone horse and rider did approach the scaffold, at which point the people cried out 'Pardon, pardon, pardon. God save the king. God save the king.' Somerset, with his cap in his hand, waited for the cries to subside. 'There is no such thing, good people,' he said, 'there is no such thing. It is the ordinance of God thus for to die.' After a few more words he composed himself and, murmuring 'Lord Jesus save me' three times, he gave his rings to the executioner and laid his head on the block for the axe. After the event many rushed to the scaffold to dip their handkerchiefs in the dead man's blood.

It is reported that the court provided many sports and entertainments for the young king during this period, to ward off any 'dampy thoughts'. Yet Edward himself seems to have been largely indifferent to his uncle's fate. He records, in his entry for 22 January 1552, 'the duke of Somerset had his head cut off upon Tower-hill, between eight and nine o'clock in the morning'. Nineteen months later Northumberland would stand on the same spot.

The affairs of the realm, too, were in a state of disarray. The debasement of the currency in the protector's regime had had the natural consequence of inflating the prices of the basic and most necessary foodstuffs. The harvest of 1551 was poor, the third such harvest in a row; and the European market for English woollens had diminished, with a glut of cloth reported at Antwerp. Money had lost half of its value since the last days of Henry. The cost of flour had doubled, for example, so that the standard halfpenny loaf was half the size; the governors of St Bartholomew's were obliged to increase the rations to those in their care. There was very little Northumberland and his colleagues could do about these matters; they were effectively helpless in the face of overwhelming misery.

In the summer of that year, compounding all the distress and woe, an epidemic illness known as 'the great sweat' or 'the sweating sickness' spread through the country. It was also known as 'Stop, gallant' on account of the fact that some people who were dancing at court at nine o'clock were dead by eleven. It came at night accompanied by chills and tremors; these were followed by a fever and vomiting. The sweat was manifest soon after the onset of the attack; stupor, and death, followed. In the course of the first few days 1,000 Londoners died, and it claimed 2–3,000 in subsequent weeks. It was said in one London chronicle that 'if they were suffered to sleep but half a quarter of an hour, they never spake after, nor had any knowledge, but when they wakened fell into pangs of death'. It was a year of horrors.

Parliament assembled for its fourth session on 23 January 1552, the day after the execution of the quondam protector, with the urgent task of once more considering religion. Its most notable achievement was the second, and revised, Book of Common Prayer in which further measures of reform were introduced. The Virgin Mary and the saints were not to be invoked. The Mass was not mentioned, since it had been replaced by a service known as the 'Lord's supper'. Vestments were reduced and simplified. Any prayer or act that did not have the warrant of the Scriptures was to be abandoned. Thus was the reformed faith firmly revealed to the English, in a liturgy that has remained essentially unchanged to the present day.

The question of kneeling, while receiving communion, was a matter of strenuous and fierce debate. Did it imply adoration of the bread and the wine? Or was it a simple gesture of piety? The bishops could not agree on the matter, and eventually an addition was made to the text which explained that the act of kneeling had no traces of superstition. Prayers for the dead were not to be said during the funeral service, and the corpse was no longer to be addressed by the priest; the dead were sealed off from the living. In a more general sense it might be said that the past no longer had any claim upon the present, a condition of liberation or forgetfulness that had enormous consequences for the direction of English life.

The new liturgy, established in the Book of Common Prayer, was then protected by a second Act of Uniformity. This was the Act that enforced the general expropriation of church plate and other valuable movables; now that the Mass had been abolished, the instruments of worship were no longer needed. The chalices and candlesticks, the monstrances and chrismatories, the pyxes and the cruets, were swept away. The chasubles and the copes, the carpets and tapestries and cushions, were all removed. Cloth of gold and cloth of silver, anything wrought in iron or embossed in copper, were confiscated. This was the furthest point reached by the English reformation. It can in fact be argued that most of the defining elements of Protestant creed and practice were formulated during the reign of Edward VI; Elizabeth I merely tinkered with them.

Compulsory attendance at church, on Sunday, was also decreed; the first offence merited six months' imprisonment, while the third relegated the offender to perpetual confinement. Yet some were disenchanted with the new service and disobeyed the order; it is likely that most received only a ministerial rebuke. Others were simply bored by the preachings and exhortations, the homilies and sermons. 'Surely it is an ill misorder,' Hugh Latimer wrote, 'that folk should be walking up and down in the sermon-time ... and there shall be such huzzing and buzzing in the preacher's ear that it maketh him oftentimes to forget his matter.'

A new Treason Act was passed specifically to protect the changes in religion; it was now considered a serious offence to question the royal supremacy or to dissent from the articles of faith that the English Church now enjoined. The conservative bishops, who had preached against the new dispensation, were already in the Tower or under house arrest.

Cranmer had just completed two works that consolidated the cause of reform, *A Collection of the Articles of Religion* and *A Code of Ecclesiastical Constitutions*. The forty-two articles which he compiled were in fact never ratified by parliament or convocation but, as they became the model for the Thirty-Nine Articles promulgated by Elizabeth in 1563, they are still the foundation of the English Church; they reflected Cranmer's mature theology, and were of a strongly Calvinist temper. Justification by faith alone, and 'predestination unto life', were affirmed. The twenty-ninth article denounced transubstantiation as 'repugnant to the plain words of Scripture' which 'has given occasion to many superstitions', and the rites of the Mass were described as 'fables and dangerous deceits'.

The code of ecclesiastical laws was drawn up by Cranmer and his colleagues as a substitute for the canon law of Rome. To deny the Christian faith is to merit death. Adultery is to be punished with imprisonment or transportation for life. The seducer of a single woman will be compelled to marry her or, if he is already married, to give her one third of his worldly goods. The code was never in fact given the force of law, and the ecclesiastical courts continued their confused course without a compass.

Yet the Edwardian reformers had completed their work. Henry's accomplishment in politics was now repeated in religion; the pope had been removed for ever. Justification by faith alone removed the intercessionary role of the Church, just as the demotion of the sacraments reduced the power of the priesthood. The denial of transubstantiation effectively destroyed the Mass. The rituals of Rome had been discarded.

In the autumn of the year Northumberland once more contemplated the menace of rebellion. In December he 'instantly and earnestly required the Lords of the Council to be vigilant for the preventing of these treasons so far as in them was possible to be foreseen'. Three months later martial law was declared in some regions of the country. The murmurings came to nothing but the danger of rebellion posed an acute threat to Edward's councillors who were never much liked by the general populace.

One of those councillors was of especial significance. William Cecil, who was to play a pre-eminent role in the reign of Elizabeth, became, at the age of thirty, a privy councillor and secretary to the king; his outstanding gifts as an administrator and 'confidential clerk' had already been recognized. He had served Somerset and, after a brief spell in the Tower in the wake of his patron's fall, he had been plucked into government by Northumberland. He wrote a state paper in the winter of 1550 in which he outlined in stark terms the prospects for the country. 'The emperor', he wrote, 'is aiming at the sovereignty of Europe, which he cannot obtain without the suppression of the reformed religion; and unless he crushes the English nation, he cannot crush the reformation. Besides religion, he has a further quarrel with England, and the Catholic party will leave no stone unturned to bring about our overthrow. We are not agreed among ourselves. The majority of our people will be with our adversaries . . .'

The last sentence is a significant admission that the acts of the reformers had not been appreciated by the larger part of the population. Cecil said that in the event of war between England

and Charles V, the majority would obey the pope rather than the king. The greater body of the peers, most of the bishops, almost all of the judges and lawyers, as well as the priests and the justices of the peace, would follow the same guide. For those who consider the Edwardian reformation to be in large part popular, this is a corrective. The people may have acquiesced in the changes, but, according to Cecil's testimony, they by no means approved of them. The habit of deference, and obedience, was combined with impotence and fear.

21

The nine-day queen

In the first days of 1552 the young king drafted 'certain points of weighty matters to be immediately concluded on by my council'. It was no longer the council, but *my* council. He was now in his fourteenth year, and he began to exercise the reality of power. At the age of fourteen Richard II had been obliged to deal with the effects of the Peasants' Revolt.

At the beginning of April, Edward fell ill of a disease that has been variously described as smallpox and the measles; yet he recovered easily enough. He told a childhood friend that 'we have a little been troubled with the smallpox, which hath letted [prevented] us to write thereto; but now we have shaken that quite away'. He had not been well enough to attend parliament but he noted in his journal for 15 April that 'I signed a bill containing the names of the acts which I would have pass, which bill was read in the House'.

After his recovery he began to sign royal warrants in his own hand rather than relying upon the signatures of his councillors. He engaged himself in foreign affairs, and in such subtle matters as the debasement of the currency. There survives a document, written in his own hand, concerning the method of proceedings in the council. Whether this was suggested to him, or was of his own devising, is not apparent. Yet he seems to have had all the makings of a good administrator. He wrote some of his notes in Greek, so that his attendants could not read them. And in the summer of the year he went on a progress, with 4,000 horse in attendance. It was the best way of displaying his power and authority to his subjects; the vast train visited Portsmouth and Southampton, among other places, before moving on through Wiltshire and Dorset.

Yet the disease and mortality of the age soon swirled around its principal figure. By the autumn of the year he seemed weaker than before, and he consulted an Italian physician who, like most doctors, also practised astrology. Hieronymus Cardano recorded that the king was 'of a stature somewhat below the middle height, pale-faced with grey eyes'; he was rather 'of a bad habit of body than a sufferer from fixed diseases. He had a somewhat projecting shoulder-blade.' Cardano also reported that he 'carried himself like an old man'.

In February 1553 Edward contracted a cold or chill that was accompanied by a fever; in the following month he was still looking 'very weak and thin'. In the spring he moved to the palace at Greenwich, and in this period the imperial ambassador reported that the young king was 'becoming weaker as time passes and wasting away'. His sputum was sometimes green and sometimes black. He was still capable of a Tudor outburst. When his will was obstructed in one matter he exclaimed to his councillors, 'You pluck out my feathers as I were but a tame falcon – the day will come when I shall pluck out yours!'

On 12 May the imperial ambassador wrote that Edward 'is suffering from a suppurating tumour on the lung'. He added that 'he is beginning to break out in ulcers; he is vexed by a harsh, continuous cough, his body is dry and burning, his belly is swollen, he has a slow fever upon him that never leaves him'. Two weeks later it was reported that 'he does not sleep except when he be stuffed with drugs, which doctors call opiates ... The sputum which he brings up is black, fetid and full of carbon; it smells beyond measure.' On 12 June he signed the Forty-Two Articles; but it was too late. They were never enforced. By the summer 'the king himself has given up hope and says he feels so weak that he can resist no longer'. He was in his sixteenth year, a dangerous period for the Tudor male. Prince Arthur, his uncle, had expired at the age of fifteen; his half-brother, the duke of Richmond, had died at seventeen.

The nature of his illness has been variously described, but it is likely to have been a pulmonary infection that led to pneumonia. Rumours at the time that he had been the victim of a poisoner are most unlikely to have been true. *Cui bono?* In the face of the growing weakness of the king, Northumberland was thrown into panic fear. The next person in line to the throne, according to Henry VIII's will, was Lady Mary, who reviled and hated him as the destroyer of the old faith. If she succeeded to the throne all the work of the reformation would be undone. It was unthinkable.

So in the early summer of the year a change in the order of succession was planned by Northumberland and the king. It has been suggested that the plot was devised by the duke alone, but there is no reason to suppose that the 'godly imp' would have calmly anticipated the reversal of religious reform. The salvation of the country depended on its survival. Northumberland himself seems to have grown tired and weary of governance. 'I have', he wrote, 'entered into the bottom of my care.'

In the early stages of the king's disease Mary was informed of his condition by Northumberland himself. In February, when her brother was kept in bed by the feverish chill, she was invited to court where she was 'more honourably received and entertained with greater magnificence' than ever before; Northumberland and a hundred horsemen welcomed her on the outskirts of the city and, when she arrived at Whitehall, the assembled council bowed their heads as if she were already on the throne of England. Yet as the death of Edward seemed to draw ever closer it became desperately important to remove Mary from the succession. There was no possibility of a Catholic queen. But who should be the beneficiary?

Jane Grey was the great-granddaughter of Henry VII by his younger daughter, Mary, and stood third in line to the throne after Mary and Elizabeth; for Northumberland, she also had the inestimable benefit of being his daughter-in-law. She was of impeccable religious credentials, as an ardent reformer. She had asked one of Mary's ladies why she curtsied to the sacrament. '"I curtsy to Him that made me." "Nay, but did not the baker make him?"' She told her tutor that it 'were a shame to follow my lady Mary against

God's word'. So she was stridently of the new faith. She was also learned. When Elizabeth's tutor, Roger Ascham, visited her he found her reading Plato's *Phaedo*. He asked her why she was not with her family hunting stag in the park. 'I think,' she replied, 'all their sport in the park is but a shade to the pleasure I find in Plato.' She would be the ideal queen, especially under the paternal eye of the duke himself.

So Edward and Northumberland, presumably working in concert, now devised a new will. Mary and Elizabeth were once more declared illegitimate, thus barring them from the throne of England. At the end of May the young king prepared what he called 'his device for the succession'. He had at first written that his crown should pass to the 'Lady Jane's heirs male' in the hope that he would live long enough to see the fruits of her marriage; he could at this stage not envisage the rule of a queen. Then, approximately three weeks later, he erased those words and inserted 'the Lady Jane and her heirs male'. He may have suffered a relapse. In any case it must have been made clear to him that he might not live.

Many of the councillors were opposed to this device, considering it illegal for an under-age king to set aside an Act of Parliament. The judges were summoned to the palace at Greenwich where, on listening to Edward's proposal, they unanimously declared that it was contrary to the law. The king was defiant and dismissive. The judges asked for more time. They returned to meet the council two days later, when they declared that to permit the alteration of the succession would incur the charge of treason.

Northumberland was absent on their arrival but, on hearing their verdict, 'he came into the council chamber, being in great rage and fury, trembling for anger . . . and said that he would fight in his shirt with any man in the quarrel'. The judges left the room. They came back on the following day, after an urgent summons, and were taken to the king's bedside. He met them 'with sharp words and angry countenance'. 'Why is my will disobeyed? There must be no delay!' The royal councillors remained silent. The judges were cowed. They asked only that their instructions should be put in writing, and that they should be pardoned if their consent was later deemed to be criminal. They argued to each other that there could be no treason in obeying the commands of their sovereign. And so it passed. The great ones of the realm eventually subscribed to the document dethroning Lady Mary.

These were the last days of the young king. On 1 July he was shown at a window of the palace, presumably to counter a rumour that he was already dead; yet he looked 'so thin and wasted' that few of the spectators were reassured. A crowd gathered on the following day, in the belief that he would appear again, but a courtier came out to declare that 'the air was too chill'.

A professor of medicine from Oxford was summoned to the palace, together with a 'wise woman' who recommended the healing powers of a mysterious liquid. Both of them were admitted to the sickroom on the strict understanding that they would reveal the king's true condition to nobody. The guard at the Tower was doubled, and wild rumours flew around the city of imminent perils. The imperial ambassador had been told that a force of 500 men had been sent to surround Lady Mary's manor house, Hunsdon, in Hertfordshire, in order to seize her person; he reported further that the princess was to be taken to the Tower, ostensibly to prepare herself for her coronation, but would then be detained indefinitely. Northumberland and his friends were purchasing all the available arms in London, and the ships upon the Thames were being prepared for the sea. It was proposed that the evangelical preachers, under the supervision of Northumberland, would declare the illegitimacy of Mary from their pulpits. It was whispered that the duke was willing to surrender England into French hands for the support of the French king. That was, perhaps, a rumour too far. He may have come to an understanding, however, about the use of French troops in case of an English revolt. Henry II, the French king, would not in any case wish the cousin of his rival, Charles V, to become the queen of England.

On 6 July the end of Edward came. Between eight and nine in the evening, according to one popular news-sheet or 'broadside', he whispered his last prayer. 'Lord God, deliver me out of this miserable and wretched life, and take me among thy chosen . . .' This is no doubt a pious fantasy of the writer purporting to witness Edward's death as a Calvinist. Another account must also be treated warily. In this version the dying king sensed, rather than saw, his attendant doctors and gentlemen of the privy chamber. 'Are you so near?' he asked them. 'I thought you had been further off.'

'We heard you speak to yourself, but what you said we know not.'

'I was praying to God.'

One of his attendants took him in his arms. 'I am faint,' he said. 'Lord, have mercy upon me and take my spirit.' The day of his death was, according to the *Grey Friars' Chronicle*, greeted by signs and wonders in the heavens. A storm broke over London and the summer afternoon became dark; great trees were uprooted, the streets turned into rivers, and the hail lay in the city's gardens as red as blood. It was said that the grave of Henry VIII had opened and that the old king had risen in protest at the defiance of his will.

Mary, alerted to all possible dangers, had fled from her manor house two days before to the relative safety of her estate at Kenninghall in Norfolk, where she was among friends and allies. The death of Edward was kept secret for three days, in order that all Northumberland's preparations could be completed. Northumberland spoke of him as if he were still alive.

Lady Jane Grey was brought to London, and on 9 July was told that the king wished to speak to her. She was taken to Northumberland's manor, Sion House, where she was greeted by the duke and certain other lords. 'The king', Northumberland told her, 'is no more.' He then explained the conditions of the new will, making Lady Jane the sovereign. Having spoken, he and the other lords fell to their knees in front of her. She received the news with alarm. The Crown could not be for her. She was unfit. But then she recovered. She raised her hands in prayer and asked God for grace to govern well.

On the same day Mary learned the fate of her younger brother. She sat down and wrote a letter to the most prominent noblemen of the kingdom. 'My lords,' she wrote, 'we greet you well and have received sure advertisement that our deceased brother the king, our late sovereign lord, is departed to God's mercy.' She went on to say that 'it seemeth strange that the dying of our said brother upon Thursday at night last past, we hitherto had no knowledge from you thereof' before demanding that 'our right and title to the crown and government of this realm to be proclaimed in our city of London'. It is reported that the lords looked into one another's faces uneasily, and that their wives sobbed. A reply was sent ordering Mary not to 'vex and molest' the people of England with her false claim.

On 10 July the heralds-at arms announced the accession of Queen Jane in Cheapside, Paul's Cross and Fleet. There is no evidence of rejoicing, or even of general acceptance. The crowds responded with silence, if not with open discontent, their faces 'sorrowful and averted'. One chronicler reports that a vintner's boy, Gilbert Potter, cried out that 'the Lady Mary has the better title'; he was seized and led away. His ears were severed at the root on the following morning.

It might have been thought that Northumberland was in a pre-eminent position. He had control of the fleet as well as the treasury; he commanded the fortresses and garrisons of the land. Mary had as yet no army at her disposal; she had only the members of her household. But all Northumberland's power was not enough in the face of her determined opposition and the evident fury of her supporters. The lawful succession to the throne of England could not be compromised by double-dealing. The crisis, of Northumberland's own making, had broken over them all. Some of the councillors secretly doubted him. Others were confused and uncertain. William Cecil armed himself and made plans to flee the realm.

Northumberland had decided to detain Mary, by force, and bring her to London. If he had acted sooner, even before Edward's death, he might have succeeded in destroying her. It was first believed that the armed party against her would be led by Jane Grey's father, the duke of Suffolk, but the new queen's protestations prevented the move. Instead Northumberland himself would march from London, by way of Shoreditch, with a retinue of 600 armed men. The citizens watched them leave. 'The people press to see us,' he remarked, 'but not one sayeth God speed us.' He had asked his colleagues to remain faithful to him, but he could not be entirely sure of their loyalty.

Mary stood her ground. She was resolute and defiant on the

model of her father; she had a stern Tudor sense of majesty, allied
with an awareness of her religious mission to save England from
heresy. It had been thought that she might flee to the emperor in
Brussels, but why should a queen abandon her realm? Supporters
flocked to her, with the earl of Sussex and the earl of Bath among
the first of them. The people from the towns and villages of the
region took up their weapons. It seemed that the whole of East
Anglia had risen for her. The city of Norwich proclaimed her as
rightful sovereign. A small navy of six ships, sent out by Northumberland to guard the seaways off the Norfolk coast, defected to
Mary's camp. When she went out to review her new troops the cry
went up 'Long live our good Queen Mary!' She removed from
Kenninghall to Framlingham Castle, in Suffolk, where she might
repel any armed force. Yet she was still in the utmost danger. If
she had been defeated and come to trial, she would have been
declared guilty of treason. The fate of the nation, and of her
religion, was now at stake.

Northumberland had taken his men to Cambridgeshire, where
Newmarket had been chosen as the rendezvous for the army made
up of tenants from various noble estates. But when the report of
the navy's defection to Mary reached that place, the men began to
mutiny; they declared that they refused to serve their lords against
Queen Mary. Northumberland sent an express message to the
council demanding reinforcements and was given 'but a slender
answer'. The members of the council, in the absence of their
presiding genius, began to entertain doubts about the wisdom of
the entire enterprise. As a contemporary chronicler put it, 'each
man then begun to pluck in his horns'.

As the radical preachers continued their pulpit campaign
against Mary, William Cecil and others began to organize a *coup
d'état*. They had been gathered in the Tower, close to Queen Jane
herself, where they remained under the observation of a garrison
loyal to Northumberland. On Wednesday 19 July, with Northumberland's forces in open rebellion, the councillors managed to leave
the Tower and gather at Baynard's Castle on the north shore of the
Thames about three-quarters of a mile above London Bridge.

They were joined here by the Lord Mayor, the aldermen and
other prominent citizens. The earl of Arundel spoke first. If they

continued to support the claims of Lady Jane Grey, civil war was unavoidable, with the distinct possibility that foreign powers would also intervene. No fate would be more unhappy for England and its people. The earl of Pembroke then rose and, taking his sword out of his scabbard, announced that 'this blade shall make Mary queen, or I will lose my life'. Not one voice was heard on behalf of Northumberland or of Jane. A body of 150 men were then marched to the gates of the Tower, where the keys were demanded in the name of Queen Mary. Lady Jane's father realized that the end had come; he rushed to his daughter's chamber and tore down the canopy of state under which she sat. Her reign had lasted for just nine days.

The lords of the council then proceeded to the cross at Cheapside, where in due state they declared Mary to be the queen of England. The crowd of spectators cried out 'God save the queen', and Pembroke tossed his purse and embroidered cap into the throng. The bells of St Paul's rang out, to be joined by all the other bells in the city. The lords then went in procession to the cathedral where, for the first time in almost seven years, the hymn of praise known as the Te Deum was sung by the choir. The apprentices gathered wood to light bonfires at the major crossroads. That evening the council wrote to Northumberland, asking him to lay down his arms.

The duke himself, now all but trapped in Cambridge, hurried to the market cross. He informed the crowds of angry spectators that he had followed the council's orders in proclaiming Jane and proceeding against Mary; now that the council had changed its opinion, he would also change his. He threw up his cap and called out 'God save Queen Mary'. He told a colleague that Mary was a merciful woman and would declare a general pardon. To which came the reply that 'you can hope nothing from those that now rule'.

Arundel came to Cambridge with orders to arrest him. 'I obey, my lord,' Northumberland said, 'yet show me mercy, knowing the case as it is.'

'My lord, you should have sought for mercy sooner. I must do according to my commandment.'

At seven in the evening of 3 August Queen Mary entered her

capital in triumph accompanied by a retinue of 500 attendants; her horse was trapped with cloth of gold, and her gown of purple velvet was embroidered with gold. She wore a chain of gold, and jewels, about her neck and her headdress was similarly covered in precious stones. She was greeted by the civic dignitaries at Aldgate and then through cheering crowds rode in procession to the Tower of London. Here, the prisoners of the old regime were waiting to greet her, among them the duke of Norfolk and the conservative bishops. She raised them from their knees, and kissed each one upon the cheek. 'You are my prisoners!' she exclaimed before returning to them their liberty. The cannons sounded 'like great thunder, so that it had been like to an earthquake'.

Less than three weeks later Northumberland was led to the scaffold at Tower Hill. He confessed to the crowds around him that he had 'been an evil liver and have done wickedly all the days of my life'. Then, perhaps to the surprise of those who watched him, he denounced radical preachers for turning him away from the true religion. 'I beseech you all,' he declared, 'to believe that I die in the Catholic faith.' The day before he had heard Mass in the chapel of St Peter ad Vincula in the Tower. It was said that he had made his conversion in a desperate attempt to avert death or, perhaps, to save his family from further punishment. Yet his return to Catholicism may have been entirely genuine.

As the end came he recited a prayer and the psalm *De Profundis*. The executioner, according to custom, now begged his pardon; the man wore a white apron, like a butcher. 'I have deserved a thousand deaths,' Northumberland told him. He made the sign of the cross in the sawdust around him and laid his head upon the block. One stroke of the axe was enough. Some little children mopped up the blood that had fallen through the slits of the scaffold.

22

In the ascendant

The imperial ambassador declared that Mary's triumphant reclamation of the crown had been a miracle of God and a token of the divine will. The new queen herself saw her accession as part of a sacred dispensation. It was her destiny, and duty, to bring her country back to the old faith. On the secular level it could also be said that a popular rebellion had overthrown an established regime. She had, in addition, gained the throne largely as a result of the loyalty of the Catholic nobility; no overtly Protestant lord had supported her. As soon as she heard that she had been proclaimed queen in London, she ordered that the crucifix be once more set up in her chapel at Framlingham.

When Mary first rode into the capital, after her triumph, many households placed images of the Virgin and of the saints in their windows as a token of the change. News of her accession reached the congregation gathered in Exeter Cathedral to hear a sermon by the reformer Miles Coverdale; the report was whispered around the assembly and, one by one, the people stood up and walked out. Only a few of the 'godly' remained. All over the country the Mass was once more chanted in Latin. Without any statutes or proclamations, the images and altars of the old faith were quickly restored. The crucifixes were set up, and the statues of the Virgin and the saints were put in their familiar places. When a justice tried to prosecute some priests in Kent for saying Mass, he himself was imprisoned. Six or seven Masses were, in any case, now being sung every day in the royal chapel at Whitehall. It had once again become the centrepiece of true faith.

On the matter of her brother's funeral Mary was hesitant. She did not want to use the reformed burial service. 'She could not', she said, 'have her brother committed to the ground like a dog.' She was advised that it were best for a heretic king to have a heretic funeral, thus avoiding public controversy. So she compromised. Reluctantly she agreed that he could be buried according to the rite that he had favoured during his reign, but she tried to safeguard his soul and her principles by having a Latin Mass for the dead sung the night before his funeral and a solemn requiem a few days later.

On 18 August 1553 Mary issued a Proclamation Concerning Religion in which she forbade the use of opprobrious terms such as 'papist'; she also commanded that no one 'shall henceforth under pretext of sermons or lessons either in Church, publicly or privately, interpret the Scriptures, or teach anything pertaining to religion, except it be in the Schools of the university'. She had, in other words, banned all radical or reformed preachers. She had asserted that she had no thought of religious compulsion, but with the ominous proviso 'until such time as further order by common consent may be taken'.

Yet, in certain quarters, resistance to the reintroduction of the old faith could be fierce. Some preachers, righteous in their generation, proclaimed the true doctrine of King Edward's reign. London was as ever the centre of religious radicalism. When one Catholic chaplain preached at Paul's Cross, a large crowd cried out 'Thou liest!' and 'Pull him out! Pull him out!' A dagger was thrown at the pulpit, and he had to be hurried away through the school-house close by. Nevertheless, the European reformers, who had made the capital their home, now quickly made their way back to Zurich or Geneva or Strasburg. The colony of Walloon weavers, settled in Glastonbury, was happy to go home.

Other incidents of insurrection took place. A church in Suffolk was set on fire as Mass was being said. One radical, Thomas Flower, pulled out a wooden knife from his belt at the time of communion and repeatedly stabbed at the officiating priest. The reformers were soon obliged to meet in secret; they went into fields, or ships moored on the Thames, under cover of darkness. The bishop of London, Edmund Bonner, was determined to root out the heretics. 'Yes, yes,' he said to one of them, 'there is a brotherhood of you, but I will break it, I warrant you.' He had been condemned to perpetual imprisonment in the Marshalsea by Northumberland's council; soon enough he became known as 'Bloody Bonner' for his determined persecution of reformers.

Another restored bishop, Stephen Gardiner, was fresh from the Tower when he confronted another heretic. 'My lord,' the man said, 'I am none heretic, for that way that you count heresy, so worship we the living God.'

'God's Passion!' bellowed the bishop. 'Did I not tell you, my lord deputy, how you should know an heretic? He is up with the "living God" as though there were a dead God. They have nothing in their mouths, these heretics, but "the Lord liveth, the living God ruleth, the Lord Lord" and nothing but "the Lord"'. At this point he took off his cap, and rubbed to and fro, and up and down, 'the fore part of his head, where a lock of hair was always standing up'. His final words were 'Away with him! It is the stubbornest knave that ever I talked with.' He dispatched another radical preacher with the words 'carry away this frenzy-fool to prison'. His arch-deacon at Westminster was equally vehement; when disputing with a disciple of Arianism, whereby the Son of God is inferior to God the Father, he spat in the man's face. Just as 'Catholic' now became used as a term of triumph, so 'Protestant' entered the language in the course of this reign as a mark of opprobrium.

To gauge the true faith of the English is impossible. It is clear enough that only a minority of the people were committed to the new faith, and that a slightly larger number now espoused full Catholicism. The changes in direction of religious policy, the attack upon the rituals of the old faith, the stripping of the churches, must have had devastating consequences for the piety of the people. The bonds of the sacred had been loosened. It is possible, then, that there was no drift from Catholicism to Protestantism (or vice versa) but rather a movement from the fervent or instinctive piety of the medieval period to bland conformism and even indifference. This would be entirely consistent with a reformation that was less about the assertion of faith and principle than about the redistribution of power and wealth. Habit and custom, rather than faith or piety, were the determinants of English religion.

Mary was the first woman, apart from the ill-starred Jane Grey, to be proclaimed queen regnant of England. Her one possible predecessor, Matilda, had never been crowned and was known only as *domina*, or lady. But Mary had one precedent; her grandmother, Isabella, had ruled as queen of Castile and had maintained all the panoply of a royal court. No doubt Katherine of Aragon had discoursed with her daughter on the rituals and splendours of a reigning queen. Mary's great-grandmother, Margaret Beaufort, had been the power behind the throne of her son Henry VII. And her cousin, Margaret, had been ruling as queen-regent of Flanders for the last twenty years. As a child she had been brought up to be a queen; no subject could kiss her, except on the hand, and in formal rituals those about her knelt. There was a tradition of female power upon which she could draw.

She employed the members of her own household as her first advisers, but she could not wholly dispense with the councillors of the previous reign; only they had the knowledge, and skill, to maintain the system of government. Two days before her coronation she had summoned them; when they assembled she sank to her knees before them and spoke to them of the duties that, as a sovereign, God had imposed upon her. 'I have entrusted my affairs and person to you, and wish to adjure you to do your duty as you are bound to your oaths.' According to the Spanish ambassador, who became her principal confidant, they were deeply moved and did not know how to reply. But hers was a politic move. She knew that many of them had been hostile to her in the past, having signed the device barring her from the succession, and she distrusted them. She declared to the ambassador that 'she would use their dissimulation for a great end, and would make their consent prevent them from plotting against her'.

It was a large and in some ways unwieldy council, composed of some fifty members. Mary herself was infuriated by the divisions among them; they were continually 'chopping and changing', blaming one another and exculpating themselves. Some had always been loyal to her, while others had been disloyal to the last possible minute; some were conservative bishops, newly released from prison, while others were great magnates who had done well out of the confiscation of monastic lands. She said, on a later occasion, that she spent most of her time shouting at them. Yet from this council a small inner circle of six or seven men was soon formed. Most notable among them was the old bishop of Winchester, Stephen Gardiner; the bishop, previously confined to the Tower, was appointed to be lord chancellor. Most of the others were professional administrators who had served under the old regime.

Mary set about the business of governing with a will. She rose at dawn, when she prayed and heard a private Mass; she then went to her desk where she stayed until one or two in the afternoon. She took a light meal and then returned to her desk where she worked until midnight. She wrote letters; she granted audiences to her subjects; she conferred with her council. Yet it was still commonly believed that she needed a husband. A female monarch was considered to be unnatural, an aberration that could be countered only by a male figure of authority at her side.

When parliament assembled on 5 October, in the first year of her reign, the question of her marriage was a pressing issue. The vast majority, of both Lords and Commons, wished her to take an Englishman as her consort. At her formal coronation, four days before, she had worn her hair loose as a symbol that she was a virgin.

Matters of a more general purport were also debated. Parliament passed a bill affirming the validity of Henry VIII's marriage to Katherine of Aragon, legitimizing Mary's claim to the throne. An Act was also passed to enforce the religious settlement as it had stood in the last year of Henry VIII, thus abolishing all the Edwardian innovations; the matter caused protracted deliberation, over a period of four days, and was eventually agreed by 270 over 80 votes. A significant minority, therefore, still supported the Edwardian reforms. The members of parliament, however, let it be known that there were two topics on which they were united. There was to be no restitution of Church property, and no restoration of papal authority.

In the following month the Speaker of the House of Commons

came before the queen and her council. He presented her with a petition on the question of her marriage and then, in a long and prolix speech, he urged the queen to choose one of her own subjects as her spouse. It would not be fitting to choose someone from abroad, since a foreign prince would have other interests and other priorities. She started to her feet and in the course of a hasty and improvised reply she stated that 'if you, our Commons, force upon us a husband whom we dislike, it may occasion the inconvenience of our death; if we marry where we do not love, we shall be in our grave in three months . . .'

Yet others were already involved in the matter of marriage. Just nine days after her proclamation as queen the Spanish ambassador raised the question with her. Mary replied that she would willingly follow the advice of her cousin, Charles V, which meant that in practice she would have no hesitation in marrying a member of the Spanish royal family of which she was already a part. She was, indeed, half-Spanish. The most suitable of the male candidates was inevitably Philip, the eldest son of the king. This is what the Lords and Commons feared.

Mary summoned the ambassador to her private chapel in the autumn of 1553, just as parliament was meeting; this was the sanctuary where she kept the Holy Sacrament and where she told the ambassador that 'she had continually wept and prayed God to inspire her with an answer to the question of marriage'. She went down upon her knees and began to recite 'Veni Creator', a hymn from the Gregorian chant. It seems to have been at this point that she resolved to marry Philip. He was, in a sense, the natural choice. How could the queen marry an English subject?

One possible English candidate had emerged. Edward Courtenay, great-grandson of Edward IV and heir to the House of York, had been imprisoned for the last fifteen years on trumped-up charges of treason; his Plantagenet blood was always a threat to the Tudor dynasty. Mary had released him, as a matter of honour, but had no intention of marrying him. 'I will never, never marry him,' she had told her council, 'that I promise you, and I am a woman of my word. What I say, I do.' He was not to her taste. Long imprisonment had rendered him feeble and supine. She had irrevocably turned to Spain.

One evening the Spanish ambassador was received at court and, as he bowed to her, he whispered in her ear that he had credentials from the emperor to deliver to her. At the same time he passed her a letter that she quickly concealed. On the following evening he was brought in state by barge to the palace, bearing the official proposal for Mary to wed Philip. Some days later, as the queen was being led towards the royal chapel for Vespers, someone in the court shouted out 'Treason!' to general alarm. Mary was unperturbed but her younger sister was seized with fear and trembling.

Princess Elizabeth had largely been a spectator in these marital proceedings. She had followed Mary in her sister's triumphant entry into London, as a way of advertising their accord in rebutting the claims of a rival family, but the two were not united in any other way. Elizabeth was seen tacitly to represent the Protestant influence, and as such she soon came under suspicion. The French ambassador reported that 'Elizabeth will not hear Mass, nor accompany her sister to the chapel'. She was considered to be of a proud and fiery spirit, like the other members of her family. The imperial ambassador, another conduit of news and rumour, decided that 'the princess Elizabeth is greatly to be feared; she has a spirit full of incantation'.

But she knew when to bend. On hearing that her refusal to hear Mass was being treated as insurrection, she fell upon her knees before the queen and begged to be given instruction in the Catholic faith. Yet her sincerity was doubted; it was said that she was too ready to consort with heretics. When she attended her first Mass, in the autumn of the year, she complained all the way to the chapel that she was tormented by a stomach ache, 'wearing a suffering air'. She never wore the gorgeous rosary that her sister had given her. Mary let it be known that she did not want Elizabeth to succeed to the throne, but her only remedy was of course to bear her own children. The queen was now thirty-seven years old, spare and lean, with a thin mouth and commanding gaze; Elizabeth was twenty, with youth and beauty on her side. She might be a threat.

That threat seemed to emerge in a rebellion at the beginning of 1554. When the envoys from Spain had arrived in January to

seal the terms of the marriage treaty with Philip, the Londoners
'nothing rejoicing, held their heads down sorrowfully'. Schoolboys
pelted the Spanish delegation with snowballs. The terms of the
treaty were announced on 14 January and, although they restricted
Philip's role in the determination of policy, a chronicler reported
that 'almost each man was abashed, looking daily for worse matters
to grow shortly after'. Religious, as well as political, discontent was
in the air. By the end of 1553 the Mass and the Latin offices were
decreed to be the only legal forms of worship. In December, at the
close of parliamentary proceedings, a dead dog was thrown through
the window of a royal chamber; it had been shaved with a tonsure
like a monk. On another occasion a dead cat was found hanging in
Friday Street, wearing Romish vestments; it had between its paws
a piece of bread like a 'singing cake' or sacramental host.

The leaders of the Protestant cause now began to act in concert;
among them was Sir Thomas Wyatt, the son of the poet, and the
duke of Suffolk together with his three brothers. Suffolk himself
was of course the father of Jane Grey, the queen of nine days.
Edward Courtenay, perhaps angry at his rejection by Mary, joined
them. They were in league with the French ambassador, whose
country was much affronted by the queen's decision to marry the
heir of the Spanish crown. Some insurgents were simply opposed
to the Spanish presence, while others were convinced reformers
who were dismayed at the return to Catholicism. A party of the
rebels had in fact been members of the military establishment under
Northumberland and Edward VI. Cornwall and Devonshire were
supposed to be the first regions to rise; Wyatt would carry his
native county of Kent, and Suffolk would stir the Midlands. All of
the armies would then converge upon London, where they hoped
for a happy welcome.

The conspirators remained in London for the first two weeks
of the year, but in that period Edward Courtenay gave signs of
indecision. He professed to believe that the queen was about to
marry him, after all, and he lingered in the purlieus of the court;
then he ordered a lavish costume of state, and spoke unwisely about
what he knew. The chancellor, Stephen Gardiner, interviewed him
and discovered much about the plot. Gardiner summoned one of

the insurgents, Sir Peter Carew, to London. Carew fell into a panic
and tried to incite his native city of Exeter; Exeter did not rise, and
Carew fled to France.

Wyatt, thrown into confusion by this unanticipated and unwelcome news, called the people of Kent to rebellion. On 25 January
the church bells of the county rang with the signal for alarm, and a
proclamation was issued to the effect that the Spanish army was
crossing the seas to conquer England. Wyatt seized the cannon
from the ships moored in the Medway and brought them into his
stronghold at Rochester. The queen had professed no unease in
the first days of the revolt. 'Let the prince come,' she said, 'and all
will be well.' But her position was not safe. She had no army, and
she feared that many of her council were secretly eager that the
rebellion might succeed. The city agreed to give her 500 men from
their trained bands, as much to preserve the capital as to safeguard
the queen.

The king of France had promised to send eighty vessels to
assist the insurgents, and the news somehow reached the English
court. The French ambassador was closely watched and one of his
couriers was arrested. He was carrying some coded messages from
the ambassador himself, and a copy of a letter from Lady Elizabeth
to her sister. There was no treason here, but it was nonetheless
suspicious. Why should the French king be interested in one of the
princess's letters?

The duke of Norfolk led the trained bands of London against
Rochester but, as he approached the bridge, he saw to his horror
that his men were deserting to Wyatt's side. They cried out 'A
Wyatt! A Wyatt!' This was the familiar phrase of acclamation.
'We are all Englishmen!' Norfolk and a few commanders galloped
off in fear of their lives. Wyatt then appeared on the bridge. 'As
many as will tarry with us,' he said, 'shall be welcome. As many as
will depart, let them go.' So he gained 300–400 men, together
with their weapons. The rebellion seemed set to succeed. If Wyatt
had marched to London immediately, the gates might have been
opened to him.

The queen, in her defenceless position, remained resolute and
defiant. She rode through the streets of the city to the Guildhall,

where she met an assembly of citizens. She had a deep voice, often compared with that of a man, and piercing eyes that could command respect as well as fear. She spoke to them from the steps of the hall. She was the lawful queen of England. She appealed to the love and loyalty of Londoners against a presumptuous rebel who intended 'to subdue the laws to his will and to give scope to rascals and forlorn persons to make general havoc and spoil'. She also promised to call a parliament that would consider the suitability of Philip as her consort; if the Lords and Commons rejected him, then she would think of him no more.

Her courage and her bearing impressed the Londoners. On the following day 25,000 armed citizens came to her defence against the encroachments of Wyatt and his men. He had come up to Greenwich from Rochester but, on arriving on the south bank by London Bridge, he found the gates closed against him. He was declared to be a traitor and a ransom of £100 was placed on his head. In response he wore his name, in large letters, upon his cap.

He could derive no comfort from the position of his confederate, the duke of Suffolk, whose attempt to raise the Midlands had ended in failure; he had fled to one of his estates, but his hiding-place was betrayed by his gamekeeper. His ally in the Midlands rebellion had been Lord John Grey, uncle of the unfortunate Jane Grey; he had concealed himself for two days, without food or drink, in the hollowed trunk of an ancient tree. He, too, was discovered. The Greys were undone.

Wyatt stood irresolute before London Bridge, now barred, while the guns on the Tower were trained against him. There was no way to cross the river. After much hesitation and diversity of counsel Wyatt determined to ride with his host to Kingston Bridge, from where he could then march back on London; his friends in the city had promised him a welcome. So on the following morning he rode out with 1,500 men, together with some cannon from the Medway ships, and at four in the afternoon he reached Kingston. He found the bridge to be in part broken down, with a small guard on the opposite bank; the guard fled, and Wyatt caused the bridge to be repaired with moored barges. Then he marched once more upon London.

The queen was woken at two or three in the morning, and told that her barge was waiting to take her to the safety of Windsor Castle. 'Shall I go or stay?' she asked those closest to her. The Spanish ambassador offered the best advice. 'If you go,' he told her, 'your flight will be known, the city will rise, seize the Tower and release the prisoners. The heretics will massacre the priests, and Elizabeth be proclaimed queen.' Mary saw the force of his argument.

At nine in the morning Wyatt led his now exhausted men up the hill at Knightsbridge, but a force of the queen's cavalry divided them near Hyde Park Corner. Wyatt had lost his rearguard but he pushed forward along the road that is now Pall Mall; some citizens were gathered to watch him, and made no sign. They parted to let the insurgents through their midst. Some of the courtiers were alarmed at this acquiescence, and cries of 'Treason!' were soon ringing through the palace at Whitehall. 'Lost! Lost! All is lost!' The queen replied that, if some would not fight for her, she would go out and fight for herself. She would be happy to die with those who served her.

It did not come to that. Wyatt and the remnant of his forces made their slow way along the Strand and Fleet Street towards the old city. Yet the gates of Ludgate had been closed against him. 'I have kept touch,' he said in his despair. He sat down upon a bench outside Belle Sauvage Yard (now known simply as Bell Yard) while his companions scattered in the side streets and alleys off Ludgate Hill. When a part of the queen's cavalry galloped towards him, he surrendered his sword and was taken into custody.

In the days after the rebellion, gallows were erected in all the principal sites of London from Smithfield to Tower Hill. Some of the rebellious soldiers were hanged outside their doors. 'There has never been such hanging,' the French ambassador wrote, 'as has been going on here every day.' Yet mercy sometimes prevailed amid the slaughter. On 22 February some 400 men were brought before the queen with halters around their necks, whereupon she pardoned them all.

Lady Jane Grey had remained in the Tower ever since the accession of Mary and in other circumstances could no doubt also have been spared. The treachery of her father changed her situation with dramatic effect. The queen had hardened her heart against her and all her family. The old abbot of Westminster tried to convert the young woman to the Roman communion, but she withstood all of his appeals. She was taken to Tower Green, quietly praying until she reached the scaffold; she calmly ascended the steps and told the spectators that she had broken the law by accepting the crown but that she was innocent of any evil intention. She recited the Miserere psalm, 'Have mercy upon me, O God', and then let down her hair, while making sure that her neck was uncovered. 'I pray you, dispatch me quickly,' she said to the executioner. And as she knelt she asked him, 'Will you take it off before I lay me down?'

'No, madam.'

She tied a handkerchief about her eyes, and then began feeling for the block. 'What shall I do? Where is it?' One of the bystanders guided her to it, and she laid down her head. Her husband, her father and her uncles were also beheaded.

There was one who had invited suspicion but had as yet escaped punishment. Princess Elizabeth had remained out of harm's way at Ashridge House, in Hertfordshire, where she awaited events. It had become clear that Wyatt's rebellion had been intended to set her upon the throne in the place of her sister, but there was no clear evidence of her involvement in the plot. Her confidential servants were interrogated in the Tower with the threat of the rack hanging over them. She herself was summoned to London, after pleading illness, and on 18 February she was carried in a litter to the capital. She passed through the streets of London dressed entirely in white, as a token of her innocence, and her pale face was described by the Spanish ambassador as 'proud, lofty and superbly disdainful'. He, as well as his master, was pressing for her execution. Sensational news spread of a miraculous voice in a London wall. When anyone called 'God save the queen' there came no response; but if the cry of 'God save the Lady Elizabeth' was made, a voice replied 'So be it'. The credulity of crowds is never-ending. Of course it was a hoax concocted by a serving girl.

The queen refused to see her sister, and Elizabeth was given a suite of closely guarded rooms in the palace at Whitehall. She remained in this state of confinement for some weeks, but at the beginning of April she was interviewed by the royal council. The

councillors accused her of complicity in the rebellion, to which
charge she made an indignant denial; in this defiance she never
once wavered. It was finally agreed that she should be removed
from Whitehall to the Tower and, when the news was broached to
her, she fell 'in heavy mood'. It is not hard to understand the
reasons for her desolation. Her mother had been taken to the
Tower as a prelude to execution, and it seemed more than likely
that Elizabeth would share her fate. She begged time to compose
a letter to the queen in which she lamented that she should be
'condemned without answer and due proof, which it seems that I
now am: for that without cause proved, I am by your council from
you commanded to go unto the Tower, a place more wonted for
a false traitor than a true subject'. She went on to declare that
'I never practised, counselled, nor consented to anything that might
be prejudicial to your person any way'.

Mary did not reply. 'Very well then,' Elizabeth is reported to
have said. 'If there be no remedy I must be contented.' She was
taken by barge to the Tower and came ashore by the drawbridge.
'Here landeth as true a subject,' she declared to her guards and her
gaolers, 'as true a subject, being prisoner, as ever landed at these
stairs.' It was a day of heavy rain and in her dejection she sat down
upon a stone.

'Madame,' the lieutenant of the Tower said, 'you were best to
come out of the rain; for you sit unwholesomely.'

'It is better sitting here than in a worse place, for God knoweth,
I know not whither you will bring me.'

She was escorted within the fortress, as all the doors were
locked and barred behind her. She could not be sure that she would
ever see the outer world again. At a later date she told the French
ambassador that she was in such despair that she considered writing
to her sister with the request that she should be beheaded with a
sword, like her mother, rather than an axe. The rigours of her
confinement were soon relaxed a little; by the middle of April she
was allowed to walk on the 'leads' of her prison house and enjoy
the Tower garden. Two guards always walked behind her, and two
before her. The other prisoners were enjoined 'not so much as to
look in that direction while her grace remained therein'.

She was interrogated five days after her confinement. What

was her connection with Wyatt and the other rebels? Had she received letters or messages from them? She denied all knowledge of them and of their activities. She proclaimed her innocence and demanded to see proof of her treason. There was none. 'My lords,' she said, 'you do sift me very narrowly.' She preserved her calm and authoritative demeanour; danger had taught her to dissemble and prevaricate.

On 18 May she was released from the Tower and removed to Woodstock in Oxfordshire, where she came under the custody of Sir Henry Bedingfield. She is reputed to have carved, with one of her diamonds, some lines on a glass window pane of the mansion:

> Much suspected by me,
> Nothing proved can be.
> *Quod* Elizabeth the prisoner.

And she was still a prisoner. A force of soldiers was encamped on a hill overlooking the house, and no one could enter without Bedingfield's permission.

On 20 July Philip landed at Southampton. When he set foot on English ground he drew his sword and carried it in his hand; this was not considered to be a good omen. He was accustomed to the sunshine of his native land, and was greeted in England by thunderous rain that lasted several days; many of his entourage caught colds. Three days after his arrival he was received at the door of Winchester Cathedral and in the bishop's palace, after supper, he was first received by the queen, 'each of them merrily smiling on other, to the great comfort and rejoicing of the beholders'. She could understand Spanish, but could not speak it; the first and last time Philip ever used English was on that same evening to the assembled courtiers. He was supposed to say 'Good night, my lords all', but he only managed 'God ni hit'. It is most likely that they spoke French with each other. The Spanish were not necessarily impressed by the queen, who was described by one of them as 'rather older than we were led to believe'; she was of relatively modest height, and slender to the point of thinness. At the age of twenty-seven Philip was eleven years younger than Mary.

On 25 July they were married in Winchester Cathedral, where

the heralds proclaimed them to be king and queen of England, France, Naples, Jerusalem and Ireland. Philip had been given the crown of Naples by his father the night before, so that the English queen could be sure of marrying an equal. During the Mass of celebration it was noticed that the queen entirely fixed her gaze upon the jewelled crucifix. At the wedding feast, to the dismay of the Spanish entourage, Mary was served on gold plates while Philip deserved only silver. In the various royal palaces Mary used the chambers reserved for a king, while Philip stayed in those of a queen consort. He was in a most ambiguous position. He was never crowned and could not be a source of patronage in England; he was not permitted to fill English offices with his own men, and the queen never delegated authority to him.

On 18 August the royal couple made their way through London, to respectful if muted rejoicing. In a sermon at Paul's Cross Stephen Gardiner exhorted the citizens 'to behave themselves' so that Philip 'might tarry still with us'. Soon after this, twenty cartloads of Spanish gold were drawn through the streets of the city.

Yet all the treasure in the world would not allay the fears and suspicions of the citizens. It was rumoured that a great Spanish army would invade the country and that Spanish friars would take over the churches. It was feared that England would no longer be an independent country. One chronicler reported that 'the English are so bad, and fear God so little that they handle the friars shamefully, and the poor men do not dare to leave their quarters ... the crowd tried to tear the cloaks off the backs of Don Pedro and Don Antonio his nephew asking what they meant by wearing crosses and jeering at them'. Religion and xenophobia were a potent mixture.

The Spanish in turn treated the English with disdain. It will be profitable here to examine the general reputation of the nation, described by the French ambassador as 'this nasty island'. The women were deemed to be beautiful, while the men were handsome and of ruddy complexion. The language was considered to be uncouth, but what could you expect from people living at the extremity of the world? They were, essentially, barbarians. Englishmen swore with a vehemence that shocked foreigners; even the children swore great oaths. All the people drank too much with the favoured 'double beer', as strong as whisky, leaving them 'stark staring mad like March Hares'. It may have been the beer that encouraged the belching, in which sport all the English participated; every meal ended with a belching contest. Dinner was eaten at any time between ten and twelve, with supper at six in the evening.

And what did these barbarians eat? The Spanish noblemen with Philip were astonished by the variety of the food. 'These English have their houses made of sticks and dirt, but they fare commonly so well as the king.' They feasted on great shins of beef, on mutton and veal, on lamb and pork; they ate brawn, bacon, fruit pies, fowls of every sort. This could not have been a universal diet, however, and the poorer sort would have eaten the 'white meats' of the dairy, such as butter and cheese, as well as beans, peas, onions and garlic.

The Spanish courtiers described their hosts as 'white, pink and quarrelsome'. It was a violent world, where every man went armed. The English were quick to take offence. They were fit for nothing except eating and drinking; their dances were all 'strutting or trotting about'; their women were 'of evil conversation'; they were all thieves. The courtiers moved among the local people 'as if they were animals, trying not to notice them'. Fights and brawls erupted in the streets, and even broke out in the halls of the palace at Whitehall. In one battle 500 Englishmen were involved; it ended with six dead and three dozen badly wounded. More innocent misunderstandings also took place. When the duchess of Alva visited the queen neither lady would allow the other to take a lower seat; the elaborate courtesies ended with both of them sitting on the floor.

In the autumn of the year it seemed possible, even likely, that the fruit of the royal marriage would soon be ripe. The queen believed that she had conceived, and in this belief she was supported by her doctors. If that were indeed the case then her immediate problems, among them the popular reception of her husband, would be resolved. The Te Deum was sung in the churches of the realm, where prayers were also offered for the safe birth of an heir to the throne. Some of course were horrified at the prospect of a Catholic succession. A sheet of writing was nailed to the gate of the palace at Whitehall. 'Will you be such fools, oh noble Englishmen, as to believe that our queen is pregnant? And of what should she be, but of a monkey or a dog?' The nation waited.

23

Faith of our fathers

The failure of Wyatt's rebellion, and the subsequent arrival of Philip, lent confidence to the queen. The pace of religious reform, or perhaps of religious reversal, now intensified. The Mass was celebrated throughout the kingdom. On Palm Sunday of 1554 palms were once more held aloft in procession, and the ceremony of 'creeping to the cross' was renewed on Good Friday; the old rite of resurrection was performed on Easter Sunday. The quotations from Scripture, which had taken the place of images and pictures, were wiped away or whitewashed. At St Paul's Cathedral the choir went up to the steeple to sing the anthems, reviving a custom that had long been in disuse. Edmund Bonner, bishop of London, decreed that every church in the city must have among other instruments of devotion 'a cross for procession with candlesticks, a cross for the dead, an incenser, a ship or vessel for frankincense, a little sanctus bell . . .' There must be a high altar, with all its cloths and hangings. He asked if, at the time the host was raised, any of the congregation hung their heads or hid behind the pillars or even left the church. Church music was in due course restored.

Certain individuals suffered from these changes. Married priests were deprived of their livings. The vicar of Whenby, in Yorkshire, proceeded in front of his congregation wearing a surplice and carrying a lighted candle. 'Masters,' he began, 'I have been seduced and deceived, thinking that I might lawfully marry . . .' He then proceeded to beg pardon. Of the twenty-two bishops in the Edwardian regime, only seven retained their sees. The old reformers – Cranmer, Ridley and Latimer – were sent to Oxford where they were to be interrogated by the bishops and clergy of the convocation. They were taken from the Tower, where they had been detained, to the Bocardo; this was Oxford's prison, in a watchtower by the north gate of the town. The queen had a particular dislike for Archbishop Cranmer, who had been instrumental in the degradation of her mother. Bonner used to call him in derision 'Mr Canterbury'.

They were given what might be called a show trial before a committee of the convocation. On being questioned about transubstantiation Cranmer was often hissed down, so that he could not be heard at all; he was described as 'unlearned', 'unskilful' and 'impudent'.

Ridley was called on the following day for his interrogation. 'You see the obstinate, vainglorious, crafty and inconstant mind of this man,' his inquisitor concluded, 'but you see also the force of truth cannot be shaken. Therefore cry out with me, truth has the victory!' The clergy responded as if with one voice. Throughout his appearance 'there was great disorder, perpetual shoutings, tauntings and reproaches' so that the school of divines resembled a beargarden.

When Latimer came in, old and frail, he was permitted to sit; a pair of spectacles was hanging by a string at his breast, and he carried a staff. He was finally judged to be a heretic and accepted his fate as a means of glorifying God. 'If you go to heaven with this faith,' one of his interrogators told him, 'then I will never come thither.'

Some 800 reformers fled to the Protestant centres of Europe, among them many clerics and scholars from the universities. The dowager duchess of Suffolk departed with many servants, among them her laundress and her fool. Eight English communities were established, in cities such as Frankfurt and Zurich, from where a stream of pamphlets was issued in general condemnation of Mary and the Marian settlement. The exiles were hoping, naturally enough, for the assassination of the idolatress. She was the queen of all evil. In the meantime they thought of themselves as an embattled minority, a little flock of the faithful under the perpetual shadow of persecution. This image had a long life and helped to shape the discourse of the stricter sort of Calvinism. The anonymous author of *Humble Supplication unto God* blamed England's 'unthankfulness and wicked living' for the return of popery. The religious refugees left a more enduring legacy with their Geneva Bible, the text for which Shakespeare had an abiding affection. A bishop in the more accommodating reign of Elizabeth remembered with fondness his years of exile. 'Oh Zurich, Zurich, I think more of Zurich in England than ever I thought of England when I was in Zurich.'

A cleric of quite another stamp was coming to England in the winter of 1554. Reginald Pole, cardinal and papal legate, was returning home after an exile of twenty-two years. He came back eagerly, with the pious intention of bringing his country once more into the fold of Rome. England was still under papal interdict, perhaps consigning all its inhabitants to the peril of damnation. It was he whose family had been executed on the orders of Henry VIII; his mother, Margaret Pole, had been beheaded in a botched and painful death. He considered himself to be the son of a martyr. He was a solemn and pious man, grave and earnest.

On a day in late November his barge, with a great silver cross upon its bow, passed under London Bridge on its way to Whitehall. On his arrival at the palace Philip embraced him, while the queen waited at the head of the grand staircase. When Cardinal Pole came up to her she threw herself upon his breast. 'Your coming', she said, 'causes me as much joy as the possession of my kingdom.' He replied in Latin with the words that Gabriel had uttered to the Virgin. '*Ave Maria, gratia plena, Dominus tecum, benedicta tu in mulieribus*' – 'Hail Mary, full of grace, the Lord is with you, blessed are you among women.' At this point the queen felt her baby leap in her womb. It was a moment of benediction.

Four days later the Lords and Commons assembled in the Great Chamber at Whitehall where the cardinal, at the right hand of the queen, addressed them. It was noted that the queen tried to make her supposed pregnancy very clear. Pole told parliament that he had come to return the keys to the kingdom of heaven, on condition that all acts directed against the papacy were repealed. 'I come to reconcile,' he said, 'not to condemn. I come not to compel but to call again.' Some of the members were observed to weep. When the Lords and Commons met at Westminster on the following day they all agreed – with only two dissentient voices – to make their submission. The schism of two reigns was thereby ended.

On 30 November, St Andrew's Day, the cardinal sat on a raised platform at the upper end of Westminster Hall. As he rose to his feet Mary and Philip fell to their knees, as did the whole of the assembly. With the authority of Jesus Christ and the most holy lord Pope Julius III, he then proceeded to absolve 'this whole realm and the dominions thereof from all heresy and schism, and from all and every judgement, censure and pain for that cause incurred; and we do restore you again into the unity of our Mother the Holy Church, in the name of the Father, of the Son and of the Holy Ghost'.

The queen could be heard to sob; the most solemn and sacred intention of her life had been fulfilled. Many in the hall called out 'amen, amen' before also breaking into tears. Some members threw themselves weeping into one another's arms. Slowly they processed into the chapel where the choir sang the Te Deum. When the news reached Rome the cannon of Castel Sant'Angelo were fired. In a portrait of the queen, painted in this year, she is wearing a large Tau cross upon a choker of pearls around her neck; from her waist hangs an enamel reliquary adorned with the emblems of the four evangelists. She loved jewellery, but it was jewellery with a message.

Pole's central purpose was to restore order and direction to a battered faith. He tried to refurbish the finances of the Church; he appointed twenty bishops; he established seminaries where young priests could be trained. He had long been a resident in Rome and was therefore eager to embrace papal supremacy; but the Lords and Commons had gone beyond that point. It was not practical. He had also wanted to take back the monastic lands that had been expropriated in Henry's reign, but there were too many vested interests to make that course feasible. What lord or gentleman would surrender what they had owned for thirty years? The imperial ambassador remarked that in any case 'the Catholics hold more church property than the heretics'.

After the solemn ceremony of absolution, parliament then proceeded to deal with the matter of church lands. A bill declared such land had always been subject to statute law, and that no other authority could meddle with the matter. A supplication was addressed to the pope, requesting that church property should be allowed to remain in lay hands. In the same parliament Stephen Gardiner fought successfully to pass his Revival of the Heresy Acts; the medieval statute *de heretico comburendo*, on the burning of heretics, was thereby restored.

Other elements of Catholic practice also returned to life. The Carthusian monks were sent to Sheen and the Benedictines were returned to Westminster; the Dominicans were reunited at St Bartholomew's in Smithfield and the Franciscans at Greenwich. The Bridgettine nuns, many of whom had crossed the Channel in Henry's time, flocked back to Syon.

Yet the revived Catholicism of Mary's reign did not restore the old faith in its entirety. The sacrifice of the Mass was for the queen the single most important element of the faith to which all else was subject. The only shrine to be restored was that of Edward the Confessor in Westminster Abbey, and in her reign Mary never went on pilgrimage. St Thomas of Canterbury and Our Lady of Walsingham remained unhonoured. Some of the familiar customs were also quietly ignored. There was scant interest in saints or in the Virgin. Little was said of purgatory. Mary remained the supreme head of the Church in England, and only lip service was paid to the doctrine of papal supremacy. It was pointed out at the time that almost half of the population was under the age of twenty and thus had never experienced papal domination. It simply could not be imposed once more.

The importance of Scripture was also reaffirmed in a marked departure from the practice of medieval Catholicism; the cardinal, for example, ordered an English translation of the New Testament. The power of preaching was also recognized, and an array of preachers were brought out to refute the errors of the reformed faith. A crowd of 20,000 gathered to hear the Spital sermons, held at the pulpit cross in Spitalfields during Easter week. Bishop

Bonner aided the preachers in their task by supervising a set of instructions entitled *A Profitable and Necessary Doctrine* as well as a collection of thirteen model sermons. Everything was done to reacquaint the English people with their old religion, shorn now of its more superstitious features. It may be said in general that Mary tried to re-create the Catholic faith that had existed at the end of the reign of Henry VIII, and that in a real sense she was continuing her father's work.

In a similar spirit the festivities and ceremonies associated with his rule were also revived. Church-ales, Plough Monday collections and Hocktide gatherings once more became popular; lavish church processions made their way through London on many sacred occasions. On the feast of Corpus Christi 1555, Bishop Bonner raised the sacrament in his hands at the head of a procession along Whitehall with many people 'kneeling on their knees, weeping, and giving thanks to God'. The May games of the same year in Westminster were devoted to 'giants, morris pikes, guns and drums and devils, and three morris dances, and bagpipes and viols, and many disguised, and the lady of the May rode gorgeously with minstrels'. The Lord of Misrule also returned 'with his councillors and divers other officers, and there was a devil shouting of fire, and one was like Death, with a dart in hand'. So a Londoner, Henry Machyn, recorded in his diary.

Yet not all were merry. Two weeks after the Heresy Act was passed by parliament in the early days of 1555, a secret assembly of men and women was broken up; they were gathered, in a house in Bow Churchyard, for a service in English with prayers such as 'God turn the heart of Queen Mary from idolatry, or else shorten her days'. The hunt was on.

The first to die in the course of the Marian campaign was John Rogers, a canon of St Paul's who had preached against the Catholic reaction at the cross in the churchyard. It was he who was chosen, as it was put, to 'break the ice'. He was taken the short distance from Newgate to Smithfield, and on his last journey was met by his wife and ten children, who welcomed him with cries of happiness as if he were on his way to a banquet. The spectators along his route also cheered him. As he was being tied to the stake he was offered a pardon if he recanted, but he refused. The fire was lit. He did not seem to suffer but bathed his hands in the flame 'as if it was cold water'. The burning time had come.

The bishop of Gloucester, John Hooper, was an early sacrifice. He was led from Newgate, his face muffled in a hood, and taken by his guards to his diocese where on 9 February he was tied to the stake. He suffered very badly since the green faggots were slow to burn; the fire reached only his legs and the lower part of his body; when it expired, the bishop called out 'For God's love, good people, let me have more fire!', so a fiercer flame was kindled. A bystander wrote that 'he smote his breast with his hands till one of his arms fell off; he continued knocking with the other, while the fat, water and blood dropped out at his fingers' ends . . .' He suffered torment for another three-quarters of an hour, eventually 'dying as quietly as a child in his bed'.

On the same day a weaver, a butcher, a barber, a priest, a gentleman and an apprentice were condemned to the fire by Bishop Bonner on the charge of denying the doctrine of transubstantiation. Soon enough the prisons of London were filled with other candidates for martyrdom. The legs of the priest had been crushed by irons after his conviction for heresy and so he was placed at the stake in a chair. It is reported by Foxe, in his account of the Marian fires, that 'at his burning, he sitting in the fire, the young children came about and cried, as well as young children could speak, Lord strengthen thy servant and keep thy promise – Lord strengthen thy servant and keep thy promise'.

A young farmer was burned outside the north gate of Chester. A jar of tar and pitch was put on top of his head and, as the flames reached it, the combustible material poured down his face. At Stratford-le-Bow eleven men and two women died together in a single blaze; at Lewes ten were burned at the same time. Thomas Haukes, about to die, told his friends that if the flames were endurable he would show it by lifting up his hands. He clapped his hands three times in the fire before he expired. When a fire was lit on Jesus Green, Cambridge, books were thrown in to bolster the flames. One of them happened to be a communion book in English, and the suffering man picked it up and began to read from it until the smoke and flame obscured the page. Another victim was said to 'sleep sweetly' in the fire. When a doctor of divinity proceeded on his walk to the stake he began to dance.

'Why, master doctor,' the sheriff asked him, 'how do you now?'

'Well, master sheriff, never better for I am now almost home. I lack not past two stiles to go over, and am even now at my Father's house.'

The manner of the execution may be described. A large stake or post was fixed in the ground with a step or ledge leading up to it. The victim was placed upon that ledge so that he or she might be visible to the crowd; the men were stripped to their shirts, and the women to their smocks. The victim was fastened to the stake with chains, but the arms were left free. Faggots of wood, and bundles of reed, were then piled about the stake. It was sometimes difficult to kindle or to control the fire. The wood might be too green, or the winds contrary. The friends of the victims sometimes tied little bags of gunpowder around the necks of those about to die, but on occasions they made too small an explosion and only increased the suffering.

It was customary for the victims to pray or sing before their execution. They knelt and prostrated themselves before the stake. Many of them then kissed the post or the wood piled about it. The spectators were not always or necessarily sympathetic to those who were about to die. On many occasions the victim was pelted with pieces of wood or rocks. When one dying man began to sing a psalm he was silenced by a blow to his head. 'Truly,' a religious commissioner amiably told the assailant, 'you have marred a good old song.' Street-sellers abounded and at a burning in Dartford 'came diverse fruiterers with horse-loads of cherries, and sold them'. Anyone who brought a faggot to the fire was granted forty days' 'indulgence' from the pains of purgatory; as a result parents instructed their children to bring wood for the flames.

Stephen Gardiner had believed that a few early burnings would suffice and that the terrible example would warn other heretics to be wary and remain silent. But his optimism was premature. The steadfast reaction of the martyrs, and the open sympathy of many who came to watch the proceedings, were enough to alarm him. It was said that one burning was worth more than a hundred sermons against popery. He seems to have made some effort to call a halt, but it was already too late. In truth the campaign of terror may have worked; it is sometimes supposed that it was gradually curtailed because of mounting public opposition. It is more likely that there were in the end fewer heretics to burn.

The queen and Cardinal Pole, in particular, did not see any need to reverse their policy. Heretics were the breath of hell, a noxious danger to the health of the body politic. Anyone whom they corrupted would be damned eternally. In a pastoral letter to London, Pole wrote that 'there is no kind of men so pernicious to the commonwealth as they be'. The queen herself considered them to be guilty of treason and of sedition, two of the greatest crimes imaginable to her. The tainted wether may infect the whole flock. She was, with this belief, in good company. The great reformer, Calvin, had declared that it was a Christian duty to destroy the preachers of false gods; he did indeed burn the Spanish theologian Servetus for his views concerning the Trinity. Cranmer had celebrated the burning of the Anabaptist Joan Bocher. Nobody really doubted the merit of burning, therefore, only its convenience in an already unsettled society.

In the four years of the stake almost 300 men and women perished, the preponderance coming from the south-east of England where religious reform had been most welcome. Under the auspices of Bishop Bonner 112 Londoners were killed, but only one man was burned in Yorkshire. This may be a sign of the incidence of the new faith in the north of England, but it may also reflect the unwillingness of the authorities there to persecute unto death. The majority of those who suffered were artisans and tradesmen, the independent workers of the community.

The great question put to them by their interrogators was 'How say you to the sacrament of the altar?' If they did not believe that Christ's body and blood were physically as well as spiritually present in the bread and the wine, they were condemned for heresy. Bishop Bonner came to a judgment with the phrase, 'for thou must needs be one of them'. To which the prisoner replied, 'Yea, my lord, *I am one of them*.' Another man spoke out with defiance: 'Thought is free, my lord,' he said. It was ordained that the more recalcitrant of them could be put to the torture. Three months before her death the queen sent a letter of complaint to the sheriff of Hampshire; his offence was to cancel the burning of a man who had recanted at the first lick of the flame. It was thus that she earned the soubriquet of 'Bloody Mary'.

John Foxe, in *Foxe's Book of Martyrs*, created a narrative of suffering that for centuries acted as a Protestant folk legend after its publication in 1563; he evoked a series of tableaux in which wicked priests and dissemblers destroyed the practitioners of the true religion. Yet these martyrs were not all of the same faith; among them were those who denied the divinity of Christ or who condemned the practice of infant baptism or who questioned the doctrine of the Trinity. When they were incarcerated in the same prison they often refused to pray together. It should be noted, in passing, that in the succeeding reign of Elizabeth some 200 Catholics were strangled or disembowelled. Many of those who died would also have been burned under the religious policy of Henry VIII.

Yet Foxe's book effectively demonized Catholicism in England in the latter part of the sixteenth century; it would always after that date be fringed with fire.

24

An age of anxiety

Mary had not felt a baby leap in her womb at the moment of the cardinal's benediction. There was to be no blessed fruit. In April 1555, Elizabeth had been summoned under close guard from Woodstock to Whitehall, so that the heir presumptive might be present at the birth of the heir apparent. It was also a sensible precaution if the queen should die in the course of childbirth. Philip visited the princess two or three days after her arrival, and it was reported that subsequently he asked his wife to show forgiveness to her sister. The king also gave Elizabeth a diamond valued at 4,000 ducats. She claimed in later life that Philip had fallen in love with her, but it is more probable that he feared for his own safety in the event of his wife's death. The people might rise up in revolt against him.

Mary was not in good health. The Venetian envoy reported that 'she is not of strong constitution, and of late she suffers from headache and serious affection of the heart, so that she is often obliged to take medicine and also to be blooded. She is of very spare diet.' He also reported that a young man had proclaimed himself to be the true Edward VI and thus 'raised a tumult among the populace'; he was whipped through the streets and his ears cropped, but the incident could have done little for the queen's serenity. Unrest was in the air. Any crowd that gathered in the streets of London was dispersed. The summer of the year was bleak and wet; the crops failed and the fields were turned to mud. In the sixteenth century this was a natural disaster. The prices of staple commodities doubled and even tripled. There was the genuine prospect of death by starvation.

The happy moment of royal birth was supposed to arrive at the end of April. Mary retired to the relative peace of Hampton Court. The bells rang, and the Te Deum was sung in St Paul's Cathedral; nothing transpired. Mary still professed herself to be confident, however, and said that she felt the motions of the child. The priests and choirboys continued to process through the streets of London, at the head of the poor men and women from the alms-houses who were telling their beads on behalf of their sovereign. The Holy Sacrament was paraded along Cheapside in a blaze of candlelight. Yet all the prayers were in vain. There was to be no child. She remained in seclusion throughout the month of May; she sat upon the floor, her knees drawn up to her face, in an agony of despair.

She wept and prayed. She believed that God had punished her. And her sin? She had failed in her duty to extirpate all the heretics in the realm; the beast of schism still endured. She came to believe that she would not safely be delivered of a child until all the heretics in prison were burned. On 24 May she directed a circular to her bishops urging them to show more speed and diligence in their pursuit of 'disordered persons'. A holocaust of burnt offerings might bring fertility to her.

The affairs of the realm were in suspense. The imperial ambassador wrote to his emperor that 'I foresee convulsions and disturbances such as no pen can describe'. He also repeated the rumours that Mary had never been pregnant or, more damagingly, that a convenient newborn male child would be conveyed to her bed. There were also fears that the queen was in fact barren, and would never produce an heir. It was possible that a cyst or tumour had provoked this phantom pregnancy, in which case her condition might prove fatal.

Elizabeth was summoned to Hampton Court from Woodstock, where much to the displeasure of the queen the courtiers knelt and kissed her hand. She was pressed to ask for pardon from her sister, but she acknowledged no offence. A week later the two women met for the first time in almost two years. Two chroniclers, Foxe and Holinshed, have left reports of this encounter. 'You will not confess,' the queen told her, 'you stand to your truth. I pray God it may so fall out.'

'If it does not,' Elizabeth replied, 'I desire neither favour nor pardon at your hands.'

The queen asked her if she would spread reports that she had been wrongfully punished by her imprisonment at the Tower and at Woodstock. Elizabeth denied any intention of so doing. 'I have borne the burden,' she said, 'and I must bear it.'

The queen merely muttered, in Spanish, '*Dios sabe*' – 'God knows'. Her sister then withdrew from her presence. Yet Elizabeth now remained at liberty.

Philip could not endure a longer stay in England; his anxious and disheartened wife was for him a dead failure. No son of his would now ascend to the throne. 'Let me know,' he wrote to an adviser, 'what line I am to take with the queen about leaving her and about religion. I see I must say something, but God help me!' His departure was made all the more urgent by the decision of his father, Charles V, to abdicate and to seek solace in a monastery. Philip informed his wife that he would leave her for only two or three weeks, but he was dissembling. At the end of August they parted at Greenwich, since the long journey to Dover would trouble the queen's health.

The Venetian ambassador was, as always, in attendance. The queen was entirely composed as she accompanied her husband through all the halls and chambers of the palace just before his departure; she stood at the head of the staircase clothed 'in royal state and dignity' as he went out of the door towards the water. She then retired to her private chambers overlooking the Thames where 'thinking she was not observed, she gave scope to her grief in floods of tears'. She watched as the barge slowly disappeared from sight, Philip raising his hat in farewell.

The weeks passed. The queen spent her evenings, after the work of government was done, writing long epistles to her absent husband. He tended to reply with short letters on matters of business. She even went to the trouble of writing to the emperor himself, expressing her 'unspeakable sadness which I experience because of the absence of the king'. She may also have been receiving news of his dissipations at the imperial court of Brussels; he was feasting and dancing with a joy he had never shown in London. He was also visiting Madame d'Aler, a beautiful woman of whom he was much enamoured. He had other companions. He relished eating lumps of bacon fat, and it was said that his taste in courtesans was not much higher.

In the autumn of 1555 he assumed the leadership of the Spanish territory of the Netherlands and, when Mary wrote asking him to return to her, he replied that he could only come back to England if he were given some role in its governance. It was essentially a polite refusal. England had become for him an expensive distraction. Mary is reported to have told her ladies that she would now revert to the life she had led before her marriage. According to reports she looked ten years older.

The parlous situation of the queen of course encouraged the ambitions of others. Parliament was divided and obstinate, with the queen herself complaining of 'many violent opposition members'; her advice, in the election of the autumn of 1555, for the return 'of the wise, grave and Catholic sort' had not necessarily been followed. No parliamentary parties or groups existed in the modern sense, only a shifting aggregate of discontented individuals. Mary's administration suffered another blow with the death in November of the chancellor, Stephen Gardiner, from 'suppression of urine'. The archdeacon of Winchester wrote, from his prison cell, that 'although the cockatrice be dead, yet his pestilent chickens, with the whore of Babylon, still live'.

An armed conspiracy against the queen was detected at the end of 1555. 'I am sure you hear,' Sir Henry Dudley told a friend in confidence, 'they go about a coronation.' He was referring to the rumour that Mary was about to crown Philip as king, which would be an intolerable threat to the safety and independence of England. It was enough to stir the 'western gentlemen' who now, in secret conspiracy, proposed to march on London and give the crown to Elizabeth; Mary would be sent packing to Brussels and the arms of her husband.

A further refinement came from Sir Henry Dudley himself, who intended to bring in the French. The French king had promised to supply ships and money, with the crews made up of western privateers. The captain of the Isle of Wight was prepared to surrender his island and Dudley undertook to attack Portsmouth, where he would find the cannon out of action. At a midnight audience the French king, Henry II, handed a large sum of money to Dudley and advised him to reconnoitre the coast of Normandy in preparation for an invasion.

The walls of a royal court have ears and eyes. The English ambassador in Paris had been informed of the interview immediately after it had taken place, and he passed on the information to Mary in the form of a cipher. One of the conspirators, in panic fear, betrayed the names of his colleagues to the council. They were arrested and imprisoned; some of them were tortured.

Yet even after their execution Mary could not rest. The French ambassador, recalled at this time of tension, described her 'dreading every moment that her life might be attempted by her own attendants'. She was 'deeply troubled' and saw conspiracies in every corner. The palaces at Whitehall and Greenwich were filled with armed men. She did not appear in public, and slept no more than three hours each night.

The name of Elizabeth had been invoked by the Dudley conspirators, but there was no clear evidence that she was involved in the rebellion; nevertheless, the suspicion was there. The constable of France had written to the French ambassador ordering him to 'restrain Madame Elizabeth from stirring at all in the affair of which you have written to me, for that would be to ruin everything'. Five of her household servants were arrested, and one of them was found guilty of treason; he was later pardoned. The princess was now heir apparent, and had to be treated with circumspection. Mary tried to dissemble her real feelings but in private she was said always to talk of Elizabeth with scorn and hatred. The atmosphere was further clouded by the persistent rumours that Philip was about to invade the country with an imperial army.

At the beginning of May 1556, a blazing comet appeared in the London sky; it was half the size of the moon and was 'shooting out fire to great wonder and marvel to the people'. It could be seen flaring for the next seven days and seven nights, thus signifying great changes in the affairs in the world. A gang of twelve men went about the streets predicting the end of the world, but the tumult they caused was a screen for their robberies. More generally the rumours of riot and rebellion grew ever more numerous.

In this age of anxiety Mary now relied primarily upon the counsels of Reginald Pole. At his behest the most celebrated burnings of Mary's reign were performed at Oxford. The three great bishops of reform – Ridley, Latimer and Cranmer – had been stripped of their rank and solemnly degraded. The worst disgrace was reserved for the archbishop of Canterbury. He had been clothed in his full pontifical robes – except that they were made of rough canvas. As each strip of clothing was pulled from him Bishop Bonner made a speech. 'This is the man', he said, 'that despised the pope, and is now judged by him. This is the man that pulled down churches, and is now judged in a church. This is the man that condemned the sacrament, and is now condemned before it.' One of those presiding pulled Bonner by the sleeve several times, begging him to stop the abuse of this grave old man. Bonner paid no heed. A barber clipped the hair around the old man's head and then Cranmer was forced to kneel before Bonner, who began to scrape the tips of the archbishop's fingers to desecrate the hand that had administered extreme unction. 'Now,' he said, 'are you lord no longer.' Cranmer was then given a threadbare gown and a townsman's greasy cap before being surrendered to the secular authorities.

The stake was raised in a ditch outside Balliol College. Ridley and Latimer were the first to die. 'Oh, be ye there?' Ridley called out on seeing his colleague.

'Yea, have after as fast as I can follow.'

When they reached the stake they both knelt down and kissed it. To his friends Ridley gave the small gifts in his possession – some pieces of ginger and nutmeg, his watch. Latimer had nothing to give, but stood meekly as he was stripped to the shroud he wore as a mark of his fate. Ridley was given a small bag of gunpowder to tie around his neck. 'Have you any for my brother?'

'Yes, sir, that I have.'

'Then give it unto him betime, lest you come too late.'

They were tied on opposite sides and, when the lighted faggot was placed at Ridley's feet, Latimer called out to him: 'Be of good comfort, Master Ridley, and play the man. We shall this day light such a candle, by God's grace, in England, as I trust shall never be put out.' These words have become perhaps the most celebrated in the entire history of Reformation but they may be the invention of John Foxe in the second edition of *Foxe's Book of Martyrs*. The truth of the matter cannot be determined.

As the flames leapt up Ridley cried: '*In manus tuas, Domine, commendo spiritum meum*' – 'Into your hands, Lord, I commend my spirit.' Latimer cried: 'Oh Father of heaven receive my soul!' Latimer seemed to embrace the fire and 'after that he had stroked his face with his hands, and as it were bathed them a little in the fire, he soon died . . .' Ridley was less fortunate. The fire stalled and proceeded only slowly. In his agony he cried out 'I cannot burn! I cannot burn! Lord have mercy upon me! Let the fire come unto me! I cannot burn!' The flames were stoked and as they rose higher the bag of gunpowder around his neck exploded. His time had come.

Thomas Cranmer, quondam archbishop of Canterbury, had witnessed the burning of his colleagues from the tower of Bocardo and was of course much moved by the sight. It is reported that he fell to his knees in tears. Some of the tears may have been for himself. He had always given his allegiance to the established state; for him it represented the divine rule. Should he not now obey the monarch and the supreme head of the Church even if she wished to bring back the jurisdiction of Rome? In his conscience he denied papal supremacy. In his conscience, too, he was obliged to obey his sovereign.

Soon after the burning of his colleagues he was removed from Bocardo to the house of the dean of Christ Church, where he was more at ease. He was visited there by a Spanish friar who tried to persuade him of the merits of the Catholic faith. He did indeed issue a series of recantations; whether out of deference to the arguments of the friar, or from fear of a painful death, was soon to be ascertained. He wrote a declaration in which he acknowledged the pope to be supreme head of the Church in England;

this was his duty to queen and parliament. In another submission he stated that he believed in all the articles of faith promulgated by the Catholic Church; in particular he accepted the power of the sacraments. On 18 March 1556, in a sixth submission, he confessed himself to be an unworthy sinner who had persecuted the holy Church and stripped the realm of true faith. His was the most significant religious statement in the realm. It was said that one salmon was worth a thousand frogs.

These six statements of belief might have been considered enough to earn him a pardon, or at least a respite from the fire. Yet Cranmer had been the father of schism in England, the most energetic promoter of reform. Mary could not forgive him as the master of heresy any more than she could forget his role in the persecution of her mother. On 20 March he was told that he would be tied to the stake on the following day.

On that last morning he was brought to St Mary's Church, where he stood on a platform as a sermon was directed against him. He looked 'the very image of sorrow'. He sometimes raised his face to heaven, and sometimes stared at the ground; he was in tears. He was then expected to deliver a short address in which he would repeat his acceptance of the truths of the Catholic Church. He began by declaring himself to be a miserable penitent who had set forth many sinful writings. It was now believed that he would repeat his belief in the sacraments. But instead he proceeded to recant his recantations and deny the six statements he had previously made. The audience murmured and called out. He had written them, he said, 'for fear of death'. The university church was now in commotion, and Cranmer had to shout to be heard. 'And as for the pope. I refuse him, as Christ's enemy, and Antichrist, with all his false doctrine.'

An attendant lord called out to him 'Remember yourself, and play the Christian.'

But Cranmer could not be restrained: 'And as for the sacrament, I believe as I have taught in my book against the bishop of Winchester!' He did not, in other words, accept the Catholic doctrine on transubstantiation.

The officials pulled him down from the platform and, amid the noise and confusion, hustled him into the rain; he was led towards the stake as the Spanish friar repeated over and over again '*Non fecisti?*' – 'You didn't do it? You didn't do it?'

He knelt before the stake where he prayed; after he was bound the flames came up quickly, and he put his right hand into the middle of them, saying 'my unworthy right hand' for composing the recantations. In the heat he wiped his forehead with his un-burnt hand. He died quietly enough, praying 'Lord Jesus receive my spirit' as the fire rose around him. On that day Cardinal Pole became archbishop of Canterbury.

25

Nunc Dimittis

On 20 March 1557 Philip returned to England. He was met at Greenwich with a thirty-two-gun salute; the fire of arms was a suitable greeting for a man who had come to talk of war. He had already declared war against Henry II, in defence of imperial interests in France and the Low Countries. Now he wanted the support of his adopted nation. He claimed only that he had come to discuss fresh supplies of grain, but he was in fact looking for arms and men. The queen's council was not disposed to help him. The country was impoverished, and the people of England were not directly involved in maintaining the interests of the Habsburgs.

Yet the queen was naturally eager to support her husband and actively promoted the cause of war against the larger part of the council who did not wish to intervene in the affairs of Europe. In the presence of Philip she told her councillors that it was her duty to obey her husband in the prosecution of war against a country 'which was already menacing the whole world'. She summoned the councillors individually to her, and threatened them with depriva-tion or even death if they did not consent. As the French ambas-sador commented at the time, Mary would oblige 'not only men, but also the elements themselves, to consent to her will'. She was as wilful and as imperious as her father or her sister.

Her case was in fact made for her by an attack on Scarborough by two French ships towards the end of April; under the command of an errant nobleman, Sir Thomas Stafford, a small force of men landed and seized the garrison of the castle there. Stafford then declared that the defences of the country were about to be 'delivered to 12,000 Spaniards before the king's coronation'.

The invasion was not a success. Stafford and his men were surrounded and captured within three days, but the damage to French interests had been done. It has since been speculated that Stafford had in fact been lured to the English shore by a 'double agent' who desired a confrontation with France. Certainly it was a highly convenient attack for those who favoured conflict. War was thereupon declared in June: 7,000 men were to be transported across the Channel to fight the French in the Low Countries. Philip left England in the following month to assume command of his forces.

All seemed to be set fair. The Spanish achieved a remarkable victory outside St Quentin and the English forces arrived two days later to assist in the storming of the city itself; they had not been victorious in battle but at least they had been on the winning side. Bonfires were lit in London and the churches rang with hymns of celebration.

Yet soon enough the fortunes of war changed. A Scottish army came down to the border in a campaign of fire and destruction in support of their traditional ally, and an English force had to be dispatched against them. By the middle of December, the French were also gathering about the neighbourhood of Calais, the last English garrison town in their country. A council of war in the town sent an urgent letter to London for reinforcements; they had few supplies and could not withstand a siege. The queen commanded men to be raised but two days later, on 31 December, countermanded the order on the grounds that 'she had intelligence that no enterprise was intended against Calais or the Pale'. The Pale was the immediate neighbourhood under English control, covering 120 square miles of territory.

The intelligence given to the queen had been wrong. A French army under the duke of Guise gradually broke down the defences of the English territory and proceeded to besiege Calais itself. Its governor sent a message that he was 'clean cut off from all relief and aid which he looked to have'. In the first week of the new year, 1558, the town was taken. Its 5,000 inhabitants were shipped back to England. Calais had once been called 'the brightest jewel in the English crown'. It had been a centre of commerce between England and Europe; a reminder of the Plantagenet empire, it had been held for 211 years. The catastrophe was complete.

It can be argued in hindsight that the French recapture of Calais was in fact a benefit. It had required constant finance for its garrison. At a later date the English historian Thomas Fuller wrote that 'now it is gone, let it go. It was a beggarly town, which cost England ten times yearly more than it was worth.' Its loss deterred the English from any further needless meddling in French affairs, and national attention was slowly turned towards the west and the New World. Only a year before, Sebastian Cabot became the director of a new company formally sanctioned by Philip and Mary under the title of 'Merchant Adventurers of England for the Discoveries of Lands, Territories, Isles and Signories unknown'.

Yet at the time the surrender of Calais was considered to be a calamity. The queen was prostrate with grief and anger. She was used to finding divine providence at work in her affairs and, after this dishonour, it seemed that God had deserted her. One of her household reported later to John Foxe that he had found her sighing. 'When I am dead and opened,' she told him, 'you shall find Calais lying in my heart.'

It was widely believed that the French, now emboldened, would launch an invasion. Parliament voted that a large subsidy should be imposed upon an impoverished and unwilling nation for the purpose of improving the defences. Philip himself proposed to lead a joint army of English and Spanish forces to recapture the town. The council declined the offer on the grounds that there was only 'a wan hope of recovering Calais' and that 'inconveniences might follow' if the campaign failed. The Spanish connection had in any case proved to be a disaster.

Could it still bear fruit by other means? At the time of the loss of Calais, the queen had persuaded herself that she was pregnant at last. She delayed telling her husband until she was absolutely certain. At the end of March she made her will, 'foreseeing the great danger which by God's ordinance remain to all women in their travail of children'. Yet once more it was a delusion born out of hope and fear. By the beginning of May it was clear enough that there was no child. The last hope had gone. Indeed the false signs of an impending birth may have been a symptom of the illness that soon enough would destroy her. From this time forward reports and rumours of her 'malady' became ever more common.

Illness was one of the defining features of her reign. In the early months of 1558 an epidemic disease, called the 'new ague', descended upon the people; it seems to have been a virulent form of influenza and combined with the prevailing incidence of plague and sweating sickness it cut a vast swathe through the people. The year witnessed the highest mortality rates of the century. This is the vast setting of suffering, from what were called 'hot burning fevers', behind the last troubled period of Mary's rule.

It was still a time for burning in more than one sense. Fewer were left to bring to the stake but the queen still clamoured for their deaths. A congregation of radicals was discovered at a prayer meeting in a field outside London, and thirteen were promptly detained. Seven of them were burned together at Smithfield, on 28 June, while the other six were burned on Bishop Bonner's orders at dead of night in Brentford. Mary had sent out a proclamation forbidding anyone to approach, touch, comfort, or speak to a heretic on the path to the stake; the penalty for doing so was death.

In the summer of the year Mary removed from Hampton Court to Whitehall, where she was reported to be in a state of profound depression. 'The truth is,' one ambassador related, 'that her malady is evidently incurable, and will end her life sooner or later, according to the increase or decrease of her mental anxieties, which harass her more than the disease, however dangerous it may be.' Those anxieties must have been exacerbated by her realization that she was slowly losing the love and trust of her subjects. The loss of Calais had emphasized the fact that she was an unlucky queen; in the sixteenth century fortune, or providence, was seen as the evidence of divine judgment. Philip was told that, after Calais, only a third of the previous number of worshippers went to Mass. The religious exiles vented their anger and malice from the cities of Europe, none more vituperative than John Knox in *The First Blast of the Trumpet against the Monstrous Regiment of Women*. 'I fear not to say,' he stated, 'that the day of vengeance which shall apprehend that horrible monster Jezebel of England, and such as maintain her monstrous cruelty, is already appointed in the council of the eternal.'

By the beginning of September it was clear that she was mortally ill. There were times when she lay in a state of torpor. She contracted a fever, perhaps part of the epidemic that was passing across the country. In the following month Philip was informed that his wife was about to die.

The attention of the realm and its councillors now turned towards Elizabeth. She knew that the crown would soon be hers. When an envoy from Philip called upon her, to remind her of the favour shown to her by his master, she was noticeably cool. She would inherit the kingdom without any help from him, and went on to inform the ambassador that her sister had lost the loyalty of the country when she married a foreigner. In that supposition, she may have been correct. In any event she did not intend to make the same mistake. The envoy concluded that 'she is a very vain and clever woman'.

On 5 November Parliament had sent an urgent request to the council that its members should persuade the queen to 'accept Madam Elizabeth as her sister and heiress, and to inform her of this in loving terms'. The queen assented to the statement and asked only that her successor should pay her debts and make no changes in the national religion. Elizabeth of course chose to ignore this, just as she ignored all the provisions of Mary's formal will. By the time the message was conveyed to her at Hatfield House she was already assembling her court. She had also taken the precaution of soliciting military help, if and when it should prove necessary.

When a Spanish envoy arrived on 9 November, it was clear that Mary could not recover. According to her closest household servant, Jane Dormer, she comforted those who attended her; she told them that she had dreamed of 'seeing little children like angels play before her singing pleasing notes, giving her more than earthly comfort'. She must have hoped, too, that she would soon be received by angels. She died at six o'clock on the morning of 17 November during the celebration of Mass.

Cardinal Pole received the news at Lambeth; he himself was close to death, as a consequence of the epidemic of fever, and it must be assumed that this further blow was enough to destroy him. He died twelve hours later, at seven o'clock in the evening. When the message of her sister's death reached Elizabeth she sank to her knees and called out '*O domino factum est istud, et est mirabile in oculis nostris*' – 'It is the work of the Lord, and it is marvellous in our eyes'.

At eight o'clock, two hours after Mary's death, parliament was summoned with an announcement that Elizabeth was now 'queen of this realm'. The Commons answered with 'God save Queen Elizabeth, long may she reign over us'. The bells rang out and the bonfires blazed; tables were set outside the houses of the richer citizens, where ale and wine were distributed.

Yet some mourned Mary's passing. In his funeral sermon the bishop of Winchester praised the dead queen for her many virtues and her piety, mentioning the fact that her knees had hardened with her incessant kneeling. Yet the new queen was 'a lady of great virtue whom we are bound to obey, for you know, "a living dog is better than a dead lion"'. For that injudicious remark he was deprived of his see. Meanwhile the English court was buying up all the cloths of silk at Antwerp in readiness for the coronation.

26

A virgin queen

Elizabeth began her progress to London in the last week of November, attended by a grand concourse of lords and ladies and gentlemen. A procession of bishops met her at Highgate and knelt in homage; she gave each one of them her hand to kiss, with the notable exception of Bishop Bonner. The reputation of 'Bloody Bonner' had preceded him. The queen had given an early sign of her true religious allegiances.

She remained at the Charterhouse for five days before taking formal possession of the Tower as the preliminary to her coronation. She rode in state along the streets of the city, where she was greeted by choirs of children and the salutations of scholars. As she entered the Tower itself she remarked to those standing about her that 'some have fallen from princes of this land to be prisoners in this place. I am raised from being prisoner in this place to be prince of this land.' It is reported that she went immediately to the apartment in which she had been confined, and fell to her knees in prayer.

The great scholar and magus John Dee was asked to cast a horoscope for the most propitious day of coronation. He hit upon Sunday 15 January 1559, and so the preceding day was chosen for her grand procession through the streets of London from the Tower towards Westminster. Accompanied by 1,000 horsemen she was carried in an open litter covered with gold brocade; she wore a rich robe of state, made out of cloth of gold and lined with ermine.

It was a day of high ceremony in which the queen performed her part with great skill and relish. She waved at the spectators and called out greetings to them. 'God bless you, my people!' She raised her hands in surprise and delight; she listened with great seriousness as a child prattled a short oration, 'with a perpetual attentiveness in her face and a marvellous change of look, as if the child's words touched her person'. She accepted with grace the little nosegays and branches of rosemary that the poor women of London pressed upon her. Her expressions of joy and amusement were marked by everyone. 'God save you all!' 'I thank you with all my heart!' When passing through Cheapside she was observed to smile broadly. 'I have just overheard one say in the crowd,' she confided to an attendant, 'I remember old King Harry the eighth.' She had retained her father's ability to embody the national spirit. When an English Bible was lowered into her chariot on a silken string she received it with both her hands, kissed it and clasped it to her chest. 'I thank the city for this present, and esteem it above all others.' When prayers were said for the return of true religion she raised her eyes to heaven and cried 'Amen!'

Many pageants were set up on stages along her path. The allegory of Time and Truth had been erected at the Little Conduit in Cheapside. She asked for the identity of an old man holding a scythe and an hourglass, but of course she already knew the answer. 'Time,' she was told. 'Time!' she declared. 'And time has brought me here!' As she passed through Temple Bar, she called out to the populace 'Be ye well assured, I will stand your good queen.'

There was, however, a problem concerning the coronation. The archbishop of Canterbury was dead. The archbishop of York refused to crown her as supreme head of the Church, and the surviving Catholic bishops followed his example. The bishop of Carlisle was eventually persuaded to play the part at the abbey, however, on the understanding that the queen would take the ancient oath used by her Catholic predecessors. The controversies in matters of faith were only just beginning.

Another obstacle could have been found. According to canon law Elizabeth was illegitimate and therefore barred from the throne.

The most considerable candidate for the throne therefore became Mary Stuart, the queen of the Scots, who was the great-grand-daughter of Henry VII and who conveniently enough happened to be a Catholic. Mary was married to the dauphin of France, soon to become crowned as Francis II; it was at this time that the young couple began to quarter the English arms with those of France as a token of proprietorship. Elizabeth and Mary would ever after be engaged in a duel that would end in death.

On the day of Elizabeth's coronation she made the journey from Westminster Hall to the abbey on foot. She trod upon a rich crimson carpet and, as soon as she had passed, it was cut away by the spectators. Her hair hung loose as a token of her virginity. As she arrived at the portals of the church all the bells of London rang out in unison. When the members of the congregation were asked if they wished Elizabeth to be their queen, they cried out 'Yes!' Then the organs and the fifes, the drums and the trumpets, resounded. The coronation banquet in Westminster Hall began at three o'clock in the afternoon and ended at one o'clock of the following morning.

She had met her privy council at Hatfield even before her entry into London. Twenty-nine of Mary's appointed men soon with-drew or were asked to resign; only six powerful nobles remained at the table, among them the earls of Arundel and Bedford, together with certain bureaucrats whose experience was invaluable. The clerics and the Catholics had gone. The members of the council represented a lay body, drawn from the nobility and from the elite trained at Cambridge and the Inns of Court; they were also largely interrelated and, at a slightly later date, eighteen out of twenty-five were related to each other and to Elizabeth herself.

One of her most important appointments was that of Robert Dudley, later earl of Leicester, as her master of the horse. He came from a great, if tainted, family. He was the son of the duke of Northumberland, who had tried to place Lady Jane Grey on the throne, and became a childhood friend of Elizabeth at the age of seven or eight; they may subsequently have met in the Tower, where both were for a while incarcerated. 'I only show him favour,' she is reported to have said, 'because of his goodness to me when I was in trouble during the reign of my sister.' In any event they established an enduring and affectionate relationship that subsequently became the source of much scandal.

The women about the queen were her distant relatives from suitably noble families. She was always accompanied by seven ladies of the bedchamber and by six maids of honour, all of them dressed in black or white or a medley of the two. She did not wish any of her attendants to mar the effect of her brightly coloured gowns. Strict rules were imposed upon them. They were never to speak to her about affairs of state and they were never, ever, to be betrothed or to marry without her permission. Some of them were consigned to prison for their disobedience in the matter. She herself naturally stood out. She had a somewhat swarthy complexion, like that of her mother, but she plastered her face with egg-white, alum and other agents so that it attained in time a luminous whiteness; she had a face considered too long to be entirely beautiful, but her eyes were large and expressive. She had the reddish-golden hair of her father, and the high cheek-bones of her mother. Her nose was slightly hooked, lending her an eagle-like appearance.

She had appointed Sir William Cecil as her principal secretary of state, telling him that 'without respect to my private will, you will give me that council which you think best'. On that account she was not to be disappointed. Cecil remained by her side until the end of his life. She called him her 'spirit' and addressed him as 'Sir Spirit'. He had first served in the reign of Edward VI and had managed to retain the favour even of Mary as the most able and industrious administrator of the day. It was his habit to draw up elaborate analyses of a particular problem, with the arguments for and against a policy summarized in two columns. He favoured a middle course in affairs of state and religion, and in this respect he was closely attuned to the wishes of his mistress. The Elizabethan historian William Camden wrote that 'of all men of genius he was most a drudge; of all men of business the most a genius'. He was also, in every sense, a survivor.

He knew well enough that the problems and dangers facing the queen were severe. A former clerk of the council under Edward VI sent an address to the new council with his own summary of the nation's affairs. 'The queen poor; the realm exhausted; the nobility poor and decayed; good captains and soldiers wanting; the people out of order; justice not executed; all things dear; excesses in meat, diet and apparel; divisions among ourselves; war with France; the French king bestriding the realm, having one foot in Calais and the other in Scotland; steadfast enemies, but no steadfast friends.'

That is why the new ministers about her urged for caution above all else – caution in religious policy and caution in foreign affairs. One of Cecil's aphorisms was to the effect that the realm gains more from one year of peace than from ten years of war. Elizabeth shared his belief, knowing well that war was an expense she could not afford; the treasury was bare. It was necessary to accept the loss of Calais, therefore, and come to peace with France. It was also wise to reach some agreement with Scotland for the safety of the northern border. Some said that there was not a wall in England strong enough to stand a cannon shot.

Yet in some matters she was quick. When the Fellows of King's College Cambridge wrote to her asking for advice on the election of a new provost, she replied with a name by return of post.

In the winter of 1558, even before Elizabeth's coronation, a paper was drawn up with the title 'Device for the Alteration of Religion'. It is likely to have been the work of William Cecil; he was himself a supporter of the reformed faith. In the document he urges a full restoration of the 'true religion' as it existed in the reign of Edward VI, with all the risks this 'alteration' implied. The pope would excommunicate the queen, and the French would be able to attack the English as heretics as well as enemies. The Catholic power of Scotland might also be levied against the realm. Internal rebels would be no less dangerous than external foes; the bishops, and many of the judges, would be against the change. A majority of the people might also become discontented and rebellious. Yet the cause of God had to be maintained. Only then would Elizabeth and her nation be secured and glorified. At the end of the year, in this spirit, it was proclaimed that the litany and the Lord's Prayer might be recited in English.

In practice the 'alteration' would prove difficult to implement. Parliament met eleven days after her coronation. When the royal procession entered Westminster Abbey, for the customary Mass before the parliamentary session, the queen was met by a group of monks bearing lighted candles. 'Away with these torches,' she called out, 'we see very well.' In the succeeding sermon the preacher denounced monks in particular for their part in the Marian persecution of heretics, and he urged the queen not to countenance 'idolatry' in her country. It was also well understood that the service in the royal chapel was predominantly Protestant in spirit, doing away with the elevation of the host. She would never countenance the demands of Rome. How could Elizabeth have embraced a faith that had denounced her mother as a prostitute and herself as a bastard? And she abhorred the smell of incense.

She had no affection for theological niceties. Although she once stated that she had studied divinity from childhood, she believed that controversies over religion were 'as ropes of sand or sea-slime leading to the moon'. 'There is only one Jesus Christ,' she told the French ambassador, 'the rest is a dispute over trifles.' Her own religious opinions are difficult to discern; she had a liking for elaborate choral music and appreciated much of the ritual of the Roman communion; she called herself a Protestant, but kept a small crucifix in the royal chapel which the more radical members of the new faith deemed to be idolatry. She also had a strong dislike for married priests.

A succession of bills was passed in the early months of 1559. The religious laws of the time of Edward VI were reintroduced and the English service was resumed. Private bills were passed returning to lay owners certain lands that had been seized by the Marian bishops. The second Edwardian prayer book was once more deemed to be the key to public worship, but it was subtly altered to avoid offending Catholic sensibilities. A reference to the 'detestable enormities' of the pope was removed, for example, and the real presence of Christ in the sacrament was tacitly allowed. In practice the priest would be allowed to wear the same vestments, and stand in the same position, as he had in the previous reign. Elizabeth was content to style herself 'supreme governor' rather than 'supreme head' of the Church in England. Christ was the head.

The Elizabethan 'settlement', as it later became known, was designed to pursue a middle course. Yet it was by no means wholly popular. The Catholic bishops in the Lords were opposed to the measures and eventually the Act of Uniformity, designed to reinforce the Book of Common Prayer, was passed by only three votes. A debate between Catholics and Protestants in Westminster Hall settled nothing. One of the disputants was described as 'turning himself towards all quarters, and into every possible attitude, stamping with his feet, throwing his arms, bending his sides, snapping his fingers, alternately elevating and depressing his eyebrows'. After the debate Elizabeth was obliged to imprison two Catholic bishops, in order to prevent them from excommunicating her in public. This was also a means of diminishing the opposition to her proposals in the Lords. The Commons were committed to the measures, but many of the Lords were defiantly hostile. In the end it was a close-run thing.

The queen wished to calm any form of disputation; she set herself the task of creating a broad consensus with which both the reformers and the orthodox could live in peace. The settlement, if such it was, did not in fact please either party. The Catholics lamented the reversal of Mary's policies, while the reformers were inclined to believe that the English Church was still papistical. A Puritan broadside described the Book of Common Prayer as 'an unperfect book, culled and picked out of that popish dunghill, the Mass book full of all abominations'. This was in fact a mixed religious polity that relied upon compromise and accommodation. The constitution of the Church remained largely unchanged while the liturgy contained ancient, medieval, Lutheran and Calvinist aspects; it was Protestant in regard to preaching but Catholic in its attention to ritual. It was perhaps the least reformed of all the reformed faiths and promulgated no uniform theology. This ramshackle contraption was designed to hold as many passengers as before. So Elizabeth had remained cautious. Towards the end of her reign Francis Bacon, the philosopher and statesman, declared that she had no wish to peer into any subject's soul. She required only outward conformity to the English Church for the sake of order. All the English were obliged to attend their parish churches every Sunday and holy day; the fine for absence was one shilling. The nation had changed its faith four times in twenty years, and the time had come for an end to innovation.

She never allowed anyone to meddle with the order she had established and, with a brief period of interregnum in the seventeenth century, it has remained largely unchanged ever since. One of her advisers remarked that she had 'placed her Reformation as upon a sure stone to remain constant'. It was a very English settlement; it was practical rather than speculative; it brought together materials that might otherwise have been considered incompatible; it introduced compromise and toleration as well as a fair amount of ambiguity. Its very lack of clarity saved it. In London the reformers preached predestination and justification by faith alone while in York the faithful prayed still on their strings of beads. 'The difference between Catholics and Lutherans', the queen told the Spanish ambassador, 'is not of much importance in substance.' She required only a settlement that would maintain order and would bring unity to her subjects. More politic reasons for her caution can also be found. She did not wish to lose the support of the Lutheran princes in Germany, nor did she wish to antagonize the Catholic kings of Europe. The religion of the people had a significant foreign context.

Just before the end of the parliamentary session the Speaker of the House of Commons asked permission to present a petition to the queen that was of vital importance to the realm; it contained the wish, or entreaty, that she should marry and bear an heir to the throne. Only then could the peace and stability of the realm be maintained, and the throne itself protected from foreign enemies. She paused before making a long reply in which she expressed her wish to remain in 'this virgin's estate wherein you see me'. She alluded mysteriously to the danger that any issue might 'grow out of kind and become ungracious'. A male heir, in other words, might try to supplant her; this was always the danger for a female sovereign.

She then drew from her finger the coronation ring. She said that she had received the ring on the solemn condition that she was bound in marriage to the realm and would take no other as a partner. It would be quite sufficient if, on her tomb, were inscribed the words 'Here lieth Elizabeth, which reigned a virgin, and died a virgin'. In that supposition she was to prove correct. The experiences of her mother and of her sister would have warned her of the dangers of the married state, and it was suggested by one of her doctors that her body might not be able to withstand the strain of childbirth. And of course, as she said, she may have feared a male heir. The Spanish king, Philip, her brother-in-law, had in fact proposed marriage to her already; the offer was for a while graciously evaded rather than denied. The direct refusal came later, when she declared that she could not marry him because she was a Protestant.

When parliament finally rose in the second week of May a Spanish bishop summarized the nature of the change. 'The Holy Sacrament was taken away yesterday from the royal chapel, and Mass was said in English. The bishops who will not swear [the oath of supremacy] will lose their sees; and when they have been deprived the queen will go on progress and institute their successors.' All except one were indeed deprived of their bishoprics and replaced with more convenient men. The monks and nuns had been scattered to the winds, and the statues of the Virgin and the saints were once more removed from their niches just as the crucifix was banished from the rood loft. The new liturgy was slowly, if grudgingly, accepted; yet within a generation it became the heart of English religion. The heretics of Mary's realm had been long since freed from their prison cells. Yet not all was peace and light. The people of the north did not care for the new Book of Common Prayer, and whispers of rebellion could once more be heard.

The queen herself had managed her parliament well. With the help of Cecil and other councillors she had successfully manoeuvred between the papists and the more radical clergy newly returned from exile under Mary. In a sense she had already become a symbol of the emerging nation. Her private experiences had directly reflected the travails of the nation. She had been in peril during the reign of Mary and Philip; she had suffered privation and had lived among manifest dangers. She had been a prisoner. Now she had triumphed.

She had gained her ascendancy despite her sex. At court she presided over a largely masculine community of some 1,500 persons, and she had to learn how to dominate her wholly male council. She was a natural diplomat, in turn serpentine and obstinate. She had no need for an army of translators since she herself spoke Latin, Italian, French, Spanish and German. Her intelligence and her quick wit were invaluable; her wilfulness and imperiousness also assisted her in the never-ending battle with the world. The

Spanish envoy remarked that she was infinitely more feared than her sister, and gave her orders with as much authority as her father. She once said that she had a great desire 'to do some act that would make her fame spread abroad in her lifetime and, after, occasion memorial for ever'. No specific act was necessary. It was enough, and more than enough, to be herself.

We may trace from this date, in fact, the beginning of the cult of Elizabeth. She would eventually be hailed as Deborah of fiery spirit from the book of Judges; she was Judith and she was Hester. She was Gloriana and Pandora. She was Astraea, the Greek virgin-goddess of justice who had in the age of gold dwelt among mortals upon the earth; Astraea retired into the sky as the constellation Virgo. The days of the queen's birthday and accession were treated as national celebrations marked by parades and banquets and music.

Many signs of providence could be found in her destiny. Her birthday, 7 September, was also the feast day of the Nativity of the Virgin Mary. On that day her champion at the tilt, Henry Lee, erected a pavilion 'like unto a church, wherein were many lamps burning'. The paintings and miniatures and woodcuts portrayed her as an allegorical figure in circumstances of glory. Whether the people of England were wholly dazzled and deceived by these fabrications is another matter. Deep reserves of apathy, and even of cynicism, must have resisted many of the blandishments. It is impossible to gauge the sensibilities and opinions of the English people in the middle of the sixteenth century, but no doubt they were as unruly and as disaffected as every other generation.

Yet Elizabeth came to be defined as the virgin queen (with connotations of another Virgin), whose motto was '*semper eadem*' or 'always the same'. That would in time become the truism, and perhaps the tragedy, of her reign.

27

Two queens

In the summer of 1559 Elizabeth issued a series of injunctions in matters concerning religion. The liturgy was to be recited in English, and an English translation of the Bible be placed in every church. Images and monuments 'of feigned miracles, pilgrimages, idolatry, and superstition' were to be removed from walls and windows, but the fabric of the church was to be repaired or restored. No more wholesale iconoclasm was permitted. The cult of the saints, and prayers for the dead, were abolished.

The processions of Rogationtide, when the people beat the bounds of their parish and invoked blessings on the fields and the folk, were still to be performed. The congregation was ordered to uncover and bow on the pronunciation of the name of Jesus, and to kneel during the reading of the litany. Clergy were to continue to wear their traditional habits, complete with square hats. Wafers, rather than portions of ordinary bread, were to be provided for the time of communion. 'Modest and distinct' songs were permitted. All opprobrious names, such as 'heretic' or 'papist', were forbidden. The injunctions were, in other words, an attempt to compose differences and to soften the acrimony and recrimination attendant on the further change in religion.

Yet the differences were evident at the consecration of the archbishop of Canterbury. Matthew Parker had not wanted to become archbishop. He considered the burden to be too great to bear, and he wrote to inform Cecil that he wished to remain in a private station 'more meet for my decayed voice, and small quality, than in theatrical and great audience'; he wished to be 'quite forgotten'. Yet the queen insisted; he had, after all, been her mother's chaplain. He was told that 'her pleasure is, that you should repair up hither [to London] with such speed, as you conveniently may'. At the consecration itself only one bishop wore the legally stipulated vestment of the cope; two bishops refused to put on the Romish attire and wore surplices; a fourth believed the surplice to be going too far and wore only the black gown of Geneva. The disagreement did not augur well. All of the fourteen surviving bishops of Mary's reign had, in the interim, been deprived; some of them spent the rest of their lives in prison for refusing to take the oath of supremacy. Bishop Bonner, for example, was taken to the Marshalsea. He tried to befriend some of the criminals incarcerated there, calling them 'friends' and 'neighbours'. But one of them answered, 'Go, you beast, into hell, and find your friends there.'

And then there was the matter of the queen's silver crucifix. For those of reformed faith the crucifix was a papistical idol, in which reverence for an object had been substituted in place of reverence for God. Yet one stood in the queen's private chapel, with candles burning before it. It was, in the words of one reformer, 'a foul idol' placed on 'the altar of abomination'. Such was the dismay among the clergy that a debate among four bishops was held before the council but, despite their best endeavours, it remained. When the dean of St Paul's preached to her on the iniquity of crosses, she became very angry. 'Do not talk about that,' she called to him. When he returned to the theme she remonstrated with him. 'Leave that! Leave that! It has nothing to do with your subject and the matter is threadbare.' He brought his sermon to an abrupt close, and she walked out of the chapel.

On two later occasions the crucifix was attacked and broken up, much to the delight of the bishop of Norwich. 'A good riddance of such a cross as that! It has continued there too long already, to the great grief of the godly.' On both occasions a crucifix was restored to the same position. For Elizabeth it was a token of her belief in ritual and order, as well as a way of maintaining her relations with Spain and the Vatican. She told the Spanish ambassador that 'many people think we are Moors or Turks here, whereas we only differ from the Catholics in things of small importance'. It was also of course a benevolent gesture towards her more orthodox subjects. Soon enough the Catholic requiem for the dead came back in altered guise, with 'the celebration of the Lord's supper at funerals'.

In the same spirit of religious conciliation the queen went in the spring of this year on procession to St Mary Spital, in the east of the city, to hear a sermon. She was attended by 1,000 men in full armour, but she was also accompanied by morris dancers and two white bears in a cart. Religion was no longer to be removed from festival. The animals were baited to death after the sermon. Elsewhere in London psalms were being sung in English for the first time since the reign of Edward VI; it was reported that, at Paul's Cross, some 6,000 people sang together.

> He shall be like the tree that groweth
> > fast by the river side:
> Which bringeth forth most pleasant fruit
> > in her due time and tide.

The new injunctions were followed by a series of visitations in the late summer to make sure that they had been given practical effect. Some 125 inspectors were chosen, to travel on six separate 'circuits' of the country, but the peers and gentry nominated for this task were unable or unwilling to perform it. So the more eager lawyers and clerics were given the job; naturally enough they were keen reformers who anticipated a general cleansing of the churches. All the evidence suggests that in most regions the arrival of the visitors was quickly followed by the removal of altars and images. The bonfires of the Catholic vanities could be seen in London, Exeter, York and other cities. Vestments, statues, banners and ornaments were thrown into the flames. The archbishop of York hailed the destruction of the 'vessels that were made for Baal' and the 'polluted and defiled altars'. It seems that the visitors were more rigorous in the pursuit of superstition than the queen herself would have liked. That is why Elizabeth soon issued a proclamation denouncing the 'negligence and lack of convenient reverence' in the maintenance of the churches, citing 'unmeet and unseemly tables with foul cloths for the communion of the sacraments, and generally leaving the place of prayers desolate of all cleanliness and of meet ornaments for such a place'. It was no doubt left to the clergy to decide of what a 'meet ornament' might consist.

In some parts of the country resistance to the changes was still strong, albeit in disguised form. Pictures and images were sometimes merely covered, and the other vestiges of the old faith concealed. Various reasons, apart from piety, can be adduced for this. The most pressing and practical of them concerned the succession. If Elizabeth died without an heir, the Catholic Mary Stuart might become queen and reverse all the previous changes.

The presence of Mary Stuart in the French court emphasized the larger diplomatic problem with which Elizabeth and her council had to deal. Mary was now queen of France, her husband having ascended to the throne as Francis II in 1559, and she also styled herself queen of England. In her absence Scotland was ruled by her mother, Mary of Guise, who had asked for more troops from her home country to defy the Protestant lords of Scotland. French troops had been assembled in Normandy, while the French forts on the north bank of the Tweed were in offensive or defensive array. Invasion was to be feared.

The French court was supposed to be alive with plots to assassinate the English queen. It was claimed that Mary's uncles, the brothers Guise, had devised a scheme 'to poison her by means of an Italian named Stephano, a burly man with a black beard, about forty-five years of age, who will offer his services to the queen as an engineer'. Stephano did not arrive. She was in any case surrounded by precautions. No dish arrived at her table untasted, no glove or handkerchief could be presented to her without being carefully examined. She was dosed every week with antidotes against poison.

Another Scottish complication presented itself. The Protestant lords had sent an envoy to the court of Elizabeth, asking for an army to help them remove the French from their country. Elizabeth did not like war. Since the rebellion would effectively injure the status of Mary Stuart, queen of Scotland, it was not necessarily to be assisted or even welcomed. Elizabeth, naturally enough, supported very strongly the claims of a rightful queen. It was not proper to renounce an anointed sovereign. She also had no real affection for the Protestantism of the Scots. The people of that faith were led by John Knox, the reformer who had aimed a cannon of vituperation and malice against the idea of a female sovereign.

William Cecil was a more ardent Protestant and a bolder statesman. He set out a policy that included the invasion of Scotland by an English army and, if necessary, the removal of Mary Stuart from the throne. 'Anywise kindle the fire,' he wrote, 'for, if quenched, the opportunity will not come in our lives.' It was clear to him that the forces of European Catholicism might now be confronted and defied. He feared a French conspiracy to subvert the English state and the English religion.

The queen hesitated and resisted. She told her council that 'it was a dangerous matter to enter into war'. Cecil, declaring that the faint hearts and the flatterers were supporting her policy of prevarication, threatened to resign. The leading faint heart, Sir Nicholas Bacon, had asserted 'safety in moderation'. Secretly she sent money; then she sent a fleet into the Firth of Forth. Eventually, by the end of the year, she was persuaded to send a force of troops into the territory of her northern neighbour; much to the fury and resentment of the queen it failed in its attack upon the French fortress of Leith. The scaling ladders had been too short. The English settled down to a siege, a most unsatisfactory state of affairs. 'I have had herein such a torment with the Queen's Majesty,' Cecil wrote, 'as an ague hath not in five fits so much abated.'

It was Cecil who had supported the war; it was Cecil who would be obliged to conclude it. The queen ordered him to arrange a peace with the Scots and the French. Much to his dismay he was obliged to obey. The eventual Treaty of Edinburgh, signed in the summer of 1560, was an honourable truce. Both sides agreed to withdraw their troops from the country, with the additional promise that Mary and Francis would surrender their claim to the English throne. England had confronted France and survived the ordeal. This was the lesson which all parties adduced from the affair. Such was the rivalry between Spain and France, also, that Philip was in a certain sense obliged to support the heretic Elizabeth in any rivalry with her neighbour. It could be said that his benign inaction helped to ensure the triumph of the Protestant cause in England.

The treaty was perhaps more than Cecil and Elizabeth had expected, but it had one serious imperfection; Mary herself never signed the document. Mary of Guise had died in that same summer and, with the removal of the French troops, the parliament of Scotland professed the Protestant faith; again the decision was not ratified by the queen, and the dispute between doctrines continued as before. Mary Stuart might have been forgiven for thinking that the rival queen, by means of the treaty, had tried to rob her of the allegiance and loyalty of her subjects. Yet her ushers at the court in Paris still called out, as she passed, 'Make way for the queen of England!' Her claim to the throne of England would become the single source of the calamities that would one day descend upon her.

The question of Elizabeth's marriage remained the most important matter of the realm. The pursuit of Philip II for her hand was copied by other great men of Europe. It was always an advantage to marry a queen. By the autumn of the year ten or twelve eminent suitors were in contention. Two kings, two archdukes, five dukes and two earls vied for mastery. Principal among them were archdukes Charles and Ferdinand of Austria; gambolling up in the rear was Eric of Sweden, the Swedish king's eldest son. Elizabeth did not disguise the fact that she enjoyed the attention, but she always fell back upon coquetry and dissembling. She had never said that she would *never* marry but, still, she proposed to remain a virgin. What she said she wanted, she did not want; her stated intentions were always at odds with her real designs. Her settled policy was that of delay and prevarication. The Spanish ambassador wrote that 'you will see what a pretty business it is to have to treat with this woman, who I think must have a hundred thousand devils in her body, notwithstanding that she is forever telling me that she yearns to be a nun and to pass her time in a cell praying'. It was of course always useful, in an uncertain and dangerous world, to have the grandees of several nations competing for her charms.

In the autumn of the year a Scottish theologian sent to her an account of the fall of her mother, including the scene where Anne Boleyn held up the infant Elizabeth in supplication to her irate husband: a timely reminder of the perils of matrimony. It is likely that it was always her desire to remain single. Had she not already said that she was married to her parliament and to her nation? This was the mystical marriage of state, in which she was made whole by incorporating the male world. It might be termed the body politic. Yet in the circumstances of the age it was a brave and even astonishing decision. It was inconceivable that a woman, let alone a queen, would not choose to marry. Great social prejudice was directed against unmarried females. It flouted the divine, as well as the human, order. An unmarried queen would be subject to 'dolours and infirmities' attendant upon the celibate condition. At a later date the archbishop of Canterbury, together with the bishops of London and York, sent her a pastoral letter in which they feared 'this continued sterility in your Highness's person to be a token of God's displeasure towards us'. It imperilled the safety and even the existence of the nation.

There was another player in the pack. Robert Dudley, master of the horse, was part of her close entourage. He was handsome and flamboyant; it was clear that the queen had a great liking and affection for him. In the spring of 1560 it was rumoured that she was visiting his chamber both by day and by night, and the rumours were soon fashioned into a scandal that was even being reported by the foreign envoys at the court. It was whispered that if Dudley's wife were to die, Elizabeth would marry him. A woman from Brentford was arraigned for claiming that the queen was pregnant with his child. On a progress in the summer of that year, just after the success in Scotland, she travelled along the southern bank of the Thames. Dudley was her constant companion, riding and hunting with her every day. Cecil, seeing that his influence had declined, was considering his position. He told the Spanish ambassador that 'the queen was conducting herself in such a way that he was about to withdraw from her service. It was a bad sailor who did not make for a port when he saw the storm coming . . .'

Then, on 8 September 1560, Amy Dudley died in a mysterious manner. She had broken her neck after falling down a staircase. The convenient death of Dudley's wife provoked 'grievous and dangerous suspicion and muttering'. Had she been pushed? Had she, perhaps, committed suicide? The queen sent Dudley to his house in Kew, where he seems to have lingered in a state of shock and anxiety. He told one of his servants, Sir Thomas Blount, that 'the greatness and suddenness of the misfortune doth so perplex me . . . as I can take no rest'. He knew well enough what 'the malicious world' would make of the affair.

When a coroner's jury was convened to consider the evidence, the verdict was one of death by misadventure. The judgment did not of course silence the rumours of conspiracy, and even of the queen's participation in a plot to murder Amy Dudley. The rumours were most unlikely. It would have been politically impossible for the queen to have married Dudley after such an event. Those who favour conspiracies might even speculate that Cecil arranged for Amy Dudley to be killed, thus wrecking any chance of marriage and damaging the reputation of Dudley himself.

The nature of the relationship between the favourite and the queen is unknown. Elizabeth had been formed by experience and adversity; she was always cautious and ever watchful. Would she have courted disaster by engaging in a love affair with one of her subjects? The queen was rarely, if ever, alone. She was surrounded by the ladies of her bedchamber and her maids of honour even as she slept; any departure from the rigid ceremonial of her life would have been instantly observed. 'My life is in the open and I have so many witnesses,' she said, 'I cannot understand how so bad a judgement can have been formed of me.'

At this juncture Cecil drew up a memorandum for his own use, in which he summarized the relative attractions of Archduke Charles of Austria, still the favourite candidate for Elizabeth's hand, and Robert Dudley, master of the horse. The balance sheet is all on the archduke's side. He reports that 'in wealth' Charles had 'by report three thousand ducats by the year' whereas Dudley has 'all of the queen, and in debt'. In 'friendship' the archduke had the emperor and the king of Spain as well as various dukes; Dudley had 'none but such as shall have of the queen'. In reputation Charles was 'honoured of all men' whereas Dudley was 'hated of many. His wife's death.' As far as Cecil was concerned, the case was closed. But, as he said, 'what the queen will determine to do, God only knows'.

At the beginning of 1561 a close companion of Dudley approached the Spanish ambassador with a proposal. He suggested that if Philip II were to approve and assist the marriage of Dudley and the queen, Elizabeth herself might look more favourably on reunion with Rome. On hearing of this manoeuvre Cecil reacted swiftly by discovering a popish conspiracy; he arrested and imprisoned several Catholic priests and gentry on suspicion of attending Mass. The public enthusiasm for his measures was so great that it sent an unmistakable message to Dudley that any proposals for a papal reconciliation would be rejected. 'I thought it necessary,' Cecil wrote, 'to dull the papists' expectations by discovering of certain Mass-mongers and punishing them.' A projected visit from the papal nuncio was refused.

It seems most unlikely that Elizabeth herself was party to Dudley's plan; she had more than enough wit and common sense to know that such a course would be foolish in the extreme. It was in fact in this period that she expressed her most vehement comments about the married state. The archbishop of Canterbury told Cecil that the queen had spoken with such 'bitterness of the holy estate of matrimony that I was in a horror to hear her'. The context may have been a proposal for the possibility of married clergy, but her wider purport is clear enough. 'I will have here but one mistress,' she declared, 'and no master!' In her married state she would be a queen; unmarried, she was both king and queen. When an ambassador from one of the German states referred to marriage as a 'desirable evil', she laughed. 'Desirable?' she asked him. She would rather be a beggar-woman and single than a queen and married.

A further complication had arisen over the succession. Lady Katherine Grey was a younger sister of the unfortunate Jane Grey;

as such she could be considered a legitimate heir to the throne if her cousin, Mary Stuart, was denied any claim. But in November 1560 she entered a clandestine marriage with Edward Seymour, son of the late Lord Protector Somerset. As possible heiress and lady of the privy chamber, she had a double duty to ask permission from the queen before any wedding could take place. In fact she had concealed her affair with Seymour, no doubt fearing that Elizabeth would prohibit any further contact. The queen was harsh in matters of the heart, let alone of the succession.

Her reaction, when the news inevitably reached her, was predictably furious. She consigned the young husband and wife to the Tower, to be detained indefinitely. When Katherine Grey gave birth to a son while in confinement, her anxieties increased; the possibility of a male heir materially weakened Elizabeth's position. She was determined to declare the infant as illegitimate, thus debarring him from the crown. In a display of alarming incompetence, Katherine Grey had in fact lost the marriage documents and had forgotten the name of the cleric who had married them; the one witness to the ceremony had recently died. Fate, or providence, was against her. The child was declared to be a bastard, and Katherine was taken from the Tower and placed under house arrest until her death seven years later. The queen herself believed that 'there had been great practices and purposes' behind this dynastic marriage, and it was rumoured by some that Katherine Grey and Edward Seymour were being set up as a possible alternative to her rule.

When Katherine Grey's younger sister, Mary, also married without official permission she was placed under house arrest; her husband was incarcerated for some years in the Fleet. The marriage was at the time a subject of ribaldry as well as consternation. Mary Grey was a dwarf who was 'crookbacked and very ugly' while her husband was 6 feet 8 inches in height and a commoner. They posed no true threat to the queen. Yet it was said at the time that she resented those natural pleasures of others which she denied to herself.

The Crown was indeed surrounded by cares, for once more Mary Stuart came back as a cause of alarm and anxiety. The death of Francis II in December 1560 left her a childless widow in a country which might not welcome her presence among rival factions at the court; her formidable mother-in-law Catherine de Medici, who had become regent of France during the minority of the ten-year-old Charles IX, had 'a great misliking' for Mary. Mary Stuart in turn dismissed the lady as no more than the daughter of a merchant. Yet the death of her husband had left the Scottish queen with little status and less authority. It was time to consider a return to her own realm where her position would be more assured.

The Catholic and Protestant parties of Scotland sent envoys to her, asking her to come again into her inheritance. The Catholics urged her to land on the north-east coast of the country where the house of Gordon, a family of ardent Catholics, would welcome her and accompany her to Edinburgh in triumph; the Protestants also wished her to return and come to some accommodation with their religion as a safeguard for the throne. It was clear, in any event, that she would receive an enthusiastic reception.

She sent her own envoy to the court of Elizabeth, asking her cousin for permission to land at an English port on her way to Scotland. The queen of England addressed him in a loud voice in a crowded assembly. She refused the request, adding that Mary should ask for no favours until she had signed the Treaty of Edinburgh in which her claim to the English throne was removed. 'Let your queen ratify the treaty,' she said, 'and she shall experience on my part, either by sea or by land, whatever can be expected from a queen, a relation and a neighbour.'

The English ambassador at Paris was then summoned for an audience with Mary. 'It will be thought strange,' she said, 'among all princes and countries, that she should first animate my subjects against me; and now that I am a widow, hinder my return to my own country.' She then made an indirect threat. 'I do not trouble her state or practise with her subjects; yet I know there be in her realm [some] that be inclined enough to hear offers.' The threat was followed by an insult. 'Your queen says I am young, and lack experience. I confess I am younger than she is.' Mary was then only nineteen, but already a practised exponent of sarcasm and innuendo. It was clear that there would be two queens in Albion. John Knox had occasion to meet Mary Stuart. 'If there be not in her', he said afterwards, 'a proud mind, a crafty wit, and an indurate heart against God and his truth, my judgement faileth me.'

She began her journey to Scotland on 15 August 1561. As her ship left the harbour at Calais, another vessel had fallen foul of the soundings and currents of the sea; it began to sink, with the loss of its passengers and crew. 'Good God!' Mary cried. 'What an omen for a voyage!' What an omen for a reign. On landing at Leith she and her party were dismayed by the poor state of the horses on which they were obliged to ride. Already she lamented the passing of the pomp and splendour of the French court. When she rested that night at the palace of Holyrood a crowd of some 500 Calvinists sang psalms outside her window. On the following morning they threatened her Catholic chaplain, whom they regarded as little more than a priest of Baal. 'Such', said the queen, 'is the beginning of welcome and allegiance from my subjects: what may be the end I know not, but I venture to foretell that it will be very bad.' These are the words, at least, that she is supposed to have used. There may be an element of hindsight, however, in even the best-conducted histories.

In the summer of 1561, just before Mary returned home, a great prodigy startled London. The medieval spire of St Paul's Cathedral stood 520 feet from the ground, and 260 feet from the tower; it was constructed out of wood and cased with lead, rising, as it might seem at the time, into the empyrean. On 4 June a thunder cloud descended over the city, rendering it as dark as night. At about two in the afternoon a lightning flash broke out from the depths of the cloud, and a streak of light touched the highest point of the cathedral. It seemed to pass but, early in the evening, a blue mist or smoke was seen to be curling around the ball. Within a minute the cross and the eagle at the summit of the spire crashed down through the roof and onto the floor of the south transept; the lead casing melted and ran down the tower, and soon enough the whole structure was in flames.

It was said that 'all London rushed to the churchyard' in consternation. The queen had seen the fire from the windows of her palace at Greenwich. Some sailors moored on the Thames and set up an impromptu line of water-buckets from the river;

they then climbed onto the roof with damp hides to suppress the flames. By midnight the fire was extinguished, leaving the cathedral as a blackened and roofless ruin. It was widely considered to be an omen, portending great changes in the affairs of men, but as ever it remained unclear. As for the cathedral itself, the tower was repaired but the spire was never rebuilt.

Some believed that conflagration was caused by papists, using gunpowder or employing the more elusive methods of magic. A commission of inquiry had already been set up in the spring of the year to investigate 'Mass-mongers and conjurors', and certain Catholic gentry were arrested for necromancy; various conjurors confessed to using black arts against the queen before they were paraded through the streets of London and placed in the pillory. So the isle was full of rumours. The prophecies of Nostradamus were invoked, and in 1562 twenty booksellers were fined for selling one of his prognostications. In that year, too, various other marvels were announced. The body of a child born with a ruff around its neck, and with hands 'like a toad's foot', was carried to the court. Pigs were born with the noses of men:

> The calves and pigs so strange
> With other more of such misshape,
> Declareth this world's change.

It was an unfortunate time, perhaps, for Elizabeth to fall sick. In the autumn of 1562, at the end of a letter, she added a postscript. 'My hot fever prevents me writing more.' She was at the time resting at the palace of Hampton Court. She took a bath to alleviate the effects of the fever, but instead she caught a chill and quickly succumbed to illness. She was in fact afflicted by the smallpox, from which it was likely that she might die. At a later date she recalled that 'death possessed almost every joint of me, so as I wished then that the feeble thread of life, which lasted (methought) too long, all too long, might by Clotho's hand have quietly been cut off'. (Clotho was one of the Fates who presided over human destiny.) Elizabeth lapsed into unconsciousness, 'without speech'.

Cecil had been summoned as soon as the queen fell ill, and was told that she might have only a few days to live. The members of the council were called down from London and met at all times of night and day to consider the calamity that was facing them. All the doubts and divisions of the nation now came to a head as they debated the matter of the succession. Mary Stuart was not to be thought of. There could be no second Catholic queen. Of all the candidates Lady Katherine Grey, still in disgrace after her clandestine marriage, was the most favoured. She was, at least, of the reformed faith.

When the fever had cooled sufficiently, the queen returned to consciousness. She believed that she was dying and, as the council crowded around her bed, she asked them to make Dudley the protector of the realm. She told them that she loved him dearly but, invoking God as her witness, declared that 'nothing unseemly' had ever taken place between them. Yet the crisis had passed; her native good health reasserted itself, and she remained among the living. The fact of her mortality, however, was now evident to all the nation and to the lady herself. In later years the queen never wished to be reminded of her illness.

28

The thirty-nine steps

The religion of England had always possessed a vital European aspect. At the beginning of the 1560s, for example, it bore a part in the wars of religion that divided France. In matters of faith no nation was an island. In the regency of Catherine de Medici the Catholics and the Huguenots vied for mastery, with the Guise family supporting the Catholics and the house of Bourbon allied with the Protestants. Catherine herself was obliged to maintain some kind of balance between them to preserve the unity of the kingdom. Into this uneasy struggle were in turn drawn the rulers of the other European states, Catholic and Protestant alike; among the former were the Holy Roman Emperor, Ferdinand I, and Philip II of Spain. Elizabeth could not stand apart. To have done so would look like weakness. The balance of the members of her council, who favoured the reformed religion, were also likely to support the Protestant cause.

Elizabeth, as always, vacillated. She never made a decision when one could be avoided. Procrastination was her policy in all the affairs of state. She was no friend to the Calvinist Huguenots, having hated the doctrines of Calvin in the shape of John Knox and *The First Blast of the Trumpet against the Monstrous Regiment of Women*; she had an aversion to spending her much needed money in European wars; she had far more cause to watch the affairs of

Mary Stuart in Scotland. In any case the prospect of a general religious war in Europe promised manifold perils. It could draw England itself into senseless slaughter. Rich prizes, on the other hand, might be won. One of her advisers wrote to her that 'it may chance in these garboyls [broils] some occasion may be offered as that again you may be brought into possession of Calais'. Still she remained irresolute. She sent an envoy to Catherine de Medici, promising her help in any mediation.

At the same time Mary Stuart was pressing for a meeting with her English cousin, in which she hoped that Elizabeth would recognize her claim to the throne. Elizabeth herself welcomed the opportunity of seeing her close relative and neighbouring queen. It might also help to pacify the House of Guise, to which Mary was allied through her marriage to the former French king, and promote a truce in France. Yet here, too, infinite dangers threatened. The council voted, without one dissenting voice, against any such interview between the two queens. They believed Mary to be a secret enemy, still pursuing the interests of the Catholic cause on behalf of France. The prospect of another Catholic queen of England was in any case too dreadful to consider.

Elizabeth persisted in her wish to meet the queen of Scots, and promised that she would receive her in Nottingham at the beginning of September 1562. Letters were sent to the authorities of that city, ordering them to prepare for the retinues of two sovereigns amounting to some 4,000 people. News now came, however, that Spanish troops were advancing towards the French border in order to assist the pretensions of the House of Guise. The Protestants might be overwhelmed; Elizabeth's offers of mediation were now worthless, and any meeting tactless in the extreme. So she cancelled the proposed encounter with Mary. On receiving this news the queen of Scots took to her bed for the whole day.

In desperation the leader of the Huguenot cause, the prince of Condé, appealed to Elizabeth for men and for money. He still controlled Normandy and, in return for her assistance, he promised her Le Havre and Dieppe as securities for the eventual restoration of Calais into English hands. She could no longer hesitate; her reluctance to help the Protestants was ruining her credit on the bourse at Antwerp. On 22 September a treaty was concluded with

Condé's legation at Hampton Court. The queen agreed to send 6,000 troops into France, while also granting a large loan. She wrote to Mary arguing that it was necessary 'to protect our own houses from destruction when those of our neighbours are on fire'. Need knows no law.

On 2 October an English force left Portsmouth for France and, two days later, had taken possession of Le Havre. This was to be the first step in the repossession of Calais. It is likely that the queen was more interested in that town than in the Protestant cause. Against her express orders a smaller force of English troops had also joined the Protestants in defence of Rouen. The affairs of war are, as she knew well enough, uncertain. Rouen was taken by the Catholic forces of the Guises, and its defenders put to the sword. A bloody battle at Dreux in north-west France, in which thousands were slain on either side, led to an uneasy interval. Catherine de Medici then arranged a truce between Catholics and Protestants, in which the prince of Condé was offered a moderate form of religious toleration. It seemed likely then that, in the saying of the time, the English interest was 'to be left out at the cart's tail'.

The English forces in Le Havre were defiant. They wanted 'to make the French cock cry cuck', and they promised the queen that 'the least molehill should not be lost without many bloody blows'. Condé and Guise now marched together against the ancient enemy, while Elizabeth railed against the prince as 'a treacherous inconstant perjured villain'. She insisted that Calais was given over to her before she would think of leaving Le Havre. She ordered her ships to sea, and a force was raised from the prisons of London; the thieves and highwaymen were enrolled as soldiers as a means of escaping the gallows.

Yet death came in other forms. A 'strange disease' broke out among the English garrison at Le Havre. In the heat of June it was soon known to be the plague. By the end of the month sixty men fell each day. The French besiegers had cut off water from the town; no fresh meat, or vegetables, could be obtained. By the beginning of July only 1,500 men were left, and French cannon were devastating the streets. The queen and council sent more and more men across the water, but they were wasted; the polluted and pestilential air was more lethal than the weaponry of the French.

The commander of the garrison, the earl of Warwick, came to terms with the enemy. Effectively he surrendered. Le Havre was returned to the French, and the remainder of the English were allowed to embark upon their ships.

It had been a disaster, but it was prelude to another calamity. The returning soldiers brought the plague to England with them. Throughout the rest of the summer 'the death' raged in the towns and villages through which they passed. The symptoms were those of fever; fits of shivering were followed by violent headaches, which in turn were succeeded by a great desire to sleep. The languor commonly resulted in death. In August the mortalities in London rose from 700 to 2,000 a week. Only when the heavy rains of November and December cleansed the streets was the epidemic eventually stilled.

The queen had learnt two harsh lessons from the disaster of Le Havre. It was not wise to rely upon the promises of princes. It was dangerous to meddle in wars not of her own choosing. In a subsequent treaty Elizabeth gave up all claim to Calais.

A parliament had been summoned at the beginning of 1563 to consider these great matters of state and, in particular, to finance what was then the ongoing French war. But the members of both Lords and Commons were more exercised over the problem of the succession; the recent illness of the queen only emphasized the precarious state of the nation in the event of her death. The debate was considered to be so important that Mary Stuart sent her own ambassador to observe the proceedings and to press her interests.

The Commons dilated on the perils of the single life. If no marriage was contemplated, or if no heir was chosen, the entire country was in a sense barren; this increased the risk of infinite mischiefs, among them civic conflict and foreign invasion. The queen answered their petition in a direct but not unambiguous speech in which she declared that she understood the dangers as well as, if not better than, they did. She had read of a philosopher whose custom was to recite the alphabet before applying his mind to a delicate problem (the same story was told of the emperor Augustus); in similar fashion she would wait and pray before making her deliberation. Yet 'I assure you all that though after my death you may have many step-dames, yet you shall never have a more natural mother than I mean to be unto you all'. This might be interpreted as the reply courteous.

To the petition sent by the Lords a few days later, she was more blunt. She had hoped that they would show more foresight than their colleagues in the Commons, where there were 'restless heads in whose brains the needless hammers beat with vain judgment'. She asserted that to declare a successor would lead to civil unrest and bloodshed. The marks on her face were not the wrinkles of old age but the scars of smallpox. In any case, like the mother of the Baptist, she might bear fruit in her advanced years. She was in fact only twenty-nine years old.

In a final address to both the Lords and Commons, read out by the lord chancellor, she admitted that she had not resolved *not* to marry. 'And if I can bend my liking to your need, I will not resist such a mind.' 'If' might prove only a very slender undertaking. She promised to consult the learned of the land, 'so shall I more gladly procure your good after my days than with my prayers whilst I live be mean to linger my living thread'. As a masterwork of obfuscation, this could mean anything or nothing.

She had also been asserting herself on another front. It is likely that William Cecil, and certain other members of the council, had been helping to promote the petitions of parliament. They could not be seen directly to intervene in its argument with the queen, but indirectly they could bring pressure to bear upon her. 'The matter is so deep,' Cecil wrote, 'I cannot reach into it. God send it a good issue!' Yet it was clearly his belief that parliament should consider and advise on the matter of the succession, even at the cost of diminishing the queen's prerogative.

It was also his belief that she should be guided, if not ruled, by the members of her council. She required wise, male advice in order to forward the godly rule of the nation. One of her councillors, Sir Francis Knollys, explained to her that she should set aside 'such affections and passions of your mind as happen to have dominion over you. So yet the resolutions digested by the deliberate consultations of your most faithful counsellors ought ever to be had in most price.' The council were the 'watchmen' or 'the fathers of the country'. Elizabeth could not have become a tyrant.

Yet she remained the mistress of her parliament. Her immediate predecessor had called five parliaments in four years, but in the first thirty years of her reign she summoned it only seven times. 'It is in me and my power,' she once told the Speaker, 'to call parliaments: it is my power to end and determine the same: it is in my power to assent or dissent to anything done in parliaments.' The legislation came from the council, or was introduced into parliament at the express wish or with the connivance of the council. Her ministers, such as Knollys and Hatton, sat among the Commons. The Speaker himself was chosen by the sovereign as an instrument of her rule. Occasions of restlessness and discontent of course emerged in the course of the long reign, but in general she managed to curb them with gracious speeches, politic negotiations, or the selective imprisonment of recalcitrant members. In the battle of wits she was never defeated.

The question of 'free speech' was raised but never resolved, and the confusions attendant upon it were resurrected in the next reign. In general parliament was considered to be an extension of royal government, on the supposition that the source of all law, according to one political philosopher, 'standeth in diverse statutes made by the king, the Lords and the Commons'.

In 1563 Cecil also drafted a succession bill in which he advised that, in the event of the queen's death without an heir, the authority of government would pass for the immediate future to the privy council. For a time England would become an oligarchy or aristocratic republic not unlike that of Venice. Cecil proposed that it would then become the responsibility of parliament to elect a new monarch. The idea of an hereditary elected monarchy was new and startling; it was a denial of the whole structure and spirit of the Tudor dynasty. It was of course a measure of Cecil's anxiety and frustration that he was forced to this expedient. Yet the bill itself was never put forward for discussion. If Elizabeth had seen it she would undoubtedly have quashed it; Cecil may have realized that he had overreached himself.

Parliament passed two bills of more than usual significance. Among the measures proposed by the Statute of Artificers was the concept of a minimum wage to be assessed by the local justices of the peace. Workmen were to be hired on a yearly contract.

Apprentices were to follow the custom of London and serve for seven years. All able-bodied men could be compelled to work in the fields at the time of harvest. It may have been a provisional device, designed to meet the needs of the moment, but this adventitious and only loosely coherent statute remained in force for the next 250 years.

Another Act considered the problem of 'sturdy beggars' and of the unemployed. It was further decreed that each parish must support the 'impotent, aged and needy' out of communal funds. The relief of the poor was no longer the preserve of the Church, as had been the custom of many centuries, but had become a local and secular matter. Gifts to the poor had been called 'donations' and the food spared from the rich man's table had been known as 'Our Lady's bread'; they had of course disappeared. The dissolution of the religious houses, in the reign of Henry VIII, may also have prompted the search for fresh remedies.

We might say in general that the Reformation created a wider space in which the lay authorities could regulate and control the nation at large. The first workhouse in England, Bridewell, was established in 1553; a workhouse was set up in Exeter in 1579. The authorities of London had already established five 'hospitals' that took over from their medieval spiritual equivalents. The hospitals of St Thomas and St Bartholomew were designed for the sick and for the old; they exist still. Christ's Hospital sheltered orphan children, while Bedlam served the insane. An Act of 1572 instituted the first local Poor Law tax. Other Acts and statutes followed. Not until the close of the sixteenth century, however, did the term 'state' emerge with its modern connotations.

It can be said with some confidence, therefore, that these two Acts were signal measures in the social and economic construction of English society. Yet the measures of parliament were not meant to be benevolent but were, rather, strict and authoritarian. The penalties for vagabondage, for example, were increased. The ordinary vagrants were to be whipped and then imprisoned until a master could be found for them; the dangerous among them were to be banished from the realm and, if ever they returned, consigned to the gallows or the galleys.

In 1563 the convocation of the bishops and senior clergy met, as usual, in conjunction with parliament. Since this was the first convocation called since the re-establishment of the reformed faith, it was considered important to frame suitable legislation on behalf of the Church. A document entitled 'General Notes of Matters to be Moved by the Clergy in the Next Parliament and Synod' expressed the desire for a 'certain form of doctrine to be conceived in articles'. The grounds of the English faith were to be defined.

So, by a process of consultation and debate, the Thirty-Nine Articles of Religion were compiled. Some of them were not drawn up in time for parliament to pass the necessary legislation, and had to wait for the assembly called three years later; the document itself only became the official doctrine of faith in 1571. But the essential work had now been done. The convocation of 1563 established the most important doctrinal statement in the history of the Church of England and, in its essential form, it remains in force to this day. The language of the liturgy must be in the vernacular; the Mass is not to be allowed, and adoration of the Eucharist is blasphemy; the papist doctrines of transubstantiation and purgatory are denied; there is to be no invocation of the saints. The monarch's role, as the supreme head of the Church, is emphasized.

The full measure of the Thirty-Nine Articles has been deemed to be moderately Calvinist in tone, but there is not one article that is incompatible either with Lutheranism or with Calvinism. The articles represent as wide a definition of the reformed faith as was possible in the sixteenth century. They were believed to be the thirty-nine steps towards broad domestic agreement. The more precise reformers were not necessarily happy with the outcome, and in the course of time they would become identified as the 'Puritan' tendency. 'I confess,' the bishop of Durham wrote, 'we suffer many things against our hearts; but we cannot take them away, though we were ever so much set upon it. We are under authority; and we can innovate nothing without the queen; nor can we alter the laws; the only thing left to our choice is whether we will bear these things, or break the peace of the Church.' These words can be seen as a harbinger of later divisions.

The religion of the vast majority of people must have been mixed and variable, neither wholly old nor completely new. The reformed faith was a recent development, while the Catholic religion was a long time dying. It was estimated by two contemporaries that at the time of the queen's accession only 1 per cent of the population was actively and determinedly Protestant in inclination. In 1561 a professor of divinity at Oxford, Nicholas Sander, drew up a document entitled 'How the Common People of England are disposed, with regard to the Catholic faith' in which he declared that 'the farmers and shepherds are Catholic'; they of course represented a large proportion of the people. He said that the artisans did not accept the reformed faith 'except those engaged in sedentary tasks, weavers, for example, and cobblers'. Of the overwhelmingly Catholic areas he named Wales, Devon, Cumberland, Northumberland and Westmorland. In time, over the next few decades, the doctrines of Protestantism were better received in Kent, Essex, Suffolk, Norfolk, Sussex and of course London.

In the summer of 1561 the bishop of Carlisle reported that in many of the churches of his diocese the Mass was still being said with the connivance of the local lord. In the same summer the justices of Hereford commanded the observance of St Lawrence's Day as a holy day or holiday; no butcher sold meat, and no trader dared open his shop, on that day. A party of recusant priests was welcomed in Devonshire and they were so 'feasted and magnified, as Christ himself could not have been more reverentially entertained'. The bishop of Winchester complained that his people were 'obstinately grovelled in superstition and popery, lacking not priests to inculcate the same daily in their heads'. Among the city council of Hereford there was 'not one favourable to this [reformed] religion'. Only six practised it in Ludlow. As late as 1567, seventeen churches in East Yorkshire still possessed Catholic fittings, while seven years later more than a dozen churches in Northamptonshire contained the rood lofts that had been forbidden. In the course of this reign seventy-five recusant priests were active in Lancashire, and one hundred more in Yorkshire.

Yet if the majority of the population were still inclined to the old faith, few of them were willing to disobey the authorities by openly practising it, at least in London and the south-east of England. Some averred that if by going to Protestant worship they sinned, then the sin would redound upon the queen. As long as they attended church once a week and followed the newly proclaimed rites of the reformed faith, they were free to believe what they wished. They may have believed anything or nothing. It was easier, and safer, to serve and obey rather than to rebel.

That is why the reformed services were rendered elastic, if not ambiguous, by openly proposing only what all Christians agreed in believing; the rubric and ceremonial could be subtly changed to match the inclinations of the congregation. Thus Cecil was informed of the multiplicity of worship in 1564 so that 'some perform divine service and prayers in the chancel; others in the body of the church ... some keep precisely to the order of the book, some intermix psalms in metre ... some receive the communion kneeling, others standing; some baptize in a font, some in a basin; some sign with the sign of the cross, others not'.

Confusion also reigned in the wardrobe, with 'some ministers in a surplice, some without; some with a square cap, some with a round cap, some in a button cap, and some in a round hat; some in scholar's clothes, and some in others'. Many complaints were made about inattention, and token worship, in the churches. With the interiors stripped bare of their former ornamentation, there was nothing to look at. The alehouses were reported to be full on Sundays, and the people would prefer to go to a bear-baiting than to attend divine service. With the great rituals gone there were many who, in the words of one cleric, 'love a pot of ale better than a pulpit and a corn-rick better than a church door; who, coming to divine service more for fashion than devotion, are contented after a little capping and kneeling, coughing and spitting' to sing a psalm or slumber during the sermon. There was also a shortage of reformed ministers, with only 7,000 ordained clergy for 9,000 livings.

It would be unwise, however, to exaggerate the fervency of the Catholic cause. The Venetian ambassador, some eighteen months even before the accession of Elizabeth, had suspected that very few of those under the age of thirty-five were truly Catholic. They did not espouse the new faith but they had lost interest in the old. They had become what one Benedictine called 'neutrals in religion'. We must suspect, therefore, a very high level of indifference. A man or woman of that age would hardly remember a time when the monarch was not head of the Church, yet such a fact was not likely to inspire devotion.

To indifference might be added uncertainty and confusion. The bishop of Salisbury, preaching before the queen herself, lamented that 'the poor people lieth forsaken, and left as it were sheep without a guide ... they are commanded to change their religion, and for lack of instruction they know not whither to turn them: they know not neither what they leave nor what they should receive'. Many were simply ignorant. When an old man was told that he would be saved through Christ he replied, 'I think I heard of that man you spake of once in a play at Kendal called Corpus Christi play, where there was a man on a tree and blood ran down.'

Some, however, knew precisely what they were supposed to believe. As late as 1572 an anonymous chronicler stated that, outside London, fewer than one in forty were 'good and devout gospellers'. This small and fervent minority, however, was greatly encouraged by the publication of *Foxe's Book of Martyrs* in the spring of 1563. It offered a vivid and in many respects horrifying account of those who had burned for their new faith in the previous reign of Mary. Foxe described the plight of a woman, for example, who gave birth while being consumed by flame in Guernsey; the newborn babe was tossed into the fire with its mother. This was once widely dismissed as a fabrication, but other contemporary documents suggest that it did take place as Foxe described. The book's woodcuts were in themselves a tour de force of hagiography. The work furnished a new litany of saints for a nation that was bereft of them.

Foxe also created a new history of the Reformation in which the English Church had restored the 'old ancient church of Christ' that had been all the time concealed within the Roman communion. 'The time of Antichrist', beginning in approximately AD 1100, had at last been purged. He declared that 'because God hath so placed us Englishmen here in one commonwealth, also in one church, as in one ship together, let us not mangle or divide the ship'. In this period the commonwealth had connotations of the body politic and the general good; it was the vision of a community that transcended self-interest and the bitterness of faction, with an idealized and productive union between all of the estates of the realm. The aim was a 'godly commonwealth'.

The English were once more an elect nation. By creating a

Protestant historiography Fox had effectively given form and meaning to the newly established religion. The book went through five editions in the reign of Elizabeth and became, after the Bible, the most popular and indispensable of all books of faith. Eventually the order came that it should be placed in every parish church alongside the *Paraphrases* of Erasmus.

Many of the more avid reformers were dissatisfied with the settlement of religion and waited for a day when further reforms were implemented. One of them, the dean of Wells Cathedral, trained his dog to snatch off the papistical square caps from any conforming clerics who chose to wear them. In the 1560s these radicals still formed part of the restless and dissatisfied Elizabethan Church, but they were already beginning to assert their identity. It was in this period, for example, that the Puritan movement began to be distinguished from the broader Church. One hundred London clergymen had been convoked at Lambeth where a clergyman was paraded before them in the orthodox dress of four-cornered cap, tippet and scholar's gown. When asked if they would wear the same dress, they were dismayed. 'Great', says one observer, 'was the anguish and distress of those ministers.' They exclaimed: 'We shall be killed in our souls for this pollution!' Eventually sixty-one agreed to don the vestments, and the other thirty-nine were suspended from their duties and given three months to conform.

Other measures were now taken, at the queen's command, against the stricter Protestants. No licence to perform divine service would be given to anyone who refused to sign a declaration of conformity. As a result many godly preachers retired into private life as lawyers or even doctors; some migrated to the more welcoming air of Scotland, or travelled once more overseas to Zurich or to Geneva. A number of pamphlets and books of sermons espousing the Puritan cause prompted an injunction from the Star Chamber forbidding, on pain of three months' imprisonment, the publication of any treatise 'against the queen's injunctions'.

The radical sectarians, believing themselves to be persecuted, clung more tightly together. They adopted the book of service used by the Calvinists at Geneva as their model, discarding the conventional English liturgy used by what they called 'the traditioners'. They were especially active in London. John Stow wrote, in 1567, that 'a group who called themselves puritans or unspotted lambs of the lord . . . kept their church in the Minories without Aldgate'. At various times the godly met on a lighter in St Katherine's Pool, in Pudding Lane, and in a goldsmith's house along the Strand.

They entertained various opinions on such matters as baptism and predestination but they were united in their fervour for preaching and for the propagation of the Word; they stressed the paramount importance of Scripture; they detested the relics of popery still present within the established religion, and pressed hard for the sanctity of the Sabbath while denouncing the general licentiousness of the age. The essence lay in individual faith mediated by grace and not by any priest. It might be said that the godly emphasized a spiritual, while the traditionalists preferred a visible, Church.

In June 1567 a group of the godly hired Plumbers' Hall in Chequer Yard, London, ostensibly to celebrate a wedding; in reality they wished to enjoy a day of sermons and of prayers. Word of their plans had reached the city authorities; they were surrounded and some of them were arrested by the sheriffs and taken before the bishop of London. Twenty-four were committed to prison, where they remained for some time. Here perhaps we may glimpse the origin of those religious quarrels that were eventually to divide the nation.

The godly had supporters among the highest in the land. Many of the bishops were naturally sympathetic to their cause. The earl of Leicester was only the most prominent among the nobles who supported the radical reformers; William Cecil was believed to be of the same party, together with other of the queen's councillors. At the university of Cambridge, too, a prominent group of Puritans began to gather. The queen herself was unmoved. She did not intend to impose orthodoxy, but she demanded conformity. In this, she believed, the peace of the realm consisted. She would not be pushed into doctrinal reform. She did not relish religious change of any kind.

Others were equally sanguine. In *The Apology of the Church of England* John Jewel, bishop of Salisbury, declared in 1562 that 'we are come as near as we possibly could to the ancient apostolic faith'. He rested this trust upon the fact that 'we have searched out of the Holy Bible, which we are sure cannot deceive, our sure form of religion'. These modest reformers believed that they had recovered an ancient truth long lost in the quagmire of popery. Slowly, in the course of this reign, Protestantism became the acquired faith of the majority of the people; they may have conformed out of fear or indifference, but that conformity became by degrees the traditional religion of England. Within a few years none had known any other form of worship. This uniquely monarchical Church was at the turn of the century given the name of Anglican, the product of England.

There was a further reformation for which the queen and her council can claim a certain credit, the reformation of money. Elizabeth called in the debased coin and reduced the quantity of cheap metal used in minting it; for the first time in many years the worth of the coin was now equivalent to its face value. The queen had reversed the decline that had begun in her father's reign, and such was the achievement that it was commemorated on her tomb. In her epitaph it is listed as her third greatest success after the religious settlement and the maintenance of peace. Piety, peace and prosperity were not to be separated.

29

The rivals

The queens of Scotland and of England were still single, and that unusual state presented complications to both women. Mary Stuart was now actively seeking a French or Spanish match; it was rumoured that she might marry Don Carlos, the son of the Spanish king, or even her brother-in-law, Charles IX of France. The power of her country would thereby be redoubled and the threat to her neighbour increased. In an extraordinary act of audacity Elizabeth suggested to the Scottish commissioners at her court that their queen might consider marriage to her own earlier suitor, Robert Dudley; it was even proposed that the two queens might then share a household, with Elizabeth providing the funds. Mary considered the offer for a moment, as another way to the English throne, but she was never really prepared to take up that which Elizabeth had cast off. She was happy to appease her rival with vague promises, but in reality she was looking for a foreign prince.

This led Elizabeth in turn to revisit the question of her own marriage. Once more the prospects of Archduke Charles of Austria were revived, and at the beginning of 1564 she wrote to the Habsburg court that 'she was ever in courtesy bound to make that choice so as should be for the best of her state and subjects'. She had taken the words of parliament to heart. The great difficulty lay, however, with the archduke's religion; he was a devout Roman

Catholic who would brook no impediment to the practice of his faith. Robert Dudley was created earl of Leicester in the autumn of 1564 but his new status did not materially assist his suit. He was still the great favourite of the queen, her true knight 'without fear and without reproach'. At the ceremony itself, in which Dudley received the honour, it was noted by the Scottish ambassador that 'she could not refrain from putting her hand in his neck to tickle him'. If the queen should take a husband, however, this intimacy would of course be severely curtailed.

So he seems to have determined to thwart the queen's possible alliance with the archduke. He intrigued with the French to put forward the young Charles IX, but the disparity in age between the fourteen-year-old boy and the thirty-one-year-old woman would have caused only ridicule and disquiet. She said that it would take only a few years for him to desert her, leaving her a discontented old woman. When the Spanish ambassador asked her if she was about to marry the French king, she 'half hid her face and laughed'.

On the failure of this plan Leicester objected to the archduke on the grounds of his religion, and it is perhaps no coincidence that in this period he emerged as the protector of the true Protestant faith; he supported 'godly' ministers, for example, in their remonstrance against the papistical elements of the Book of Common Prayer. In his stance against the marriage he was opposed by Cecil as well as the duke of Norfolk and the earl of Sussex; Sussex himself had travelled to Vienna in order to expedite the union. So there was a division at the heart of the court and of the queen's council. The retainers of Sussex and of Leicester carried arms 'as if to try their utmost'; the Sussex party wore yellow ribbons while the supporters of Leicester sported purple. The queen ordered them 'not to meddle with' one another and to lay down their weapons. Nevertheless, Leicester continued to gather 'great bands of men with swords and bucklers'. There came a point when the two great nobles exchanged 'hard words and challenges to fight', at which point the queen ordered them to ride together through the streets of London in a show of amity. Sussex was eventually created lord president of the council of the north, thus removing him to York. The fracas is a reminder, however, of the tensions between the great nobles that had been so prominent in previous centuries.

The court was still in part a medieval institution. It is probable, too, that the presence of a female queen encouraged the greater nobles around her to assert their masculine power; they were still warlords but they were also in a sense putative lovers competing for her favour.

The negotiations between the courts of London and Vienna continued at a painfully slow pace; but the delays and disputes over religion were acceptable to Elizabeth if they deferred any final decision. It meant also that she was still on conciliatory terms with both branches of the Habsburg empire, represented by Philip II of Spain and the new emperor Maximilian II. Philip himself was assured of her suitability as a bride to his cousin; his ambassador bought information from the queen's laundresses about her menstrual cycle.

At this time, too, attempts were made to standardize her painted image. At the end of 1563 William Cecil had drafted a proclamation which criticized the depiction of the queen 'in painting, graving and printing'; these unflattering or unsophisticated portraits provoked 'complaints among her loving subjects'. It had been decided that 'some cunning [skilful] person' would create a great original on which all other portraits might be modelled. Since portraits were also often used in marriage negotiations, the queen might have desired a more perfect image. In this decade, too, she began to entertain hopes of an alchemical elixir of life that would maintain her youth and beauty; William Cecil noted in his diary that Cornelius Lanoy, a Dutchman, 'was committed to the Tower for abusing the queen's majesty, in promising to make the elixir'.

Yet her negotiations with the Habsburgs were overshadowed by the devices of Mary Stuart. The Scottish queen's attention had turned to a young man, Henry Stuart, Lord Darnley; he had been born in Leeds, but his father was the fourth earl of Lennox, a prominent Scottish nobleman who had been forced into exile by a rival faction. Yet more pertinently Darnley was the grandson of Margaret Tudor, the sister of Henry VIII, and cousin to Mary Stuart herself. On the Scottish side, he was directly descended from James II. Any alliance with him would immensely strengthen Mary Stuart's claim to the throne after the death of Elizabeth. Darnley was also a Catholic, and the clergy of the Scottish kirk feared above all else the renewed prospect of Catholic supremacy. The young man was given a passport to visit Scotland, where of course he paid his respects to his cousin the queen. She saw him 'running at the ring', a chivalric game for horsemen, and soon enough they became inseparable. Mary had become genuinely infatuated with him, almost at first sight. She was in many respects quixotic and impulsive, relying upon her instinct rather than her judgement; she did not have her rival's gift of calculation.

In the course of these marital games the Scottish ambassador, Sir James Melville, was obliged to haunt the court of Elizabeth in search of information or gossip. In his memoirs, written in the early years of the seventeenth century, he left certain vignettes concerning the conversation and behaviour of the queen that throw an interesting light upon her character. She discussed with him the female costume of different countries, and told him that she possessed the 'weeds' of every civilized country. She proved the point by wearing a fresh set of clothes every day.

She asked him 'what coloured hair was reputed best, and whether my queen's hair or hers was the best, and which of the two was the fairest'? He replied, in the manner of the Sibylline oracle, that 'the fairness of both was not their worst fault'. She pressed for a more direct response. 'You are the fairest queen in England and ours the fairest queen in Scotland.' Still she was not satisfied with his answer. He was obliged to make a judgement. 'You are both the fairest ladies in your courts; you are the whitest, but our queen is very lovely.'

'Which of us,' she now asked him, 'is of the highest stature?'

'Our queen.'

'Then she is over high, for I am neither too high nor too low.'

When Elizabeth asked him about Mary's pastimes, he told her that his mistress liked sometimes to play on the lute or virginals. She then asked him whether the Scottish queen played well.

'Reasonably well,' he replied, 'for a queen.'

There then followed a contrived piece of showmanship. After dinner the queen's cousin, Lord Hunsdon, invited Melville to a retired gallery where he promised him some enchanting music. He whispered, as if imparting a secret, that it was 'the queen playing on her virginals'. The ambassador listened for a moment and then very boldly put aside a tapestry that hung before the doorway of a recess, to see the great queen at her virginals. Her back was to him but she turned her head and seemed surprised to find him there; she rose from her instrument, affecting embarrassment and alleging that 'she used not to play before men, but when she was solitary, to eschew melancholy, and asked "How I came there?"'

Melville replied that he had been drawn by the sweetest melody, which gracious answer pleased the queen. She sat down upon a cushion, while he knelt. She then provided him with a cushion to place beneath his knee. It was a breach of etiquette but the queen insisted. She demanded to know 'whether she or the Queen of Scots played best?' Melville gave the palm to her. She then spoke to him in French, Italian and Dutch as a sign of her proficiency.

Two days later she decided that the ambassador must see her dance. At the end of the performance she once again wished to know which queen danced best. He replied that 'my queen danced not so high or disposedly as she did'. By this he meant that Elizabeth's dancing was more mannered and deliberate than that of Mary.

It is not at all clear that Melville's recollections are always accurate. Yet he is surely right to have emphasized the implicit rivalry or jealousy between the two queens. When he returned to his native country, Mary asked him if he believed that Elizabeth's words of affection for her were genuine. He replied that 'in my judgement there was neither plain dealing nor upright meaning, but great dissimulation, emulation and fear that [Mary's] princely qualities should over soon chase her out and displace her from the kingdom'.

In the early spring of 1565 Mary was so enamoured of Darnley that she helped to nurse him through an attack of measles that may in fact have been a manifestation of syphilis. An English envoy wrote to Elizabeth that 'The matter is irrevocable. I do find this Queen so captivate either by love or cunning – or rather to say truly by boasting and folly – that she is not able to keep promise with herself, and therefore not able to keep promise with your Majesty in these matters.' Her desire and wilfulness had outrun her discretion. Darnley was twenty, and she three years his senior.

By May they had made a secret engagement and, in July, they

were married without waiting for the papal dispensation from Rome allowing the first cousins to unite. She then proclaimed him king of Scotland without asking the advice of her parliament. She had married in haste, but she would soon repent it. Darnley was as vain as he was unbalanced; he was arrogant and dissolute; he was weak-willed; within a short time he had managed to offend most of the Scottish nobility. 'The bruits here are wonderful,' the English envoy wrote at the time, 'men's talk very strange, the hatred towards Lord Darnley and his house marvellous great, his pride intolerable, his words not to be borne . . .' He added that in token of his 'manhood' Darnley is eager to 'let blows fly where he knows they will be taken'. He was, in other words, an egregious bully.

The young queen was herself no stranger to conflict. Her illegitimate half-brother, James Stuart, first earl of Moray, espoused the Protestant cause and sought to lead a group of rebels against her. Mary summoned 5,000 of her supporters, and from summer to autumn of 1565 mercilessly harried her enemies in a series of skirmishes that became known as the Chaseabout Raid. 'I defy them,' she said, 'what can they do, and what dare they do?' She rode fast and furiously; she wore a steel helmet and carried a brace of pistols at her side. Eventually she chased her half-brother over the border into England, and in her triumph declared that she could lead her troops to the walls of London. She was a formidable opponent.

The marriage of the two Catholics posed an immediate problem for the English queen and her council. It seemed that their union was a plain hint of their right to the succession of the English throne. The Catholics of England would consider them to be their natural and proper leaders. If the young couple also produced a son and heir, which seemed most likely, an already complicated situation would become infinitely worse. In the face of Elizabeth's refusal to marry, many other of her subjects were also prepared to countenance Mary and Darnley as the least bad alternative to a virgin queen. One day in the spring of this year the French ambassador had come upon Elizabeth playing chess.

'Madam, you have before you the game of life. You lose a pawn; it seems a small matter; but with the pawn you lose the game.'

'I see your meaning. Lord Darnley is but a pawn, but unless I look to it I shall be check-mated.'

Another reported conversation can be added to this account. Mary Stuart was discussing with some courtiers a portrait of the queen of England and debating whether it resembled the great original. 'No,' said Mary, 'it is not like her. For I am queen of England.'

The members of the council discussed the matter endlessly. They even prepared for war, but in the end nothing was done. Elizabeth declared that Mary 'doth look for my death'. In this period the queen of England became seriously ill with a fever commonly known as 'the flux'. The strain of her perilous situation, perhaps, was beginning to affect her.

Yet by the end of the year it was apparent that all was not well with the marriage of Mary and Darnley. She had expected him to be pliant and tractable; instead he revealed himself to be foolish and obstinate. He carried himself like a king in role as well as name, and therefore became intolerable. Mary would not allow anyone to usurp her place, and by degrees began to demote him. He was now known as 'the queen's husband' rather than king, and he was forbidden the use of the royal arms. He was drinking excessively and, when she once tried to remonstrate with him, he 'gave her such words as she left the place in tears'. His demand for the matrimonial crown was refused. 'I know for certain', an English agent at the Scottish court wrote, 'that this queen repents her marriage – that she hates him and all his kin.'

A further complication arose in the shape of Mary's Italian secretary, David Rizzio or Riccio, a gentleman of charming and persuasive manners. He was an accomplished musician who enchanted her with love-songs; he soon became her closest adviser and confidant. It was he, perhaps, who counselled the queen to maintain a distance from Darnley. He had also offended many Scottish nobles, perhaps on the sole grounds that he was a foreigner who had more influence with the queen than did they. As a Catholic, too, he was cause of offence to the Protestant nobility. Those who had been chased out of Scotland by Mary, with the earl of Moray at their head, were seeking revenge.

They decided to enlist the help of Darnley; he was, at least, of

Scottish stock. They informed him that Rizzio was the sole cause of his decline in influence, and that the secretary had 'done him the most dishonour that can be to any man'. He entered a bond of association with them where, in exchange for his support and assistance in the murder of Rizzio, they would assert his claim to the throne. In particular Moray and his followers were to be pardoned for their rebellion of the previous year. After the murder Mary was to be consigned to Stirling Castle; the queen was in fact already six months pregnant, but the noblemen seem to have convinced Darnley that the child was fathered by Rizzio.

On the evening of Saturday 9 March 1566 Mary was entertaining Rizzio and some other friends in a small room next to her bedchamber in the royal palace of Holyrood; just after they had assembled Darnley led his fellow conspirators into the presence of the shocked company by means of his private staircase. When they thrust the queen aside and laid hands on Rizzio he cried out 'Justice! Justice! Save me, my lady!' He tried to cling to Mary's skirts but the men dragged him away and hustled him into an adjoining room, where he was dispatched with fifty-six dagger wounds. His body was then dragged down a staircase and left at its foot.

When Mary asked her husband why he had committed this crime he repeated the slander that Rizzio 'had more company of her body' than he did. She stayed in her private chambers for the next few hours but, within a short time, had managed to convince Darnley that he would be the next victim of the nobles. She had divined their malevolent intent very well. They had planned all along to lay the blame for Rizzio's murder on Darnley alone, and to inform the queen that her husband had decided to commit the murder in front of her; he wished to disable her and perhaps the unborn child.

Darnley was by now thoroughly alarmed, and at midnight on 11 March he and Mary left the palace by means of the servants' quarters and fled on horseback to Dunbar. The other nobles, deserted by Darnley, dispersed; many of them took shelter across the border in Berwick. Mary returned in triumph to Edinburgh where she meditated vengeance on her feckless and unstable husband. But revenge would have to wait upon the birth of her child.

That child was itself the subject of whispered report; it was claimed by some that Rizzio was the real father. The somewhat unattractive features of James VI of Scotland, who was to become James I of England, were enough to guarantee the longevity of such rumours.

Elizabeth was shocked at the outrage of murder committed in the presence of a reigning queen. 'Had I been in Queen Mary's place,' she told the Spanish ambassador, 'I would have taken my husband's dagger and stabbed him with it.' As she was at the same time negotiating a marriage with the archduke Charles with the connivance of the Spanish, she hastened to add that she would not take any such action against *him*.

In the early summer of the year Mary Stuart gave birth to a son. A messenger arrived at the palace of Greenwich in the course of a grand party; he went up to Cecil and whispered in his ear. Then Cecil went over to his mistress. She is reported to have slumped into a chair and told those around her that 'The queen of Scots is lighter of a fair son, and I am but a barren stock.' The party came to an end. This at least is the story of Melville's *Memoirs*. As Thomas Fuller once observed, 'when men's memories do arise, it is time for History to haste abed'. But if the queen's words have been improved in the telling, they perfectly suit the situation.

Only two months earlier Elizabeth had fallen sick of a strange disease and had grown so thin that 'her bones may be counted'. It was whispered that she might be consumptive. 'Her Majesty', Cecil wrote to the English envoy in France, 'suddenly sick in the stomach and suddenly relieved by a vomit. You must think such a matter would drive men to the end of their wits, but God is the stay of all that put their trust in Him.' Despite the confident and indeed imperious demeanour of the queen, her first years of rule were undermined by a constant note of insecurity and danger.

Yet she recovered and in the late summer of 1566 went on a progress to Oxford, stopping off at Woodstock, where she had been held prisoner during the reign of her sister. The dons came to meet her before she came into the town, calling out '*Vivat regina!*' She gave them thanks in Latin. Then she listened to a loyal address in Greek before replying to that oration in the same ancient tongue. She was as learned as any Oxford scholar.

Her arrival at the university was the occasion for further orations and sermons, public lectures and public disputations, plays and debates. While she watched one drama, *Palamon and Arcite*, the stage collapsed; three people were killed and five were injured. She sent her own barber-surgeon to care for the afflicted, but then laughed heartily when the performance was resumed. She also expressed her instinctive dislike for the more doctrinaire reformers. On meeting one noted sectarian, of Puritan persuasion, she remarked 'Mr Doctor, that loose gown becomes you mighty well. I marvel that you are so strait-laced in this point [of religion] but I come not now to chide.' He had made the mistake of praying, in public, that the queen would allow further change within the Church. This was a subject on which her mind was closed. At the end of her visit she made another speech in Latin, on the dignity and worth of learning, and her litter was accompanied for 2 miles by a body of scholars and local worthies.

The birth of James Stuart had alarmed Elizabeth, since the prospect of an heir materially increased Mary's following in England. The Scottish ambassador in England told his mistress that many shires were ready to rebel and that the nobility had named the captains of the enterprise. Elizabeth's envoy wrote to Cecil from the French court that 'both the pope's and the king of Spain's hands be in that dish further and deeper than I think you know . . . I have cause to say to you *vigilate!*' The ambassador was acute. Six months later Philip II wrote to the Vatican that the time would soon come 'to throw off the mask and bestir ourselves'. He and the pope must consider the way in which they could assist Mary Stuart and promote the cause of God; the queen of Scots was the 'gate by which religion must enter the realm of England'.

It is probable, then, that Cecil helped to orchestrate the pressure placed upon Elizabeth by the parliament of 1566. He left a paper, or memorial to himself, in which he wrote that 'to require both marriage and the stabilizing of the succession is the uttermost that can be desired'. Parliament assembled in the autumn of that year, unaltered since the last meeting of 1563; it had then been prorogued rather than dissolved. The clamour for the queen's marriage had become more intense during the interval, and it was rumoured that the Commons would refuse to vote her 'supplies', or finances, unless she revealed her commitment to matrimony or at least named her successor. The debate went on for two mornings, in the course of which several members traded blows. The Lords then agreed to join the Commons in a petition to her.

Elizabeth was furious with her councillors, who were suspected of collusion. She vented her anger first on the duke of Norfolk and, when another councillor tried to defend him, she said that he spoke like a swaggering soldier. Then she turned upon Leicester, her favourite. She accused him of abandoning her. He swore that he was ready to die at her feet. What, she asked him, has that to do with the matter? Before venting some further insults on those present, she left the room. Of the Commons she was disdainful. She told the Spanish ambassador that she did not know what those 'devils' wanted.

She summoned a delegation of fifty-seven members of the Lords and Commons to Whitehall, and forbade the presence of the Speaker. It was only the queen who would talk. They presented her with a petition in which they expressed their wish that she marry 'where it should please her, with whom it should please her, and as soon as it should please her'. She opened her harangue by accusing 'unbridled persons in the Commons' of contriving a 'traitorous trick'. Then she accused the Lords of supporting them. 'Whom have I oppressed?' she asked them. 'Whom have I enriched to other's harm?' But then she turned to the subject. 'I have sent word that I will marry, and I will never break the word of a prince said in a public place, for my honour's sake.' A prince's honour is of course a flexible commodity. There then followed what might be called an Elizabethan moment. 'I am your anointed queen,' she told them. 'I will never be constrained to do anything. I thank God I am endued with such qualities that if I were turned out of the realm in my petticoats I were able to live in any place in Christendom.'

Cecil read an edited version of her speech to the Commons in their chamber, and he was greeted with silence. The members were not impressed, and almost at once further calls for a petition on the marriage were being heard. The queen demanded to see the Speaker and commanded him to instruct parliament that 'there should be no further talk of the matter'. When they remonstrated with her on the infringement of their 'lawful liberties' she wisely yielded. But it was in no sense a triumph. At the end of the session, in January 1567, Elizabeth rose from the throne and made her concluding speech. It was already dusk. 'I have in this assembly', she said, 'found such dissimulation where I always professed plainness that I marvel thereat; yea, two faces under one hood, and the body rotten.' She finished her peroration with 'beware how you prove your prince's patience as you have now done mine . . . My Lord Keeper you will do as I bid you.'

The lord keeper rose in the fading light. 'The Queen's Majesty doth dissolve this parliament. Let every man depart at his pleasure.' The queen proceeded to the royal barge and returned to the palace. Parliament would not meet again for another four years. Cecil noted 'the succession not answered, the marriage not followed, dangers ensuing, general disorientations'.

It may be noted, in parenthesis, that in this period the coach was introduced to England. John Taylor, the popular 'water poet', believed that it had been brought to England by the queen's coachman, a Dutchman named William Booner. 'A coach', he wrote, 'was a strange monster in those days, and the sight of it put both horse and foot in amazement. Some said it was a great crab-shell brought out of China; and some thought it one of the pagan temples in which the cannibals adored the devil. Soon an outcry was raised about the scarcity of leather, from the quantity used in coach building.' So in the 1560s the monstrous carriage, as well as the queen's marriage, was the talk of London.

30

The rites of spring

Having alienated both his wife and the Scottish nobility, Henry Stuart, Lord Darnley, had every reason to leave Scotland; he spoke of escaping into England, although he would hardly have been welcomed at the court of Elizabeth. She would not even recognize him as king of Scotland, and he was deluded enough to believe that he had some claim upon the English throne. After the safe birth of her son Mary turned her face against him, believing him to be responsible for the murder of her Italian secretary. Mary neither ate nor slept with him and on one occasion, according to the English ambassador in Scotland, 'used words that cannot for modesty nor with the honour of a queen be reported'.

At the beginning of 1567 Mary was reliably informed that Darnley was proposing to kidnap their son and rule as regent in his name; the queen herself was to be confined in a secure castle. It was important that all his movements and meetings should be watched. When he fell ill, perhaps from a recurrent bout of syphilis, she visited his sickroom and remained with him for the next two or three days. At the end of January she brought him to Edinburgh in a horse litter.

James, the fourth earl of Bothwell, now enters the plot. At the age of twenty-one he had become Lieutenant of the Border, and had served Mary's mother during her regency of Scotland. He had

337

been one of the lords who had accompanied the newly widowed Mary on her journey from Paris; soon enough he had caught the young queen's attention. He had already become one of her principal counsellors, and one of those whose antipathy to Darnley was as great as that of the queen.

He was part of a small group who now planned permanently to remove Darnley, and a bond or deed was drawn up between its members. It was later reproduced in Robert Pitcairn's *Ancient Criminal Trials in Scotland* (1833). The conspirators stated that 'such a young fool and proud tyrant [as the king] should not bear rule of them – for diverse causes therefore they had all concluded that he should be put forth [dispatched] by one way or the other'; they pledged to be true to one another, and all would take on the guilt of murder. It is uncertain what the Scottish queen knew of this, even though her own half-brother was aware of the plot. At a later date she asserted that she had told them to do nothing 'to touch her honour and conscience'. Yet even if she had refused her consent to these proposals, by her own confession she had listened to them without reacting violently to the putative murderers of her husband. She could have accused them of treason, but she remained silent.

As Mary and Darnley moved towards Edinburgh, Bothwell met them on the road. Their intended destination had been Craigmillar Castle, but now the earl directed them to new lodgings at the house of the provost of St Mary's known as the 'Kirk of Field' or 'Kirk o' Field'. Darnley's chambers had been properly furnished for a king in the west wing of the house, and it was here that Mary watched over her husband's convalescence; she did not sleep in the house but in the evening retired to the more palatial surroundings of Holyrood. An apartment was in fact made ready for her after a few days, directly beneath that of her husband, and she took particular care to have the bed situated. 'Move it yonder,' she said to her attendant, 'to the other side.' She spent the nights of Wednesday 5 and Friday 7 February there. It was later rumoured that this was part of her design, so that people might suspect the target of the conspirators was herself.

At approximately ten o'clock on Sunday night two or three men brought some sacks of gunpowder into Mary's chamber at

Kirk o' Field. Mary herself was with her husband in the chamber above, and at this juncture remembered that she was supposed to attend a masque and dance at Holyrood. As she left the room she said, as if as an afterthought, 'It was just this time last year that Rizzio was slain.' Darnley turned to an attendant and asked, 'Why did she speak of Davie's slaughter?'

At two o'clock on the Monday morning a 'crack' was heard throughout Edinburgh. The old provost's house of Kirk o' Field was in ruins. Darnley had not perished in the explosion. His corpse and that of his page were found 40 yards away beneath a tree, on the other side of the town wall, with 'no sign of fire on them'. Close by them was a chair, a rope and Darnley's furred cloak. A dagger was also found, but neither victim had been stabbed.

The mystery of their last moments persists. They may have been smothered in their sleep; they may have been pursued and taken in the garden. Or they may have lowered themselves from the first-floor window, after discovering that the doors to their chamber were locked, only to be dispatched near the scene of the crime. Within hours of the explosion placards had been fixed to the Tolbooth in Edinburgh accusing Bothwell and his associates of the crime. Bothwell's antipathy to Darnley was notorious. Two days later Mary issued a proclamation in which she offered £2,000 for information against her husband's murderers. But she knew well enough that the name of Bothwell was on everyone's lips. His portraits were posted on the gates and walls of the city with the legend 'Here is the murderer of the king'.

On hearing the news of Darnley's death, and of Bothwell's involvement in it, Elizabeth sent an urgent letter to Mary. 'Madame,' she began, 'my ears have been so deafened and my understanding so grieved and my heart so affrighted to hear the dreadful news of the abominable murder of your mad husband and my killed cousin that I scarcely have the wits to write about it . . .' She professed to be more grieved for Mary than for her husband but she added that 'I will not dissemble what most people are talking about; which is that you will look through your fingers at [dispense with] the revenging of this deed'. Mary, in other words, was already rumoured to be complicit or at least acquiescent in the deed. The queen of England exhorted her to lay these reports to rest by taking action; she urged her 'to touch even him whom you have nearest to you if the thing touches him'. Mary was so angered by this message that she refused to reply to it.

The courts of Europe were now alive with speculation about Mary's role in the murder of her husband. Some were already denouncing her, while her Catholic supporters were divided on the matter. 'Should it turn out she is guilty,' an envoy at her court wrote, 'her party in England is gone, and by her means there is no more chance of a restoration of religion.'

The day after the explosion Mary attended the wedding feast of one of her female attendants; she should have put the court in mourning immediately, but delayed that decision for five days. Her husband was buried without any solemnity in the chapel of Holyrood. It was clear enough that she was relieved by his sudden removal from her life. Mary and Bothwell were now being seen together. The queen gave him her husband's horses and fine clothes, a gesture which further alienated popular opinion. It was rumoured that, although already married, Bothwell was now actively seeking the queen's hand.

The father of Darnley, the earl of Lennox, had brought charges against Bothwell that had to be heard in open court. The trial was to take place on 12 April, at the Tolbooth, but the presiding officers were supporters of Bothwell; at the same time the palace bodyguard was increased by 300 cavalry. Bothwell himself rode to the courtroom with an entourage of 4,000 retainers. The earl of Lennox was too apprehensive to risk any appearance in Edinburgh. It was only to be expected that, after more than eight hours of deliberation, Bothwell was acquitted.

Yet the course of events was now so precipitate that no one could feel safe. Mary had ridden to Stirling Castle nine days after the trial to collect her infant son, but the boy's guardian, the earl of Mar, refused to give him up. He had a horror of yielding him to Bothwell, the murderer of the infant's father. Three days later, on 24 April, the queen was riding from her birthplace at Linlithgow to Holyrood when Bothwell abducted her and took her to Dunbar. It was here that she was 'ravished'. Yet she remained in his castle for twelve days, and made no serious effort to escape or resist him.

On 26 April Bothwell rode to Edinburgh in order to expedite the divorce from his first wife. On the following day the queen formally asked for an annulment of that marriage from the archbishop of St Andrews.

Some great nobles of the realm had by now become so incensed and alarmed that they bound themselves in a confederacy against Bothwell, whom they described as 'that barbarous tyrant' and 'cruel murderer'. When he and Mary returned in procession to Edinburgh they were met by silent and sullen crowds. Nevertheless the queen raised her champion as duke of Orkney and lord of Shetland. The confederate lords now assembled in Stirling Castle, where they created an alternative royal court around the infant James. On 14 May 1567 Mary Stuart and James Bothwell were married in the great hall of Holyrood Palace. On hearing the news Elizabeth remonstrated with her cousin. 'How', she asked, 'could a worse choice be made for your honour?' On the gates of Holyrood a placard was nailed with the verse:

> As the common people say,
> Only harlots marry in May.

William Cecil wrote that Scotland was 'in a quagmire; nobody seemeth to stand still; the most honest desire to go away; the worst tremble with the shaking of their conscience'.

The result of these bewildering events was civil war. The Scottish earls marched against Bothwell under a banner that portrayed Darnley lying dead beneath the tree, with the infant prince kneeling beside him. In the middle of June Mary rode with her new husband to the security of Dunbar Castle, but then led her forces to Carberry Hill outside Edinburgh. Inconclusive negotiations were undertaken between the two sides, but it became clear that Mary's soldiers did not wish to fight their compatriots in a civil war. As the day wore on they joined the army of the confederate lords or simply went their own way. Delaying only long enough to allow Bothwell to ride back to the castle, she gave herself up to the forces of her lords.

She had been wearing male attire for her entry into battle but now she put on a borrowed dress and was led downhill on horseback. She was noticeably pregnant, which suggested to all observers that she had consorted with Bothwell before her abduction and marriage. When she rode among the soldiers some of them cried out, 'Burn the whore!' She was smuggled out of Edinburgh at night, but the mob was waiting for her with words of fury. 'Burn her, burn her, she is not worthy to live, kill her, drown her!' She had never known the openly expressed anger of her subjects before. She was taken 20 miles to the north, and was then rowed across to the island prison upon Loch Leven, where she remained for the better part of a year.

Elizabeth had been shocked by her cousin's behaviour, but she was even more dismayed by her treatment at the hands of her lords and people. It was against all laws of heaven and earth to treat with disrespect a sovereign queen. To expose her to the infamous jeers of the populace, and then to imprison her, were unforgivable offences. She wrote that 'we assure you that whatsoever we can imagine meet for your honour and safety that shall lie in our power, we will perform the same that it shall well appear you have a good neighbour . . .' She sent an ambassador to Edinburgh, but the lords prevented him from visiting Mary. He did learn, however, that her loyalty to Bothwell was undiminished. He wrote to Elizabeth that she 'avows constantly to live and die with him'.

It is unlikely that the English queen was sympathetic to such passionate statements. For her, love and loyalty were all matters of statecraft. The disgrace of Mary meant that her chances of the English throne were severely reduced; thus the whole weary problem of succession once more raised itself. There was a further difficulty. If the French royal family were able to adopt the infant prince James, the power of Scotland might be used against England. Thus in the summer of this year Elizabeth resumed negotiations for the hand of the archduke Charles of Austria. It would be wise to have the Habsburgs as allies, or at least not to rule out the possibility of such an alliance.

So in the summer of the year, as Mary was being held prisoner on the island, Elizabeth's envoy, the earl of Sussex, set out for Vienna. As the archduke espoused the Catholic faith, religious difficulties could be anticipated. It would be preferable, and advisable, for him to accept the English liturgy. The Spanish ambassador had already indicated that the first Mass said publicly in England would be the signal for a general rebellion. These were delicate matters.

It seemed better, therefore, that the archduke should come to England for a personal interview with the queen. Charles considered the idea to be beneath his dignity; what if he should arrive and then be rejected on the ostensible grounds of religion? He demanded that all hindrances should be cleared in advance, and in turn agreed that as the spouse of the queen he would hear Mass only in private. Sussex urged Cecil to entreat the queen to accept the compromise since, without it, 'I foresee discontent, disunion, bloodshed of her people'.

The queen prevaricated, and seemed set upon delay. It was perhaps her duty to the nation to accept him, but her innate aversion to matrimony and her affection for Leicester caused her to hesitate. 'The hatred that this queen has of marriage', the Spanish ambassador wrote to Philip, 'is most strange.' Eventually she sent her suitor a letter in which she affirmed the unity of religion in her kingdom but permitted him the free exercise of his religion, on the proposed visit to England, 'so far as should be found possible'. The clause could be variously interpreted, and the archduke replied that it was too vague. The negotiations were once more allowed to falter and finally to fade.

The international situation became more difficult when, in August 1567, Philip II sent the duke of Alva into the Netherlands with a force of 10,000 Spanish troops. The presence of a great army in the middle of Europe, with the western reaches of the Netherlands only 100 miles away from the mouth of the Thames, was a matter of great concern to Elizabeth and her advisers. The Netherlands comprised many states, provinces and duchies that had come by inheritance to the Habsburg dynasty; they included most of modern Belgium, part of northern France, Holland and Zeeland. It was not likely that these predominantly merchant states would acquiesce for ever in the rule of a Spanish Catholic king. The Spanish army had been sent to quell large-scale rioting that had broken out in Antwerp and other cities, where a combination of economic grievances and religious discontents stirred a mixed population of Calvinists, Lutherans and

Anabaptists. The Calvinist weavers of Ypres, for example, attacked the Catholic churches of that region and smashed the religious statuary.

It was rumoured that Philip II had already set sail for the Low Countries and might divert to Portsmouth on his way. This set the court into an alarm. Should the king be treated as a welcome guest or as a potential enemy? In the event he did not arrive, but the problems of religion remained. The coincidence of the failure of the negotiations for marriage and the suppression of the Protestant revolt further emphasized the rift between England and Spain. The two countries were already on course for the collision that would occur twenty years later.

The situation of Europe was further vexed by a revival of civil and religious wars within France, where the Huguenots under the prince of Condé were contesting the Catholic regime of Charles IX; 3,000 French Protestants then joined the cause of their fellow reformers in the Netherlands. Elizabeth and her councillors were inclined to favour their co-religionists across the sea, and did indeed offer them clandestine support; English agents contrived to raise Protestant forces and English money helped to finance them. The seamen of the West Country joined forces with a Huguenot fleet in a Calvinist offensive against Spanish shipping. One sceptical naval chaplain wrote that 'we could not do God better service than to spoil the Spaniard both of life and goods, but indeed under colour of religion all their shot is at men's money'. The importance of English sea power was becoming manifest.

Towards the end of 1568 five Spanish frigates, carrying money for the duke of Alva's forces, took temporary refuge in Falmouth and in Plymouth; Elizabeth ordered the ships to be impounded and seized the money on the grounds that it belonged not to Philip but to Genoese bankers. She would pay the requisite interest and use the money for her own purposes. The duke of Alva promptly took control of the English warehouse or 'factory' in Antwerp and confiscated its goods. In retaliation the property of all Spanish subjects in England was taken. Elizabeth, and her councillors, wished to prove that they could confront the great power of Europe. Yet it was a war without battles. Negotiations and conferences, meetings and audiences, continued over the next four years.

The confrontation did represent, however, a change in English policy. Cecil was trying to advance the cause of Protestantism by confronting Spain, but only at the cost of turning rivals into enemies. The sovereigns of Spain and of France distrusted the English queen to the extent that Cecil feared a grand Catholic alliance was about to be formed against her. If Spanish forces could be dispatched to the Netherlands, they could also be sent to England.

Mary remained incarcerated in her prison of Loch Leven, where she miscarried of twins in the early summer of 1567. The Protestant lords of Scotland presented her with a letter of abdication which, in her weakened state, she duly signed. It was said that she had been threatened with death. Her son was proclaimed James VI of Scotland. She had few attendants, and was allowed even fewer visitors. Her powers of persuasion were believed to be marvellous, and charm might succeed where guile failed. She must not be allowed to escape.

Her captivity lasted for a little over ten months. On the evening of 2 May 1568 a young page, in a predetermined plan, smuggled out the keys of her chambers in the round tower of the castle; she was waiting, dressed in the simple garb of a maidservant. The two of them, together with a young girl designed to waylay suspicion, sprang into a waiting skiff and within a few minutes they were on shore. She was met there by a group of horsemen and taken to her supporters gathered at Hamilton Castle; they were a band of Catholic loyalists in a predominantly Protestant country. She dispatched envoys as well as letters to Paris and to London, pleading for assistance. Elizabeth characteristically chose a middle course, offering to mediate between the Scottish queen and her subjects. William Cecil in turn wrote to the regent ruling Scotland in the young king's name, the earl of Moray, urging 'expedition in quieting these troubles' by defeating the queen. So England spoke with two voices. Two heads, in a phrase of the period, were under one hood. Cecil could therefore countenance policies that Elizabeth could later disown. He was more avowedly

Protestant than the queen and could fight her battles for her without any express command to do so.

On 13 May Mary's small army was defeated at Langside Hill, outside Glasgow; Mary had watched the fortunes of the battle from a hillside, half a mile distant, and had now determined to flee. She was in continual danger of detention and even death; in desperation, she crossed the Solway into England and made her way to the safety of the castle at Carlisle. She was now in Elizabeth's kingdom. If Elizabeth refused to receive her, she would at least give Mary free passage to France. 'I fear', the archbishop of Canterbury wrote, 'that our good queen has the wolf by the ears.' There was an additional connotation; an outlaw was known as a 'wolf's head that anyone might cut down'.

In a letter to Elizabeth, Mary vented her fury against the rebels who, as she implied, had been tacitly supported by English policy. She also hinted that she had friends and allies elsewhere who would come to her aid; it is clear enough that she meant the Catholic sovereigns of France and Spain. The intervention of those nations in Scottish affairs was not to be endured. Elizabeth had already written to Mary that 'those who have two strings to their bow may shoot stronger, but they rarely shoot straight'.

What was to be done with her? Elizabeth had at first considered inviting her to the English court, but was quickly persuaded otherwise. It would afford her too much prominence, and her presence at Whitehall or Greenwich would greatly boost her claim to the throne. Already the northern Catholic lords were paying court to her, and it seemed likely that a Catholic party would congregate around her. The Scottish lords themselves would not look favourably on the support that Elizabeth would give her; it might drive them in the direction of France, with the infant king as the prize. Mary herself must not be allowed to travel to France, where she could provoke infinite troubles.

So the Scottish queen continued in what might be described as honourable captivity. From Carlisle she was transferred to Bolton Castle in North Yorkshire. She had said defiantly that she would have to be carried there but, after many scenes of passion and demonstration, she eventually consented to her removal. Thereupon it was decreed that an inquiry should be established into the events surrounding the murder of Darnley. Elizabeth herself determined to be the ultimate judge and mediator in the matter. If Mary was proven to be innocent, she should in theory be instantly restored to her throne. If she were found to be guilty, it would be impossible for Elizabeth to receive her. 'Oh Madam!' Elizabeth wrote, 'there is not a creature living who more longs to hear your justification than myself; not one who would lend more willing ear to any answer which will clear your honour.' She added an important proviso, however. 'But I cannot sacrifice my own reputation to your account.' Elizabeth sent her councillors to York, where they were instructed to arrange a settlement between Mary, Elizabeth and King James's supporters that would precede Mary's return. Elizabeth could then be seen as the benign healer of Scotland's ill. It did not quite go to plan.

The queen, meanwhile, went on a progress in the summer of the year. A 'progress' was a long peregrination through the more accessible counties of England, in the course of which the queen would graciously consent to accept the hospitality of the greater nobles whose large houses lay along her route. For them, it was an expensive business; for her, it was an opportunity to live more cheaply while at the same time showing herself to selected groups of people. It was a complex and cumbersome undertaking, the queen's belongings alone requiring 400 wagons. She was also accompanied by approximately 500 courtiers and servants.

Sometimes she travelled in the newly fashionable royal coach, although two years before she had been a little shaken and bruised when it was driven too fast. But more often she was carried in an open litter or rode on horseback, her route lined with her welcoming subjects calling out 'God save your grace!' while she replied with 'God save my people!' Sometimes she called a halt to the process so that a suitor might present a petition or even speak to her. 'Stay thy cart,' Serjeant Bendlowes of Huntingdonshire called out to her coachman, 'stay thy cart, that I may speak to the queen!' Elizabeth laughed and listened to what he had to say; then she offered him her hand to kiss.

And so it went on. The Spanish ambassador reported that, on

this summer progress, 'she was received everywhere with great acclamations and signs of joy'. She pointed out to him the love and affection in which she was held by her subjects while her neighbours (naming no names) 'are in such trouble'. If she was in danger of assassination she showed no signs of apprehension; she even took up food and drink without waiting for the precaution of a taster in case of poison.

The towns along her route were cleansed and freshly painted, with the vagabonds and other unsightly persons removed from sight. It was customary to present her with a silver cup, preferably filled with coin, that she gladly accepted. Her remarks were recorded for the sake of posterity. 'Come hither, little recorder,' she said to the recorder of Warwick, 'it was told me that you would be afraid to look upon me or to speak boldly; but you were not so afraid of me as I was of you.' A schoolmaster of Norwich seemed nervous before addressing her in Latin. 'Be not afraid,' she said. At the conclusion of his speech she told him that 'it is the best that ever I heard, you shall have my hand'. As she left Norwich she declared that 'I shall never forget Norwich' and, as she rode away, she called out 'Farewell, Norwich!'

An orator at Cambridge was enumerating her virtues, at which she modestly shook her head, bit her lip, and expressed a brief disclaimer. Then he began to praise virginity. 'God's blessing of thine heart,' she called out, 'there continue.' During her reign of forty-four years she organized more than twenty such ritual journeys and when, at the age of sixty-seven, she embarked on yet another some of the more elderly courtiers were heard to grumble, at which she commanded 'the old stay behind and the young and able to go with me'. Yet she never ventured too far, confining her perambulations largely to what became known in the nineteenth century as the home counties; she never travelled to the north or to the south-west.

The inquiry into Mary's behaviour opened at York in the beginning of October 1568. Elizabeth had sent Thomas Howard, fourth duke of Norfolk, to be the principal English commissioner; since he was suspected of having Catholic sympathies, it was believed

that he had been dispatched in order to assist Mary's cause. Yet
she had found more than an ally in the duke of Norfolk; she had
found a possible husband. Norfolk, three times a widower at the
early age of thirty-two, was now available for marriage once more;
as the foremost nobleman in England he was a most suitable
match. If the queen of Scots were to marry him her succession to
the English throne would become easy and almost inevitable. It
seems likely that Norfolk himself, together with a number of his
allies, had contemplated this arrangement even before his journey
to York; it can safely be said, however, that Elizabeth herself was
quite unaware of any such plan.

The regent of Scotland and Mary's half-brother, the earl of
Moray, threw the proceedings into disorder by bringing with him
eight letters and twelve 'adulterous' sonnets allegedly written by
Mary to Bothwell; they had been discovered in the possession
of one of Bothwell's servants after the decisive battle of Carberry
Hill. They became known as the 'casket letters' and did more to
damage Mary's reputation than even the killing of Darnley. 'I do
here a work that I hate much,' she had written to Bothwell, 'but
I had begun it this morning . . . You make me dissemble so much
that I am afraid thereof with horror, and you make me almost
to play the part of a traitor . . . Think also if you will not find
some invention more secret by physick, for he is to take physick
at Craigmillar and the baths also.' The inference must be that she
was meditating with her lover the means of killing her husband.

The authenticity of the letters has been a cause of controversy
ever since. The originals have long since disappeared, perhaps
destroyed, and the material can only be read in translation or
transcription; some of the transcripts have Cecil's annotations in
the margin, testifying to the care with which he pored over them.
The general assumption must be that genuine passages have been
interpolated with fabricated words and phrases, no doubt planted
by Moray to incriminate his half-sister, but no certainty in the
matter is possible. It can only be said that they achieved their
purpose at the time.

The duke of Norfolk confessed himself horrified by their
content. He wrote to Elizabeth that the letters contained 'foul
matter and abominable, to be either thought of or to be written by

a prince'. Yet his disgust did not alter his intention of marrying the lady. The complication of the case was such that the tribunal was moved from York to Westminster, where, towards the end of the year, the commissioners entered what one observer called 'the bowels of the odious accusation'. The letters were produced in court and read in the privy council. Mary was herself defiant, stating that 'the charges against her were false because she, on the word of a princess, did say that they were false'.

There followed days and weeks of meetings and conferences between the various interested parties, rendered even more un-certain by the hesitancy and vacillation of Elizabeth. She had promised to support Mary in her distress but had in fact started proceedings that placed the Scottish queen in an undesirable light. Mary still protested her innocence but there was no one at court who believed her; Mary herself refused to discuss the letters, except in an audience with the English queen. Yet Elizabeth could not receive Mary while she was under suspicion of murder. It was a tangled web.

Elizabeth did not wish to condone the behaviour of the earl of Moray in overthrowing his lawful sovereign, but it was he who could bring peace and stability to Scotland. So she informed the regent that he could depart with his delegation 'in the same estate in which they were before their coming into the realm'. Nothing had been resolved. These affairs of state were in any case too sensitive to bear much further examination. Elizabeth demanded absolute secrecy in the matters discussed. The whole imbroglio had ended inconsequentially, yet had still managed severely to damage the reputation of the queen of Scots. Mary herself was soon removed to Tutbury Castle, in Staffordshire, where she endured conditions of genteel confinement; her imprisonment lasted for another eighteen years.

Cecil was reduced to despair by Elizabeth's hesitation and indecision. He wrote in a private memorandum that 'her majesty shall never be able to raise her decayed credit, nor pluck up the hearts of her good subjects, nor prevent and escape the perils that are intended towards her, unless she do utterly give over the government of her most weighty affairs unto the most faithful councillors . . .' It was the central dilemma of her reign, with the strength and solitariness of one woman pitched against a phalanx of men.

The movements of the larger world went largely unremarked and unreported in the accounts of the struggles and rivalries at court. In the reign of Elizabeth the commerce of England was greatly increased with spices and perfumes from India, ermine and steel from Russia. England sent woollen cloths and calf-skins to Turkey, and in return purchased silks, camblets, rhubarb, oil, cotton, carpets, galls and spices. From the New World came gold and silver. They were part of the great exfoliation of life that slowly covered the globe, as the power of European finance and trade pushed its way forward. This was the age of the great commercial companies of merchants that planned their ventures from Muscovy and Persia to Cathay. By the end of the queen's reign English traders had reached the Gulf of Guinea and the Indian Ocean. One of the first travellers upon that ocean, Thomas Stevens, remarked that 'there waited on our ship fishes as long as a man, which they call Tuberones. They come to eat such things as from the ship fall into the sea, not refusing men themselves if they light upon them.' In February 1583 Elizabeth wrote letters to the kings of Cambaia (now Gujarat) and of China, asking leave for her representatives to trade. As a result of all these activities London was fast overtaking Antwerp as the European capital of trade and finance. When the shah of Persia asked a merchant, Arthur Edwards, the name of the place from which he had come the answer puzzled him. 'England,' the man said. No one had ever heard of that land. Edwards then ventured on 'Inghlittera'. 'Ah,' one courtier said, 'Londro.' So London was better known than the nation.

The Turkey merchants brought their wares from the Levant while the mariners of England sailed down the western coast of Africa and the eastern coastline of the New World. In the 1560s Sir John Hawkins made three successful voyages to the African continent, where he opened the unhappy trade in slaves, and crossed the Atlantic to Hispaniola and the Spanish colonies in America. At the beginning of the next decade Sir Francis Drake made three journeys to the West Indies. On his last expedition, from a summit of a mountain on the Isthmus of Darien, he caught sight of the great Pacific. So the map of the world was slowly being unrolled.

A Company of the Mines Royal was created in 1568 in order to promote the mining and distribution of copper, and in the same decade the industries for window and crystal glass were successfully established. England was growing more luxurious, at least for those with full purses. Some lamented 'the over quantity of unnecessary wares brought into the port of London' and Cecil himself complained about 'the excess of silks' as well as 'the excess of wine and spices'.

In this context we may view the miracles of Tudor architecture, many of which survive still. It is marked by wreathed chimneys and oak-panelled rooms, by mullioned bay-windows and vertiginous gable roofs. The ornamental plaster ceiling also became characteristic. The size and complexity of the windows prompted a comment upon one great Elizabethan house, 'Hardwick House, more glass than wall'. Eltham Palace and Hampton Court furnish evidence for the Tudor halls with open timbered roofs at a great height. The private chambers of the richer sort were furnished with tapestries, hangings and curtains; high stools, covered chairs, cabinets, chests and cupboards were everywhere apparent. Cushions could be found in most rooms.

The appetite for luxuries materially increased over the course of Elizabeth's reign; sugar and pearls came from the New World, while lemons and pomegranates and scented soap came from the Old. In previous times no flesh had ever been eaten on fish days; now the people of London scorned fish as a relic of papistry. William Camden noted that 'our apish nation' had grown so rich that its citizens engaged in a 'riot of banqueting' and 'bravery in building'. Even the ploughman, according to Thomas Lodge, 'must nowadays have his doublet of the fashion with wide cuts, his garters of fine silk of Granada'. Fine lace became a new 'craze' among both sexes, with its application to cuffs and ruffs, aprons and handkerchiefs. The style of male and female costume, at least in London, was as changeable as the wind. One woodcut shows a semi-naked Englishman with a pair of tailors' shears in his hand, saying 'I will wear I cannot tell what'. Samuel Rowlands, the sixteenth-century pamphleteer, made out an inventory of

> ... the French doublet and the German hose;
> The Muff's cloak, Spanish hat, Toledo blade,
> Italian ruff, a shoe right Flemish made.

The latter part of Elizabeth's reign, in particular, witnessed the greatest extravagance of fashion. New silks and velvets were introduced; great ruffs and farthingales became common. The queen herself left, at the time of her death, approximately 3,000 dresses.

The industry of England advanced as strongly as its commerce. The investment in looms, furnaces and forges increased, while parliamentary Acts were passed to promote the trade in leather. More coal was needed for the manufacture of glass and for soap-boiling. The production of pig iron rose threefold in the space of thirty years.

William Harrison, in his *Description of England* of 1577, amplified the changes with some local detail. One was 'the multitude of chimneys lately erected', while another was 'the exchange of vessel, as of treen [wooden] platters into pewter, and wooden spoons into silver or tin'. Timber and clay had given way to stone and plaster; pallets of straw had been replaced by feather beds, and logs of wood by pillows. The rise of the stricter forms of Protestantism had not yet inhibited the lavish materialism that seems to characterize Elizabethan society. This might be described as the first secular age.

31

Plots and factions

The confinement of Mary, queen of Scots, rendered her even more desperate and dangerous. She began a correspondence with the duke of Norfolk that might seem to suggest collusion against Elizabeth. Elizabeth herself had by now heard the rumours about a possible alliance and berated Norfolk for even considering the notion. 'Should I seek to marry her,' he responded, 'being so wicked a woman, such a notorious adulteress and murderer?' He added that Mary still pretended a title to the English throne; any marriage with her 'might justly charge me with seeking your crown from your head'. Elizabeth did not need to be reminded of that fact. In January 1569 Elizabeth sent a confidential letter to Mary in which she wrote that 'those do not all love you who would persuade your servants that they love you. Be not over confident in what you do. Be not blind nor think me blind. If you are wise, I have said enough.'

An alliance of the more conservative councillors was ready to support the project of uniting Mary and Norfolk; it would provide the neatest possible dynastic solution to the problem of the succession. The marriage between Mary and Bothwell could easily be annulled, with Bothwell himself soon to be imprisoned in a Danish dungeon from which he would never escape. In their happy vision Mary would be pronounced to be the heir, and all help would be withdrawn from the Protestant rebels of Europe. This policy would be the exact opposite of that pursued by Cecil, who distrusted Mary as much as he despised European papistry. The councillors found an unlikely ally in the earl of Leicester, who had long hated Cecil for his role in wrecking his hopes of marriage with the queen.

So a concerted attack was mounted against the queen's principal councillor. Leicester told the queen that Cecil was so badly managing the affairs of the nation that he ought to lose his head; it was he who had managed to alienate both the French and the Spanish, thus endangering the realm. Elizabeth in turn berated Leicester for questioning Cecil's judgement and by extension her own.

Norfolk also lent his voice against Cecil, knowing that he was the principal obstacle in the pursuit of marriage with Mary. In the queen's presence he turned to the earl of Northampton. 'See, my lord,' he is supposed to have said, 'how when the earl of Leicester follows the secretary he is favoured and well regarded by the queen, but when he wants to make reasonable remonstrances against the policy of Cecil, he is frowned on and she wants to send him to the Tower. No, no, he will not go there alone.' Elizabeth made no comment.

It was rumoured that a plan was formed to arrest Cecil, but like many such schemes it came to nothing. The loyalty of the queen to her faithful servant was adamantine. Cecil himself, aware of the threat, tried to mend relations with Norfolk. He deferred to his judgement and offered to consult the other councillors more widely and openly. He bent to the storm.

The duke himself was already stepping further and further into the sea of Mary's troubles. Letters of an affectionate nature passed between them. The earl of Leicester was also pressing the suit in the belief that he might gain from it. At worst he would earn the gratitude of a future queen and, at best, Elizabeth might decide to marry him as a counterpoise to Norfolk. Elizabeth herself was aware of the rumours from a hundred mouths. She asked the duke one day what news was abroad. He was aware of none. 'No?' she replied. 'You come from London and can tell me no news of a marriage?'

It is likely that he was too much afraid of her wrath to venture upon the subject, and as a result his silence deepened. But if it had become a secret matter, then it might come close to treachery. Some of his supporters deserted him. The earl of Leicester, thoroughly discomfited by the queen's growing displeasure, retired to his sickbed from where he told Elizabeth all he knew. The queen then summoned Norfolk, who was forced to confess to the marital arrangement; whereupon she commanded him to give it up.

Norfolk left the court, whilst in the middle of a summer progress at Titchfield in Hampshire, without formally taking leave of the queen before returning to his house in London. In Howard House he met an envoy from Mary. The Scottish queen was complaining about all the delays in the negotiations for their marriage. When the envoy asked him about the intentions of the queen, he replied that 'he would have friends enough to assist him'. This was dangerous talk. Some of these friends were the Catholic lords of the north who were prepared to rise in arms for the Scottish queen.

Elizabeth, fearing something very much like an uprising, ordered that the guard on Mary be strengthened. She then sent a message to Norfolk ordering him to return to the court, now at Windsor. The duke was already beset by rumours that he was in fact about to be sent to the Tower. He pleaded illness in response to the queen's command, but then promptly retired to his estate at Kenninghall in Norfolk. This was the centre of his power with land, wealth and a loyal tenantry. The name of Kenninghall itself is derived from the Anglo-Saxon words for king and palace. If he married Mary, could he perhaps then become king in reality?

Elizabeth later told Leicester that, if the two had married, she feared that she would once again be dispatched to the Tower. When some of her council were of the opinion that Norfolk's intentions were not necessarily treacherous, it is reported that the queen fainted. These were not the wiles of court. Elizabeth knew the situation intimately for, in the reign of Mary Tudor, she had been in the same state of hapless imprisonment that she had now imposed upon Mary, queen of Scots. In a panel Mary was then embroidering she wove the image of a tabby cat in orange wool with a crown upon its head; Elizabeth was red-headed. Then Mary placed a little mouse beside the cat.

Norfolk wavered between defiance and despair. He wrote to

23. Mary I, stubborn and imperious.

24. Philip of Spain, Mary's unwilling husband who deserted her at the first opportunity.

25. An allegory of Stephen Gardiner, the papist Bishop of Winchester. This was painted during Edward's reign when papists were considered to be the spawn of the devil.

26. Cranmer burning in Oxford – one of Mary's many victims.

27. Elizabeth I as a young princess. Her early life was fraught with danger.

28. Elizabeth's glorious signature in which she reveals her forceful and magisterial character.

29. Elizabeth in coronation robes, the image of splendour.

30 (*below*). Robert Dudley, earl of Leicester. He was always Elizabeth's favourite and their affectionate relationship caused much scandal.

31. Thomas Howard, fourth duke of Norfolk, executed for plotting against Elizabeth.

32. Elizabeth in Parliament, a body which she alternately appeased and bullied.

33. Mary Queen of Scots, the perpetual conspirator.

34. The execution of the Scottish queen, who believed that she died a martyr.

In nomine Domini incipit omne malum.

The Popes bull against the Queene.

Fridericus Hulsius Inuent. et sculp.

35. The pope's bull against Elizabeth in 1570, in which he excommunicated her as a heretic.

36. The arrival of Elizabeth at Nonesuch Palace, 'none such like it' in the kingdom.

PALATIVM REGIVM IN ANGLIÆ REGNO APPELLATVM NONCIVTZ,
Hoc est nusquam simile.

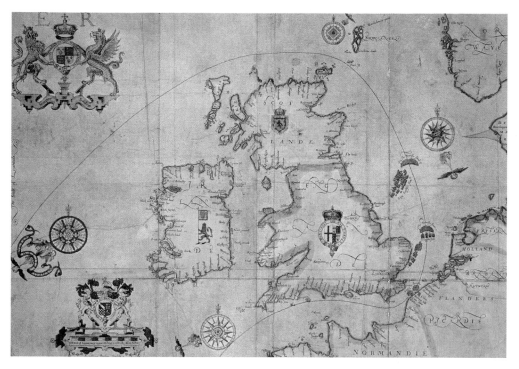

37. The unhappy route of the Armada, trapped by the sea no less than by English ships.

38 (*left*). Sir Francis Drake, captain victorious and navigator extraordinaire.

39. *Ark Royal*, the English fleet's flagship against the Armada.

40. William Cecil, Elizabeth's principal councillor, known to her as 'Sir Spirit'.

41. Francis Walsingham, spymaster general and confidential councillor.

42. Robert Cecil, the great survivor, known to the queen as 'my pigmy'.

43. James VI of Scotland, who would eventually become James I of England.

the queen protesting his loyalty and declaring his fear that he might be unjustly imprisoned. At the same time he wrote to his principal supporters in the north – among them Thomas Percy, earl of Northumberland and Charles Neville, earl of Westmorland – urging them not to stir and thereby risk his head. Another royal summons followed with a peremptory command. The duke decided to obey the command but he was diverted into the place he most feared; the doors of the Tower were locked behind him. The ports were closed for fear of foreign intervention.

The earls of Northumberland and Westmorland were now summoned to court by Elizabeth. 'We and our country were shamed for ever,' Westmorland's wife lamented, 'that now in the end we should seek holes to creep into.' Her advice, therefore, was to stand firm and to confront the queen in what would be a 'hurly-burly'. At Topcliffe, the estate of Northumberland, the bells were rung in reverse order as the well-known call to arms. The earls rose in November 1569, in the name of the old religion. They rode to Durham Cathedral with their men, where they pulled down the communion table; then they ripped to pieces the English Bible and the Book of Common Prayer before demanding that the Latin Mass be once more performed. It was the most serious test that Elizabeth had yet faced, with the prospect of civil war dividing the realm made infinitely more dangerous with the introduction of the religious question. The Spanish ambassador played a double part, promising much to the conservative cause but delivering very little. The French ambassador in turn was delighted at the prospect of England's collapsing into the same religious turmoil as his own country.

Two days later the rebellious earls rode through Ripon in the traditional armour of the Crusaders, wearing a red cross; they were in procession behind the banner of the Five Wounds of Christ, another emblem of the old faith. This was how the Pilgrims of Grace had ridden against Henry VIII thirty-three years before. It was the sign of the north, which had remained predominantly Catholic; in fact many of the northern rebels were the sons of those who had participated in the earlier movement. The father of Northumberland himself, Sir Thomas Percy, had been attainted and executed after the failure of the Pilgrimage of Grace. After the earls had arrived in Ripon, Mass was celebrated in the collegiate church, where a proclamation was addressed to those of 'the old, Catholic religion'. The queen's evil councillors had attempted to destroy 'the true and Catholic religion towards God' and had thus thrown the realm into confusion. The candles were lit and the organ pealed out.

Yet on 28 November 1569 the earls sent forth another address in which the issue of the succession took the place of religion. It was a way of rallying more support, but it was only partly successful in its purpose. Many of the great northern lords refused to join them in insurrection. The earl of Cumberland, for example, could not be moved. In contrast most of the English nobility rallied about the queen, prominent among them the earl of Sussex. Lord Hunsdon was sent north, while the earl of Bedford was dispatched to the west of England in case of danger there. Mary herself was taken to Coventry, where she was securely placed behind the red sandstone city wall. If Mary had been able to reach the rebels, a general insurrection might have ensued. It was said that the Spanish had a fleet, with guns and powder, waiting at Zeeland in the Netherlands. But 'if' is not a word to be used by historians. As a result of the Catholic threat, the Act of Uniformity was more strictly enforced, including the compulsory swearing of the oath of supremacy.

Elizabeth said at the beginning of the troubles that 'the earls were old in blood, but poor in force', and in that respect her judgement proved to be correct. They had expected popular support, but none was evident. They remained at Tadcaster in the north of Yorkshire for three days, and then retraced their steps. Their armies were demoralized and began to break up even as they were being pursued by the queen's soldiers. The only battle of the campaign was fought at Naworth, in February 1570, where Hunsdon defeated a rebel force under the command of Lord Dacre.

The northern rebellion, known as 'the Rising of the North', was in effect already at an end. The earls of Northumberland and Westmorland had fled across the border into Scotland, and the remaining insurgents were quickly arrested. The lowlier of them were hanged, and almost 300 suffered death in Durham alone. Scarcely a local town or village did not boast a gibbet. It is estimated that approximately 900 were executed for treason, making it the single most fatal act of reprisal in Tudor history. It was a measure of the queen's fury, but also of her fear. She had already made it clear that 'you may not execute any that hath freeholds or noted wealthy'. She wanted their money rather than their lives; the lands and estates of the mightier or most prosperous were therefore confiscated. Northumberland was sold to England by the Scots for £2,000 and subsequently executed, while Westmorland sought sanctuary in the Spanish Netherlands.

This was the last of what may be called the traditional rebellions led by the feudal warlords of the old faith. The great lords, the Percys and the Nevilles, had once been considered to be the de facto rulers of their territories where they exercised more power and authority than the monarch. Yet now they had failed to ignite the northern lands in open revolt. Many of the Catholics of the region had no wish to challenge the political and social order of the country. Even the tenantry of the great families were reluctant to rise. The crisis that Cecil had most feared had been overcome, with the old faith now associated with treason and force. It was described as 'a cold pie for the papists'. The loyalty of the majority of the realm had been reaffirmed. The northern rebellion represented one of the great and silent transitions in the nation's history.

Just after the revolt was suppressed a further challenge to the queen's authority was mounted in Rome. In early 1570, Pope Pius V issued a bull in which he excommunicated Elizabeth as a paramount heretic and tyrant. It stated that 'the pretended queen of England' could no longer command allegiance, and that she was 'the servant of iniquity'. Its denunciation covered any person who obeyed her laws and commands. The queen herself was now a legitimate object of attack by any assassin of the old faith; her death would speed his way to heaven. It was the last stand of medieval religion, the final occasion when a pope would try to depose a reigning monarch.

Yet it might be considered a blow against English Catholics more than against the English queen. They were now being urged to depose their sovereign just after the signal failure of the northern earls to do so. It was, to say the least, bad timing. If the bull had been released at the time of the northern rising it might have persuaded some of the fainter hearts. But it was now possible to claim that the Catholics of England could no longer be good and loyal subjects.

A copy of the papal bull was nailed to the gates of the palace of the bishop of London. The offender, John Felton, was put on the rack to determine the names of his accomplices or associates; he said nothing, but he suffered the gruesome death of the traitor. Just as he mounted the scaffold, however, he drew out a diamond ring and sent it to Elizabeth – 'the pretender' – as a last gift. He was beatified by a later pope as Blessed John Felton. Yet his militant cause was already lost at the time he was quartered and disembowelled. It is no accident that in this year the great book of Protestant faith, *Foxe's Book of Martyrs*, was reissued in a much more elaborate second edition. A memorandum from the privy council to the two archbishops declared that this was a 'work of very great importance and necessary knowledge both touching religion and other good offices, the matter whereof being very profitable to bring Her Majesty's subjects to good opinion, under-standing and dear liking of the present government'. Rarely have religion and politics been so closely aligned.

It is also significant this was the first year in which Elizabeth's accession day, 17 November, became the object of celebration. It was named as 'the queen's holy day', and became an annual event that had no precedent in earlier reigns. The church bells rang in every parish; there were bonfires, and candles, and bread, and beer. It became a Protestant equivalent to the sacred festivals of the medieval Church, conflating Elizabeth with the Virgin Mary. On 'Crownation Day', as it came to be known, there was scarcely a spot in England where bells could not be heard.

It was now possible that England would be invaded by the great Catholic powers, in solemn unity with Rome, and it was said that the English were beginning to fear their own shadows. The English fleet was mobilized, and the sheriffs were obliged to enrol local men in the service of home defence; shooting practice was organized on the village greens of southern and eastern England. In the summer of the year much anxiety, therefore, was aroused at the sight of a great Spanish fleet; yet it was sailing to Antwerp in order to escort the new bride of Philip II. The Spanish had in any case no desire to fight a war against England, and Philip remonstrated with the pope for not consulting him before issuing the bull. The French king, Charles IX, made a similar protest. The papal bull had the indirect consequence of facilitating trade between England and Turkey; the infidel queen was happy to come to terms with the infidel Ottomans.

The rebellious earls were still colluding with their Scottish hosts in plotting against Elizabeth, and as a result the border was troubled by alarms or incursions. In the spring of 1570 an English force was sent into southern Scotland both as a punishment and a warning; in the course of this venture ninety strong castles, houses and dwelling places, as well as towns and villages, were utterly destroyed. The position of the queen of Scotland was still in doubt. She was effectively under house arrest but many of the nobility of England wished to see her restored to her throne; Cecil, and some other councillors, did not. Elizabeth herself was hesitant and indecisive.

In this febrile atmosphere talk of marriage was revived, with Prince Henry, the duke of Anjou, raised as a possible favourite. He was seventeen years younger than Elizabeth but, as the brother of the king of France, he was a most acceptable offering. It had been rumoured that his family wished to marry him to the queen of Scots and it is possible that Elizabeth stepped forward to prevent that union. She would now need all of her arts of guile and deceit infinitely to prolong the negotiations. It is unlikely that she ever really considered marrying him, but matters of state might still have overturned her personal predilections. A union between France and England would have thwarted the power of Spain.

Anjou's mother, Catherine de Medici, was enthusiastic for the match. 'Such a kingdom for one of my children!' she explained to the French ambassador in England. But the young prince himself proved refractory. He was, according to one of the English negotiators sent to Paris, 'obstinate, papistical and restive like a mule'. The fact that he was 'papistical', at least in theory, did not bode well for the peace of England; Elizabeth, having only recently been threatened by the earls of the old faith, was reluctant to make any concessions on the matter of private Masses or Catholic confessors.

Another and more private impediment was discovered. In this

period the queen suffered from an ulcer on the shin of her leg, a painful condition difficult to cure. Her father had also contracted ulcers. The young prince came to hear of this, and referred to her publicly as 'an old creature with a sore leg'. He also called her a 'putain publique' or common whore. This was not promising. Yet still the discussions continued, growing warmer or becoming chillier according to the general temperature of European affairs. Elizabeth ordered her principal negotiators to delay and defer decisions; they were asked to tell Catherine de Medici 'not to be over-anxious as desiring so precise an answer until the matter may be further treated of'. In circumlocution, and prevarication, Elizabeth was pre-eminent. The affair was drawn out for some months on a very fine line, and in desperation the queen was eventually offered the hand of Anjou's younger brother, Francis, duke of Alençon. Yet the duke of Alençon was disfigured by pockmarks. It was believed that the price of accepting the pockmarks would be the return of Calais to England, but once more the proposals got precisely nowhere. The queen delayed and hesitated, seeming not to know her own mind from one day to the next. In truth there was never any real likelihood that she would marry.

The duke of Norfolk was released from the Tower in the summer of 1570, humiliated but not necessarily humbled. He sent Elizabeth a document vowing 'never to deal in that cause of marriage of the Queen of Scots', but soon enough he was drawn into another conspiracy against the throne. The plot was engineered by a banker from Florence, Roberto di Ridolfi, who had lived in London for some years and who had the full confidence of the Spanish ambassador. Ridolfi communicated with Norfolk and the Scottish queen, on the understanding that certain lords would rise up and set Mary free; at this point Mary's supporters would come over the border in force.

It was the merest fantasy, and it is hard to credit the serious involvement of any of the alleged conspirators. The duke of Alva, Philip's representative in the Spanish Netherlands, dismissed it as foolish nonsense. Yet there were some in England who favoured the scheme, among them the duke of Norfolk. He shrank from signing any incriminating documents but gave his verbal support. The duke's 'instructions' to Ridolfi were read over to him, and he assented to their contents. 'We commission you to go with all expedition, first to Rome and then to the Catholic king, that you may lay before his Holiness and his Majesty the wretched state of this island, our own particular wrongs . . . and an assured mode by which our country and ourselves can obtain relief.' It was his dearest wish 'to advance the title of the queen of Scots, to restore the Catholic religion'. Eight peers and four knights were then named, who together would command an army of 45,000 men. Their purpose would be to depose Elizabeth and proclaim Mary as queen. Spain was to send an army of 6,000 men and, after landing at Harwich or Portsmouth, they would join themselves with the insurgent English forces. It is very likely that Ridolfi himself wrote the letter but by listening to these details, and not rejecting them, Norfolk had committed high treason. It seems that he had uttered only one word when he heard them: 'Well.' It would be enough to condemn him.

The queen of Scotland added to the thickness of the mist by announcing that she had a secret that she could impart only to Elizabeth in person. 'You have caused a rebellion in my realm,' Elizabeth replied, 'and you have aimed at my own life. You will say you did not mean these things. Madam, I would I could think so poorly of your understanding.' She then declared that 'those who would work on me through my fears know little of my character. You tell me you have some mystery which you wish to make known to me. If it be so, you must write it. You are aware that I do not think it well that you and I should meet.'

Just as the plot was reaching its climax, in the spring of 1571, a parliament was summoned. Elizabeth had already reigned for thirteen years, and in that period only three sessions were held. She had no affection for its members, despite her protestations, because they dealt in grievances rather than remedies. She was still unmarried and, without a named heir or successor, the kingdom was in peril. The religious differences within the realm had also been emphasized by the late rebellion. Yet she needed the money that only parliament could authorize. So at the opening of the session she appeared in the robes of state with the golden coronal on her head. At her right hand sat the dignitaries of the Church and on her left hand were the lords of the realm; the privy councillors sat in the centre while the knights and burgesses of the lower house crowded at the back.

The Commons were more interested in religion than in finance. This was the first parliament, after all, from which all Catholics were excluded. A bill was introduced that would compel Sunday attendance and twice-yearly communion. The queen hated religious debate and sent a message to the Commons forbidding them to discuss matters that did not concern them and 'to avoid long speeches'. This was an order they chose to ignore. A bill was introduced, for example, proposing the reformation of the Book of Common Prayer. Elizabeth would not be permitted to behave like a tyrant or, in the phrase of the period, 'like the Great Turk'.

Some notice had to be taken of the papal bull, and it was agreed that it would be high treason 'to affirm, by word or writing, that the queen was not queen' or 'that the queen was a heretic, schismatic, tyrant, infidel, or usurper of the crown'. Any Catholic priests travelling in disguise or posing as serving men in noble households were to be whipped or set in the stocks as 'vagrants or Egyptians'. It also became treason to import any writings from 'the bishop of Rome', as the pope was called, or to introduce any crosses, pictures, or beads blessed by that bishop. With their righteous wrath appeased, parliament voted £100,000 for the queen's treasury.

The plot against Elizabeth was now beginning to unwind. Its leader, Ridolfi, was a great talker who did not always guard his words; he was also an inept conspirator. He confided messages in cipher to a courier who was arrested and searched when he arrived at Dover. Other secrets were obtained from the unfortunate man as he lay helpless upon a rack in the Tower. As a result the details of the conspiracy soon became known to Cecil. 'I am thrown into a maze at this time,' he wrote, 'that I know not how to walk from dangers.' The Spanish ambassador reported that Cecil was so alarmed that he had made preparations to flee the kingdom; he had urged his wife to pack her jewels and to be ready to leave at a moment's notice. This report, however, may simply be the ambassador's wishful thinking. Cecil himself was secure enough in council that, at the beginning of 1571, he was ennobled as Lord Burghley. Soon enough he was also appointed to be lord high treasurer.

Mary denied any involvement in the conspiracy but she was at least complicit in the proposals, with a letter of agreement to the invasion ratified by her signature. Whether she knew all the details is uncertain. But she was described by one member of parliament as 'the monstrous and huge dragon, and mass of the earth'. Elizabeth, on the revelation of the plot, no longer concerned herself with Mary's restoration to the Scottish throne; from this time forward she seems to have concluded that the queen of Scots could never regain her liberty. The duke of Norfolk was in an even more pitiable state. The chance discovery of another coded letter led to his ruin, when searchers found the key to the code hidden between two tiles on the roof of Howard House. They also came upon a letter from Mary Stuart in the duke's possession. In the early autumn of 1571 he was once more consigned to the Tower. Burghley also sent a letter to the earl of Shrewsbury, Mary Stuart's custodian, that was marked as 'sent from the court, the 5th of September, 1571, at 9 in the night'; it also had the familiar superscription for urgency, 'haste, post haste, haste, haste, for life, life, life'. Mary was planning to escape and flee to Spain. The guard around her was redoubled.

Under interrogation Norfolk denied knowing Ridolfi, but then conceded that he had indeed met the man; he then stated that the Florentine banker had suggested treason to him but that he had refused to listen. One by one his falsehoods were exposed. The earls of Southampton and Arundel were also arrested, together with the lords Cobham and Lumley and associated gentry. Burghley had flushed out the Catholics at court.

On 16 January 1572 the duke of Norfolk was put on trial. He was charged with the crime of 'imagining and compassing the death of the queen'. He denied the charge but, in the sixteenth century, it was very difficult to withstand the prosecution of the Crown. He was denied counsel and deprived of all books and papers. From his chamber in the Tower he wrote that he was as crushed 'as a dead fly' or 'a dead dog in this world'.

He was duly convicted but the queen prevaricated over the

sentence. Twice she signed the warrant for execution but then at the last moment revoked it. Norfolk was the premier nobleman in England, after all, and closely related to her. She told Burghley that 'the hinder part' of her brain did not trust 'the forward sides of the same'; her passion, in other words, overruled her judgement. She was in such distress of mind that she collapsed in pain; Burghley and Leicester sat by her bedside for three nights. The same indecision and nervous perplexity had ruined the negotiations for her marriage to the duke of Anjou.

Eventually she signed the third warrant in the early summer and, after much earnest persuasion by her councillors, she did not rescind it. Norfolk went to the scaffold. It was the first execution of a nobleman, by beheading, in the whole course of Elizabeth's reign; the scaffold on Tower Hill was derelict, and another had to be raised in its place. When told of the news Mary, queen of Scots, burst into tears; she was said to be inconsolable for days. But she was still plotting, ever plotting. Burghley would now direct his attentions towards the lady. It was his opinion that the axe should strike at the root.

The whole plot had been so clumsily handled that some historians have concluded that Ridolfi himself was a double agent in Burghley's employment chosen to entrap Mary, Norfolk and the other Catholic conspirators. It is an unlikely, but not wholly implausible, scenario. Ridolfi himself had already fled to Paris, after the arrest of his messenger at Dover, and never returned to England; he died in his native city more than forty years later.

A new parliament assembled in May 1572, just after the Ridolfi plot had been uncovered. The Commons were indignant at the likely role of Mary in the affair. The advice of one speaker was 'to cut off her head and make no more ado about her', an opinion to which the majority assented. Another member, Thomas Digges, urged 'the shunning of that sugared poison bearing in outward show the countenance of mild pity'. Beware of pity. It was not her 'private case' but one that affected the safety of the entire realm. It was then agreed with the Lords, in committee, that Mary should be attainted with treason. The convocation of the senior clergy reached the same decision, arguing that the 'late Scottish queen hath heaped up together all the sins of the licentious sons of David – adulteries, murders, conspiracies, treasons and blasphemies against God'. Yet Elizabeth, in an unrecorded speech, managed to turn away their murderous wrath.

The Lords and Commons then proposed a bill that took away Mary's title to the throne and made it a treasonable offence to advocate the same. The queen refused to sanction it, employing the ancient formula '*La royne s'advisera*' – the queen will consider the matter, the queen will think of it, the queen will advise upon it. It meant that the queen was likely to do nothing at all. She may have felt some remaining sympathy with her relative; Elizabeth had once been in confinement, too. So she took counsel, and all was lost in a mist of words.

Just before the parliament of 1572 was prorogued a pamphlet was addressed to its members that dared to question the constitution of the church. *An Admonition to the Parliament* declared that 'we in England are so far off being rightly reformed, according to the prescript of God's word, that as yet we are not come to the outward face of the same'. The authors, John Field and Thomas Wilcox, wished to found all church teaching and organization on the basis of Scripture. The Book of Common Prayer was 'an unperfect book, culled and picked out of the popish dung-hill, the Mass-book of all abominations'. There should be no archbishops and no bishops; an 'equality' of ministers should govern the Church with 'a lawful and godly seignory' in every congregation. Field and Wilcox were promptly sentenced to a year's imprisonment for violating the Act of Uniformity, but their words reached more attentive ears; in the early 1570s we can trace the rise of the Presbyterian movement.

Just as parliament was becoming more radical, with the entire absence of Catholic members from the Commons, so also were others in authority. At Cambridge, two years before, the Lady Margaret Professor of Divinity had given a set of lectures in which he propounded the same measures as those laid out in the *Admonition*; he had been deprived of his chair and had gone into exile at Geneva, but his followers still remained in the universities. 'I am no parson,' a Cambridge graduate exclaimed after his ordination.

'No, I am no vicar. I abhor these names as Antichristian. I am *pastor* of the congregation there.' The Puritan clergy of England were largely created at the universities.

In London and elsewhere, individual congregations also set up a cycle of preaching and catechizing on the Puritan model; certain popular preachers were immune to the wrath of the bishops and continued to pronounce 'God's truth', often with the support of noblemen and gentry. The earl of Leicester was known to favour the Puritan cause. Lord Burghley himself, at a slightly later date, said of the Puritan clerics that 'the bishops, in these dangerous times, take a very ill and unadvised course in driving them from their cures'.

The rudiments of a system known as the 'classis' soon began to emerge, with the ministers and lay elders of the churches in assembly. A republican union of ministers was established south of London, in the neighbourhood of Wandsworth, and called itself a 'presbytery'; Wandsworth then became known as a haven for religious refugees, from the Protestant Dutch of the 1570s to the Huguenots who fled there in the early seventeenth century. The example had already been set by the 'refugee churches' established in the capital where Protestant exiles were also accustomed to worship. Yet it was not always safe to be one of the 'stricter' sort. In this year a young carpenter from Sussex, Noah by name, walked 6 miles from his village of Hailsham to Warbleton, where he intended to remove the maypole on the village green as a symbol of idolatry; one of the locals then killed him by shooting him through the neck.

Burghley was soon joined in the queen's counsels by Francis Walsingham, a subtle and resourceful finder of secrets; it was said of him that he heard, at his house in Seething Lane, what was whispered in the ear at Rome. He became one of the first in a long line of 'spymasters' in the world of European diplomacy. He had begun his career as Elizabeth's envoy at the French court, but in 1573 she appointed him to be one of her secretaries of state.

A group of men had now emerged about the throne who were

firmly allied to the Protestant cause and, with their business managers in parliament, were opposed to the pretensions of Mary Stuart and to the Catholic powers of Europe; it may be supposed that they had guided the anti-papist measures of the last parliament. The most illustrious of them were Lord Burghley, the earl of Leicester and Francis Walsingham. They had the full confidence of the queen but they were not afraid to question her judgement and, if necessary, to nudge parliament in their direction. It was said that they listened to the queen's commands, but then quietly proceeded as before. Elizabeth herself seems to have been genuinely fond of them; she called Walsingham 'Moor', perhaps because of the darkness of his clothes, and Burghley was her 'Spirit'. Leicester was her 'Eyes'.

Another favourite, Sir Christopher Hatton, emerged in this period. He was primarily a courtier of handsome address, with a genius for dancing. In that capacity he attracted the attention of the queen. He became a gentleman pensioner and then captain of her bodyguard before rising ever higher until he was appointed chancellor of Oxford and lord chancellor of England. It was said that he had danced his way into office. His nickname was 'Lids' or 'Sheep' that soon became 'Mutton'.

A measure of the queen's attentiveness can be found in a peremptory letter that she wrote to the bishop of Ely. Hatton was covetous of some garden-land owned by the bishop, on Holborn Hill and Ely Place, but the divine was not willing to give way to the courtier. The queen insisted, however, and sent the following message to him. 'PROUD PRELATE, You know what you were before I made you what you are now. If you do not immediately comply with my request, I will unfrock you, by God. ELIZABETH.' The bishop then of course surrendered his lands, with the proviso that he and his successors could have free access to the gardens and leave to gather 20 bushels of roses every year.

A much stranger transfer of land is noticed by the chroniclers of the period. A piece of ground in Hertfordshire, 26 acres about an eminence known as Marlech Hill, 'burst from its station, and moved with a groaning noise, carrying with it cattle, sheepcotes, trees etcetera full forty paces the first day'. After four days it ceased to move, forming a hill of 72 feet in height. It had overturned a local chapel in its progress and left a hollow 30 feet in depth, 160 yards wide and 400 yards in length.

Another marvel was reported. At the beginning of 1572 the earl of Leicester presented Elizabeth with a jewelled bracelet in which was set a miniature timepiece. The queen of England wore the first-ever wristwatch.

32

The revels now are ended

As part of her summer progress Elizabeth often visited the home of the earl of Leicester, Kenilworth Castle in Warwickshire. It was here that in succeeding years she was entertained with pageants and with plays. On her procession through the park gates one summer, the porter came attired in the robes of Hercules and delivered to her a speech of welcome. A large pool acted as a moat for one side of the castle, where the queen was greeted by nymphs who seemed to walk on the water. The greatest pageant of welcome was conducted in the base court of the castle, where seven pairs of pillars had been constructed from which the gods and goddesses of Greece offered her various gifts. When she entered the inner court and alighted from her horse, all the clocks of the castle were stopped; no one was to be aware of the time while the queen stayed at Kenilworth.

On the following day, Sunday, she went to church; but the afternoon was filled with music and dancing. The queen was not of the stricter sort.

In particular she loved dancing. One painting shows her engaged with a courtier, thought to be Leicester, in La Volta. In this dance the male partner takes the female and twirls her around in the air, as her feet swing out. She also danced the galliard. She took five steps, leapt as high into the air as she might, and then beat her feet together on returning to the floor. Elizabeth insisted that the dance should become more intricate and challenging, in which pursuit her older or more staid councillors did not follow her.

Other diversions were followed at the castle over successive summers. A 'wild man' from the Indies sang her praises while the goddess Echo redoubled them. Italian allegories, Roman myths and chivalric romances were heaped one upon another. She was shown the local prodigies, such as a giant boy and a monstrous sheep. She enjoyed the hunt and rode with the men in pursuit of the hart. She was delighted by bear-baitings, where twelve or thirteen bears would be set upon by a pack of dogs. Tumblers and fireworks were mingled. In the hot weather she drank wine mixed in equal parts with water. While on progress she also touched for 'the king's evil' by laying her hands on the throat or jaw of the person afflicted with scrofula.

So it was that, in the summer of 1572, she was diverted by an entire world of Tudor entertainment in which the pastoral and the classical were mixed with all the prodigality of an English romance. Peace was in the air. A treaty between France and England had been agreed only five months before. The Treaty of Blois was the indirect result of the long process of unsuccessful negotiations over a French marriage for the queen. It was essentially a defensive treaty against the power of Spain but it had the additional merit of putting an obstacle to further French meddling on behalf of Mary. A painting attributed to Lucas de Heere, *The Family of Henry VIII: An Allegory of the Tudor Succession*, is most likely to be a celebration of the treaty. It was presented by Elizabeth to the man who more than any other had fashioned the agreement, Francis Walsingham, and on a panel at the bottom edge of the work was the inscription:

THE QUENE TO WALSINGHAM THIS TABLET SENTE
MARK OF HER PEOPLES AND HER OWNE CONTENTE

The painting shows in allegorical form the Tudor line, from Henry to Elizabeth herself, but it also shows the queen leading forward the figure of Peace who is carrying an olive branch in her left hand while trampling underfoot the weapons of war.

Yet the tidings of war were never far away. In the earlier part
of this year the people of the Netherlands rose up against their
Spanish overlords and the forces of the duke of Alva; they were
led by William, prince of Orange, whose admiral had previously
taken refuge in England among his co-religionists. In the spring
of 1572 the admiral had sailed from Dover with a small fleet and
had overpowered the town of Brielle at the mouth of the Meuse.
The other ports of Zeeland, Holland and Utrecht all rose up
and expelled the Spanish garrisons. Their sailors became known
as the 'sea beggars', at a time when piracy and patriotism were
often conflated. The prince of Orange himself raised an army in
Germany while the forces of the French, animated by hostility to
Spain, seized Hainault.

The fervour in London grew as the European Protestants and
their French allies began to win victory after victory over the
Catholic forces of Philip of Spain. This was the conflict that the
English reformers had been waiting for; collections of money in
the churches were soon turned into guns and powder while many
volunteers crossed the North Sea to join the offensive. Parliament,
and many of the bishops, urged Elizabeth herself to participate
and to declare war upon the Spaniards in the United Provinces.
A blow would be struck for England but also for God.

Yet Elizabeth was not so sure. She disliked the fact that the
people of the United Provinces had risen against their lawful
sovereign, and she had no reason to welcome the substitution of
Spanish forces by French ones. Her policy, as always, was one of
caution touched by compromise. If the duke of Alva seemed likely
to prevail, or at least to avoid defeat, then she should allow the
protagonists to fight on; it suited her policy to have her neighbours
at each other's throats. As Lord Burghley put it in a paper of
advice to her, 'let both sides alone for a time'. But if the French
began to take over the entire coast and the frontiers, under cover
of their alliance with the Netherlanders, then Elizabeth would
assist Philip 'in the defence of his inheritance' and even join with
him on condition that he restore religious liberty to his subjects
and 'deliver them from the fear of the Inquisition'. To this policy
she adhered. The Spanish ambassador at the English court even
reported that the queen was ready to take possession of Flushing,

in apparent support of the Orange cause, and then surrender it back to the Spanish.

Her deliberate ambiguity was not to the taste of those who espoused the cause of radical Protestantism but it reflected the pragmatism which she brought to all the affairs of state. It was not necessarily with displeasure, therefore, that she heard news of victories by the duke of Alva against the rebels; the French had fallen back in disorder, and Charles IX faced the unwelcome prospect of war against Spain without the help of any ally.

In these difficult circumstances the providential alliance between the French Catholics and the Protestants of the United Provinces could not endure. When the French leader of the Huguenots, Gaspard de Coligny, became the victim of an attempt at assassination, the queen regent, Catherine de Medici, took fright at the possible retaliation of his supporters. So she ordered the pre-emptive destruction of the Huguenot leaders, among them Coligny himself, whose body was thrown out of the window of his lodgings. Unfortunately the bloodshed was contagious and on that same St Bartholomew's Day, 24 August 1572, the mobs of Paris began their murderous work on any Huguenots they could find. They believed that they were attacking the enemies of God; neighbour turned upon neighbour in an atmosphere of frenzy as the Huguenots were stabbed, hanged or beaten to death. It was said that some of the boys of Paris strangled babies in their cradles. The bodies were piled into carts and taken down to the Seine; it was in flood that day and by the grace of God, as the Catholics said, it was better able to wash away the traces of heresy. The emblem of St Bartholomew was the knife as a symbol of his murder by flaying; the knife now ruled.

Cardinal Orsini had told the French king that not one Huguenot should be left alive in France and, although the advice could not be followed in practice, thousands died in Paris and in the provinces. The country was now divided by a religious hatred far outweighing that within England. The occasion itself became known as the Bartholomew's Day Massacre, and did more than any other event in sixteenth-century history to discredit the Catholic cause. It showed the people of England, for example, their possible fate if a Catholic queen once more reigned over them. In Rome the bells rang in celebration, however, and Pope Gregory walked with his cardinals from shrine to shrine in grateful procession.

The queen was still at Kenilworth, enjoying the festivities that Leicester had displayed in her honour, when news of the massacre came to her. She had been discussing with the French ambassador the never-ending question of her marriage to a French prince. Then, on 3 September, a messenger arrived from Paris while she was out hunting. His report broke off any negotiations with the ambassador. A Spanish agent in London informed the duke of Alva that the queen has 'sent all her musicians and minstrels home, and there are no more of the dancers, farces and entertainments . . .' The pageants were suddenly ended, leaving not a rack behind.

The earl of Leicester, eager to support the Protestant cause in Europe, wrote that 'I think no Christian since the heathen time has heard of the like . . .' It was partly his urgent persuasions that moved Elizabeth to come to the aid of William of Orange; privately she sent him £30,000, and permitted 6,000 men to be raised in his cause. She now feared that the massacre was only a prelude to a general assault by the Catholic powers against herself and the other Protestant princes. The people feared this also. The bishops sent her a message requesting that any Catholic priests held in prison should immediately be put to death. The bishop of London urged Burghley to rid the court of all Catholics and to send Mary Stuart to the block.

In the middle of September the French ambassador was allowed to return to court, by now resident at Woodstock. The queen was dressed in mourning, as were all the members of her council and her principal ladies; they were standing in a semicircle and they received the envoy in silence. Elizabeth took him over to a window and asked him if the deplorable reports happened to be true. He replied that there had been a conspiracy against the French king, orchestrated by Coligny himself. So the king had in effect sanctioned the massacre in retaliation for a plot against his life? The envoy could only bluster. After a few more words, she left him.

Nevertheless she maintained her policy of careful neutrality in public. She dispatched the earl of Worcester, a notably Catholic nobleman, to Paris for the baptism of the French king's daughter; Elizabeth herself had agreed to be the infant's godmother, much to the dismay of her Protestant councillors. How could an English earl go in an official capacity to the city that had been the scene of the most appalling massacre in sixteenth-century Europe? The queen also claimed that she could take no part against her dear brother, the king of Spain, despite the fact that she had sent troops and money to his enemies. One Spanish courtier, in a letter to the duchess of Feria at the beginning of 1573, established the facts very well when he informed her that 'the queen has promised to supply funds for six thousand men in the coming spring. If it be so, you can force his Majesty to see the profound cunning with which she is acting. She pretends to be unresolved upon her answer, when she had already consented to what the States [the United Provinces] ask of her . . .'

So Elizabeth was playing a double part, dexterously trying to contrive to keep in balance with all of her neighbours. Yet genuine hesitation also held her hand. This hesitation, close to procrastination, emerges in small as well as in great matters. She was urged to give a small royal manor, Newhall, to the earl of Sussex. She listened kindly to the proposal, said that she would like to give it to him, but then changed her mind. All things considered, it was proper to let him possess it but then, on the other hand, her father had built it at such expense. Burghley asked her if she had a final reply but 'she would give no resolved answer, yea or nay'. She was in any case rarely in the giving mood. When Mary Stuart sent her a present of nightcaps she remarked that 'when people arrive at my age, they take all they can get with both hands, and only give with their little finger'.

A courtier complained to Cecil, on another matter in the same period, that 'it maketh me weary of my life . . . I can neither get the other letter signed nor the letter already signed permitted to be sent away, but day by day and hour by hour deferred, till "anon, soon, and tomorrow"'. Her godson, Sir John Harrington, wrote that 'when the business did turn to better advantage she did most cunningly commit the good issue to her own honour and understanding; but when aught fell out contrary to her own will and

intent, the council were in great strait to defend their own acting
and not blemish the queen's good judgement'. She was happy to
accept the praise, in other words, and refused to shoulder the blame.

In most of the affairs of state, her preferred stance was one of
inaction. And who was to say that this was not the wisest policy?
Doing nothing is better than acting foolishly. When chance or
fortune largely determined the ways of the world, what point was
there in moving forward too quickly? Despite the blandishments
of Cecil and Leicester, therefore, she refused to place herself at the
head of a Protestant League in Europe. It would expose her to too
many risks. In any case she was in sympathy with established
monarchs and with the prevailing regimen of law and order; she
saw no reason to endanger it.

It may also be that she did not comprehend the fierce religious enthusiasms of the Calvinists in the Netherlands or of the
Catholics in France; as far as she was concerned, all such matters
could be resolved by calculation or compromise. She could profit
from the pious zeal of others, however. With the Spanish engaged
in protracted hostilities against the Netherlanders, and with the
French close to civil war, England could be regarded as a place of
safeguard and stability. It might even be able to act as an arbiter
in the fortunes of Europe. Elizabeth decided to remove the English
volunteers from the Netherlands, in a gesture of goodwill towards
Philip, and in the spring of 1573 a treaty with Spain was agreed.
Commercial benefits were bound to follow. By the middle of
April the ports of Spain and of the Low Countries were formally
open to English merchants who were no longer obliged to fear the
attentions of the Inquisition.

More distant events were to play a part in larger and longer
conflicts. In the previous year Sir Francis Drake had landed on
Panama, the strategic bridge between the silver mines of Peru and
the ports of the Caribbean from where the Spanish ships set sail.
It was feared by Spain that Drake and his men would form an
alliance with the runaway slaves of Panama, and thus control all
of the traffic of the isthmus. If Madrid were to be deprived of
its gold and silver, it could not afford to fight in the Netherlands
or anywhere else.

In 1578 John Hawkins, the quondam slave-runner, was enrolled as treasurer of the navy, in which capacity he laboured hard to prepare an ocean-going fleet; the ships were no longer to resemble floating fortresses but to be slimmer and faster, with the emphasis upon guns and cannon for long-range battle. Within fifteen years of his appointment the country possessed twenty-five fighting ships and eighteen ocean-going pinnaces.

At the end of 1577 Drake set sail once more with a fleet of five ships led by the *Golden Hind*, then known as the *Pelican*; he sailed down the coast of Africa, taking such foreign vessels that came in his way, and then sailed across the Atlantic to the New World before passing through the Strait of Magellan and entering the Pacific. He became the first Englishman to circumnavigate the globe. In that same year John Dee, Elizabeth's favourite astrologer, published *General and Rare Memorials Pertaining to the Perfect Art of Navigation*; its title page displayed an English fleet embarking from a well-defended shore under the benediction of the queen. Dee advocated the formation of a British empire founded on sea power, and his work heralded all of England's imperialist aspirations among the merchants and the more adventurous courtiers. Martin Frobisher, for example, was the English seaman who joined forces with Sir Christopher Hatton and John Dee in a deeply laid scheme to discover the North-West Passage that he believed would lead him to Cathay.

It has been said of Richard Hakluyt, the great memorialist of English sea voyages, that the span of his life from 1552 to 1616 matched the rise of a greater England – 'an England stretching fingers of empire to East and West'. Hakluyt himself wrote that 'in this famous and peerless government of her Majesty, her subjects, in searching the most opposite corners and quarters of the world, have excelled all the nations and people of the earth'. The first English colony in America, Roanoke, was established in modern North Carolina by 1585. This is not the 'empire' that Henry had envisioned when he wore the imperial crown, but it derived ineluctably from the same ambition, drive for power and pursuit of profit. Yet so far the struggles between Spain and England on the seas were confined to the New World rather than the Old.

*

A religious complication now further embarrassed relations between Spain and England. At the beginning of 1574 the first seminarians arrived. A seminary of English Catholic priests had been established at Douai, in the Spanish Netherlands, and from here three priests sailed secretly to England to begin work among the faithful. The Catholics of England had by this date organized a network of connections, with their own priests to provide them with the sacraments, all the time hoping for assistance from the Catholic exiles abroad. Some Catholic priests had become private chaplains; others had compromised by accepting the introduction of the new faith while at the same time celebrating the Mass in secret with the chosen few.

After the arrival of the three priests, more followed across the sea; over the next twenty-five years some 600 were sent to England. They were not missionaries. They came only to sustain the adherents of the old faith rather than to convert those who had embraced Protestantism. Nevertheless they were a potent source of unrest in the kingdom, largely because they opposed the claims of one whom they considered to be an unlawful monarch. The leader of the community at Douai, William Allen, told his superiors in Rome that the priests were commanded 'to preach and teach (though not openly but in private houses, after the old example of the Apostles in their days) the Catholic faith, and administer the sacraments to such as had need . . .' The seminarians were to hear confessions, absolve schismatics and strengthen the faith of those tempted to conform. In previous years the authorities had treated the Catholics with a certain amount of caution, maintaining Elizabeth's wish to preserve peace and order at all costs, but the presence of the priests was considered to be an unwarrantable intrusion into domestic affairs. A harsher policy soon prevailed.

The pious of another persuasion were also provoking trouble. In the spring of 1575 a congregation of Anabaptists was discovered in Aldgate. This was the sect most despised and most feared. Although they were of Dutch nationality they were tried before the bishop of London in St Paul's Cathedral for the most horrible offences of heresy and blasphemy; five recanted and were saved. They paraded with lighted faggots in their hands and abjured the doctrines that Christ had not 'taken flesh' of the Virgin Mary, that infants ought not to be baptized, that a Christian ought neither to be a magistrate nor bear a sword, and that no Christian should take an oath. Fifteen of their companions were shipped overseas, and five were condemned to death by burning. Only two of them were in fact consigned to the fire, John Weelmaker and Henry Toorwoort, and at Smithfield they died 'in great horror with roaring and crying' as the concourse of people applauded their punishment. It was the first blood spilt for religion in the reign of Elizabeth.

No burnings had taken place for seventeen years and John Foxe, the historian of the martyrs under Mary, remonstrated with the queen in a letter about their unhappy return. Elizabeth called him 'my father Foxe' and so he had some licence to preach to her. 'I have no favour for heretics,' he wrote, 'but I am a man and would spare the life of man. To roast the living bodies of unhappy men, erring rather from blindness of judgement than from the impulse of will, in fire and flames, of which the fierceness is fed by the pitch and brimstone poured over them, is a Romish abomination . . . for the love of God spare their lives.' The call was not heeded.

The death of Archbishop Parker in May 1575 led to a change in the general direction of the Church. Parker had left behind great wealth, and it was believed that he had been generally corrupt in the duties of his office. His successor, Edmund Grindal, was known for his piety as much as for his learning; he had been favoured by Lord Burghley and was indeed of a stricter sort. An anonymous admirer wrote to persuade him that 'there may be consultation had with some of your brethren how some part of those Romish dregs remaining, offensive to the godly, may be removed. I know it will be hard for you to do that good that you and your brethren desire. Yet (things discreetly ordered) somewhat there may be done.' The task was 'hard' because Elizabeth herself much disliked any further change or meddling. She was a religious conservative, and soon enough Grindal would earn her displeasure.

Elizabeth was alarmed, for example, by the rise in events that became known as 'prophesyings' or exercises. These were meetings, attended by the lesser as well as the more senior clergy, in which passages of Scripture were discussed and the lesser clergy were instructed in the art of the sermon and other matters. The laity were sometimes allowed to attend the sessions, and the day usually ended with a supper at a local inn when points of doctrine were pronounced and debated. The term 'prophesyings' derived from St Paul's First Letter to the Corinthians in which he urged that 'the prophets speak two or three, and let the other judge ... for ye may all prophesy one by one, that all may learn and all may be comforted'.

These events were welcomed by those of an evangelical persuasion. The attendance of all ranks of clergy did much to erase the hierarchical degrees of the established Church, and the emphasis on preaching and debate also offered ample opportunity for the more open and informal discussion of doctrine beyond the confines of the Sunday service. The prophesyings in fact became popular among the general population and were soon being attended in the Midlands, East Anglia, London, Devon, Kent and Surrey.

The queen came to hear of the matter as a result of some local quarrels between conformists and nonconformists. She had also been told that certain priests, suspended from their duties for their more radical opinions, had participated in the events. So she asked Archbishop Grindal to bring them to an end; with an inveterate dislike for any form of religious zeal, she also ordered him to restrict the number of preachers in each shire to three or four. In response the archbishop proposed a code of practice, an offer of compromise that she rejected. He then wrote her a letter, in which he quoted the example of the biblical prophets who had not scrupled to offend or rebuke the kings.

It was his solemn duty to speak plainly to her. Without the preaching of the Word of God, the people would perish. The prophesyings had been introduced for 'the edification, exhortation and comfort of the clergy', and he went on to say that 'I cannot with a safe conscience and without the offence of the majesty of God give my consent to the suppressing of the said exercises'. He was willing to disobey the queen who was also the governor of his Church. 'Remember Madam,' he wrote, 'that you are a mortal creature.' The somewhat impertinent letter was met with royal silence. Five months later a decree was issued from the court forbidding 'inordinate preachings, readings, and ministerings of the sacrament'; the people had left their parishes in order to attend 'disputations and new devised opinions upon points of divinity, far unmeet for vulgar people'. The prophesyings thereby came to an end.

Archbishop Grindal himself had incurred the severe displeasure of the queen. She had wanted to chase him from office, but Cecil and Walsingham persuaded her that this would create an unhappy precedent. Any open scandal would also bring comfort to the Catholics. So she excluded him from any real authority and confined him to his palace at Lambeth, where he was allowed to perform only the most routine duties. A time came when he was ready to resign, by mutual agreement, but his death prevented that further compromise.

Parliament was summoned in February 1576, and almost at once a supporter of the Puritan cause, Peter Wentworth, delivered what was considered to be a most indelicate address. He demanded freedom of speech in parliament, especially in matters of religion, even at the risk of incurring the queen's displeasure. He argued that parliament was the guardian of the laws, and that it ought to be able to discharge the trust with impunity; even the monarch was constituted as such by the law. It was intolerable that religious debate was curtailed because of a rumour that 'the queen's majesty liketh not of such a matter; whosoever preferreth it, she will be much offended with him'. It was equally intolerable that 'messages' could be sent from the court inhibiting debate. 'I would to God, Mr Speaker, that these two were buried in hell: I mean rumours and messages.' And he went on to say that 'none is without fault; no, not our noble queen . . . It is a dangerous thing in a prince unkindly to entreat and abuse his or her nobility and people, as Her Majesty did the last Parliament. And it is a dangerous thing in a Prince to oppose or bend herself against her nobility and people.'

His colleagues in the Commons immediately denounced him for promoting licence rather than liberty, and in particular condemned him for introducing a question about the prerogatives of the sovereign. He was sequestered from the chamber and committed as a prisoner to the sergeant-at-arms. He was then brought before a committee of the council, and excused his references to liberty of speech on the grounds that the queen's 'messages' to parliament explicitly forbade debate on the vital matters of religion. This was not a tolerable position. Wentworth was confined for a month before the queen, by special 'grace and favour', restored him to his liberty. There was as yet no presumption of free speech in parliament.

Once more the business of the queen's marriage was introduced, in this parliament, and once more she demurred with an ambiguous reply. In her speech at the end of the session she declared that 'if I were a milkmaid with a pail on my arm, whereby my private person might be little set by, I would not forsake that poor and single state to match with a monarch ... yet for your behalf, there is no way so difficult that may touch my private person, which I will not content myself to take'. She preferred to remain unmarried, in other words, but would bow to the consideration of the great matters of state.

The queen thought so much of this speech that she sent a copy of it to her godson, John Harrington, with a covering letter. 'Boy Jack,' she wrote, 'I have made a clerk write fair my poor words for thine use, as it cannot be such striplings have entrance into the Parliament House as yet ... so shalt thou hereafter, perchance, find some good fruits thereof, when thy godmother is out of remembrance.' Her undertaking, to respect the greater matters of state, would soon enough be put to the test.

33

The frog

Towards the close of 1576 the Netherlands were exposed to what became known as 'the Spanish fury', when many of the unpaid Spanish forces mutinied against their officers; a massacre of the civilian population was the consequence, with 8,000 murdered in Antwerp alone. That city never regained its former prominence. The outrage deeply disturbed the people of the Netherlands, then comprising what is now Holland and Belgium, and even the Catholic provinces joined forces with the rebellious provinces of Holland and Zeeland in their determination to curtail the powers of their Spanish overlords. Hence arose the Pacification of Ghent signed just four days after the massacre; this was a proposal grudgingly accepted by the new governor, Don John of Austria, younger half-brother of Philip II, among the terms of which was the demand that all of the Spanish troops should be removed. There was now a common front among the provinces of the Netherlands, ratified by the Union of Brussels at the beginning of 1577.

Elizabeth was once more enmired in caution and hesitation. Sir Walter Raleigh is reported to have said of her that she 'does everything by halves'. Yet this was for England a time of peace. It lasted for twenty-six years, from 1559 to 1585, and, as the chancellor of the exchequer, Sir Walter Mildmay, told the Commons, 'we be in quietness at home and safe enough from troubles abroad'. There was no room for complacency, however, and he warned that 'we ought in time to make provision to prevent any storm that may arise either here or abroad'. So why then should the queen risk raising any 'storm' by meddling directly or militarily in the affairs of the Spanish Netherlands?

She sent £20,000 to the Netherlands and arranged for the later dispatch of a similar sum, on condition that she was repaid in full within eight months; she justified this action to the Spanish on the grounds that she was merely providing funds to pay for the arrears of the Spanish army. By the summer of the year the occupying army was on its way home. Then, at the beginning of 1578, all was changed. The army of the Low Countries was destroyed in an engagement at Gembloux, when Don John's forces poured back over the frontier. The United Provinces looked to Elizabeth at this juncture for much-needed aid, but they looked in vain. The queen did nothing.

'If Her Majesty do nothing now,' her envoy wrote a week after the defeat, 'it will in the judgement of the wisest bring forth some dangerous alteration.' A month passed without any sign of action from Elizabeth. It was rumoured that she was about to send an army under the earl of Leicester to fight the Spanish, but this was wishful thinking on the part of the Protestants. The envoy wrote once more that 'hesitation is cruel and dishonourable. If she say no, she will not escape the hatred of the papists. If she say yes, she still has great advantages for the prosecution of the war; but it must be one or the other and swiftly.' Elizabeth was the last person on earth to whom such advice would be profitable or welcome. Instead she sent a further £20,000, with terms for prompt repayment. William Camden, a contemporary, wrote that 'thus sate she as an heroical princess and umpire betwixt the Spaniards, the French and the States; so as she might well have used that saying of her father, *cui adhaereo praeest*, that is, the party to which I adhere getteth the upper hand. And true it was which one hath written, that France and Spain are as it were the scales in the balance of Europe, and England the tongue or the holder of the balance.'

Her influence upon France was further strengthened by another bout of matrimonial politics, when once more she invited

the attentions of Francis, duke of Anjou. He was the unfortunate youth, then duke of Alençon, the reports of whose personal
attractions were the object of many jokes at the English court; his
face was pitted with the scars of smallpox, and he had a slight
deformity of the spine which belied his nickname of 'Hercules'. He
was also twenty-one years younger than the English queen, which
might leave Elizabeth herself open to ridicule. In these unpromising
circumstances the negotiations began once more. Her resolve might
have been further strengthened by her discovery that her favourite,
the earl of Leicester, had remarried. In the spring of 1578, at a
secret ceremony in Kenilworth, he had joined himself with the
countess of Essex; it was said that 'he doted extremely on marriage',
and he purchased for her a manor house at Wanstead, in Essex,
where he might see her away from the eyes of the world.

Leicester then came to London but declared himself too ill to
attend the court. But the queen was informed of his arrival soon
enough. The Spanish ambassador reported that, on 28 April, while
she was taking the air in the royal garden, she found a letter that
had been left in the doorway. After reading it she went at once to
Leicester House, and remained there until ten in the evening. It is
possible that Leicester had written the letter, hoping to turn away
the royal wrath. Or it may have been an anonymous denunciation
of his marriage. Whatever the cause, the effect was the same. It
was said that she had wished to commit Leicester to the Tower of
London, but then relented. In the following month, however, she
opened negotiations for her marriage to the young duke.

The French were suspicious of her motives. It may be that she
wished only to draw Anjou away from a possible alliance with the
rebels of the Low Countries; the duke was possessed by an appetite
for greatness in military affairs, and the prospect of the English
crown was the only means of diverting him. Together the French
and the English might then be powerful enough to bring Spain
and the rebels to peace. So the French court was cautious. The
king of France believed that there was more artifice than desire in
the proposal. Anjou himself entertained her offer but urged speed
and expedition. To the French ambassadors she was benign if not
exactly coquettish; she even professed to be unconcerned about the
difference in age between herself and the young duke. She would

treat him as a son as well as a husband. No one knew if she was sincere in these blandishments; perhaps even she was not sure of her own intentions.

It is characteristic that her progress in the summer of 1578 was beset by confusion. In May it was reported that 'Her Majesty will go in progress to Norfolk this year, but there is no certain determination thereof as yet'. Leicester was concerned that his good friend, Lord North, would have no time 'to furnish his house according to his duty and honourable good will'; yet Kirtling Tower, near Newmarket, was refurbished for the occasion. A new inn had to be hastily constructed to cope with the unanticipated numbers of her entourage.

The man chosen to oversee the pageants and revels to take place at Norwich, on the occasion of the queen's visit to the city, believed that the local magnates had received 'but small warning' of the events. In mid-July, even as the progress unrolled, the lord keeper was not sure that Elizabeth would venture into Suffolk, while another courtier reported that it was not clear that the queen would even go to Norwich 'if the bird sing truly that I heard this day'. On the following day the earl of Northumberland was asking Burghley for confirmation of 'the certainty of her Majesty's progress'.

These confusions reflect the divisions within the council, as the various aims and ambitions of the most prominent members clashed. In the pageants themselves carefully coded political messages were introduced into the entertainments, some of them advising against the marriage with the duke of Anjou. It was no accident that, in the pageants of Norwich, the image of Elizabeth the Virgin Queen was first presented to the people. In the course of the tableau Chastity presented the queen with Cupid's bow as her own special possession since 'none could wound her highness's heart':

> Then since O Queen chaste life is thus thy choice
> And that thy heart is free from bondage yoke . . .

It is believed that Leicester was the moving spirit of these designs, opposed as he was to the Anjou marriage. All was not sweetness and light; behind the veneer of entertainment and spectacle can be glimpsed fierce conflicts and partisan hostilities.

The queen was also travelling into a most disordered diocese, where Catholics and Protestants – or, as it might be expressed, recusants and reformers – vied for mastery. On the journey to Norwich the queen stopped at Bury St Edmunds where two radical preachers were associated with the practice of prophesying. One of them was interrogated by the council that accompanied the queen; he was left unmolested, and some of the Puritan gentry of the town were knighted.

The queen then went on to stay with a prominent Catholic, Edward Rokewood, at Euston Hall. She granted her favour to this recusant household but, at the end of the visit, an image of the Virgin Mary was found in the hay-house. Elizabeth ordered that the image be burned 'which in her sight by the country folks was quickly done, to her content, and unspeakable joy of everyone but some one or two who had sucked of the idol's poison milk'. It is an odd episode. Had the image been planted by those who wished to harm Rokewood? Or was it all part of a planned theatre to emphasize the queen's distaste for papal superstitions? Rokewood himself was arrested and consigned indefinitely to prison.

While touring the cathedral at Norwich she was informed that the duke of Anjou had invaded the Netherlands and had devised a treaty with the Protestant states in which he was declared to be 'Defender of the Liberties of the Low Countries against Spanish Tyranny'. She was incensed by this unwelcome alliance and exploded with rage against her councillors, although it was her neglect and prevarication that had persuaded the Netherlanders to court the French duke. She sent a letter of support to Philip of Spain while at the same time continuing the marriage proposal to Anjou himself. Soon enough the northern provinces joined in an association or contract. It was only a matter of time before they formally renounced Philip of Spain, with Anjou likely to be their next sovereign.

So the affairs of the court, like the progress, continued by means of inconstant resolutions, turns and half-turns. It is no wonder that some were discontented. Sir Philip Sidney, poet as much as courtier, told friends that, weary of a jaded and servile court, he was 'meditating some Indian project'; he was considering the voyage to the New World. Walsingham wrote that he wished 'if I may conveniently, I mean, with the leave of God, to convey myself off the stage and to become a looker on'. Another courtier, Sir Thomas Heneage, complained that 'neither counsel nor fore-cast can prevail; if we prosper it must be, as our custom is, by miracle'.

These men lived at the full pitch of responsibility and anxiety, rendered infinitely worse by the unreliability of the queen. The perils of ambition and high position were sometimes dreadful. On 4 April 1578 the earl of Bothwell, Mary Stuart's tempestuous husband, died; he ended his days raving, while tied to a pillar in the dungeons of Dragsholm Castle in Denmark. His mummified body could until 1976 be seen in a church close to the castle.

The queen was prone to ailments in this period. At the age of forty-five she was once more subject to the leg ulcer that had afflicted her eight years before. In the autumn of the year she suffered from what John Dee called a 'fit' that lasted for four hours; on the following day a 'sore fit' lasted for three hours. The nature of these fits is unknown but they were described as 'grievous pangs and pains by reason of the ache and the rheum'. In December she was beset by toothache that was so painful that it kept her without sleep for forty-eight hours. A meeting of the privy council was called to consider the matter, and a tooth-drawer named Fenatus outlined the safest method of removing the offend-ing tooth.

The councillors waited on the queen, together with a surgeon who would perform the operation. Elizabeth herself was fearful and drew back from the ordeal. The bishop of London then stepped forward and volunteered to calm her nerves by losing one of his own few remaining teeth. The surgeon extracted it without the least sign of distress on the bishop's part and, following his example, the queen submitted with good grace.

The negotiations with Anjou were conducted with even more fervour. Despite the fits and the ulcer her doctors 'foresaw no difficulty' in her successfully bearing a child. At the beginning of 1579 the duke's envoy, Jean de Simier, arrived at court with an entourage of sixty gentlemen; he was perhaps not himself the model of a courtier, having recently murdered his brother for an affair with his wife, but Elizabeth was charmed by him. She called him 'Monkey' and 'the most beautiful of my beasts'. She gave a court ball in his honour and lingered in his company until it might have seemed that Simier himself was the proper suitor. He was even admitted into the royal bedchamber, where he claimed her nightcap as a love token for his master.

The earl of Leicester was violently opposed to the proposed marriage and accused Simier of practising the black arts of enchantment upon the queen. Even the sermons at court were directed against the French connection, and on the first Sunday of Lent a preacher invoked the evil example of the queen's half-sister, Mary, and proclaimed that 'marriages with foreigners would only result in ruin to the country'; Elizabeth stormed out of the royal chapel.

In this year John Stubbs composed a violently anti-Gallican tract, *The discovery of a gaping gulf*, which accused certain evil 'flatterers' and 'politics' of espousing the interests of the French court 'where Machiavelli is their new testament and atheism their religion'. He described the proposed union as a 'contrary coupling' and an 'immoral union' like that of a cleanly ox with an uncleanly ass; the danger of a papist heir was too great to be endured. Elizabeth was in any case too old to bear children, so the marriage was without purpose. The pamphlet was formally burned in the kitchen stove of Stationers' Hall, but Stubbs was destined for further punishment. He was tried at Westminster and was found guilty of 'seditious writing'. The queen had wished for the death penalty, but was persuaded that the punishment was too extreme. Instead it was decreed that the offender should lose his right hand. Just before the sentence was carried out he cried 'My calamity is at hand', one of the few occasions when a pun has accompanied a violent assault. When the right hand was severed Stubbs took off his hat with his left hand and called out 'God save the queen!' before fainting.

Another incident more closely touched Elizabeth. When she and Simier were sailing upon the Thames in the royal barge, one of her bargemen was wounded by a shot from another boat in the river; immediate hysteria followed, with fears of an assassination plot directed against Simier or even against the sovereign herself. Yet it proved to be an accident, and Elizabeth pardoned the innocent perpetrator with the words that 'she would believe nothing of her people which parents would not believe of their children'.

The young Anjou himself arrived in the middle of August, so early in the day that he roused Simier from his bed. The duke was eager to begin his courtship at once, but Simier persuaded him to rest. The envoy wrote a letter to the queen, however, in which he explained how he soon 'got him between the sheets, and I wish to God you were with him there as he could then with greater ease convey his thoughts to you'. Anjou was not yet officially in the country and at a court ball in the following week he was concealed behind an arras; the queen danced and made a number of gestures towards him that the courtiers pretended not to notice. He was gone four days later, on hearing of the death of a close friend, but he had made an impression. She called him her *grenouille* or 'frog'.

A parliament was due to meet in October, but the queen prorogued it in order to avoid unseemly debate on the matter of her marriage; she was accustomed to the meddling of Lords and Commons, but on this occasion declined to encourage it. Instead she assembled her council in solemn session for the purpose of giving advice; in fact the councillors sat for several days, and on one occasion remained in the council chamber from eight in the morning until seven in the evening without stirring from the room. They were deeply divided, with seven of them against the marriage and five for it; so they attended the queen, and asked for her real opinion on the matter. Only then could they resolve the issue.

Elizabeth burst into tears. She had wanted them to arrive at a definite decision in favour of the marriage, but now she was once more lost in uncertainty. She defended the idea of her union with Anjou and later that day argued cogently on its merits. But she knew well enough that it divided the country just as surely as it divided the council; without the full support of her councillors, moreover, it would be very difficult to gain the acquiescence of a more stridently Protestant parliament. That parliament itself was prorogued for a further three months, but not without much hesitation and indecision. She even signed the articles of marriage, with a proviso that she had two months in which to win over her subjects or give up the attempt.

It seems likely that her tears in front of her councillors were genuine, and that they were evidence of her frustration and unhappiness; her last chance of a married life had been snatched from her. In this period a portrait of her, commissioned by Christopher Hatton and attributed to Quentin Metsys, depicts her beside a pillar that is decorated with medallions of Dido and Aeneas from Virgil's *Aeneid*. On her other side stands a globe, displaying the maritime ventures of the English. The moral is clear enough. Just as Aeneas must desert Dido in order to fulfil his imperial destiny, so the queen must forfeit the love of Anjou to establish her own empire. This was the time when complex allegorical portraits of the queen, in which virginity and empire stood in equipoise, began to appear. Between 1579 and 1583 no fewer than eleven 'sieve' paintings of the queen were finished; the sieve was a symbol of virginity. The perpetually youthful and unassailable queen was thus the emblem of a vigorous and invincible body politic.

Her natural frustrations, however, may have taken a peculiar form. She was incensed that certain of her subjects dared to match the height and dimensions of the royal ruff, at the neck of a shirt or chemise; so an Act of Parliament was passed that permitted certain officers of the court to stand at street corners and, brandishing a pair of shears, to clip all ruffs above the permitted size. She also forbade the rapiers of gentlemen to exceed a certain length. Her own tastes could still be exotic. She purchased six Hungarian horses, to draw the royal coach, before dyeing their manes and tails bright orange.

The English chronicler Raphael Holinshed has another story about the ruffs of 1580 that throws a curious light on the period. A Sussex boy, of eleven years, lay in a trance for ten days; when he awoke he had acquired the character of a divine or moralist. He rebuked a serving man for wearing 'great and monstrous' ruffs about his neck, saying that 'it were better for him to put on sackcloth and ashes than to prank himself up like the devil's darling'; whereupon the servant wept, took out a knife and tore the ruff from his neck before cutting it into pieces.

*

In the first week of April 1580, a powerful earthquake shook the whole of south-eastern England; the citizens of London ran from their houses into the streets, in panic fear, while some of the cliffs at Dover were dislodged and fell into the sea. A pinnacle tumbled from Westminster Abbey, and two children were killed by stones dislodged from the roof of Christ's Hospital. Thomas Churchyard wrote, in a contemporaneous pamphlet, that 'wonderful motion and trembling of the earth shook London and Churches, Pallaces, houses, and other buildings did so quiver and shake, that such as were then present in the same were tossed too and fro as they stoode, and others, as they sate on seates, driven off their places'. It was supposed to be a sign of divine retribution on a luxurious and wasteful people.

This was the period, in the spring and early summer of the year, when the first Jesuits arrived in England on their mission to maintain, if not to restore, the old faith. They came six years after the first Catholic priests had re-entered the country, but the Jesuits were perhaps more determined. An order, after all, established precisely to combat the Reformation, they were as disciplined as they were devout, with an overpowering desire to proselytize their faith; they became known as 'the black horsemen of the pope'.

Edmund Campion and Robert Parsons, together with seven other colleagues, were among the first to return. Campion had studied at the English College in Douai, but his earlier education had been more impressive. He had been a fellow of St John's College, Oxford, and such were his gifts of scholarship and oratory that he was chosen to welcome the queen on her visit to that university in 1569. He gained the patronage of both Leicester and Lord Burghley, and seemed likely to gain preferment in the established Church; he was considered likely to be one day archbishop of Canterbury.

Yet he suffered from what he called 'remorse of conscience and detestation of mind', as a result of which he returned to his own old faith; he fled to Douai where he received the Eucharist and was reconciled to the Catholic communion. He was, therefore, an able and worthy representative of the cause. He had friends, and acquaintances, at Westminster; he may even have had secret friends in the queen's council.

He was of course in danger, since he was mixing with those who detested Elizabeth as a heretic and favoured the cause of Mary Stuart. Yet the peril was part of the enterprise; it had occurred to his superior, William Allen, that the Catholics of England might be stirred out of their complacence by the spectacle of burnings or worse. Campion was ordered to refrain from any discussion of politics and to say nothing injurious to the queen. He was to concentrate solely on religious matters so that, if he died for the faith, he would die as a martyr rather than a traitor.

It was not so easy, however, to contain the doubts and desires of the English Catholics. Some papers were scattered in the streets of London, declaring Elizabeth to be a schismatic and unlawful queen. The council thereupon reissued the statutes against Catholics. A gentleman caught hearing Mass would be imprisoned. Any English family found to be harbouring Jesuit priests would be prosecuted for maintaining rebels. The problem was compounded when a detachment of Catholic soldiers from Italy, under a Spanish general, landed in Ireland; it was considered to be the likely preparation for an invasion commanded by the king of Spain. It was also widely reported that the pope had acquiesced in plans for the assassination of the queen.

Walsingham, the catcher of spies, now became the hunter of Jesuits. By the end of the year, six or seven young Jesuits had been arrested and taken to the Tower. It is said that, to this day, no dog will enter the Salt Tower where they were imprisoned. On the walls of that tower were engraved a pierced heart, hand and foot as a symbol of the wounds of Jesus together with a cross and an 'H' that are the emblem of the Jesuits. After a time the prisoners were led to the rack which was housed in a vaulted dungeon beneath the armoury. Which gentlemen had welcomed them? Where were their leaders concealed? Every turning of the winch increased their agony.

Yet Parsons and Campion were still at large, and more Jesuits were returning to England. They landed secretly at night, avoiding any dwellings and even barking dogs; they spent the first night in the woods, whatever the weather, and at daybreak they separated and made their own way. They avoided the high roads, where strangers might question them. They might be disguised as gentlemen, or as military captains, or as journeymen. One of them, Father Gerard, cut across the fields and asked anyone he met if they had seen his escaped falcon.

A secret printing press was established in Stonor Park, at Henley-on-Thames, where the printers dressed up as gentlemen – complete with swords and ruffs – to disguise their occupation. It is from the Jesuits that the word 'propaganda' comes. Campion and Parsons went on a tour of the country, visiting most of the shires where they preached and administered the sacraments; they were welcomed by gentlemen and noblemen in every place to which they travelled. They generally stayed only one night, for fear of discovery.

In the summer of 1581 Parsons described the danger to a fellow priest. 'Sometimes,' he wrote, 'when we are sitting merrily at table, talking familiarly about points of religion (for our talk is mostly of matters of this sort), there comes the insistent rapping at the door we associate with the constables; all start up and listen, hearts beating, like deer who hear the hunters' halloo; we leave our food and commend ourselves to God in a brief moment of prayer; not a word is spoken, not a sound is heard, until the servant comes in to say what it is. If it is nothing, we laugh – all the more merrily because of our fright.'

'The enemy sleeps not,' Sir Walter Mildmay told the Commons on behalf of the council. 'A sort of hypocrites, Jesuits and vagrant friars, have come into the realm to stir sedition, and many of those who used to come to church have fallen back and refused to attend . . . it is time to look more strictly to them.' Campion was for a time concealed in London. He often visited a friend who lived along the road to Harrow and on his walk there he would pass the gallows at Tyburn; whenever he passed by, he touched his hat to the machine that might one day destroy him.

In the summer of 1581 he was discovered within a secret 'priest's hole' in a manor house at Lyford, near Abingdon. He was taken to London, still wearing his lay disguise of a buff jerkin and velvet hose; his feathered cap was put on his head, and his legs were tied beneath the belly of a horse. On his head a sign was fastened, 'Campion, the seditious Jesuit', and he rode through crowds of jeering spectators to find his place in the dungeon of

Little Ease in the Tower; with dimensions of just 4 square feet this chamber was itself a form of torture.

On the following day the earl of Leicester sent for him, and on being taken into a private chamber Campion found himself in the presence of the queen. She remembered the learned young man whom she had met and was determined, if possible, to save his life. She asked him whether he regarded her as his lawful sovereign; to which proposition he assented. The pope had permitted this. She then asked him if the bishop of Rome could lawfully excommunicate her. He replied more equivocally, saying that such matters were beyond his judgement. He was sent back to the Tower and, on refusing to answer his interrogators, he was put on the rack for two successive days.

Torture had in previous centuries been applied only to those who refused to plead and were then slowly 'pressed to death', but in the reign of the Tudors it became a royal prerogative in cases of national safety or security. In 1580 Burghley himself wrote a short narrative in praise of the practice. The most notorious of the interrogators was Richard Topcliffe, a lawyer from Yorkshire who came to specialize in the refinements of torture upon priests. One Jesuit wrote from his prison cell that 'the morrow after Simon and Jude's day I was hanged at the wall from the ground, my manacles fast locked into a staple as high as I could reach upon a stool: the stool taken away where I hanged from a little after 8 o'clock in the morning till after 4 in the afternoon, without any ease or comfort at all, saving that Topcliffe came in and told me that the Spaniards were come into Southwark by our means: "For lo, do you not hear the drums" (for then the drums played in honour of the lord mayor). The next day after also I was hanged up an hour or two: such is the malicious minds of our adversaries.' Any form of barbarity became known as a 'topcliffian custom' and 'topcliffizare' was the verb for hounding to ruin or death. It was said that there were men in the world who would drink blood as easily as beasts drank water.

Weak though Edmund Campion was from his treatment, he was not demoralized. He called for a public debate on matters of religion, and the chapel of the Tower was used as the chamber for a contest between him and two Protestant divines. They argued on three separate occasions but inevitably there was no settled conclusion. The matter was one concerning the stability of the realm rather than the truths of religion. He was tortured once more but, remaining defiant, he was sent for trial. He was brought to Westminster Hall, his limbs dislocated from the rack. He could not raise his arm to proclaim his response of 'not guilty'; two of his fellow defendants held it up, and kissed the broken joint as they did so. There could only be one outcome. 'We are charged with treason,' Campion declared. 'We are no traitors.' He went on to say that 'we are men dead to the world, and we travailed for the salvation of souls'.

Campion, and fourteen other Jesuits, were condemned to death by the conventional punishment of hanging, drawing and quartering. On the first day of December he and two others were led from the Tower for their journey to Tyburn. It was noticed that Campion's fingernails had been torn off by his torturers. When he came up to the gallows he declared that 'we come here to die, but we are not traitors'. The ropes with which he met his death are preserved at Stonyhurst College. As the butchery commenced a drop of his blood spurted upon a spectator, Henry Walpole; Walpole was converted on the spot, and himself became a Jesuit. He, too, would meet the same fate at Tyburn.

It has been calculated that some 200 Catholics suffered death in the course of Elizabeth's reign, among them 123 priests, compared with the 300 Protestant martyrs who perished during Mary's much briefer rule. In the reign of Henry VIII 308 people were executed as a result of the Treason Act of 1534. The historian here often pauses to deliver a lament on human bigotry, but the temptation should be resisted. It is not possible to judge the behaviour of one century by the values of another. It was in any case a high crime to refuse to conform to the religious imperatives of the state.

An alternative to execution was found in incarceration, and a special prison was established for priests and Catholic laymen at Wisbech Castle on the Isle of Ely. It would in more recent times be described as an internment camp for approximately thirty-five prisoners. The conditions were not harsh, however; scholars were among the number, and Wisbech became a form of seminary.

The ancient castle of Beaumaris, on the island of Anglesey, was another such centre. More conventional detention was also in place and it was said that 'the prisons are so full of Catholics that there is no room for thieves'. When parliament assembled at the beginning of 1581 further measures were taken against them; the fine for recusancy was raised from 1 shilling each Sunday to £20 per month, two hundred times higher. Anyone attempting to absolve a subject from his or her allegiance to the queen was guilty of treason.

In this spirit the Cheapside Cross was assaulted, to 'a great shout of people with joy'. It was considered to be a pagan idol from the dark days of superstition. On the night of 21 June 1581, certain young men 'did then fasten ropes about the lowest images' of the Cross but they could not dislodge them; they did take the picture of Christ, however, and struck off the arms of the Virgin Mary. The cross itself, on the top of the monument, was also pulled down.

The image of the cross could also be put to secular use. When builders were repairing or restoring parts of the palace at White-hall, they painted red crosses on the new plaster. This was to prevent the common practice of pissing anywhere. It was believed that no one would dishonour the cross by urinating upon it.

The Jesuit missionaries claimed that they had made 140,000 converts; the figure may be slightly exaggerated, but in any case they were not converted from Protestantism to Roman Catholicism. They represent those who were now ready to confess their adherence to the old faith, and of course they were considerably outnumbered by the 'church papists' whose Catholicism was disguised by their attendance at the orthodox services. It has been estimated, however ingeniously, that the country harboured some 200,000 Catholics; if that figure is correct, they made up some 5 per cent of the population.

It was not necessary to be a Catholic, however, to be named as a recusant. There were heretics of quite another colour. In 1581 Robert Browne established in Norwich the first religious organization that considered itself to be independent of the Elizabethan settlement. Its members became known indiscriminately as Brownists, Independents or Separatists; they rejected the established Church of England as unscriptural and were attached to the more severe forms of Puritan doctrine. Their churches became known as 'gathered' churches because they relied upon a gathering of people. The Brownists were as a result harried and persecuted by the authorities. They retreated from Norwich to Bury St Edmunds, and then fled overseas to Holland; those caught in England were likely to be imprisoned or hanged.

The proponents of another sectarian faith, the Familists or the Family of God, believed that a man or woman might be 'godded with God' and thus be responsible for a fresh incarnation. They rejected the notion of the Trinity and repudiated infant baptism; they refused to carry arms or to take oaths. Henry Barrowe, in 1581, left Gray's Inn and retired to the country, in which retreat he formulated the creed known as Barrowism; he believed that the Elizabethan Church was polluted by the relics of popery, and that only complete separation from it could guarantee a true faith. These men and women were of truly heroic fortitude; they challenged all the principles of the society in which they lived, and were willing to endure the scorn and punishment of those whom they offended. No account of sixteenth-century England would be complete without them.

34

The great plot

The duke of Anjou had returned to England at the time of Campion's arrest and trial. It might have been unfortunate timing for a Roman Catholic duke to be seeking the queen's hand once more, but he was immune from such embarrassments. Anjou was on the tennis court, about to begin a game, when a French *abbé* approached him and asked him to intercede with the queen on Campion's behalf. He hesitated for a moment and stroked his face; then he turned away and called out 'Play!'

This was his last chance to win the game. He had already been appointed as sovereign of the Netherlands, as a result of his intervention against Spanish rule, but now he was after a larger prize. If he could also gain the crown of England his power might be a match for that of his brother, the French king, and even for Philip. Yet the queen was as irresolute as ever. He stayed for three months, after his arrival in the autumn of 1581, and there was much closeting and whispering. The French court painter arrived to execute a full-length portrait of the queen. 'You must', she said, 'paint me with a veil over my face.' Veils were, in these negotiations, in plentiful supply.

Anjou required money to pursue his campaign against Spain in the Netherlands; she promised him £60,000 but paid him £10,000. She wanted at all costs to stay clear of any explicit involvement whereby she might provoke war with Philip. Yet at the same time she wanted to alarm the Spanish king with the threat of an Anglo-French alliance, so that he might cease his meddling in Ireland. It was an infinitely difficult balancing act.

'What shall I do?' she asked the archbishop of York. 'I am between Scylla and Charybdis. Anjou grants all that I ask. If I do not marry him he will be my enemy and if I do, I am no longer mistress within my own realm.' She would eloquently announce her intention to marry, but it was believed that her sincerity could only be judged by the tone of her voice; if she spoke in a low and unimpassioned way, she was being serious. By this standard she was not being serious about Anjou. She was practising what the Spanish ambassador, Bernadino de Mendoza, called her 'gypsy tricks'.

On one occasion the queen kissed the duke on the lips and promised in public to marry him, but many considered her to be acting a part. She may have made the espousal before witnesses as a way of conciliating the French court before making it clear that the opposition to the marriage, in the council and in the nation, was too powerful for her to withstand. The duke's frustration was immense. At the end of 1581 he declared that, sooner than leave England without her, he would prefer that they both perished. The queen was alarmed and entreated him not to threaten 'a poor old woman in her own kingdom'. This is reported by the Spanish ambassador.

'No, no, Madame, you mistake; I meant no hurt to your blessed person. I meant only that I would sooner be cut in pieces than not marry you and so be laughed at by the world.' With these words he broke down in tears, and Elizabeth was obliged to lend him her handkerchief. 'Try to think of me,' she said, 'as a sister.' Philip of Spain, to whom this drama was narrated, wrote '*Ojo*' in the margin of the letter. This meant 'Pay attention' or 'Look out!'

It was clear enough to all that Anjou had become something of an embarrassment in the English court. Elizabeth would not marry him. 'I am an old woman,' she told her courtiers, 'to whom paternosters will suffice in place of nuptials.' She was forty-nine years old. When in February 1582 he eventually parted from her at Canterbury, tears were plentiful. But it was said that she danced for joy in her private chamber.

The European imbroglio was further complicated by the ascension of Philip to the throne of Portugal; his navy was thus at a stroke greatly enlarged. Philip was already displeased with Elizabeth for the assaults of Sir Francis Drake upon Spanish ships, and for the plunder of Spanish treasure, in the Pacific Ocean and the Caribbean Sea. It was likely that the booty would eventually arrive in England and Philip ordered his ambassador to 'advise me instantly when you hear the pirate has arrived'.

The merchants of London were anxious that their trade with Spain would be curtailed, but they were told by the privy council that Drake was a single adventurer and could not bring the wrath of Spain upon England. The queen invited the ambassador to a bear-baiting where, in the intervals, she discussed with him the affairs of Europe. Was it true that Philip had taken up 6,000 more seamen? *'Ut quid tot sumptus?'* – 'What can such an expense be for?' Mendoza had a ready reply. *'Nemo novit nisi cui Pater revelavit'* – 'No man knows except he to whom the Father has revealed it.' 'Ah,' the queen said, impressed by his Latin, 'I see you have been something more than a light dragoon.' Mendoza was Philip's master of the horse.

The rumours of invasion and war were still circulating, and the fleet was being prepared at Chatham. Mendoza once more was received by the queen. 'I found her in such alarm of his Majesty's fleet, and so conscience-stricken by her own complicity [in the seizure of plunder], that when I entered her cabinet she bounded half a dozen paces from her sofa to receive me. Before I could say a word she enquired if I was come as a king-at-arms to declare war.' He believed her to be 'timid and pusillanimous' in private, whatever her bravura in public.

Just as Philip helped to promote rebellion in Ireland, so Elizabeth decided to match him by fomenting dissent in his newly acquired kingdom of Portugal. 'We think it good,' she wrote, 'for the king of Spain to be impeached both in Portugal and also in the Low Countries; whereto we shall be ready to give such indirect assistance as shall not be a cause of war.' Covert hostilities, accompanied by effusive diplomatic gestures, were the order of the day.

Mary Stuart was of course still waiting in the wings, engaged in clandestine intercourse both with Madrid and with Rome; she was the likely successor to Elizabeth, and it was only natural for her to press her suit. But there was no great appetite for her rule, even among the Catholics. The Spanish ambassador told his master that 'on no account should any declaration be made to them, and they should not even be sounded, as they are quite paralysed with fear, and no good end would be gained by doing so'. Only on the death of Elizabeth might an attempt be made. Even the faithful and favoured courtier Sir Christopher Hatton sent word that on the instant of his mistress's demise he would ride to Sheffield, where Mary was imprisoned, and declare her to be queen.

In the summer of 1583 John Whitgift was appointed archbishop of Canterbury; unlike his predecessor, Edmund Grindal, he had set his face against the Puritan tendency that had been manifested at its extreme end by the Brownists and Barrowists. Walsingham's secretary, Nicholas Faunt, himself of a Puritan persuasion, wrote that 'the choice of that man at this time to be archbishop maketh me to think that the Lord is even determined to scourge his Church for their unthankfulness'. In his inaugural sermon, preached at Paul's Cross in the centre of London, he inveighed against the three kinds of disobedience manifested by papists, Anabaptists and 'our wayward and conceited persons'; in the latter class he would have placed the stricter type of Puritan. Faunt reported that Whitgift had launched all his bitterness and vehemence against 'such as loved reformation'.

The archbishop promulgated six articles to which all of the clergy were obliged to assent, among them strict adherence to the Thirty-Nine Articles and to the Book of Common Prayer; as a result of his order 200 ministers were suspended or obliged to resign. New laws were also set in place against Catholic recusants. He relied for his investigation and his discipline on the High Commission, an ecclesiastical court that worked swiftly and secretly in pursuit of heresy and schism, error and vice. It demanded an oath that obliged anyone brought before the court to answer all questions, in defiance of the principle that no one is obliged to accuse himself or herself. 'This corporal oath', wrote one Puritan, 'is to inquire of our private speeches and conferences with our dearest and nearest friends . . .'

Those 'conferences' had a more precise meaning. The parish church in the village of Dedham, in Essex, was already known as a place for 'schismatic sermons and preachings'. In the autumn of 1582 approximately twenty ministers of the neighbourhood organized an assembly or 'conference' in which a time was devoted to preaching and a time to scriptural exposition; parochial business was also discussed. Should the child of an unmarried couple be baptized? Should one of the ministers accept a chaplaincy in a great house?

The 'members' gathered for three hours on the first Monday of each month; they met in secret, moving from house to house in order to avoid discovery. They sometimes consulted their learned brethren at Cambridge, but they were in general completely separate from other churches. They became, however, an inspiration for other such conferences. 'Let's go to Dedham,' the people of Ipswich said, 'to get a little fire!' This early assembly, therefore, can have some claim to shaping the Presbyterian movement that was to bear such unexpected fruit in the next century of English history. Neither Whitgift nor the High Commission proved an impediment.

Henry Barrow, the founder of the sect that bore his name, was himself summoned before the commission.

> Lord Chancellor [pointing to Whitgift]: Who is that man?
> Barrow: He is a monster, a miserable compound, I know not
>   what to make [call] him; he is neither ecclesiastical nor civil,
>   even that second beast spoken of in the Revelation.
> Lord Treasurer: Where is that place, show it.

Ten years later Barrow would be executed for publishing seditious literature. Whitgift himself was implacable. When a Kentish delegation of ministers came to remonstrate with him on the severity of his measures he impugned them as 'boys, babes, princocks, unlearned sots'. He shouted down one more assertive complainant with 'thou boy, beardless boy, yesterday bird, new out of shell'.

Burghley, quietly sympathetic to the Puritan cause, remonstrated with Whitgift about his articles of examination which were 'so curiously penned, so full of branches and circumstances, as he thought the inquisitors of Spain used not so many questions to comprehend and to trap their preys'. At a time when there was such a lack of learned clergy, and with the threat of resurgent Catholicism, he believed that the bishops 'take a very ill and unadvised course in driving them from their cures'.

Whitgift's methods, however, were entirely congenial to the queen; she called the archbishop 'my little black husband'. She had been alarmed by the spread of preachers calling for more reform, and appreciated all of Whitgift's efforts to curb nonconformity. The archbishop himself declared that she had given 'straight charge' for his policy. Whitgift, the first of what might be called the truly Elizabethan bishops, was eventually obliged to curb his attacks upon the more moderate of the Puritans; but he did succeed in imposing order and uniformity upon the Church, largely by removing the Catholics and the stricter Puritans from the embrace of the state religion.

Some of the clerics of a more severe persuasion often continued their ministry, for fear that their flock might otherwise be lost or scattered. We must, as one said, labour on 'bearing so much as with a good conscience we may'. A text from Revelation was set up beside the royal arms in the parish church of Bury St Edmunds, with the words 'I know thy works, that thou art neither cold nor hot: I would thou wert cold or hot. So then because thou art lukewarm, and neither cold not hot, I will spew thee out of my mouth.' So much for Elizabeth.

When on Sunday 12 January 1583 a stand of the bear-pit in Paris Garden collapsed, killing many spectators, it was deemed to be a judgement of God on the profanity of London. In the summer of that year a comet appeared above the city and was supposed to be the portent of the death of a great person. Many pointed to the queen. She was in her palace at Richmond at the time. She ordered the windows to be thrown open so that she might more clearly see the ominous light. She called out *Jacta est alea* – 'The dice are thrown'.

In the following month an attempt was made upon her life. John Somerville resided with an old Catholic family, the Ardens of Park Hall in Warwickshire; he seems to have been of an excitable disposition and fervently supported the cause of Mary Stuart. There had been more than one plot devised against the queen on behalf of that lady, but Walsingham had managed to foil them all. Somerville began to speak of the queen as a witch and a spawn of the devil, and he told friends that he was riding to London to assassinate her; he hoped 'to see her head set upon a pole, for she was a serpent and a viper'. He wore the emblem of the lamb of God as an amulet, and then set out for the capital. Touched by insanity, perhaps, he bragged to people on the road concerning his divine mission and word of his conduct reached London before he did; he was intercepted and taken to the Tower. He confessed to his intent upon the rack and at the same time incriminated his father-in-law, John Arden, and their house-priest. Arden was hanged at Tyburn, while Somerville managed to strangle himself in his cell; the priest agreed to act as a spy in other Catholic families.

At the same time another conspiracy had been formed against Elizabeth. Francis Throgmorton, of an old Cheshire family, owned a house in London at Paul's Wharf; here he acted as an intermediary between Mary Stuart and the Spanish ambassador. He was often seen leaving the ambassador's house by the secret agents of the Crown, and Walsingham waited for the right moment to arrest him and search his house. In the middle of writing a ciphered letter to Mary when the officers arrived, he managed to destroy the incriminating document. But other papers were found, among them a list of prominent English Catholics and the sketched plans of harbours suitable for the landing of a foreign force. A treatise in defence of the title of the queen of Scots was also seized together with 'six or seven infamous libels against Her Majesty, printed beyond seas'.

Throgmorton had the opportunity to write a few words to the Spanish ambassador, in which he said that he had denied all knowledge of the writings and claimed that they had been planted in his house by one who wished to destroy him. He declared that he would be faithful and silent to the death, but he was sent to the Tower and to the persuasions of the rack. Elizabeth, faced with a serious conspiracy, agreed that he should be subject to 'the pains'.

On his first racking he confessed nothing but, when he was tied to the frame for a second time, he broke down and confessed all the details of the plot. The founder of the Catholic League, Henry I, duke of Guise, had intended to land with an invasion force on the Sussex coast near Arundel; at which time the Catholic gentlemen and noblemen would rise up on behalf of Mary, queen of Scots. Philip of Spain 'would bear half the charge of the enterprise'. Throgmorton also declared that Mary herself had known every detail of the plan. After he had made his confession, according to the official account, he collapsed in tears. 'Now,' he said, 'I have disclosed the secrets of her who was the dearest queen to me in the world . . .' He was hanged a few months later, when his testimony was no longer of any use.

On the news of his arrest and confession many prominent Catholics fled the country; others were suspected and placed under arrest. It has been estimated that 11,000 were confined to prison cells or, at best, to their own houses. The Inns of Court, long considered to be a haven of papists, were visited; conformity of religion now became essential for all lawyers. The queen at once realized the extent of Spanish hostility against her. At any minute the duke of Guise might reach English shores with the forces of the Catholic League; the navy was sent to guard the coast in the Downs, the Isle of Wight and the Scilly Islands. Most of the fleet would be sent to the west, which faced the greatest danger of a Spanish invasion, but in the event of an attack from the Channel the enemy would be followed and confronted. Money was urgently needed to restore forts and garrisons; trenches would have to be dug 'to impeach landing'. Burghley also wrote a note to himself, 'to have regard to Sheffield', by which he meant Sheffield Castle. That was now the home, or prison, of Mary.

It was here she remained, plotting and planning in her relatively comfortable confinement. Her principal purpose was to regain her freedom and to ascend to the thrones of Scotland and of England. In this, she was tenacious and resourceful. There were many, Walsingham and Burghley among them, who were waiting for the opportunity to destroy her. Elizabeth was not yet of their mind. It was suggested that she might now recognize Mary's son, James, as the lawful king of Scotland. Walsingham also proposed an alliance with the Protestants of the Low Countries, in a situation where England needed all the allies it could find.

Some commissioners were sent to the queen of Scots. They found her in a fury, eager to tell once more the story of her wrongs 'using bitter speeches of her misery'. One of the English delegation remarked, respectfully, that foreign observers believed her treatment to be one of 'singular mercy'. The queen's reply (here paraphrased) was royal: 'Mercy? What had mercy to do with it? I am as much an absolute prince as her Majesty. I am not, and have never been, her inferior. I have been a queen from my cradle. I have been proclaimed queen of France, the greatest realm in Christendom. Mercy is for subjects. I am not a subject.' The delegation reported that 'all this was said with extreme choler'.

She calmed herself and went on to describe 'her grief and her woeful estate'. She was younger than Elizabeth, she said, but suffering had made her look older. The leader of the delegation, Sir William Wade, then asked her about the plots and intrigues and conspiracies of which she was a part. 'May I not ask my friends to help me? I have meant innocently and, if they have done wrong, they alone are to be blamed.' Wade mentioned the proofs of her involvement. At which she flared out with 'you are not of calling [rank] to reason with me'. Eventually peace was restored, and Mary sang to the English delegation. Yet she remained stubborn and defiant, convinced both of the justice of her cause and of her ultimate success. Any traveller in the neighbourhood of the castle was questioned, and no one could enter the stronghold without especial permission from the council. Whenever she rode out for the air, she was accompanied by an armed guard.

The prognostications became ever more gloomy on the news of the assassination, in the summer of 1584, of the leader of the Dutch Protestants. William of Nassau, prince of Orange, had been killed on the orders of Philip II. Who could doubt that Elizabeth would be next? The duke of Guise, the leader of the Catholic League, had also become more dangerous. Elizabeth's once determined suitor, the duke of Anjou, had died of a fever after a miserable failure in the Netherlands; when the queen heard news of his death, she cried for many days afterwards. She wore black for six months and put the court into mourning. 'I am a widow woman,' she told the French ambassador, 'who has lost her husband.' His comment was that she was 'a princess who knows how to transform herself as suits her best'. It was more significant that Anjou's demise left the royal succession to a Protestant, Henry of Navarre, and Guise concluded a treaty with Philip to prevent that possibility. They had also entered an alliance against Elizabeth.

In the autumn of the year the queen posed two questions to her council. Should she protect and defend the Low Countries from the tyranny of Spanish rule? And, if she decided so to do, 'what shall she do to provide for her own surety against the king of Spain's malice and forces?' The majority of her councillors were in favour of intervention, but still she hesitated. She wanted the support and co-operation of the French king. Otherwise England would be utterly alone.

This was the moment when Burghley and Walsingham drew up a document that became known as the Bond of Association; those who subscribed to it gave a solemn oath that they would defend Elizabeth's life and guarantee a Protestant succession. The signatories promised that they 'would pursue as well by force of arms as by all other means of revenge' anyone who threatened the queen. It was also declared that no 'pretended successor by whom or for whom any such detestable act shall be attempted or committed' was to be spared. If Elizabeth were assassinated, Mary would be executed. It was a direct appeal to force. This was the time when portrait cameos of the queen were manufactured in quantity, creating a sacred image of majesty that would challenge those of the Virgin Mary on the continent.

Burghley went to further lengths to ensure that a Protestant would inherit the throne. He drew up a document proposing that, in the event of the queen's death, a Grand Council would be called. This council would act as the governing body while at the same time summoning a parliament to consider the succession; since parliament was wholly Protestant, Catholics being excluded, their choice was not in doubt. 'The government of the realm shall still continue in all respects,' Burghley wrote in a memorandum. 'This cannot be without an interreyne [interregnum] for some reasonable time.' The queen was not happy with her principal minister. It was unpardonable of him to meddle in such matters and to question the principle of hereditary rule. To imagine the queen's death was, in any case, itself an act of treason. It may have seemed to her that a group of males, with shared religious and ideological convictions, was springing up around her. That is why she preferred to see her councillors individually, or in twos and threes. It may also be the reason she often seemed to listen more attentively to foreign ambassadors than to her own men. The novel situation may serve to elucidate the latter part of her reign.

The parliament of November 1584 met in a state of some excitement. The members confirmed the details of the Bond of Association by passing an Act for the Queen's Safety. The arrangements for the 'interreyne' were never discussed, and it is likely that Elizabeth's severe displeasure prevented their being taken any further. The importance of the Bond of Association, however, was immediately emphasized at the beginning of 1585 in a further conspiracy against the queen's life that was engineered by a curious double agent, William Parry, who was supposed to act as a spy against English Catholics. Instead he turned against his mistress and lay in wait in her garden at Richmond; eventually, when she appeared, he was so daunted by her majesty that he gave up the attempt. That is one story. Another records that he had gained an audience with the queen and came into her presence with a knife concealed in his shirt. Once more his nerve failed him.

Nevertheless he was seized before being questioned by Walsingham. He was dispatched to the Tower and afterwards sent to the gallows. 'It makes all my joints to tremble,' one member of parliament wrote after his arrest, 'when I consider the loss of such a jewel [Elizabeth].' Parry himself wrote a confession to the queen that ended on a tender note. 'And so farewell, most gracious and the best natured and qualified Queen that ever lived in England. Remember your unfortunate Parry, overthrown by your hard hand. Amend that in the rest of your servants, for it is past with me if your grace be not greater than I look for. And last and ever, good madam, be good to your obedient Catholic servants. For the bad I speak not.'

Parliament had made one significant change to the Bond of Association; on the orders of Elizabeth herself, they had expressly exempted Mary's son, James, from the threat of reprisals. At the same time the queen opened negotiations with the young man, with the prospect of her recognizing him as James VI of Scotland. This also implied that he might have some claim to the English throne in the event of her death. Of course James had already inherited the crown of Scotland, since at the age of thirteen months he had ascended the throne after the forced abdication of his mother. Yet the formal acceptance of his position by Elizabeth would immensely strengthen his rule. The queen herself would appreciate the support of the Protestant monarch in the event of Spanish intrigue or invasion.

James now wrote to his mother, assuring her that she would always be honoured with the title of 'queen mother'. She fell into a rage. 'I pray you to note,' she wrote in reply, 'I am your true and only queen. Do not insult me further with this title of queen mother ... there is neither king nor queen in Scotland except me.' She threatened to disinherit and to curse him if he signed any separate agreement with England, but that was precisely the decision he took. Mary herself was removed to the stricter confinement of Tutbury, where she might be able to reflect upon her diminished sovereignty. Soon after this a young Catholic priest was also confined in the castle, where after three weeks he managed to hang himself in his cell. The next morning Mary found him suspended in front of her own windows. She believed this to be a presage of her own death, and wrote once more to Elizabeth with a desperate plea for her life and liberty.

Her Catholic allies were meanwhile in retreat. Philip Howard, the earl of Arundel, had for a long time been suspected of recusancy; when finally he was privately reconciled to the Catholic Church he wrote a long letter to the queen in which he enumerated his woes and his failure to gain friends at court. He knew well enough the fate of his father, the fourth duke of Norfolk, who had been executed as a traitor. He had now come to that point where he must 'consent either to the certain destruction of my body or the manifest endangering of my soul'. He had therefore decided to leave the realm without royal licence.

He gave the letter to a messenger and then proceeded to embark on a boat off the coast of Sussex. He did not know that his servants had been in the pay of the privy council, or that the master of the ship in which he travelled was also a spy of the government. He was followed by two ships and was obliged to surrender after a short fight. He was then taken to the Tower, where he remained for the rest of his life.

The arrest of Howard was followed by the death of Henry Percy, eighth earl of Northumberland; he had been consigned to the Tower after being implicated in the plot of Francis Throgmorton against the queen, and had remained for a year in his cell without trial. On the evening of 20 June 1585 he was found dead in his bed with three pellets in his heart. It was concluded that, in fear of the shame of public execution, he had determined to kill himself. If he did not suffer the death of a traitor, then at least his inheritance would be preserved. He was supposed to have cried out that 'the bitch shall not have my estate'. Others believed, however, that he had been assassinated for want of evidence against him.

In the summer of 1585 Elizabeth finally signed a treaty with the Netherlands, pledging her support for their cause against the Spanish. She agreed to send 4,000 men, their wages paid for three months, on the understanding that she would eventually be recompensed. In return she had been given possession of the sea towns of Ostend and Sluys, Brielle and Flushing. A long declaration announced that 'our next neighbours, the natural people of the Low Countries, being by long wars, and persecution of strange [foreign] nations there, lamentably afflicted, and in present danger to be brought into a perpetual servitude' had to be assisted.

The agreement came too late, however, to save Antwerp; the city had fallen to the duke of Parma three days before. In the previous months the duke had occupied Flanders and much of Brabant, while Bruges and Ghent had surrendered to him. The queen had finally come out into the open, however, after years of covert negotiation and secret alliances. Yet she did not wish to become queen of the Low Countries; that would open her to fresh dangers and fresh expense. She merely wished to uphold their liberties under Spanish rule. She would be their protector rather than their sovereign.

In the early autumn of the same year she also helped to finance Sir Francis Drake in a voyage to the West Indies, with the purpose of rifling Spanish vessels and Spanish-held towns of the region. His force numbered twenty-nine ships and 2,300 men. He captured St Domingo on the island of Hispaniola, with the pillage from that town filling the holds of his vessels. He then went on to Cartagena, on the Spanish Main, and held it to ransom for 107,000 ducats. He was about to set sail for Panama, when an epidemic of yellow fever among his men prevented him.

The conflicts of the Old World had therefore been transferred to the New and, although it would be anachronistic to speak of a global strategy, there is no doubt that Drake and his fellow adventurers knew that Philip might be seriously weakened in the Netherlands by the capture of his shipments of gold. It was said by Philip's secretary, at the time of the Armada, that the object of the invasion was 'no less the security of the Indies than the recovery of the Netherlands'. Open warfare with Spain, therefore, could not now be indefinitely delayed. The new pope, Sixtus V, declared that Elizabeth 'is certainly a great queen, and were she only a Catholic she would be our dearly beloved. Just look how well she governs! She is only a woman, only mistress of half an island, and yet she makes herself feared by Spain, by France, by the empire, by all.' In this year Burghley commissioned a painting of the queen, known as the 'Ermine' portrait, which displays a sword placed beside her on a table. As lord treasurer, he was in charge of the finances of war.

On 17 November 1585, the twenty-seventh anniversary of the proclamation of her sovereignty, the queen rode in a gold coach through London; it was an open coach but it carried a canopy embroidered with gold and pearls. She was dressed entirely in white, and at frequent intervals she would call out 'God save my people!' The people knelt as she passed and replied 'God save your Grace'. Behind the coach rode the earl of Leicester, while it was preceded by Burghley and Walsingham. Leicester and Burghley had been with Elizabeth from the beginning of her reign, while

Walsingham had joined them eleven years later. She exemplified her motto *'semper eadem'* – 'always the same'.

In the following month the earl of Leicester was sent to the Low Countries as her lieutenant general. He was eagerly awaited as the 'new messiah', one of the leaders of the international Protestant cause, and so great were the expectations that he was offered the post of governor-general; much to the queen's fury and consternation, he accepted the title. When at the beginning of 1586 he was confirmed as 'absolute governor' she became incandescent with rage. It would seem to the world that she was indeed queen and that Leicester was her viceroy; her 'storms' and 'great oaths' alarmed her councillors, some of whom she accused of being part of the plot to undermine her purposes. She threatened to make peace with the duke of Parma, thus emasculating Leicester in turn.

When her choler had subsided she left Leicester in command of the English forces, in alliance with those of the Netherlands; but his campaign did not prosper. He found it hard to co-ordinate the counsels of the allies, and was obliged to request more money and more men. One commander wrote to Burghley that 'the havoc which has been made of the soldiers is lamentable, which must be supplied and enlarged presently before my Lord can do anything'. He could not contain the quarrels between the various states, such as Holland and Zeeland, nor could he satisfy their suspicions of his actions. Although he had been warned by Walsingham to beware 'charges', he increased the pay of his officers (including his own) and overlooked the problems of bribery and general corruption. The war had led also to a marked diminution of English exports, with the consequent loss of employment; the situation was exacerbated by a disastrous harvest in 1586 that led directly to malnutrition, disease and death. When we turn from the affairs of the great to the smaller lives of England, we often find misery and discontent.

It was no wonder, in any case, that the queen had grown alarmed at the costs of conflict. She was fundamentally averse to war; she had no skill or interest in it. It was rumoured now that she would make peace with Spain, and recall Leicester from the ill-starred enterprise; it was also reported that one of the conditions of that peace was her surrender of the sea-towns to Philip II. Religion was not to be a difficulty. If Spain could guarantee the Low Countries their 'ancient liberties', it would be enough. Burghley believed that any peace granted on these terms would be a lasting dishonour. He told her that he wished to resign his office and retire into private life; she was for the moment moved by him, but then continued on the course which he described as 'very absurd and perilous'. Walsingham agreed with him, fearing that everyone would say that 'there is no court in the world so odious and uncertain in its dealings as ours'. So with the council at variance, and Elizabeth herself uncertain, the war in the Low Countries continued. The whole ill-starred enterprise was rendered more dramatic by the death of Sir Philip Sidney after a skirmish at the siege of Zutphen. He had taken off his leg armour, in heroic emulation of a fellow soldier, but then received the arrow wound that killed him; it was an example of the romance and bravado that characterized him. 'I am weary,' Leicester wrote to Walsingham, 'indeed I am weary, Mr Secretary.'

By the summer of 1586, however, the queen was once more on intimate terms with her favourite. In one letter she reveals her affection for him with 'Rob: I am afraid you will suppose from my wandering writings that midsummer moon hath taken possession of my brains this month.' She concluded with 'now I will end that do imagine I talk still with you and therefore loathly say ô ô [her symbol for Eyes, his nickname] though ever I pray God bless you from all harm and save you from all foes with my million and legion of thanks for all your pains and cares. As you know, ever the same, E.R.' Her moods were as always mercurial and mysterious.

With Elizabeth braving the wrath of Spain, however, this was a time of maximum peril. She feared the machinations of Mary, and in February 1586 it was reported in the French court that she had fainted; it was said that she had remained unconscious for two hours. In the early summer of that year she had been walking to the royal chapel in stately progress when suddenly she was 'overcome by a shock of fear'; she went back to her apartments, according to a Spanish agent, 'greatly to the wonder of those present'.

She was perhaps wiser than they knew. A conspiracy was even then being formed against her, guided by a Jesuit priest, John Ballard, and by Mary's agent in Paris. They had courted a rich young Catholic, Anthony Babington, and he had in turn recruited six courtiers who at the appropriate moment would rise up and assassinate Elizabeth. Walsingham was, meanwhile, closely watching Mary. The queen of Scots was moved to another house, Chartley Manor. It can be said with some certainty that Cecil was happy to allow the conspiracy to develop, disorganized and chaotic as it was. It was to be hoped that Mary would enter a traitorous correspondence that would end her life. And so it proved. On 12 July Babington wrote to Mary Stuart outlining the plan for her liberation and for her ascension to the throne. They must choose a landing place for the invading Spanish troops. The 'usurping competitor' would then have to be 'dispatched', and he had nominated the men to undertake 'that tragical execution'.

The letter had of course been diverted to Walsingham before it was sent on to Mary; he employed a code-breaker to help him decipher the clandestine correspondence. An elaborate scheme had been set up by the spymaster, by means of which a double agent had persuaded Mary to smuggle out letters concealed at the bottom of beer barrels. Mary pondered on her response to Babington. Her guard, Sir Amyas Paulet, wrote to Walsingham that 'she could see plainly that her destruction was sought, and that her life would be taken from her, and then it would be said that she had died of sickness'. What, then, had she left to lose?

A few days later Mary replied to Babington's message. She went through his plan in detail and wrote that 'when all is ready, the six gentlemen must be set to work, and you will provide that on their design being accomplished, I may be myself rescued from this place'. Walsingham received this epistle, also, but before sending it on to its intended recipients his code-breaker forged a postscript in Mary's hand asking for the names of the six assassins.

And then they waited, wanting to test the Scottish queen to destruction. Elizabeth now knew of the plot and had been told that 'the beast was to be removed that troubled the world'. It is said that Babington was so sanguine of his chances that he commissioned a portrait of himself in the company of the six courtiers.

They and their supporters were seen drinking and eating in taverns, quite unaware that they were being followed. In August 1586, Walsingham ordered that John Ballard be arrested on the charge of being a covert priest. The others, taking fright, fled London; yet fourteen were arrested. Babington, his face 'sullied with the rind of green walnuts', was found concealed in St John's Wood; 300 of the most prominent recusants in the north of England were then taken to London under guard.

One more significant conspirator remained. Mary Stuart was arrested and detained while her rooms at Chartley were searched. A key to sixty different ciphers was discovered, together with the lists of her supporters in England; there was, for example, a record of all the nobles who had pledged allegiance to her. This list was shown to Elizabeth who, after reading it, burned it. '*Video taceoque*,' she said. 'I see and I am silent.'

The conspirators were slaughtered in the usual manner of traitors, Babington being one of the first. But one notable plotter had not yet been brought to the scaffold. It was clear enough now that Mary had been involved in schemes against the queen's throne, and therefore the queen's life, for the past eighteen years. In the summer of this year, by the Treaty of Berwick, Elizabeth and James VI of Scotland were bound in a permanent embrace; the two monarchs agreed to maintain the Protestant religion in their separate realms, and to help each other in the event of an invasion. James also received a pension of £4,000 per year and it was clear enough that he was the favourite to succeed to the English throne. His mother was no longer considered. What was to be her fate now?

35

The dead cannot bite

When Mary Stuart was led back to Chartley Manor, after her most secret documents had been taken from her apartment, she was greeted by a crowd of beggars. 'I have nothing for you,' she cried out to them, 'I am a beggar as well as you. All is taken from me.' She turned to her escort and, weeping, said to them 'Good gentlemen, I am not witting or privy to anything intended against the queen.' Many had good reason to doubt that. Her gaoler, Paulet, was asked to keep her in as much isolation as possible. The privy council met each day at Windsor to ponder the situation, but it seemed inevitable that the queen of Scots would be obliged to stand trial for her intrigue against Elizabeth. In the autumn of 1586, in her forty-third year, she was taken from Chartley to Fotheringhay Castle.

Mary had at first protested against her removal. Since she was not an English subject, she could not be brought before the jurisdiction of an English court. To her protest Elizabeth sent a firm reply that 'you have in various ways and manners attempted to take my life and to bring my kingdom to destruction by bloodshed. These treasons will be proved to you and all made manifest. It is my will that you answer the nobles and peers of the kingdom as if I myself were present . . . Act plainly without reserve and you will then sooner be able to obtain favour of me.'

Burghley made a rough sketch of the chamber of presence at Fotheringhay Castle, where Mary was tried on 14 and 15 October. The earls, barons and privy councillors – those who would act as judges in the matter – were seated around the walls. Mary was given a chair in the middle of the hall, immediately opposite a throne beneath a cloth of estate; the empty throne represented the absent queen. It was of course a trial for her life, the parliamentary Act for the Queen's Safety having declared that any attempt to injure the queen was to be 'pursued to the death by all the Queen's subjects'. Mary knew this well enough, and declared to the duke of Guise that she was ready to die in the cause of her religion. She would not be a murderer, but a martyr. In that respect her death would be sanctified.

She may in any case have secretly relied upon Elizabeth's reluctance to impose upon her the extreme penalty; that was why the English queen held out the possibility of 'favour' to her. The lawyers had no precedent for her case; she was an anointed queen who did not recognize the court to which she had been taken. She was also a rightful claimant to the English crown. So she had some cause for confidence. She relied, too, upon her personal presence before her judges. She had a sharp wit and a ready tongue; she also had the aura of majesty. She would not easily be put out of countenance. Burghley and a small party of the commissioners went to her privy chamber at Fotheringhay. 'I am an absolute queen,' she told them. She would not bargain with them. 'My mind is not yet dejected, neither will I sink under my calamity.' Then she warned them to 'remember that the theatre of the whole world is wider than the kingdom of England'. She was reminding them that the Catholic princes of Europe might revenge her death.

She entered the chamber of presence, on the morning of 14 October, in a gown of black velvet and sat down upon the seat offered to her: the commissioners took off their hats as a mark of respect to her rank. She was described as a 'big-made' woman with a face 'full and fat, double-chinned and hazel-eyed'; after years of imprisonment, her plumpness was only to be expected. The charges against her were read out, in which she was accused of conspiring for the destruction of the queen and her country. She replied that she had come to England as a suppliant, but had been held in confinement ever since. She was an anointed queen and could be judged by no earthly tribunal. She was, however, ready to refute any falsehoods made against her. Babington's letters to her were then read aloud. 'It may be that Babington wrote these letters,' she replied, 'but let it be proved that I received them.' The confessions of her two private secretaries were also recited, in which they confirmed her complicity in the writing of ciphered letters. Once more Mary simply repeated her denials of any involvement in a conspiracy against the queen. She also claimed that the word of a prince could not be challenged. She was entirely calm and self-possessed; Paulet wrote to Walsingham that 'she was utterly void of all fear of harm'.

It was clear to all others that she could not be allowed to evade the charge. On the second and final day of the trial, Burghley told her that she should not complain of her imprisonment. Only her own mistakes had kept her in confinement. 'Ah,' she told him, 'I see that you are my adversary.' 'Yes, I am adversary to Queen Elizabeth's adversaries.' Burghley then prorogued the commission for ten days, on the express command of the queen. She did not wish to be seen to rush to judgment.

The commissioners met in the Star Chamber at Westminster on 25 October, where, in the absence of Mary, they reviewed the evidence. The queen of Scots was then found guilty. When she received the news, Elizabeth knelt down in prayer for fifteen minutes. She demurred at any public declaration. She was not yet certain of her next move. When Mary heard the verdict she lifted up her eyes to heaven and thanked God for it. The stage was set for her final scene.

When parliament assembled four days later, the Lords and the Commons bayed for Mary's blood. Burghley had so arranged matters that it rang with accusations against her. On 3 November one of the queen's favourites, Sir Christopher Hatton, denounced the practices of Mary as 'most filthy and detestable'. A commission of the Lords and Commons was appointed, while at the same time a petition for her execution was drawn up. After the queen had heard it, in her chamber of presence, she responded very carefully. She warned those assembled that 'we princes, I tell you, are set on stages in the sight and view of all the world duly observed'. Just as Mary had warned the commissioners about the possibility of the vengeance of Catholic princes, so now Elizabeth warned her parliament that there were large matters at stake. If she and Mary had been only milkmaids, 'with pails on our arms', she would not consent to her death in the same circumstances. But the queen of Scots had her 'favourers' in a pattern of alliances and interests that were ready to act against England; it was not the person of Mary, but what she represented, that threatened the country.

On 24 November Elizabeth once more prevaricated with them. 'I have strived more this day, than ever in my life,' she told them, 'whether I should speak or use silence.' As for their petition 'I shall pray you for this present, to content yourselves to an answer without answer; your judgement I condemn not, neither do I mistake your reasons, but pray you to accept my thankfulness, excuse my doubtfulness, and take in good part my answer answerless . . .' She allowed her speech to be published, in a copy approved by her.

The queen had indeed fallen into agonies over the decision. It was whispered to her that 'the dead cannot bite', but did she have the right to execute an anointed queen? Could she execute her cousin? The kings of France and Scotland, near to Mary in blood, were eager to rescue her from death; she had, after all, once worn the crown of France and was the mother of the Scottish sovereign. Philip of Spain had the highest interest in her as a Catholic princess and, however remote the chance, still a potential successor to Elizabeth. It was also possible that her execution would dissolve the bonds that held together the Protestants and Catholics of England in a frail unity. Might her death precipitate the civil war that was always to be feared? So Elizabeth told the Lords and Commons that 'I am not so void of judgement as not to see mine own peril, nor yet so ignorant as not to know it were in nature a foolish course to cherish a sword to cut mine own throat'. Her dilemma could not have been better expressed. William Camden, Elizabeth's first historian, relates that she sat many times 'melancholic and mute'. Two phrases occurred to her: *Aut fer, aut feri* – 'Bear with her or smite her' – and *Ne feriare, feri* – 'Strike lest thou be stricken'.

In the first week of December the news of Mary's guilt was finally proclaimed in London to the sound of trumpets. Bonfires were lit in the streets and the church bells tolled for twenty-four hours. After the delivery of the verdict the chair of state, and the canopy above it, was removed from her. Writing to Scotland, she said that the act was 'to signify that I was a dead woman, deprived of the honours and dignity of a queen'. She feared that, according to the articles of the Bond of Association, any loyal Englishman had the duty to kill her. This may also have been the private wish of the queen, who would thereby be relieved of the responsibility of ordering her execution. So in these final weeks Mary went in constant fear of assassination. In a last letter to Elizabeth she requested that her corpse be taken to France, where she might lie beside her mother, Mary of Guise, at the convent of Saint-Pierre at Rheims.

Parliament had reassembled on 2 December, two days before the reading of the proclamation, but now Elizabeth prorogued it until the middle of February. She wanted ten weeks to steady her nerve for the final decision. Rumours and counter-rumours flew around London in January 1587; it was whispered that Mary had escaped confinement, and that the Spaniards had launched an invasion. The council may have encouraged such false reports, however, in order to force Elizabeth's hand. A 'plot' was revealed to Walsingham, involving a poisoned saddle to be given to Elizabeth; the enterprise is likely to have been concocted further to frighten the queen. She could afford no more delay; the feelings of the country could not with impunity be ignored. All of her councillors declared that Mary must be executed.

At the beginning of February the queen was at Greenwich. She asked her secretary, Sir William Davison, to carry to her the warrant for Mary's execution. He brought it to her chamber, mixed with other papers. She commented to him on the brightness of the morning, and signed the papers given to her without paying any particular attention to the warrant. But then she mentioned it to him. She had delayed for so long in the matter to demonstrate her unwillingness to act against Mary. Was he not sorry to see such a paper signed? He replied that it was best that the guilty should suffer before the innocent.

Elizabeth then told him to get the warrant sealed by the chancellor as quickly and as quietly as possible; it was then to be sent, without proclamation of any kind, to the commissioners. She asked him to inform Walsingham, who was then lying sick; the grief, she said sarcastically, would probably kill him. Davison was about to leave her presence when she called him back. What if a loyal subject, a member of the Bond of Association, would commit the deed? She mentioned two such subjects, one of whom was Mary's gaoler, Amyas Paulet. By these means she might be able to avoid censure and the unfavourable attention of rival powers. She did not wish to incur the guilt of regicide. She asked Davison to raise the matter with Walsingham; he agreed reluctantly to do so but told her that it was a labour lost. No official would contemplate such an act without the queen's express commandment.

Burghley summoned the council and informed his colleagues that Elizabeth had at last signed the warrant. It was now necessary to act secretly and swiftly. The warrant was quickly on its way to Fotheringhay, and the necessary letters were sent to the principal commissioners. Elizabeth did not mention the matter. She asked no questions. When she read Paulet's response to her letter, refusing her request to kill Mary without a warrant, she exploded in rage; she called him a 'precise' fellow who pledged himself to her but would do nothing to protect her safety.

Her caution and her patience, two days later, had worn thin. Had Davison expedited the matter? Was the warrant sealed? Davison, in his own narrative, described her as 'swearing a great oath, it was a shame for them all that it was not already done'. Mary's self-confidence had returned. She had sent another letter to Elizabeth protesting her innocence and asking for a private inter-view; she received no reply but Leicester said that her letter 'hath wrought tears'. On 4 February the principal executioner travelled to Fotheringhay Castle dressed as a serving man; the axe was concealed in his trunk. On Tuesday 7 February, the commissioners arrived at Fotheringhay and, when they were admitted into Mary's presence, they informed her that they had received an instruction under the Great Seal; she was to be executed on the following morning.

She refused to believe them at first; then she became agitated. She called for her physician and began to discuss money owed to her in France. At that point she broke down. She asked to see her

Catholic chaplain, but the commissioners did not want to turn her execution into the martyrdom she so much wished for; instead they offered her the presence of a Protestant dean. She sent a note to her confessor and asked him to pray for her that night; in the morning, when she was led to her death, he might see her and bless her.

At eight o'clock, on the morning of 8 February, the provost-marshal of Fotheringhay Castle knocked on the door of her apartments; there was no response at first, prompting fears that the queen of Scots had taken her own life. Suicide was a mortal sin, however, and Mary did not wish to stain her personal glory. The door was opened. She stood on the threshold, wearing a robe and jacket of black satin trimmed with velvet. Her hair was arranged in a coif; over her head, and falling over her back, was a white silk veil. A crucifix of gold hung from her neck. In her hand she held another crucifix of ivory.

As she passed into the chamber of presence, where she had been tried, the master of her household knelt and wept. 'Melville,' she told him, 'you should rejoice rather than weep that the end of my troubles is come. Tell my friends I die a true Catholic.' She asked for her chaplain; he had been forbidden to attend, for fear of some religious demonstration. Then she looked around for her women. They also had been kept back as a precaution against unseemly scenes; they might scream, or faint. Yet Mary needed her courtiers to send an authentic account of her death to her admirers, at home and abroad; in the end it was agreed that she could choose six of her closest followers to attend her. '*Allons donc*,' she told them when they were assembled. 'Let us go then.' She descended the staircase to the great hall.

The hall had been cleared of its furniture, and at the upper end stood the scaffold, 12 feet square and 2½ feet in height; it was covered with a black cloth, and railed. A black cushion had been placed before it, together with a black chair. The axe had been put against the rail. A wood fire blazed in the chimney. Present in the hall were 300 knights and gentlemen of the neighbourhood, to witness the memorable occasion, and thousands had gathered outside the castle. The news of her imminent execution had soon spread.

Quite calm and giving no sign of fear, she sat down in the chair made ready for her, in front of the block, and listened to the reading of the warrant against her. The earl of Shrewsbury approached her. 'Madam, you hear what we are commanded to do.'

'You will do your duty.' She then prepared herself to kneel and to pray, when the dean of Peterborough tried to forestall her; but he stuttered his words. 'Mr Dean, I am a Catholic, and must die a Catholic. It is useless to attempt to move me, and your prayers will avail me but little.' There was a slight altercation. When she knelt down he began to call out an English prayer in which the assembly joined. So she recited in a loud voice the penitential psalms in Latin, striking the crucifix against her bosom.

The executioners, dressed in black, stepped forward to ask her forgiveness for the duties they were obliged to perform. 'I forgive you,' she told them, 'for now I hope you shall end all my troubles.' They began to arrange her dress for the final scene, and she looked at the earls close to her. 'Truly, my lords, I never had such grooms waiting on me before.' She laid her crucifix on the chair; the principal executioner took it up, as a prize of his office, but was commanded to leave it. Her silk veil was then removed, together with the black robe and the black jacket. Beneath them she was wearing underclothes of crimson velvet and crimson satin. She was now blood-red, the colour of the martyr.

She knelt upon the cushion as her ladies sobbed around her. '*Adieu,*' she said, '*au revoir.*' One of her entourage then bound her eyes with a handkerchief. She recited the psalm *In te, Domine, confido,* before feeling for the block, 'I trust in you, my Lord God.' She whispered, '*In manus tuas, Domine, commendo animam meam*' – 'Into your hands, O Lord, I commend my spirit.' As she stretched forward one of the executioners held her while the other raised the axe. But his aim was awry and the blade fell on the knot of the handkerchief. He raised the axe again and, this time, he was successful; he severed the head, with the exception of a small shred of skin. The coif and the false hair fell off, and when he picked up the head to show to the spectators it was that of a withered and nearly bald grey-haired old woman.

The dean stepped forward. 'So perish all enemies of the queen.' The assembly called out 'Amen'. It was over. Then a lapdog was found concealed in her clothes and, yelping, it slid in her blood. It was taken away and carefully washed. Anything touched by Mary – the scaffold, the handkerchief, even the beads of her rosary – was now burned in the great hall. No relics were allowed to survive. Yet she had played her final part to perfection, and the story of Mary, queen of Scots, has remained in the public imagination ever since.

On the morning of 9 February Elizabeth went out riding and, when she returned to the palace at Greenwich, she heard the bells of London ringing. She asked for the reason. 'I never saw her fetch a sigh,' Elizabeth's young cousin, Robert Carey recalled, 'but when the queen of Scots was beheaded.' It was more than a sigh. It was a rant, an explosion of guilt and rage. She became almost hysterical, accusing those closest to her of deceit and duplicity. She had never intended that her dear cousin should die. She commanded Burghley from her presence, and refused to allow him back to the court for two months. She admitted to signing the warrant but claimed that she had asked Davison to keep hold of it. Now she wanted Sir William Davison's life in revenge. She was persuaded out of this impolitic course, and instead Davison was tried in the court of the Star Chamber for abusing the confidence of the queen; he was committed to the Tower, but was released a year later. He, too, had played his part.

Within four days of Mary's execution Elizabeth had written to James VI, denying any involvement in the act. 'My dear brother,' she wrote, 'I would you knew (though not felt) the extreme dolour that overwhelms my mind, for that miserable accident which (far contrary to my meaning) hath befallen . . .' It is true that she had been placed under intolerable pressure by her councillors, principal among them Walsingham and Burghley, and she may have persuaded herself that she had acted against her will. Her ministers had conspired behind her back to hasten Mary's death. But her distress may also have been caused by the pangs of an awakened conscience.

The threat to her reign now grew stronger. By the spring of 1587 reports reached the court of Spanish preparations at Cadiz and at Lisbon; a squadron of ships was then assembled at Plymouth under Sir Francis Drake's command with orders to sail to Spain. Knowing the inconstancy of his mistress, Drake made haste to leave the shores of England before she could countermand her previous orders. Sure enough the order to cease and desist came through but, by then, Drake was far away. He sank many store-ships and transports at Cadiz before moving on to Cape St Vincent, where he might confront any Spanish invasion force.

Thwarted of this goal he sailed to Corunna, where he cleared the harbour of the store-ships assembled there; he destroyed half of the stores accumulated for the Armada against England. It had been said previously that there was enough bread and wine to feed 40,000 men for a year, but those preparations were now wasted. Drake then completed a triumphant campaign by seizing a carrack loaded with booty from the East Indies. The Spanish had reason to feel themselves humiliated, while the confidence of the English was thereby increased.

The debacle delayed Philip's plans for an invasion of England a further year. Elizabeth had been granted more time for what was now the inevitable struggle with Spain.

36

Armada

The depredations of Sir Francis Drake had been swiftly repaired and by the winter of 1587 a great Spanish fleet, the greatest ever seen in Europe, was floating out to sea by the mouth of the Tagus. At the same time the Spanish army in the Netherlands, under the command of the duke of Parma, had been further strengthened. It was planned that the navy, under the command of the marquis of Santa Cruz as lord high admiral, would make for the Thames estuary and anchor by Margate; the Spanish ships would then command the Strait of Dover, giving the duke of Parma time and opportunity to land his forces at Thanet. Their path to London would then lie clear. Yet the naval forces were not adequately prepared and the autumn winds began to blow. Philip of Spain had reluctantly to postpone the expedition for more clement weather.

The duke of Parma had not been informed of the delay, and his troops suffered in the rain and freezing conditions upon the hills above Dunkirk. When a letter arrived from the king, remonstrating with him for not launching an invasion, he was naturally irate. He had been told to wait for the arrival of the Spanish fleet. 'To write to me as if I should have acted already in direct contradiction to your instructions is naturally distressing to me. Do me the signal kindness to tell me what to do, and no difficulty shall stop me, though you bid me cross alone in a barge.' The disagreement did not bode well for the enterprise. The finances of Spain were ailing. The troops were on short rations. To compound an already difficult situation, Santa Cruz died. His successor, the duke of Medina Sidonia, knew next to nothing about service at sea. Delays and frustrations once more bedevilled the proposed Armada.

News reached England in the spring, however, that the vast preparations were almost complete; the Spanish authorities let it be known that the fleet was destined for the West Indies, but no one was deceived.

On 18 May 1588 the Spanish fleet finally sailed out of the Tagus; but it was scattered by a heavy storm. Medina Sidonia recommended that the expedition be once more postponed. Philip replied that 'I have dedicated this enterprise to God ... Get on then, and do your part.' So on 12 July the Spaniards set sail again. The church bells of Spain rang out. On board were printed copies of the papal bull confirming Elizabeth's excommunication and calling on all faithful Catholics to rise up against her. The Armada consisted of approximately 130 large ships of war, carrying 19,000 soldiers and 8,000 sailors. The Spanish, the Italians and the Portuguese made up the various contingents, with the Spanish themselves divided into squadrons of Gallicians, Andalusians, Catalans and Castilians. There were also 600 monks on board, to maintain religious devotion and to care for the wounded. Gambling and swearing were forbidden. All of the Spanish forces were confessed and then received holy communion, in this religious crusade against the heretics. The royal standard of the Armada had, as its motto, '*Exsurge, Domine, et judicia causam tuam!*' – 'Rise up, oh Lord, and avenge Thy cause!' As the fleet sailed for England Philip remained kneeling before the Holy Sacrament, without a cushion, for four hours each day.

The English were now fully aware of the imminent danger. A division of the fleet was watching the harbours under the control of Parma while the principal body made itself ready at Plymouth. The Elizabethan navy consisted of twenty-five fighting galleons, but at this time of peril it was enlarged by other vessels furnished by the city of London and by private individuals. Some other ships and coasters had to be hired. The queen had relied upon Sir Francis Drake and other privateers. It has been estimated that the English fleet consisted of 197 various vessels (not all of which were suitable for combat).

The trained bands and the county militia of England were as prepared as their somewhat rickety organization allowed; they would be joined by the surviving retinues of the nobles, drawn from their major tenants. It was said that 100,000 men were ready to fall to arms, but that may be an overestimate. If they had encountered the duke of Parma and his men, in any case, they would have met the finest military force in Europe. The coastal companies were told to fall back where the enemy landed, removing the corn and the cattle; they were to wait until reinforcements from other companies had arrived. The musters of the Midland armies, 10,000 strong, were to form a separate force in defence of the queen herself.

On 19 July the Spanish fleet was sighted off the Lizard in the Channel. 'The Spanish Armada,' Camden wrote, 'built high like towers and castles, rallied into the form of a crescent whose horn was at least seven miles distant, sailing very slowly though under full sail, as the winds laboured and the ocean sighed under the burden of it.' When it was sighted from the topmast of the *Ark Royal*, the crew shouted for joy. The moment of battle between Spain and England had arrived.

The story goes that Drake received the news while playing bowls at Plymouth, only remarking that 'we have time enough to finish the game and beat the Spaniards too'. The words are probably apocryphal but he may have said something quite like it; he would have to wait for the tide to turn before he made his way out of the harbour. A contemporary observer noted that 'the country people, forthwith, ran down to the seaside, some with clubs, some with picked staves and pitchforks . . .' It is perhaps fortunate that their fighting skills were not tested.

The rest of the world remained neutral, looking on with interest. The Venetians believed that the English would win, and the French merely suggested that they would be able to hold off their enemies at sea. 'For the love of God,' the vice-admiral wrote to Whitehall, 'and our country, let us have with speed some great shot sent us of all bigness.' On 21 July William Hawkins, mayor of Plymouth, wrote that 'the Spanish fleet was in view of this town yesterday night and my lord admiral [Lord Howard] passed to the sea before our said view and was out of sight'. The English fleet had the wind on their side and on that Sunday morning a skirmish ensued between the two parties that lasted two hours. Philip's treasure ship was badly damaged, and was taken by its captors into Dartmouth.

On 23 July the two fleets were off Portland Bill and were engaged in a general struggle; the English had the advantage, with their smaller ships and larger guns. The Spanish vessels wished to close up and grapple with their adversaries, allowing their soldiers to take over the fight. But they were not allowed to come too close. The English relied largely upon seaworthiness and speed. Eventually Medina Sidonia broke off and resumed course to his supposed meeting with the duke of Parma. In the fighting of that day Howard had almost run out of ammunition; there was only store enough for one more large engagement. The Spanish were in worse case; they too were running low on bullets, and their vessels had been more severely damaged. A galleon and a flagship drifted as wrecks to the French coast. For three days, sailing towards Calais, Medina Sidonia sent increasingly urgent messages to the duke of Parma. Meanwhile the English forces were receiving reinforcements from the coastal ports and castles. 'The enemy pursue me,' Sidonia told Parma. 'They fire upon me most days from morning till nightfall; but they will not close and grapple. I have given them every opportunity. I have purposely left ships exposed to tempt them to board; but they decline to do it, and there is no remedy, for they are swift and we are slow.' So the English were able to drive the Spanish forward 'like sheep' until Medina Sidonia reached the haven of Calais.

Yet it was not a haven for long. At midnight on Sunday 28 July, Howard directed eight fire-ships upon the Spanish fleet at anchor; the vessels frantically cut loose their cables before drifting into the sea and the night. On the following morning the Spanish commander collected his fleet together, just off Dunkirk; the English, now seizing their good fortune, went on the attack. The battle of Gravelines was decisive. The English went in among the Spanish, and wrought havoc with their guns and cannon. Three galleons were sunk or captured, along with a host of smaller ships.

'I will not write unto her majesty before more be done,' Howard wrote to Walsingham. 'Their force is wonderful great and strong; and yet we pluck their feathers by little and little.'

The feathers were indeed plucked. The Spanish had already lost eight galleons in the course of the conflict, and many men were dead or dying. No English vessel had suffered any serious harm. The duke of Parma could not move; he was marooned in Nieuport, and the Armada was in no condition to make a rendezvous. The Dutch navy, hostile to Parma, also kept him enclosed. The wind then changed to west-south-west, sending the Spanish fleet away from the shoals into the North Sea. The English had no ammunition left to hinder them but instead 'put on a brag countenance' by pursuing them up the coast. On 31 July Sir Francis Drake wrote that 'we have the army of Spain before us and mind . . . to wrestle a pull with him . . . I doubt it not but ere it be long so to handle the matter with the duke of Sidonia as he shall wish himself at St Mary Port among his orange trees.'

It was at this moment that the queen came down from London for the review of the army at Tilbury. She arrived by barge and, as she landed at the blockhouse, the cannon were sounded in her honour. She was met by an escort of 1,000 horse and 2,000 foot, and on the following day she took part in the formal review when she passed among the men 'like some Amazonian empress'. In her speech she told them that she had been advised to take care of her person, but she scorned any such protection; she could rely on the trust and devotion of her people. She is then supposed to have said that she was resolved 'to live and die among you all, to lay down for my God and for my kingdom and for my people, my honour and my blood, even in the dust. I know I have the body of a weak and feeble woman, but I have the heart and stomach of a king, and of a king of England too.' It is a matter of debate whether she used these precise words but the gist of the speech, recounted later, is no doubt accurate. There was a great shout from her soldiers at the end of the oration. She then retired to Leicester's tent at noon for her dinner.

The Spanish fleet, battered and defeated, was even then making its way along the Scottish coast. It was noted at the time that the Scottish king had kept his word to the queen and had not even covertly supported Spain; James had told the English ambassador at his court that 'all the favour he expected from the Spaniards was the courtesy of Polyphemus to Ulysses, that he should be devoured the last'.

When they reached the north coast of Scotland the commanders were ordered to make the best way they could to Spain. Four or five men died each day from starvation, and all the horses were thrown overboard to save water. When the Spanish ships reached the Irish Sea a great storm blew up and threw them against the coast of Ireland. The loss of life by shipwreck was enormous but it was compounded by the loss of life on shore. One Irishman, Melaghin McCabb, boasted that he had dispatched eighty Spaniards with his gallowglass axe. The English ambassador in Paris told his Venetian counterpart that nineteen vessels had been wrecked, with the loss of 7,000 men; other reports put the fatalities higher. Only half of the Armada returned to Spain, less than half of the men. Philip himself remained calm, or impassive. It was, he said, the Lord's will. Secretly he raged, and vowed on his knees that one day he would subdue England even if he reduced Spain to a desert by the effort.

The celebrations attendant on victory had a more sombre note. In the streets of the Channel ports thousands of sailors were dying of typhus or the scurvy; they had conquered the enemy but they could not vanquish disease. The lord admiral wrote to Burghley, after the destruction of the Armada, that 'sickness and mortality begins wonderfully to grow among us' and asked for the resources to purchase food and clothing. But, after the expense of warfare, Elizabeth's purse was now closed. She left her men to their fate.

Another casualty of the war touched her more deeply. The earl of Leicester, worn out by his campaign in the Netherlands, was 'troubled with an ague' that became 'a continual burning fever'. His death was not greatly mourned by anyone except the queen herself. He was considered incompetent and vainglorious; a contemporary historian, John Stow, wrote that 'all men, so far as they durst, rejoiced no less outwardly at his death than for the victory lately obtained against the Spaniard'.

Elizabeth kept the last letter he had written to her in a little wooden casket; it was found by her bed after her death. Yet distress at his death did not mitigate her practical temper. He had died indebted to her exchequer and so she ordered his goods to be sold at public auction to reimburse her for loss. There were other rewards. When she sat for her famous 'Armada' portrait by George Gower, where she exults in the victory with an imperial crown beside her, she is wearing the pearls that Leicester had bequeathed to her.

On 26 November she was drawn by two white horses in a richly decorated chariot to St Paul's Cathedral for the final celebration; there had not been such a spectacular procession since her coronation almost thirty years before. In the following year Edmund Spenser completed the first three books of his verse epic *The Faerie Queene*, in which Elizabeth herself is transmuted into Gloriana.

Towards the end of 1588 a young man ran down the Strand calling out to the people, 'If you will see the queen, you must come quickly.' It was said that she was about to appear in the courtyard of Somerset House. So the crowd rushed to the area. It was five in the evening, and already dark, but then in a blaze of torchlight Elizabeth suddenly appeared.

'God bless you all, my good people!'
'God save your Majesty!'
'You may well have a greater Prince, but you shall never have a more loving Prince!'

The queen had been raised to new heights of glory and prestige, but the defeat of the Armada wrought other wonderful consequences. The myth of English sea power now became a more striking aspect of national consciousness, linked as it was to the defeat of Catholicism and the defence of true religion. Drake and Hawkins were new types of Protestant hero, fighting on behalf of national liberty. The papal curse had been lifted in the most striking possible manner. Elizabeth herself wrote to the duke of Florence that 'it is as clear as daylight that God's blessing rests upon us, upon our people and our realm, with all the plainest signs of prosperity, peace, obedience, riches, power and increase of our subjects'.

The pope tried to excuse himself by saying that he always knew the Spaniards would be defeated. The Spanish ambassador then congratulated him on his gift of prophecy. The pope merely 'turned up the whites of his eyes and looked piously towards heaven'. Spain could no longer be considered to be the resolute champion of Catholicism in the world, and the papacy mitigated its own pretensions. The Catholics of England now accommodated themselves to the established Church or were the object of more determined persecution.

The death of Leicester helped to forward the career of another court favourite. Robert Devereux, second earl of Essex, was twenty-two years old at the time of the Armada. He had been the ward of Burghley ever since the untimely death of his father in Ireland; Sir Walter Devereux had died of dysentery in 1576. Two years later Leicester had married the widow, the countess of Essex. Leicester was then the stepfather, as well as the godfather, of the young man. So the young Essex was doubly blessed.

He was always restless and ambitious, striving for power as well as for glory. It was said that 'he was entirely given over to arms and war'; yet he was also eloquent and highly intelligent. He believed, or professed to believe, in the importance of 'virtue' in both a martial and an ethical sense; manliness was to be joined with piety, valour with clemency and justice. He pursued what he later called 'the public use for which we are all born'. He supported the Protestant cause, naturally enough, and was known to favour the more godly sort. He was impulsive and energetic, too, making a contrast with the older and more staid councillors of Elizabeth's realm. He was 'soft to take offence and hard to lay it down'; he could 'conceal nothing' and 'carried his love and hatred on his forehead', and was sometimes the victim of nervous prostration. It has been said that the court was now so changed that it seemed to herald a new reign. In truth it was simply entering a darker and more sequestered phase, of which Essex himself would eventually become the victim.

37

Repent! Repent!

It had not gone unnoticed that a large proportion of the forces that fought the Armada were of a Puritan persuasion. The Jesuit Robert Parsons wrote that 'the puritan part at home in England is thought to be most vigorous of any other, that is to say, most ardent, quick, bold, resolute, and to have a great part of the best captains and soldiers on their side, a point of no small moment'.

The Puritans could now muster a considerable following in the country, especially after the defeat of the papists at sea, and it is certain that they commanded the loyalty of many members of the Commons. Their strength had already emerged two years previously, in the parliament of 1586; the Commons introduced several bills to curb the power and authority of the bishops, at which point the archbishop of Canterbury wrote in alarm to the queen. She had many times in the past warned parliament not to meddle in religious affairs. She now sent a message to the Commons reprimanding them for disobeying her and for venturing upon her supremacy. She commanded the Speaker 'to see that no bills concerning reform in ecclesiastical causes be exhibited and, if they were exhibited, not to read them'. 'Specifically,' the Speaker told the Commons, 'you are commanded by Her Majesty to take heed that none care be given or time afforded the wearisome solicitations of those that commonly be called Puritans . . .'

But the Commons refused to be cowed and introduced a petition to abolish all existing laws that concerned ecclesiastical government. A 'new directory for prayer' was also proposed as a replacement for the familiar liturgy. No more sweeping measure had ever been put forward by a parliament, and it suggested that the Puritan cause was now being asserted in a more forceful and methodical manner. Yet it had reached its apogee and would now recede.

On a motion for the reading of the new directory the Speaker declared that the sovereign had already commanded the members to keep silence on religion. He predicted her severe displeasure and, sure enough, another message from the palace reached him. She ordered him to send her the petition and the book, but she also dispatched several of the more zealous MPs to prison. 'I fear me,' one of the members complained, 'we shall come shortly to this, that to do God and her Majesty good service shall be accounted Puritanism.' It was another phase in the relationship between sovereign and parliament.

The Puritan cause was further advertised in a series of tracts. The Martin Marprelate tracts, as they came to be known, were written anonymously; 'Martin' launched a series of attacks, in seven separate works, upon 'petty antichrists, proud prelates, intolerable withstanders of reformation, enemies of the gospel and covetous wretched priests'. Yet 'Martin' was witty and animated as well as being pugnacious; he addressed the ecclesiastical hierarchy as 'right poisoned, persecuting, and terrible priests. My horned masters, your government is anti-christian; your cause is desperate; your grounds are ridiculous.' He wished to undermine the bishops by portraying them as simply absurd. 'I will spare [bishop] John of London for this time, for it may be he is at bowls and it is pity to trouble my good brother, lest he should swear too bad . . .'

In response the supporters of the established Church published tracts with titles such as 'A Sound Box on the Ear for the Idiot Martin to hold his Peace' and 'A Whip for the Ape. Martin Displayed'. One of them was reported to be 'printed between the sky and the ground, within a mile of an oak, and not many fields off from the unprivileged press of the ass-signees of Martin junior'. Richard Bancroft, treasurer of St Paul's who was later to become archbishop of Canterbury, accused the Puritan party of promoting schism and dissension within the Church. 'Her majesty is depraved [abused]. Her authority is impugned and great dangers are threatened. Civil government is called into question. Princes' prerogatives are curiously scanned.' The Puritan party was close to becoming a Church within the Church, with all the rivalries that implied.

The Martin and anti-Martin texts represented the high point of acrimony in Protestant debate, and we may date from this time the portrayal of Puritans on the Elizabethan stage as figures of fun; in Shakespeare's *Twelfth Night* Malvolio, a 'sort of Puritan' according to Maria, anticipates by twelve years Zeal-of-the-Land Busy in Ben Jonson's *Bartholomew Fair*. 'Down with Dagon, down with Dagon . . . I will no longer endure your profanations . . . that idol, that heathenish idol, that remains, as I may say, a beam, a very beam, not a beam of the sun, nor a beam of the moon, nor a beam of a balance, neither a house-beam, nor a weaver's beam, but a beam in the eye, in the eye of the brethren; a very great beam; an exceeding great beam; such as are your stage-players, rhymers, and morris-dancers . . .'

The Marprelate texts in particular soon became the talk of London, while enormous efforts were made to hunt down the writer and the printer. One secret press was discovered in Northamptonshire, but others escaped detection. Some of those involved were found before being fined or imprisoned, but the identity of 'Martin Marprelate' is still not certainly known. His high spirits and inventiveness, however, may have been a mark of desperation. There now seemed to be little chance that the principles of Puritanism would have any effect upon the Elizabethan polity. Marprelate's levity may have been a sign that there was little left to lose.

The godly found in Archbishop Whitgift a profound and determined enemy. 'The name Puritan', he wrote, 'is very aptly given to these men not because they be pure . . . but because they think themselves to be *mundiores ceteris*, more pure than others.' Throughout 1589 and 1590 the leaders of the Puritan cause were arrested and silenced. Some were even imprisoned for refusing to take the ex-officio oath; they refused to swear that, in a court of religion, they would answer all questions truthfully. It was a form of self-entrapment. In the spring of 1589 the members of the High Commission, the authorities on religious matters, delivered an injunction that no London parish should allow the preaching of the stricter sort. One of the leading Puritans, Thomas Cartwright, was imprisoned in the Fleet and eventually came before the Star Chamber. As a contemporary noted in the following year, 'these sharp proceedings make that sect greatly diminish'.

So it had come to this. The Puritans in parliament had proved unable to advance their cause and to secure further reformation. The Puritan presses were one by one closed down, and the hunt for the Marprelate presses had become a general pursuit of the Puritan movement. There followed a decade which has been called one of stabilization or normalization, in which orthodox pieties came to the fore, but it may be more accurately seen as a time of secret and silent antagonism played out in various churches and meeting places. Puritanism ceased to be a public movement or campaign, but instead retreated to the confines of the household or the soul of the individual in the hope that better times might follow. The cause of the godly was indeed revived at the beginning of the next reign.

Yet the religious aspirations of the minority must be set against the neutrality or indifference of the population. A report was sent from Lancashire to the privy council in which it was asserted that the churches were still largely empty and that the county contained 'multitudes of bastards and drunkards'. This could be the condition of England at any time. The preachers were few, and the parsons unlearned, but in any case the preachers were not needed for lack of auditors. The churches 'generally lie ruinous, unrepaired, and unfurnished' while the chapels of ease, built for those who could not easily attend the parish church, 'are many of them utterly destitute of any curates, and thereby grow into utter ruine and desolation'. The people 'swarm in the streets and alehouses during service-time'. Many of these people were in fact unreformed Catholics who delighted in 'wakes, ales, greenes, May games, rushbearings, bearbaits, doveales etcetera'. Those who did attend the services were often prompted by convention rather than devotion; they talked, made jokes, or slept during the ceremonies.

Others were simply weary of religious dissension and doctrinal debate; they were secularists in the sense that they wished for stability and security above all else. Immune from enthusiasm of any kind, they were not particularly interested in any new form of Protestant spirituality. If they conformed to the current religion it was simply because they were obliged so to do. Thus the Anglican Church, as it would become known, was slowly being established.

'Repent! Repent!' The call went up in the streets of London. A yeoman named Hackett had proclaimed himself to be king of Europe and the New Messiah. 'Tell them in the City that Christ Jesus is come with his fan in his hand to judge the earth. And if any man ask you where he is, tell them he is at Walker's house by Broken Wharf!' He also said that Elizabeth had forfeited her crown. He soon reached the gallows where he cried out with his dying breath for God to deliver him from his enemies. 'If not,' he said, 'I will fire the heavens and tear Thee from Thy Throne with my hands.' The spectators, horrified, called out for his disembowelment to be protracted. It is a vignette of the Elizabethan world.

Philip II, despite the destruction of the Armada, was still a most powerful enemy. He controlled an empire that must count as one of the most splendid in human history; he ruled Spain, Portugal and much of the Netherlands; he commanded Milan and Sicily while many of the states of Italy were wholly dependent upon him. He was the sovereign of the Philippines as well as the coastal settlements of Malabar and Coromandel. He was lord of the spice islands of Indonesia. And of course he was the master of the New World on both sides of the equator. The gold of the Americas meant that his revenue was ten times as large as that of Elizabeth. He had a standing army of 50,000 men, where Elizabeth had none. The emperor of Germany was a member of Philip's House of Habsburg. France was divided by religious schism.

Sir John Puckering, the lord keeper, addressed both Houses of Parliament on the naval power of the Spanish king five years after the Armada; he warned the members that 'how great soever he was before, he is now thereby manifestly more great ... He keepeth a navy armed to impeach all trade of merchandise from England to Gascoigne and Guinea.'

Yet this was the power that England now dared to provoke and abuse. In the spring of 1589 Drake conceived a scheme to strike at Portugal. Elizabeth became a shareholder in what was essentially a joint-stock company; she had neither the money nor the men to equip an armada of her own. The fleet was supposed to sail against Santander but instead made its way to Corunna, where it delayed for a fortnight. Its commanders also failed to provide adequate supplies.

In May they set sail for Lisbon, against orders, and were joined on the way by the young earl of Essex; the English were hoping that the Portuguese would rise against their new Spanish masters. But the attack on Lisbon proved to be a failure, and the anticipated insurrection never took place. It was reported at the time that 6,000 men had perished on 'this miserable action', as one captain called it; of the 1,100 gentlemen on board, only 350 returned. Elizabeth was by now thoroughly displeased and ordered the recall of Essex.

The expedition, promising so much and achieving so little, made its way back to Plymouth. Drake remained in disgrace for some years. He had alarmed Philip of Spain without causing him much damage, thus achieving the worst of both worlds. The maritime future for the rest of the queen's reign was confined to private raids for the capture of booty; privateering thereby became a business, with syndicates of shareholders and freely available capital resources.

Sir Richard Hawkins has left a very interesting set of notes on the campaign against the Spanish navy; his *Observations* recall a journey into the South Sea in 1593. Of the scurvy, for example, he reports that the disease can be deduced 'by the swelling of the gums, by denting of the flesh of the legs with a man's finger . . . others show it with their laziness, others complain of the crick of the back etcetera'. He records 'the seething of the meat in salt water' and the corruption of victuals by 'the vapours of the sea'.

By means of his observations we get closer to the real nature of sea warfare in the sixteenth century. He notes, for example, the obstinacy of the English sailors who 'apprehending a conceit in their imaginations, neither experiment, knowledge, examples, reasons nor authority can alter or remove them from their conceited opinions'. When he labours to convince them they were wrong in wishing to attack two Spanish ships, they 'break out, some into vaunting and bragging, some into reproaches of want of courage, others into wishings that they had never come out of their country'.

Hawkins warns other commanders not to trust their men in the extremities of battle. Too much wine, for example, 'infused desperate and foolish hardiness in many who blinded with the fume of liquor, considered not of any danger, but thus and thus would stand at hazard; some in vainglory vaunting themselves; some others railing upon the Spaniards; another inviting a companion to come and stand by him, and not to budge a foot from him; which indiscreetly they put in execution, and cost the lives of many a good man'.

It is the folly of the English sailor to prefer to fight without armour. The Spaniard, being of more temperate and sober disposition, was happy to don armour in order to protect himself. But the English cast it off, 'choosing rather to be shot through with a bullet, or lanced through with a pike, or thrust through with a sword, than to endure a little travail and suffering'. In some sea battles, Hawkins reports, 'I have seen the splinters kill and hurt many at once, and yet the shot to have passed through without touching any person'.

He condemns those who denounce the English sailors as pirates, since 'the English have neither peace nor truce with Spain; but war; and therefore not to be accounted pirates. Besides Spain broke the peace with England, and not England with Spain; and that by Embargo, which of all kinds of defiances is most reproved and of least reputation . . .'

The temporary disgrace of Essex did little to calm the fevered atmosphere at court, and in the summer of 1589 one observer remarked that 'there was never in court such emulation, such envy, such back-biting as is now at this time'. Still in the ascendant was Burghley. As a clerk of the signet put it to a suitor, 'Old Saturnus is a melancholy and wayward planet, but yet predominant here, and if you have turn thus to do, it must be done that way; and whatsoever hope you have of any other, believe it or not.' Burghley was also actively and assiduously promoting the prospects of his son, Robert Cecil, who at the times of his father's incapacity through illness took on much of the business of government. He was of uncommon appearance. One contemporary described him as 'a slight, crooked, hump-back young gentleman, dwarfish in stature, but with a face not irregular in feature, and thoughtful and subtle in expression, with reddish hair, a thin tawny beard and large, pathetic greenish-coloured eyes, with a mind and manners already trained to courts and cabinet'. The queen called him 'my elf' or 'my pigmy'.

Cecil and Essex had both been brought up in the household of Lord Burghley, one as son and one as ward, but they continually quarrelled with each other. Their rivalry became all the more strenuous after the death of Elizabeth's trusted servant Walsingham, in the spring of 1590. Essex favoured an aggressive foreign policy that supported the cause of international Protestantism; Cecil and his father preferred to pursue a more defensive strategy, with the aim of keeping Spain at arm's length. Essex represented noble and martial valour; Cecil was essentially a career courtier. War for Essex was a form of sport or game; for Cecil it was a source of expense and danger.

So they were rivals for power and for the queen's favour. It was not a competition that the impulsive Essex could ever win. One of his retainers wrote that 'Sir Robert Cecil goeth and cometh very often between London and the Court, so that he comes out with his hands full of papers and head full of matter, and so occupied passeth through the presence [chamber] like a blind man, not looking upon any'. This was a courtier upon whom the queen could rely. Soon enough he was knighted and appointed as a member of the privy council. More than any other man he would control the last years of her reign.

38

The setting sun

The queen asked her carver, at dinner, what was in a certain covered dish. 'Madame,' he replied, 'it is a coffin.' A 'coffin' was then the word for a certain type of pie.

'Are you such a fool,' she shouted at him, 'to give a pie such a name?' She was now approaching her sixtieth year, and becoming fearful of her mortality. Her eyes had sunk a little, and she had lost teeth on the left side of her mouth that sometimes made her diction blurred and indistinct; her skin was plastered white and her wigs were a deep red. In 1593 she began to translate from sixth-century Latin *The Consolation of Philosophy* by Boethius, perhaps as an antidote to the signs of weariness and age all around her.

Over the years she had acquired more expertise than anyone around her. When one of her servants ventured to speak to her about the affairs of the Netherlands, she rebuked him: 'Tush, Brown! I know more than thou doest.' And when he made a remark about France she again interrupted him: 'Tush, Brown! Do not I know?'

The earl of Essex had at last been called to her privy council. He had recruited two very brilliant brothers, Francis and Anthony Bacon, to advise him on matters of state. Anthony Bacon had previously been in the employ of Walsingham, and had established a network of agents across the continent working in the Protestant cause. So Essex could supply the queen with useful information. He believed that astute patronage materially increased his power. Yet he found it impossible to break into the inward circle of influence represented by Burghley and his son. In time this would breed resentment and suspicion.

Elizabeth had governed for the last four years without a parliament, but her depleted treasury needed the supply of fresh revenue. So she summoned an assembly for the middle of February 1593, when she told them through the mouth of her chancellor 'that they were not called together to make new laws, or lose good hours in idle speeches, but to vote a supply to enable her Majesty to defend her realm against the hostile attempts of the king of Spain'.

The Commons then made their customary request for freedom of speech as well as liberty from arrest. She granted the request with the significant comment that 'wit and speech were calculated to do harm, and their liberty of speech extended no further than "ay" or "no"'. The Commons then proceeded to defy her attempt to silence discussion by framing a petition that she should settle the question of royal succession. She sent the two members responsible to the Fleet prison. As she grew older, she became more despotic.

Parliament now bowed to the inevitable, and voted the subsidies to her exchequer as well as passing a bill 'for keeping her Majesty's subjects in better obedience'. Having demonstrated the power of her will, she dismissed them on 10 April with a speech in which she mentioned the proposed invasion by the king of Spain. 'I am informed, when he attempted this last measure, some upon the sea-coast forsook their towns, leaving all naked and exposed to his entrance. But I swear unto you, by God, if I knew those persons, or may know them hereafter, I will make them know what it is to be fearful in so urgent a cause.' In her contempt, she could be magnificent.

She also made an important statement about her purpose in the management of foreign affairs: 'It may be thought simplicity in me that all this time of my reign I have not sought to advance my territories and enlarge my dominions; for opportunity hath served me to do it ... And I must say, my mind was never to invade my neighbours, or to usurp over any; I am contented to reign over mine own and to rule as a just prince.' She was making an implicit contrast between herself and the Spanish king. Her central aim was simply peace at home and security from foreign threat.

The bill that parliament had passed for 'better obedience' was designed to curb the activities of papists and sectaries. Attendance at conventicles and unlawful assemblies was now considered to be the equivalent of hearing Mass, so that Catholic recusants and the more fervent Protestants were equally liable to imprisonment. It was also enacted that anyone over the age of sixteen who refused to attend public worship over the space of a month should be imprisoned; a second offence would result in banishment from the realm; a refusal, or a return from banishment, would be punished by death. It was further enacted that no Catholic should stray more than 5 miles from his or her residence. For papists England had become a kind of open prison.

This assault upon Catholics and Puritans alike is the appropriate context for the most important religious treatise of the period. Richard Hooker's *Of the Laws of Ecclesiastical Polity* – the first four books of which were published in 1594 – is an eloquent and magisterial account of what may be described as the middle way of England's settlement.

He declared that much religious controversy was over things of no account. He rebuked the Puritans for their excessive reliance on Scripture, which was a standard for doctrine but not a rule for discipline. It was not necessary to follow the practice of the apostles as an invariable model. The English Church, like other forms of human society, may make the laws for its own government as long as they are not contrary to Scripture, and human authority may intervene where Scripture is silent. The Puritan belief in *sola scriptura* – that the Bible contains all that is needed for salvation – was unwarranted. The Church may therefore institute its own ceremonies. All those born within the domain or district of an established Church should conform to it. It was the mother of all.

The visible Church was not perfect – it must of necessity contain sinners as well as saints – but it existed in an imperfect world. The pursuit of certainty on matters that could not be adequately understood in this life was not fruitful; debates on predestination were unnecessary and harmful, since the truth could never be revealed on earth. The congregation of worshippers must depend upon prayer, and the sacraments, as the fortifications of their faith. These were the foundations of the community.

As to the Calvinism of Geneva, Hooker remarked that 'our persuasion is, that no age ever had knowledge of it but only ours; that they which defend it devised it; that neither Christ nor his Apostles at any time taught it, but the contrary'. He granted that the Church of Rome was still part of the family of Jesus Christ but one defiled 'by gross and grievous abominations'; the English Church was the true Church purged of this dross.

He stated further that Church and State make up the fundamentals of the Commonwealth, and that both must accord with the natural law of God as understood by the general reason of humankind. The doctrine of the Trinity, for example, is not explicitly announced in the Bible, and must be deduced from the act of reasoning. These interacting societies, of Church and State, may thereby both be ruled by the Christian prince. The community of Christians is a visible Church, held together by prayer and sacramental worship. Hooker, then, provides the foundation for the Church of England. Anglicanism really did not exist before the advent of his work.

Thomas Fuller, in his *Church History of Britain*, written two generations later, remarked that 'Mr Hooker's voice was low, stature little, gesture none at all; standing stone-still in the pulpit, as if the posture of his body were the emblem of his mind, immovable in his opinions'.

Essex, with the assistance of the brothers Bacon, was now in command of all intelligence. He was in fact instrumental in uncovering another plot against the queen. António, the claimant to the Portugese throne, had taken refuge in England. When it was discovered that some of his supporters were selling secrets to the Spaniards, Essex was asked to investigate. In the course of his enquiries he discovered, or professed to discover, that Rodrigo Lopez, the queen's Portuguese physician, was seeking to poison her. Although Lopez outwardly conformed as a Protestant, he was in fact a Jew; the suspicion of him was therefore part of that anti-Semitic atmosphere in which Christopher Marlowe's *The Jew of Malta* thrived.

Robert Cecil, who in important matters was not inclined to support Essex, informed the queen that there was no evidence against her doctor. Whereupon Elizabeth called Essex 'a rash and temerarious youth'. In the face of this reproof Essex redoubled his efforts in the determination to justify himself. That is when he uncovered the plot. Lopez was taken to the Tower where, under torture, he confessed his guilt. He was sentenced to death. Essex had therefore acquired the additional glory of saving the life of his mistress; in the words of a contemporary, he had 'won the spurs and saddle also'.

Yet all the glory in the world could not conceal a rising sense of disquiet at Elizabeth's councillors. In the last five years of the sixteenth century a disastrous series of harvests was responsible for an extraordinary rise in the price of essential commodities. The four successive years from 1594 witnessed the worst living conditions of the Elizabethan era, and the price of flour tripled from 1594 to 1597. In the latter year real wages plunged lower than at any time since 1260. The proportion of families without sufficient land to feed themselves was growing all the time; the number of vagrants, forced to wander in order to find work, also increased. Many people did not have enough money to buy food; the dearth caused famine, and created the conditions for diseases such as typhus and dysentery on a wider scale than had previously been seen in the country. The records for the city of Newcastle, in the autumn of 1597, record the burial at municipal expense of twenty-five 'poor folks who died for want in the streets'. This is the context for Titania's complaint to Oberon in *A Midsummer Night's Dream*, performed at some point in 1595 or 1596:

> The ox hath therefore stretch'd his yoke in vain,
> The ploughman lost his sweat, and the green corn
> Hath rotted ere his youth attain'd a beard;
> The fold stands empty in the drownèd field,
> And crows are fatted with the murrion flock.

It was therefore a time of general unrest and disaffection. The mayor of Norwich received an anonymous letter in 1595 warning

him that 60,000 London craftsmen were waiting for the call to
rise in revolt. In the summer of that year Sir Thomas Wilford was
appointed as provost-marshal of London with orders to seize any
riotous people and, according to the justice of martial law, to
execute them openly and speedily on the gallows. This was a case
of the royal prerogative overturning the principles of common law.

An Essex labourer was arrested for complaining that corn was
being taken on ships and sold to the enemy. 'I will be one of them
that shall rise and gather a company of eight or nine score and will
go to fetch it out ... and if we were such a company gathered
together, who can withstand us?' A Kentish man said that 'he
hoped to see such a war in this realm to afflict the rich men of this
country to requite their hardness of heart towards the poor'. In the
autumn of 1596 the earl of Bath wrote to the privy councillors
that they should order the gentry of Devon to return to their
estates 'to be at hand to stay the fury of the inferior multitude, if
they should happen to break out in a sudden outcry for want of
relief, as without good circumspection they may and will do'.
A rising in Oxfordshire, in 1596, was led by an instigator who
declared 'it will never be well until the gentry are knocked down'.

With the genuine fear of insurrection in the air, a steady
increase in criminal indictments is evident in the 1590s. The
'inferior multitude' was regularly being castigated now for being
feckless and idle, with the threat from below adding to a general
mood of pessimism that is evident in the last years of the queen's
reign. By the end of the decade a body of Poor Law legislation
had been enacted that placed the burden of responsibility for the
poor upon the parish, with the costs of maintaining the distressed
and the unemployed to be provided by a parish poor rate. The
justices of the peace were to nominate 'overseers' of the poor who
were also to run the parish workhouse. This framework of social
legislation became an important aspect of national life for 250
years, remaining in place until the new Poor Law of 1834. It may
have been one of the principal reasons for the absence of a social
or political revolution; it represented a bedrock of stability.

The queen and her council were nevertheless at the time
blamed for indecision and misgovernment. Thomas Wilson, in a
collection of papers entitled *The State of England Anno Dom. 1600*,

complained that the privy councillors 'suffer very few to be acquainted with matters of state for fear of divulging it, whereby their practices are subject to be revealed, and therefore they will suffer few to rise to places of reputation'. And in truth the queen was growing old. In this year, 1596, she reached the feared climacteric of sixty-three years. Bishop Rudd, of St Davids, preached the Lenten sermon before her, in which he congratulated her for her good fortune in living so long. He delivered some reflections on sacred arithmetic, with seven times nine leading to sixty-three. He also quoted the passage describing old age in Scripture 'when the grinders cease because they are few and those that look out of the windows be darkened'.

Elizabeth was not amused. She opened the window in her private oratory when the sermon was over and told him that 'he should have kept his arithmetic to himself'. But then, she added, 'I see that the greatest clerks are not the wisest men.' A few days later, at court, 'she thanked God that neither her stomach, nor strength, nor her voice for singing, nor fingering for instruments, nor, lastly, her sight was any whit decayed'. She refused to allow court painters to use shade in any portraits of her since shade 'was an accident and not naturally existent in the face'. The privy council now forbade the circulation of any unauthorized portraits. Any paintings that depicted her as in any sense old, 'to her great offence', were cast into ovens. Nicholas Hilliard was commissioned to produce a formalized or mask-like visage that could be copied by those less skilful. English art was still essentially conservative. The mood is caught in Francis Davison's poetical rhapsody:

> Time's young hours attend her still,
> And her eyes and cheeks do fill,
> With fresh youth and beauty . . .

Still the shadows were growing longer. Her long-serving courtiers were dying around her; in this year, for example, Puckering, the lord keeper, Sir Francis Knollys, and Lord Hunsdon, were taken from her service to the grave. It was against this background that Essex helped to plan a great expedition against Cadiz, in order to singe the beard of the king of Spain once more. It was said that he had grown tired of life at court, surrounded by old men. His sister described him as 'the Weary Knight', since he was 'always weary and longing for the change'. It was within his power to renew the energy, and revive the honour, of the court.

At the beginning of June 1596, a large English armada left England for Spanish waters; a total of eighty-two ships was under the command of three men, one of whom was Essex. The French king, Henry IV, joked that Elizabeth would not want Essex to be very far from her petticoats. There was some truth in that. She was never very convinced by his assertion of martial prowess. But in fact the expedition to Cadiz was a great success; the Spaniards were taken entirely by surprise, and the city was seized in a swift assault. Essex had intended to remain there indefinitely but the problem of supplies obliged him to return with his forces to England.

Another prize was won. The authorities of Cadiz were forced to sink the Spanish fleet in their harbour, for fear of its falling into the hands of the enemy; the cost to Philip of Spain amounted to 12 million ducats. It had been a great victory, reinforcing England's claim to mastery of the sea. Essex became the hero of the hour to everyone except the queen, who remarked that the expedition had been more of an 'action of honour and victory against the enemy and particular spoil to the army than any profitable to ourself'. She was not at all interested in martial glory; she wanted the Spanish gold that had been distributed among the successful English troops, and she was furious that Essex had not reserved it for her. She was heard to remark that previously she had done his pleasure, but now she would teach him to do hers.

So Essex was still sensitive to the point of distraction. When Lord Howard of Effingham was created earl of Nottingham, with a citation of his services in Cadiz, Essex perceived a slight to himself. He raged furiously at the honour and asked the queen to rescind it. His protégé, Francis Bacon, counselled him to mitigate his temper. The queen would otherwise regard him as 'a man of nature not to be ruled, that hath the advantage of my affection and knoweth it'. That is why she continued to favour his great rival. At the very time of the Cadiz operation, Robert Cecil was appointed to be her secretary of state.

It became clear that Essex was no longer her pre-eminent

favourite, but just one among her councillors in a court that was described as 'dangerously poisoned with the secret stings of smiling enemies'. Her principal councillor was still Lord Burghley, but he was growing old. He was reported by the French ambassador to be 'very proud and presuming in his words'; he possessed 'a kind of crossing or wayward manner' with 'a tone of choler'.

Elizabeth herself seems naturally to have become more irate. In the spring of 1597 one courtier, William Fenton, reported that the queen 'seemeth more forward than commonly she used to bear herself towards her women, nor doth she hold them in discourse with such familiar matter, but often chides for small neglects, in such wise as to make these fair maids often cry and bewail in piteous sort'.

One of these 'fair maids', Lady Mary Howard, had a gown that threatened to rival those of the queen in its finery. Elizabeth sent for the dress and secretly put it on. It was too short for her. She went into one of the household chambers and asked the ladies 'how they liked her new-fancied suit'. She was met by an embarrassed silence, and she went up to Lady Mary herself and asked her 'if it was not made too short and unbecoming'. The lady agreed. 'Why then,' she said, 'if it become not me, by being too short, I am minded it shall never become thee, as being too fine; so it fitteth neither well.' The gown was never worn again.

She showed her anger, too, against the ambassador from Poland at an audience in 1597. In an address to her he seems to have been more bombastic than suited the company, and as a result she stormed at him. Cecil reported to Essex that 'her Majesty made one of the best answers *ex tempore* in Latin that ever I heard'. She began with '*Expectavi orationem, mihi vero querelam adduxisti!*' – 'I expected an oration. But you have brought a complaint against me!' 'Surely,' she went on to say, 'I can hardly believe that if the king himself were present, he would use such language!' And so she harangued him. At the end she paused and then turned to her court. 'God's death, my lords, I have been enforced this day to scour up my old Latin, that hath long lain rusting.' 'God's death' was an oath she used frequently in these days.

A French envoy from Henry IV was given an audience with her, and he reported that 'all the time she spoke she would often rise from her chair and appear to be very impatient with what I was saying; she would complain that the fire was hurting her eyes, though there was a great screen before it and she six or seven feet away, yet did she give orders to have it extinguished'. Yet still she maintained her regimen of daily exercise. She would ride or walk every day, even in the rain or frost. Her ladies, careful of their own health as well as that of their mistress, asked Whitgift to intervene. The archbishop implored the queen to stay within doors during inclement weather, but she paid no regard to his advice.

The Spanish danger had not passed with the success of the mission against Cadiz. Philip of Spain dispatched a new armada a month or two after that city's fall; it was supposed to sail to Ireland where it would assist the rebels there. But the storms of Cape Finisterre ended the expedition. Elizabeth was now thoroughly discomfited and in 1597 ordered a new attack, led by Essex and the newly ennobled Nottingham, designed to scatter the Spanish fleet and to intercept the treasure ships in the Azores. The expedition did not altogether go as planned, however, and the English never came near the Spanish gold that escaped them with impunity. They returned in October, but were able before reaching shore to turn back another armada against England that Philip had launched in a last gamble. Her relief that the threat of invasion had been lifted was matched only by her anger with Essex for failing to take the treasure. He was caught in a cycle of defeat and dismay that would soon have disastrous consequences.

39

A disobedient servant

One day in the summer of 1598 a few close courtiers were closeted with the queen, discussing who should be the next lord lieutenant of Ireland; that country was in a state of revolt, and needed careful handling. In the royal closet that day were Essex, Howard, Cecil and one or two others. Elizabeth named Sir William Knollys for the post. Essex, knowing that the choice had been suggested by Cecil, opposed it with great bluster and vehemence. The queen made a sarcastic comment of some kind and Essex, offended and with a contemptuous expression upon his face, gave mortal offence by turning his back upon her. The queen, telling him to 'go and be hanged', boxed his ears.

Essex then grasped his sword-hilt. Howard rushed between them, and thereby prevented the earl from drawing his sword against his sovereign; it would have been a capital offence. Essex swore an oath, however, 'that he would not have taken that blow from King Henry, her father, and that it was an indignity that he could nor would endure from anyone'. He muttered some words about 'a king in petticoats' before rushing from the royal presence and withdrawing from the court.

The chancellor, Egerton, implored him to write a letter of submission to the queen. But he demurred, stating that 'if the vilest of indignities is done to me, does religion enforce me to sue for pardon? Cannot princes err? Cannot subjects receive wrong? Let Solomon's fool laugh when he is stricken . . .' He now raged even more furiously against Robert Cecil, demanding of Lord Cobham, for example, 'to declare myself either his only or friendly to Mr Secretary, and his enemy; protesting that there could be no neutrality'. To create factions, however, was to risk the dangers of isolation.

This was the period in which Lord Burghley was dying. Elizabeth sent one of her ladies for news of him every day, bearing with her a cordial. She said that 'she did entreat heaven daily for his longer life, else would her people, nay herself, stand in need of cordials too'. Her 'saucy godson', John Harrington, observed that 'the lord treasurer's distemper doth marvellously trouble the queen'. He died, at the age of seventy-seven, on 4 August. Harrington also reports that 'the queen's highness doth often speak of him in tears, and turn aside when he is discoursed of, nay, even forbiddeth his name to be mentioned in the council'.

In the following month Philip II, king of Spain, died covered with putrefying sores. So in quick succession the two men who helped to define Elizabeth's reign were gone. Elizabeth, however, did not necessarily replace her deceased councillors. They had now been reduced to ten, only half the number who had surrounded her at the beginning of her rule. Essex himself did not appear at court for five months after his precipitate withdrawal; he returned, in the autumn of the year, when he wished once more to display his martial skills. Ireland was in the balance. A native revolt, led by Hugh O'Neill, second earl of Tyrone, had ambushed an English army sent out to defeat him; as a result the territory held by the English was left undefended. No English estate was safe and most of the settlers fled. Only Leinster remained to the English Crown. It was considered to be 'the greatest loss and dishonour the queen hath in her time'.

Essex now saw his opportunity of redeeming himself in her eyes, and he sent her a letter offering his services. Before he received a reply he had hurried to London, but the queen refused to see him. 'I stay in this place,' he said, 'for no other purpose but to attend your commandments.' 'Tell the earl,' she replied, 'that I value myself as at great a price as he values himself.' A period of silence was followed by tense negotiations in which Essex finally received the post he had requested, that of lord deputy of Ireland. One courtier wrote that 'if the Lord Deputy performs in the field what he hath promised in the council, all will be well . . .'

The relations between the sovereign and the earl were still strained, however, and the easy affection of earlier years did not return. They argued over the size of the army to be sent to Ireland. At one moment of low spirits he wrote that 'how much so ever Her Majesty despiseth me, she shall know she hath lost him who, for her sake, would have thought danger a sport and death a feast'. True to his mercurial temper, he even thought of abandoning the idea of Ireland altogether. Yet he knew well enough that 'his honour could not stand without undertaking it'.

At the end of March 1599, he set off with an army of 16,000 men, the largest ever to be dispatched to Ireland. He had decided to attack Tyrone in the north, both by sea and by land; unfortunately both ships and horses were in short supply and so, while awaiting reinforcements, he launched an expedition against Munster and Limerick. He occupied two months in this pursuit but achieved very little. Elizabeth was now growing impatient; time, for her, meant money. She was also angry at Essex for appointing the earl of Southampton to be the general of his horse, against the queen's express order; he had also exercised his right of making knights, which she deemed to be a privilege reserved for herself. Was he trying to become a king? Elizabeth sent a peremptory letter to him, ordering him to seek out the principal enemy. Why was Tyrone, 'a base bush kern', now accounted to be 'so famous a rebel'?

So at her instigation he marched north with 4,000 men to confront Tyrone. The Irish leader countered with a much larger force and, at a ford on the River Lagan, Essex agreed to meet him for a private conference without the presence of witnesses. It is therefore not known what was discussed or agreed but, when the reports of the meeting reached London, the enemies of Essex were only happy to spread rumours of treachery. Tyrone and Essex had indeed agreed a truce, but the rest is silence. He now persisted in disobeying her commands. He had been ordered to remain with his men, but on 24 September he left Dublin and sailed back to England.

As he had feared and anticipated, his ill-omened expedition had been beset by rumour and suspicion at court. His enemies had taken advantage of his absence to spread malicious reports about his conduct. Even before he left Ireland he wrote a querulous letter to his mistress. 'But why do I talk of victory or success? Is it not known that from England I have received nothing but discomfort and soul's wounds? Is it not spoken in the army that Your Majesty's favour is diverted from me and that already you do bode ill both to me and to it?'

It was said that he planned to stay in Ireland at the head of his troops until the queen's death; he could then return as the conquering hero. The queen herself believed that he had colluded with Tyrone. She told Francis Bacon that 'his proceedings were not without some private end of his own'. Some of the rivals of Essex had also prospered in his absence. The queen promoted Robert Cecil to be master of the Court of Wards, a lucrative post that Essex himself had hoped to occupy. Cecil's older brother became president of the council in the north, another enviable position.

Essex was anxious to reach the court, now at Nonsuch Palace in Surrey, as quickly as possible. Four days after his departure from Dublin he arrived at the palace and ran to the privy chamber, where Elizabeth was 'newly up, her hair about her face'. Essex knelt before her while they conducted a conversation that seemed to comfort him. Yet her mood changed to anger after his departure. When her godson, John Harrington, knelt before her she complained 'By God's Son, I am no queen! That man is above me! Who gave him command to come here so soon? I did send him on other business.'

Essex was summoned before the privy council and questioned by Robert Cecil about his conduct in Ireland. The councillors accused him of disobeying the queen's direct orders and deserting his command in Ireland; he was berated for making too many 'idle' knights, and for intruding without permission into the queen's bedchamber. His responses were then relayed to the queen, who said that she 'would pause and consider of his answers'. He was meanwhile committed to the charge of the lord keeper at York House while the queen herself removed to Richmond. A contemporary, Rowland Whyte, wrote that the servants of Essex 'are afraid to meet in any place, to make merry, lest it might be ill taken'. Meanwhile the enemies of Essex dined happily together.

A courtier wrote, in the autumn of 1599, that 'it is a very dangerous time here, for the heads of both factions being here a man cannot tell how to govern himself towards them. For here is such observation and prying into men's actions that I hold them happy and blessed that live away.' It was Whyte again who named the members of the factions. With Sir Robert Cecil were the earls of Shrewsbury and Nottingham and the lords Howard and Cobham, together with Sir Walter Raleigh and Sir George Carew. With the earl of Essex were the earls of Southampton, Worcester and Rutland, together with the lords Mountjoy and Rich. It might be surmised, therefore, that the queen's grasp upon the life of her court was not as firm as it once had been. The courtiers were no longer a coherent body following her will.

By the beginning of 1600 the temperature of the court was rising. Somebody had scrawled on Cecil's door 'here lieth the Toad'. Sir Walter Raleigh wrote a letter to Cecil in which he warned him not to be 'mild' with Essex. 'The less you make him, the less he shall be able to harm you and yours; and if her Majesty's favour fail him, he will again decline to a common person . . .' Essex in turn wrote to Elizabeth that 'as if I were thrown into a corner like a dead carcass, I am gnawed on and torn by the basest creatures upon the earth'. When in February Mountjoy was sent to Ireland in place of Essex, Francis Bacon argued to the queen that his master was still the person most fitted for the service. 'Essex!' she replied. 'When I send Essex back into Ireland, I will marry *you*. Claim it of me.'

In June 1600, a special court met at York House to examine the case of the earl of Essex. He was asked to kneel at the lower end of the council table; after a while he was allowed a cushion; he was then permitted to lean against a cupboard and eventually he was granted leave to sit upon a stool with his hat lying beside him on the floor. One courtier wrote that 'it was a most pitiful and lamentable sight to see him that was the minion of fortune, now unworthy of the least honour he had of so many. Many that were present burst out into tears at his fall to such misery.'

He was charged with 'great and high contempts and points of

misgovernance' in Ireland; he was acquitted of disloyalty but found guilty of 'contempts'. Whereupon he was suspended from his offices and ordered to remain a prisoner in his own house at Her Majesty's pleasure. He now seemed destined to remain in private life for the rest of the queen's reign. On an ally's pleading with him to seek her pardon he replied that his enemies would 'never suffer me to have interest in her favour'. When at a dance in the summer of the year one of the ladies took on the role of 'Affection', Elizabeth said to her 'Affection! Affection's false.' In that summer, by order of the privy council, all engravings of Essex and of other noblemen were called in. A further command ordered 'that hereafter no personage of any nobleman or other person shall be ingraven and printed to be put to sale publicly'.

On Michaelmas, at the end of September, the licence that Essex held for the customs revenue from imported sweet wine fell due; it was not renewed, thus depriving him of a substantial income. Elizabeth is reported to have said that 'an unruly horse must be abated of his provender, that he may the more easily and better be managed'. He was already deeply in debt, with his creditors waiting to claim the money from any of his servants. He fell into a fury in which, according to Harrington, he 'shifteth from sorrow and repentance to rage and rebellion so suddenly as well proveth him devoid of good reason . . .'

The word 'rebellion' was a dangerous one. Essex wrote to James VI of Scotland proposing that they act together to remove from England Robert Cecil and Walter Raleigh; he told the Scottish king that 'now am I summoned on all sides to stop the malice, the wickedness and madness of these men, and to relieve my poor country that groans under their burden'. James seems to have responded with caution. It is likely that Elizabeth and Cecil had some warning of these manoeuvres, but they did nothing; they were waiting, perhaps, for more open treason. Essex heard, for example, that the council was already interrogating certain prisoners in the Tower who had been allied with him. Elizabeth danced the coranto at court that Christmas.

At the beginning of 1601 Essex began to draw up further plans with the more vainglorious of his supporters whom he met at Drury House, the London residence of the earl of Southampton.

He had conceived a plan whereby he and his followers would seize the guard of the palace at Whitehall in order to allow him to enter the queen's presence; Essex would then, with the threat of force behind him, ask her to remove his enemies from the court. If this were not successful he would demand the recall of parliament to give him justice.

Elizabeth and her councillors watched events with some trepidation. Would Essex strike more quickly than they anticipated? Harrington reported that 'the madcaps are all in riot, and much evil threatened . . . she is quite disfavoured and unattired, and these troubles waste her much. She disregards every costly cover that comes to the table, and takes little but manchet [fine wheat bread] and savoury pottage. Every new message from the city disturbs her, and she frowns on all her ladies.' He reported on a later occasion that 'she walks much in her privy-chamber, and stamps with her foot at ill news, and thrusts her rusty sword, at times, into the arras, in great rage'. The last touch is worthy of Shakespeare.

On 7 February Essex was summoned to appear before the privy council, but he declined the invitation. On the following morning, a Sunday, he gathered 300 of his supporters at Essex House; his plan was to proceed with them to Paul's Cross, where the Londoners were accustomed to hear sermons on this day. He hoped to persuade the citizens and apprentices to join his forces, no doubt on the cry that he would 'save the queen from her evil councillors'. To his intimates he had said that 'the old woman was grown crooked in her mind as well as in her body'. There was a spy in his camp, one Ferdinando Gorges, who betrayed the scheme to Cecil. The lord mayor of London was ordered to keep the people of London within their houses, and the palace of Whitehall was given a double guard.

At approximately ten o'clock in the morning the lord chancellor and other royal officers arrived at Essex House and demanded admittance; after a delay, they were allowed to enter. Essex was asked why his supporters were gathered in arms, and he replied with an account of the wrongs to which he had been subject. 'You lose time,' his supporters urged him. 'Away with them! They betray you.' Essex then took the unfortunate step of imprisoning them within his house and, with his allies, of riding out into the streets.

They wielded pistols and rapiers, calling out 'England is sold to Spain by Cecil and Raleigh! Citizens of London, arm for England and the queen!'

The citizens of London did not respond. The streets were quiet. Essex rode to Ludgate Hill, where he ordered a charge. Yet now his supporters, realizing their desperate plight, began to desert him. The queen had been given news of the tumult, and reacted calmly. While her attendants were in some disarray she proposed that she should go into the city and confront her opponents and that 'not one of them would dare to meet a single glance of her eye'.

The confrontation was not necessary. Discomfited by his failure to raise the citizens, Essex rode on to Queenhithe, where he took a boat to Essex House; he then discovered that Ferdinando Gorges had released his prisoners. The house was soon surrounded by the royal forces and, after some tense negotiations from the leads of the mansion, he surrendered himself to the lord admiral. He and his principal supporters were taken to Lambeth Palace and on the following day were removed downriver to the Tower. Elizabeth told the French ambassador that 'a senseless ingrate had at last revealed what had long been in his mind'. She issued a proclamation on the day after the failed rebellion, thanking the people of London for their loyalty.

Some residual support for Essex still existed in the purlieus of the court. Thomas Leigh, who had served under him in Ireland, proposed that four or five resolute men should force themselves into the queen's presence and obtain from her a warrant for the release of Essex and Southampton. Leigh was denounced and arrested that night outside the queen's supper room. On the following day he was tried, convicted and executed. In the middle of February the queen issued another proclamation in which she ordered all vagabonds, idlers, newsmongers and tavern frequenters to leave London on pain of death.

On 19 February Essex and Southampton were tried by their peers in Westminster Hall. Both men denied the charge of treason, but their guilt was taken for granted. They argued with their prosecutors, but to no avail. Essex, dressed all in black, declared 'I have done nothing but that which by the law of nature and the necessity of my case I was enforced into.' These were not concepts recognized by common law, and seem to be borrowed from what might be called the chivalric code. They could not save him. After sentence of execution was passed against him, he remained calm enough. 'Although you have condemned me in a court of judgment,' he told his judges, 'yet in the court of conscience you would absolve me.' Two days later Cecil and some other councillors were asked to visit Essex in the Tower. They found him much changed, declaring himself to be 'the greatest, most vilest and most unthankful traitor that has ever been in the land'. He admitted that, while he lived, the queen would not be safe.

It was the last of the aristocratic risings of England, like that of the Percys in the early fifteenth century; Essex did not have the same level of regional or territorial support, but the complex motives of honour and of valour were the same. It was almost a medieval event. As the earl of Southampton had said to Sir Robert Sidney in the final siege of Essex House, 'You are a man of arms, you know we are bound by nature to defend ourselves against our equals, still more against our inferiors.' A band of brothers, many of them related by blood, Essex and his supporters were aroused by the old and noble code of honour but, in the court of Elizabeth, it was no longer enough.

The admission of Essex that he had committed treason came too late. Elizabeth graciously consented to his private execution by beheading, and at the same time she commuted Southampton's sentence to that of life imprisonment. On 25 February Essex was brought to a scaffold that had been erected in the courtyard of the Tower. He was wearing doublet and breeches of black satin, covered by a black velvet gown; he also wore a black felt hat. He always played his part. At the last moment he turned his neck sideways and called out, 'Executioner, strike home!' It took three strokes to sever his head from his body. 'Those who touch the sceptres of princes,' the queen observed, 'deserve no pity.'

40

The end of days

After the execution of the earl of Essex, some criticized the queen for her hardness of heart. It was said that the people were weary of an old woman's rule and that her public appearances were not greeted with the old jubilation. One Kentish man was summonsed for saying that it 'would never be a merry world until Her Majesty was dead'. When a constable told a yeoman to obey the queen's laws, the man replied, 'Why dost thou tell me of the queen? A turd for the queen!'

When she summoned her last parliament in the autumn of 1601, it became notable for its fractiousness and confusion. The customary calls of 'God save your majesty' were subdued. When passing a group of irritable members of parliament, she moved her hand to indicate that she needed more room.

'Back, masters,' the gentleman usher called out.

'If you will hang us, we can make no more room,' one member replied. Elizabeth looked up at him, but said nothing.

The matter of taxation was the cause of much turmoil. The cost of Mountjoy's campaign against Tyrone in Ireland was high, compounded by the dispatch of Spanish troops to that country in the rebel cause. The subsequent financial burden on the English was considered onerous, with the poor having to sell their 'pots and pans' to meet the price of the subsidy. When one member remarked that the queen 'hath as much right to all our lands and goods as to any revenue of her crown' the commons proceeded to 'hem, laugh and talk'. Bad temper was in the air. Speakers were 'cried or coughed down' and the voting provoked pulling and brawling. In the end, however, Elizabeth received the subsidy she had asked for.

The other contentious issue was that of monopolies. These were patents granted to individuals which allowed them to manufacture or distribute certain named articles for their private profit. It was a device by which Elizabeth could confer benefits on favoured courtiers without putting her to any personal expense. 'I cannot utter with my tongue,' one member said, 'or conceive with my heart the great grievances that the town and country which I serve suffereth by some of these monopolies.' Another member began to list the articles so protected, from currants to vinegar, from lead to pilchards, from cloth to ashes:

'Is bread not there?'

'Bread?'

'Bread?'

'This voice seems strange.'

'No, if order be not taken for these, bread will be there before the next parliament.'

The queen had heard of these complaints and summoned the Speaker. She told him that she would reform the procedure on monopolies; some would be repealed and some suspended. None would be put into execution 'but such as should first have a trial according to the law for the good of the people'. She had anticipated a crisis and had resolved it.

Parliament sent a deputation to thank her, and at the end of November she addressed her grateful Commons in the council chamber at Whitehall. She told them that 'I never was any greedy, scraping grasper, nor a strait fast-holding prince, nor yet a waster; my heart was never set on worldly goods, but only for my subjects' good'. She added that 'it is my desire to live nor reign no longer than my life and reign shall be for your good'. It was not the last of her public speeches but it was one of the most memorable.

There was little, if any, mention of the succession during this parliament. It is likely, to put it no higher, that she had come to believe that James, the son of Mary, queen of Scots, should ascend the throne after her. She may not have known that Robert Cecil, now her most prominent councillor, had been engaged in secret negotiations with him; she must have suspected, however, that he was now the favoured heir. But she kept her silence. Although she was often accused of indecision or prevarication, there were occasions when she simply wished to conceal her intentions.

In April 1602, at the age of sixty-eight, the queen took part in the energetic dance known as the galliard. At the beginning of the following month she rode out to Lewisham for 'a-Maying'. She told the French ambassador that 'I think not to die so soon, and am not as old as they think'. She continued to ride as often as the opportunity occurred. When one of her relations, the second Lord Hunsdon, suggested that she should no longer ride between Hampton Court and Nonsuch, she dismissed him from her presence and refused to speak to him for two days.

Yet the signs of ageing were unmistakable. Her eyesight was becoming weaker and she was growing more forgetful. She could remember faces, but sometimes not names. After she had gone riding her legs were often 'benumbed'. Sometimes she needed help to mount her horse or to climb stairs. She told one of her ladies, Lady Scroope, that one night she had seen a vision of 'her own body, exceedingly lean and fearful in a light of fire'. 'I am tied with a chain of iron about my neck,' she told the earl of Nottingham. 'I am tied, I am tied, and the case is altered with me.'

When in the early spring of 1603 another of her relations, Sir Robert Carey, came to greet her he found her in chastened state. 'No, Robin,' she told him, 'I am not well.' She described her indisposition to him, a narrative that was punctuated with many sighs. On 19 March the French envoy told his master that for the last fourteen days she had eaten very little and slept very badly. Another contemporary reported that she 'had fallen into a state of moping, sighing, and weeping melancholy'. She was asked by one of her attendants whether she had any secret cause for her grief. She replied that 'I know of nothing in this world worthy of troubling me'.

For four days she sat upon cushions in her privy chamber,

gazing down at the floor and rarely speaking. She was by now unclean and emaciated. 'I meditate,' she said. Robert Cecil remonstrated with her.

'Madam, madam, to content the people you must go to bed.'

'Little man, little man, the word *must* is not to be used to princes.'

On the third day she put her finger in her mouth and rarely removed it. Eventually she grew so weak that her doctors were able to take her uncomplaining to her bed. When an abscess burst in her throat she recovered a little and sipped some broth. But then she declined once again and lay without seeming to see or notice anything. Knowing that the end was coming, the councillors asked her if she accepted James VI of Scotland as her successor. She had lost the power of speech and merely made a gesture towards her head which they interpreted as one of consent.

At six o'clock on the evening of 23 March the archbishop of Canterbury was summoned to her deathbed. He prayed for half an hour beside her and then rose to depart; but she gestured for him to continue. He continued his prayers for another hour and, whenever he mentioned the joys of heaven, she would clasp his hand. She lost consciousness soon after, and died in the early hours of the following morning. Her coronation ring, deeply sunk into the flesh of her finger, had to be sawn off.

As soon as he heard the sounds of her women weeping, Sir Robert Carey took horse and galloped towards the Great North Road. He was on his way to Edinburgh, where he would break the news to James VI that he was now king of England. Thomas Dekker, in *The Wonderful Year*, wrote that 'upon Thursday it was treason to cry God save king James of England and upon Friday high treason not to cry so. In the morning no voices heard but murmurs and lamentation, at noon, nothing but shouts of gladness and triumph.' The long rule of the Tudors had come to an end.

41

Reformation

We return to the great theme of this volume. The reformation of the English Church was, from the beginning, a political and dynastic matter; it had no roots in popular protest or the principles of humanist reform. No Calvin or Luther would have been permitted to flourish in England. Reformation was entirely under the direction of the king. The English Reformation had other unique aspects. In the countries of continental Europe that espoused Protestantism, all the rituals and customs of Catholicism were abolished; there was to be no Mass, no Virgin Mary and no cult of the saints. Yet Henry, in all matters save that of papal sovereignty, was an orthodox Catholic. The monasteries may have been destroyed, and the pope replaced, but the Mass survived. Nicholas Harpsfield, the historian and Catholic apologist, described Henry as 'one that would throw down a man headlong from the top of a high tower and bid him stay when he was half way down'. Yet somehow the king managed this miracle of levitation. He carried out the work of change piece by piece so that no one could contemplate or guess the finished design; that was the reason it worked. Henry himself may not have known where he was going.

Those who supported the king's cause were, in large part, of a practical persuasion; they wanted the lands and revenues of the Church for themselves. They were lawyers and courtiers. They were members of parliament, which voted in accordance with the king's will throughout this period. Only for a few scholars and divines was the theology of the Reformation important. The arch-bishop of Canterbury, Thomas Cranmer, was a man of piety rather than of principle; he was as much an ecclesiastical lawyer as a divine who saw his way forward through compromise and conciliation. The refining of Church doctrine under Edward, and the reversal of practice under Mary, serve only to emphasize the slightly incoher-ent framework of the religious polity.

The Elizabethan settlement created what Lord Burghley called a 'midge-madge' of contradictory elements that was soon to pass under the name of Anglicanism. It was as alien to the pure spirit of Protestantism, adumbrated in Zurich or Geneva, as it was to the doctrines of Rome. The English liturgy contained elements old and new, and the perils of religious speculation were avoided with a studied vagueness or ambiguity. The Book of Common Prayer is also animated by a spirit of piety rather than dogmatic certainty.

England therefore became Protestant by degrees, and by a process of accommodation and subtle adjustment. The people acquiesced in the new dispensation. Time and forgetfulness, aided by apathy and indifference, slowly weakened the influence of the old religion beyond repair. If, by the beginning of the seventeenth century, England had become a Protestant nation, therefore, the nature of that Protestantism was mixed and divided; we may only say, perhaps, that England was no longer Catholic. The passage of time had accomplished what the will of men could not work.

We may see the enduring effects of the Reformation in the emphasis upon the individual rather than upon the community. Private prayer took the place of public ritual. Manuals addressed to the personal devotional life abounded. Justification by faith alone, one of the cardinal tenets of the new religion, was wholly private in character. The struggles of individual consciences, with the constant awareness of sin, now became the material of the religious pamphlets of the period. We may suspect the influence of the reformed religion, too, on the conditions that made possible the birth of the modern state; the word itself emerged towards the end of the reign of Elizabeth. The Protestant calendar was devoted to the celebration of a new national culture, with such holy days as the queen's birthday and the defeat of the Armada. It became a civic and courtly, rather than a religious, timetable.

The separation from Rome and from continental Catholicism also encouraged the belief that England was in some sense an 'elect' nation; this in turn led to a redefinition of Englishness that excluded, for example, the Catholics of the nation. Bishop Gardiner, in *De Vera Obedientia*, composed immediately after the executions of John Fisher and Thomas More, declared that 'in England all are agreed that those whom England has borne and bred shall have nothing whatever to do with Rome'. Popular preachers such as Hugh Latimer apostrophized the entire nation. Oh England! England! Latimer wrote also that 'verily God hath showed himself God of England, or rather the English God'.

The belief in divine providence, one of the blessings of the Protestant spirit, led to submission and obedience to the secular authorities. Where once the monks had taken responsibility for the indigent, their place had been taken by parish officers; the overseers of the poor, and the workhouses, became the solutions to what was now regarded as a social problem rather than an ordinance of God. When the House of Commons took over the former royal chapel of St Stephen's in 1549, it was the mark of a larger transition; the law of God ultimately gave way to the statutes of parliament. The idea of good governance emerges most fully in the sixteenth century, and the state itself was deemed to have a formative role in social and economic policy.

The cultural effects of the Reformation were no less profound. New forms of history were composed after the demise of the monkish historians; Hall's *Chronicle*, devoted to the Tudor cause and in spirit anti-clerical, replaced Ranulph Higden's *Polychronicon*. In a more general sense the destruction of church buildings, and the stripping of church art, led to an indifference towards the past among many people. The sense of continuity and kinship was broken just as the old ties of the community were severed. In a society that had previously been heavily dependent upon custom and tradition, the effects must have been profound. It might be said that the memory of history was erased in order to take the next leap forward.

The demise of the mystery plays and the whole panoply of

religious drama, which had possessed so strong a hold over England for many centuries, led ineluctably to the secularization of the drama and the rise of the London playhouses. The great efflorescence of the English drama in the sixteenth and seventeenth centuries can be regarded as one of the consequences of the Reformation. In literature, too, the translation of the Bible into English inspired writers as diverse as Shakespeare and Milton and Bunyan. In a more general sense the new place of the English language encouraged the growth of literacy among the population. This may in turn help to account for the great increase in educational provision through the period; in the 1550s forty-seven new school foundations were made, and in the following decade a further forty-two.

The abolition of the rituals of the Catholic faith may have had more profound, although less easily observed, consequences. The Rogationtide processions, in which the boundaries of the parish were delineated with bells and crosses, had been an important element in the English sense of sacred place; the land was, in a sense, now secularized. The holy wells and springs of the landscape were largely forgotten, and land itself became a commodity rather than a communal possession. Just as the communion of the living and dead enshrined in the old Church was being dissolved, so the common fields of the realm became the property of private individuals. When Christopher Saxton produced his series of maps in the 1570s the old shrines and paths of pilgrimage were omitted; his maps were primarily designed as surveys for the new landowners. Yet the commercial spirit claimed its own victims, and William Cobbett once wrote that the wretchedness of the landless labourer was the work of Reformation.

The abandonment of public rituals in the streets and open places of the towns led in the course of time to social fragmentation. When popular pastimes were curtailed and despised, the richer sort tended to think of themselves as a class apart. Seats were soon supplied in churches for families of local stature. We may see the change from another perspective. It has been estimated that the number of alehouses doubled in the fifty years after 1580; with the demise of the guild fraternities, the pageants and the church-ales, there had to be an alternative source of refreshment.

Yet arguably all of these matters – the growing emphasis upon the individual, the dissolution of communal life, the abrogation of custom and tradition – were the necessary conditions for the great changes in the spirit and condition of the nation that were still to come.

THE END OF THE SECOND VOLUME

Further reading

This is by no means an exhaustive list, but it represents a selection of those books the author found most useful in the preparation of this second volume.

THE REFORM OF RELIGION

Aston, Margaret: *England's Iconoclasts* (Oxford, 1988).
—— *Faith and Fire* (London, 1993).
Baskerville, Geoffrey: *English Monks and the Suppression of the Monasteries* (London, 1937).
Beard, Charles: *The Reformation of the Sixteenth Century* (London, 1883).
Bernard, G. W.: *The King's Reformation* (London, 2005).
Betteridge, Tom: *Literature and Politics in the English Reformation* (Manchester, 2004).
Bossy, John: *The English Catholic Community* (London, 1975).
Brigden, Susan: *London and the Reformation* (Oxford, 1989).
Burnet, Gilbert: *The History of the Reformation of the Church of England*, three volumes (Oxford, 1829).
Carlson, Eric Josef (ed.): *Religion and the English People* (Kirksville, Miss., 1998).
Chadwick, Owen: *The Reformation* (London, 1964).
Collinson, Patrick: *The Religion of Protestants* (Oxford, 1982).
—— *Godly People* (London, 1983).
—— *The Birthpangs of Protestant England* (Basingstoke, 1988).
Constant, G.: *The Reformation in England* (London, 1934).
Davies, Horton: *Worship and Theology in England* (Princeton, 1996).
Dickens, A. G.: *The English Reformation* (London, 1964).

Doran, Susan and Durston, Christopher: *Princes, Pastors and People* (London, 1991).

Duffy, Eamon: *The Stripping of the Altars* (London, 1992).

—— *The Voices of Morebath* (London, 2001).

—— *Marking the Hours* (London, 2006).

Elton, Geoffrey (ed.): *The Reformation* (Cambridge, 1958).

—— *Reform and Reformation* (London, 1977).

Gairdner, James: *A History of the English Church in the Sixteenth Century* (London, 1902).

—— *Lollardy and the Reformation in England*, two volumes (London, 1908).

Gasquet, F. A.: *Henry VIII and the English Monasteries* (London, 1906).

Haigh, Christopher (ed.): *The English Reformation Revised* (Cambridge, 1987).

—— *English Reformations* (Oxford, 1993).

Heal, Felicity: *Reformation in Britain and Ireland* (Oxford, 2003).

Heath, Peter: *English Parish Clergy* (London, 1969).

Hughes, Philip: *The Reformation in England*, three volumes (London, 1956).

Hurstfield, Joel (ed.): *The Reformation Crisis* (London, 1965).

Hutton, Ronald: *The Rise and Fall of Merry England* (Oxford, 1994).

King, John N.: *English Reformation Literature* (Princeton, 1982).

Knappen, M. M.: *Tudor Puritanism* (London, 1939).

Knowles, David: *The Religious Orders in England* (Cambridge, 1959).

Lake, Peter and Dowling, Maria (eds): *Protestantism and the National Church* (Beckenham, 1987).

MacCulloch, Diarmaid: *Thomas Cranmer* (London, 1996).

—— *The Later Reformation in England* (London, 2001).

—— *The Reformation* (London, 2003).

Maitland, S. R.: *Essays on the Reformation in England* (London, 1849).

Marshall, Peter: *The Catholic Priesthood and the English Reformation* (Oxford, 1994).

—— (ed.): *The Impact of the English Reformation* (London, 1997).

McConica, James Kelsey: *English Humanists and Reformation Politics* (Oxford, 1965).

Morgan, John: *Godly Learning* (Cambridge, 1986).

O'Day, Rosemary: *The Debate on the English Reformation* (London, 1986).

Pollard, A. E.: *Thomas Cranmer* (London, 1905).

Powicke, Maurice: *The Reformation in England* (Oxford, 1941).

Randell, Keith: *Henry VIII and the Reformation in England* (London, 1993).

Read, Conyers: *Social and Political Forces in the English Reformation* (Houston, 1953).

Rex, Richard: *Henry VIII and the English Reformation* (London, 1993).

Rosman, Doreen: *From Catholic to Protestant* (London, 1996).

Rupp, E. G.: *The Making of the English Protestant Tradition* (Cambridge, 1966).

Scarisbrick, J. J.: *The Reformation and the English People* (Oxford, 1984).

Shagan, Ethan H.: *Popular Politics and the English Reformation* (Cambridge, 2003).

Smith, H. Maynard: *Pre-Reformation England* (London, 1938).

—— *Henry VIII and the Reformation* (London, 1948).

Walker, Greg: *Persuasive Fictions* (Aldershot, 1996).

Whiting, Robert: *The Blind Devotion of the People* (Cambridge, 1989).

Wooding, Lucy: *Rethinking Catholicism in Reformation England* (Oxford, 2000).

Youings, Joyce: *The Dissolution of the Monasteries* (London, 1971).

The reign of Henry

Anglo, Sydney: *Images of Tudor Kingship* (London, 1992).

Bernard, G. W.: *Power and Politics in Tudor England* (Aldershot, 2000).

—— *Anne Boleyn* (London, 2010).

Brewer, J. S.: *The Reign of Henry VIII* (London, 1884).

Brigden, Susan: *New Worlds, Lost Worlds* (London, 2001).

Brown, Andrew D.: *Popular Piety in Late Medieval England* (Oxford, 1995).

Byrne, M. St Clare (ed.): *The Letters of Henry VIII* (London, 1936).

Coby, J. Patrick: *Henry VIII and the Reformation Parliament* (London, 2006).

Coleman, Christopher and Starkey, David (eds): *Revolution Reassessed* (Oxford, 1986).

Davies, C. S. L.: *Peace, Print and Protestantism* (London, 1977).

Dodds, Madeleine Hope and Dodds, Ruth: *The Pilgrimage of Grace and the Exeter Conspiracy*, two volumes (Cambridge, 1915).

Elton, Geoffrey: *Policy and Police* (Cambridge, 1972).

Erickson, Carolly: *Great Harry* (London, 1980).

Fox, Alistair and Guy, John: *Reassessing the Henrician Age* (Oxford, 1986).

Froude, James Anthony: *History of England from the Fall of Wolsey to the Death of Elizabeth*, twelve volumes (London, 1862–70).

Galton, Arthur: *The Character and Times of Thomas Cromwell* (Birmingham, 1887).

Graves, Michael A. R.: *Henry VIII* (London, 2003).

Guy, John: *The Cardinal's Court* (Hassocks, 1977).

—— *The Tudor Monarchy* (London, 1997).

Gwyn, Peter: *The King's Cardinal* (London, 1990).

Hoak, Dale (ed.): *Tudor Political Culture* (Cambridge, 1995).

Hoyle, R. W.: *The Pilgrimage of Grace* (Oxford, 2001).

Hutchinson, Robert: *Thomas Cromwell* (London, 2007).

Ives, E. W.: *Anne Boleyn* (London, 1986).

Jones, Whitney R. D.: *The Tudor Commonwealth* (London, 1970).

Lingard, John and Belloc, Hilaire: *The History of England*, eleven volumes (New York, 1912).

MacCulloch, Diarmaid (ed.): *The Reign of Henry VIII* (Basingstoke, 1995).

Pickthorn, Kenneth: *Early Tudor Government* (Cambridge, 1951).

Pollard, A. F.: *Wolsey* (London, 1929).

—— *Henry VIII* (London, 1934).

Randell, Keith: *Henry VIII and the Government of England* (London, 1991).

Rosenthal, Joel and Richmond, Colin (eds): *People, Politics and Community in the Later Middle Ages* (Gloucester, 1987).

Scarisbrick, J. J.: *Henry VIII* (London, 1968).

Smith, Lacey Baldwin: *Henry VIII* (London, 1971).

Starkey, David (ed.): *Henry VIII: A European Court in England* (London, 1991).

—— *The Reign of Henry VIII* (London, 2002).

—— *Henry, Virtuous Prince* (London, 2008).

Watts, John L. (ed.): *The End of the Middle Ages?* (London, 1998).

Weir, Alison: *The Six Wives of Henry VIII* (London, 1991).

—— *Henry VIII* (London, 2001).

Williams, C. H.: *England under the Early Tudors* (London, 1925).

—— *The Tudor Despotism* (London, 1928).

Williams, Penry: *The Tudor Regime* (Oxford, 1979).

Wooding, Lucy: *Henry VIII* (London, 2009).

Zeeveld, W. Gordon: *Foundations of Tudor Policy* (Cambridge, Mass., 1948).

THE REIGN OF EDWARD

Alford, Stephen: *Kinship and Politics in the Reign of Edward VI* (Cambridge, 2002).

Aston, Margaret: *The King's Bedpost* (Cambridge, 1993).

Beer, Barrett L.: *Rebellion and Riot, Popular Disorder in England during the Reign of Edward VI* (Kent, Ohio, 2005).

Bush, M. L.: *The Government Policy of Protector Somerset* (London, 1975).

Constant, G.: *Introduction of the Reformation into England, Edward VI* (London, 1942).

Gasquet, Francis Aidan and Bishop, Edmund: *Edward VI and the Book of Common Prayer* (London, 1890).

Heard, Nigel: *Edward VI and Mary* (London, 1990).

Hoak, D. E.: *The King's Council in the Reign of Edward VI* (Cambridge, 1976).

Jones, Whitney R. D.: *The Mid-Tudor Crisis* (London, 1973).

Jordan, W. K.: *Edward VI, the Young King* (London, 1968).

—— *Edward VI: The Threshold of Power* (London, 1970).

Loach, Jennifer: *Edward VI* (London, 1999).

Loach, Jennifer and Tittler, Robert (eds): *The Mid-Tudor Polity* (London, 1980).

MacCulloch, Diarmaid: *Tudor Church Militant, Edward VI and the Protestant Reformation* (London, 1999).
Mackie, J. D.: *The Earlier Tudors* (Oxford, 1952).
Pollard, A. F.: *England under Protector Somerset* (London, 1900).
Skidmore, Chris: *Edward VI* (London, 2007).

THE REIGN OF MARY

Duffy, Eamon: *Fires of Faith* (London, 2009).
Duffy, Eamon and Loades, David (eds): *The Church of Mary Tudor* (Aldershot, 2006).
Edwards, John and Truman, Ronald (eds): *Reforming Catholicism in the England of Mary Tudor: the achievement of Friar Bartolome Carranza* (Aldershot, 2005).
Erickson, Carolly: *Bloody Mary* (London, 1978).
Loach, Jennifer: *Parliament and the Crown in the Reign of Mary Tudor* (Oxford, 1986).
Loades, David: *Mary Tudor* (Oxford, 1989).
Miller, James Arthur: *Stephen Gardiner and the Tudor Reaction* (London, 1926).
Porter, Linda: *Mary Tudor: the First Queen* (London, 2007).
Prescott, H. F. M.: *Mary Tudor* (London, 1940).
Richards, Judith M.: *Mary Tudor* (London, 2008).
Schenk, W.: *Reginald Pole* (London, 1950).
White, Beatrice: *Mary Tudor* (London, 1935).
Whitelock, Anna: *Mary Tudor* (London, 2009).

THE REIGN OF ELIZABETH

Adams, Simon: *Leicester and the Court* (Manchester, 2002).
Alford, Stephen: *The Early Elizabethan Polity* (Cambridge, 1998).
—— *Burghley* (London, 2008).
Archer, Jayne Elisabeth, Goldring, Elizabeth and Knight, Sarah: *The Progresses, Pageants and Entertainments of Queen Elizabeth I* (Oxford, 2007).
Black, J. B.: *The Reign of Elizabeth* (Oxford, 1936).

Collinson, Patrick: *Elizabethan Essays* (London, 1994).
—— *The Elizabethan Puritan Movement* (London, 1967).
Doran, Susan: *Monarchy and Matrimony* (London, 1996).
—— *Queen Elizabeth I* (London, 2003).
Doran, Susan and Freeman, Thomas S. (eds): *The Myth of Elizabeth* (London, 2003).
Dunn, Jane: *Elizabeth and Mary* (London, 2003).
Elton, G. R.: *The Parliament of England, 1559–1581* (Cambridge, 1986).
Graves, Michael A. R.: *Burghley* (London, 1998).
Greaves, Richard L. (ed.): *Elizabeth I, Queen of England* (London, 1974).
Guy, John (ed.): *The Reign of Elizabeth I* (Cambridge, 1995).
—— *My Heart is My Own* (London, 2004).
Haigh, Christopher (ed.): *The Reign of Elizabeth I* (London, 1984).
—— *Elizabeth I* (London, 1988).
Hammer, Paul E. J.: *The Polarisation of Elizabethan Politics* (Cambridge, 1999).
Haugaard, William P.: *Elizabeth and the English Reformation* (Cambridge, 1968).
Hibbert, Christopher: *The Virgin Queen* (London, 1990).
Hurstfield, Joel: *Freedom, Corruption and Government in Elizabethan England* (London, 1973).
Jenkins, Elizabeth: *Elizabeth the Great* (London, 1958).
Jones, Norman: *The Birth of the Elizabethan Age* (Oxford, 1993).
Levin, Carole: *The Reign of Elizabeth I* (Basingstoke, 2002).
Levine, Joseph M. (ed.): *Elizabeth I* (London, 1969).
MacCaffrey, Wallace: *The Shaping of the Elizabethan Regime* (London, 1969).
—— *Elizabeth I* (London, 1993).
McClaren, A. N.: *Political Culture in the Reign of Elizabeth I* (Cambridge, 1999).
Mears, Natalie: *Queenship and Political Discourse in the Elizabethan Realms* (Cambridge, 2005).
Meyer, Arnold Oskar: *England and the Catholic Church under Queen Elizabeth* (London, 1967).
Neale, J. E.: *Queen Elizabeth I* (London, 1934).
—— *Essays in Elizabethan History* (London, 1958).
Palliser, D. A.: *The Age of Elizabeth* (London, 1983).

Rex, Richard: *Elizabeth I* (Stroud, 2003).
Strickland, Agnes: *The Life of Queen Elizabeth* (London, 1906).
Strong, Roy: *Gloriana* (London, 1987).
Weir, Alison: *Elizabeth the Queen* (London, 1998).
Williams, Penry: *The Later Tudors* (Oxford, 1995).

Society

Bindoff, S. T.: *Tudor England* (London, 1950).
Bindoff, S. T., Hurstfield, J. and Williams, C. H. (eds): *Elizabethan Government and Society* (London, 1961).
Byrne, M. St Clare: *Elizabethan Life in Town and Country* (London, 1925).
Chambers, J. D.: *Population, Economy and Society in Pre-Industrial England* (Oxford, 1972).
Cheyney, Edward P.: *Social Changes in England in the Sixteenth Century* (Pennsylvania, 1895).
Clark, Peter (ed.): *The Early Modern Town* (London, 1976).
—— *The Cambridge Urban History of England*, Volume Two, *1540–1840* (Cambridge, 2000).
Clay, C. G. A.: *Economic Expansion and Social Change, England 1500–1700*, two volumes (Cambridge, 1984).
Collinson, Patrick (ed.): *The Sixteenth Century* (Oxford, 2002).
Coward, Barry: *Social Change and Continuity in Early Modern England* (London, 1988).
Cressy, David: *Birth, Marriage and Death* (Oxford, 1997).
Dodd, A. H.: *Life in Elizabethan England* (London, 1961).
Ellis, Steven G.: *Tudor Frontiers and Noble Power* (Oxford, 1995).
Elton, G. R.: *England Under the Tudors* (London, 1955).
Guy, John: *Tudor England* (Oxford, 1988).
Jack, Sybil M.: *Trade and Industry in Tudor and Stuart England* (London, 1977).
James, Mervyn: *Society, Politics and Culture* (Cambridge, 1986).
Polito, Mary: *Governmental Arts in Early Tudor England* (Aldershot, 2005).
Ramsey, Peter H. (ed.): *The Price Revolution in Sixteenth-Century England* (London, 1971).

Robertson, H. M.: *Aspects of the Rise of Economic Individualism* (Cambridge, 1933).

Rowse, A. L.: *The England of Elizabeth* (London, 1950).

—— *The Expansion of Elizabethan England* (London, 1955).

Sharpe, Kevin: *Selling the Tudor Monarchy* (London, 2009).

Simon, Joan: *Education and Society in Tudor England* (Cambridge, 1967).

Sommerville, C. John: *The Secularisation of Early Modern England* (Oxford, 1992).

Tawney, R. H.: *The Agrarian Problem in the Sixteenth Century* (London, 1912).

Thurley, Simon: *The Royal Palaces of Tudor England* (London, 1993).

Walsham, Alexandra: *The Reformation of the Landscape* (Oxford, 2011).

Wernham, R. B.: *Before the Armada* (London, 1966).

Williams, Penry: *Life in Tudor England* (London, 1964).

Index

abbots: and dissolution of monasteries, 118–19; translated to diocesan bishoprics, 120; executed, 123

Absolute Restraint of Annates Act (1534), 79

Acton, John Emerich Edward Dalberg, 1st baron, 69

agriculture: changes, 22–4

alehouses: numbers increase, 470

Alençon, Francis, duke of *see* Anjou, Francis, duke of

Aler, Madame d', 275

Alesius, Alexander, 143

Allen, Cardinal William, 379, 394

Alva, Ferdinand de Toledo, duke of: command in Netherlands, 343; seizes English warehouse in Antwerp, 344; on Ridolfi plot, 362; and Netherlands revolt, 373–4; and Elizabeth's reaction to St Bartholomew's Day massacre, 375

Alva, Maria, duchess of, 260

Amadas, Mrs, 6

Ambsworth, Margaret, 141

Ammonius (Andrea Ammonio), 8

Anabaptists, 133, 379–80

Anglican Church *see* Church of England

Anjou, Francis, duke of (*earlier* duke of Alençon): as Elizabeth's suitor, 362, 386–7, 389, 400–1; invades Netherlands, 388, 400; visits England, 391, 400; death, 408

Anjou, Henry, duke of *see* Henry III, king of France

Anne Boleyn, queen of Henry VIII: Henry meets and courts, 35, 40–2; and Henry's divorce, 44, 51; gives Simon Fish pamphlet to Henry, 58–9; religious liberalism, 59; popular hostility to, 63, 66–8, 71, 75, 77, 98; made marquess of Pembroke, 71; pregnancy and birth of Elizabeth, 71, 76; marriage to Henry, 72, 74; crowned queen, 74–5; and Henry's infidelity, 76, 92–3; succession settled on children, 80; on Mary's refusing oath of Succession, 82–3; miscarries male child, 92; threatens Mary, 92; accused of infidelity, 93–7; deteriorating relations with Henry, 93; executed, 96–9

Anne Boleyn (ship), 40

Anne of Cleves, queen of Henry VIII: marriage and divorce from Henry, 145–7; separation from Henry, 146–7; and Cromwell's fall, 149; on Henry's marriage to Katherine Parr, 162

Anne, Queen, 159

Anselm, St, archbishop of Canterbury, 83

anti-Semitism, 447–8

António, Don (pretender to Portuguese throne), 447

Antwerp: trade, 39; unrest, 343; Spanish massacre in, 384; falls to Parma, 412

Aquinas, St Thomas, 2–3

architecture, 352

Arden family, of Park Hall, 405–6

Arden, John, 406

Ardres, treaty of (1546), 171–2

Arthur, prince (Henry VIII's brother), 2, 42, 53, 71, 236

Arundel, Henry Fitzalan, 12th earl of, 242, 289, 365

Arundel, Philip Howard, 13th earl of, 411–12

Ascham, Roger, 170, 238

Aske, Robert: leads Pilgrimage of Grace, 108–13; Henry meets, 114–15; tried and hanged, 116

Askew, Anne, 172–3, 179, 226

Athelney, abbot of, 122

Audeley, Lady, 124

Augmentation, Court of, 90, 196

Austin Friars, London, 122, 124, 187

Babington, Anthony, 416–17, 420

Bacon, Anthony, 444

Bacon, Francis: on Elizabeth's religious discretion, 293; recruited by Essex, 444; counsels Essex, 451; and Essex's conduct in Ireland, 457; argues for Essex's appointment to Ireland, 458

Bacon, Sir Nicholas, 301

Ball, Alice, 32

Ballard, John, SJ, 416–17

Bancroft, Richard, archbishop of Canterbury, 437–8

Barnes, Robert, 27, 48–9, 132, 151

Barrowe, Henry (and Barrowists), 399, 403–4

Barton, Elizabeth (Nun of Kent): prophecies, 67–8, 71; investigated and beheaded, 76

Bath, John Bourchier, 2nd earl of, 24

Bath, William Bourchier, 3rd earl of, 449

Beaufort, Margaret, countess of Richmond and Derby, 248

Beaumaris, Anglesey, 398

Becket, St Thomas: shrine desecrated and demoted, 91, 125–6

Bedford, Francis Russell, 2nd earl of: in Elizabeth's privy council, 289; supports Elizabeth in 1569 rebellion, 358

Bedingfield, Sir Henry, 258

Bendlowes, Serjeant, 347

benefit of clergy, 15

Bennet, Dr, 53

Berthelet, Thomas, 71

Berwick, treaty of (1586), 417

Bible, Holy: translated, 25, 46–7, 83, 131–2, 470; English version distributed, 131–2; public reading forbidden, 159; Geneva version, 264; Puritan idealization of, 446

Bigod, Sir Francis, 115

Bill of Deposition against Henry, 126

Bilney, Thomas, 26–7, 49–50

Bisham abbey, 120

bishops: draw up statement of belief for Henry, 129; appointed by king's letters patent, 197

Bishops' Book, The see *Institution of a Christian Man, The*

Blois, treaty of (1572), 372

Blount, Elizabeth (Bessie), 34

Blount, Sir Thomas, 304

Bocher, Joan see Joan of Kent

Boethius: *The Consolation of Philosophy*, 444

Boleyn, Mary: liaison with Henry VIII, 34

Bolton Castle, 346

Bond of Association, 409–10, 422–3

Bonner, Edmund, bishop of London ('Bloody Bonner'): interrogates Anne Askew, 172–3; protests at religious reforms, 192; abuses Cranmer, 247, 263; persecutes reformers, 247, 268, 270, 284; decrees Church forms and services, 262, 267; absent from Elizabeth's arrival in London, 287; imprisoned, 298

Book of Common Prayer: provokes Western Rising, 209, 212–13; publication (1549), 209–11; overrides other prayer books, 225; revised (1552), 231, 292; in Elizabeth's reign, 293; unpopularity in North, 295; proposed reform, 364; criticised, 367; clergy required to assent to, 403; piety, 468

Booner, William, 336

Bothwell, James Hepburn, 4th earl of: in plot to murder Darnley, 337–9; relations with Mary Stuart, 340–1; tried and acquitted, 340; made duke of Orkney, 341; marriage to Mary, 341; and inquiry into Darnley's murder, 349; Mary's 'casket letters' to, 349; imprisoned in Denmark, 354; death, 389

Boulogne: siege of (1544), 165–6; Henry occupies for eight years, 172; Somerset plans to reclaim, 194; Henry II of France besieges, 219; returned to French, 226

Boxley Abbey, Kent, 125

boy bishops, 191

Bradford, John, 186

Brereton, William, 94

Brocke, Edward, 106

Browne, Robert (and Brownists), 398–9, 403

Brussels, Union of (1577), 384

Bryan, Sir Francis, 52

Bucer, Martin, 212

Buckingham, Edward Stafford, 3rd duke of, 5, 36

Bunyan, John, 470

Burghley, Sir William Cecil, baron: on popular unrest, 233–4; as privy councillor under Edward VI, 233; and accession of Mary Tudor, 241–2; as Elizabeth's principal secretary of state, 290–1; supports reformed faith, 291, 301, 323, 345, 369; and Parker's reluctance to accept archbishopric, 298; negotiates treaty of Edinburgh, 301; threatened by Elizabeth's relations with Dudley, 303–4; on Elizabeth's suitors and marriage prospects, 304–5, 326, 334–6; on Elizabeth's ill health, 309–10, 333; promotes parliament's petitions to Elizabeth, 315; drafts succession bill (1563), 316; and multiplicity of religious practices, 320; informs Elizabeth of birth of Mary Stuart's

son, 333; and threat of Mary Stuart's succession, 334; on state of Scotland at marriage of Mary and Bothwell, 341; confronts Spain, 345; writes to Moray on escape of Mary Stuart, 345; annotates Mary Stuart's casket letters, 349; and Elizabeth's vacillations over Mary Stuart, 350; complains of excess of luxury goods, 352; distrusts Mary Stuart, 355; opposition to, 355; and end of Rising of the North, 359; learns of Ridolfi plot, 364; and arrest of Catholic plotters, 365; ennobled, 365; and Elizabeth's nervous collapse, 366; on war in Netherlands, 373; and popular reaction to St Bartholomew's Day massacre, 375; and Elizabeth's procrastinations, 376; and Elizabeth's refusal to head Protestant League, 377; favours Edmund Grindal as archbishop, 380; dissuades Elizabeth from dismissing Grindal, 382; as patron of Campion, 393; praises torture, 396; rebukes Whitgift, 404–5; hopes to destroy Mary Stuart, 407; and threat of invasion, 407; drafts Bond of Association and ensures Protestant succession, 409; accompanies Elizabeth on 27th anniversary of accession celebrations, 413; commissions portrait of Elizabeth, 413; and financing of force in Netherlands, 414; opposes peace proposals for Netherlands, 415; and trial of Mary queen of Scots, 419–20; and Elizabeth's signing Mary's death warrant, 423; Elizabeth ostracizes after death of Mary, 426; dominance at court, 442, 452; ageing, 452; death, 455; on religious changes, 468

Burning of Heretics, Act for (1414): revoked, 197

burnings at the stake: described, 269; revived under Elizabeth, 380

Bury St Edmunds, 388

Butts, Margaret, Lady (*née* Bacon), 163

Index

Cabot, Sebastian, 283

Cadiz, 426–7, 450–1

Caius, Dr John, 20

Calais: in English hands, 4; and English invasion of France (1544), 165; French besiege and capture (1557–8), 282–4, 291; English attempt to repossess, 313; Elizabeth gives up claim, 314; Spanish Armada reaches, 431

Calvin, Jean: doctrines and practice, 188–9, 270, 311

Calvinism, 264, 318, 322, 377, 447

Cambridge: colleges founded, 196

Camden, William, 290, 352, 385, 421, 430

Campeggio, Cardinal Lorenzo, bishop of Salisbury, 44, 50–2, 54

Campion, Edmund, 393–7, 400

canon law: subordination to common law, 73

Canterbury: Becket's shrine dismantled and plundered, 90, 125

Carberry Hill, battle of (1567), 341, 349

Cardano, Hieronymus, 236

Carew, Sir George, 458

Carew, Sir Peter, 253

Carey, Sir Robert, 426, 465–6

Carlisle: Mary Stuart flees to, 346

Carlos, Don, prince of Asturias, 325

Carthusian friars: refuse oath upon Act of Succession, 82; executed, 85, 87; properties destroyed, 119–20; emigrate to continent during Edward VI's reign, 190

Cartwright, Thomas, 439

'casket letters', 349

Castle Acre priory, Norfolk, 120, 121

cathedrals: survive after dissolution of monasteries, 122

Catherine de Medici, regent of France, 307, 311–13, 361–2, 374

Catholic Church: flourishes in England, 6–7; calls for reform, 8, 17; and heretics, 15, 50; and king's jurisdiction, 16–17; and anti-clericalism, 17, 26, 59; reforms, 26, 28; Wolsey controls in England, 30;

attacked in parliament, 58; and Henry's claims to supremacy, 63–5; Commons petition against, 68; offers concession to Henry, 69; and transubstantiation, 141; Henry wishes for reform, 171; members emigrate during Edward VI's reign, 190; seasonal festivities silenced under Edward VI, 191; revival under Mary Tudor, 245–6, 262–3, 266–7; and persecution of Protestants, 267–71; followers persecuted under Elizabeth, 271, 397–8; subordinated under Elizabeth, 293, 295, 318; popular following, 319; and excommunication of Elizabeth, 359–60; discredited by St Bartholomew's Day massacre, 374–5; extremism in France, 377; seminarians in England, 379; English statutes against, 394; members restricted in movement, 446; Hooker on, 447; and Protestant reformation, 467; rituals abolished, 470; see also religion

Catholic League, 407

Cavendish, George, 9, 35

Cecil, Sir Robert (*later* earl of Salisbury): career and appearance, 443; rivalry with Essex, 443, 445, 451, 459; supports Lopez, 448; appointed secretary of state, 451; Essex abuses, 455; as master of Court of Wards, 457; questions Essex on conduct in Ireland, 457; heads court faction, 458; imprisoned by Essex, 460; informed of Essex's rebellion plan, 460; in negotiations with James VI of Scotland over succession, 465; Elizabeth rebukes for personal advice, 466

Cecil, William *see* Burghley, Sir William Cecil, baron

Chancery, court of, 21

chantry foundations, 197

Charles V, Holy Roman Emperor: succeeds Ferdinand as king of Spain, 17; conflicts with Francis I, 18;

succeeds as emperor, 31; Wolsey negotiates with, 31; meets Henry in England, 32; Pavia victory, 35; Mary Tudor betrothed to, 36–7; Henry makes treaty against Francis I, 37; released from betrothal to Mary, 40; and Henry's seeking divorce from Katherine of Aragon, 43, 53; sacks Rome and imprisons pope, 43; Henry's breach with, 71; as potential threat to Henry, 92; Henry warns of Cardinal Pole, 134; invasion threat to England, 139; proposes duchess of Milan as wife for Henry, 145; fails to form alliance with France, 149; Henry forms alliance against France, 157, 163–4; relations with papacy, 157; treaty with France (1544), 165–6; persecutes Protestants, 187, 189; and plot to depose Somerset, 219; supports Mary Tudor, 227, 229; prospective war with, 234; and Mary Tudor's prospective marriage, 250; intends to abdicate, 274

Charles IX, king of France: minority, 307; as prospective husband for Mary Stuart and Elizabeth, 325–6; and religious wars, 344; protests at bull excommunicating Elizabeth, 361; and prospective war against Spain, 374

Charles, archduke of Austria, prospective marriage to Elizabeth, 302, 304–5, 325–7, 333, 342–3

Charterhouse *see* Carthusians

Chartley Manor, 418

Chaseabout Raid (Scotland, 1565), 330

Chaucer, Geoffrey, 17

Cheapside Cross: destroyed, 398

Cheke, John, 147, 169

Christ's Hospital (school and orphanage), 123, 317, 393

Church of England: Henry declared supreme head of, 83; survey of worth (1535), 84; Ten Articles (of faith), 102, 104; bishops' statement of faith, 129–30; and Act of Uniformity (1549), 209; liturgy and practices,

210–11, 231, 297–9, 318, 468; use of English language, 211; orders of clergy, 224; statues and images limited, 225; plate and possessions expropriated, 231; compulsory attendance, 232; ecclesiastical laws, 232–3; and Thirty-Nine Articles, 232, 318; Mary heads, 266; convocation (1563), 317–18; doctrine of faith established, 318; named Anglican, 324; rules under Whitgift, 403–5; and Puritan criticism, 437; conformity to, 440; and Hooker's policies, 447; reformation, 467; *see also* Book of Common Prayer

Churchyard, Thomas, 393

Clement VII, pope: and annulment of Henry's marriage to Katherine of Aragon, 42, 44, 52–4; and Henry's marriage to Anne Boleyn, 45, 52; Henry's campaign against, 68; and Henry's pose as defender of the faith, 73–4; confirms Cranmer as archbishop, 74; threatens bishop of London, 74; declares Henry's marriage to Katherine still valid, 79; bull of interdict and deposition against Henry, 84

clergy: character of, 7; and heretics, 14–16; under law, 15–16; hostility to, 17, 26; attacked in parliament, 58; charged with *praemunire*, 62; repudiate Commons petition against grievances, 68–9; submit to Henry, 69–70, 79; self-indulgent and immoral behaviour, 85, 88–9; executed after rebellion, 118; move on dissolution of monasteries, 120; punished and executed after dissolution, 123, 126–7; in Church of England, 224; shortage of reformed, 320; obliged by Whitgift to assent to articles, 403; *see also* benefit of clergy

Clyst St Mary, Devon, 213–14

coach: introduced to England, 336

Cobbett, William, 470

Cobbler, Captain, 106

Cobham, Henry Brooke, 11th baron, 458

Cobham, William Brooke, 10th baron, 365

coinage: debased, 163, 206, 207; debasement reversed, 227

Colchester abbey, 123

Colet, John, 8, 10

Coligny, Gaspard de, 374–5

Collectanea satis copiosa, 59

Commons, House of *see* parliament

Company of the Mines Royal, 352

Condé, Louis, prince of, 312–13, 344

Confession of Augsburg, 88

consubstantiation, 141

convents: dissolved, 124

Corunna, 427

countryside: changes and decay, 22–3

Courtenay, Lord Edward (*later* earl of Devonshire), 136, 250

Coventry cathedral, 122

Coverdale, Miles, 83, 131, 245

Cox, Richard, 147

Cranmer, Thomas, archbishop of Canterbury: meets at White Horse tavern, 27; supports Henry in divorce negotiations, 54–5; and relations between king and pope, 59, 63; sees portent in sky, 67; on Elizabeth Barton, 68, 75; appointed archbishop, 73–4; and constitutional changes, 73; crowns Anne Boleyn, 75; and More's refusal to take oath, 82; on reformation, 90, 468; doubts over Anne Boleyn's guilt, 95; draws up articles of faith, 102; and Pilgrimage of Grace, 112; on Henry's triumph over enemies of reform, 117; proposes collegiate school at Canterbury, 123; supervises Henry's corrected statement of belief, 129–30; letter from Melanchthon, 133; and religious reforms, 142, 187, 191, 209–10, 232; sends family into exile, 143; on Six Articles, 144; supports Cromwell, 149; as senior counsellor, 151; investigates Katherine Howard's infidelities, 153–5; supports reform and accused of heresy, 160–2; modifies beliefs, 171; and death of Henry, 178; grows beard, 187; Latimer lives with, 189; frames Act of Uniformity, 209, 211; turns against Somerset, 220; advises Edward VI to appoint reformers to council, 221, 252; detained and tried, 263; celebrates burning of Joan Bocher, 270; degraded, 277; recantations, 278–9; burnt and denies recantations, 279–80; *Book of Homilies*, 190, 192; *A Code of Ecclesiastical Constitutions*, 232; *A Collection of the Articles of Religion*, 232

crime: increase in 1590s, 449

Cromwell, Oliver, 131

Cromwell, Thomas: on affairs of parliament, 37–8; background and career, 37; opposes invasion of France, 37; devotion to Wolsey, 57; rise to power, 57, 148; and Norfolk's threat to Wolsey, 60; and constitutional changes, 73; and secrecy of Dunstable ecclesiastical court, 74; investigates Elizabeth Barton, 75; recruits Latimer, 78; system of supervision and control, 81–2; and More's refusal to take oath, 82; appointed viceregent, 84–5; supervises collection of Church revenues, 85; and fate of Fisher and More, 86–7; on visitation of monasteries, 88–9; religious reforms, 90, 142, 144, 149–50; and Henry's infidelities, 92; on commission into treason, 93; disagreements with Henry, 93; and Anne Boleyn's downfall, 96; warns Mary Tudor, 98–9; orders dissolution of monasteries, 102–4, 118–19, 150; and rebellions in North, 106, 108, 110, 112, 115–16, 118; Aske attacks, 114; appropriates monastic lands and possessions, 121; threatens defiant friar, 124; and burning of John Forrest, 127; decrees possession of English Bible in every church, 131;

introduces parish registers, 132; military preparations against papal threat, 140; supports Anne of Cleves as wife for Henry, 145–6, 149; arrested and charged with treason, 148–50; created earl of Essex, 148; beheaded, 150–1

Crowley, Robert: *The Way to Wealth*, 209

Culpeper, Thomas, 153–5

custom: replaced by law, 23

Dacre, Gregory Fiennes, 10th baron, 358

Darcy, Thomas, baron: opposes Pilgrim of Grace, 109–11, 113; tried and beheaded, 116

Darnley, Henry Stuart, earl of: Mary Stuart's infatuation with, 327–9; character, 330–1; marriage to Mary, 330–1; marriage difficulties, 331; plot against Mary, 337; murdered, 338–40; inquiry into murder, 347–9

Darvel Gadarn, St, 126–7

Davison, Francis, 450

Davison, Sir William, 422–3, 426

Dedham, Essex, 404

Dee, John, 287; *General and Rare Memorials Pertaining to the Perfect Art of Navigation*, 378

Dekker, Thomas: *The Wonderful Year*, 466

Denny, Sir Anthony, 178–80, 182

Dereham, Francis, 153–5

'Device for the Alteration of Religion', 291

Digges, Thomas, 366

diseases, 448

Dispensation and Peter's Pence Act (1534), 79

Displaying of the Protestants, The, 189

Dissolution of Monasteries, Act for (1536), 90, 103

Doncaster: and Pilgrimage of Grace, 111–12; Adwick le Street parish, 199

Dormer, Jane *see* Feria, duchess of

Douai, 379, 393

Douglas, Lady Margaret, 101

Drake, Sir Francis: voyages to West Indies, 351–2; in Panama, 377; circumnavigates globe, 378; attacks Spanish ships, 402; given command of squadron against Spain, 426, 428; opposes Spanish Armada, 428, 432, 434; sails against Portugal, 441

drama: development, 470

dress and costumes, 352–3

Dreux, 313

Dryffield, Revd Thomas, 14

Dudley, Amy: death, 304–5

Dudley, Sir Edmund, 4, 83

Dudley, Sir Henry, 275–6

Dudley, John *see* Northumberland, John Dudley, duke of

Dudley, Robert *see* Leicester, earl of

earthquake (1580), 393

Edinburgh, treaty of (1560), 301–2, 307

education: after dissolution of monasteries, 122–3; and English language, 470

Edward III, king, 16

Edward VI, king: birth, 136; upbringing and education, 137, 147–8, 168–70; portrait, 147; in family portrait, 168; appearance and manner, 169; religious reformism, 172, 184–7, 189–92, 199, 223–4, 232–3, 249, 468; Henry bequeaths crown to, 180; regency, 180; told of father's death, 181; coronation, 184; betrothal to infant Mary Stuart, 193; and Protector Somerset's invasion of Scotland, 195–6; founds schools, 196; Thomas Seymour attempts to influence, 203; and social divisions and unrest, 206, 208; rumoured death, 208; and Somerset's downfall, 220; attends council meetings, 222–3; relations with Dudley (Northumberland), 223; differences with Mary Tudor, 228; and Somerset's execution, 230; administration, 235–6; ill with smallpox, 235; health decline, 236–9;

Edward VI, king (*cont.*)
    succession to, 237–8; death, 239–40;
    funeral, 246
Edwards, Arthur, 351
Egerton, Sir Thomas (*later* Viscount
    Brackley), 454
Elizabeth I, queen: birth, 71, 76–7;
    paternity questioned, 97; education
    and learning, 168, 170; in family
    portrait, 168; love of music, 169; in
    succession to Henry, 180; on
    Katherine Parr's marriage to
    Seymour, 185–6; relations with
    Thomas Seymour, 186, 202, 204;
    enters household of Katherine Parr,
    202; declared illegitimate, 238; and
    Mary Tudor's accession, 251;
    Protestantism, 251, 288, 291–2, 468;
    and Wyatt's rebellion, 256–8;
    confined in Tower, 257; moved from
    Tower to Woodstock, 258; Catholics
    persecuted under, 271; relations with
    Mary Tudor, 273–4; and Dudley
    conspiracy, 276; as heir apparent to
    Mary, 276; succeeds at Mary's death,
    285–6; progress to London on
    accession, 287; coronation, 287–9; and
    privy council, 289; condition of
    England on accession, 290–1;
    relations with Robert Dudley, earl of
    Leicester, 290, 303; women courtiers,
    290; religious opinions and policy,
    292–4, 297, 299–300, 323, 334, 468;
    remains unmarried and childless,
    294–5, 302–3, 315, 334–6, 383, 391;
    ascendancy and exercise of power,
    295–6; relations with parliament, 295,
    316, 363–4, 445, 463–4; cult of, 296;
    keeps crucifix, 298–9; assassination
    plots against, 300, 405, 410; dislikes
    war, 300, 414–15; suitors and marriage
    prospects, 302, 304, 325–7, 341–3;
    smallpox, 309; hopes to meet Mary
    Stuart, 312; supports Protestant cause
    in France, 312–13; succession debated
    in parliament, 314–16; guided by
    council, 315–16; scarred by smallpox,
    315; summons parliament
    infrequently, 316; portraits, 327;
    questions Melville about Mary
    Stuart, 328–9; fluency in languages,
    329, 452; plays virginals, 329; ill with
    flux, 331; on Darnley's murder of
    Rizzio, 333; illness (1566), 333; writes
    to Mary on murder of Darnley, 339;
    deprecates Mary's marriage to
    Bothwell, 341; supports Mary on
    imprisonment, 341; on Mary's escape
    and flight to England, 345–6; and
    inquiry into Darnley murder, 347,
    350; undertakes progresses, 347–8,
    387; vacillations over Mary Stuart,
    350–1; defends Cecil, 355; and
    proposed marriage of Mary Stuart
    and Norfolk, 355–6; northern earls
    rise against (1569), 357–9;
    excommunicated by Pius V, 359–60;
    accession date celebrated, 360;
    marriage negotiations with dukes of
    Anjou, 361–2, 386–7, 389–91, 400–1;
    Norfolk supports Ridolfi plot to
    depose, 362–3; ulcerous leg, 362, 389;
    on Mary and Ridolfi plot, 365;
    nervous collapse on condemnation of
    Norfolk, 366; resists parliament's
    condemnation of Mary Stuart, 367;
    favours counsellors, 369; entertained
    at Kenilworth, 371–2; love of dancing,
    371–2, 465; touches for 'king's evil',
    372; reluctance to support war in
    Netherlands, 373–4, 385, 400–1; sends
    aid to William of Orange, 375; told of
    St Bartholomew's Day massacre, 375;
    procrastination, 376–7; ungenerosity,
    376; declines to head Protestant
    League in Europe, 377; alarmed at
    'prophesyings', 380–1; peace under,
    384–5; image as Virgin Queen, 387,
    392; suffers fits and toothache, 389;
    orders restrictions on ruffs and
    rapiers, 392; portrait by Metsys, 392;
    meets Campion, 396; relationship
    with Anjou ends, 401; favours
    Whitgift, 405; moves to recognize

James VI as king of Scotland, 407, 411; mourns death of duke of Anjou, 408–9; dislikes Burghley's plans to ensure Protestant succession, 409–10; portrait cameos manufactured, 409; selects small number of counsellors, 410; signs treaty with Netherlands (1585), 412; celebrates twenty-seventh anniversary of accession (1585), 413; 'Ermine' portrait, 413; anger at Leicester's appointment as governor of Netherlands, 414; fainting fit, 415; Babington's conspiracy against, 416–17; and trial of Mary queen of Scots, 420–1; uncertainties over decision about Mary's fate, 421–2; signs Mary's death warrant, 422–3; reaction to Mary's execution, 426; Tilbury speech (1588), 432; Gower's 'Armada' portrait, 434; forbids parliament to engage in religious affairs, 436–7; ageing, 444, 450, 465–6; on foreign affairs, 444–6; translates Boethius, 444; late portraits, 450; deprecates Essex's Cadiz expedition, 451; growing irascibility, 452–3; daily exercises, 453; assaults Essex, 454; and Essex's campaign in Ireland, 456–7; court factions, 458; and humbling of Essex, 459; and Essex's rebellion, 460–1; reforms procedure on monopolies, 464; succession to, 464–5; riding in later years, 465; decline and death, 466

Elizabeth of York, queen of Henry VII, 4

Eltham Palace, 2, 352

Ely, bishop of, 369

Empson, Sir Richard, 4

enclosure (of land), 22–3, 206–7

England: Catholic religious practices, 6–8; war with France (1513), 11–12; depopulation in counties, 22; taxation, 37–9; war against France (1523), 37–9; threat of rebellion, 39–40; treaties with France: (1525), 40–1; (1546),
171–2; (1572), 372; (1573), 377; trading development, 39; executions for treason (1534–40), 80; under supervision and control, 81–4; prophecies and portents, 106, 276–7; Franco-Spanish invasion threat against Henry, 139; war with Scotland (1542), 158; invades France (1544), 164–6; religion at time of Henry's death, 178–9; European Protestant divines visit, 187; religious reforms under Edward VI, 189–92; legislation under Edward VI, 197–8; social divisions and unrest under Edward VI and Somerset, 206–16, 233; Henry II of France declares war on, 219; food and eating, 250; described by French and Spanish, 259–60; Protestant exiles flee to Europe, 263–4; declares war on France (1557), 282; coach introduced, 336; naval development and sea power, 344, 377–8, 434; rift with Spain, 344–5; development of world trade, 351–2; material improvements, 352–3; industrial development, 353; Catholic invasion threat, 360; voyages and colonies, 378; period of peace (1559–85), 384; trade with Spain, 402; Spanish Armada and invasion threat, 428–30; strength of fleet against Armada, 429–30; seamen's behaviour, 441–2; unrest (1596), 449; *see also* North of England

English language: Bible translated into, 25, 46–7, 83, 131–3, 470; litany under Edward VI, 190–1; in Church of England, 211; used for psalms under Elizabeth, 299

Erasmus, Desiderius: opposes war, 10; on unhygienic conditions, 20; translates New Testament, 25; religious reforms, 26; on fear in England, 80; humanist learning, 85; on Becket shrine at Canterbury, 125; Mary Tudor translates, 170, 172; *De Servando Conjugio* ('On Preserving

Erasmus, Desiderius (*cont.*)
 Marriage'), 35; *Paraphrase of the New
 Testament*, 190
Erik, prince of Sweden, 302
Essex, Robert Devereux, 2nd earl of:
 character and career, 435; as
 Elizabeth's favourite, 435; on
 expedition against Portugal, 441–2;
 belligerence, 443; rivalry with Robert
 Cecil, 443, 455; as ward of Burghley,
 443; in privy council, 444–5; controls
 intelligence, 447; uncovers Lopez
 plot against Elizabeth, 447–8; leads
 expedition against Cadiz, 450–1;
 leads second attack on Spain (1597),
 453; offends Elizabeth, 454; sent to
 Ireland as lord deputy, 455–6;
 withdraws from court, 455; returns to
 England from Ireland, 456–7;
 examined by special court and found
 guilty of contempt, 458–9; disgraced,
 459; plans rebellion, 459–60;
 imprisons Cecil, 460; armed revolt
 and surrender, 461; executed, 462–3
Essex, Sir Walter Devereux, 1st earl of,
 435
Eucharist, 210, 318; *see also*
 transubstantiation
Europe: religious wars and troubles,
 311–12
Evil May Day (1517), 19
excommunication, 14
Exeter: in Western Rising, 213–14;
 workhouse established (1553), 317
Exeter, Henry Courtenay, marquess of,
 135

faith, 26–7
Familists (Family of God), 399
famine, 448
fashion, 353
Faunt, Nicholas, 403
Felton, John, 360
Fenatus (tooth drawer), 389
Fenton, William, 452
Ferdinand I, Holy Roman Emperor,
 311

Ferdinand, archduke of Austria, 302
Ferdinand, king of Aragon, 2, 9–10, 17
Feria, Jane Dormer, duchess of, 170, 285,
 376
Field of Cloth of Gold (1520), 32
Field, John and Thomas Wilcox: *An
 Admonition to the Parliament*, 367
Fish, Simon: *A Supplication for the
 Beggars*, 59
Fisher, John, bishop of Rochester: resists
 Henry's demands, 53, 58, 64, 67–8;
 proposes Spanish invasion of
 England, 71; arrested, 74; refuses oath
 on Act of Succession and consigned
 to Tower, 82; trial and execution, 86,
 469
Flodden Field, battle of (1513), 12–13,
 157
Flower, Thomas, 246
food and diet: changes, 352
Forrest, Fra John, 126–7
Foster, Thomas, 106
Fotheringhay Castle, 418–19, 423–4
Foxe, John: on killing of Hunne, 15;
 reports incidents of iconoclasm, 78;
 on Supremacy Act (1534), 83; on
 Katherine Parr, 163, 172, 174; on
 Henry's mistrust of Gardiner, 175; on
 accession of Edward VI, 184; on
 Marian persecutions, 268; and
 Elizabeth's meeting with Mary
 Tudor, 274; and martyrdom of
 Latimer, 278; recounts history of
 Reformation, 321–2; protests to
 Elizabeth at resumption of burnings,
 380; *Book of Martyrs*, 78, 174, 271, 278,
 321–2, 360
Foxe, Richard, bishop of Winchester: as
 lord privy seal, 3; promotes Wolsey, 8
France: Henry's hostility to, 4–5, 9; Holy
 League formed against, 9–10; war
 declared against (1512), 10; Henry's
 expedition against (1513), 11–12;
 Henry invades (1523), 37–8; treaties
 with England: (1525), 40–1; (1546),
 171–2; (1572), 372; (1573), 377; Henry
 visits with Anne Boleyn, 71; Henry

allies against with Charles V, 157, 163–6; alliance with Scotland, 163–4, 195, 201; invasion (1544), 163–6; renewed invasion threat from, 166; force lands at Leith (1548), 201; peace with England, 226; supports Dudley conspiracy, 275–6; ships attack Scarborough, 281–2; England declares war on (1557), 282; threatens invasion of England (1558), 283; Elizabeth seeks peace with, 291; and plots to kill Elizabeth, 300; garrison at Leith resists English, 301; rivalry with Spain, 302; troops leave Scotland, 302; wars of religion, 311–14, 344, 374; support for Mary Stuart, 346; seizes Hainault, 373; war against Spain in Netherlands, 373–4; Catholic extremism, 377; disunity, 440

Francis I, king of France: accession, 18; conflicts with Charles V, 18; Wolsey negotiates with, 31; at Field of Cloth of Gold, 32; Mary Tudor betrothed to, 36; Henry and Charles V's (1521) treaty against, 37; Henry's alliance with, 71; delays publication of pope's bull against Henry, 84; invasion threat to England, 139; fails to form alliance with Charles V, 149; detests Cromwell, 150; welcomes Scots' war with England, 158; seeks peace with Henry and Charles V (1544), 165

Francis II, king of France: marriage to Mary Stuart, 289; accession, 300; renounces claim to English throne, 301; death, 306

friaries: destroyed, 124, 126

Frobisher, Sir Martin, 378

Fuller, Thomas, 283, 333; *The Church History of Britain*, 447

Gardiner, Stephen, bishop of Winchester: chides pope, 52; on revolt in North, 107; Barnes preaches against, 151; campaign against heretics, 160; and accusations against Cranmer, 161; as Purveyor General to army in France, 164; favours peace over war, 166; Henry complains to of Katherine Parr's religious reformism, 172; in Foxe's *Book of Martyrs*, 174; investigates Katherine Parr, 174; Henry mistrusts, 175, 181; excluded from court and regency council, 176–7, 180–1; religious conservatism, 180; discounted by Edward VI, 185; protests at Edward VI's religious reforms, 192; preaches after release from prison, 200–1; rearrested and confined in Tower, 201; restored under Mary Tudor, 247; as adviser to Mary Tudor, 249; interrogates Courtenay over plot, 252–3; urges acceptance of Philip of Spain, 259; restores Act on burning of heretics, 266; death, 275; *De Vera Obedientia*, 469

Garrett, Thomas, 50

'gathered' churches, 399

Gembloux, battle of (1578), 385

Gerard, Father, SJ, 395

Germany: uprising (1525), 39; Henry seeks Protestant support from, 88, 132–3

Ghent, Pacification of, 384

Glass of the Truth, A (tract), 71

Glastonbury abbey, 123, 188

Golden Hind (earlier *Pelican*; ship), 378

Gorges, Ferdinando, 460–1

'gospellers', 47

Gower, George, 434

Gravelines, battle of (1588), 431

Great Harry (ship), 32

Greenwich Palace, 2

Gregory VII, pope: reforms, 210

Grenville, Sir Richard, 122

Grey, Lady Jane: background, 237–8; and death of Edward, 240; proclaimed queen, 241, 243; beheaded, 255–6

Grey, Lord John, 254

Grey, Lady Katherine (Countess of Hertford), 305–6, 310

Grey, Lady Mary, 306

Grindal, Edmund, archbishop of Canterbury, 380–2, 403
Guise, Francis, duke of, 282
Guise, Henry I, duke of, 407–9, 419
Guise, house of, 311–13; *see also* Mary of Guise

Habsburg dynasty: dominance, 18
Hackett (yeoman pretender), 440
Hakluyt, Richard, 378
Hall, Edward, 127, 176; *Chronicle*, 57, 469
Hallam, Henry, 197
Hambleton Hill, 107
Hampton Court, 138, 352
Hardwick House, 352
Harold Harefoot, 36
Harpsfield, Nicholas, 467
Harridaunce, John, 143
Harrington, Sir John, 376, 383, 455, 457, 459–60
Harrison, William, 198, 225; *Description of England*, 353
harvest failures: (1549), 208; (1551), 230; (1555), 273; (1586), 414; (1594–7), 448
Hatfield House, Hertfordshire, 77
Hatton, Sir Christopher: in Commons, 316; as favourite of Elizabeth, 369; scheme to discover North–West Passage, 378; commissions portrait of Elizabeth, 392; on prospect of Mary Stuart succeeding to English throne, 403; denounces Mary Stuart, 420
Haughton, John, Carthusian prior, 85
Haukes, Thomas, 268
Hawkins, Sir John, 351, 377–8, 434
Hawkins, Sir Richard: *Observations*, 441–2
Hawkins, William, 430
Heere, Lucas de: *The Family of Henry VIII: An Allegory* (painting), 372
Heneage, Sir Thomas, 389
Henry II, king of France: aims to recover Boulogne, 194, 201; alliance with Scotland, 195; declares war against England (1549), 219; and succession of Mary Tudor, 239;

promises help to English insurgents, 253, 275–6; Philip declares war on, 281
Henry III, king of France (*earlier* duke of Anjou): marriage negotiations with Elizabeth, 361–2
Henry IV (of Navarre), king of France, 409, 451
Henry VII, king: death and funeral, 1; supposed wish to marry Katherine of Aragon, 2; claim to throne, 4; bequest to Henry VIII, 5; challenges Church, 16; and Wolsey's downfall, 60
Henry VIII, king: accession and coronation, 1–2; marriage to Katherine of Aragon, 2; musicianship, 2–3; upbringing and education, 2; appearance, 3; sporting activities, 3; character and temperament, 4; hostility to France, 4–5, 9–10; infidelities and mistresses, 5–6, 34, 76, 92; inheritance, 5; pilgrimages to holy places, 6; religious faith and observance, 6, 100, 178; joins Holy League, 9; expedition against France (1513), 11–12; intervenes in Hunne heresy case, 15; and Henry Standish case, 16; birth of daughter Mary, 18–19; rivalry with French king and emperor Charles V, 18; pardons London rioters, 19; and religious controversy, 28, 467; designated Defender of the Faith (*Fidei Defensor*), 29; reads and counters Luther, 29–30; protects Wolsey, 30; in France for Field of Cloth of Gold, 32; renews claims to French crown, 32; meets and courts Anne Boleyn, 35, 40–2; and Wolsey's failure, 40; desire for legitimate son, 42; seeks divorce from Katherine of Aragon, 42–3, 51–6, 59, 63, 71; takes over administration of country, 56; claim to spiritual supremacy, 59–60, 63–4, 73, 99–100; reads Fish's *Supplication*, 59; acts against clergy, 62–3; recognized as supreme head of Church in England, 65; renounces

Katherine of Aragon, 66; accepts submission of clergy, 69–70; seeks support of parliament, 70; honours and elevates Anne Boleyn, 71; visits France with Anne Boleyn, 71; as absolute ruler, 72–3, 81; marriage to Anne Boleyn, 72, 74; marriage to Katherine declared invalid, 74; declared supreme head of Church of England, 83; Clement VII issues bull against, 84; attends Reformation Parliament (1536), 89; on death of Katherine of Aragon, 91–2; stunned in fall from horse, 92; and Anne Boleyn's infidelity and execution, 93–8; marries Jane Seymour, 97, 100; daughter Mary submits to, 99; succession question, 100–1, 180; draws up articles of faith, 102; and settlement of Pilgrimage of Grace rebellion, 112–14; meets Aske, 114–15; suppresses rebellion in North, 116–17; and dissolution of monasteries, 118; pope publishes Bill of Deposition against, 126; revises bishops' statement of belief, 129–30; opposes unorthodox religious doctrine, 133; and son Edward, 137; ulcerous legs, 137, 152, 176; and invasion threat from continent, 139; moves from religious reform, 140–4, 150; marriage to and separation from Anne of Cleves, 145–7; and Cromwell's downfall, 150, 152; supervises public affairs, 151; marriage to Katherine Howard, 152; progress to north, 152; informed of Katherine Howard's infidelities, 153, 155; obesity, 156, 176; protects Cranmer against accusations of heresy, 160–2; final marriage to Katherine Parr, 162; and invasion of France (1544), 164–6; withdraws from France, 166; in family portrait, 168; deplores differences in religion, 170–1; and Church reform, 171; deprecates Katherine Parr's religious reformism, 172; signs treaty of Ardres

(1546), 172; pardons Katherine Parr for religious views, 174; health decline and death, 176–9; rages, 176; will, 178, 180–2; funeral, 182–3; in allegorical de Heere painting, 372; executions under, 397; Harpsfield on, 467; *Assertio Septem Sacramentorum*, 29
Henry Imperial (ship), 73
Heresy Act (1555), 266–7
heretics: condemned and executed, 8, 14–15, 133–4; growing numbers, 29; suppressed, 48–50, 159–60, 171
Hertford, Edward Seymour, 1st earl of *see* Somerset, 1st duke of
Hertford, Edward Seymour, earl of (son of above), 306
Hever (house), Kent, 41
Hexham abbey, Northumberland, 103
Heywood, John, 207
Higden, Ranulph: *Polychronicon*, 469
Hilliard, Nicholas, 450
history: effect of Reformation on, 469
Hoby, Lady Elizabeth, 163
Holbein, Hans, 145, 147
Holinshed, Raphael, 274, 392
Holt Castle, Worcestershire, 203
Holy League: formed against France, 9
Hooker, John, 213
Hooker, Richard: *Of the Laws of Ecclesiastical Polity*, 446–7
Hooper, John, bishop of Gloucester, 207, 222, 224, 268
Horsey, William, 15
hospitals, 317
Hours of the Blessed Virgin, 8
Howard de Walden, Thomas Howard, 1st baron (*later* 1st earl of Suffolk), 458
Howard of Effingham, 2nd baron *see* Nottingham, 1st earl of
Howard, Lady Mary, 452
Howard, Lord Thomas, 101
Huguenots, 311–12, 344, 374
humanism, 26, 168
Humble Supplication unto God, 264
Humfrey, John, 141
Hunne, Richard, 14–15

Hunsdon, George Carey, 2nd baron, 465
Hunsdon, Henry Carey, 1st baron, 328, 358, 450

iconoclasm: early incidents, 78–9; at dissolution of monasteries, 125
imperium, 73
Inquisition, Holy, 87, 157
Institution of a Christian Man, The (The Bishops' Book), 129–31
Ireland: Catholic soldiers land in, 394; Philip promotes rebellion in, 402; lord lieutenancy, 454, 456; Tyrone's revolt (1598), 455–6, 463; Essex leads army in, 456; Mountjoy's campaign in, 463
Isabella, queen of Castile, 2, 248

James IV, king of Scotland, 12, 157
James V, king of Scotland, 139, 157–9
James VI, king of Scotland (James I of England): birth and appearance, 333–4; at Stirling Castle as infant, 340–1; as prospective successor to Elizabeth, 342, 417, 465; proclaimed king of Scotland, 345; Elizabeth moves to recognize, 407, 411; exempted from reprisals in Bond of Association, 411; and Treaty of Berwick, 417; Elizabeth writes to denying involvement in Mary's death, 426; inaction during Spanish Armada engagement, 432–3; Essex appeals to, 459; succeeds on death of Elizabeth, 466
Jane Seymour, Queen of Henry VIII: Henry courts, 92; marriage, 97; traduced in ballad, 98; in Corpus Christi procession, 102; death following birth of son, 136, 145; son Edward keeps mementoes, 147; in royal family portrait, 168
Jericho (house), Essex, 34
Jesuits: missionaries in England, 393–5, 398; captured and tortured, 396; put to death, 397

Jesus Christ: and real presence in Eucharist, 141–2
Jewel, John, bishop of Salisbury: *The Apology of the Church of England*, 323
Joan of Kent (Joan Bocher), 226, 270
John of Austria, Don, 384–5
Jonson, Ben: *Bartholomew Fair*, 438
Joye, George, 49
Julian of Norwich, Dame, 124
Julius III, pope, 265

Katherine of Aragon, queen of Henry VIII: marriage to Henry and coronation, 2; and Henry's infidelity, 5; stillbirths and false pregnancies, 5; favours war against France, 10; Henry blames for failure of Spanish expedition, 11; and defeat of Scots (1513), 12–13; Henry's disenchantment with, 35, 41; Henry seeks divorce from, 42–3, 51–3, 55–6, 59, 63, 71; popular support for, 51; Henry withdraws from and renounces, 65–6; marriage to Henry declared invalid, 74; status reduced, 75; Clement VII declares marriage to Henry still valid, 79; on execution of Fisher and More, 87; death, 91; Mary repudiates, 98–9; supported by Observant friars, 124; Edward VI requests to hand royal jewels to Somerset's wife, 185; discusses rituals with daughter Mary, 248; marriage ruled legitimate, 249
Katherine Howard, queen of Henry VIII: marriage to Henry, 152; infidelity and lovers, 153–5; executed, 155–6
Katherine Parr, queen of Henry VIII: favours religious reform, 162–3, 172; marriage to Henry, 162; as regent in Henry's absence, 168; and upbringing of prince and princesses, 168–9; influence suspected, 172; under suspicion for religious views, 174; Gardiner intrigues against, 175, 177; Henry prevents arrest, 175; nurses Henry, 175; marriage to Thomas

Seymour, 185; death, 202; Elizabeth enters and leaves household, 202; *The Lamentations of a Sinner*, 162
Kenilworth Castle, Warwickshire, 371–2, 375
Kenninghall, Norfolk, 356
Kent, Nun of *see* Barton, Elizabeth
Kett, Robert, 214–18
King's Book, the *see Necessary Doctrine, A*
Kingston, Sir William, 61, 95
Kirk o'Field (house), 338–9
Knollys, Sir Francis, 315–16, 450
Knollys, Sir William, 454
Knox, John, 158, 301, 307; *The First Blast of the Trumpet against the Monstrous Regiment of Women*, 285, 311

Lambert, John, 133–4
land: change of use and ownership, 22–4, 206–7; in Church hands, 266
Langland, William, 17
Langley priory, 124
Langside Hill, battle of (1568), 346
Lanoy, Cornelius, 327
Latimer, Hugh: preaching, 27, 78, 101, 189, 206; joins court, 78; appointed bishop of Worcester, 89; attends Reformation Parliament, 89; attacked by clergy, 101; disparages rebels, 113; encourages education of children, 123; reads sermon at John Forrest's execution, 127; resigns from Worcester, 143; released under Edward VI, 189; on Thomas Seymour in Tower, 204; on social and economic unrest, 206–7; on behaviour in church, 232; detained and interrogated, 263; degraded and burnt at stake, 277–8; on religion in England, 469
law: changes, 23; and canon law, 73
Lee, Henry, 296
Leges Anglorum, 59, 63
Le Havre, 313–14
Leicester, Lettice, countess of (*earlier* countess of Essex), marriage to Leicester, 386, 435

Leicester, Robert Dudley, earl of: appointed Master of the Horse, 289; relations with Elizabeth, 290, 303, 326, 343, 415; as prospective husband for Elizabeth, 303–5; wife Amy's death, 304; and Elizabeth's illness, 310; supports radical religious reformers, 323; Elizabeth proposes as husband for Mary Stuart, 325; earldom, 326; and Elizabeth's marriage prospects, 326; as protector of Protestant faith, 326, 369; on imprisonment of Lanoy, 327; Elizabeth attacks, 335; hostility to Cecil, 355; supports Norfolk–Mary Stuart union, 355–6; and Elizabeth's nervous collapse, 366; favours Puritan cause, 368; presents wristwatch to Elizabeth, 370; Elizabeth visits at Kenilworth, 371; on St Bartholomew's Day massacre, 375; and Elizabeth's refusal to head Protestant League, 377; dissuades Elizabeth from dismissing Grindal, 382; as prospective commander in Netherlands, 385; remarries (Lettice), 386, 435; opposes Elizabeth's Anjou marriage, 387, 390; as patron of Campion, 393, 396; accompanies Elizabeth on 27th anniversary of accession celebrations, 413; commands in Netherlands, 414; on Mary Stuart's letter to Elizabeth protesting innocence, 423; ague and death, 433–5
Leigh, Thomas, 461
Leith, Scotland: French force at, 201
Leland, John: *Itinerary*, 192
Lennox, Matthew Stuart, 4th earl of, 340
Leo X, pope, 17, 29–30
Lewes: priory destroyed, 119, 121; Marian martyrs, 268
Lewis, Hugh, 32
Leyton, Richard, 89
Lincolnshire: rebellion (1536), 106–8
Lisbon, 426, 441
Lisle, Honor, viscountess, 163
Little Waldingfield, Suffolk, 82

Lodge, Thomas, 352
Lollards, 26, 46
London: anti-clericalism, 17; radicalism and unrest, 19–20, 246; low life and conditions, 32–3; plagues, 129, 314; Marian martyrs, 270; as financial and trade centre, 351–2; damaged by earthquake (1580), 393; unrest (1595), 449
London, Dr John, 50
London, treaty of (1518), 31
Lopez, Rodrigo, 447–8
Lord of Misrule: restored under Mary, 677
Louis XII, king of France, 4
Louth, Lincolnshire, 106–7
Low Countries *see* Netherlands
Lucius I, 'king' (legendary hero), 59, 63
Lumley, John, 1st baron, 365
Luther, Martin: reform doctrines and teachings, 26–7, 56; declared heretical and books burned, 29; Henry reads and writes treatise against, 29, 36; tracts smuggled into England, 29, 46; influence on Tyndale, 47; denounced by English rebels, 117; told of Henry's indifference to religion, 132; believes in real presence, 141
Lutheranism, 132–3, 144, 151, 318
luxuries: increase in, 352

McCabb, Melaghin, 433
Machyn, Henry, 267
Malory, Thomas, 3
manorial system, 23
Manox, Henry, 153–5
Mar, James Stuart, earl of, 340
Margaret of Navarre: *The Mirror of the Sinful Soul*, 170
Margaret Tudor, queen of James IV of Scotland, 101
Marlech Hill, Hertfordshire, 369
Marlowe, Christopher: *The Jew of Malta*, 448
Marprelate, Martin: tracts, 437
Marshall, Cicely, 141
Martyr, Peter, 210

Mary I (Tudor), queen: birth, 18; childhood betrothals, 36–7; as prospective successor to Henry, 36; released from betrothal to Charles V, 40; household, 41; dances before father, 43; illnesses, 65–6, 83, 92, 272, 284–5; stripped of princess title on birth of Elizabeth, 77; refuses oath of Succession, 82–3; mother reassures, 91; Anne Boleyn threatens, 92; learns of mother's death, 92; and death of Anne Boleyn, 98; signs declaration of submission, 99; Pilgrimage of Grace demands legitimacy of, 109; frees Edward Courtenay, 136; education and learning, 168, 170; in family portrait, 168; Edward's regard for, 169; interests and activities, 169; translates Erasmus, 170, 172; in succession to Henry, 180; on Katherine Parr's marriage to Seymour, 185; hears Masses, 199; Thomas Seymour writes to from Tower, 204; rumoured involvement in Kett rebellion, 218; in plot against Somerset, 219; asked to submit to Act of Uniformity, 227; calls off flight abroad, 227; differences with Northumberland, 227; differences with Edward, 228; and Edward's health decline, 237; declared illegitimate, 238–9; and Edward's death, 240–1; accession, 242–5; promotes and restores Catholicism, 245–6, 262, 266–7; government and advisers, 248–9; as queen regnant, 248; marriage prospects, 249–51; relations with parliament, 249–50; betrothal to Philip of Spain, 250–2; piety and devotions, 250; and Wyatt's rebellion (1554), 253–5; voice and manner, 254; and Elizabeth's confinement in Tower, 257; marriage to Philip, 258–9; childlessness, 260–1, 272–3, 283–4; pregnancy, 264; welcomes Pole on return to England, 264–5; as head of Church of

England, 266; religious persecutions under, 267–71, 284, 321, 397; relations with Elizabeth, 273–4, 276; and Philip's departure from England, 274; armed conspiracy against (1555), 275–6; and burning of Cranmer, 279; supports Philip in war against France, 281–2; and fall of Calais, 283–4; makes will, 283; Knox attacks, 285; death, 286; embroiders image of cat, 356; reverses religious reforms, 468

Mary Boleyn (ship), 34

Mary of Guise, queen of James V of Scotland: as dowager queen of Scotland, 201, 300; death, 302; grave, 422

Mary Imperial (ship), 73

Mary of Portugal, 170

Mary Rose (ship), 167

Mary (Stuart), queen of Scots: birth, 158–9; betrothal to Edward as infant, 193; betrothal to French dauphin, 201; in hands of Henry II of France, 219; as successor to English throne, 289, 300, 302, 306, 403; as queen of France, 300; and renunciation of claim to English throne, 301, 307, 354–5; as threat in Scotland, 301; and death of Francis II, 306–7; character, 307–8; declines to sign treaty of Edinburgh, 307; returns to Scotland, 307–8; seeks meeting with Elizabeth, 312; and parliamentary debate of succession to Elizabeth, 314; marriage prospects, 325; infatuation with Darnley, 327–9; questions Melville about Elizabeth, 329; harries Moray in Chaseabout Raid, 330; marriage to Darnley, 330; denies Elizabeth's title as queen, 331; marriage difficulties with Darnley, 331; and murder of Rizzio, 332; pregnancy and birth of son, 332–4; ostracizes Darnley, 337; and plot to murder Darnley, 338–40; Bothwell abducts and ravishes, 340–1; marriage to Bothwell, 341–2; pregnant by Bothwell, 341; imprisoned on

Loch Leven, 342, 345; escapes, 345; miscarriage, 345; detained in England, 346–7; flees to England after Langside Hill defeat, 346; and inquiry into Darnley's murder, 347–50; and 'casket letters', 349; prospective marriage to duke of Norfolk, 349–50, 355–6; confined in Tutbury Castle, 350; corresponds with Norfolk, 354–5; moved to Coventry in 1569 northern rebellion, 358; remains under house arrest, 361; and Ridolfi plot, 362, 362–3, 365; condemned by parliament, 366–7; on execution of Norfolk, 366; sends gift of nightcaps to Elizabeth, 376; in collusion with Spain and Italy, 402–3; plots and intrigues, 406–8; and Throgmorton, 406; in Sheffield Castle, 407–8; commissioners visit, 408; plan to execute in event of Elizabeth's assassination, 409; pleads for life with Elizabeth, 411; rebukes son James, 411; returns to Tutbury Castle, 411; in Babington plot, 416; taken to Fotheringhay Castle, 418; appearance, 419; tried and found guilty, 419–22; Elizabeth signs death warrant, 422–3; told of execution plans, 423–4; executed, 425–6

Mary Tudor, duchess of Suffolk (*formerly* queen of Louis XII; Henry VIII's sister), 71

Mary, Virgin: as intercessor, 7

Matilda, queen of Henry I, 36, 248

Maximilian I, Holy Roman Emperor: Henry allies with (1513), 11–12; death, 31; Wolsey negotiates with, 31

Maximilian II, Holy Roman Emperor: relations with Elizabeth, 327

Medina Sidonia, Don Alonso, 7th duke of, 429, 431

Melanchthon, Philip, 102, 133

Melville, Sir James, 328–9; *Memoirs*, 333

Melville, Robert (*later* 1st baron), 424

Mendoza, Bernadino de, 401–2

Merchant Adventurers, 39, 283

Merlin the magician, 106

Metsys, Quentin (attrib.): portrait of Elizabeth, 392

Milan: Francis I captures, 18

Milan, Christina, Duchess of, 145

Mildmay, Sir Walter, 384, 395

Milton, John, 470

monasteries: life at, 28; visitations on, 88–9; shrines and relics, 89; dissolution, 90, 118–21; Cromwell controls, 102–3; despoiled and suppressed, 103, 110; lands and possessions appropriated and sold, 121–2; effect of dissolution on education, 122–3; images and relics destroyed, 125–6; revenues appropriated, 197

monks: and dissolution of monasteries, 124

monopolies, 464

Montague, Henry Pole, baron, 135

Moray, James Stuart, 1st earl of, 330–2, 345, 349–50

More, Sir Thomas: praises Henry VIII, 3; persecutes religious heretics, 29, 49–50, 56; as Speaker of Lower House, 37; raids Hanseatic merchants in Steelyard, 47–8; succeeds Wolsey as chancellor, 56, 58; resigns as chancellor, 70; consigned to Tower and executed, 82, 87, 469; refuses oath upon Act of Succession, 82; education of daughters, 170; religious steadfastness, 179; on corruption, 196; *Utopia*, 22, 196

Morice, Ralph, 144

Morton, Margaret, 154

Mountjoy, Charles Blount, 8th baron (*later* earl of Devonshire), 458, 463

Mousehold Heath, Norwich, 214–17

Naworth, battle of (1570), 358

Necessary Doctrine and Erudition for any Christian Man, A (the King's Book), 159

Netherlands: Spanish force in, 343; Elizabeth's reluctance to engage in, 373–4, 385, 409; revolt against Spain, 373, 377; 'Spanish fury' in, 384; Anjou invades, 388; Walsingham proposes alliance with Protestants, 407–8; Elizabeth signs treaty with (1585), 412; Leicester commands in, 414; peace proposals, 415

Netley Abbey, 121

'new ague' (epidemic disease), 284

New Testament: Erasmus translates, 25

Newhall (manor), 376

nobility: distrusts commonalty, 20

Nonsuch Palace, Surrey, 138, 457

Norfolk: popular rebellion (1549), 215–16; Elizabeth visits on progress, 387–8

Norfolk, Thomas Howard, 2nd duke of (and earl of Surrey): granted ducal title, 11; victory at Flodden Field, 12; invades France (1522), 37

Norfolk, Thomas Howard, 3rd duke of (and earl of Surrey): treats with rebels in Norfolk, 39; on Katherine of Aragon's bearing, 43; in Henry's service, 57; threatens Wolsey, 60; on commission into treason, 93; requests Mary agree to Henry's conditions, 98; and resistance of monks of Hexham, 103; opposes rebellions in North, 107, 112–17; appropriates monastic possessions, 121; in religious controversies, 142–3; quarrel with Cromwell, 144; and Cromwell's downfall, 148, 150; as senior counsellor, 151; and Katherine Howard's marriage to Henry, 152–3; on Katherine Howard's infidelities, 155; loses Henry's favour, 156; in war against Scotland (1542), 158; plots against Cranmer, 162; downfall, 177; discounted by Edward VI, 185; in Tower during East Anglian rebellion, 218; greets Mary Tudor as queen, 244; leads forces against Wyatt rebellion, 253

Norfolk, Thomas Howard, 4th duke of: and Elizabeth's marriage prospects,

326, 335; attends inquiry into
Darnley's murder, 348–9; on casket
letters, 349; as prospective husband
for Mary Stuart, 349–50, 354–6;
correspondence with Mary Stuart,
354–5, 365; opposes Cecil, 355;
confined in Tower, 357; released from
Tower, 362; supports Ridolfi plot,
362–3, 365; returned to Tower, 365;
tried, convicted and executed, 365–6,
411

Norris, Sir Henry, 94–7

North, Edward, 1st baron, 387

North of England: rebellions, 104,
106–12, 115–16; Henry visits (1541),
152; rising against Elizabeth
(1569–70), 357–9; *see also* Pilgrimage
of Grace

North-West Passage, 378

Northampton, William Parr, 1st marquis
of, 216, 355

Northumberland, Henry Percy, 8th earl
of, 387, 412

Northumberland, John Dudley, duke of
(*earlier* earl of Warwick): acquires
monastic lands, 121; at Henry's death,
179; suppresses Kett's rebellion,
217–19; plots downfall of Somerset,
219–21; dukedom, 222–3; as lord
president of council, 222; religious
convictions, 222; encourages Edward
VI, 223; administration and rule,
226–7; returns Boulogne to French,
226; differences with Mary Tudor,
227; Somerset opposes, 229; and
disarray in kingdom, 230; and threat
of rebellion, 233; and succession to
Edward VI, 237–8; and Edward's
death, 240; attempts to prevent Mary
from succeeding, 241–3; arrested and
executed, 243–4

Northumberland, Thomas Percy, 7th
earl of, 357–9

Norwich: in Kett's rebellion, 215–18

Nostradamus, 309

Nottingham, Charles Howard, 1st earl
of (*earlier* 2nd baron Howard of

Effingham): commands English fleet
against Spanish Armada, 431–2; on
sickness of seamen, 433; earldom, 451;
leads attack on Spain (1597), 453;
calms Essex in outburst against
Elizabeth, 454; in Cecil's court
faction, 458; and Elizabeth's ageing,
465

Nun of Kent *see* Barton, Elizabeth

nuns: and dissolution of convents, 124

oath: Whitgift makes compulsory, 403–4

Orsini, Cardinal Flavio, 374

Oxford: religious dissidents, 50;
Elizabeth visits, 333–4

Paget, Sir William, 179–82, 198, 208

papist: as term of contempt, 80

parish churches: design, 225

parish registers: introduced, 132

Parker, Matthew, archbishop of
Canterbury: meets at White Horse
tavern, 27; consecrated as archbishop,
297–8; and Elizabeth's distaste for
marriage, 305; on Elizabeth's
treatment of Mary Stuart, 346; death,
380

parliament: called for 1529, 57–8;
petition against Church, 68–9, 70;
Henry seeks support, 70; religious
opinions and discussions, 79, 141, 159,
171, 293, 364, 436–7, 446; supports
Henry over succession, 80;
Reformation (1536), 89; discusses
status of Mary and Elizabeth after
Anne of Boleyn's death, 100; called
(1543), 159; inaugurated with Mass
sung in English (1547), 196;
assembles (January 1552), 231; under
Mary Tudor, 249–50; Pole addresses,
264–5; demands free speech, 282–3,
445; meets after Elizabeth's
coronation, 291; Elizabeth's relations
with, 295, 316, 363–4, 445, 463–4;
debates succession to Elizabeth,
314–15; legislation under Elizabeth,
317; discusses Elizabeth's marriage

parliament (*cont.*)
  prospects, 335–6, 383; condemns
  Mary for role in Ridolfi plot, 366;
  legislates for Queen's Safety, 410;
  votes moneys to Elizabeth, 445, 464
Parma, Alexander Farnese, duke of:
  commands Spanish forces in
  Netherlands, 412, 428; awaits Spanish
  Armada for invasion of England,
  428–32
Parry, Thomas, 202
Parry, William, 410
Parsons, Robert, SJ, 393–5, 436
Paul III, pope: establishes Inquisition,
  157
Paulet, Sir Amyas, 418, 420, 423
Paulet, Sir William, 121–2
Pavia, battle of (1525), 38
Peasants' Revolt (1381), 17
Pembroke, William Herbert, 1st earl of,
  243
Percy, Sir Thomas, 357
Peto, Father William, 68, 183
Philip II, king of Spain: betrothal to
  Mary Tudor, 250–2; marriage to
  Mary in England, 258–9, 262;
  welcomes Pole to England, 264; visits
  Elizabeth, 272; leaves England, 274;
  leadership in Spanish Netherlands,
  275, 283; as invasion threat against
  England, 276; declares war against
  Henry II, 281; returns to England,
  281; proposes recapturing Calais, 283;
  proposes marriage to Elizabeth, 295,
  302; supports Elizabeth against
  France, 302; and Elizabeth's
  prospective marriage to Dudley, 305;
  and French wars of religion, 311;
  Elizabeth's relations with, 327;
  proposes assisting Mary Stuart to
  English throne, 334; sends army to
  Netherlands, 343–4; marriage (to
  Isabella of France), 360; defeats in
  Netherlands, 373; and Elizabeth's
  neutrality in Netherlands war, 376;
  Elizabeth supports over Anjou's
  invasion of Netherlands, 388;

  Elizabeth's diplomatic dealings with,
  401; and Elizabeth's relations with
  Anjou, 401; promotes rebellion in
  Ireland, 402; on throne of Portugal,
  402; finances pro-Mary plot, 407;
  orders assassination of William of
  Orange, 408; treaty with Guise
  against Henry of Navarre and
  Elizabeth, 409; ships captured by
  British adventurers, 413; and
  settlement in Netherlands, 415; and
  fate of Mary queen of Scots, 421;
  plans invasion of England, 427; and
  despatch of Spanish Armada, 429;
  and defeat and return of Armada,
  433; power, 440–1; England provokes,
  441; and Essex's expedition against
  Cadiz, 451; sends further armadas
  (1596–7), 453; death, 455
Phillips, Thomas, 56
Pilgrimage of Grace (1536), 109–13, 118,
  123
Pinkie Cleugh, battle of (1547), 195, 201
Pitcairn, Robert: *Ancient Criminal Trials
  in Scotland*, 338
Pius V, pope: excommunicates
  Elizabeth, 359
plague: (1537), 129; (1562), 313–14
Plat, Robert, 141
Plumpton, Robert, 47
Pole, Sir Geoffrey, 135
Pole, Margaret, 264
Pole, Cardinal Reginald: as papal legate,
  134; and mother's beheading, 135;
  returns to England, 264–5;
  persecutions, 270; Mary Tudor's
  reliance on, 277; made archbishop of
  Canterbury, 280; death, 286; learns of
  Mary's death, 286
Pontefract Castle: Aske threatens and
  occupies, 110, 113
Poor Catholics of the Humiliati, 25
poor laws, 317, 449
population: rural decline, 22–3; increase,
  206
portents, 67, 106, 276–7, 308–9
Portugal: Philip annexes, 401; Elizabeth

provokes unrest in, 402; Drake sails against, 441

Potter, Gilbert, 241

Poverty, Captain, 109

praemunire, 16, 62

Prayer Book *see* Book of Common Prayer

predestination, 188

Presbyterianism: beginnings, 367–8, 404

prices: rise, 163, 206, 230, 448

priests: in Church of England, 224

privateering: against Spain, 441

privy council: restored under Northumberland, 227; Elizabeth meets on accession, 289; as authority on death of Elizabeth, 316

Profitable and Necessary Doctrine, A, 267

'prophesyings' (exercises), 380–2, 388

Protestant faith: and English Bible, 131; creed and practices, 232; persecuted under Mary Tudor, 247, 267–71, 397; opposition to Mary's Catholicism, 252; under Elizabeth, 292–3; professed in Scotland, 302; persecuted in France, 311–12, 344, 374; radical activists, 322–3; spread in England, 324; influential supporters under Elizabeth, 368–9; and war against Spanish in Netherlands, 373–4; in continental Europe, 467; and submission to secular authority, 469

Provisors, Statute of (1351), 16

Puckering, Sir John, 440, 450

Puritanism: beginnings, 322–3, 368; strength in universities, 367–8; Whitgift opposes, 403; members fight against Armada, 436; strength and influence, 436–9; opposition to, 438–9; portrayed on stage, 438; parliament legislates against, 446

Queen's Safety, Act for (1584), 410, 419

Raleigh, Walter, Senior, 213

Raleigh, Sir Walter, 384, 458–9

Reading abbey, 123

rebellions and riots: (1549), 207, 209–18,

226; Wyatt's (1554), 252–6; northern (1569–70), 357–9; *see also* Pilgrimage of Grace

recusant priests, 319

Reformation: beginnings, 25–7; effect on government, 317; as political and dynastic movement, 467; effect on individual and nation, 468–70; theology, 468; cultural effects, 469–70; *see also* Protestant faith

religion: affinity with agricultural changes, 24; disputes and controversies over, 25–7, 140–2, 199, 446–7; imagery attacked, 78–9; Henry deplores differences, 170–1; in England at Henry's death, 178–9; restrictions under Edward VI, 196–200; reforms restored under Elizabeth, 292, 318; visitations under Elizabeth, 299–300; active practitioners, 319–21; and rise of extreme Puritans, 322–3; sects established, 398–9; popular indifference to, 439–40; *see also* Book of Common Prayer; Catholic Church; Protestant faith

Restraint of Appeals, Act of (1533), 72–3

Rich, Robert, 3rd baron (*later* earl of Warwick), 458

Richard II, king, 16

Richmond, Henry FitzRoy, Duke of (Henry VIII's illegitimate son): birth, 34; Katherine of Aragon and, 35; as prospective successor to Henry, 36, 100; and death of Anne Boleyn, 98; death, 101, 237

Ridley, Nicholas: meets at White Horse tavern, 27; detained and interrogated, 263; degraded and burnt at stake, 277–8

Ridolfi, Roberto di, 362–4, 366

Ripon, 357–8

Rising of the North (1569–70), 357–9

Rizzio (or Riccio), David, 331–3, 339

Roanoke colony, North Carolina, 378

Roche Abbey, Yorkshire, 119

Rochford, George Boleyn, viscount (Anne Boleyn's brother): executed, 94–7

Rochford, Jane, viscountess, 155

Rochford, Thomas Boleyn, 1st viscount (Anne's father) *see* Wiltshire, earl of, 1763

Rogers, John, canon of St Paul's, 267

Rokewood, Edward, 388

Rouen, 313

Rowlands, Samuel, 353

Rudd, Anthony, bishop of St David's, 450

Russell, John, baron (*later* 1st earl of Bedford), 214

Rutland, John Manners, 6th earl of, 458

St Bartholomew's Day massacre (14 August 1572), 374–6

St Bartholomew's hospital, London, 317

St Margaret Pattens church, London, 128

St Nicholas priory, Exeter, 103

St Paul's Cathedral, London: rood removed, 192; altar replaced, 225; damaged by lightning, 308

St Thomas's hospital, London, 317

saints: as intercessors, 7

Salisbury, Margaret Pole, countess of, 134–5

Sampford Courtenay, Devon, 212, 214

Sander, Nicholas, 319

Santa Cruz, Don Alvaro de Bazan, marquis of, 428–9

Saxton, Christopher, 470

Scarborough: attacked by French ships, 281–2

schools: founded and endowed, 123, 470

Schorne, Master John, 6

Scotland: war with England (1513), 12–13; Cromwell proposes war on (1522), 37; allies with France, 38, 163, 195, 201; dissolution of monasteries, 118; border raids into England, 157; war with England (1542), 157–8; Hertford invades and ravages, 164; Protector Somerset hopes for union

with England, 193, 201; Somerset invades (1547), 194–5; attack on England (1557), 282; Elizabeth seeks agreement with, 291; request to Elizabeth to remove French, 300–1; professes Protestant faith, 302; treaty of Edinburgh settles peace with England (1560), 302; James VI proclaimed king, 345; rebel northern earls flee to, 358, 361

Scroope, Philadelphia, Lady, 465

seminarians (Catholic): in England, 379

Servetus, Michael, 270

Seymour, Edward *see* Hertford, earl of; Somerset, 1st duke of

Seymour of Sudeley, Thomas, baron, 162; marriage to Katherine Parr, 185–6; relations with brother, 185; counsels Edward VI, 186; interest in Elizabeth, 186, 202–4; on Protector Somerset's invasion of Scotland, 195; ambitions, 202–3; arrested, charged and beheaded, 203–5

Shakespeare, William: use of English, 470; *A Midsummer Night's Dream*, 448; *Twelfth Night*, 438

Sharington, Sir Edward, 121

Shaxton, Nicholas, bishop of Salisbury, 125, 143

sheep: and change of land use, 22

Sheffield Castle, 407

Shrewsbury, George Talbot, 4th earl of, 111–12

Shrewsbury, George Talbot, 6th earl of, 425, 458

Sidney, Sir Philip, 388, 415

Simier, Jean de, 389–91

Six Articles, Act of (1539), 142–4; abolished, 197

Sixtus V, pope, 413, 434–5

Skelton, John, 12, 22

slave trade: beginnings, 351

Smeaton, Mark, 93–5

Solway Moss, battle of (1543), 158, 163

Somerset, Edward Seymour, 1st duke of (*earlier* earl of Hertford): burns Edinburgh, 164; at Henry's death,

179–81; as religious reformer, 179, 186, 188, 194, 199; as Protector in Edward's regency, 181–2, 185; tolerance, 188; hopes for union with Scotland, 193, 201; and national defence, 193; proclamations, 193–4; builds London palace, 194; invades Scotland (1547), 194–5, 202; warned of unrest in kingdom, 198–9; and arrest and execution of brother Thomas, 203–5; restores common land, 208; and Act of Uniformity, 211; and suppression of popular risings, 214–15, 219; deposed, 219–21; executed, 229–30; opposes Northumberland, 229

Somerville, John, 405–6

Southampton, Henry Wriothesley, 2nd earl of, 365

Southampton, Henry Wriothesley, 3rd earl of: in Ireland, 456; in Essex's court faction, 458; and Essex's rebellion, 459, 461–2; sentenced to life imprisonment, 462

Southampton, William Fitzwilliam, earl of, 146

Southwick, Anne, 32

Spain: in Holy League against France, 9–10; English troops in, 10; Pavia victory (1525), 38; invited to invade England, 86; invasion threat against Henry, 139–40; allies with France, 166; victory at St Quentin (1557), 282; rivalry with France, 302; force in Netherlands, 343; rift with England, 344–5; ships impounded in Falmouth and Plymouth, 344; support for Mary Stuart, 346; Netherlands revolt against, 373, 377; bullion from Latin America, 377; treaty with England (1573), 377; troops mutiny and massacre in Netherlands, 384; ships and treasure attacked by English, 402; trade with England, 402; and settlement in Netherlands, 415; prepares expedition against England, 426–7; Elizabeth orders attack on fleet (1597), 453; sends further

armadas against England (1596–7), 453; supports Tyrone's rebellion in Ireland, 463; Essex's 1596 expedition against, 551

Spanish Armada: prepared, 428; sails, 429; engagement, 431; losses, 433; retreat and return to Spain, 433

Spenser, Edmund: *The Faerie Queene*, 434

Spurs, battle of the (1513), 12

Stafford, Anne: as Henry's lover, 5, 34

Stafford, Sir Thomas, 282

Standish, Henry, 15–16

Stanford in the Vale, Berkshire, 199

Star Chamber: instituted, 21; forbids treatises against queen's injunctions, 322; tries Puritan, 439

Statute of Artificers (1563), 316

Stephano (assassin), 300

Stevens, Thomas, 351

Stonor Park, Oxfordshire, 395

Stow, John, 322, 433; *Survey of London*, 194

Strype, William, 131

Stuart dynasty, 158–9, 180

Stubbs, John: *The discovery of a gaping gulf*, 390

Submission of the Clergy, 69–70, 79

Succession, Act of (1534), 80–3

Suffolk, Henry Grey, duke of, 241, 252, 254

Suffolk, Katherine, duchess of, 163, 180, 192, 263

Suffolk, Thomas Brandon, 1st duke of: dukedom, 11; commands force against France (1523), 38; protests at delay to Henry–Katherine divorce, 54; in Henry's service, 57; appropriates monastic possessions, 121

Supremacy Act (1534), 83–4

Surrey, Henry Howard, earl of: imprisoned, 177

Surrey, Thomas Howard, earl of *see* Norfolk, dukes of

Sussex, Henry Radcliffe, 2nd earl of, 242

Sussex, Thomas Radcliffe, 3rd earl of: differences with Leicester, 326; and

Sussex, Thomas Radcliffe (*cont.*)
Elizabeth's marriage prospects, 326;
travels to Vienna to negotiate
Elizabeth's marriage with archduke
Charles, 342–3; supports Elizabeth
against northern earls, 358; Elizabeth
considers giving Newhall manor to,
376
sweating sickness: Prince Arthur dies
from, 2; in London (1517), 20; in
England (1551), 230

taxes: under Henry, 37–8, 40, 163; under
Elizabeth, 463
Taylor, John (the 'water poet'), 336
theatre *see* drama
Thérouanne, Flanders, 12
Thirty-Nine Articles (Church of
England), 232, 318, 403
Throgmorton, Francis, 406–7, 412
Tilbury: Elizabeth visits, 432
Titchfield Abbey, 121
Toorwoort, Henry, 380
Topcliffe, Richard, 396
torture: practice of, 396
Tournai, 12
transubstantiation, 141–3, 159, 171, 200,
210, 232; *see also* Eucharist
Treason Acts: (1534), 397; (1547), 197;
(1552), 232
Tunstall, Cuthbert, bishop of Durham,
100, 102, 195
Turkey: as threat, 38, 65; trade with
England, 361
Turner, William, 186
Tutbury Castle, Staffordshire, 350, 411
Tyndale, William: influenced by Luther,
26–7; New Testament translation,
46–8, 131; *The Obedience of a Christian
Man*, 60
Tyrone, Hugh O'Neill, 2nd earl of,
455–6, 463
Tyttenhanger (house), near St Albans, 45

Underhill, Thomas, 189
Uniformity, Acts of: (1549), 209–11;
(1552), 231; (1559), 292, 358

United Provinces *see* Netherlands
universities (English): reforms, 85
universities (European): involvement in
Henry's divorce proceedings, 55

Vagrancy Act (1547), 198
vagrants and vagabondage, 317, 448

Wade, Sir William, 408
Walpole, Henry, 397
Walsingham, Norfolk: Henry's
pilgrimage to, 6; Wolsey's pilgrimage
to, 20–1
Walsingham, Sir Francis: joins queen's
counsels, 368; as spymaster, 368;
Protestantism, 369; Elizabeth
presents painting to, 372; restlessness,
388–9; campaign against Jesuits, 394;
foils pro-Mary Stuart plots, 406–7;
proposes alliance with Protestants of
Low Countries, 407–8; drafts Bond
of Association, 409; questions Parry,
410; accompanies Elizabeth on 27th
anniversary of accession celebrations,
413; and cost of war in Netherlands,
414; opposes peace proposals for
Netherlands, 415; uncovers Babington
plot, 416–17; and trial of Mary queen
of Scots, 420, 426; informed of plot
against Elizabeth, 422; and
Elizabeth's signing Mary's death
warrant, 423; death, 443
Wandsworth, 368
Warham, William, archbishop of
Canterbury: as chancellor, 3; grand
manner, 21–2; death, 70, 73;
denounces legislation against Church,
70, 83
Warwick, Ambrose Dudley, earl of, 314
Weelmaker, John, 380
Wentworth, Peter, 382–3
West Indies: Drake voyages to, 351–2, 413
Western Rising (Prayer Book Rebellion,
1549), 209, 212–14
Westminster Abbey: shrine of Edward
the Confessor destroyed, 104

Westmorland, Charles Neville, 6th earl of, 357–9

Westmorland, Jane, countess of (*née* Howard), 357

Weston, Francis, 94

Wharton, Sir Thomas, 158

White Horse tavern, Cambridge, 25, 27

Whitgift, John, archbishop of Canterbury, 403–5, 436, 438, 453, 466

Whyte, Rowland, 457–8

Wilford, Sir Thomas, 449

William II (Rufus), king of England, 83

William of Nassau, prince of Orange, 373, 375; assassinated, 408

Wilson, Thomas: *The State of England Anno Domino 1600*, 449–50

Wiltshire, Thomas Boleyn, earl of (*earlier* 1st viscount Rochford; Anne's father): peerage, 34; Henry confides in, 44; mission to pope, 60; supposed attack on John Fisher, 64

Wisbech Castle, Isle of Ely, 397

Wolf Hall, 137

Wolsey, Cardinal Thomas: early career, 8–9; and Henry's expedition against France, 11–12; and inquiry into heresy case, 15, 17; and Standish case, 16; rise to power, 17, 28, 31; and London unrest, 19; contracts sweating sickness, 20; reforms judicial system, 21; appointed papal legate, 27–8, 30–1; religious reforms, 28–30; burns Luther's writings, 29; diplomacy, 31; and Anne Boleyn, 35; and execution of Buckingham, 36; and invasion of France (1523), 37, 39; raises taxes, 37–8, 40; reads Katherine of Aragon's letters, 41; negotiates divorce of Henry from Katherine of Aragon, 42, 44–5, 50–4; Henry suspects, 44–5; and suppression of religious dissidents, 48; fall from favour and dismissal, 54–8; driven north, 60; arrest and death, 60–1; interviews Elizabeth Barton, 67

Woodstock, Oxfordshire: Elizabeth in custody at, 258; Elizabeth revisits, 333

Woodstock, Thomas, 36

Worcester, Edward Somerset, 4th earl of, 458

Worcester, William Somerset, 3rd earl of, 376

workhouses, 317

Wriothesley, Sir Thomas, 121, 175

Wyatt, Sir Thomas, 94, 97

Wyatt, Sir Thomas, the younger: rebellion, 252–6, 258, 262

Wycliffe, John, 26

York: and Pilgrimage of Grace, 109–10; Mary Stuart in, 347–50

Yorkshire: rebellion (1536), 108–10